(Continued on back endsheets)

Dictionary of Literary Biography® • Volume One Hundred Forty

American Book-Collectors
and
Bibliographers
First Series

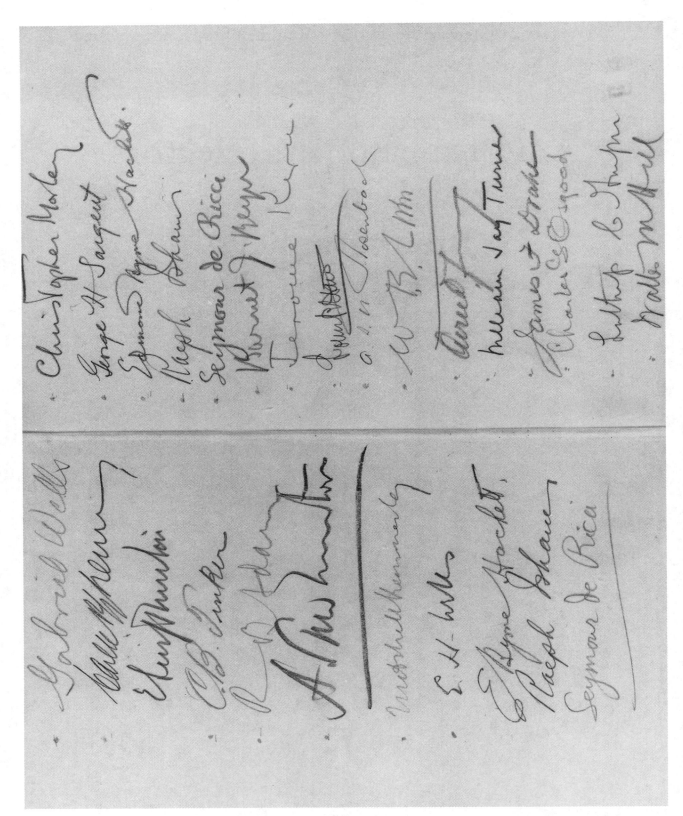

Signatures of bookmen in the catalogue of the 1926 R. B. Adam sale at the Anderson Galleries (Bruccoli Collection)

Dictionary of Literary Biography® • Volume One Hundred Forty

American Book-Collectors
and
Bibliographers
First Series

Edited by
Joseph Rosenblum
University of North Carolina at Greensboro

A Bruccoli Clark Layman Book
Gale Research Inc.
Detroit, Washington, D.C., London

Advisory Board for
DICTIONARY OF LITERARY BIOGRAPHY

John Baker
William Cagle
Patrick O'Connor
George Garrett
Trudier Harris

Matthew J. Bruccoli and Richard Layman, Editorial Directors
C. E. Frazer Clark, Jr., Managing Editor
Karen L. Rood, Senior Editor

Printed in the United States of America

Published simultaneously in the United Kingdom
by Gale Research International Limited
(An affiliated company of Gale Research Inc.)

The paper used in this publication meets the minimum requirements
of American National Standard for Information Sciences—Permanence
Paper for Printed Library Materials, ANSI Z39.48-1984. ∞™

Library of Congress Catalog Card Number 94-7047
ISBN 0-8103-5399-7

I⒯P™

The trademark **ITP** is used under license.

10 9 8 7 6 5 4 3 2 1

For my family

Contents

Contents

Plan of the Series

. . . Almost the most prodigious asset of a country, and perhaps its most precious possession, is its native literary product — when that product is fine and noble and enduring.

Mark Twain*

The advisory board, the editors, and the publisher of the *Dictionary of Literary Biography* are joined in endorsing Mark Twain's declaration. The literature of a nation provides an inexhaustible resource of permanent worth. We intend to make literature and its creators better understood and more accessible to students and the reading public, while satisfying the standards of teachers and scholars.

To meet these requirements, *literary biography* has been construed in terms of the author's achievement. The most important thing about a writer is his writing. Accordingly, the entries in *DLB* are career biographies, tracing the development of the author's canon and the evolution of his reputation.

The purpose of *DLB* is not only to provide reliable information in a convenient format but also to place the figures in the larger perspective of literary history and to offer appraisals of their accomplishments by qualified scholars.

The publication plan for *DLB* resulted from two years of preparation. The project was proposed to Bruccoli Clark by Frederick C. Ruffner, president of the Gale Research Company, in November 1975. After specimen entries were prepared and typeset, an advisory board was formed to refine the entry format and develop the series rationale. In meetings held during 1976, the publisher, series editors, and advisory board approved the scheme for a comprehensive biographical dictionary of persons who contributed to North American literature. Editorial work on the first volume began in January 1977, and it was published in 1978. In order to make *DLB* more than a reference tool and to compile volumes that individually have claim to status as literary history, it was decided to organize volumes by topic, period, or genre. Each of these free-

standing volumes provides a biographical-bibliographical guide and overview for a particular area of literature. We are convinced that this organization — as opposed to a single alphabet method — constitutes a valuable innovation in the presentation of reference material. The volume plan necessarily requires many decisions for the placement and treatment of authors who might properly be included in two or three volumes. In some instances a major figure will be included in separate volumes, but with different entries emphasizing the aspect of his career appropriate to each volume. Ernest Hemingway, for example, is represented in *American Writers in Paris, 1920–1939* by an entry focusing on his expatriate apprenticeship; he is also in *American Novelists, 1910–1945* with an entry surveying his entire career. Each volume includes a cumulative index of the subject authors and articles. Comprehensive indexes to the entire series are planned.

With volume ten in 1982 it was decided to enlarge the scope of *DLB*. By the end of 1986 twenty-one volumes treating British literature had been published, and volumes for Commonwealth and Modern European literature were in progress. The series has been further augmented by the *DLB Yearbooks* (since 1981) which update published entries and add new entries to keep the *DLB* current with contemporary activity. There have also been *DLB Documentary Series* volumes which provide biographical and critical source materials for figures whose work is judged to have particular interest for students. One of these companion volumes is entirely devoted to Tennessee Williams.

We define literature as the *intellectual commerce of a nation:* not merely as belles lettres but as that ample and complex process by which ideas are generated, shaped, and transmitted. *DLB* entries are not limited to "creative writers" but extend to other figures who in their time and in their way influenced the mind of a people. Thus the series encompasses historians, journalists, publishers, and screenwriters. By this means readers of *DLB* may be aided to perceive literature not as cult scripture in the keeping of intellectual high priests but firmly positioned at the center of a nation's life.

From an unpublished section of Mark Twain's autobiography, copyright by the Mark Twain Company

DLB includes the major writers appropriate to each volume and those standing in the ranks immediately behind them. Scholarly and critical counsel has been sought in deciding which minor figures to include and how full their entries should be. Wherever possible, useful references are made to figures who do not warrant separate entries.

Each *DLB* volume has a volume editor responsible for planning the volume, selecting the figures for inclusion, and assigning the entries. Volume editors are also responsible for preparing, where appropriate, appendices surveying the major periodicals and literary and intellectual movements for their volumes, as well as lists of further readings. Work on the series as a whole is coordinated at the Bruccoli Clark Layman editorial center in Columbia, South Carolina, where the editorial staff is responsible for accuracy of the published volumes.

One feature that distinguishes *DLB* is the illustration policy – its concern with the iconography of literature. Just as an author is influenced by his surroundings, so is the reader's understanding of the author enhanced by a knowledge of his environment. Therefore *DLB* volumes include not only drawings, paintings, and photographs of authors, often depicting them at various stages in their careers, but also illustrations of their families and places where they lived. Title pages are regularly reproduced in facsimile along with dust jackets for modern authors. The dust jackets are a special feature of *DLB* because they often document better than anything else the way in which an author's work was perceived in its own time. Specimens of the writers' manuscripts are included when feasible.

Samuel Johnson rightly decreed that "The chief glory of every people arises from its authors." The purpose of the *Dictionary of Literary Biography* is to compile literary history in the surest way available to us – by accurate and comprehensive treatment of the lives and work of those who contributed to it.

The *DLB* Advisory Board

Introduction

The term *bibliophile* derives from two Greek words: *biblio* meaning "book" (hence the Bible, long regarded as the book par excellence), and *philos,* meaning "love," as in philosopher, a lover of wisdom, and philanthropist, a lover of humanity. Both terms generally apply to bibliophiles. Eric Quayle in his *The Collector's Book of Books* (New York: C. N. Potter, 1971) defines the bibliophile as "an otherwise rational member of the community consumed by a love of books." More respectfully, in his *How To Buy Rare Books* (Oxford: Phaidon, 1985) William Rees-Mogg explains the love of books by quoting from John Milton's *Areopagitica* (1644):

> Books are not absolutely dead things, but doe contain a potencie of life in them to be as active as that soule was whose progeny they are; nay they do preserve as in a violl the purest efficacie and extraction of that living intellect that bred them. . . . A good Booke is the pretious life-blood of a master spirit, imbalm'd and treasur'd up on purpose to a life beyond life.

Though this statement is as applicable to a current paperback version of *Paradise Lost* as it is to the first edition of that work, the great collector A. Edward Newton observed that reading a reprint is like kissing a pretty woman through a pane of glass. In a first edition one is as close as one is likely to get — unless one can secure a manuscript of the text — to the author's initial intentions and thoughts. Other contemporary editions may also capture the writer's mind, of which later versions are but pale reflections. Moreover, as one reads a first or second edition of *Paradise Lost* one looks at the type, feels the paper, holds the very text that Milton's contemporaries saw, held, and felt. The physical appearance of a work conveys information. For example, the quarto format of William Shakespeare's plays published in his lifetime indicates that these works were not taken seriously as literature; important works were published in the larger folio size. The First Folio thus indicates that by 1623 Shakespeare's plays were more highly regarded, and when eighteenth-century editors added notes and a biography they showed that Shakespeare had been admitted to the pantheon of classical authors.

In his *Black Riders: The Visible Language of Modernism* (Princeton: Princeton University Press, 1993)

Jerome J. McGann argues that even for twentieth-century works the original form in which a work appears — its very typography and layout — embodies meaning. To read the poetry of William Blake without the accompanying illustrations is like listening to Ludwig van Beethoven's *Emperor* Concerto without the piano. To read eighteenth-century poetry in a twentieth-century printing is to listen to harpsichord music on the piano. Further, each reprinting is a translation, as editors intervene to determine which version to copy, which readings to ignore or relegate to footnotes — or worse, endnotes — where one may skip them and where their position and smaller typeface indicate their lesser importance. To read a modern edition of *Paradise Lost* or John Keats's "To Autumn" is to see through a glass darkly; to examine the Cambridge University manuscript of the former or the Harvard University manuscript of the latter is to see work and writer, as it were, face to face.

To this high-mindedness one must add other motives of a bibliophiliac, such as the love of fine printing, fine paper, wide margins, and beautiful leather bindings. Nor should one ignore money as a motive. The question of what books make good investments is often answered differently by collectors, dealers, and librarians. Collectible books, however, are not necessarily beautiful, old, or expensive. The 1640 *Bay Psalm Book,* the first book printed in British North America, of which only eleven copies are known, is printed on inferior paper with inferior type, the product of amateur presswork. Every new bookshop has on its shelves future collectibles priced the same as their forgettable neighbors. As such, part of the genius of the collector lies not in writing a large check for some item that many others want but in writing a small check — or in rescuing from the trash a work that others do not appreciate. As John Carter, author of *Taste and Technique in Book Collecting* (1948) and other works on the subject, has observed, "In book collecting it's not the early bird who catches the worm, but the bird who knows a worm when he sees one." Thus, the first edition of Edward FitzGerald's translation of the *Rubaiyat of Omar Khayyam* (London: Bernard Quaritch, 1859) was remaindered and found few purchasers, even for a penny. In 1979 a copy sold at Christie's in London for $8,775. At Sotheby's in

London Henry Stevens found a copy of the *Bay Psalm Book* in a lot identified as "Psalms other Editions, 1630 to 1675 black letter, a parcel." He secured the lot for nineteen 19 s. ($4.75) and sold the *Bay Psalm Book* to James Lenox for $400. In 1980 a lucky buyer secured a copy of the first edition of Edmund Spenser's *The Shepheardes Calendar* (1579), one of only seven copies known, for a few pounds at a country sale in Derbyshire. The book was resold at Christie's in London for $100,320.

Bibliophily has a long history. Barry B. Powell argues in *Homer and the Origin of the Greek Alphabet* (Cambridge: Cambridge University Press, 1991) that the first transcription of Homer, and hence the origin of the Greek alphabet, derived from someone's desire to own a copy of the *Odyssey* and the *Iliad*. In the seventh century B.C. Ashurbanipul, the last great Assyrian king, assembled a large collection of clay tablets, now housed in the British Library; he gathered these tablets in part for reasons of prestige but also in part because he loved books. Yet these are modern instances. The psychological motivations of bibliophiles are not easily traced, but one could posit that people are collectors by nature. The cave paintings at Lascaux (15,000–10,000 B.C.) reflect a desire to preserve a record of events and to possess beautiful artifacts, two key impulses that underlie bibliophily. Many bibliophiles begin as collectors of other things. Wilmarth Sheldon Lewis started with houseflies, proceeded to stamps, and concluded with Horace Walpole and eighteenth-century literature. Thomas Pennant Barton assembled a fine botanical garden as well as a library devoted to dramatic literature. Aristotle begins his *Metaphysics* by observing, "All men naturally desire knowledge," and this desire also contributes to bibliophily, as one may see in the career of Henry R. Wagner or Amy Lowell, whose libraries made possible their important contributions to learning.

While the reasons for collecting are as diverse as the collectors themselves, the methodology is fairly standard. Any book collection depends on the efforts of booksellers, bibliographers, librarians, and, of course, the collectors themselves, the four categories represented in this volume. The bookseller's livelihood depends on his or her ability to locate desirable items, a skill requiring knowledge of people as well as of books; for instance, a prime *Pickwick Papers* (1836–1837) in parts, a work that will quicken the pulse of a Charles Dickens devotee, would not interest the collector of incunabula (books printed before 1 January 1501). The bookseller must also recognize the limits of a customer's purse; interest can easily exceed ability to pay. Some booksellers, such as Gabriel Wells, seem to have been more familiar with their clients

than with the bibliographical intricacies of their wares. Others follow the example of Stevens and A. S. W. Rosenbach and succeed in large measure because of their keen bibliographic knowledge. Already noted is Stevens's recognition of a *Bay Psalm Book* among an assortment of unconsidered trifles. Rosenbach discovered the first known copy of Samuel Johnson's *Prologue Spoken at the Opening of the Theatre in Drury-Lane 1747* amid a stack of eighteenth-century poems. In the 1923 Britwell sale in London, Rosenbach spent fifty-one pounds for Philip Pain's *Daily Meditations; or Quotidian Preparations for and Considerations of Death and Eternity* (Cambridge: Marmaduke Johnson, 1668). Rosenbach's biographers Edwin Wolf II and John F. Fleming describe the volume as "a dull-sounding theological tract" that interested none of the other dealers at the auction. Even the Sotheby auctioneer was surprised that Rosenbach wanted the volume. Rosenbach was the only person in the room to know that the "Cambridge" of the imprint was in Massachusetts, not England, and that he had secured the only known copy of the first book of poetry printed in British North America.

Leona Rostenberg talks of "Finger-Spitzengefuhl," the ability to detect a treasure through some sixth sense. At the 1923 Britwell sale Rosenbach bought a copy of William Bradford's 1694 *Laws of New York,* one of the first books printed in that colony. Rosenbach felt something curious in the binding and summoned Wilberforce Eames, bibliographer of the New York Public Library, to examine the work. Eames found a dozen fragments and nearly an entire pamphlet, all printed by Bradford and some never before seen. Madeleine B. Stern tells of finding various treasures in piles of unpromising pamphlets. Yet it is bibliographic knowledge, not "finger-spitzengefuhl," that confirms the discovery. Rostenberg discovered the rare first edition of Arthur Young's *A Six Weeks Tour Through the Southern Counties of England and Wales* (London: W. Nicoll, 1768) as a Columbia University Library discard. A true bibliophile, she recognized its value where others had not.

The quest for books takes the dealer to diverse places: from the museumlike atmosphere of Maggs Brothers in Berkeley Square, London, with its glass-front oak and mahogany bookcases, to the discard shelves of Manhattan's Morningside Heights, from a country house to a cathedral library. Since the seventeenth century the auction has helped replenish the springs of book collecting. The first recorded book auction in England took place in 1676, when the library of Dr. Lazarus Seaman was dispersed. In auctions, as in all other forms of book buying, variety prevails; dealers explore boxes at estate sales or peruse an elaborately prepared catalogue describing a single item to be sold at Christie's in London or Sotheby's in New York (both houses now operate in both cities and elsewhere). Auctions afford booksellers the opportunity to add to stock or earn commissions by executing bids from customers. These sales also can generate publicity for books and dealers. George D. Smith and Rosenbach were adept at manipulating the reporting of spectacular sales at auction and at times even made the sales noteworthy by bidding extravagantly. At the 15 February 1926 sale of the Melk Abbey Gutenberg Bible at Anderson's Gallery in New York, Rosenbach was authorized by Edward S. Harkness to bid up to $75,000; Rosenbach bought the book for $106,000. Harkness gladly paid, and Rosenbach enjoyed the press coverage that resulted from his bidding a record price for a printed book. The purchase was reported in newspapers from the Barrier *Daily Truth* in New South Wales to *Die 20ste Jahr Zeit* in Stuttgart. Rosenbach's record stood for twenty years, until he broke it again with another bid exceeding his authority, when he purchased a copy of the *Bay Psalm Book* for $151,000 in 1947.

Auctions are chancy affairs. Two determined bidders can drive up the price of an item well beyond what anyone will again offer for it. In 1929 Wells paid $68,000 for Percy Bysshe Shelley's annotated copy of *Queen Mab* (London: Printed for P.B. Shelley, 1813). He never could sell it; after his death it brought a little over a tenth of what Wells had bid. At that same Jerome Kern sale in New York a first edition of Henry Fielding's *The History of Tom Jones, A Foundling* (London: A. Millar, 1749) brought $39,000, a sum that in 1993 could secure about twenty copies of that work. Conversely, when competition is not keen, a bidder can secure a bargain. Ordinarily, precisely because auctions permit competition, they serve as indicators of the rare-book market, which differs from stocks and precious metals. An ounce of gold in London or Zurich will cost virtually the same. A share of stock will not differ in price from brokerage to brokerage. However, one might facetiously but not inaccurately define a rare book as one priced identically in two dealers' catalogues. While auctions do not establish a set price for an item, they do indicate what is collectible and to what extent. The George Brinley, Jr., sales (1879–1893) encouraged an interest in Americana; the Thomas W. Streeter sales (1966–1969) reflected the extent to which prices of Americana had soared since the last quarter of the nineteenth century. On the other hand, the 1935 Seth S. Terry and 1939 John A. Spoor sales demonstrated that the high prices re-

alized by Kern's books could not be maintained during the Great Depression.

Though they are bibliophiles, booksellers can rarely afford to retain their finds. Rosenbach placed prohibitively high prices on items with which he did not want to part; some he refused to sell even when solicited. At his death he left an impressive library. The French bibliopole Edouart Rahir sequestered about 750 illustrated books and examples of fine bindings. When part of this collection was sold at auction in 1930, six years after his death, it set a three-day record of $500,000. These dealers were exceptional, since most do not compete with their customers for rarities but instead act in effect as partners with collectors for their mutual benefit. Stevens's autobiography is aptly entitled *Recollections of Mr. James Lenox of New York* (1886) because Stevens's reputation rests not only on the great books that he found and on his publications but also on the great books that he supplied to the major nineteenth-century libraries such as those of Lenox, Brinley, John Carter Brown, Edward A. Crowninshield, and George Livermore. Smith's connection with Henry E. Huntington was crucial for both men's success in the world of books. It was Charles Sessler, a Philadelphia bookseller, who initially interested Huntington in book collecting, and an engraving in Sessler's window started Lessing Rosenwald on his quest for fine prints and early illustrated books. Rosenbach was a great bookman because he supplied other great bookmen with what they wanted. Indeed, virtually all of Rosenbach's major purchases were executed either on commission or with a potential customer in mind.

In *Der Narrenschiff* (Basel, 1494) Sebastian Brant mocks the book collector, placing him at the head of what Brant calls the "dunce's dance." According to the Edwin H. Zeydel translation, Brant's foolish collector declares:

> Of splendid books I own no end,
> But few that I can comprehend.
> ***
> I, too, have many books indeed
> But don't peruse them very much;
> Why should I plague myself with such?
> My head in booklore I'll not bury,
> Who studies hard grows visionary.
> ***
> My ears are covered up for me,
> If they were not, an ass I'd be.

Indeed, the Roman satirist Lucian had also mocked bibliophiles. However, in his *Philobiblon* (Durham, 1345), the first book devoted exclusively to the love of books, Richard de Bury defends his bibliophily against satirists:

> In books I behold the dead alive; in books I foresee things to come; in books the affairs of war are displayed; from books proceed the rightful laws of peace. All things decay and waste away in time, and those whom Saturn begets he ceaseth not to devour. Oblivion would overwhelm all the glory of the world, had not God provided for mortals the remedies of books.

As this passage indicates, the collector buys books because he or she wishes to learn. Yet not every scholar or even every book buyer is a collector. The collector has a plan, a vision; the resulting library coheres. George Ticknor's collection of Iberian literature contained many choice items, but the library was greater than the sum of its parts because the works illuminated and reflected upon each other. The presence of seventy-nine First Folios in whole or in part in the Henry Clay Folger Shakespeare Library has made possible textual studies that otherwise could have been undertaken only with great difficulty if those same volumes had been dispersed in many different locations.

The collector is a preserver as well as a student of the book. Brinley recognized the importance of Americana at a time when others regarded this material as no more than wastepaper. He understood the significance of the unprepossessing sermon that might contain valuable information, the town directory or local history that would someday benefit researchers. Another New Englander, Thomas Prince, sought out manuscripts relating to the early history of his region. He intended, he declared, "to lay hold on every Book, Pamphlet, or Paper, both in Print, and manuscript, which was written by Persons who lived here, or that had any Tendency to enlighten our Heritage." Among the works he owned was William Bradford's manuscript "Of Plymouth Plantation," a work that the British took with them when they evacuated Boston during the American Revolution and which England returned to the United States largely because it contained Prince's bookplate. Prince's interest in his native state led to his acquiring five copies of the *Bay Psalm Book,* nearly half of the surviving copies, and he also preserved the journal of John Winthrop, an important source of information about the early history of Massachusetts. To compile his *History of Printing in America* (1810) Isaiah Thomas secured not only printed books but also many early newspapers and over three hundred broadsides. Carl Cannon observes in *American Book Collectors and Collecting from Colonial Times to the Present* (New York:

H. W. Wilson, 1941) that Thomas thus "preserved vital records of early American culture which must otherwise inevitably have been lost, and prepared the way for increases in the materials of our common heritage." The records of the Virginia Company that had sponsored early southern settlements lay neglected in the library of Peyton Randolph until they were rescued by Thomas Jefferson.

Even when collectors do not themselves secure an item, they can call attention to previously ignored material and so encourage others to value and preserve them. After the Brinley sales no one was likely to regard an *Eliot Indian Bible,* the first Bible printed in British North America, as scrap paper. Through his book buying and his writing Newton fostered a renewed interest in eighteenth-century British literature and so made these works collectible. Lewis's publicized pursuit of Walpoliana prompted the discovery of many previously unknown letters to and from Walpole. The publicity surrounding Charles Goodspeed's sale of a copy of Edgar Allan Poe's *Tamerlane and Other Poems* (Boston: Calvin F. S. Thomas, 1827) — one of five then known — to Owen D. Young for $17,500 led to Goodspeed's being offered yet another copy, previously unrecorded.

To paraphrase Falstaff's boast in *Henry IV, part 1,* collectors are not only learned in themselves but also are the cause of learning in others. Indeed, collectors may be regarded as the unacknowledged educators of mankind. One way in which they have filled this role is through their own research and writings that have been made possible by their collections. Prince's *Chronological History of New England* (1737-1755), Lewis's monumental edition of the correspondence of Walpole, Ticknor's *History of Spanish Literature* (1849), and Lowell's biography of Keats (1925) are examples of the intimate relationship between scholarship and collecting.

Not all collectors are scholars, and not all scholars are collectors, but many students have benefitted from libraries gathered by others. Henry Harrisse's important *Bibliotheca Americana Vetustissima* (1866), an annotated bibliography of early works relating to the New World, would have been impossible to produce without the cooperation of the works' owners, especially Samuel Latham Mitchell Barlow, who gathered an extensive library of these books. When Samuel F. Haven, librarian of the American Antiquarian Society, requested the loan of Brinley's copy of *Great Voyages* (Frankfurt, 1590-1619) by Theodore de Bry, with its accounts of early explorations of the New World, Brinley replied, "There is nothing in my library too good for you." John Hammond Trumbull of the Watkinson Library in Brinley's home town of Hartford, Connecticut enjoyed the use of Brinley's library for research. Luther Livingston's bibliography of Charles Lamb was made possible in large part by his access to the fine collection gathered by John A. Spoor. The Philadelphia collector James Logan owned a copy of Isaac Newton's *Principia*; the inventor and mathematician Thomas Godfrey and the botanist John Bartram both used Logan's library.

The collector Daniel Willard Fiske wrote in a letter from Florence that the book collector resembles the miser: "It gratifies him to see his treasures accumulating – to know that today he is richer by a score of volumes than yesterday." Yet Fiske himself, despite differences with Cornell University, gave the school his comprehensive Icelandic library as well as some four thousand volumes relating to Petrarch and an extensive Dante collection. In "The Chief End of Book Madness," which appeared in the *Library of Congress Quarterly Journal of Current Acquisitions* in 1945, Lawrence C. Wroth observed, "The question the historian of this and the last century will ask himself when he considers the libraries of the United States will not be 'What has the book collector done for these libraries?' but 'What would these libraries have been without the book collector?'" As Ruth Shephard Grannis wrote in "American Book Collecting and the Growth of Libraries," published as part of *The Book in America* (New York: R. R. Bowker, 1939), "The public libraries in America have been the outgrowth of the generosity and wise provision of private collectors of books."

Such benefactions date back to antiquity. The great Hellenistic libraries at Alexandria and Pergamum were in fact private royal collections opened to the public. Sir Thomas Bodley in the early seventeenth-century gave his name and books to the Bodleian Library, Oxford University. The oldest university in the United States takes its name from John Harvard, who, when he died at the age of thirty-one in 1638, left over three hundred volumes to the newly established college in Cambridge, Massachusetts. Prince left his collection to the Old South Church in Boston; eventually, in 1866, these books became the property of the Boston Public Library, which had been established through the efforts of, among others, Ticknor. His 1871 bequest of his Spanish and Portuguese titles and a trust fund to be used to add to the collection made the Boston Public Library one of the premier resources for the study of the literature of the Iberian Peninsula. Ben-

jamin Franklin's books enriched the American Philosophical Society, the Library Company of Philadelphia, and the Academy of Arts and Sciences.

After the destruction of the first Library of Congress in 1814, Congress acquired 6,479 volumes from Jefferson for $23,950. This new library was twice the size of the previous one. Jefferson set about rebuilding his personal collection and hoped to give it to the University of Virginia. Financial exigencies made this disposition impossible, but in 1829 the American Philosophical Society bought most of Jefferson's works dealing with Anglo-Saxon. Jefferson's sometime political rival John Adams left his books to his hometown of Quincy, Massachusetts; in 1897 what remained of this library went to the Boston Public Library. Adams's son John Quincy also left his books to Quincy. Thomas's donation of his library to the American Antiquarian Society laid the foundation for that institution's fine collections. The New York Public Library has received many bequests since its establishment, none perhaps more important than the books of Lenox, who in 1870 opened his library to scholars and so in effect created the city's first free public library. The number of libraries and public collections around the country that bear the names of bibliophiles attests to collectors' generosity and the debt owed them by the public, from the H. H. Bancroft Library at the University of California, Berkeley and the William Andrews Clark, Jr., Library at UCLA to the William L. Clements Library at the University of Michigan, the John Carter Brown Library at Brown University, the Harry E. Widener Library at Harvard, and the Chauncey Brewster Tinker collection at the Beinecke Rare Books and Manuscripts Library at Yale.

Even when private libraries have not been given to institutions, the sale of these collections have often benefitted the public. In his will Brinley left money to five libraries to allow them to buy his books being sold at auction. Thomas W. Streeter left money to eighteen institutions. Theodore Low DeVinne, master printer, assembled an extensive library of fifteenth- and sixteenth-century books as well as examples of nineteenth-century fine printing. The Newberry Library in Chicago was a major purchaser when this collection was sold at auction. While one may wish that the Brinley or DeVinne collections had been kept intact, one must recognize the need for infusions of good books into the marketplace to allow others to share the joys and creativity of collecting. Also, such dispersals through auction or private sale allow buyers, whether they be public libraries or individuals, to choose what is wanted and ignore the superfluous. Henry Raup Wagner, who donated valuable materials to libraries, believed that institutions were more appreciative of their purchases than of their gift acquisitions; libraries buy to fill gaps, and donations often include duplicates and items that did not match a library's needs. Such dispersals of collections constitute yet another contribution of the collector to book culture – the perpetuation of the process of building libraries. The French collector Edmond de Goncourt ordered in his will that his books be sold at auction "so that the pleasure which the acquiring of each one of them has given me shall be given again . . . to some collector of my own tastes."

Many factors can contribute to the forming of a collector's taste. Brinley's familial associations with his country's past probably encouraged him to collect Americana. Folger's decision to collect Shakespeare was inspired by his wife and by his reading of Ralph Waldo Emerson's observations on the playwright. Lenox's religious impulses started his collecting of Bibles. Bibliographies can also influence a collector. Booksellers may be bibliographers: the catalogues of Ernest Dawson and his sons Glen and Muir have become important references for those interested in Asiatic books, Californiana, the American frontier, and the American Southwest. Collectors, too, can contribute to bibliography. Leonard L. Mackall, who built a large collection of German literature, served as president of the Bibliographical Society of America. More often, the role of bibliographer depends upon but is distinct from that of collector or dealer. John Hammond Trumbull prepared the catalogue of Brinley's library; Rosenbach turned to Eames to analyze the pamphlets bound up in the 1694 Bradford *Laws*. Douglas C. McMurtrie's *Early Printing in New Orleans, 1764–1810* relied on the fifty-thousand volume collection of Edward A. Parsons, president of the Louisiana Historical Society. Harrisse, though he assembled an important collection of books that enriched the Library of Congress and the Bibliothèque Nationale, was primarily a bibliographer, cataloguing Barlow's library and advising him on what to buy. Harrisse was thus fulfilling the dual function of the bibliographer – helping to bring order to existing collections and at the same time pointing out what is collectible through catalogues and other publications.

In 1755 Samuel Johnson, in his *Dictionary of the English Language* (London: Printed by W. Strahan, For J. and P. Knapton; T. and T. Longman; C. Hitch and L. Hawes; A. Millar; and R. and J. Dodsley), defined "bibliography" as "the writing of books."

W. W. Greg's article, "What Is Bibliography," in volume twelve of the *Transactions of the Bibliographical Society* (1914) provided a more precise definition, dividing the bibliographer's practice into systematic (enumerative) bibliography and critical (or analytical or material) bibliography. The former Greg defined as "the classification of individual books according to some guiding principle," that is, the creation of a list, with or without annotations. The catalogues of the Dawsons and Harrisse fit into this category. Such activity dates at least as far back as the early days of the Alexandrian Library, when Callimachus of Cyrene compiled a catalogue using 120 papyrus rolls that divided the library into eight categories: drama, epic and lyric, law, philosophy, history, oratory, rhetoric, and miscellaneous. One of his successors, Aristophanes of Byzantium, drafted a selective bibliography that listed major works. He thus created a canon used by later copyists and so helped determine which works from classical antiquity would survive. Georg Wolfgang Franz Panzer's *Annales typographici ab artis inventae origine ad annum MD* (Nuremberg: J. E. Zeh, 1793–1797) listed incunabula (a term introduced by another bibliographer, Cornelis a Beughem, in his 1688 listing of fifteenth-century printed books, *Incunabula typographiae*) chronologically by city and so demonstrated the progress of the printing press across Europe.

Defending the compilation of his *Catalogue of English Printed Books* (London: Printed by John Windet for Andrew Maunsell, 1595), Maunsell wrote in his address to the "Professors of the Sciences":

> It may be thought . . . a needless labour to make a Catalogue of English printed Books: yet to men of judgment I hope it will be thought necessary, for if learned men study and spend their bodies and good to further the knowledge of their Countrymen, for the good of the common weale, methinketh it were pity their studies, and the benefit of them should be hidden.

This desire to make known to others the works that are available on a particular subject or by a certain author or in a certain place is itself an important contribution to knowledge, for, as Maunsell wrote, he compiled his work so "that those which desire to set forth more Books for the benefit of their Country, may see what is already extant upon any argument."

The systematic bibliographies compiled by Harrisse and McMurtrie interest many other than the rare-book collector. Harrisse's *Bibliotheca Americana Vetustissima* illuminates the sixteenth century.

Harrisse shows how the discoveries of Christopher Columbus, Vasco de Gama, and other explorers prompted a renewed interest in geography, as revealed by the 1508 new and revised edition of Ptolemy's *Geographia* (Rome), which includes the first engraved map of the New World. Harrisse also comments on Pantaleone Guistiniani's 1516 Polyglot Psalter (Turin: Peter–Paul–Porrus). In the margin of verse 4, Psalm 19, Guistiniani includes a biography of Columbus, implying that the explorer fulfilled the prophecy, "Yet their line goes out through all the earth, and their words to the end of the world." Harrisse thus demonstrates how the discovery of America affected even theology. Henry Raup Wagner's works fostered an interest in the American Southwest, George Watson Cole's publications include thoughts about the way books were produced in Shakespeare's day. Literary critics, historians of the book and of ideas, draw on the work of systematic bibliographers in their joint efforts to understand an age or author.

Fredson Bowers, John Cook Wyllie, and Cole exemplify the analytical as well as the systematic bibliographer. The analytical bibliographer is concerned with the book not only as an embodiment of ideas but also as a physical object: its paper; ink; type; "its printing and publishing history," in the words of Bowers; and its transmission. Edwin Eliott Willoughby, in *The Uses of Bibliography to the Students of Literature and History* (1957), writes that understanding how a book is created physically allows one "more correctly and more fully to interpret the book or other printed documents," even when individuals try to disguise important details. Greg asserted that "It is only by the application of a rigorous bibliographical method that the last drop of information can be squeezed out of a literary document," or any other written or printed work.

For example, around 1633 John Frederick Stam in Amsterdam printed six editions of the Geneva Bible, the English version favored by Puritans. To elude customs officials and agents of King Charles I, who would have seized the book for commercial and political reasons – the Geneva Bible rejected the Stuart view of the divine right of kings – Stam duplicated the 1599 London title page of the Bible. Studies of type and paper have exposed the deception and so illuminated the mentality of the English in the 1630s. One sees that the authorized version of the Bible did not supplant the Geneva Bible and its doctrines and that many continued to read the older translation.

One of the most fascinating examples of bibliographic examination concerns the fabrications of

Thomas James Wise, himself a noted bibliographer and a friend of John Henry Wrenn. Wise produced many spurious nineteenth-century first editions, including the 1847 "Reading" edition of the sonnets of Elizabeth Barrett Browning. According to the story told by Wise, Browning gave her husband, Robert Browning, the manuscript of the sonnets at Pisa in 1847. He was so impressed with the work that he sent a copy of the poems to their friend Mary Russell Mitford in England, and she oversaw the publication. John Carter and Graham Pollard revealed the deception by determining that the paper was not the kind used in 1847 and the typeface was too modern for the purported date. Gabriel Wells's failure to appreciate the bibliographical evidence of Carter and Pollard led him to accept the Wise pamphlets as authentic. The discovery interested collectors, since the Wise fabrications were commanding high prices in the guise of authentic first editions. In the case of the Browning sonnets and in other instances, the exposure also clarified aspects of biography. Elizabeth Barrett Browning did not show her sonnets to her husband until 1849, and she did so at Bagni di Lucca, not at Pisa.

Wyllie and Bowers pioneered techniques to differentiate apparently identical works. Wyllie explored differences in typography and gutter measurements; Bowers was the first to make rigorous distinctions among states, issues, impressions, and editions – and thus clarify the printing history of a book. The importance of such knowledge is evident in the case of the Shakespeare First Folio. The innermost sheets of each gathering were printed first, so that the typesetter might find himself with too much space when he got to the outermost sheets. On the last lines of the second column of page 40 of the tragedies, therefore, the printer has divided line 95 of act 3, scene 1 of *Titus Andronicus* into two lines. On page 95 of this section of the folio the typesetter has printed the opening of act 5 of *Timon of Athens* as poetry rather than prose to take up more space. Conversely, the printer of page 257 of the tragedies found himself a line short in act 1, scene 5, lines 56 to 57 of *Hamlet* and so fused two lines into one. To what extent, then, is Shakespeare's later, freer verse evidence of poetic maturity? How much of the metrical pattern is attributable to typesetters trying to make the text fit the page? A similar question arises with James Joyce's *Ulysses* (1922), set into type by non-English-speaking typesetters. How many puns attributed to Joyce are actually typographic errors?

Also represented in this volume, the librarian may be a collector, a bibliographer, even a bookseller. David Randall was head of Scribners rare-book department for twenty-one years before he became head of the Lilly Library at Indiana University in 1956. Tinker and Mackall were librarians as well as collectors and bibliographers. Like all other bibliophiles, librarians should know and love books, but their ordinary task is to acquire and then organize and make accessible the books that come under their care. The younger J. P. Morgan relied on the judgment of Belle da Costa Greene, who knew his collection at least as well as he did himself. Wyllie and Tinker promoted the growth of their institutions' libraries; Greene and Tinker also enriched their libraries with gifts of their own. Working with collectors, dealers, and bibliographers, librarians indicate what works are available and which are needed. Just as bibliographers show how books relate to each other, which works are important – and why – so librarians through their cataloguing bring order to the world of books. The four types of bibliophily combine to create the book culture of a time and place. In discussing a representative sample, this volume seeks to make their work more fully understood and to celebrate their efforts.

Acknowledgments

This book was produced by Bruccoli Clark Layman, Inc. Karen L. Rood is senior editor for the *Dictionary of Literary Biography* series. Dennis Lynch was the in-house editor.

Production coordinator is George F. Dodge. Photography editors are Edward Scott and Robert S. McConnell. Layout and graphics supervisor is Penney L. Haughton. Copyediting supervisor is Bill Adams. Typesetting supervisor is Kathleen M. Flanagan. Julie E. Frick is editorial associate. The production staff includes Phyllis A. Avant, Joseph Matthew Bruccoli, Ann M. Cheschi, Melody W. Clegg, Patricia Coate, Wilma Weant Dague, Brigitte B. de Guzman, Denise W. Edwards, Sarah A. Estes, Joyce Fowler, Laurel M. Gladden, Stephanie C. Hatchell, Rebecca Mayo, Kathy Lawler Merlette, Pamela D. Norton, Delores I. Plastow, Patricia F. Salisbury, and William L. Thomas, Jr.

Walter W. Ross and Deborah M. Chasteen did library research. They were assisted by the following librarians at the Thomas Cooper Library of the University of South Carolina: Roger Mortimer, Linda Holderfield and the interlibrary-loan staff; reference librarians Gwen Baxter, Daniel Boice, Faye Chadwell, Cathy Eckman, Gary Geer, Qun "Gerry" Jiao, Jean Rhyne, Carol Tobin, Carolyn Tyler, Virginia Weathers, Elizabeth Whiznant, and Connie Widney; circulation-department head Thomas Marcil; and acquisitions-searching supervisor David Haggard. The following librarians and book dealers generously provided material: William Cagle and Joel Silver of The Lilly Library, Indiana University; and Ann Freudenberg, Kendon Stubbs, and Edmund Berkeley, Jr., of the University of Virginia Library; and Terry Halliday at the William Reese Company, New Haven, Connecticut.

American Book-Collectors
and
Bibliographers
First Series

Dictionary of Literary Biography

Hubert Howe Bancroft
(5 May 1832 – 2 March 1918)

Annegret S. Ogden
Bancroft Library, University of California

See also the Bancroft entry in *DLB 47: American Historians, 1866–1912.*

BOOKS: *The Native Races of the Pacific States of North America,* 5 volumes (San Francisco: A. L. Bancroft, 1874–1875);

Central America, 3 volumes (San Francisco: A. L. Bancroft, 1882–1887);

History of Mexico, 6 volumes (volumes 1–5, San Francisco: A. L. Bancroft, 1883; volume 6, San Francisco: History Company, 1888);

The Early American Chronicler (San Francisco: A. L. Bancroft, 1883);

History of the Northwest Coast, 2 volumes (San Francisco: A. L. Bancroft, 1884);

California, 7 volumes (San Francisco: A. L. Bancroft, 1884–1890);

Life of Porfirio Díaz, 2 volumes (San Francisco: A. L. Bancroft, 1885);

Alaska, 1730–1885 (San Francisco: A. L. Bancroft, 1886);

History of Oregon, 2 volumes (San Francisco: History Company, 1886–1888);

British Columbia, 1792–1887 (San Francisco: History Company, 1887);

Popular Tribunals, 2 volumes (San Francisco: History Company, 1887);

Arizona and New Mexico, 1530–1880 (San Francisco: History Company, 1888);

California inter pocula (San Francisco: History Company, 1888);

California Pastoral, 1769–1848 (San Francisco: History Company, 1888);

Hubert Howe Bancroft

3

History of Utah, 1540–1886 (San Francisco: History Company, 1889);

History of Nevada, Colorado, and Wyoming, 1540–1888 (San Francisco: History Company, 1890);

History of Texas and the North Mexican States, 2 volumes (San Francisco: History Company, 1890);

History of Washington, Idaho and Montana, 1845–1889 (San Francisco: History Company, 1890);

Essays and Miscellany (San Francisco: History Company, 1890);

Literary Industries (San Francisco: History Company, 1890);

The Book of the Fair; An Historical and Descriptive Presentation of the World's Science, Art, and Industry, As Viewed Through the Columbia Exposition at Chicago in 1893, 2 volumes (Chicago & San Francisco: Bancroft Company, 1893);

Resources and Development of Mexico (San Francisco: Bancroft Company, 1893);

Achievements of Civilization; The Book of Wealth, 10 volumes (New York: Bancroft Company, 1896–1908);

The New Pacific (New York: Bancroft Company, 1900; revised, 1912);

Some Cities and San Francisco (New York: Bancroft Company, 1907);

Retrospection, Political and Personal (New York: Bancroft Company, 1912; revised, 1913);

Why a World Centre of Industry at San Francisco Bay? (New York: Bancroft Company, 1916);

In These Latter Days (Chicago: Blakely-Oswald, 1917);

History of the Life of Leland Stanford: A Character Study (Oakland: Biobooks, 1952).

OTHER: *Chronicles of the Builders of the Commonwealth,* 7 volumes, edited by Bancroft (San Francisco: History Company, 1891–1892).

"I was wound up by my mother to work," wrote Hubert Howe Bancroft in his autobiography, *Literary Industries* (1890), which chronicles his progress from bookseller to book collector, from amateur historian to producer-publisher of the mammoth history *California* (1884–1890). Published in seven hefty tomes and backed up by thirty-eight volumes of regional histories – some found in multi-volume editions of their own – it covers the territories of Central America, Mexico, Texas, and the Pacific Northwest, Alaska, and Utah and the Rocky Mountain states. To support his research, Bancroft gathered together, for over twenty-five years, a collection of sixty thousand books and manu-

scripts – the foundation for the Bancroft Library at the University of California, Berkeley.

Hubert Howe Bancroft was born in Granville, Ohio, on 5 May 1832 to Azariah Ashley and Lucy Howe Bancroft. His father was an abolitionist farmer, and his mother was a schoolteacher; they raised him in accordance with a belief in hard work, self-discipline, and intellectual curiosity – a curiosity which in Bancroft was further fed by a rebellious streak. This contributed to his low tolerance for tedious tasks, and consequently he did not do well on the family farm or in his uncle's grammar school. Realizing that she had an unusually gifted child – he had learned to read by the age of three – Lucy Bancroft taught her son at home. The family's financial difficulties forced Bancroft at the age of sixteen to forgo a college education and to earn a living. Bancroft, however, experienced as many problems with his bookkeeping job as with grammar school and farming. He was fired. But with the help of his brother-in-law, George H. Derby, he discovered his talent as a book salesman. Bancroft's career took off as soon as he was able to work independently, using his imagination, common sense, and intuitive skill.

The gold-rush West offered an opportunity for developing his book-trade acumen into the largest book-and-stationery firm west of Chicago by 1869. But his road to success was typically circuitous and arduous. His first trip to California in the spring of 1852 met with disaster. The death of George Derby left Bancroft without a solid business partner in the East, depriving the novice wholesaler of credit and confidence from western clients. His father's mining venture in California, which the younger Bancroft had dutifully joined in spite of his distaste for hard manual labor, came to naught. And Hubert Howe Bancroft found himself again out of work at a time when San Francisco was overrun with luckless miners.

By relocating to Crescent City he was able to clerk in a general store which sold stationery and books. Investing his earnings in a warehouse, Bancroft made enough to return to Ohio, having gained valuable experience for his subsequent restart in California. Backed by an investment of fifty-five hundred dollars from his widowed sister and a bank credit of ten thousand dollars, Bancroft in 1856 established the H. H. Bancroft Company on San Francisco's Montgomery Street.

Three years later he embarked on his most successful and expensive venture as collector of books and manuscripts. This endeavor was linked from the start with a publication project. It began on a modest scale in 1859, when one of Bancroft's employees was compiling a handbook and almanac about California and the Pacific Coast which Bancroft intended to publish in 1860. Aware that his California customers were not interested in general reading matter – his best-sellers were law books and legal forms – Bancroft was hoping to reach a growing market made up of new settlers and prospective immigrants. He gathered all the books he had in stock that related to California; he was surprised that there were so many – about seventy – considering the youth of the state. From then on he searched for California-related materials, making it a habit to frequent booksellers in San Francisco and on his business trips to the East Coast. He came to realize that the history of California was rooted not only in the western United States, but in Mexico, Central America, and Spain as well. He thus began to expand the scope of his search; he purchased everything he could find in print or manuscript which would lead to a history of the Pacific states. Having found an excellent partner and business manager in his younger brother, Albert, the elder Bancroft was able to absent himself from the firm for extended buying trips.

Bancroft's initial visit with antiquarian book dealers in London and Paris in 1862 held a sobering discovery that his collection of five thousand volumes was far from complete, as he had naively thought. With his wife, Emily, who had accompanied him on his previous trip, Bancroft returned once more to Europe in 1866. The yearlong book-buying spree expanded his library to ten thousand volumes. Again he believed to be at the end of his collecting endeavor.

While in London, Bancroft had engaged the owner of the *Bookseller,* Joseph Whitaker, as his agent for keeping him informed about book auctions in Europe. The Bancrofts had barely reached home when a catalogue arrived from Whitaker in the mail, publicizing one of the most important sales of Mexicana. The catalogue announced that the auction was to be held by the Leipzig firm of List and Francke in January 1869.

Although he had learned much during his recent book-hunting trip to Europe, Bancroft had known little about the literary wealth of Mexico until he saw that catalogue. Gathered by José María Andrade, a private collector in Mexico, the collection had been intended for the imperial library of Maximilian. But upon learning of the emperor's fate Andrade shipped his seven thousand books and manuscripts to Europe. As Bancroft later confessed in *Literary Industries* (1890), "A new light broke in

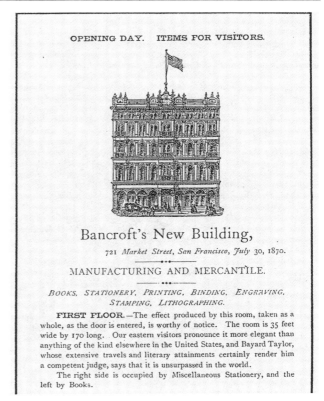

OPENING DAY. ITEMS FOR VISITORS.

Bancroft's New Building,

721 *Market Street, San Francisco, July* 30, 1870.

MANUFACTURING AND MERCANTILE.

BOOKS, STATIONERY, PRINTING, BINDING, ENGRAVING, STAMPING, LITHOGRAPHING.

FIRST FLOOR. —The effect produced by this room, taken as a whole, as the door is entered, is worthy of notice. The room is 35 feet wide by 170 long. Our eastern visitors pronounce it more elegant than anything of the kind elsewhere in the United States, and Bayard Taylor, whose extensive travels and literary attainments certainly render him a competent judge, says that it is unsurpassed in the world.

The right side is occupied by Miscellaneous Stationery, and the left by Books.

Announcement of the opening of the new building to which Bancroft moved his book and stationery store in 1870 (Bancroft Library, University of California, Berkeley)

upon me. I had never considered that Mexico had been printing books for three and a quarter centuries – and that the earlier works were seldom seen floating about book-stalls and auction rooms." Since he could not attend the sale himself, Bancroft telegraphed five thousand dollars to Whitaker, who selected and shipped to America three thousand volumes. These volumes were the basis for a part of the future Bancroft collection and second in importance only to California imprints. The following year another Andrade offering, by Puttick and Simpson in London, brought Bancroft one thousand more Mexican manuscripts and early Mexican imprints, many bearing the bookplates of Andrade and Maximilian.

In April 1870 a five-story building was erected to house the H. H. Bancroft Company's flourishing activities, from printing and publishing to the selling of books, stationery, business forms, maps, and engravings; the library occupied the top floor. The event was marred by Emily Bancroft's untimely death a few months earlier in December 1869, leaving Bancroft in charge of their young daughter, Kate.

Bancroft in 1879

As a result of Bancroft's increasing involvement with his literary bibliophilic efforts, the firm changed its name to A. L. Bancroft and Company, recognizing Albert's management role. The building was destroyed by fire in April 1886. Bancroft suffered heavy financial losses in this blaze, but by then his library had been moved to its own fireproof brick structure with iron shutters on Valencia Street. At the time of the move in 1881 the collection contained thirty-five thousand volumes. Bancroft's library eventually numbered sixty thousand volumes of books, newspapers, manuscripts, pictures, and maps. Yet he despised the amassing of books for their rarity or beauty. Nevertheless he fully recognized that his collection was bound to increase in value as more private collections disappeared from the market after having been bought by public institutions. Bancroft gathered his books for their content. The firm purpose of his library was to support the eventual publication of a series of history books.

As he expanded the geographic scope of his collection from neighboring Oregon to British Columbia and Alaska, and from his initial interest in California's Mexican past to Central America, he included promotional pamphlets and government reports about regional development as well as the handwritten accounts of the Jesuits on missionary conquests and further treasures from noted collectors. In 1876 he added a collection of Central Americana including books from the library of explorer Alexander von Humboldt which had been acquired by the American archaeologist E. G. Squier during his diplomatic career in Central America.

More treasures followed from another exiled Mexican collector, José Fernando Ramírez, former head of Mexico's national museum. One of its fine manuscripts, for instance, contains D. Vincente Castañeda's account of Viceroy Antonio de Mendoza's expedition against the tribe of Chíchímecas in central Mexico, translated from Nahuatl into Spanish in 1641 by Pedro Vazques. The bill for this purchase, arranged by London-based dealer Henry Stevens, came to thirty thousand dollars. In 1883 Bancroft traveled to Mexico and acquired some eight thousand more volumes for his collection.

Auction catalogues began to pour in from all over the world. Bancroft, lacking both the time to peruse his rapidly filling shelves and a proper command over the vast array of subjects they contained, relied on the expertise of their previous collectors. Lauriat represented Bancroft at the 1879 auction of Caleb Cushing's library in Boston. In *Literary Industries* Bancroft acknowledges the collectors whose material he acquired:

> The library of George W. Pratt was sold in New York in March, 1868; that of Amos Dean, at private sale, in New York the same year; that of W. L. Mattison in New York in April, 1869; that of John A. Rice in New York in March, 1870; that of S. G. Drake in Boston in May and June, 1876; that of John W. Dwinelle in San Francisco in July, 1877; that of George T. Strong in New York in November, 1878; that of Milton S. Latham in San Francisco in April, 1879; that of Gideon N. Searing in New York in May, 1880; that of H. R. Schoolcraft in New York in November, 1880; that of A. Oakey Hall in New York in January, 1881; that of J. L. Hasmar in Philadelphia in March, 1881; that of George Brinley in New York, different dates; that of W. B. Lawrence in New York in 1881–2; that of the Sunderland Library, first part, in London in 1881; that of W. C. Prescott in New York in December, 1881; and that of J. G. Keil in Leipsic in 1882; – from each of which I secured something.

Bancroft's rule of buying when in doubt often dictated that he go beyond what was in his time considered collectable or worthwhile. He thus took in prose works as well as poetry regardless of their literary merit as long as their themes related to western history. He copied manuscript accounts in na-

The Bancroft Library in 1881

tional or ecclesiastic archives and eventually resorted to eyewitness accounts, recorded by his assistants, when the events were too recent or too insignificant in the eyes of established writers and scholars. He canvased the Californians, the former citizens of Mexican California, who, like General Vallejo and former governor Alvarado, were writing their own histories or who possessed private archives of papers documenting the era of the preceding administration.

No historian and no publisher would have considered a project of the magnitude on which Bancroft embarked when he turned from bookseller to history writer and publisher. His scheme for utilizing the library he had gathered together was to put himself in charge of what he called his "Literary Industries," an operation that employed a staff of up to a hundred indexers, copiers, and cataloguers at a given time, none of whom had any previous training for this work. A permanent group of about twenty assistants who were qualified by education, language, and literary skills took on the tasks of abstracting and note taking from the accumulated documents as well as the actual writing of the text.

"Experience alone must be the teacher of those who strike out into new paths," Bancroft said in *Literary Industries*. "Never for a moment did I lose sight of the important work of collecting. . . . So thoroughly did I realize how ripe was the harvest and how few the laborers, how rapidly was slipping from mortal grasp golden opportunity, that I rested neither day nor night, but sought to secure from those thus passing away, all within my power to save before it was too late."

On 12 October 1876 Bancroft was married to Matilda Griffing in her parents' home in New Haven, Connecticut. Immediately after the wedding reception the couple embarked on a bookman's honeymoon. The Bancrofts called on General and Mrs. John Charles Frémont to persuade the general to submit his reminiscences, for Bancroft's proposed history of California, on Maj. John Wesley Powell, who had led the U.S. Geological Survey through western North America. In later years Matilda Bancroft assisted her husband in taking interviews from the wives of Mormon leaders in Utah. Whenever possible she continued to accompany him on his research journeys. Matilda and the children – in addition to Kate the Bancrofts had three sons and one daughter — became a constant source of support for Bancroft during his labors on the histories as well as afterward, when he had to confront his critics.

Bancroft's collecting endeavor still feeds the scholarly requirements of the academic community. His collecting principles today serve as a guide for the collection policy of the Bancroft Library: to be inclusive instead of exclusive since even library professionals cannot predict the direction of future scholarship; to treat the history of the American West as a whole, documenting the widest range of its multicultural population and its historical relationship with its Pacific neighbors from Alaska to Central America.

Like a lucky prospector Bancroft had found his treasure in California. He discovered the vein of gold hidden in dusty archives and obscure publications that no one else deemed worth retrieving. Before the study of anthropology became an academic discipline he had recognized the importance of Native American culture. Long before universities addressed the ethnic diversity of California, he had compiled information about its Hispanic and Chinese populations. To record the lives of ordinary people — miners, settlers, soldiers, and native Californians — that would otherwise remain undocumented, he resorted to such innovative methods as oral history, a technology that has only recently achieved academic status as appropriate to historical documentation. Yet, unlike California's early mining and lumber companies, Bancroft's literary industries preserved the state's unique historical resources at his own expense and at a time when they might have been lost without his vision of the future.

California may have seemed far away and of little interest to the world that Bancroft knew, and even the state of California did not feel justified in spending the $250,000 he was asking for his library. In 1905, however, the University of California bought and housed the collection; Bancroft donated $100,000 toward the purchase. On May 1973, when the university opened a new reading room after remodeling and expanding its previous facilities, President Hitch quoted from the regents' statement of September 1906: " 'The Bancroft Library is a great deal more than a department of the library of the University of California, it is a great deal more than a historical laboratory of the history department of the University, it is the indispensable nucleus of a great research library, upon which must be built the one great collection of materials for the ethnology, geography and the political, commercial and industrial history of the whole Pacific Coast.' " Hitch then added, "Except that the Bancroft has gone far beyond the Pacific Coast, this quote stands as a remarkably prescient prediction."

Hubert Howe Bancroft died in 1918 at the age of eighty-seven. One hundred thirty-five years after he began to collect his first volumes in 1859, hardly a day goes by that the manuscripts, pamphlets, newspapers, and oral histories he acquired are not perused by students and scholars from all over the globe.

Biography:

John W. Caughey, *Hubert Howe Bancroft: Historian of the West* (Berkeley & Los Angeles: University of California Press, 1946).

References:

Dale L. Morgan and George P. Hammond, *A Guide to the Manuscript Collections of the Bancroft Library* (Berkeley: University of California Press, 1963);

Reuben G. Thwaites, *The Bancroft Library: A Report Submitted to the President and Regents of the University of California upon the Bancroft Library* (Berkeley, Cal., 1905);

University of California, Bancroft Library, *Catalog of Printed Books,* volume 2 (Boston: G. K. Hall, 1964): 278–295;

University of California Library, *Spain and Spanish America in the Libraries of the University of California. II. The Bancroft Library* (Berkeley, Cal., 1930).

Papers:

Most of Bancroft's manuscript writings, business records, and correspondence are at the Bancroft Library, University of California, Berkeley.

Thomas Pennant Barton

(1803 – 5 April 1869)

Laura V. Monti
Boston Public Library

BOOKS: *Description of a Copy of the First Folio Edition of the Plays of Shakespeare, Now in the Collection of T. P. Barton* (New York: C. A. Alvord, 1860);

Thomas P. Barton's Library (New York: C. A. Alvord, n.d.).

Thomas Pennant Barton was the first major American collector of Shakespearean folios, concentrating his book-hunting efforts in both England and the United States. With dedication, knowledge, and determination he built a collection that remains among the most distinguished in the country, not so much for its completeness as for the condition of his copies, on which he insisted with a discrimination unusual in his time.

Born in Philadelphia in 1803, Thomas Pennant Barton was the son of Mary Pennington and Dr. Benjamin Smith Barton, eminent professor of natural history, botany, and medicine at the University of Pennsylvania. Little is known about Barton's childhood. The only established fact is that after his father died in 1815, he and his family moved to Europe and spent much of the next fifteen years in Paris.

In April 1833 Barton married Cora Livingston, daughter of Louise d'Avezac de Castera and Edward Livingston, who served as secretary of state (1831–1833) in the administration of President Andrew Jackson. Socially and politically prominent, the Livingstons afforded Barton entry into distinguished circles, and moreover they shared with him their love of books. Edward Livingston was a collector and avid reader, as was his wife. Cora and her mother read histories, biographies, and the Bible, as well as classical works.

In 1833 Andrew Jackson appointed Livingston minister to France to secure a settlement of the French Spoliation Claims, and Barton accompanied him as secretary of legation. In his new role as diplomat and in the company of his wife and in-laws, Barton had the opportunity to meet many prominent people in French society, and Paris was soon

charmed by the Bartons' social graces and polished French. When Livingston departed from France in 1835, Barton remained as chargé d'affaires, a post he retained until 1836, when he returned to America.

After his brief career in diplomacy, Barton and his wife went to live with her parents in Montgomery Place, the Livingston family estate on the Hudson River in Duchess County, New York. On 23 May 1836 Livingston died, leaving his son-in-law with his eleven-thousand-volume library. The Livingston collection was especially strong in the areas of politics, economics, botany, and theology.

Barton divided his time between Montgomery Place, where he dedicated much of his time to creating an arboretum, and New York City – first in an apartment on Fifth Avenue and later in one on West Twenty-second Street – where he kept his growing collection of books. During this period in his life, however, his travels in search of further acquisitions for his library were severely hampered by physical ailments. In a 1 May 1844 letter to English book dealer Horace Rodd, Barton, suffering from gout, explained that he could not cross the Atlantic to look for books in person because he was "commencing a form of medicated vapour baths which will confine" him. On 24 October 1860 Louise Livingston died, leaving Montgomery Place to the Bartons. Her death had a disastrous effect on Cora, her only child. Barton's health also continued to fail. On 30 January 1862 he wrote to his friend and book dealer John R. Smith that illness "has prevented me from paying attention to books or indeed anything else." On 5 April 1869 Barton died; he was buried in the Livingston vault under the old Methodist church in Rhinebeck, New York.

Thomas Pennant Barton might have been remembered for his interest in botany and for his arboretum, but he will always be recognized for his book collection, which he began to assemble around 1834, when he acquired some three hundred dramatic tracts that had belonged to Joseph Hasle-

Thomas Pennant Barton

wood, the English editor and antiquarian who had died in 1833. On 16 December 1833 Robert Harding Evans auctioned that collection in London. Later Barton was in England and able to buy it from dealer Thomas Thorpe. From then on Barton's enthusiasm for the English drama, especially editions of William Shakespeare published in England and America, as well as belles lettres in general, became nearly obsessive. Even when he could not be in England buying books personally, he remained in constant contact with the best-known dealers and auction houses of the time, such as William Pickering, Horace Rodd, John R. Smith, Joseph Sabin, Henry Stevens, John Pennington, and Sotheby and Wilkinson. Barton was a demanding and aggressive collector: he knew the books, he knew what he wanted, and he knew in what condition he wanted them. In an undated handwritten catalogue of Shakespeareana, Barton arranges his hierarchy of condition in the order of (1) poor; (2) indifferent; (3) fair; (4) good; (5) fine; and (6) very fine. "Let your lowest class be 'fair,'" he would say

to his agents. According to Justin Winsor of the Boston Public Library (who served as Barton's bibliographer), when Rodd sent him a *Hamlet* without a date and with pages supplied in facsimile, Barton replied that such copies should henceforth be shunned. Barton took pride in his high condition standard, and few collections in England could surpass his in that regard. He kept an eye on all the sales taking place and pressed his agents to do the same. Many of his items were bought in the Richard Heber sale (London) of 1835, and he was disappointed when he secured nothing in the 1842 Jolly sale (London). When Pickering took over as Barton's agent after Rodd's death in 1859, Barton urged him to procure the Shakespeare quartos he lacked. The Halliwell sale at Sotheby's (London) on 21 May 1857 offered an unusual chance, and Pickering took advantage of it. The competition for Shakespeareana had greatly increased. In New York James Lenox had begun collecting in 1835, and in England fourteen libraries were interested in the sale. But Barton was determined to acquire as much

Shakespeare material as possible. Following a want list, in a nota bene he wrote, "The above, I wanted for a Shakespeare collection formed upon a plan which is almost unlimited. Nothing is of nature too slight to be admitted into it . . . my only fear is the person collecting for me might reject as too trifling some matter which would be of some interest to me, if it enables me an approach, though even small, toward completeness." Despite the competition at the Halliwell sale, Barton secured many choice items, including nine early quartos, the 1802 Boydell edition of Shakespeare, and the 1685 Fourth Folio.

Barton was particular not only about the condition of the copies he bought but also about the bindings, of which he was a connoisseur. In an order sent to Rodd he included a letter for Clarke and Bedford, binders, giving the rules for the binding of his books. Dark calf should be used for books of a serious nature and light calf for those less serious. For the endpapers he advised a variety of marbled papers, preferring for old books and their reprints the old-fashioned papers and plain colors with light calf. He also included his ideas on how the bindings should be decorated. As a result there are beautiful bindings in the collection, many of them done by the best binders of the time, such as Roger Payne, Bedford, Hayday, and others from England; Derome, Padeloup, and Thouvenin from France.

The Bartons did not have children, so their name lives in the great collection Thomas accumulated during his lifetime. It was left to his widow, Cora, to do what she pleased with it, with the only requirement being that it be kept together. In the summer of 1869 F. W. Christern, with whom Barton had maintained a relationship as a client, contacted Justin Winsor, superintendent of the Boston Public Library, to let him know that Cora Barton wanted to dispose of her husband's library. Negotiations continued until 27 March 1870, when a contract was signed by both parties. Cora agreed to sell the collection for thirty-four thousand dollars upon certain conditions: that no book should be removed from it and that the Boston Public Library would publish a catalogue of the books. She died two days after the books were transferred to Boston.

A catalogue of the Shakespeare works was published in 1878 by order of the Trustees of Boston Public Library. In 1880 a catalogue of the complete collection was published, compiled by James Mascarene Hubbard. When it was issued it included 12,108 volumes plus correspondence, autographs, and plates. The collection is divided into two major sections. The Shakespeare works num-

bering about 2,000 volumes and the works of English dramatists in their first or early editions, another 2,000 volumes, make up the first part. The second part embraces works in history, geography, voyages and travels, biographies and antiquities, literary history, bibliography, belles lettres, grammar, rhetoric, poetry, drama, fiction, and philology. Some 6,000 volumes are in this class.

The Barton collection remains one of the most distinguished in the field of Shakespeare and Shakespeareana. It contains the Four Folios. The first, dated 1623, is a perfect copy that Barton succeeded in obtaining from Rodd in 1845. Several letters exchanged between these two men refer to the First Folio, and Barton privately printed a description of it. The Second Folio of 1632 is represented in two fine copies; the Third Folio is represented by two copies, one dating from 1663, the other from 1664. The Fourth Folio (1685) is a large copy with broad margins. Besides the original folios there are famous reprints of the first. Present too is the Nicolas Rowe edition of 1709, the first octavo edition as well as the first to carry illustrations and an important biography of the playwright. Barton owned forty-two eighteenth-century editions of Shakespeare, among them the one edited by Alexander Pope (1723–1725). The Samuel Johnson edition of 1765 also is in the collection. The library contains more than a hundred different Shakespeare editions published after 1800. The Barton collection, with twenty-eight of the Shakespeare quartos, is among the most impressive in this area. All of Barton's quartos are in good condition and elegantly bound.

Some of the doubtful and spurious Shakespeare works are present, such as the quartos of *Pericles* (1609, 1619, 1630), *Sir John Oldcastle* (1600), and *The Yorkshire Tragedy* (1619). There are seventeenth-century adaptations of Shakespeare's plays by Sir William Davenant, John Dryden, Thomas Otway, and Nahum Tate, and imitations of Shakespeare by John Milton, Francis Beaumont, and Nicholas Rowe. The collection includes works about Shakespeare and translations in eleven languages, including seven in German, three in French, one in Danish, one in Swedish, and one in Italian. Among the illustrated editions is John Boydell's *Collection of Prints from Pictures Painted for the Purpose of Illustrating the Dramatic Works of Shakespeare, by the Artists of Great Britain*. Published in two royal folio volumes in 1805, this was the culmination of nearly twenty years' work executed by the leading British artists of the day and converted into engravings for the publication. Though intended to supplement Boydell's 1802 edition of the plays, this title is distinguished in its own right as a magnificent example of the book arts. Also represented are sources of Shakespeare's plays.

The largest category in Barton's library is that of belles lettres, with several thousand volumes devoted to rhetoric, drama, poetry, and philology. In the field of poetry are first editions of works of English poets, such as Edmund Spenser's *Daphnaïda* published by W. Ponsonby of London in 1591; early French poetry such as *Le Roman de la Rose* in the 1529 Paris edition published by Galliot du Pre; and even a few rare works in Spanish such as the *Cancionero General* published by P. Nucio of Anvers in 1573. Dante, Petrarch, and Torquato Tasso are represented in choice copies of the best editions. The dramatic section, excluding Shakespeare, includes more than fifteen hundred volumes in English. Shakespeare contemporaries Ben Jonson, Christopher Marlowe, Robert Greene, and George Chapman are represented, together with plays by minor dramatists of the seventeenth, eighteenth, and nineteenth centuries. The French dramatists also are well represented. Besides the classics — Pierre Corneille, Jean Racine, and Molière — there are many works by lesser figures of the French stage. Nor are Spanish and Italian playwrights neglected. In fiction the library contains works by English novelists, the rare poetic version of Giovanni Boccaccio's *Decameron* in Vincenzo Brugiantino's *Cento novelle* (Venice: F. Marcolini, 1554). French fiction includes the *Nouvelles* of Marguerite de Valois in the Berne edition of 1780–1781, and the Spanish section contains eight editions of Miguel de Cervantes' *Don Quixote,* among them the version printed by Ibarra in Madrid in 1780.

One of the most noteworthy items in Barton's library is the collection of *Voyages* published by the eminent French engraver Theodore De Bry, who began the publication of his great work in 1590, when he issued the first part of the American series: Thomas Hariot's *Briefe and True Report of the New Found Land of Virginia,* which had been published separately in London in 1588. To take full advantage of the plates, De Bry printed the text in four languages: English, German, Latin, and French. By the time of his death in 1598 De Bry had published six parts on America in Latin, seven parts in German, and one each (the first) in English and French. The publication was continued by his widow and two sons, Johann Theodore and Johann Israel De

Bry, and later by Matthew Merrian, another member of the family.

Barton did not own a complete set of the fifty-seven volumes but did have the America series complete in thirteen volumes in Latin and the complete India series in Latin bound in twelve volumes. The plates are exquisite, and the text is filled with information about the New World and the Orient.

Since Barton's death the collection has continued to grow. With the possible exception of the bequest of George Ticknor, Barton's books constitute the greatest gift the Boston Public Library ever received, for the thirty-four thousand dollars paid for the collection was a nominal fee. These works continue to assist students of Shakespeare everywhere.

Bibliographies:

James M. Hubbard, *Catalogue of the Works of William Shakespeare, Original and Translated, Together with the Shakespeariana Embraced in the Barton Collection of the Boston Public Library* (Boston: Trustees at Boston Public Library, 1880);

Boston Public Library, Barton Collection, *Catalogue of the Barton Collection, Boston Public Library in Two Parts: Part I, Shakespeare's Works and Shakespeariana; Part II, Miscellaneous* (Boston: Trustees of Boston Public Library, 1888).

Biographies:

Charles Havens Hunt, *Life of Edward Livingston with Introduction by George Bancroft* (New York: Appleton, 1864);

Louise Livingston Hunt, *Memoir of Mrs. Edward Livingston, with Letters Hitherto Unpublished* (New York: French, 1880).

Reference:

James Wynne, *Private Libraries of New York* (New York: French, 1860).

Papers:

The Barton collection at the Boston Public Library contains Barton's correspondence with book dealers, his agents, and other collectors of William Shakespeare's works. The collection also contains Barton's manuscript catalogue of all his books except those in his Shakespeare collection; his manuscript list of Shakespeareana, or all works relating to Shakespeare; and his manuscript general index to Joseph Haslewood's collection.

Fredson Thayer Bowers

(25 April 1905 – 11 April 1991)

George Walton Williams
Duke University

See also the obituary tributes to Bowers in *DLB Year-book 1991.*

BOOKS: *The Dog Owner's Handbook* (Boston: Houghton Mifflin, 1936);

Elizabethan Revenge Tragedy 1587–1642 (Princeton, N.J.: Princeton University Press, 1940);

Principles of Bibliographical Description (Princeton, N.J.: Princeton University Press, 1949);

On Editing Shakespeare and the Elizabethan Dramatists, Rosenbach Fellowship in Bibliography Publications (Philadelphia: University of Pennsylvania Library, 1955);

Textual and Literary Criticism (The Sandars Lectures in Bibliography 1957–58) (Cambridge: Cambridge University Press, 1959);

Bibliography and Textual Criticism (The Lyell Lectures, 1959) (Oxford: Clarendon, 1964);

Hamlet: An Outline Guide to the Play (New York: Barnes & Noble, 1965);

Essays in Bibliography, Text, and Editing (Charlottesville: University Press of Virginia for the Bibliographical Society of the University of Virginia, 1975);

Hamlet as Minister and Scourge and Other Studies in Shakespeare and Milton (Charlottesville: University Press of Virginia, 1989).

VIDEOTAPES: *Death in Victory: Shakespeare's Tragic Reconciliations,* Eminent Scholar/Teachers Videotape (Detroit: Omnigraphics, 1990);

Hamlet as Minister and Scourge, Eminent Scholar/Teachers Videotape (Detroit: Omnigraphics, 1990).

OTHER: *A Fary Knight or Oberon the Second; A Manuscript Play Attributed to Thomas Randolph* (Chapel Hill: University of North Carolina Press, 1944), editor;

The Dramatic Works of Thomas Dekker (Cambridge: Cambridge University Press, 1953–1961), editor;

Whitman's Manuscripts: Leaves of Grass (1860), A Parallel Text (Chicago: University of Chicago Press, 1955), editor;

The Centenary Edition of the Works of Nathaniel Hawthorne (Columbus: Ohio State University Press, 1962–1975), general editor;

William Shakespeare: The Merry Wives of Windsor (Baltimore: Penguin, 1963), editor;

The Dramatic Works in the Beaumont and Fletcher Canon (Cambridge: Cambridge University Press, 1966–), general editor;

John Dryden: Four Tragedies (Chicago: University of Chicago Press, 1967), editor;

John Dryden: Four Comedies (Chicago: University of Chicago Press, 1967), editor;

The Works of Stephen Crane (Charlottesville: University Press of Virginia, 1969–1975), editor;

The Complete Works of Christopher Marlowe (Cambridge: Cambridge University Press, 1973), editor;

Stephen Crane The Red Badge of Courage: A Facsimile Edition of the Manuscript (Washington, D.C.: Bruccoli Clark/NCR Microcard Editions, 1973), editor;

Tom Jones; The History of a Foundling, by Henry Fielding (Middletown, Connecticut: Wesleyan University Press; Oxford: Oxford University Press, 1974), editor;

The Works of William James (Cambridge: Cambridge University Press, 1975–), textual editor;

Vladimir Nabokov, *Lectures on Literature* (New York: Harcourt Brace Jovanovich/Bruccoli Clark, 1980), editor;

Nabokov, *Lectures on Russian Literature* (New York: Harcourt Brace Jovanovich/Bruccoli Clark, 1981), editor;

Nabokov, *Lectures on Don Quixote* (New York: Harcourt Brace Jovanovich/Bruccoli Clark, 1983), editor;

Leon Kroll: A Spoken Memoir, with Nancy Hale Bowers (Charlottesville: University Press of Virginia, 1983), editor;

13

Fredson Bowers at the University of Virginia following his naval service in World War II

F. Scott Fitzgerald, *The Great Gatsby* (Cambridge: Cambridge University Press, 1991), textual consultant.

Fredson Bowers was a man of wide interests, tireless energy, and many skills. He will be remembered primarily for his extensive contributions to the theoretical study of descriptive bibliography, analytical bibliography, and textual criticism, and for the practical application of his research in specific studies and editions. Though these three specialities are separable, their coordination in his work will render it of permanent value.

His extraordinary accomplishments were recognized and honored at home and abroad. They take their justification from his inspirational teaching, his many writings, his services to the profession, and, particularly, from the series *Studies in Bibliography,* the Papers of the Bibliographical Society of the University of Virginia, established in 1948 on the base of the Bibliographical Society of the University of Virginia, which in company with others he founded in the previous year. Of this series, published annually, he was named editor, a position he held continuously for forty-three volumes, until the time of his death. In 1949 he published his monumental *Principles of Bibliographical Description.*

In recognition of these and other accomplishments he was elected Corresponding Fellow of the British Academy (1968), Fellow of the American Academy of Arts and Sciences (1972), and Honorary Member of the Bibliographical Society of America (1986). He received the Bicentennial Medal of Brown University (1964), the Gold Medal of the Bibliographical Society (1969), the Thomas Jefferson Award of the University of Virginia (1971), and the Julian Boyd Award of the Association for Documentary Editing (1986). He was awarded honorary degrees by Clark University (1970), Brown University (1970), and the University of Chicago (1973), and fellowships from the Fulbright Commission (1952–1953), the Guggenheim Foundation (1958–1959, 1970), the Rockefeller Foundation at the Bellagio Study and Conference Center (1971, 1972), All Souls College, Oxford (1972, 1974), and Churchill College, Cambridge (1975).

He was chairman of the Department of English (1961–1968) and Dean of the Faculty (1968–1969) at the University of Virginia, Phi Beta Kappa Visiting Scholar (1961–1962), member of the Executive Council of the Modern Language Association of America (1962–1966), and President of the South Atlantic Modern Language Association (1969).

Fredson Thayer Bowers was born in New Haven, Connecticut, on 25 April 1905. He graduated from Brown University in 1925 and took his Ph.D. at Harvard in 1934; his dissertation director was the redoubtable George Lyman Kittredge, and he also studied under Hyder Rollins. His field was the English Renaissance, and his revised dissertation was published as *Elizabethan Revenge Tragedy, 1587–1642* (1940). After two years as an instructor at Princeton University he moved to the University of Virginia in 1938. In 1942 he married author Nancy Hale, and they were an impressive couple. He was promoted to professor in 1948, following wartime naval service as a cryptographer.

Bowers began his publishing career in 1930 while still a graduate student at Harvard. Before he had received his doctorate he had published seven articles. These treated literary topics, and some of them appeared in two of the prestigious journals of the profession, *Modern Language Notes* and *Studies in Philology*. In 1936 his first paper appeared in the *Library;* it was followed by other papers in 1937, 1938, and 1939. After the war his productivity expanded enormously; the complete record of his achievement includes the execution as author, editor, or general editor of over sixty volumes as well as of more than 250 reviews, articles, and separate essays. (To these should be added many writings of a professional caliber on Irish wolfhounds, postage stamps, mobile post offices, and music recordings.)

Prewar articles in the *Library* and his papers on "The Headline in Early Books" in *English Institute Annual 1941*, the postwar "Notes on Standing Type" and "Criteria for Classifying Hand-Printed Books" (*Papers of the Bibliographical Society of America*, 1946 and 1947), and "Proof Correction in *Lear*" (*Library*, 1947) clearly demonstrated the direction in which his inexhaustible mind was turning. W. W. Greg had published in 1939 the first volume of his detailed descriptive *Bibliography of the English Printed Drama to the Restoration* (four volumes, the last pub-

Bowers as an undergraduate at Brown University

lished in 1959). Inspired as he must have been by this commanding example, Bowers set himself the task of continuing that analysis from the Restoration to 1700. In 1948 he described himself as involved in writing this project, and it remained a lifelong concern of his; he worked on it intermittently, regarding its completion as the cap to his career. He died before he could finish the project, but his papers in the Alderman Library, the University of Virginia, contain a mass of data in various stages of completeness which await the finishing touches to be provided by another hand. Although Bowers was unable to finish this bibliography, his determination to continue Greg's work provided the material and the stimulus that produced the *Principles of Bibliographical Description*. Greg's great achievement, represented immediately on the appearance of the first volume of his "monograph," was a model, a pattern,

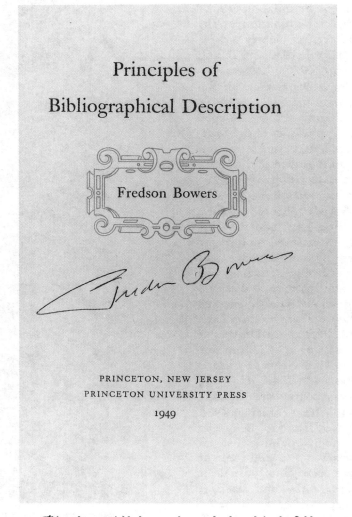

Principles of

Bibliographical Description

Fredson Bowers

PRINCETON, NEW JERSEY
PRINCETON UNIVERSITY PRESS
1949

This volume quickly became the standard work in the field.

and a challenge for Bowers – even though he did not always agree with Greg's methodology.

Though Bowers did not succeed in providing the "Drama of the Restoration," which was to illustrate the application of his *Principles,* he did produce on a small scale the model of what was almost the perfect descriptive bibliography. This was his collaboration with Richard Beale Davis, *George Sandys: A Bibliographical Catalogue of Printed Editions in England to 1700* (1950), a project which had a Virginia connection. This catalogue fell short of a complete "descriptive bibliography" because Bowers had not been able to examine for variants as many copies of the several books as he would have wished to require for a full description, but even with this incompleteness, the catalogue was clear evidence of what could and should be done. It exhibited, early

in his career, the techniques demanded in the *Principles* and his magisterial understanding of the problems involved in descriptive bibliography and how they were to be solved and then described in specific detail.

Because *Principles* appeared so commandingly and so unexpectedly from a scholar trained in literary matters rather than in library cataloguing or from the antiquarian book trade, it received a mixed reception, many critics finding it too scientific and excessive in its rigor. The revolutionary effect of this study and of its "principles" was demonstrated most dramatically at the annual meeting of the Bibliographical Society in London on 17 March 1953. At an earlier meeting on 18 November 1952, Bowers had presented a paper entitled "Purposes of Descriptive Bibliography with Some Remarks on

Nancy Hale Bowers and Fredson Bowers, Woodburn, Charlottesville, Virginia

Methods," in which he described not only the methods but also the philosophy behind the writing of *Principles*. When, four months later, Sir Geoffrey Keynes delivered at the meeting the presidential address which he had entitled "Religio Bibliographici," members of the society were alert to the possibilities of an ideological confrontation, as Keynes was the primary expositor of the form of casual "bio-bibliography" to which Bowers was specifically objecting. Keynes recalls in his autobiography that his address "contained what was intended to be a friendly attack on the Bowers school of analytical bibliographers who considered the work which had given me so much enjoyment 'impure bibliography' and therefore inadequate." As many of the members of the society knew that Bowers was present in the room, the address was greeted with polite applause and an awkward silence, while the membership waited for Bowers to respond. Prompted by a friend to reply, Bowers, who had been – as he later

wrote – "keeping my mouth shut," rose "to compliment Keynes on the felicity of his title." Keynes remembered that "I was glad that he accepted the address in the spirit in which it was meant." Bowers records – but Keynes does not – that John Hayward subsequently gave Keynes "an almost embarrassing going over at his Presidential address." Personal interests and differences aside, the annual meeting of 1953 has gone down in history as the symbolic moment when the new school of descriptive bibliography replaced the old.

Time has shown the vices that critics and reviewers from the old school saw in the *Principles* to be its virtues, not its defects; and time has also shown that this volume, as one reviewer described it on its publication, is "one of the most important and, implicitly, one of the most provocative volumes produced by literary scholarship within our generation." Forty-four years after the publication of *Principles*, Bowers's biographer G. Thomas Tan-

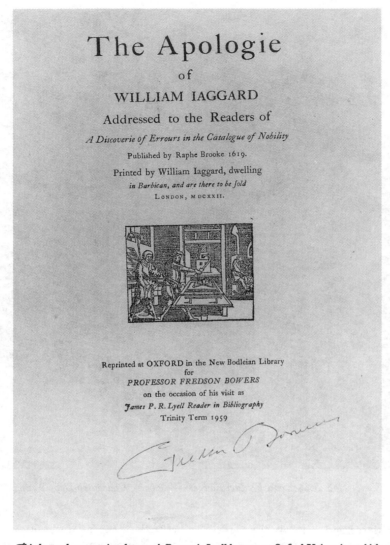

The Apologie
of
WILLIAM IAGGARD
Addressed to the Readers of
A Discoverie of Errours in the Catalogue of Nobility
Published by Raphe Brooke 1619.
Printed by William Iaggard, dwelling
in Barbican, and are there to be sold
LONDON, M DC XXII.

Reprinted at OXFORD in the New Bodleian Library
for
PROFESSOR FREDSON BOWERS
on the occasion of his visit as
James P. R. Lyell Reader in Bibliography
Trinity Term 1959

This keepsake was printed to mark Bowers's Lyell lectures at Oxford University, which were published as Bibliography and Textual Criticism *(Bruccoli Collection).*

selle termed the work "one of the great achievements in modern scholarship . . . not likely ever to be superseded."

The study, which Bowers himself described as "almost an accident," derived from his inquiries into the printed exemplars of the drama of the Restoration. "The state of affairs was a mess," Bowers wrote, "and from starting the play examinations and recording, I began to see that I could learn enough, with some special reading, to begin to put some order into a mushy situation." The materials for that "special reading" were few; in articles he published in *Papers of the Bibliographical Society of America,* the *Library,* and in other studies, Bowers developed and sharpened the methodology that was to define the achievement of the volume. He perceived

from the lack of analysis in the work of his predecessors, that such "order" was necessary and he found from his own work that it was possible. He sought from his investigation of exemplars of the printed books and the discovery of the physical facts of their mechanical production to build a foundation which he deemed a prerequisite for textual criticism, particularly "as the evidence may turn on the relation of the printed text to the manuscript copy" — that is to reveal something of the intention of the author.

The foreword to the volume identifies the three purposes of descriptive bibliography: (1) to describe the physical characteristics of a book, (2) to order the facts of that description so as to form a basis for textual criticism, and (3) to use those facts to understand "literary and printing and publishing history." These three purposes move straightforwardly from the practical to the theoretical — from close scrutiny of specific objects to literary criticism of the intellectual content of those objects which is to be founded on that scrutiny — and on to the philosophical, the history of human thought and development. One of the surest foundations of the volume is Bowers's unwavering insistence that the minute details of physical objects contribute to the understanding of the broadest abstract considerations. Three hundred fifty pages of the five-hundred page volume address the descriptions of hand-printed books (fifteenth- to seventeenth-century books); one hundred pages discuss machine-printed books. Though scholars had given careful attention to the details of incunabula, little serious, scholarly research had addressed the forms of books printed since 1800. The volume directly attacked, with no little force, the complacency and dilettantism that had marked the treatment of volumes published in recent history. "I am conscious," Bowers observed in his first chapter, "of attempting to set a standard for descriptive bibliography which is not customarily thought to be necessary and hence has been seldom observed." That standard showed itself in the most detailed treatment that had ever been given to the subject, in rationale and in procedure developing a coherent structure for the descriptions that Bowers would have used in his projected "Drama of the Restoration" and which his followers will use for many years to come. The volume offered for the first time the clear, exacting, and demonstrable distinctions that can and must be made among *state* (and variant states), *issue* (and *reissue*), *printing* (or *impression*), and *edition*:

> In its purest sense an *edition* of a book consists of all copies printed at any time or times from one setting of type, or its equivalent in the form of plates or monotype rolls; *i.e.*, it is the sum of all impressions from one setting. According to this pure meaning, a new major edition is not created except by a complete resetting of the type. Resetting is sufficient; there need be no alterations in the text. All the copies of any single edition are not necessarily printed at any one time but may accumulate from a series of separate *impressions* removed from each other in date; that is, the original type-pages or their equivalents may be placed on the press at any time and fresh copies of the book printed as demand warrants. On each occasion when a complete run of sheets is made in this manner, a different impression of the book is formed.

> Copies of each impression compose a part of an edition; therefore, the tenth impression of a book (the tenth time the type or plates have been imposed and printed from as a separate and complete *total* operation) is as much a part of the first edition of a book as is the original first impression.

> ISSUE: *A re-issue is a special form of the original sheets of an impression, this form resulting from post-publication-date alterations made intentionally on order of the publisher or issuer to the form or forms of the sheets as originally printed in the impression concerned or as subsequently altered in state or in issue. These alterations go beyond attempts to fulfill the standards for an 'ideal copy' in completeness or proof correctness intended but not achieved at publication. To cause re-issue of the sheets the changes must represent alterations in contents or form not envisaged on publication as necessary for an 'ideal copy'; hence they constitute a definite effort to improve or change the import of a part of the sheets in a manner justifying a re-issue of the unsold sheets. Re-issue is caused only by alterations to the sheets and is not affected by variations in the publishers' binding or any of its parts. A re-issue cannot comprise a complete impression but only a part of an impression.*

Since *state* must be discussed in relation to *issue*, its definition follows:

> STATE: *As it relates to the sheets of a book, a state is a variant form of the type-setting or makeup of one or more sheets of an impression or any of its issues, the variants resulting from alterations of any kind (a) made during the impression of the sheets, (b) made after impression but before publication, or (c) made after initial publication providing the alterations are attempts to create a form of 'ideal copy' as envisaged at the time of publication. Alterations to the sheets of an impression form a state if they result from the binder's initiative and not as a publishing effort by order of the publisher. As it relates to binding, all variations of publishers' binding or its parts used to case the sheets of an impression (including its issues) comprise state of the binding whether occurring before or after the date of initial publication.*

Bowers's definitions of the four key bibliographical terms as applied to nineteenth- and twentieth-century books challenged the anarchistic usage whereby each cataloguer applied the terms idiosyncratically or even interchangeably.

Another highly significant event at the turn of the postwar decade was the appearance of an article by Greg, "The Rationale of Copy-Text," solicited by Bowers for the conference held in 1949 by the English Institute and published in volume three of *Studies in Bibliography*. This article, presenting a new approach to the methodology of editing, Bowers rightly perceived as the foundation for the modern editing of texts: chiefly texts of the English drama in the sixteenth and seventeenth centuries. But though the article addresses specifically the problems of those early English texts, it maintains an attitude that is readily transferable to the editing of texts from other times and other cultures. It clearly marshaled Bowers the way that he was going, and its

Bowers on the occasion of being awarded the degree of Doctor of
Humane Letters at the University of Chicago, 1973

precepts confirmed the move from descriptive to analytical bibliography and textual criticism that Bowers made in the early 1950s.

First evidence of this move was the appearance of the first volume of *The Dramatic Works of Thomas Dekker,* published by Cambridge University in 1953 (three later volumes appearing in 1955, 1958, and 1961). The second evidence was the parallel-text edition of *Whitman's Manuscripts: Leaves of Grass (1860), A Parallel Text,* published by the University of Chicago Press in 1955. These two undertakings initiated the succession of studies and editions of both English and American authors that was to occupy Bowers for the rest of his career. The *Dekker* was followed by two volumes of John Dryden's plays, *Four Tragedies* and *Four Comedies,* edited in collaboration with Lester Beaurline and published by the University of Chicago in 1967 and by Christopher Marlowe's *Complete Works:* a two-volume work published by Cambridge University Press in

1973 and revised in 1981. In addition, Bowers was participating editor and general editor of the series of ten volumes of *The Dramatic Works in the Beaumont and Fletcher Canon,* of which the first volume appeared in 1966 and the tenth and last, still under his (posthumous) general editorship will appear in 1995 or 1996. He was also consulting textual editor for six of the volumes of the *Works of Henry Fielding* (1967–).

Meanwhile, he served as textual editor of the twenty volumes of *The Works of Nathaniel Hawthorne* (Ohio State University Press, 1962–1988), of the ten volumes of *Stephen Crane* (University Press of Virginia, 1969–1976), of the twenty volumes of *John Dewey* (Southern Illinois University Press, 1967–1983), and of the nineteen volumes of *William James* (Harvard University Press, 1975–1988). A European interest appears in his supervisory textual work on the three volumes of the lectures of Vladimir Nabokov (Harcourt Brace Jovanovich/Bruccoli Clark, 1980–1983).

Bowers described the editorial principles of analytical bibliography and textual criticism underlying these editions in three volumes, which may be considered a parallel to the single volume on descriptive bibliography already published. Each of these three volumes derived from an invitation to deliver a series of lectures on bibliography, these series surely representing the most distinguished and important lectureships in the field. The first was the Rosenbach Lectures delivered in 1954 at the University of Pennsylvania and published by the University of Pennsylvania Library as *On Editing Shakespeare and the Elizabethan Dramatists* (1955). The second was the Sandars Lectures in Bibliography at Cambridge University delivered in 1958 and published by that university press as *Textual and Literary Criticism* (1959). The third was the Lyell Lectures delivered in 1959 at Oxford University and published by that university press as *Bibliography and Textual Criticism* (1964). Taken together this trio records and displays the principles on which Bowers had been editing both English and American texts and, at the same time, setting and declaring the standards which others should follow. The universal significance of these volumes is demonstrated by the appearance of *Textual and Literary Criticism* in a Japanese translation (by Sachiho Tanaka) in Tokyo in 1983. From his many essays on bibliographical topics, Bowers selected twenty-six for reprinting in *Essays in Bibliography, Text, and Editing,* a volume conceived by three of his former students in 1973 and published, under the supervision of one of them, Irby B. Cauthen, Jr., by the Bibliographical Society of the University of Virginia in 1975 in Bowers's honor.

The intellectual life of Fredson Bowers, richly productive in studies bibliographical, has shaped and directed the minds and work of a generation of students and will guide generations more who are concerned with the accuracy and thoroughness of descriptions and editions. His accomplishments in the area of descriptive bibliography include for theory the magisterial *Principles* and for practice the *Sandys* "bibliographical catalogue" and the data for the "Printed Drama of the Restoration"; similarly, in the areas of analytical bibliography and textual criticism they include for theory three substantial series of lectures delivered at prestigious institutions and published separately and for practice scores of editions of manuscripts and printed books spanning five centuries of human thought. It is a notable, and noble, record.

Bibliography:

Martin C. Battestin, "Fredson Thayer Bowers: A Checklist and Chronology," in *The Life and Work of Fredson Bowers,* by G. Thomas Tanselle (Charlottesville: The Bibliographical Society of the University of Virginia, 1993), pp. 155–186.

Biography:

G. Thomas Tanselle, *The Life and Work of Fredson Bowers* (Charlottesville: The Bibliographical Society of the University of Virginia, 1993).

Reference:

Ross Harvey, ed., "Fredson Bowers Commemorative Issue" of the *Bulletin of the Bibliographical Society of Australia and New Zealand,* 15 (1991).

Papers:

A large collection of papers assembled by Bowers and supplemented by the additions of others has been deposited in the Alderman Library, University of Virginia. Books from Bowers's personal collections and gifts from others constitute a memorial collection housed in the Department of English, University of Virginia.

George Brinley, Jr.

(15 May 1817 – 16 May 1875)

Joseph Rosenblum

University of North Carolina at Greensboro

WORKS: Preface to *The Laws of Connecticut: An Exact Reprint of the Original Edition of 1673* (Hartford, Conn.: Privately printed, 1865);

"The First Charter of Massachusetts Bay," *Daily Evening Transcript* (Boston), 8 December 1845, p. 3.

In a paper presented in conjunction with a Grolier Club exhibition of books from the library of George Brinley, Jr., Marcus A. McCorison observed, "Over a period of thirty-five years, Brinley accumulated a private library of Americana that remains to this day unrivalled in its extent and richness within his self-imposed limits." By the time of his death in Hamilton, Bermuda, on 16 May 1875, one day after he turned fifty-eight, he had acquired nearly fifty thousand titles relating to the history and literature of the United States.

Brinley was hardly the first to pursue this interest. Carl L. Cannon's *American Book Collectors and Collecting from Colonial Times to the Present* (New York: H. W. Wilson, 1941) gives pride of place to Thomas Prince (1687–1758); the nineteenth-century Harvard librarian Justin Winsor called Prince the "father of American bibliography." At one point he owned five of the eleven surviving copies of the *Bay Psalm Book;* one of these copies would find its way into the Brinley library. Isaiah Thomas (1749–1831), whose library provided the foundation for that of the American Antiquarian Society, was another precursor of Brinley, and, at about the same time that Brinley began assembling his library, John Carter Brown (1797–1874) and James Lenox (1800–1880) also entered the field of American book collecting.

Nonetheless, Brinley deserves the title of premier Americanist because his was the largest, and in many ways the finest, collection of Americana assembled in the nineteenth century. In his *Three Americanists: Henry Harisse, Bibliographer; George Brinley, Book Collector; Thomas Jefferson, Librarian*

(1939) Randolph G. Adams compares the auction catalogues of the leading Americanists of Brinley's era: 2,667 items were offered in the John A. Rice sale of 1870; 2,205 in the William Menzies sale of 1875; 1,050 in the Almon W. Griswold sale of 1876; 3,142 in the Henry Cruse Murphy sale of 1884; and 2,741 in the Samuel Latham Mitchell Barlow sale of 1889. The five sales of the Brinley library held between 1879 and 1893 contained 9,501 lots. Although the Lenox collection at the time it was acquired by the New York Public Library held approximately 11,870 titles, Lenox's library, unlike Brinley's, was not exclusively devoted to Americana. Even the Robert Hoe sales of 1911–1912, with their 14,588 lots, probably did not include more books relating to the United States.

If it is the case that some are born book collectors, others achieve this state, and still others have bibliomania thrust upon them, then Brinley would be classified in the latter category. His father, George Brinley, Sr., a self-made, self-educated merchant, collected works dealing with the Indian and American revolutionary wars. Charles Brinley, son of George, Jr., recalled that the family house at 33 Asylum Street in Hartford, Connecticut, contained many books, and he remembered his grandfather to be an avid reader.

Brinley's paternal ancestors came to Rhode Island in the 1650s, and family members lived in Boston for over a century prior to the revolution, when their Tory sentiments led to their departure from the city, destroying the family fortune. In 1836 Brinley's father moved the family from Boston to Hartford due to the poor health of his wife, Catherine Putnam, granddaughter of the Revolutionary War hero Gen. Israel Putnam. Despite having gained refuge from the cold, wet Boston winters, Catherine died on 2 October 1842. On 15 May 1839 Brinley had married Frances Terry, granddaughter of Col. Jeremiah Wadsworth, commissary general of the Continental army. Brinley began to establish himself as an im-

George Brinley, Jr.

portant landowner in the Hartford area and enjoyed the fruits of his father's labors. In 1843, at the request of Brinley's sister Elizabeth, Brinley, Sr., wrote "a brief sketch of my pilgrimage through life," in which he traced his rise from relative poverty to "a goodly share of prosperity" that allowed his children to be educated in the best schools and at home by a tutor and to live comfortably (and to collect books) without working. According to Charles Brinley's unpublished memoir dated 1910, however, the income of his father never exceeded two thousand dollars a year. This figure is probably not accurate. While not as wealthy as Lenox or Brown, during the 1870s Brinley did pay three thousand dollars in real-estate taxes in Worcester, Massachusetts; he also owned property in Boston and Hartford.

In his memoirs Charles described his father to be "a man of leisure" and recalled that at Gravel Hill Farm, the family estate, Brinley left it to his children to perform "the hard and dirty work." Charles also remembered his father as

> a man of strong prejudice.... His temper was autocratic. He had no little personal distinction, which showed itself in his manners, his handwriting, and in his dress. At home he was given to prolonged silences, with an implication of disapproval, which were often inconvenient and uncomfortable.... There was something touching about his moody reticence, which appeared to be born of unhappiness.

McCorison notes that photographs show Brinley to have been "of a melancholy mien, with hooded eyes and a drooping mouth." Charles added that "those he desired to please found him winning and convincing, [and he] had a fine feeling for all forms of beauty whether in nature or in art." Brinley appeared to have shared his mother's delicate constitution, and in 1874 he went to Saint Augustine, Florida, for his health. While there he contracted

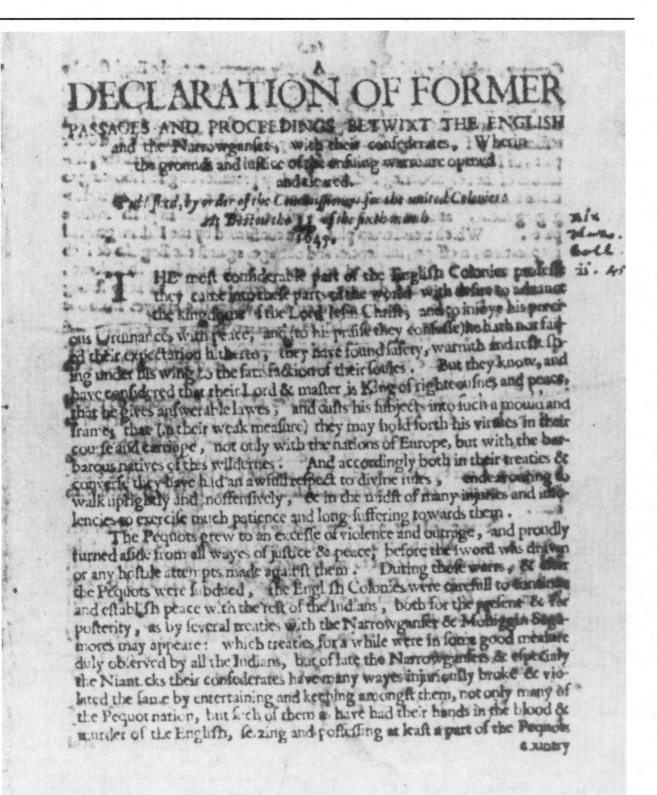

A Declaration of Former Passages, *for which Brinley paid fifty dollars in 1868*

malaria, however, and in May of the following year he died in Hamilton, Bermuda.

Though often melancholy and in general averse to exertion greater than that required to make a morning visit, in pursuit of Americana he was determined, energetic, and sagacious. At the age of twenty-eight Brinley acquired Samuel G. Drake's collection dealing with American Indians. Drake's books were to be sold by auction, but Brinley bought them shortly before the sale was to take place, thus securing 1,517 lots en bloc. In November 1852 he sold the duplicates at auction. In 1846 Brinley added to his collection at the Gabriel Furman and John Pickering sales, and in 1856 he was an important buyer when the E. B. Corwin library was sold at Bangs's auction rooms in New York. At the 1870 Rice Sale at Bangs he paid $825 for a copy of the Eliot Indian Bible (Cambridge, Mass.: Samuel Green and Marmaduke Johnson, 1663) in Algonquin, the first Bible printed in the British colonies.

Many of Brinley's acquisitions required more effort to locate than money to purchase. Charles recalled that in the early days of his father's collecting Brinley would "drive through New England, calling on country ministers and at old houses in quest of 'nuggets,'" for which he would exchange the new pots that he carried with him. On one occasion, according to Charles, Brinley

> found a coveted psalm book belonging to an old lady who resisted all his blandishments, not that she read the psalm book any more than my father expected to, but it had belonged to someone for whose sake she treasured it. My father did not despair; he wrote every now and then to the old lady and sent her presents. She remained obdurate until, one cold winter, he had made for her a particularly handsome flannel petticoat. He received the psalm book with a note of thanks.

He made an equally felicitous exchange to acquire the diary of Samuel Sewell, a work offering insights into the Puritan mind as well as details about such important historic events as the Salem witch trials, in which Sewell was an active participant. A Sewell descendant showed Brinley the manuscript, interleaved in seventeenth-century almanacs. The owner was seeking a complete run of the *Gentleman's Magazine,* which Brinley assembled and traded for Sewell's work. As Charles noted, those whom Brinley desired to please found him winning and convincing.

During the Civil War the price of paper rose sufficiently to prompt an extensive cleaning out of attics. Brinley made an arrangement with the mills receiving the paper, allowing him to examine the refuse before it was converted to pulp, and he thus acquired various treasures for the price of scrap. His granddaughter Katherine Brinley confirmed George Watson Cole's story of Brinley ordering a load of waste paper deposited in his front yard, much to the chagrin of his family. Perhaps they were at least partially placated by Brinley's discovery of an Eliot Bible in the trash; he would eventually own nine copies of this rarity.

Brinley also patronized the booksellers. In New York he frequented the shop of William Gowans. From Moses Polock, uncle of Dr. A. S. W. Rosenbach, he acquired seventeenth-century Boston and Philadelphia imprints, including William Bradford's 1691 Philadelphia reprint of George Whitehead's *Christian Epistle to Friends in General* and Bradford's reprint of George Keith's *The Christian Faith of the Quakers* (Philadelphia, 1692), as well as James Logan's translation of *Cato's Moral Distichs,* printed by Benjamin Franklin in Philadelphia in 1735. Polock also sold him *The Laws & Acts of the Assembly for Their Majesties Province of New York* (New York: William Bradford, 1694), at the time regarded as the first product of Bradford's press after the printer had relocated to New York from Pennsylvania. The price was sixteen dollars; at the second Brinley sale it fetched a hundred times that sum. According to William Brotherhead, "The mention of this fact operate[d] on Polock's mind as if he had taken bitter gall for his breakfast," and the experience may have contributed to Polock's famed reluctance to sell.

Brinley's most important supplier was Henry Stevens, who as a native of Vermont liked to refer to himself as the Green Mountain Boy and who had moved to Trafalgar Square, London. One of the gems of the Brinley collection was the *Bay Psalm Book,* which Edward A. Crowninshield had acquired from the Thomas Prince library in return for providing a binding for another book. As that binding may have cost as little as one dollar, Crowninshield stands guilty of sharp practice, neither unprecedented nor unrepeated in the annals of bibliomania. Brinley came by the copy in a more conventional manner. Stevens had bought the Crowninshield library en bloc, largely, he claimed, to get that one book of psalms, the first book printed in British North America. Having sold a complete though sophisticated copy to Lenox in 1854, Stevens offered this perfect volume to the British Museum for £150, or $750. For several years the trustees hesitated, and in 1868 the copy returned to New England, Brinley having agreed to pay Stevens's

The cover of Brinley's prized copy of the 1624 large-paper edition of John Smith's
General History of Virginia

price in guineas (one guinea equaling a pound plus one shilling) rather than in pounds. For the additional sum he received a binding by Francis Bedford "in his best style," as Stevens wrote. Though modern collectors shudder at the sacrilege, the nineteenth-century bookman generally preferred elegance to original state, and a binding by Bedford elevated the status of an amateurishly produced American imprint to that of the more attractive and more sought-after examples of British and Continental presswork. This volume was acquired by Cornelius Vanderbilt in the first part of the Brinley sale in March 1879 for $1,200 and remained in the family until Dr. Rosenbach bought it for Yale in 1947 for $151,000, then a record sum for a printed book sold at auction.

Brinley was not only a good customer of Stevens but also a friend; when the bookseller came to Hartford he visited the Brinley home. Yet Stevens did not confuse friendship with business; he gave first refusal of his American nuggets to Lenox and Brown. During a visit to Hartford in 1868 Stevens mentioned to Brinley that a collection of 275 works by the various Mathers, together with *A Declaration of Former Passages and Proceedings betwixt the English and the Narrowgansets, with Their Confederates* (Cambridge, Mass.: Stephen Daye, 1645), had been rejected by the British Museum, Lenox, and Brown. The *Declaration* was then regarded as unique; three other copies are now held in American libraries. Brinley bought Stevens's book for $50. In 1879 the Lenox Library repented and paid $215 for it at the first Brinley sale. At the Hoe sale Henry Huntington paid $10,000 for his, and the Brown copy cost $15,000.

Another item that initially slipped through the hands of Lenox and into Brinley's was a large paper copy of John Smith's *General History of Virginia* (London: Printed by I. D. and I. H. for Michael Sparkes, 1624). Lenox took great interest in this work and published two bibliographical essays on the *General History* in *Norton's Literary Register* (1854). Lenox had asked Stevens to locate a large paper copy for him. After a twenty-year search Stevens wrote to Lenox on 1 March 1873, describing his find:

> It is not only large paper, but is in the original binding in dark green morocco, very richly tooled all over, and in excellent preservation. It is the *Dedication* copy, and no doubt belonged to the Duchess of Richmond and Lenox. The Richmond and Lenox arms, very large and elaborate, with her quarterings, are on the side. The binding alone is, I think, the finest I ever saw of Charles I's time, and would readily bring £100 without the book. . . . The price of the Smith is 250 guineas, a large sum for a Smith; but when you see the book I trust you will not think — or rather will think it not best to pass it.

Stevens also wrote to Brinley about his find on 22 March 1873, stating that he thought it unlikely that Lenox would forgo the opportunity to secure the book; Stevens added that if Lenox did pass it, "he is more of a . . . than I ever took him for." Lenox, however, refused even to look at the volume. Brinley paid Stevens's price, about $1,275. At the first Brinley sale Lenox bought it for $1,800. Though it no longer is regarded as the dedication copy, it is a fine and rare specimen.

In 1874 Lenox similarly declined John Brereton's *A Briefe and True Relation of the Discovery of the North Part of Virginia* (London: George Bishop, 1602) and James Rosier's *A True Relation of the Most Prosperous Voyage Made This Present Year 1605, by Captain George Waymouth* (London: George Bishop, 1605); Brinley acquired the pair for $1,250. At the Samuel Latham Mitchell Barlow sale the Lenox Library paid $1,125 for a second edition of the former and $1,825 for a copy of the latter. The 1647 English reprint of the *Bay Psalm Book,* rarer than the original — only two copies are known — also came to Brinley after Lenox refused it. When Stevens offered it to Lenox in 1867 the collector wrote back, "I do not wish to retain your offer even for 24 hours. I cannot give you 100 guineas for the Bay Psalm Book of 1647." Brinley could. The John Carter Brown Library acquired Brinley's copy for $435 in 1879. The New York Public Library still does not own this edition; the only other copy resides in the British Library.

Toward the end of his life Brinley flirted for a time with incunabula, though he acquired only one example — the Gutenberg Bible. The Brinley copy of the Bible, lacking seventeen leaves, had been found in Erfurt, Germany. In 1870 Albert Cohn of Berlin offered it for sale for 4,000 talers. In a letter dated 18 January 1873 Stevens described how he secured the book for Brinley. Asher of Bedford Street had four other orders for it, but all the other prospective buyers wanted to look first. Stevens offered to take it unseen and promised prompt payment. Brinley quibbled a bit about the price but paid the £637.15.0.

The list of American firsts in the Brinley collection includes, besides the *Bay Psalm Book,* the first book issued for private distribution rather than for sale in America (John Eliot, *Communion of Churches,* Cambridge, Mass.: Marmaduke Johnson, 1665), the first book printed in Boston (Increase Mather, *The Wicked Man's Portion,* Boston: John Foster, 1675), the first book printed in Connecticut (*Saybrook Platform,* New London: Thomas Short, 1710), one of only two copies of the first book printed in Pennsylvania (Samuel Atkins, *Kalendarium Pennsilvaniense,* Philadelphia: William Bradford, 1685), the first book printed in New York (George Keith, *New England's Spirit of Persecution Transmitted to Pennsylvania,* New York: William Bradford, 1693), the first American edition of the Book of Common Prayer (New York: William Bradford, 1710), the only copy of the first surviving book printed in Maryland (Thomas Bray, *The Necessity of an Early Religion,* Annapolis: Thomas Reading, 1700), and the first Florida imprint (*The Case of the Inhabitants of East Florida,* Saint Augustine: John Wells, 1784).

He owned the only known copies of the almanacs printed at Cambridge, Massachusetts, between 1646 and 1649; the unique *Rhode Island Almanac* (Newport: James Franklin, 1728) — an important precursor to a more famous work by the publisher's brother, Benjamin Franklin's *Poor Richard's Almanac;* and the only copy of Cotton Mather's elegy on the death of Nathaniel Collins, *An Elegy on the Much-To-Be-Deplored Death of that Never-To-Be Forgotten Person, the Reverend Nathanael Collins . . .* (Boston: Richard Pierce for Obadiah Gill, 1685). Brinley's library included over two hundred Franklin imprints, more than fifty of William Bradford's, as well as products of the presses of Andrew Bradford (William's son), Daniel Fowle (the first printer of New Hampshire), Judah Padock Spooner (the first printer of Vermont), James Parker (who established the first permanent press in New Jersey), Lewis Timothy (one of the first printers in South Carolina), and James Davis and James Johnston (the first printers in North Carolina and Georgia, respectively). Association copies in the Brinley collection included Rich-

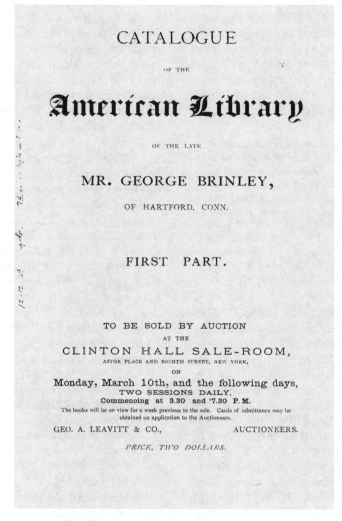

CATALOGUE

OF THE

American Library

OF THE LATE

MR. GEORGE BRINLEY,

OF HARTFORD, CONN.

FIRST PART.

TO BE SOLD BY AUCTION

AT THE

CLINTON HALL SALE-ROOM,

ASTOR PLACE AND EIGHTH STREET, NEW YORK,

ON

Monday, March 10th, and the following days,

TWO SESSIONS DAILY,

Commencing at 3.30 and 7.30 P. M.

The books will be on view for a week previous to the sale. Cards of admittance may be
obtained on application to the Auctioneers.

GEO. A. LEAVITT & CO.,   AUCTIONEERS.

PRICE, TWO DOLLARS.

*Cover of the first volume of the Brinley sale catalogue issued in
1879. The first volume included three of five parts of the sale.*

ard Eden's copy of his translation of Peter Martyr's
Decades (London, 1555) and a copy of *Chronological
History of New England* (Boston, 1736) that had be-
longed to the author, Thomas Prince. Also on
Brinley's shelf was Cotton and Samuel Mather's
copy of Erasmus's *Praise of Folly*.

Brinley did not confine his interest to highly
sought-after materials, however. He recognized the
value of the unconsidered trifle, such as Martin
Moore's *Sermon, January 5, 1817; Containing a History
of the Town of Natick, Massachusetts from 1651* (Cambridge, Mass.: Hilliard & Metcalf, 1817). This title
brought only a dollar at the Brinley sale, but it is
one of only two copies listed in the *National Union
Catalog* and includes useful information about the
early history of the New England town. Charles
Carroll Spalding's *Annals of Kansas City* (Kansas

City: Van Horn and Abeel's Printing House, 1858)
brought three dollars; it is now worth at least that
many thousands. In commenting on his wide-ranging tastes as a book collector, William S. Reese
states that Brinley appreciated "the entire range of
material printed in America — historical works, sermons, chapbooks, textbooks, psalm books of less
exalted stature, and pamphlets of every sort."

When the Brinleys were living at 33 Asylum
Street the library was housed in rooms behind the
Wadsworth Atheneum. After the death of Brinley's
father in 1857 the family relocated; Brinley acquired a large house at the southwest corner of
Pearl and Wells Streets and converted its third-floor
ballroom into a library . Charles Brinley described
the transformation: "All the wall space, and that of
a smaller room adjoining, [were] covered with

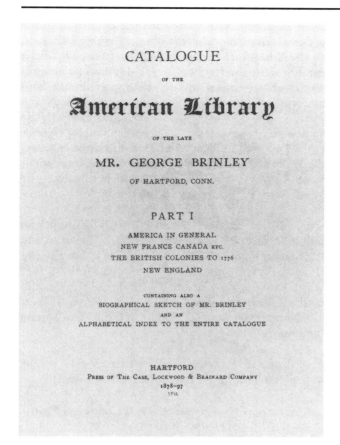

CATALOGUE

OF THE

𝔄merican 𝔏ibrary

OF THE LATE

MR. GEORGE BRINLEY

OF HARTFORD, CONN.

PART I

AMERICA IN GENERAL.
NEW FRANCE CANADA ETC.
THE BRITISH COLONIES TO 1776
NEW ENGLAND

CONTAINING ALSO A
BIOGRAPHICAL SKETCH OF MR. BRINLEY
AND AN
ALPHABETICAL INDEX TO THE ENTIRE CATALOGUE

HARTFORD
PRESS OF THE CASE, LOCKWOOD & BRAINARD COMPANY
1878-97

CONTENTS.

Title page and contents page for part 1 of the catalogue

shelving; up and down the center of the main room were a double row of old fashioned standing bookcases with cupboards and drawers below and shelves above behind glass doors." The front and back halls of the third story, a small room on the first floor, the bedrooms, and even the dining room received shelving. The two horsehair sofas in the dining room were "piled high with books. . . . Spare dining room chairs had often the same burden."

Brinley could be generous with his books. When Samuel F. Haven, librarian of the American Antiquarian Society from 1838 to 1881, requested the loan of Theodore de Bry's rare, self-published account of early explorations, *Great Voyages* (Frankfort, 1590–1619), Brinley replied, "You are quite too ceremonious in asking for De Bry. There is nothing in my library too good for you and I hereby present you with the freedom of it in a golden box: — barring a pleasant fiction about the box." In 1854 Brinley gave the society the council chamber copy of the 1726 edition of the laws of Massachusetts, *Acts and Laws of His Majesty's Province of the Massachusetts-Bay in New England* (Boston: B. Green, 1726), though he had gone through much trouble to acquire the vol-

ume. John Hammond Trumbull, librarian of the Watkinson Free Library at Hartford, Connecticut, enjoyed free run of Brinley's collection, which he used repeatedly for his research. Trumbull prepared the catalogues of the first four Brinley sales; Frank B. Gray, also of the Watkinson Free Library, prepared the final list.

In successfully getting their hands on Brinley's books, Haven and Trumbull were in a fortunate minority, for Brinley did not indulge the merely curious when granting access to his collection. According to the 12 February 1879 issue of the *Hartford Daily Courant*, Trumbull "was . . . the only person besides its owner who had access to [the] volumes." Indeed, Brinley voiced his attitude toward the notion of public access to private collections upon learning of Lenox's decision to convert his personal collection to a public reference library. In a letter from Stevens to Lenox dated 10 February 1870, Stevens paraphrases Brinley's comments: "Mr. Lenox had at last like Sampson brought the whole fabric down upon himself, meaning that the great meddlesome public would be down upon you and worry you to death."

Those excluded from Brinley's library during his life were able to see it when it was sold at auction. The books constituted a significant portion of Brinley's estate, so his decision to sell them rather than donate them to an institution is not surprising. In a memorandum housed in the Connecticut Historical Society he set down four other reasons for dispersing the collection:

1st. Because I am not satisfied with the loose way in which such trusts are managed in this country and do not believe that any directions I might impose would be observed according to my will.

2nd. After a careful survey of the principal collections of books in this country, it is my opinion that all are in danger of destruction by fire, none of them being housed in fireproof buildings and therefore if my library was in the possession of one institution it would, in case of fire, be entirely destroyed.

3rd. Consequently, I prefer to have it distributed by a public sale among many institutions or individuals who may choose to buy the books and hoping that the books being thus dispersed they may escape destruction for a longer period than if all were exposed to be destroyed by fire at one and the same time.

4th. Moreover, if the entire library had been left to anyone of the institutions ... that institution would be surrounded with many books which were already upon their shelves and which therefore they did not want; or many books which they did not want under any circumstances.

To help institutions acquire the books they did want, Brinley allotted generous grants to seven libraries: ten thousand dollars to Yale, which had awarded him an honorary master of arts degree in 1868; five thousand dollars each to the American Antiquarian Society and the Watkinson Free Library; and twenty-five hundred dollars each to the Boston Public Library, the Library of Congress, the New York Historical Society, and the Historical Society of Pennsylvania. Brinley died intestate, as did his wife (1877). Their son George together with Trumbull were responsible for organizing the sale of the Brinley collection, and they altered Brinley's bequests somewhat, allowing no subvention to the Boston Public Library and the Library of Congress and reducing by five hundred dollars the grant to the Historical Society of Pennsylvania. Justin Winsor objected to grants altogether, claiming that they would drive up prices. They do not appear to have done so, however, and Winsor's comments may have been influenced by his association with Harvard and the Boston Public Library – neither of which received any of Brinley's largesse.

Trumbull had catalogued the collection in the order in which it was arranged on Brinley's shelves, so the 2,619 lots representing the first part of the catalogue in the first sale were devoted to general works about America, books about Canada, and material dealing with prerevolutionary North America and New England. The Lenox Library, the largest buyer at the sale, was represented by George H. Moore and Mr. Key. The Boston Public Library, the American Antiquarian Society, the Connecticut State Library, the Chicago Public Library, the Watkinson Free Library, Yale, the Wisconsin Historical Society, and the Library of Congress (represented by the auctioneer's son, Joseph Sabin, Jr.) all sent delegates. Private collectors were also drawn to the books. Ogden Goelet of New York, Levi Leiter (Marshall Field's partner) of Chicago, Brayton Ives (another New Yorker and a founder of the Grolier Club), Charles H. Kalbfleisch of Brooklyn, Cornelius Vanderbilt, Jr., and Hamilton Cole were among the important buyers.

The 16 March 1879 issue of the *New York Times* described the results of the first Brinley sale, noting how public libraries in particular had benefited:

The American Antiquarian Society's Library has filled many gaps that marred its collection of seventeenth-century American books. The Lenox Library ... has largely increased its store of this class of books – the writings of the Mathers, witchcraft literature, &c. ... The J. Carter Brown Library at Providence has been vastly strengthened in Mather books through the liberal and judicious purchases of Mr. J. R. Bartlett. The Library of Congress has expended about $3000 and has secured a very desirable mass of literature from all departments of the catalogue.

Other large purchasers were the Chicago Public Library, the Watkinson Free Library (five thousand dollars), Yale (four thousand dollars), the Brooklyn Historical Society, and the Connecticut Historical Society (twenty-five hundred dollars).

This first sale was filled with gems and produced more than a third of the $127,138 total earned in the five Brinley sales – a record that stood until the Hoe sales. Each of the other four sales offered attractive items as well. The second sale, held in 1880, concentrated on the Middle Atlantic states and the American Revolution; it brought in $32,690. The third, which added $23,716, contained books about the American South and West and the American Indians, as well as editions of Bibles, including the Gutenberg. The fourth and fifth sales (1886 and 1893) yielded $7,364 and $14,644, respectively. These included fifteen Franklin imprints, two Eliot Bibles, the first-known chart of Boston Harbor (circa 1686), and the account books of Jeremiah Wadsworth, commissary-general of the Continental army, together with two thousand letters addressed to him. These manuscripts provide invaluable information about the history of the American Revolution.

In his *Bibliography and Pseudo-Bibliography* (1936) Alfred Edward Newton called the five Brinley auctions "the first great book sale in the country." Similarly, R. W. G. Vail, in his *The Literature of Book Collecting* (1936), of the American Antiquarian Society described them as "the greatest sale of Americana ever held." The sale sent two-thirds of Brinley's books to institutional libraries, and many more have since found their way there. Many of these works might not have survived had Brinley not rescued them from paper mills and attics. The Brinley sales called attention to neglected materials and stimulated others to share his enthusiasm for a wide range of Americana, not just the few glamorous items.

As Carl L. Cannon noted in *American Book Collectors* (1941), "Brinley was the first of the great collectors to see that a book about Oregon was as true a piece of Americana as a Columbus letter, and that an American imprint has a special interest for American collectors. He broadened the field of collecting by despising nothing." The sale of his library also allowed both winners and losers to share in the thrill of the preoccupation that had delighted Brinley for thirty years.

References:
Randolph G. Adams, "George Brinley, Book Collector," in his *Three Americanists: Henry Harisse, Bibliographer; George Brinley, Book Collector; Thomas Jefferson, Librarian* (Philadelphia: University of Pennsylvania Press, 1939), pp. 35–67;

William Brotherhead, *Forty Years among the Old Booksellers of Philadelphia, with Biographical and Bibliographical Remarks* (Philadelphia: A. P. Brotherhead, 1891);

Donald B. Engley, "George Brinley, Americanist," *Papers of the Bibliographical Society of America,* 60 (1966): 465–472;

Marcus A. McCorison, "George Brinley, Americanist," *Gazette of the Grolier Club,* new series 32 (1980): 4–23;

Kenneth Nebelzahl, "Reflections on the Brinley and Streeter Sales," *Papers of the Bibliographical Society of America,* 64 (1970): 165–175;

William S. Reese, "George Brinley and His Library," *Gazette of the Grolier Club,* new series 32 (1980): 24–39;

Joseph Rosenblum, "George Brinley and His Sales," *American Book Collector,* 6 (September–October 1985): 13–23;

Henry Stevens, *Recollections of Mr. James Lenox of New York,* edited by Victor Hugo Paltsits (New York: New York Public Library, 1951), p. 156;

James Hammond Trumbull and Frank B. Gray, *Catalogue of the American Library of the Late Mr. George Brinley, of Hartford, Conn.,* 5 volumes (Hartford, Conn.: Case, Lockwood & Brainard, 1878–1893).

Papers:
The bulk of the Brinley papers are at the William L. Clements Library, University of Michigan. The American Antiquarian Society also holds some of his letters.

William Byrd II

(28 March 1674 – 26 August 1744)

Kevin J. Hayes
University of Central Oklahoma

See also the Byrd entry in *DLB 24: American Colonial Writers, 1660–1734.*

BOOKS: *A Discourse Concerning the Plague, With Some Preservatives Against It. By a Lover of Mankind,* attributed to Byrd (London: Printed for J. Roberts, 1721);

The Westover Manuscripts: Containing The History of the Dividing Line Betwixt Virginia and North Carolina; A Journey to the Land of Eden, A.D. 1733; and A Progress to the Mines. Written from 1728 to 1736 . . . , edited by Edmund Ruffin (Petersburg, Va.: Printed by Edmund & Julian C. Ruffin, 1841);

History of the Dividing Line and Other Tracts . . . , 2 volumes (Richmond, 1866); revised as *The Writings of "Colonel William Byrd of Westover in Virginia, Esqr.,"* edited by John S. Bassett (New York: Doubleday, Page, 1901);

Description of the Dismal Swamp and A Proposal to Drain the Swamp, edited by Earl G. Swem (Metuchen, N.J.: Printed for C. F. Heartman, 1922);

A Journey to the Land of Eden and Other Papers, edited by Mark Van Doren (New York: Macy-Masius, 1928);

The Secret History of the Line, in *William Byrd's Histories of the Dividing Line betwixt Virginia and North Carolina,* edited by William K. Boyd (Raleigh: North Carolina Historical Commission, 1929);

The Secret Diary of William Byrd of Westover, 1709–1712, edited by Louis B. Wright and Marion Tinling (Richmond: Dietz Press, 1941);

Another Secret Diary of William Byrd of Westover, 1739–1741, With Letters & Literary Exercises, 1696–1726, edited by Maude H. Woodfin, translated and collated by Tinling (Richmond: Dietz, 1942);

The London Diary (1717–1721) and Other Writings, edited by Wright and Tinling (New York: Oxford University Press, 1958).

Collection: *The Prose Works of William Byrd of Westover: Narratives of a Colonial Gentleman,* edited by Louis B. Wright in a collated edition with a modernized text (Cambridge: Harvard University Press, 1966).

William Byrd II created the most diverse library in colonial America. His collection of belletristic literature was unsurpassed. His collection of law books rivaled that of John Mercer's, generally considered the largest in colonial Virginia. He owned the best art-book collection in America prior to the nineteenth century, the best architectural library prior to 1750, the greatest medical library in colonial Virginia, the largest collection of Anglican works in the colonies, and, prior to Benjamin Franklin, the best collection of histories and travels in colonial America. With over twenty-five hundred titles in over thirty-five hundred volumes, the Byrd collection was one of the two largest private libraries in colonial America. Although the Mather collection has been estimated to have been the larger of the two, much less is known about it.

Born in Virginia on 28 March 1674, the son of William Byrd and Mary Horsemanden Filmer, William Byrd II was sent to England for his education. At the Felsted School in Essex, he learned Latin with the help of John Langston's *Lusus Poeticus Latino-Anglicanus* (1675), a collection of pithy sayings from the classical poets which taught students as they competed against one another "capping verses": one student would provide a quotation; the next would follow it up with a corresponding quotation. His schooling also included studies in French, German, and Italian. Byrd left Felsted in early 1690 and made his way to Holland, where he began studying the merchant trade and continued his bookish learning. The Netherlands had an active French-language press, and Byrd acquired such Amsterdam imprints as Jean Racine's *Oeuvres* and Car-

Portrait of William Byrd II, circa 1692–1695, by unknown artist (Colonial Williamsburg Collection)

dinal Richelieu's *Testament politique.* Byrd acquired copies of Henry Hexam's and William Sewel's English/Dutch dictionaries and many Dutch imprints including Johan van den Sande's history of the Netherlands' wars of independence, Emanuel Van Meteren's history of the Netherlands, and a Dutch translation of John Lyly's *Euphues.* Byrd continued his study of other languages as well, reading such works as Giovanni Veroni's introduction to Italian and the posthumous works of Janus Erasmius, which were printed in Latin and Flemish.

Byrd abandoned the merchant profession, and in 1692 he returned to London and began studying law at the Middle Temple. During this period he also began to build his law library, acquiring many reports of cases and legal treatises as well as several works concerning natural law. In 1696, at the age of twenty-two, Byrd was elected to the Royal Society, and his colleagues there helped foster his burgeon-

ing curiosity in medicine and natural history. Byrd owned several works by colleagues at the Royal Society such as Sir Isaac Newton, John Evelyn, Alexander Pitfield, and Martin Lister. Later that year Byrd returned to Virginia at the request of his father and entered the House of Burgesses, beginning a lifetime of political activity in the colony. Byrd was soon back in England, however. (Living in England five separate times, Byrd spent nearly thirty years of his life abroad.)

In 1701 Byrd traveled around England with Sir John Percival, and books became an integral part of the trip. They brought along Thomas Smith's *De republica Anglorum* and John Brome's *Historical Account of . . . Three Years Travels over England and Wales* as guidebooks. During their journey Byrd and Percival toured Burghley, the earl of Exeter's seat. The earl had an excellent library, which Percival described as "one of the finest in England, for

Westover, the Byrd family home (Virginia State Chamber of Commerce)

the number of Books, the choice of them & the ornamentary part being all curiusly guilt and plac'd in exact order." Byrd's decision to have his books specially gilt may have been inspired by what he saw at Burghley, and the "exact order" of the earl's books may have influenced Byrd's organizational scheme. The two travelers visited many other libraries, and Byrd would come to own works by men he met during the journey such as Humphrey Prideaux; Simon Patrick, bishop of Ely; and Richard Cumberland, bishop of Peterborough.

Back in London Byrd read, bought books, wrote, attended the theater, and made daily rounds of the coffeehouses. His time spent socializing was balanced by periods of quiet study in the morning, a daily practice he continued throughout his life. In his self-characterization, "Inamorato L'Oiseaux," Byrd argues for his routine of daily study:

Too much company distracts his thoughts, and hinders him from digesting his observations into good sence. It makes a man superficial, penetrateing no deeper than the surface of things. One notice crowds out another, haveing no time to sink into the mind. A constant hurry of visits & conversation gives a man a habit of inadvertency, which betrays him into faults without measure &

without end. For this reason he commonly reserv'd the morning to himself, and bestow'd the rest upon his freinds.

After his father's death in 1705, Byrd returned to Westover in Virginia, received his inheritance, and became a Virginia councillor. Soon after his return to Virginia, Byrd found that certain titles in his law library were in demand; at the 2 November 1705 meeting of the Virginia Council, it was recorded that the governor authorized payment to Byrd for law books for the use of the governor and the council. Most likely, after he inherited his father's library, Byrd found redundant works and sold the duplicates to the council. He also may have donated books to the College of William and Mary. Byrd settled into a quieter life than he had known in England. His fond memories of London society, however, faded somewhat when he met Lucy, daughter of Gen. Daniel Parke. They were wed in May 1706.

Byrd's diary provides an extended look into how he used and cared for his library. After his regular morning study, he would read once or twice during the day and again in the evening. During the summer of 1709 Byrd designed and built a separate

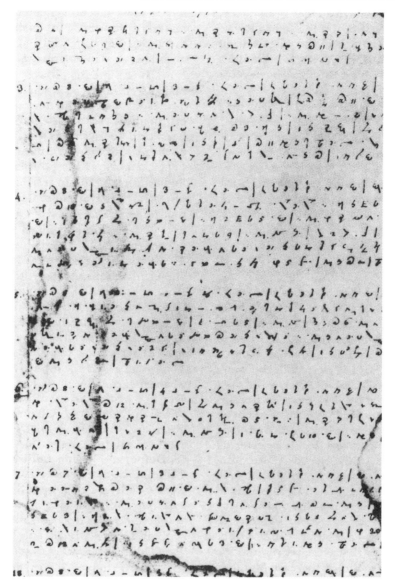

13–17 March 1718 entries in Byrd's diary. Written in shorthand, the diary offers a detailed record of his book collecting and reading habits (Virginia Historical Society).

structure to house his books at his Westover home. He spent several hours a day for five or six days in August removing his books into the new library, a long, spacious gallery which would eventually house twenty-three walnut bookcases with up to seven shelves per case. As Mary Willing Byrd later described it to a correspondent: "The library would delight you. It contains a fine collection of books in cases; the room is very long – ten couples might dance in it very well – and there is a fine spinet & harpsichord." Byrd made the library as aesthetically pleasing as possible. He had many of his books uniformly gilt and decorated the gallery with the por-

traits of friends and family members. The library was sparsely furnished, however; Byrd used the room as a place to exercise during inclement weather. The building which housed the library was burned during the Civil War.

The diary also shows how he acquired many of his books. Although book purchases from the families of the deceased account for a relatively small part of Byrd's acquisitions, his collection of medical books most likely grew when Byrd purchased titles from the estate of his friend and neighbor Dr. William Oastler two months after the doctor's death in 1709. In the spring of that year,

Virginia planter Benjamin Harrison died at Berkeley, the Harrison family plantation on the James River. Byrd visited the widow Harrison and acquired several books from her husband's library. He got most of his books in the same fashion his father had, however — from London friends and merchants.

Byrd recorded in his diary that he spent time in July and August of 1709 "settling his books." Since the time spent "settling" his library was approximately equal to the time spent the previous summer removing his books, the settling must have involved a major reorganization. He subdivided the collection into seven categories: history and travel, law, medicine, belles lettres, French, the classics, and a large miscellaneous group which included books on a wide range of topics such as geometry, architecture, and astronomy.

In the first three bookcases and on the top part of the fourth, Byrd shelved his histories and travel books. He enjoyed reading about voyages from every part of the world, but many of the titles he owned dealt specifically with travels in America and were by such authors as Peter Martyr, Samuel Purchas, John Ogilby, Lionel Wafer, William Dampier, Baron La Hontan, Jonathan Dickinson, and Thomas Gage. Most of the Byrd volumes do not survive, and the 1752 manuscript catalogue does not always allow for precise identification of the editions that Byrd owned. Although Byrd derisively referred to Americanist colonists to the north as "New England Saints," titles in his library suggest that he took a greater interest in the region than he was willing to reveal. Byrd owned histories of the New England colonies such as Cotton Mather's *Magnalia Christi Americana* (London: for Thomas Parkhurst, 1702). Other books in the Byrd library that were representative of New England culture included Increase Mather's *Diatriba de signo filii hominis* (Amsterdam: apud M. Browning, 1682), a meditation on the second coming of Christ and the conversion of the Jews; the *Confession of Faith* from the 1680 Boston synod; John Eliot's Algonquin translation of Lewis Bayly's *Practice of Piety;* and Eliot's American-Indian translation of the Bible, the first Bible printed in British North America. Byrd owned histories of Virginia by Capt. John Smith, Hugh Jones, and Robert Beverley.

In the lower part of the fourth, fifth, and sixth bookcase, Byrd kept his law collection. Mercer, a practicing Virginia lawyer, had three times as many "Reports" as Byrd; but the number of ancient legal treatises, continental law treatises, and books on legal and political theory in the Byrd collection was unsurpassed. Like other categories in his library,

Byrd's law collection encompassed a broad range of materials; his collection included works describing the underlying historical and theoretical basis of English law, as well as practical legal texts.

Byrd's medical library was the finest in colonial Virginia. Byrd owned the popular practical guides, as well as the most ancient and most modern medical treatises. Fellow Royal Society members kindled Byrd's fascination with the study of anatomy and the workings of the human body. He kept a record of his physical health in his diary. Soon after writing in his diary that his "head was out of order," for example, Byrd read the anonymous *Treatise of Diseases of the Head, Brain and Nerves.*

The eighth and ninth bookcases and the top part of the tenth contained "Entertainment, Poetry, Translations &c.," the most loosely organized of the subject divisions. Along with belletristic works, the category included gardening books and art treatises. Also shelved under this category was the finest drama collection in colonial America. It included Francis Beaumont and John Fletcher's *Works,* Colley Cibber's *Plays,* two Ben Jonson folios, William Congreve's *Works,* John Dryden's *Plays,* and a Shakespeare folio, probably the 1685 Fourth Folio. Byrd owned a variety of other belletristic writers: *Works* by Geoffrey Chaucer, Edmund Spenser, François Rabelais, John Denham, William Davenant, Abraham Cowley, Sir Thomas Browne, Daniel Defoe, and Joseph Addison. Byrd's collection of Milton included *Paradise Lost; History of Britain; Artis logicae;* Milton's edition of Sir Walter Ralegh's *Arts of Empire;* William Hog's Latin translation of *Paradise Lost, Paradise Regained,* and *Samson Agonistes;* John Toland's *Life of Milton,* and Joseph Addison's *Notes upon the Twelve Books of Paradise Lost.*

Byrd shelved his gardening books alongside his art books, and he kept both among the belletristic works. In closely associating gardening with the arts, Byrd was not unusual; Jefferson, for instance, grouped his books similarly. Byrd had the greatest collection of historical and theoretical art treatises in colonial America, with many of his art books preceding the next recorded American copies by forty to a hundred years. After permanently moving to Virginia, Byrd told a London correspondent that gardening and caring for his library were among the innocent pleasures with which he diverted himself. Byrd had the finest garden in Virginia, in large part due to his fine collection of gardening books. He owned practical horticulture books by John Evelyn, Jean de la Quintinie, Henrick van Oosten, Moses Cook, Richard Bradley, and Philip Miller.

The bookplate of William Byrd II (Library of Congress)

The lower part of the tenth and eleventh bookcases contained works collected under the "Divinity" category. Byrd owned the greatest collection of Anglican works in colonial America, as well as a wide variety of tracts pertaining to other denominations; the breadth of his divinity collection extended from early religious titles to contemporary theoretical treatments of religious meditation and study. His religious interests pervade his own writing. In the diaries, he meticulously recorded his daily reading of the Hebrew *Bible* and his frequent attention to the Greek *Testament*. He read sermons and works dealing with "the nature of the spirit" and wrote prayers and articles of faith. His copy of Jeremy Taylor's *Worthy Communicant* (London: R. H. for Awnsham Churchil, 1683) contains his personal creed written inside the back cover. The *London Diary* describes his eagerness to act as ship's chaplain during the 1719–1720 ocean crossing. One of the lengthiest entries in Byrd's commonplace book is a reflection on William Wollaston's *Religion of Nature Delineated*. Byrd expressed some skepticism regarding Wollaston's work but was nevertheless fascinated with the enlightened ideas.

In the twelfth bookcase and in the bottom part of the thirteenth, Byrd shelved his French works, which included poetry, romances, courtier books, histories, and travel books. Byrd generally saved his French collection for purposes of entertainment rather than of edification; even the French histories, he believed, contained more fiction and romance than fact. In a 10 October 1735 letter to an English correspondent Byrd wrote, "it would not be possible for one of us anchorites to carry on a tolerable correspondence, but like French historians, where we don't meet with pretty incidents, we must e'en make, & lard a little truth with a great deal of fiction." His weighty Dictionary of the French Academy also reveals how entertaining the French language was to Byrd. The recto of the back flyleaf of the dictionary contains the lengthiest annotations in any of Byrd's surviving books, and Byrd's manuscript supplement to the dictionary lists obscene French words the Academy did not see fit to include. For each entry, Byrd wrote the French word, provided the Latin definition, and then used the word in a sentence.

The books in the top part of case thirteen and cases fourteen and fifteen are titled "Classicks" in the library catalogue, but philology might more appropriately describe the collection. Besides the standard Greek and Latin histories and verse, the collection contained critical treatments of classical literature and dictionaries for Latin, Greek, Hebrew, Spanish, and Italian. He attempted to learn Middle Eastern languages from Valentin Schindler's *Lexicon Pentaglotton: Hebraicum, Chaldaicum, Syriacum, Talmudico-Rabbinicum & Arabicum.*

The remainder of the books shelved in cases labeled "A" through "H" are unclassified, although certain subject groupings can be discerned. Case B contained large folio volumes of prints. Books on mathematics and science, many of which attempted to reconcile science with religion, were grouped together in case G. He owned works describing the most up-to-date experiments including the seminal works in the study of electricity, although experiments in electromagnetism did not significantly develop until after Byrd's death.

In early 1715 Byrd left Virginia for England to attend to personal and governmental matters, leaving behind his daughter Erie and his pregnant wife. Byrd had planned to return home some time before the end of 1716, but in the middle of that year his wife came to London after having given birth to another daughter, Whilhelmina, or "Mina" as Byrd would call her. With her arrival, Byrd decided to stay another winter. He was proud of his wife and enjoyed seeing her well received in London society. While in England, however, Lucy contracted smallpox in the autumn and died shortly afterward.

Byrd remained in London and sent for his two daughters in Virginia. On 9 May 1724 Byrd married Maria Taylor. After the marriage Byrd returned to Virginia with his family. Maria would bear one son and four daughters during the next five years.

Having returned to Virginia to settle permanently, Byrd spent the following years devoting his attentions to his writing as well as to his library. In 1728 Byrd was chosen to lead a surveying trip to settle the boundary between Virginia and North Carolina. Traveling through "the most charming country" he had ever seen, Byrd began to recognize in the American land not only a new and tremendous economic source, but also a new source for symbol, humor, and even myth. The trip provided Byrd with the opportunity to write his greatest works. Both the *Secret History of the Line,* published in 1929, and the *History of the Dividing Line Betwixt Virginia and North Carolina . . . ,* first separately published in 1841, draw on his familiarity with the classics and contemporary travel narratives, as well as his interest in natural history and his understanding of life in America.

During the last fifteen years of his life, Byrd acquired many contemporary books to educate his children. The Westover library shelved multiple copies of several of these textbooks. Since Byrd had only one son who survived beyond infancy, the multiple copies suggest his daughters were also taught Latin, classical history, astronomy, and mathematics. Byrd's surviving diary indicates that he devoted much time to helping them with their lessons.

After Byrd's death in 1744, the library descended to his son, William Byrd III. Byrd III turned out to be a drunk, a profligate, and a gambler. He committed suicide in 1777. The will of Byrd III stipulated that the Westover library be sold to pay his gambling debts. Virginian Isaac Zane purchased the entire collection and carted it to Philadelphia where the books were sold piecemeal. Of the original collection, which numbered more than twenty-five hundred titles, fewer than four hundred survive.

Letters:

The Correspondence of the Three William Byrds of Westover, Virginia, 1684–1776, 2 volumes, edited by Marion Tinling (Charlottesville: University Press of Virginia, 1977).

Biographies:

Richmond Croom Beatty, *William Byrd of Westover* (Boston: Houghton Mifflin, 1932); republished, with an introduction and an annotated bibliography by M. Thomas Inge (Hamden, Conn.: Archon, 1970);

Pierre Marambaud, *William Byrd of Westover 1674–1744* (Charlottesville: University Press of Virginia, 1971).

References:

Wyndham B. Blanton, *Medicine in Virginia in the Eighteenth Century* (Richmond: Garret & Massie, 1931);

William Hamilton Bryson, *Census of Law Books in Colonial Virginia* (Charlottesville: University Press of Virginia, 1978);

Herbert A. Johnson, *Imported Eighteenth-Century Law Treatises on American Libraries, 1700–1799* (Knoxville: University of Tennessee Press, 1978);

Helen Park, "A List of Architectural Books Available in America before the Revolution," *Journal of the Society of Architectural Historians,* 20 (October 1961): 115–130;

St. George L. Sioussat, "The *Philosophical Transactions* of the Royal Society in the Libraries of William Byrd of Westover, Benjamin Franklin, and the American Philosophical Society," *Proceedings of the American Philosophical Society,* 93 (1949): 99–113;

Mark R. Wenger, *The English Travels of Sir John Percival and William Byrd II: The Percival Diary of 1701* (Columbia: University of Missouri Press, 1989);

Edwin Wolf II, "The Dispersal of the Library of William Byrd of Westover," *Proceedings of the American Antiquarian Society,* 68 (1958): 19–106;

Wolf II, "Great American Book Collectors to 1800," *Gazette of the Grolier Club,* new series 16 (June 1971): 1–70;

Wolf II, "More Books from the Library of the Byrds of Westover," *Proceedings of the American Antiquarian Society,* 88 (1978): 51–82.

Papers:

The largest collections of Byrd's books are at the Pennsylvania Hospital and the Library Company of Philadelphia. Byrd's manuscripts are at the Huntington Library in San Marino, California; the American Philosophical Society in Philadelphia; and the Virginia Historical Society.

George Watson Cole
(6 September 1850 – 10 October 1939)

Donald C. Dickinson
University of Arizona

BOOKS: *A Catalogue of Books Relating to the Discovery and Early History of North and South America, Forming a Part of the Library of E. D. Church,* 5 volumes (New York: Dodd, Mead, 1907);

Bermuda in Periodical Literature (Boston: Boston Book Company, 1907);

A Catalogue of Books Consisting of English Literature and Miscellanea Forming a Part of the Library of E. D. Church, 2 volumes (New York: Dodd, Mead, 1909);

Check List or Brief Catalogue of the Library of Henry E. Huntington — English Literature to 1640 (New York: Privately printed, 1919);

An Index to Bibliographical Papers Published by the Bibliographical Society and the Library Association, London, 1877–1932 (Chicago: University of Chicago Press, 1933).

OTHER: Ben Jonson, *The Gypsies Metamorphosed,* edited by Cole (New York: Century, 1931).

SELECTED PERIODICAL PUBLICATIONS – UNCOLLECTED: "An Easy Method of Measuring Books," *Library Journal,* 10 (March 1885): 49–50;

"A Quicker Method of Measuring Books," *Library Journal,* 12 (September 1887): 345–349;

"American Bibliography, General and Local," *Library Journal,* 19 (January 1894): 5–9;

"Compiling a Bibliography," *Library Journal,* 26 (November 1901): 791–795; (December 1901): 859–863;

"The First Folio of Shakespeare," *Papers of the Bibliographical Society of America,* 3 (1908): 65–83;

"Book Collectors as Benefactors of Public Libraries," *Papers of the Bibliographical Society of America,* 9 (1915): 47–110;

"Bibliographic Problems, with a Few Solutions," *Papers of the Bibliographical Society of America,* 10 (1916): 119–142;

"Bibliographic Pitfalls – Linked Books," *Papers of the Bibliographical Society of America,* 18 (1924): 12–30;

"Bibliographic Matters of Passing Interest," *New York Herald Tribune,* 5 April 1925, p. 15;

"Early Library Development in New York State," *Bulletin of the New York Public Library,* 16 (November 1926): 849–857; (December 1926): 917–923;

"Lewis Hughes, Militant Minister of the Bermudas," *Proceedings of the American Antiquarian Society,* 37 (October 1927): 247–311;

"A Survey of the Bibliography of English Literature 1475–1640," *Papers of the Bibliographical Society of America,* 23 (1929): 1–95;

"Do You Know Your Lowndes?," *Papers of the Bibliographical Society of America,* 33 (1939): 1–22.

Those who knew George Watson Cole best agreed that he was an ambitious, talented professional. First as a teacher and lawyer, then as a librarian, bibliographer, and writer he made significant contributions to several disciplines. To all of these endeavors Cole brought intense intellectual curiosity, a high level of energy, and a strong belief in humanistic scholarship. When Margeret Stillwell dedicated her monumental study, *Incunabula in American Libraries* (1940), to Cole she referred to him as a "Friend of books and all the world of books, learned in all that touched the manuscript or printed word, insistent on thoroughness and accuracy in himself and others . . . unselfish, untiring, unafraid."

Cole was born in Warren, Connecticut, on 6 September 1850, the only child of Munson and Antoinette Taylor Cole. Munson Cole provided his family with a steady but modest income as a shingle maker and a real-estate salesman. To supplement his income he made children's toys, some of which he patented. Cole attended elementary school in Warren and then was sent to Phillips Academy at Andover, Massachusetts, to prepare himself for uni-

George Watson Cole (Henry E. Huntington Library and
Art Gallery)

versity study. As a result of a disciplinary problem he was asked to leave the academy before the end of his second year. He taught in a one-room elementary school for two years in Litchfield County, Connecticut, but when teaching failed to meet his financial needs he decided to prepare himself for a legal career. He read the law in the evenings and on weekends and in 1876, after passing the qualifying examinations, was admitted to the county bar. He opened a practice in Torrington, Connecticut, and from 1880 to 1885 served that area as county prosecutor for liquor violations. It was not an appointment calculated to win friends. The earnest young attorney took his position seriously and prosecuted anyone he found operating an illegal still or engaged in bootlegging. As a diversion from his stressful professional duties, Cole became active on the Torrington Public Library board and volunteered to help reorganize the library catalogue. He knew nothing about libraries as such, but he had trained

himself in Takygraphy, a form of shorthand, which he thought might be useful in library work. In his readings about Takygraphy, Cole had come upon the name of another enthusiast, Melville Dewey, the librarian at Columbia College, who had created a new classification system for books. Cole wrote asking for advice on cataloguing procedures and after meeting Dewey in New York produced a well-organized fifty-page catalogue of the library's holdings. This was the beginning of a friendship that was to have a profound effect on Cole's future.

In August 1885 Cole accepted Dewey's advice and left his law practice to take a temporary position in the Fitchburg, Massachusetts, Public Library where, again, a catalogue was needed. In September, at Dewey's urging, Cole attended the Lake George (New York) Conference of the American Library Association and while there got further help on his cataloguing project from such distinguished members of the profession as Charles A. Cutter,

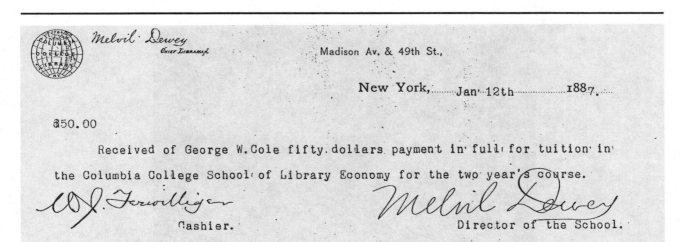

Cole's Columbia College tuition receipt (American Antiquarian Society)

Justin Winsor, and William F. Poole. After thirteen months in Fitchburg, Cole produced a meticulous seven-hundred-page author, title, and subject list for the sixteen-thousand-volume collection. While working in the Fitchburg library he, with Dewey's support, wrote several articles on classification and book measurement for the *Library Journal*. In one he described what came to be known as the Cole Size Card, a lined card used for measuring books according to rules established by the American Library Association. Eventually the Library Bureau marketed the Cole Size Card for general use throughout the country.

In 1887 Dewey urged Cole to move again – this time to Brooklyn, New York, where he was employed as a cataloguer by Charles Pratt, then organizing a library for the Pratt Institute. The appointment had the additional advantage of allowing Cole to attend classes at Dewey's newly formed School of Library Economy at Columbia College. In the spring of 1888, after two years of study, Cole graduated as a member of Dewey's first class. He immediately took a position as assistant to Poole in the Newberry Library in Chicago. At the time the Newberry was just beginning to develop its reputation as a distinguished rare-book archive with specialties in American and British history and literature. One of Cole's first assignments was to organize the twenty-five hundred incunabula, jeweled bindings, and early Bibles received from the Cincinnati collector Henry Probasco.

Cole had never before experienced handling such a treasure trove of materials, and he found the detailed work involved in cataloguing the rare books stimulating. It was the kind of work that was to occupy the greater part of his professional life for the next forty years.

In 1891 Cole became head librarian at the Jersey City, New Jersey, Public Library. Although the job involved a heavy administrative schedule he found time to work on American Library Association committees and to assume the office of treasurer in that organization. He also continued to publish articles in the *Library Journal* on various aspects of public library service and bibliography. In an 1894 article, "American Bibliography, General and Local," Cole praised R. R. Bowker's plan for a universal bibliography of nineteenth-century American imprints and further asserted that it was the duty of librarians to create guides of this kind. He made practical suggestions for organizing such a work and spoke of the "intense pleasure and satisfaction" to be found in the resulting product. Cole believed that librarians should look at the compilation of bibliographies as a hobby turned to for rest and relaxation at the end of a busy day. With typical optimism he declared that successful bibliographic projects required only three ingredients: enthusiasm, time, and financial support. For those with a strong will, Cole believed, these ingredients should be easy enough to come by.

Cole resigned from his position with the Jersey City Public Library in the fall of 1895 on his physician's advice after a serious bout with typhoid fever. He recuperated in Bermuda and while there started to compile a massive bibliography of the island's history and culture. He continued the project back in New York, working intensively in the Lenox Library. At the Lenox he became acquainted with the head of collections, the ascetic and learned

The letter that resulted in Cole's compilation of the E. D. Church catalogues published
in 1907 and 1909 (American Antiquarian Society)

bibliographer Wilberforce Eames. The two men shared many interests and quickly became close friends. It was Eames who spoke to Robert Dodd and suggested that Cole would be the ideal person to take on a major bibliographic project then under consideration by the Dodd, Mead bookselling and publishing firm. The project would result in the 1907 publication of a detailed catalogue of the rare-book and manuscript collections owned by Brooklyn businessman Elihu D. Church.

In New York book circles prior to 1907 little was known about the contents of the Church library. A reticent man, Church had avoided fanfare in making his purchases of rare material, and he never loaned his books for public display. It *was* known, however, that the library consisted of some of the finest copies of rare Americana and English literature ever gathered by one collector in the

United States. When Cole started work on the Church catalogue in 1901, he sought to create a meticulous and scholarly piece of work. Included in the description of each book Cole planned to provide a full collation, detailed pagination, facsimile reproduction of significant title pages, colophons and printer's marks, location and description of other copies, and, whenever appropriate, historical notes. The publication of the five-volume catalogue, *A Catalogue of Books Relating to the Discovery and Early History of North and South America, Forming a Part of the Library of E. D. Church* (1907), was well received by reviewers, who were astounded at the list of riches contained in the Church library. For his meticulous efforts, Cole was praised for having elevated bibliography to a new level of scientific excellence. The 1907 catalogue was followed in 1909 by two companion volumes titled *A Catalogue of Books Consisting*

A CATALOGUE OF
BOOKS
RELATING TO
THE DISCOVERY AND EARLY HISTORY OF
NORTH AND SOUTH
AMERICA
FORMING A PART OF
THE LIBRARY OF E. D. CHURCH

COMPILED AND ANNOTATED
BY
GEORGE WATSON COLE

VOLUME I
1482–1590

NEW YORK
PETER SMITH
1951

*Cover for the first volume of the catalogue of the E. D. Church
Library, compiled and annotated by Cole*

*of English Literature and Miscellanea Forming a Part of
the Library of E. D. Church.*

Over the next few years Cole spent considerable time traveling and writing. In a major article, "The First Folio of Shakespeare," published in the *Papers of the Bibliographical Society of America* in 1908 he explained his theories on the arrangement of the preliminary leaves in William Shakespeare's First Folio. Cole argued that seventeenth-century binding and printing practices account for the different sequence of preliminary leaves in various copies of the First Folio. In 1915 he published another important contribution to bookmanship, "Book Collectors as Benefactors of Public Libraries," in the *Papers of the Bibliographical Society of America.* This fifty-page essay includes extended comments on Hubert Howe Bancroft, Thomas Grenville, E. D.

Church, Aldolph Sutro, Robert Huth, James Lenox, and other American and English collectors, praising their efforts in support of learning. By his use of the term *public libraries* Cole intended to include all libraries public or private that provided scholars with access to their materials. Cole concluded his article by agreeing with John Hill Burton, who in his work *Book Hunter* (Edinburgh and London: Blackwood, 1862) argued that the creation of a library for the preservation of literature was, for those with means, nothing less than a public duty.

The year before the publication of his article on book collectors Cole had paid a call on Dodd. During their visit Dodd introduced him to the wealthy railroad entrepreneur Henry E. Huntington. It was a meeting that would have an important effect on Cole's future. Cole and Huntington had

AMERICANA

MELA, POMPONIUS. (*fl.* A. D. 40.)

POMPONIJ MELLAE COSMOGRAPHI GEOGRAPHIA. VENETIJS, *Erhardus Ratdolt*, 1482. [1]

Small 4to. Printed in gothic; no title-page.

COLLATION BY SIGNATURES : A, B, C, D, E, F, each 8 leaves; total 48 unnumbered leaves.

COLLATION BY PAGINATION : [blank], recto of [A 1]; — [map of the world], verso of [A 1]; — [text, in three books, the first page of the first book, as reproduced; *See* No. 1 *a*], recto of A 2 to recto of B 4; — | Pomponij Melle de situ orbis liber secundus. |, recto of B 4 to recto of [C 6]; — | Pom-

ponij Melle cosmographi liber Tertius. |, recto of [C 6] to recto of [D 6]; — | Ptisciani cesarienfis Interpretatio | ex Dionysio de orbis Situ. |, verso of [D 6] to recto of [F 8]; — [colophon, as reproduced; *See* No. 1 *b*], recto of F 8 ; — [blank], verso of [F 8].

CONDITION : Size of leaf, 8¼ x 5¾ inches. Bound in half brown morocco ; lettered | POMPONII MELLAE. DE SITUS ORBI. RAD. 1482 |, lengthwise along the back. Manuscript notes, in ink, on some pages.

On the verso of leaf A 1 is a modified Ptolemaic Map of the World engraved on wood, which shows Europe, Asia, and the northern portion of Africa. On the latter we find the Nile, with its sources in two lakes, one directly on the equator, and the other just south of it. These lakes correspond in place with those now called the Albert and Victoria Nyanza, showing that their location was surmised, if not actually known to geographers, at least four centuries before their late re-discovery. At the south streams rising in mountains flow into these lakes. The Niger in western Africa is also laid down. This map is a very early example of true chiaroscuro printing.

Of Pomponius Mela nothing whatever is known, but he is believed to have lived in the time of the Emperor Claudius. This is one of the earliest geographical works, the *editio princeps* of which appeared in 1471. It is written in a clear and simple style and notwithstanding its conciseness is enlivened with interesting descriptions of manners and customs.

OTHER COPIES : British Museum ; Bodleian ; University Library, Cambridge ; John Carter Brown ; and Lenox Libraries.

REFERENCES : Redgrave, *Erhard Ratdolt* (Bibliographical Society, *Illustrated Mono-*

graphs, No. 1; 1894), p. 35, No. 28 ; Winsor, 2 : 181 ; Proctor, No. 4385 ; Graesse, 5 : 400 ; Brunet, 4 : 800 ; Hain (and Copinger), No. *11019.

AMERICANA. VOL. I.—1 [1] CHURCH CATALOGUE

The first page of the catalogue of the E. D. Church Library

much in common — they were the same age, they had been born in small towns in the East, they had worked their way up in their chosen fields without benefit of college educations, and they both had a deep respect for scholarship. At the time, Huntington was in the process of building one of the most important rare-book and manuscript collections in the country. Between 1911 and 1914 he had purchased the entire Dwight Church collection, acquired the major items offered in the Robert Hoe sale at the Anderson Auction Company of New York, and dominated the buying at the Robert Huth sales at Sotheby, Wilkinson and Hodge in London. He had purchased Beverly Chew's literary collection as well as the Chatsworth Library, formerly owned by William Cavendish, sixth Duke of Devonshire. Books and manuscripts had accumulated in Huntington's Fifth Avenue mansion to such an extent that it was no longer possible for the secretarial staff to organize and list them with any degree of accuracy. Huntington was in need of a professional staff of bibliographers.

In the spring of 1915 Huntington called on Cole in California and asked him to take on the job of cataloguing the books and manuscripts. Cole moved to New York and started to work for Huntington in October 1915. He found an accumulation of approximately forty thousand volumes, some shelved in Huntington's private third-floor library and some still stored in crates in a basement workroom. By December he had hired three assistants and set up a formal system for recording the con-

THE BIBLIOGRAPHICAL SOCIETY

President : SIR D'ARCY POWER, K.B.E., F.S.A.

Hon. Treasurer :
R. FARQUHARSON SHARP,
British Museum,
W.C. 1

Hon. Secretaries :
A. W. POLLARD, C.B., *40 Murray Road,*
Wimbledon, S.W. 19
R. B. McKERROW, *Enderley, Gt. Missenden, Bucks.*

1 June 1927

Dear Dr. Cole,

I have much pleasure in informing you that at its meeting this afternoon the Council in gratitude for your great services to the Short Title Catalogue, and in recognition of all you have done for bibliography, unanimously conferred on you the Honorary Membership of this Society — the only honour which it is at present in its power to bestow.

Yours very sincerely,

A. W. Pollard

Cole's position at the Huntington Library enabled him to make significant contributions to the monumental Short Title Catalogue.

tents of the library. During the next five years, as Huntington continued to buy large private libraries en bloc, the collection doubled in size. For the staff the task was twofold: first, they were expected to record and catalogue the day-to-day acquisitions; second, and of paramount interest to Cole, they were required to create a detailed bibliographic catalogue of all items held by the library printed in the British Isles before 1641. According to Cole's scheme, this catalogue, or as it was formally called, *Check List or Brief Catalogue of the Library of Henry E. Huntington — English Literature to 1640,* would rival the Church catalogue, upon which it was modeled, for accuracy and detail. But in the richness of materials to be included Cole hoped it would surpass its predecessor. The first printing of the catalogue in 1919 was applauded by librarians and bibliographers, who hailed it as a major work of meticulous bibliographic scholarship and an important contribution to book culture.

Although he was busy with the Huntington collections, Cole found time to write a series of scholarly articles on bibliography, many of which were published in the *Papers of the Bibliographical Society of America.* In "Bibliographical Problems, With a Few Solutions" (1916), Cole argued that a model bibliography should be based on a full and accurate description of a perfect copy, including size by fold, signature marks, and full pagination. In this essay, as in many of his other writings, Cole urges bibliographers to bring to their work a scientific approach similar to that employed by physicians. The proper role for the bibliographer is, in Cole's words, to act as "the anatomist of the book." If this close attention to detail were followed, Cole claimed, then bibliography would be elevated to its proper place among other disciplines recognized as intellectually challenging and rewarding. In his devotion to the cause of bibliography Cole not only wrote scholarly articles but took an active interest in the affairs of the Bibliographical Society of America. In 1906 he served as secretary of the Organization Committee, and from 1916 to 1921 he held the office of president of the society.

In addition to supervising the day-to-day activities of Huntington's library and carrying out his responsibilities as president of the Bibliographical Society of America, Cole found himself absorbed in planning the relocation of Huntington's entire book and manuscript collection. Since 1918 Huntington had worked with his architects in California on plans for a library building to be located on his San Marino estate. By the summer of 1920 the building was nearly completed. The details of moving eighty

thousand books and manuscripts as well as twelve staff members and their families necessarily occupied much of Cole's time. By the middle of September the major portion of the library had been moved. For the next four years, until the time of his retirement, Cole was absorbed with the organization of the materials in the new building. With the move to California, Huntington had to shift his attentions away from the business of cataloguing pre-1641 English imprints and toward the more practical tasks involved in the housing, preservation, and administration of the collection as a whole — a bitter disappointment for Cole since it meant dropping the project closest to his heart. Also, as the number of staff members increased, Cole found himself increasingly involved in managerial decisions, further removing him from his bibliographic work. At the age of seventy-four, he decided that he did not want to spend his remaining professional years in a mostly administrative role, and in September 1924, after writing a closely documented two-hundred-page summary report on the history and progress of the library, Cole retired as director.

For the two years immediately following his retirement, Cole returned happily to his favorite activity — detailed bibliographic scholarship. A major project suited to his skills was at hand. He had been a member of the Bibliographical Society (London) since 1894 and had closely followed that organization's activities, especially their work toward compiling and publishing *A Short Title Catalogue of Books Printed in England, Scotland & Ireland and of English Books Printed Abroad, 1475–1640.* In the course of his duties he had regularly supplied the editors, Alfred W. Pollard and Gilbert R. Redgrave, with information on titles in the Huntington library. Now, with more time to give, Cole took on additional editorial and proofreading tasks. In the preface to the catalogue published in 1926 the editors praised Cole for the "immense help" he and his successors at the Huntington had provided. In recognition of his contributions, the officers of the Bibliographical Society made Cole an honorary member, the fifth American to receive such a tribute.

Well into his seventies Cole continued to write provocative essays on bibliography and on early English printing and publishing. Working in a historical rather than a bibliographic vein, Cole in 1926 published a long essay in the *Bulletin of the New York Public Library* titled "Early Library Development in New York State." In the October 1927 issue of the *Proceedings of the American Antiquarian Society* he traced the career of Lewis Hughes, the so-called militant minister of the Bermudas. In 1929 Cole traveled to Rome as representative for the Bibliographical Society of America and read two papers at the first meeting of the World Congress of Bibliography. In 1929 his annotated "Survey of the Bibliography of English Literature 1475–1640" came out in the *Papers of the Bibliographical Society of America.* When at the age of eighty-two Cole produced the lengthy and carefully edited *Index to Bibliographical Papers Published by the Bibliographical Society and the Library Association, London, 1877–1932,* a reviewer in the 13 February 1933 issue of the *Library Journal* referred to him as an "indefatigable bibliographer" whose production remained prodigious in his advanced years.

Cole was a loyal and productive member of the Bibliographical Society of America, the New York Library Club, the Bibliographical Society (London), the American Library Association, the American Antiquarian Society, and the Grolier Club. He and his wife traveled widely, making a total of nine trips to Europe between 1914 and 1929. For recreation Cole collected picture postcards, rode his bicycle, and composed light verse. One of his published efforts, "The Five Foot Shelf," appeared in the 1 May 1923 issue of the *Library Journal* as a satire on the Harvard Classics, a set popularized by Charles W. Eliot as a complete storehouse of knowledge.

In 1937 Cole suffered a stroke and was forced to give up writing for the last two years of his life. At the time of his death he was a recognized leader in his chosen field and, as Lawrence Thompson asserts in a biographical sketch in *Grolier 75 . . .* (1959), "a major force in humanistic scholarship in the early twentieth century." Throughout his career he promoted bibliographic study as a serious discipline. In "Bibliographic Matters of Passing Interest," published in the 5 April 1925 issue of the *New York Herald Tribune,* Cole had claimed that librarians lacked proper appreciation for bibliographies, failed to produce them as they should, and used them only in emergencies. No matter how little they are appreciated, Cole concluded, there are those whose "happiness in life" consists of compiling bibliographies for the use of scholars and librarians. Obviously, Cole was one who had achieved such happiness.

Biography:
Donald C. Dickinson, *George Watson Cole 1850–1939* (Metuchen, N.J.: Scarecrow Press, 1990).

References:
Leslie Bliss, "George Washington Cole," *Pacific Bindery Talk* (November 1939): 35–37;

Harold Carew, "Toiler in the Vineyard of Books," *Touring Topics* (February 1929): 32–34, 48–49;

T. J. Damon, "George Watson Cole," *Proceedings of the American Antiquarian Society,* 45 (October 1939): 215–223;

Stella Haverland, "George Watson Cole," *Pacific Bindery Talk* (November 1936): 39–43;

Victor Paltsits, "George Watson Cole," *Papers of the Bibliographical Society of America,* 33 (1939): 22–24;

Margaret Stillwell, *Incunabula in American Libraries* (New York: Bibliographical Society of America, 1940).

Papers:
The major collection of Cole's papers, including correspondence, diaries, essays, photographs, manuscripts, cash-account books, and newspaper clippings, is located at the American Antiquarian Society Library in Worcester, Massachusetts. A file of correspondence, reports, and articles is located at the Henry E. Huntington Library in San Marino, California.

Edward Augustus Crowninshield

(25 February 1817 – 20 February 1859)

Joseph Rosenblum
University of North Carolina at Greensboro

Edward Augustus Crowninshield was a major collector of Americana in the first half of the nineteenth century. Although his collection did not rival that of John Carter Brown or James Lenox in size, it was rich in rarities that would later enhance many public and private libraries. Through commissions and encouragement Crowninshield also was instrumental in establishing the career of Henry Stevens, purveyor of Americana to the gentry, and he served as a mentor in cultivating Charles Deane's bibliophily.

Crowninshield was born in Salem, Massachusetts, on 25 February 1817 to Benjamin William and Mary Boardman Crowninshield. Benjamin, a businessman and politician, served as president of the Merchants Bank of Salem, prospering sufficiently enough to allow his son a life of leisure, and held the post of secretary of the navy under Presidents James Madison and James Monroe. He also served four terms in the U.S. House of Representatives and in both branches of the Massachusetts state legislature.

Edward attended the Round Hill School in Northampton, where he studied under the institution's founders, Joseph G. Cogswell and George Bancroft. Both were learned bibliophiles. Cogswell later became librarian of the Astor Library. Bancroft, dubbed "the Critter" by his students, would become a noted historian of the American colonial period, an interest which Crowninshield shared. From the Round Hill School Crowninshield went on to Harvard, graduating in 1836. He then studied law as an apprentice to Franklin Dexter and William H. Gardiner of Boston, though he never practiced. On 15 January 1840 he married Maria Welsh, daughter of Francis Welsh, and the couple settled in Boston at 78 Beacon Street. Of their three boys only one, Frederic, lived past his twenties; Frederic became an important artist and teacher in the latter half of the nineteenth century.

Largely because of the influence of Cogswell and Bancroft, Crowninshield assembled an impressive library dealing with American history. The chief supplier of Crowninshield's volumes, which at his death numbered between twenty-five hundred and three thousand, was Stevens. In November 1844 Gurley and Hill of New York conducted the only American sale of books from the libraries of Augustus, Duke of Sussex, and Robert Southey; Stevens executed commissions for several Bostonians, including Crowninshield, who acquired the duke's 1611 edition of *Coryat's Crudities* (London: Printed by William Stansby) among other choice items. From the duke's library also came a Dutch account of the English civil wars, *England's Memorial* (Amsterdam, 1649), and a fifteenth-century Book of Hours on vellum. Crowninshield's copy of Hernando de Soto's *A Relation of the Invasion and Conquest of Florida* (London: Printed for J. Lawrence, 1686) came from the Southey library, as did a set of Jeremy Belknap's *History of New Hampshire* (Philadelphia and Boston, 1784–1792).

Crowninshield encouraged Stevens to move to England and become a bookseller. In the summer of 1845 Stevens arrived in London carrying book orders from Crowninshield. From the expatriate American Obadiah Rich, a London bookseller, Stevens bought £650 worth of Americana that had belonged to Henri Ternaux-Compans, compiler of the *Bibliotheque Americaine* (Paris: Arthus–Bertrand, 1837), an important early listing of 1,153 works on the New World that were published before 1700. Rich had secured a large share of the Ternaux collection in 1844 and resold the books to Stevens. Brown received first choice of these items, but Crowninshield bought whatever was left along with duplicates that Stevens located for him. Ternaux's books are especially desirable because of the Frenchman's learned annotations.

Among the items that Stevens sent Crowninshield on 20 May 1846 were Thomas Mante's *History of the Late War in North America* (London: Printed for William Strahan and T. Cadell, 1772),

Letter from Henry Stevens to Edward A. Crowninshield reporting on a visit to Grenville library (William L. Clements Library, University of Michigan) purchased for £2 6s. 6d., and *New England's First Fruits in Respect of the Conversion of Some* . . . (London: Printed by R. O. and G. D. for H. Overton, 1643), the first of a series of ten publications known as "Eliot's Indian Tracts" (for the missionary John Eliot) that dealt with the Christianizing of Native Americans in New England. In the same lot was the third pamphlet in this series, Thomas Shepard's *The Clear Sun-Shine of the Gospell* . . . (London: Printed by R. Cotes and J. Bellany, 1648) purchased for £1; Crowninshield ultimately owned seven of the ten tracts. For £2 2s. Stevens also acquired for Crowninshield a copy of William Vaughan's *The Golden Fleece* (London: Printed for Francis Williams, 1626), containing a map of Newfoundland by Capt. John Mason; for £1 3s. John Cotton's *Abstract of the Lawes of New England* (London: Printed for F. Cowles and W. Ley, 1641), which the auction catalogue of Crowninshield's books (prepared by Leonard and Company of Boston) describes as "the first collection of laws for New England"; and for 16s. John Phillips's *The Tears of the Indians* (London: Nathaniel Brook, 1656), a translation of Bartholomé de Las Casas's accounts of Spanish atrocities in the Americas. Later that year Stevens sent Crowninshield a copy of *New England's Teares for Old England's Feares* (London: John Rothwell and H. Overton, 1641), by William Hooke.

By far the most important piece of Americana in Crowninshield's library was a perfect copy of the *Whole Booke of Psalmes Faithfully Translated into English Metre* (Cambridge: Printed by Stephen Day, 1640). Better known as the *Bay Psalm Book,* it is the earliest surviving work printed in British North America. The history of Crowninshield's copy illustrates the truth of the observation by the second-century grammarian Terentianus Maurus: "Habent sua fata libelli" (Books, too, have their destinies). The book had belonged to the great eighteenth-century Boston collector Thomas Prince, one of five copies of the *Bay Psalm Book* he owned and donated to the Old South Church in Boston. Of these five copies, three passed into private hands. Dr. Nathaniel B. Shurtleff acquired a perfect copy in 1859; it now resides at the John Carter Brown Library. Ten years earlier George Livermore had secured an imperfect copy, which later was rendered still more defective when twelve of its leaves were taken to replace those missing from the *Bay Psalm Book* that Stevens sold to Lenox. Crowninshield's perfect copy had the most interesting history of the three. Indeed, Stevens would later compare the Crowninshield acquisition to Thomas Frognall Dibdin's "Lincoln

Nosegay," a transaction in which the English bibliographer defrauded the Lincoln Cathedral Library of early English imprints of William Caxton, Wynkyn de Worde, and Richard Pynson in exchange for far less valuable books. Crowninshield secured his *Bay Psalm Book* in exchange for rebinding another volume in cardboard and imitation leather at the cost of about a dollar, according to Zoltan Haraszti in his *The Enigma of the Bay Psalm Book* (1956). Some historians have claimed that Crowninshield acquired his copy by having exchanged books of equal value. Haraszti's account is more likely, however, given Stevens's description of the exchange.

Crowninshield owned many other early American works, produced by the Cambridge Press, including the twenty-three-page sermon *A Brief Recognition of New England's Errand into the Wilderness* . . . (Cambridge, Mass.: Printed by Samuel Green and M. Johnson, 1671), by Samuel Danforth I, and the 1685 second edition of *The Eliot Indian Bible.* Crowninshield also owned an imperfect copy of the *General Laws and Liberties of the Massachusetts Colony* (Cambridge, Mass.: Printed by Samuel Green, for John Usher, Boston, 1672). The *General Laws* is important not only because of its printer's imprint but also because it contains the first copyright law in America, an order from the Massachusetts General Court establishing ownership of exclusive rights to the book: "no printer shall print any more copies than are agreed and paid for by the owner of the copy or copies, nor shall he make any other reprint or make sale of any of the same without the said owner's consent."

Although strongest in examples of early New England presses, Crowninshield's collection of early American imprints included works such as William Stith's *History of the First Discovery and Settlement of Virginia,* printed by William Parks of Williamsburg, Virginia, in 1747. Numbered among Crowninshield's holdings printed outside of New England were publications by Benjamin Franklin, including a long run of the *Pennsylvania Gazette,* from October 1739 to January 1742, and his *Account of the New-Invented Pennsylvania Fireplaces* (1744), which tells of the creation of the Franklin stove, as well as John Estaugh's *Call to the Unfaithful Professors of Truth* (1744).

Crowninshield also held an impressive collection of titles relating to voyage and discovery in the New World. This collection contained works by Richard Hakluyt, including *Divers Voyages Touching the Discoverie of America* (London: Thomas Woodcooke, 1582), the first edition of *Principall Navigations*

☞ PRESERVE THIS CATALOGUE FOR THE SALE.

CATALOGUE

OF THE

Valuable Private Library

OF THE LATE

EDWARD A. CROWNINSHIELD,

EMBRACING IN THE COLLECTION

A LARGE NUMBER OF VALUABLE AND RARE BOOKS;

CHOICE EDITIONS, OR ELEGANT LARGE PAPER COPIES OF

STANDARD ENGLISH AUTHORS;

RARE WORKS ON THE EARLY HISTORY OF AMERICA;

Early Voyages and Travels,

INCLUDING FIRST EDITIONS OF

PURCHAS AND HAKLUYT;

THE FIRST BOOK PRINTED IN NORTH AMERICA,

"THE BAY PSALM BOOK;"

Elliot's Indian Bible; Mather's Magnalia;

SUPERB COPIES OF WORKS ON BIBLIOGRAPHY,
INCLUDING THOSE OF DIBDIN AND BRYDGES;
WORKS FROM THE STRAWBERRY HILL AND LEE PRIORY PRÆSSES;
EARLY PRINTED BOOKS;
RARE COPIES OF FIRST EDITIONS, INCLUDING THE POEMS OF

SHAKSPEARE AND MILTON;

HISTORICAL AND LITERARY SOCIETY COLLECTIONS;

Choice Works in other departments of Literature,

GENERALLY IN ELEGANT BINDINGS, MANY OF THEM BY HAYDAY,
AND A SMALL COLLECTION OF AUTOGRAPH LETTERS,

TO BE SOLD BY AUCTION,

ON TUESDAY, NOVEMBER 1, 1859, AND THREE FOLLOWING DAYS,

IN THE LIBRARY SALESROOM OF

LEONARD & CO.,

CHAPMAN HALL, (Chapman Place,) SCHOOL STREET,

☞ Sale to commence each day at 10 o'clock.

BOSTON:
ALFRED MUDGE & SON, PRINTERS, 34 SCHOOL STREET.
1859.

☞ The Auctioneers will execute faithfully all Orders for the Purchase of Books.

Cover for the catalogue of Crowninshield's library

(London: George Bishop and Ralph Newberie, deputies to Christopher Barker, 1589) — with the six separately published leaves, sometimes found between pages 643 and 644, that deal with the voyage of Sir Francis Drake — as well as the 1598–1600 edition of the same title, and *Virginia Richly Valued* (London: M. Lownes, 1609), describing Hernando de Soto's conquest of Florida. Crowninshield also owned Samuel Purchas's *Hakluyt Posthumus* (London: Henry Fetherstone, 1625–1626), which continues Hakluyt's account of voyages to the Americas. Purchas's work is of particular interest because, according to Samuel Taylor Coleridge, it influenced the writing of "Kubla Khan." Crowninshield owned two titles by Peter Martyr: *The Decades of the New Worlde or West India* (London: William Powell, 1555), translated by Richard Eden, and *De Rebus Oceanicis et Novo Orbe, Decades Tres* (Cologne: Gervinum Calenuim and haeredes Quentelios, 1574). Crowninshield's 1537 edition of *Novus Orbis Regionum ac Insularum Veteribus Incognitarum* (Basel: John Hervagius), compiled by John Huttich and edited by Simon Grynaeus, had belonged to the poet Thomas Gray and contained his autograph and annotations. This volume includes accounts of the first three voyages of Christopher Columbus, the four voyages of Amerigo Vespucci, an excerpt from Martyr's *Decades,* and a letter written by Maximilian of Transylvania describing Ferdinand Magellan's circumnavigation of the globe. Crowninshield also owned a copy of the 1516 *Polyglot Psalter* (printed in Turin by Peter-Paul Porrus), an important example of early printing, and early Americana that includes a biography of Columbus by Augustine Giustiniani of Genoa. The library held a fine copy of Jan Huygen Van Linschoten's *Discours of Voyages into the Easte and West Indies* (London: Printed by John Wolte and translated from the Dutch by William Phillip, 1598), with all twelve maps present, as well as Daniel Denton's *A Brief History of New York* (London: John Hancock and William Bradley, 1670), the first English account of the former Dutch settlement. The most prized titles in this collection, however, were three by John Smith: *Description of New England* (London: R. Clerke, 1616), the first book to use that geographical designation instead of North Virginia and, bound together, perfect copies of the *Generall Historie of Virginia, New England, and the Summer Isles* (London: Printed by I. D. and I. H. for Michael Sparkes, 1627) and *The True Travels, Adventures, and Observations of Captaine John Smith* (London: Thomas Slater, 1630), bound together. Stevens

acquired this composite volume in 1846 for eleven guineas.

Almost daily Crowninshield made a noon trip to the Little and Brown bookstore in Boston to look at and discuss books with George Livermore and Rev. Alexander Young, one of Crowninshield's closest friends. Crowninshield shared with Young an interest in the early history of Massachusetts and collected such works of local interest as *Historical Sketch of the First Church in Boston* (Boston: Munroe and Francis, 1812), by William Emerson, father of Ralph Waldo. An item of particular interest in Crowninshield's library was Roger Williams's *A Key into the Language of America* (London: Printed by Gregory Dexter, 1643). Though primarily a dictionary of Narraganset speech, it includes verses that offer an idealized portrait of the Native Americans:

When Indians hear the horrid filths
  Of Irish, English men,
The horrid oaths and murders late,
  Thus say these Indians then,

"We wear no clothes, have many gods,
  And yet our sins are less.
You are barbarians, pagans wild,
  Your land's the wilderness."

Crowninshield had a small but choice selection of works by three generations of the Mathers — Richard, Increase, and Cotton — including the last's *Magnalia Christi Americana* (London: T. Parkhurst, 1702) and *The Wonders of the Invisible World* (London: John Dunton, 1693). Crowninshield also owned a copy of John Josselyn's *New England's Rarities Discovered* (London: G. Widdowes, 1672), the first natural history of the region, and Nathaniel Morton's *New England's Memorial* (1669), of interest in part because it was the first book published by John Usher of Boston, though printed at Cambridge by Green and Marmaduke Johnson. Crowninshield's interest in local history led to his election as a resident member of the Massachusetts Historical Society in December 1858, a few months before his death.

Crowninshield owned a few choice titles in early American poetry and fiction, such as the first edition of Anne Bradstreet's *The Tenth Muse Lately Sprung Up in America . . .* (London: Stephen Bowtell, 1650); Phyllis Wheatley's *Poems* (London: A. Bell, 1773); the second (Boston: E. G. House, 1809) edition of William Cullen Bryant's *The Embargo . . . with Other Poems;* and *Salmagundi* (London: J. Limbrid, 1824), *Sketch Book* (London: J. Murray, 1821), and *Works* (fifteen volumes, New York: Putnam, 1855), by Washington Irving. Typical of his era, however, Crowninshield took greater interest in American history than in American literature.

Nationalistic pride was creating a market for histories of the country and fostering the writing of such works, yet Americans still felt culturally inferior and thus valued English over American letters. As such, Crowninshield's collection of British literature was strong. He had the first printing of Roger Ascham's *The Schoole Master* (London: John Daye, 1570). His shelves also housed the 1761 three-volume set of Ascham's works edited by Samuel Johnson – though the name of James Bennet appears on the title page. Other authors of the English Renaissance represented in the Crowninshield library include Francis Beaumont and John Fletcher. In addition to a modern eleven-volume edition of their works (London: E. Moxon, 1843–1846), Crowninshield also acquired the second (London: Printed by N. O. for I. S., 1635) edition of *The Knight of the Burning Pestle.* He had Horace Walpole's copy of *Lucasta* (London: T. Ewster, 1649), by Richard Lovelace; a fine set of John Milton first editions, including *Paradise Lost* (London: Peter Parker and Peter Boulter, 1667) and *Paradise Regained* (London: John Starkey, 1671); and the 1640 second edition of William Shakespeare's sonnets (London: Printed by Thomas Cotes to be sold by John Benson).

Though not as strong as his Renaissance collection, Crowninshield's eighteenth-century British holdings included some desirable items: the second (Edinburgh, 1787) edition of Robert Burns's *Poems;* the sixty-eight-volume set of English poets with Johnson's prefaces (London: C. Bathurst and others, 1779–1781); the first appearance of Thomas Gray's *Odes* printed at Strawberry Hill in 1757; and the London 1730 quarto edition of James Thomson's *Seasons* (printed by Samuel Richardson). The collection contained three first editions of works by Samuel Rogers – two copies of *Italy* (London, 1830), one of which had been owned by the duke of Sussex, and a copy of the *Poems* (London: T. Cadell and E. Moxon, 1834). From George Livermore, Crowninshield secured a copy of Michael Drayton's *Works* (London: Robert Dodsley, 1748) owned by Charles Lamb, and from the library of the Shakespearean actor and collector William Burton he secured Lamb's only black-letter book, the 1598 edition of Geoffrey Chaucer.

Like virtually all of his contemporaries, Crowninshield preferred fine bindings to original condition. In *A Glance at Private Libraries* (1855) Luther Farnham observes that Crowninshield's "books are most elegantly bound." Deane, in his "Memoir of Edward Crowninshield," quotes George S. Hillard as saying that Crowninshield "wanted the best editions of the best books, and not only that, but that they should be bound in the nicest and most appropriate manner." Such bindings were attractive, but they also conferred status on the contents. Among the binders represented in Crowninshield's collection was Christian Samuel Kalthoeber, whom Howard M. Nixon in *Five Centuries of English Book Binding* (1978) described as a "leader of the numerous German binders working in London in the second half of the eighteenth century." The work of Charles Lewis and James Hayday also graced Crowninshield's shelves, and he owned an example of the embroidered bindings produced by the Anglican community established by Nicholas Ferrar at Little Gidding in the seventeenth century. Fine printing and limited editions also appealed to Crowninshield. One noteworthy limited edition in his collection was *The First Plymouth Patent* (Cambridge, Mass.: Privately printed), one of four copies printed for Deane in 1854. The first example of a book printed on vellum in the United States, the book was presented to Crowninshield by Deane.

Crowninshield also owned a small, but choice, selection of manuscripts, the most important of which was Samuel Gorton's response in a 30 June 1669 letter to Nathaniel Morton's *New England's Memorial;* the document, written on both sides of four folio leaves, had belonged to Prince. Crowninshield made it available to Peter Force, a major collector of Americana and a prominent historian, who published it. Crowninshield also owned a 25 September 1776 letter from Jonathan Trumbull to his son that discusses sending Franklin, John Adams, and Edward Rutledge to negotiate with British general William Howe and a 27 September 1779 letter from George Washington to Count Charles-Henri-Theodat D'Estaing that speaks of cooperation between French and American forces. The letters and documents Crowninshield assembled included those of many signers of the Declaration of Independence.

Throughout the 1850s Crowninshield suffered from poor health, which repeated trips to Europe did nothing to improve, and he died in Boston on 20 February 1859. Crowninshield's library was catalogued, not altogether accurately, by Leonard and Company of Boston in anticipation of their auctioning the contents on 1–4 November 1859. Stevens, however, had anticipated the sale and bought the collection en bloc. He wanted Crowninshield's copy of the *Bay Psalm Book,* but he also wanted to demonstrate that Americana was worth collecting.

Before shipping the books to England Stevens, through his brother Frank, offered the choicest items to Lenox, Brown, and Deane. Deane secured the 1582 Hakluyt and Robert Cushman's *A Sermon Preached at Plimouth in New England December 9, 1621* (London: John Bellamy, 1622), the first sermon delivered in British North America to be printed. American purchasers secured about $2,000 worth of material before Stevens resold them, along with other books from stock, through Puttick and Simpson's auction house in London on 12–20 July 1860.

The sale realized £4,450 – less than Stevens had hoped but still yielding a profit – and the prices that many of Crowninshield's books fetched indicated an increased interest in Americana in England and on the Continent. Stevens had assisted Crowninshield in his bibliophily, and the sale of the Crowninshield library in turn helped Stevens in his effort to create an enthusiasm for books dealing with American history.

References:

Carl Cannon, *American Book Collectors and Collecting from Colonial Times to the Present* (New York: H. W. Wilson, 1941), pp. 110–111;

Catalogue of the Valuable Private Library of the Late Edward A. Crowninshield . . . (Boston: Alfred Mudge & Son, Printers, for Leonard, 1859);

Charles Deane, "Memoir of Edward Crowninshield," *Publications of the Massachusetts Historical Society,* 17 (1880): 356–359;

Luther Farnham, *A Glance at Private Libraries* (Boston: Crocker & Brewster, 1855), pp. 31–32;

Howard M. Nixon, *Five Centuries of English Bookbinding* (London: Scolar, 1978), p. 172;

Wyman Parker, *Henry Stevens of Vermont* (Amsterdam: N. Israel, 1963);

Henry Stevens, *Recollections of Mr. James Lenox of New York* (London: Henry Stevens & Son, 1886).

Ernest Dawson

(1 December 1882 – 15 November 1947)

Glen Dawson
Dawson's Book Shop

BOOKS: *Dawson's Book Shop, Catalogues 1–518* (Los Angeles: Dawson's Book Shop, 1907–1993);
Soviet Russia as I Saw It (Los Angeles: Epic News, 1937);
A Visit with Dr. R. (Los Angeles: Muir Dawson, 1948);
Ernest Dawson and Jake Zeitlin: Two Letters (Pasadena, Cal.: Juniper, 1992).

SELECTED PERIODICAL PUBLICATIONS –
UNCOLLECTED: "What's Wrong with the Rare Book Trade," *Publishers' Weekly* (1931);
"The Rare Book Trade," *Publishers' Weekly,* 119 (18 April 1931): 1989–1993;
"Are Booksellers' Conventions the Bunk?," *Publishers' Weekly,* 119 (16 May 1931): 2415–2417;
"Soviet Russia and the Collaboration to Keep the Peace," *World Affairs Interpreter,* 14 (Winter 1944): 367–372;
"Los Angeles Booksellers of 1897," *Historical Society of Southern California Quarterly,* 29 (June 1947): 84–92.

In 1905 Ernest Dawson established Dawson's Book Shop in Los Angeles, a meeting place for authors, artists, librarians, and collectors. Dawson was the first to issue antiquarian book catalogues in southern California and the first in the area to import antiquarian books from England on a large scale. His business was buying and selling old and rare books, but his interests were diverse and included the outdoors, religion, and politics.

Ernest Dawson was born to Mary Ann Grosvenor and Thomas Dawson in San Antonio, Texas, on 1 December 1882, the third of eleven children and the oldest boy. His sisters were named for plants: Lily, Rose, Violet, Daisy, Myrtle, Ivy, Pansy, and Althea. His brothers were Albert ("Bob") and Frank. His father was a carpenter, builder, and wanderer; he had been born in the United States of English parents, had married in England, and had moved to Texas in 1881. In about 1885 the Dawson family moved to a remote ranch near Cholame in eastern San Luis Obispo County, California. Later they moved to the mission town of San Luis Obispo. While there Ernest Dawson attended public school but dropped out at the age of thirteen to work full time in the town's bookstore, which was owned by J. A. Goodrich.

In 1897 the Dawson family went by ship to Los Angeles, where Ernest found work first as a gift wrapper in the Broadway department store and later as a dealer in secondhand books for bookseller Henry Ward and Company. At the age of eighteen Ernest Dawson had not completed seventh grade but was given permission to enter Los Angeles High School. Henry Ward arranged a work schedule so that Dawson could keep his full-time job while attending school full time. He graduated in the winter of 1905.

In April of that year, with a total capital of about $100, Dawson entered the book business, renting part of a store at 713 South Broadway for $40 a month. He shared the store with a printing company, A. K. Tate and Son. Dawson used his personal library and stamp collection for stock, and he sold books and stationery on consignment from wholesalers. His first major purchase was from the Salvation Army: twenty-three hundred books at one cent each delivered in about fifty sacks. One of these books was a copy of Otis Tufton Mason's *Aboriginal Indian Basketry* (Washington, D.C.: Smithsonian Institute, 1902). The first sale of Dawson's Book Shop, the book had been purchased by Dawson for 1¢ and sold for $2.50 to the attorney LeComte Davis. Another early customer of Dawson's was Hubert Howe Bancroft, publisher, historian, and founder of the Bancroft Library.

An aggressive dealer, Dawson would take a suitcase of books and travel by Pacific Electric railroad to sell Californiana to the Pasadena Public Library. He also offered books by mail to collectors,

Ernest Dawson

librarians, and other dealers. In April 1906 San Francisco was struck by earthquake and fire, causing a scramble to replace lost books, especially titles pertaining to the American West; western Americana has been an important part of the stock of Dawson's Book Shop ever since. In October of that year Dawson entered into a partnership with Henry W. Collins. Knowledgeable about rare books, art books, and bibliography, Collins had worked for Parsons, a London bookshop.

In December 1907 Dawson's Book Shop issued the first catalogue of rare books in Los Angeles. Shortly afterward both Dawson's Book Shop and A. K. Tate and Son moved to 518 South Hill Street in the Portsmouth Hotel opposite Central Park, now Pershing Square. In this new location the partners abandoned their emphasis on occult books,

which had comprised a large part of the stock taken on consignment. On 24 June 1909 Dawson married Sadie Alena Roberts. They had two sons, Glen and Muir, who would carry on the Dawson book business, and two daughters, Fern and June.

In 1911 Dawson traveled to London, Paris, and Rome on a book-buying expedition, his only luggage an extra pair of socks in his pocket. He shipped the books he acquired, packed in wooden crates, to America, and upon his return to California proclaimed his finds as constituting "the greatest collection of rare and fine books ever offered for sale in Los Angeles." Catalogue 12, issued in November 1911, featured some choice folio volumes, including Hogarth works (circa 1822), for fifty dollars; *Gallerie de Florence et du Palais Pitti,* a four-volume set elegantly bound in tree calf and published

The interior of Dawson's Book Shop at 518 South Hill Street

in Paris between 1789 and 1807, for seventy-five dollars; and Sir William Hamilton's *Etruscan Vases* (Naples, 1766–1777) for fifty dollars. The partners continued to issue catalogues in 1912, staying open until eight or nine at night five days a week and working half days on Saturday. In that year Collins died in London, having traveled to England to buy books for stock.

In April 1913 Dawson became a trustee of the Voluntary Cooperative Association (VCA), an organization that advocated utopian socialism. Dawson served as editor of the VCA periodical *Voluntary Cooperator* and drove a horse and wagon to make pickups for the association's salvage store. Dawson sold the bookshop to an employee, E. H. Barring; between catalogues 16 and 17 there is consequently a five-year gap – 1912 to 1917 – representing Dawson's career as a socialist. In April 1917 Dawson left the VCA and was able to borrow enough money to buy back the bookstore.

Dawson's Book Shop moved to 627 South Grand Avenue in January 1922 and remained there for thirty years. When in 1930 Wiltshire Boulevard was cut, the store became a corner of Grand and Wiltshire. Swedish-born artist Carl Oscar Borg sug-

gested a mural, which was painted on the Wiltshire side of the building by Gile McLaury Steele and repainted several times with names of Dawson's customers on some of the books in the mural.

Beginning in June 1924, long before antiquarian book fairs were held regularly, Dawson's Book Shop held several rare book exhibits in San Francisco. One such fair, held 19–24 January 1925 at the Saint Francis Hotel, offered a special catalogue listing notable bindings, extra-illustrated books, first editions, association copies, and color-plate books. Prices ranged from five dollars for a first edition of John Muir's *The Mountains of California* (New York: Century Company, 1894) to three hundred dollars for a book bound by Bateman, the royal binder. Later exhibits were held at the library of the fine printer John Henry Nash (May 1926) and at the studio of Dorothy True Bell (2–14 November 1931).

There were many buying trips to New York and Europe during this period. A notable excursion occurred in 1928, when Dawson and his son Glen undertook a tour of antiquarian bookshops in the United States and abroad. They met and bought books from many of the legendary figures in the trade on both sides of the Atlantic, including Ben

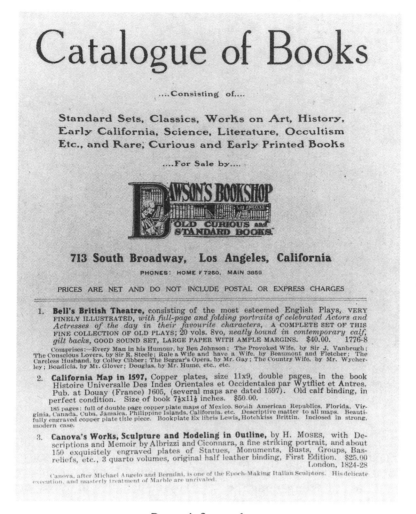

Dawson's first catalogue

Marks and Mark Cohen in London. A close working relationship, as well as a friendship, was struck between Dawson and the famous book dealers. Beginning in 1928 Marks and Cohen served as London agents for Dawson's Book Shop, buying in quantity at auction and privately sending large wooden crates packed with books through the Panama Canal to California.

At the beginning of the Depression Dawson's Book Shop continued to prosper. There were several good customers who had money, including Mrs. Estelle Getz, who paid her bills in cash with crisp one-hundred-dollar bills, and Mrs. Estelle Doheny, who collected fore-edge paintings, first editions listed in Merle Johnson's *High Spots of American Literature* (1929), and Californiana. The Estelle Doheny sale catalogue credits Ernest Dawson with selling to Doheny her first incunable, Saint Augustine's *De Civitate Dei* (Mainz: Peter Schoeffer,

1473). As the 1930s wore on, however, the Depression began to effect store operations. Although Dawson never had to lay off employees or miss a payday, he was forced to reduce salaries, as well as renegotiate rent. Employees and proprietor were loyal to each other. After Tom Neal had worked at the bookshop just two weeks in February 1933, Dawson wrote him a note to say that Neal would have to leave. Neal offered to work for free, and Dawson let him remain. Neal eventually worked at Dawson's longer than any other employee.

From 1928 to 1938 Dawson sent members of the staff to Europe to buy books for stock. In 1935–1936 Glen Dawson spent fourteen months traveling around the world. He returned with a small suitcase filled with early Chinese and Japanese block-printed books, Nara picture books (colorful manuscripts with hard-style paintings), and woodcut botanical works. Impressed with his son's findings, Dawson

A. Edward Newton with Geraldine Kelly and Dawson in 1931

and his wife also went on an extended book-buying trip in 1937, stopping first to buy stock in Tokyo, Shanghai, and Peking and then traveling along the Trans-Siberian Railroad. Dawson secured early printings of Russian books in Moscow and anti- quarian materials in England. In his heaviest buying trip since 1928, Dawson filled two hundred large wooden crates with his acquisitions. Catalogue 122 offered some of these purchases, such as for $150 a Slavonic New Testament printed at Ostrog in 1580; for $300 a Chinese printed Charm dating from 938; and incunabula priced from $10 to $100. Also in this catalogue was a collection of twenty-six colored lithographs of Mexico, dated 1848, by Phillips and Rider and priced at $40.

During World War II Marks and several other dealers sent valuable books to Dawson on consignment to protect this material from German bombs, and Dawson was able to sell most of it. He had built his business on the basis of quick sales and small returns, believing that "a quick nickel is better than a slow dime." Books in the 1940s remained plentiful and inexpensive. In 1942, for example, Dawson listed a mint-condition, leather-bound copy of Edward S. Curtis's *North American Indians,* in

twenty volumes with twenty portfolios, for $450. From noted New York dealer Lathrop C. Harper, Dawson bought a hundred incunabula for $15 each.

The war caused many changes in personnel. Muir and Glen Dawson were serving in the army; cataloguer Ellen Shaffer, though termed "irreplace- able," went to the South Pacific with the Women's Army Corps; and buyer Tom Neal left to work at Lockhead. Dawson, however, continued to run the bookstore and amass a stock of collectibles. In 1941 he acquired the library of the cowboy artist Charles M. Russell from Earl C. Adams, executor of the Russell estate, and the library of Hamlin Garland. Catalogue 183, issued in January 1944, announced the purchase of the library of A. Gaylord Beaman, whom Dawson had regarded as one of his best cus- tomers and best friends. In 1945 Dawson secured the ten-thousand-volume collection of Olive Perci- val and the western Americana library of Dr. Her- bert M. Evans.

Sales to Henry E. Huntington were slight and only through the good offices of Leslie Bliss and Robert Schad. Dawson's Book Shop had many noted visitors such as the authors Edwin Markham, Christopher Morley, and Hugh Walpole; the artist

Dawson in his North Larchmont Boulevard shop

Rockwell Kent; and noted authority on the history of books Douglas McMurtrie. Major collectors counted among Dawson's customers included Robert Ernest Cowan, Ernest DeGolyer, John Goodman, Everett Graff, George Harding, Jean Herholt, W. J. Holliday, William Kerr, Charles Lummis, William McPherson, Thomas Streeter, Julius Wangenheim, Carl I. Wheat, Robert Woods, William Wyles, and John I. Perkins, a Dawson customer from 1909 to his death in 1942. Of his relationship with Perkins – and with book collectors in general – Dawson wrote, "His faith in me increases my respect for my own calling. Collectors make booksellers just as truly as booksellers make collectors."

At the home of Ansel Adams on 8 December 1930 and at the Mark Hopkins Hotel in San Francisco on 9 November 1931, Dawson formally addressed the Roxburghe Club – northern California's select group of book lovers – on issues of buying and selling in the rare-book market. Although not himself a member of the Zamorano Club, southern California's band of bibliophiles, he numbered most of its members among his customers. In 1945 he spoke to that club on "Forty Years of Book Selling." He was highly active in the American Booksellers Association and was elected its western vice-president.

A many-sided, complex personality, Dawson had multiple and wide-ranging interests. From his youth he loved the land of California. After graduating from high school in 1905 he celebrated by taking a solitary biking trip to Dana Point in Orange County. By 1916 he was chairman of the Committee on Local Excursions for the Sierra Club, and remained chairman of the Local Walks Committee until 1928. He served as a director of the Sierra Club almost continuously from 1922 to 1937, was the first to hold the post of fifth officer (1923 to 1925), was vice-president from 1933 to 1935, and was president from 1935 to 1937.

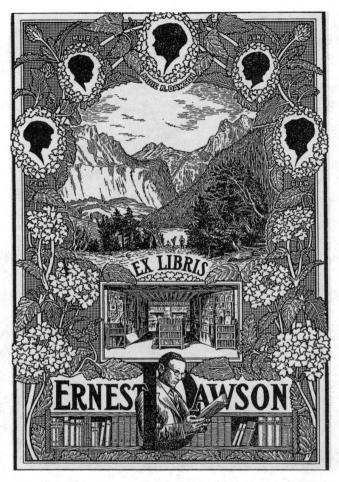

Dawson's bookplate, which illustrates three of his interests: family, books, and the outdoors

Brought up in a strongly religious family, Dawson was keenly interested in the spiritual life – an interest that was reflected in his work. In the early years of the bookshop, he handled occult books – even publishing in 1905 a paperback on astrology, Raphael's *A Key to Astrology* – as well as Christian Science rarities, which he advertised in several special catalogues. Between 1908 and 1930 Dawson sold fifty copies of the first edition of Mary Baker Glover's *Science and Health* (Boston, 1895) at prices ranging from $100 to $750.

Dawson was also politically active, although his political attitudes often underwent radical change. He supported Job Harriman when Harriman ran for mayor of Los Angeles on the Socialist ticket in 1911, yet as a registered Republican he supported both of Herbert Hoover's bids for the presidency. By 1934 Dawson had become a Democrat and campaigned actively for Upton Sinclair, who was running for the governorship of California. Later in the decade he supported Culbert Olson, who was elected governor. Olson appointed Dawson to the State Parks Commission in 1938, but Dawson soon resigned because he objected to the governor's interference with the commission's activities.

His health failing, Dawson published his final letter to his employees in catalogue 220, issued in October 1947. He shared his last days with his family and died on 15 November 1947 in a little frame house on York Boulevard, near York Junction in Highland Park, next to the house in which he had been married.

A collection of his letters and ephemera was given to the Department of Special Collections at the University of California, Los Angeles. His importance in shaping the book world of southern California was recognized when the first endowment fund for the UCLA library was named for him. The fund was sponsored by many of the region's leading book people, among them the

UCLA librarian Lawrence Clark Powell, the printer Ward Ritchie, and the bibliographer Henry R. Wagner.

In an appeal for the creation of an Ernest Dawson memorial fund, George Petitt had written an apt and loving tribute to Dawson, observing,

> He made of his work an avocation, and in the course of his life he brought literally hundreds of thousands of volumes to his home State which have given substance to its culture, and direction to its development. There is probably no one on the Pacific Coast who has had a greater influence on readers and collectors of books over quite so long a period of time as Mr. Dawson. He made friends of his customers, and one could scarcely be his friend without gaining something of his enthusiasm and becoming a customer. He was simple, honest, and personally concerned in all his book dealings. He generated respect, loyalty, and lasting affection in the minds and hearts of all who worked for him or knew him.

Jake Zeitlin, another major figure in the California book world and a competing bookseller, was also an admirer. In a letter dated 23 December 1944 he wrote a tribute to Dawson:

> Since I don't owe you any money and do not contemplate asking any favors of you I feel free to write you this letter without questions of motive. For some time I have had the urge to tell you how much I admire and respect all of the things for which you stand. While I have never had the background which would enable me to emulate you and must work out my destiny in my own terms I have come to appreciate more and more the combination of idealism and realism with which you are endowed. And the realization has slowly ripened in me that for a person to live so well as you do in relation to your family, your economic and cultural environment, and your political times is a rare thing. It takes energy and courage and great human understanding. There are many who distinguish themselves in some single art like music or letters or painting but those who master the art of living are very few.

Dawson's philosophy of living combined with his enthusiasm for bibliophily have deeply influenced his children and have contributed to the survival of Dawson's Book Shop, an enduring monument to a great bookman.

Biographies:
Mary Patricia Dixon, *Ernest Dawson* (Los Angeles: Dawson's Book Shop, 1967);

Anna Marie Hager, *Ernest Dawson and his Wonderful Shop. A Reminiscence* (Pasadena, Cal.: Grant Dahlstrom, 1968);

Glen Dawson, "'Father' Ernest Dawson," *Hoja Volante,* 177 (May 1992): 2–8.

References:
Thomas A. Neal, *Farewell My Book* (Los Angeles: Dawson's Book Shop, 1983);

Ward Ritchie, *Bookmen & Their Brothels: Recollections of Los Angeles in the 1930s* (Los Angeles: Zamorano Club, 1970);

Ritchie, *Of Bookmen & Printers, A Gathering of Memories* (Los Angeles: Dawson's Book Shop, 1989);

Warren S. Rogers, *My Own Los Angeles* (Los Angeles: Dawson's Book Shop, 1982);

Rogers, comp., *The Family of Thomas Dawson* (Los Angeles: Dawson's Book Shop, 1977);

Fern Dawson Shochat, *The Fiftieth Anniversary of Dawson's Book Shop: 1905–1955* (Los Angeles: Dawson's Book Shop, 1955);

Shochat, "The Voluntary Cooperative Association of Los Angeles, 1913–1922," *Southern California Quarterly,* 45 (June 1963): 169–180;

Madeleine B. Stern, *Antiquarian Bookselling in the United States: A History from the 1940s* (Westport, Conn.: Greenwood Press, 1985).

Papers:
A collection of Ernest Dawson's letters and ephemera, including much on his changing religious, economic, and political views, are in Special Collections at the University of California, Los Angeles, library. Letters and photographs are also at Dawson's Book Shop in Los Angeles. An oral history of the bookshop is recorded in *Dawson's Book Shop, An Oral History Memoir,* 2 volumes (Claremont, Cal.: Oral History Program, Claremont Graduate School, 1986).

Carrie Estelle Doheny

(2 August 1875 – 30 October 1958)

Monsignor Francis J. Weber
Archdiocese of Los Angeles

and

Josephine Arlyn Bruccoli

The reputation of Carrie Estelle Doheny as a book collector has grown considerably since her death in 1958. Although the Doheny name appears in many textbooks of American history because of the activities of oil tycoon Edward Laurence Doheny, fifty years after his death the name of his widow has become as familiar as his. Since 1987, when the decision was made to return many of the treasures of Carrie Estelle Doheny to the market, a new generation has become aware of the marvelous collection this determined woman assembled.

Carrie Estelle Betzold was born on 2 August 1875 in Philadelphia, the older of two daughters of German immigrants John E. and Susan Schultz Betzold. In 1876 the Betzold family moved to Marshalltown, Iowa, and in about 1890 they took up residence in Los Angeles, where John found employment as a streetcar motorman.

Upon graduation from high school Estelle was employed at the Petroleum Exchange Center as a telephone operator. The warmth of her voice captivated Edward Laurence Doheny, whose offices were in the same building. His first marriage ended, and Edward and Estelle were married in Albuquerque, New Mexico, on 22 August 1990 aboard the oilman's private railroad car, which was thereafter named "Estelle." The Dohenys and Edward's seven-year-old son, Ned, first lived in New York City. In 1901 they took up residence in the former Posey mansion at 8 Chester Place in Los Angeles, where Mrs. Doheny was to live for the next fifty-seven years.

Mrs. Doheny became a Catholic on 25 October 1918, when she and her husband were received into the church by Bishop Joseph S. Glass at Saint Patrick's Cathedral in New York City. During her lifetime Mrs. Doheny was honored by two popes: in 1931 she and her husband were made members of the Equestrian Order of the Holy Sepulchre by Pius

XI, and eight years later Estelle was given the rare title of papal countess by Pius XII.

The Doheny name became unalterably associated with the Teapot Dome scandal when Edward was accused of bribing Secretary of the Interior Albert Fall. Mrs. Doheny testified at a series of trials beginning in 1923 and ending with her husband's acquittal in 1930. In the years following the death of her husband on 8 September 1935, Mrs. Doheny assumed control of his petroleum business, which she managed successfully until its eventual liquidation.

Edward Doheny had given liberally to charitable and educational causes, establishing the pattern on which his wife based her own benefactions in later years. Projects attributed wholly to Mrs. Doheny were the Edward Laurence Doheny Memorial Library at Saint John's Seminary in Camarillo, California (1940); the Edward L. Doheny Memorial Vincentian House of Studies in Washington, D.C. (1941); the Carrie Estelle Doheny Eye Foundation (now the Doheny Eye Institute) in Los Angeles (1947); the Carrie Estelle Doheny Foundation (1949); the chapel and two other buildings at Maryvale (1952); the Estelle Doheny Hospital (1956); and the chapel and three other buildings at Saint Vincent's Seminary in Montebello (1958). In 1954 she was chosen Woman of the Year by the *Los Angeles Times*.

Mrs. Doheny began her collection of rare books and manuscripts in the 1920s with the encouragement of the Dohenys' legal counsel, Frank J. Hogan, a leading bibliophile. She was also assisted by A. Edward Newton, A. S. W. Rosenbach, and California dealer Alice P. Millard. In 1929 Mrs. Doheny decided to gather the titles mentioned by Merle Johnson in his *High Spots of American Literature* (1929). Eventually she assembled two complete sets, one for herself and the other for her daughter-

Carrie Estelle Doheny

in-law, Lucy. She also collected books featured in other bibliographies, including A. Edward Newton's "One Hundred Good Novels" (in his *This Book-Collecting Game,* 1928) and the Grolier Club's *One Hundred Books Famous in English Literature* (1903). In cases where signed books were unavailable, Mrs. Doheny frequently inserted letters by the authors.

The riches of the Doheny collection were in illuminated manuscripts and incunabula. Mrs. Doheny bought her first incunabulum, Saint Augustine's *City of God* (Peter Schoeffer, 1473), in 1931. Her second major incunabulum, Thomas à Kempis's *Imitation of Christ* (Gunther Zainer, 1473), was purchased the same year. This period was also represented in her collection by another great treasure, the *Moralia* by Pope Gregory the Great, mostly an exegesis on the Book of Job. While religious works dominated her collection, which covered

every aspect of the field from fine examples of early German monastic books to late calligraphic works, there were some notable exceptions, including the *Portolan Atlas* (1544) by Battiste Agnese. Three secular incunabula were acquired in 1932: the *editio princeps* of Homer (1488), the *Nuremberg Chronicle* (1493), and *Hypnerotomachia Polophili* (1499). The illuminated manuscript *In Unum ex quartuor* of Zacharias Chrysopolitanus was acquired in 1933.

As her collection increased, Mrs. Doheny faced the problem of housing and displaying her books. In 1940 at the suggestion of the archbishop of Los Angeles, Mrs. Doheny made the decision to turn over her collection of rare books and manuscripts to Saint John's Seminary in Camarillo, California, in memory of her husband. The Edward Laurence Doheny Memorial Library, designed by Wallace Neff in the style of early Mexican religious architecture, was erected to

The Edward Laurence Doheny Memorial Library in Camarillo, California

house the seminary's working library on the first floor and Mrs. Doheny's collection on the second floor. There were two exhibitions of the Doheny collection at the library. The first was held on 12–18 September 1932. The second exhibition, "The Book as a Work of Art," was held two and a half years later. The Treasure Room of Los Angeles Junior College also held an exhibition of Doheny books in December 1936.

Estelle continued to add to the collection even though she experienced a physical setback. On her birthday in 1944 while attending mass in her private chapel, she suffered an ocular hemorrhage, which left her left eye sightless and her right eye severely impaired. Within a few years she was completely blind.

From the outset of her collecting days Estelle was attracted to various editions of the Bible. Her activities in that area culminated in 1950 with the purchase of the Dyson-Amherst-Perrins copy of the Gutenberg Bible. Estelle was the last private collector to own one of the forty-eight extant

copies of the Gutenberg Bible. Acting for her in 1947, Dr. A. S. W. Rosenbach was the underbidder on the copy of volume one at Sotheby's. In 1950 David Randall attempted to buy the copy held at General Theological Seminary of New York for Mrs. Doheny, but it was withdrawn from the sale. That year the Dyson-Perrins copy again came on the market, and she bought it at $70,093.75; this price would increase seventy-seven-fold in 1987 during the sale of the Estelle Doheny Collection.

Among the other categories housed at Saint John's Seminary were the largest collection of fore-edge paintings in the world, papal bulls, presidential letters, a complete set of the signers of the Declaration of Independence, oil paintings, Currier and Ives prints, porcelain, antique furniture, and oriental jade.

Mrs. Doheny was methodical in her collecting of western Americana, using as her chief guide the three volumes of Robert Ernest Cowan's *A Bibliography of the History of California 1510–1930*. In addition, she was attentive to the suggestion of such

Doheny examining her Gutenberg Bible in 1950

local book dealers as Glen Dawson, Jake Zeitlin, and Harry Levinson. Although no private collector had managed to gather a complete set, the Estelle Doheny Collection at one time had seventy-seven of the titles listed in *The Zamorano 80*. These books, dealing with the history of the West, include the most important titles in western Americana.

Titles other than those enumerated in Cowan's bibliography were added over the years, until the printed Californiana holdings represented a balanced selection of source materials on the period of colonization, the period of transition, and the period of American visitors. As a supplement to the Californiana, which includes a rich assortment of broadsides, pamphlets, and other ephemera, Mrs. Doheny amassed what was probably the most complete collection of books printed by the noted California typographer John Henry Nash, together with 130 volumes from the Grabhorn Press.

The Estelle Doheny Collection of books and manuscripts was auctioned by Christie, Manson and Woods in six sales that took place between 1987 and 1989. (There was a seventh sale of antiques.) The 2,370 lots brought a total of $37,842,758 — an extraordinary average of $15,967. Part 1, sold in New York, was restricted to incunabula. The first item, appropriately, was the Gutenberg Bible, which reached $5,390,000. Two other items passed a million dollars: the *Epistulare* (Peter Schoeffer, 1470) at $1,045,000 and the *Biblia Pauperum* (block book, circa 1460–1470) at $2,420,000. The 136 lots totaled $13,602,765.

Part 2, sold in London, was restricted to medieval and Renaissance manuscripts. The top items were *Zacharias Chrysopolitanus* (circa 1170–1180) at £1,320,000, a *Book of Hours* (circa 1528) at £880,000, and *Battista Agnese: Portolan Atlas* (1544) at £660,000. The forty-six items brought £5,787,595 ($10,475,546).

Part 3, sold at Camarillo, consisted of books and manuscripts including western Americana. A

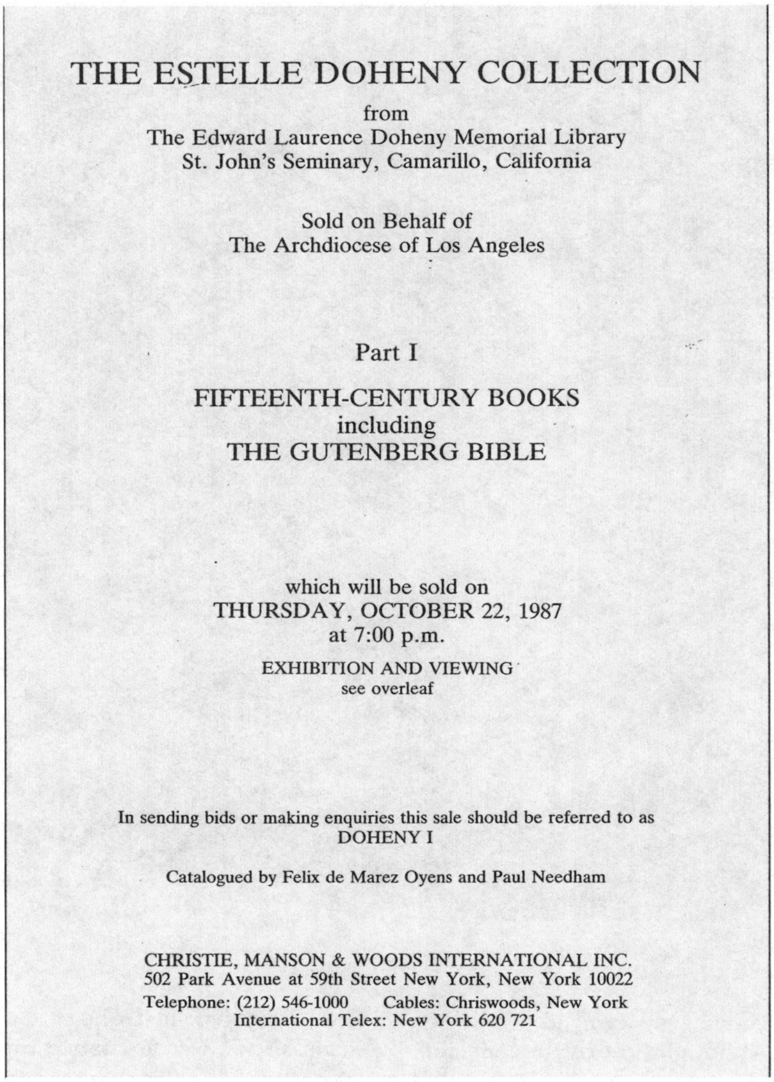

THE ESTELLE DOHENY COLLECTION

from
The Edward Laurence Doheny Memorial Library
St. John's Seminary, Camarillo, California

Sold on Behalf of
The Archdiocese of Los Angeles

Part I

FIFTEENTH-CENTURY BOOKS
including
THE GUTENBERG BIBLE

which will be sold on
THURSDAY, OCTOBER 22, 1987
at 7:00 p.m.

EXHIBITION AND VIEWING
see overleaf

In sending bids or making enquiries this sale should be referred to as
DOHENY I

Catalogued by Felix de Marez Oyens and Paul Needham

CHRISTIE, MANSON & WOODS INTERNATIONAL INC.
502 Park Avenue at 59th Street New York, New York 10022
Telephone: (212) 546-1000   Cables: Chriswoods, New York
International Telex: New York 620 721

The Doheny Library was dispersed in six sales held in New York, London, and Camarillo, California.

strong group of fifty-seven Mark Twain items (of 125 in the collection) featured the copy of *Adventures of Huckleberry Finn* (New York: Webster, 1885) that Samuel Clemens inscribed to his wife ($82,500) and the 65-page manuscript of "A Family Sketch" ($93,500). This sale included 118 fore-edge paintings of the 233 in the collection. The 828 lots totaled $2,761,400.

Part 4, in New York, featured early printing, literature, and fine bindings. The 1502 Aldus Manutius Sophocles reached $198,000; two atlases — Blaeu's *LeGrand Atlas, a Cosmmographie Blauiane* and Janssonius's *Theatrum Urbium* — brought $176,000 and $187,000 respectively. The 662 lots realized $4,104,177.

Part 5, New York featured Americana, literature, and fine bindings. The Eliot Indian Bible (the first bible printed in America, 1705) brought $330,000. There were eleven William Blake pieces: *Songs of Innocence* (1789) reached $330,000, and Blake's drawing *The Infant Jesus Saying His Prayers* made $352,000. The signers of the Declaration of Independence included a Caesar Rodney letter dated 4 July 1776 referring to the adoption of the declaration; the star item in this sale, it brought $440,000. The 559 lots totaled $4,162,202.

The final part, also in New York, featured 112 books and manuscript lots for William Morris and the Kelmscott Press. Just as the Doheny sale opened with a supreme book, it closed with one: Virgil's

EX

LIBRIS

ESTELLE

DOHENY

Carrie Estelle Doheny's bookplate

Aeneid, described as "William Morris's Unfinished Calligraphic Masterpiece," which brought $1,320,000. The 139 lots totaled $2,340,668.

The accomplishments of Estelle Doheny as both a philanthropist and a bibliophile are tremendously impressive. Through what began as an interest in religious books, manuscripts, and art, she amassed one of the most thorough collections in this field. Her success in that area led her to acquire her incredible Americana collection. With the funds from the sale of her collection benefiting the Catholic church, her great philanthropic work continued even after her death in 1958.

Despite the dispersal of the Estelle Doheny Collection of rare books, manuscripts, and works of art, historical and western American enthusiasts can take consolation in the knowledge that a substantial part of the overall holdings continues to serve researchers. That part of the western Americana section retained at the Archival Center, Archdiocese of Los Angeles, as the Estelle Doheny Collection of Californiana, accounts for about three-fourths (887 titles) of the volumes Doheny had collected in the field.

References:

The Book as a Work of Art: An Exhibition of Books and Manuscripts from the Library of Mrs. Edward Laurence Doheny (Los Angeles: Printed by W. Ritchie, 1935);

Catalogue of Books and Manuscripts in the Estelle Doheny Collection, 3 volumes (Los Angeles: Ward Ritchie Press, 1940–1955);

One Hundred Manuscripts and Books from the Estelle Doheny Collection in the Edward L. Doheny Memorial Library (Los Angeles, 1950).

Wilberforce Eames

(12 October 1855 – 6 December 1937)

Joel Silver
Indiana University

BOOKS: *Bibliographic Notes on Eliot's Indian Bible and on his other Translations and Works in the Indian Language of Massachusetts* (Washington: Government Printing Office, 1890); reprinted in *Bibliography of the Algonquian Languages,* edited by James C. Pilling (Washington: Government Printing Office, 1891), pp. 127–184;

Early New England Catechisms. A Bibliographical Account of Some Catechisms Published before the Year 1800, for Use in New England. Read in Part, before the American Antiquarian Society, at its Annual Meeting in Worcester, October 21, 1897 . . . (Worcester, Mass.: Charles Hamilton, 1898);

The First Year of Printing in New-York, May, 1693 to April, 1694 (New York: Printed by the New York Public Library, 1928).

OTHER: Joseph Sabin, *Bibliotheca Americana. A Dictionary of Books Relating to America, from Its Discovery to the Present Time* (New York, 1868–1936), part of volume 14, all of volumes 15–20, and parts of volumes 117–121, edited by Eames (New York, 1868–1936);

The Letter of Columbus on the Discovery of America: A Facsimile Reprint of the Pictorial Edition of 1493 . . . , prepared with an introduction and translation by Eames (New York: Printed for the Trustees of the Lenox Library, 1892?).

SELECTED PERIODICAL PUBLICATIONS –

UNCOLLECTED: "Illinois and Miami Vocabulary and Lord's Prayer," *United States Catholic Historical Magazine,* 3 (1980): 278–286;

"The First American Edition of Wither's Poems and Bacon's Essays," *The Bibliographer,* 1 (January 1902): 11–21;

"Two New York Views of about 1650," *Bulletin of the New York Public Library,* 28 (September 1924): 679–681;

"The Antiqua Press and Benjamin Mecom, 1748–1765," *Proceedings of the American Antiquarian Society,* new series 38 (October 1928): 303–348.

Wilberforce Eames is regarded today as the greatest of Americanists and one of the most remarkable of bibliographers. Although he lacked a formal education and never traveled outside of North America, Eames attained a facility with a variety of languages and an almost overwhelming knowledge of books and their histories — especially in the area of Americana. As a collector he assembled a series of sizable libraries, ranging in content from books on Native American linguistics to histories of Asia and Africa. As a librarian he was responsible for the custodianship of the collection built by James Lenox; he oversaw its operation during a period of transition from private library to a part of the New York Public Library. As a bibliographer he played an instrumental role in the compilation and publication of Joseph Sabin's *Bibliotheca Americana. A Dictionary of Books Relating to America From Its Discovery to the Present Time* (1868–1936), wrote articles and studies, was one of the founders of the Bibliographical Society of America, and more important, served as an invaluable resource of bibliographical and historical information for countless authors of scholarly works. Few publications with which he was involved bear his name; yet Eames spent his life largely in gathering knowledge and disseminating it to those who sought his help, earning him an esteemed place at the heart of the bibliographic community.

Wilberforce Eames was born in Newark, New Jersey, on 12 October 1855, the son of Nelson Eames and Phoebe Harriet Crane. When Eames was six years old, his family moved to Brooklyn, New York, where Eames lived for the rest of his life. His father, a former schoolteacher, saw to it that Eames learned to read, and the young Eames pursued his studies at home until he

Eames early in his career

entered public school at the age of nine. Like many children in his neighborhood, Eames also began to work at an early age. By the time he was twelve years old, he was holding odd jobs, including working as a delivery boy for a local grocer. A dog bite suffered on one of his deliveries led to a period of recuperation at home, which was spent reading Edward Gibbon's *The History of the Decline and Fall of the Roman Empire* (1776–1788). Eames used Gibbon as a source in compiling a historical chronology – an ongoing project during much of his youth – and he also recorded Gibbon's references to other works; for the next several years Eames used these as the nucleus of a reading and acquisition list.

Eames left school at the age of thirteen and eventually found full-time employment at a newly established local newspaper, the *East New York Sentinel*. Although the newspaper operated for only six months, Eames learned the practical side of printing, and this experience in the composition of type and in presswork later became invaluable in his bibliographical studies. After the demise of the newspaper, Eames worked as a clerk and messenger in the East New York post office. One of his regular duties was to take the mailbag to the Brooklyn central post office, where he waited an hour for the return bag. Eames regularly spent this hour in the nearby bookshop operated by Edward R. Gillespie, and in 1873 Eames gave up his job at the post office to work for Gillespie.

From the time he began to work in Gillespie's shop until his death more than sixty years later, Wilberforce Eames never left the world of books. He worked for Gillespie for six years, performing the various duties of a bookseller's clerk. During this period Eames continued to build his own library. His most extensive purchase was a sixty-four volume set of the second edition of the *Universal History* (1747–1766), which he used in augmenting and extending his chronology. Working at Gillespie's also brought Eames in contact with many collectors of the day, including Thomas Warren Field, a noted collector and bibliographer of books about the American Indian, and Daniel G. Treadwell, collector of Oriental books.

Eames left Gillespie in 1879 and accepted a position with the New York religious book-selling firm, N. Tibbals and Sons. Eames's work with Tibbals was varied and included ordering new books from publishers, assisting in the preparation of an 1882 edition of the Bible published by the firm, and acting as the firm's sales representative at camp meetings at Sing Sing. Work at the Tibbals firm was followed by stints at the shops of Henry Miller and Charles L. Woodward.

Eames had an ability with languages, and if in researching bibliographical and historical inquiries he came across an unfamiliar language, he engaged in the study of that language. His interest in the history of the world led Eames to a familiarity with ancient and modern European languages, Oriental languages, and various languages and dialects of Africa and North America, and to the acquisition of books in these areas. Eames became well acquainted with James Constantine Pilling of the Bureau of American Ethnology, who was compiling a bibliography of the languages of North American Indians. Eames was of great assistance to Pilling in his bibliographical work, and Eames's contribution was acknowledged by Pilling in the preface of his *Proof-Sheets of a Bibliography of the Languages of the North American Indians* (1885):

> Almost from the beginning of the type-setting, the catalogue has had the benefit of his aid and advice. His thorough knowledge of the class of books treated, his interest in the subject itself, his fine library, rich in bibliographical authorities, his scrupulous care and accuracy with the minutiae which compose so large a part of a work like this, and his judgment in matters of arrangement, have all rendered his cooperation invaluable. The frequent mention of his name throughout shows but imperfectly the extent of my obligations to him.

This acknowledgment was typical of the kind of tribute Eames's bibliographical work received over the years. The vast majority of his research appeared in the works of others, and he never saw a need to publish regularly under his own name. During the next few years, Eames also assisted Pilling with bibliographies of individual language groups, including detailed contributions relating to the Algonquian languages in general and to the Eliot Indian Bible (1663) in particular.

At Woodward's shop, Eames had also come into contact with Joseph F. Sabin, the son of bookseller and bibliographer Joseph Sabin who had died in 1881. The elder Sabin had begun the compilation and publication of *A Dictionary of Books Relating to America . . .* , of which thirteen volumes had been organized in alphabetical order by entry and issued at the time of his death. No one had continued Sabin's work, and in 1883 Eames offered to assume editorial supervision of the *Dictionary,* with the Sabin firm continuing to publish it. As Eames wanted no remuneration for the work, the arrangement was agreeable to Joseph F. Sabin.

The first part of the *Dictionary* to be published under Eames's editorship began with the entries for "Pennsylvania" in volume fourteen, which appeared in 1884. For the next eight years Eames oversaw the production of five more volumes and brought a high degree of bibliographical accuracy to his entries.

Eames's reputation for sound bibliographical judgment and hard work was widespread. As a bookseller's clerk he spent his leisure time answering bibliographical queries from around the world in addition to pursuing his own research.

In 1885 George Henry Moore, superintendent of the Lenox Library, asked Eames to be his personal assistant. By the time of his death in 1880 James Lenox had built an extensive collection of rare books, with particular strength in Americana. In 1870 the Lenox Library was incorporated as a separate legal entity, and a new building was constructed to house the collection, a treasure trove of source material for the study of American history. Eames accepted the position and left the bookselling world to spend the rest of his career as a librarian.

After three years as Moore's assistant, Eames became a full member of the Lenox Library staff in 1888, and following Moore's death in 1892 Eames was named librarian. The increased workload of his new position forced him to give up his work on Sabin's *Dictionary,* although he would return briefly to the project in 1906 and would resume editorship in 1925. (In 1930 Eames turned the editorship of the *Dictionary* over to Robert William Glenroie Vail, who completed it in 1936.)

The next few years were a period of intensive work for Eames. Although the Lenox Library was supposed to serve as a gift to the city of New York, it had operated with limited hours open to the public and few finding aids for the collections; the library had a reputation as an unfriendly institution.

Eames's personal books were sold in a series of auctions in 1905, 1906, and
1910–1911

Eames was determined to make the collections more accessible while still giving them the protection and care that they deserved. He had begun this work under Moore's supervision, and now with greater authority Eames was able to implement a card catalogue, increase the public exhibition activities of the library, prepare more detailed and readable annual reports, and greatly improve the library's relations with the public and the press. Eames also saw to it that the Lenox Library was a significant participant in the events of 1892 commemorating the four-hundredth anniversary of the voyage of Christopher Columbus. He prepared a facsimile edition and a new translation of the Columbus Letter, which the library issued as a commemorative publication.

In 1895 the Lenox Library joined the Astor Library and the Tilden Trust to form the New York Public Library. The Lenox collections remained physically separate, and Eames remained in charge of the Lenox Library, overseeing its transition and working with the director of the New York Public Library, John Shaw Billings. In 1911 the Lenox collections were moved to the new building at Fifth Avenue and Forty-second Street, and Eames was made chief of the American History Division of the New York Public Library.

In addition to attending to the moving of the collection, Eames purchased a camera and began a program of the application of photography and photostatic copying to bibliography. Although the value of this study had been proposed by Henry Stevens nearly forty years before, few scholars had applied it to the close study of the characteristics of printed books. In 1916 Eames was named Bibliographer of the Library. The position entailed no time-consuming administrative duties, allowing him to concentrate on bibliographical questions and to deal with his voluminous correspondence. Eames held the position of bibliographer until his death of cancer in 1937 at the age of eighty-two.

Books were never merely the tools Eames used in his work; they were his passion and occupied the center of his life. Eames collected books relentlessly from the time he could first buy them, and he viewed his gradually increasing salary first and foremost as a means to acquire more books. Eames's personal life was simple. He lived his life in the Brooklyn house in which he was raised; never marrying, he shared the house with his parents until his mother's death in 1892 and his father's death ten years later. His meals were usually taken with a neighboring family, and someone was hired to clean the house regularly (with instructions not to touch the books). Like many collectors, Eames used whatever funds not required for his immediate needs for the purchase of books. Bookcases were constructed everywhere, and books were shelved three deep; the foundations of the house were reinforced to accommodate the increased load. Eames was rumored to sleep in a hammock, since any available floor space that might have been taken up by a bed was otherwise occupied.

Eames's collection of books covered the full range of his interests. Bibliographical reference works; American and world histories; Asian, African, and Native American linguistics studies; and scholarly periodicals all contributed to the more than twenty thousand volumes that he had amassed by 1904. These had not come from bulk purchases, but from careful individual selection, constant visits to bookshops, and scouring of catalogues; he continuously weeded and upgraded his copies.

At the age of fifty, Eames realized that his life had been a sedentary one, completely devoted to books. His love of books never changed, but an attack of appendicitis – and a subsequent hospital stay – coupled with bouts of insomnia caused Eames to reexamine his routines. A period of recuperation at the Westchester County health resort of William Muldoon instilled in him an appreciation for outdoor exercise, and he began to take long daily walks and to go on an occasional fishing trip.

A desire to simplify and improve his life also led to the decision to reduce the size of his library. Between 1905 and 1907 portions of Eames's library were sold in a series of five sales, totaling more than ten thousand lots, at the Anderson Auction Company in New York. While these sales included significant collections on printing and the book arts, as well as on British, European, and western and central Asian history, literature, and linguistics, Eames retained among other books his Chinese, Japanese, and Korean collections. He also kept his materials on American Indian linguistics. During the next decade Eames donated or sold at cost to the New York Public Library some five thousand volumes on American Indian and African linguistics, while additional sales at auction, including more than twenty-five hundred lots, disposed of other parts of the collection.

In addition to these transactions, Eames sold to various institutions his remaining Oriental collections, as well as his holdings of classical literature and commentaries. As was the case with many collectors, Eames used the proceeds to begin collecting again. He had retained many of his bibliographical tools, and to these he added a focused collection of American imprints. Eames began to work on his American-imprints collection in earnest after he was named bibliographer in 1916. The lack of a required schedule allowed him to make the rounds of the bookshops each day and to obtain for relatively little money American books and pamphlets of the eighteenth and nineteenth centuries.

When organized by state, territory, town, and printer, Eames's collection provided the raw material for serious study of the development and spread of printing in the United States. By 1923 the collection had grown to well more than twelve thousand items, and Eames decided to sell. The American imprints were sold en bloc through A. S. W. Rosenbach to Henry E. Huntington. Eames was to receive more than fifty thousand dollars upon the delivery of the collection to Huntington. At Eames's request, however, delivery was delayed to allow him to do final research, as well as to organize and inventory the collection. The research took another two years, and with all of the books finally delivered and Eames in good financial position he began to collect again.

Eames had long been attracted to all forms of written communication, and ancient languages held a particular appeal. Although he pursued his work in Americana, in the last decade of his life he concentrated much of his collecting on ancient Oriental languages and written records. This collection, on which Eames was estimated to have spent between twenty and thirty thousand dollars, encompasses

some fourteen hundred items, including more than seven hundred ancient tablets and seals, primarily Sumerian and Assyrian. Eames spent a good part of his final years transcribing and translating these cuneiform records, as well as researching other such objects in New York City collections.

As a bibliographer Wilberforce Eames is best remembered for his contributions to Sabin's *Dictionary,* and much of Eames's most detailed work appeared in his Sabin entries. Several of his most significant contributions to Sabin were also issued in small numbers as separate publications, including the sections on Ptolemy's Geography, Sir Walter Ralegh, John Smith, and Amerigo Vespucci. Eames also regularly contributed articles to the *Bulletin of the New York Public Library* and would occasionally

write for other bibliographical or historical publications.

Eames's published output, when compared to that of other noted Americanists of his day such as Charles Evans and José Toribio Medina, is relatively small, however. His dedication to bibliographical endeavors was without regard for credit to himself. In matters of Americana he was a constant source of information. He cared far more about the usefulness of the information he provided to others than for publishing a newly discovered bibliographical point himself. Eames's carefully recorded notes on thousands of books and his well-stocked memory came to the aid of thousands of bibliographers and historians around the world, and the great bulk of Eames's work was published by others, acknowledged and unacknowledged in countless bibliographies, catalogues, and studies.

Despite a retiring personality, Eames did receive honors during his lifetime. He was elected to the American Antiquarian Society, was made an honorary member of the Grolier Club, and received the gold medals of the New York Historical Society and the Bibliographical Society of London. He also received three honorary degrees – in 1896 an M.A. from Harvard University and in 1924 an LL.D. from the University of Michigan and a Litt.D. from Brown University. He was also the recipient of a 1924 Festschrift, *Bibliographical Essays: A Tribute to Wilberforce Eames,* organized by George Parker Winship and Victor Hugo Paltsits, among others; contributors included Lawrence C. Wroth, Henry R. Wagner, and Lathrop C. Harper. In presenting the secretly produced volume to Eames on 19 December 1924, Winship said, "Dr. Eames, I have in my hand a book about which every one in this room knows more than you do. This is the first time such a thing has happened, and it is certain that it can never happen again."

At Eames's death in 1937, his Oriental collection, an extensive bibliographical library, early manuscripts and incunabula, and a large collection of Americana remained as part of his estate. The Oriental collection was eventually purchased at far below its original cost by the New York Public Library. Other than a few specific bequests, the remainder of the estate was bequeathed to the New York Public Library to establish a "Wilberforce Eames Americana Fund" for the purchase of Americana before the year 1801. Those who knew him best expressed repeatedly their praise for Eames's selfless devotion to bibliography and for his vast knowledge of books. He is considered the dean of Americanists, a collector of enormous scope, and a leading example of the scholar-librarian, committed to making irreplaceable resources available to all and acquiring knowledge for the sake of the love of learning and of service to others.

Bibliographies:

Victor Hugo Paltsits, "Works and Contributions," in "Wilberforce Eames: A Bio-Bibliographical Narrative," in *Bibliographical Essays: A Tribute to Wilberforce Eames,* prepared by Paltsits and others (Cambridge, Mass.: Harvard University Press, 1924), pp. 23–26;

Lewis M. Stark, "The Writings of Wilberforce Eames," *Bulletin of the New York Public Library,* 59 (October 1955): 515–519.

References:

Harry Miller Lydenberg, "Wilberforce Eames As I Recall Him," in *Proceedings of the American Antiquarian Society,* prepared by Paltsits and others, 65 (20 April–19 October 1955): 213–233;

Victor Hugo Paltsits, "Wilberforce Eames: A Bio-Bibliographical Narrative," in *Bibliographical Essays: A Tribute to Wilberforce Eames,* prepared by Paltsits and others (Cambridge, Mass.: Harvard University Press, 1924), pp. 1–26;

Paltsits, "Wilberforce Eames, American Bibliographer," *Inter-American Review of Bibliography,* 3 (September–December 1953): 252–263; reprinted in *Bulletin of the New York Public Library,* 59 (October 1955): 505–514;

Proceedings and Addresses at the Presentation of the New York Historical Society's Gold Medal to Dr. Wilberforce Eames (New York: New York Historical Society, 1932);

George Parker Winship, "Wilberforce Eames: Bookman," *Bulletin of the New York Public Library,* 42 (January 1938): 3–9.

Papers:

The papers of Wilberforce Eames are at the New York Public Library.

Eugene Field

(2? September 1850 – 4 November 1895)

Alison M. Scott

Bowling Green State University

See also the Field entries in *DLB 23: American Newspaper Journalists, 1873–1900* and *DLB 42: American Writers for Children Before 1900.*

SELECTED BOOKS: *Tribune Primer* (Denver, Colo.: Tribune Publishing Company, 1881); republished as *The Model Primer* (New York: Tredwell, 1882); republished as *Eugene Field's First Book: The Tribune Primer* (New York: Marion, 1900); republished as *The Complete Tribune Primer,* with drawings by Frederick Opper (Boston: Mutual Book, 1901);

Culture's Garland, Being Memoranda of the Gradual Rise of Literature, Art, Music and Society in Chicago, and Other Western Ganglia (Boston: Ticknor, 1887);

A Little Book of Profitable Tales (Chicago: Wilson, 1889; London: Osgood, McIlvaine, 1891);

A Little Book of Western Verse (Chicago: Wilson, 1889; enlarged edition, New York: Scribners, 1890; London: Osgood, McIlvaine, 1891);

Echoes from the Sabine Farm, Being Certain Horatian Lyrics Now for the First Time Discreetly and Delectably Done into English Verse, by Field and Roswell M. Field (New Rochelle, N.Y.: Wilson, 1891; revised edition, Chicago: McClurg, 1893);

With Trumpet and Drum (New York: Scribners, 1892);

Second Book of Verse (Chicago: Stone, 1892; revised edition, New York: Scribners, 1893);

The Holy-Cross and Other Tales (Cambridge & Chicago: Stone & Kimball, 1893; enlarged edition, New York: Scribners, 1896);

Love-Songs of Childhood (New York: Scribners, 1894);

The House: An Episode in the Lives of Reuben Baker, Astronomer, and of his Wife Alice (New York: Scribners, 1896);

The Love Affairs of a Bibliomaniac (New York: Scribners, 1896; London: Scribners/Lane, 1896);

Songs and Other Verse (New York: Scribners, 1896);

Second Book of Tales (New York: Scribners, 1896);

Florence Bardsley's Story: The Life and Death of a Remarkable Woman (Chicago: Way, 1897);

Sharps and Flats, 2 volumes, collated by Slason Thompson (New York: Scribners, 1900);

A Little Book of Nonsense (Boston: Mutual, 1901);

A Little Book of Tribune Verse: A Number of Hitherto Uncollected Poems, Grave and Gay, edited by Joseph G. Brown (Denver: Tandy, Wheeler, 1901);

Hoosier Lyrics, edited by Charles Walter Brown (Chicago: Donohue, 1905);

John Smith, U.S.A., edited by Brown (Chicago: Donohue, 1905);

The Poems of Eugene Field (New York: Scribners, 1910).

OTHER: *First Editions of American Authors: A Manual for Book-Lovers,* compiled by Herbert Stuart Stone, introduction by Field (Cambridge, Mass.: Stone & Kimball, 1893).

Highly regarded by his contemporaries as a poet, journalist, humorist, and raconteur, Eugene Field also built a reputation for himself as a bibliophile – although he did not accumulate a notable collection of books or establish a great library. His significance to the history of book collecting lies in his having successfully popularized book collecting as an avocation and in having helped create a middle-class ideal of civic and self-improvement based on books. His own writings, widely distributed during his lifetime through newspaper, magazine, and book publication, remain collectible for their sharp, affectionate, and witty portrayals of bibliophilia.

Eugene Field was born in Saint Louis, Missouri, the eldest of the two surviving children of Roswell Martin and Frances Reed Field, both of whom were natives of Vermont. In his later years Field claimed he had two birth dates – 2 and 3 September 1850 – so if friends forgot the first day they could celebrate his birthday on the second. At the time of Eugene's birth, his father, an attorney, was pursuing the legal appeals which he had begun in 1847 on behalf of the fugitive slave Dred Scott. After his mother's death in 1856, Field and his brother Roswell, Jr., were sent to Amherst, Massachusetts, to be raised by their paternal

Eugene Field

cousin, Mary Field French. After receiving classical training (he corresponded with his father and uncle in Latin), he attended Williams College in 1868, Knox College in 1869, and the University of Missouri at Columbia from 1870 until 1872, when he left on a European tour which lasted until 1873. After returning to the United States, Field married sixteen-year-old Julia Sutherland Comstock. During their twenty-two-year marriage the couple had eight children, of whom five survived to adulthood.

Field's career as a journalist began in 1873 when he went to work for the *St. Louis Evening Journal.* Through the following decade he worked for the *St. Joseph Gazette,* the *St. Louis Times-Journal,* the *Kansas City Times,* and the *Denver Tribune.* Field's first book, *The Tribune Primer* (1881), modeled after *The New England Primer* (1689), was a collection of some of his sardonically humorous and caustic observations on Denver so-

ciety and politics. The flavor of his early writing — irreverent, biting, even coarse — clearly emerges from such short pieces as his remarks upon politicians:

> Here is a Statesman. He makes speeches about the poor Tax-Payer and Drinks Whisky. . . . He picks his Teeth with a Fork and Wipes his Nose on the Bottom of Sofas and Chairs. If you Neglect your Education and Learn to Chew plug Tobacco, maybe you will be a Statesman some time. Some Statesmen go to Congress and some go to Jail. But it is the Same Thing, after all.

In 1883 the *Chicago Daily News* hired him as an editorial columnist. He spent the rest of his newspaper career writing a two-thousand-word daily column, "Sharps and Flats," for the paper (which merged with the *Chicago Record* in 1892); the last appeared on 2 November 1895, two days before his death at the age of forty-five.

Field in his library

In his early columns for the *News,* Field focused on the political, cultural, and business activities of Chicago – which he whimsically dubbed "Porkopolis" – civic-improvement schemes, as well as state and national politics. A merciless critic of shortcuts to cultural attainment, he also wrote humorous attacks on the cultural pretensions of midwestern businessmen, targeting in particular their lack of understanding or appreciation of the cultural objects they purchased and exploited for social purposes. In one such piece, collected in *Culture's Garland . . .* (1887), Field wrote,

Our esteemed fellow-townsman, Mr. Charles F. Gunther, the well-known candy-manufacturer, is indefatigable in collecting rare old curiosities. Not very long ago he discovered a genuine autograph of William Shakespeare, and he paid five thousand dollars for it; subsequently he found and bought a volume of Ella Wheeler Wilcox's poems containing the autograph of Dante Alighieri written in a clean round hand on one of the fly-pages.

Field illustrated *Culture's Garland* himself, drawing a wreath of sausages labeled "A Chicago Literary Circle," as the frontispiece.

Throughout his time in Chicago, Field regularly recommended books for purchase as gifts and discussed the various bookstores in the city and region, asserting that even the most inexperienced book buyers need not be intimidated by the range of choices facing them. Following the publication of *Culture's Garland,* Field increasingly devoted his column to poetry, short stories, and bibliographic gossip. He featured news of historical or literary interest, such as the discovery of a fourteenth-century manuscript of Aristotle's work in 1887, and he also began regular publication of what he called "paraphrases" – free translations into a modern American idiom – of the poetry of Heinrich Heine, Pierre-Jean de Béranger, François Villon, Johann Ludwig Uhland, Virgil, and Horace.

After 1889 Field's column began to report on the activities of the "Saints and Sinners," a mythical

Field, James Whitcomb Riley, and Bill Nye, Indianapolis, 1886 (Denver Public Library)

group of bibliophiles made up of prominent local businessmen, professionals, and ministers created by Field. Field's description of their meetings in the Old Book Department of McClurg's Bookstore became prominent features. Primarily inventive anecdotes about Field's friends and assorted public figures, interpolated with poetry and anecdotes about books, the Saints-and-Sinners pieces served to acquaint Field's readership with book-collecting interests and coveted items. The meeting recorded on 21 February 1891 ended with the singing of "The Extra-Illustrator's Hymn":

> I love to tear my self away
>   From sorrows and vexations,
> And, in dark nooks, from ancient books,
>   Tear out the illustrations. . . .

Only one "in the flesh" meeting of the Saints and Sinners was held – on 31 December 1890, at which

Field recited the poem "Dibdin's Ghost." A witty evocation of the spirit of the great English bibliographer Thomas Frognall Dibdin, the poem later appeared in "Sharps and Flats" on 30 August 1892:

> Dear wife, last midnight whilst I read
>   The tomes you so despise,
> A specter rose beside the bed
>   And spoke in this true wise:
> "From Canaan's beatific coast
>   I've come to visit thee,
> For I am Frognall Dibdin's ghost!"
>   Says Dibdin's ghost to me. . . .

It should be noted that in describing the practice of book collecting, Field routinely asserted that women were almost uniformly opposed to it, particularly as it distinguished their husbands' interests from their own and drew men away from domestic concerns. Part of Field's aim in the Saints-and-Sinners pieces was indeed to rehabilitate the genteel

The Love-Affairs of a Bibliomaniac.—XIV.

The manuscript for **The Love Affairs of a Bibliomaniac,** *Field's most widely known bibliophilic work (from Eugene Field,* The Love Affairs of a Bibliophile, *1905)*

[2

My publications have been, chronologically, as follows:

1 — The Tribune Primer; Denver, 1882. (Out of print and very, very scarce)

2 — Culture's Garland; Ticknor; Boston; 1887. (Out of print.)

A Little Book of Western Verse; Chicago; 1889. (Large paper, privately printed, and limited)

A Little Book of Profitable Tales; Chicago; 1889. (Large paper, privately printed and limited)

3 — A Little Book of Western Verse; Scribners; New York; 1890.

4 — A Little Book of Profitable Tales; Scribners; New York; 1890.

5 — With Trumpet and Drum; Scribners; New York; 1892.

6 — Second Book of Verse; Scribners; New York; 1893

7 — Echoes from the Sabine Farm *; Translations of Horace; McClurg; Chicago; 1893.

8 — Introduction to Stone's First Editions of American Authors; Cambridge; 1893

9 — The Holy Cross and Other Tales; Stone & Kimball; Cambridge, 1893.

———

Ill health compelled me to visit Europe in 1889; there I remained fourteen months, that time being divided between England, Germany, Holland and Belgium. My residence at present is in Buena Park, a north-shore suburb of Chicago.

I have a miscellaneous collection of books numbering 3500, and I am fond of the quaint and curious in every line. I am very fond of dogs, birds and all small pets — a passion not approved of by my wife. My favorite flower is the carnation. My favorites in fiction are Hawthorne's "Scarlet Letter", "Don Quixote" and "Pilgrim's Progress." I greatly love Hans Christian Andersen's tales and I

———

* In collaboration with my brother, Roswell Martin Field.

Field's autobibliography, with a description of his library (from Eugene Field, Verse and Prose, *1917)* pursuit of books as a fraternal and intellectual avocation for "real men."

During an extended trip to Europe with his family in 1889–1890, Field pursued his own literary interests and filled his column entirely with poetry, short stories, essays, and bibliographical commentary – reporting, for instance, on the sales of William Makepeace Thackeray and Dante Gabriel Rossetti manuscripts and rare editions of William Shakespeare's plays in London. His work increased his reputation among his contemporaries as a sentimental poet and bibliophile, while at the same time moving him farther from the role of social and cultural satirist which had brought him early fame.

Field returned to Chicago after the death of his son Melvin and once again began regularly to chronicle the activities of the Saints and Sinners and the hoopla surrounding the World's Columbian Exposition. The founding of the University of Chicago in 1891 and the activities of William F. Poole – the Newberry Library's head librarian since its founding in 1885 and prominent member of the Saints and Sinners – also provided Field's column with a wealth of material. Going less and less often to the *Daily News* downtown offices after 1890, Field did most of his writing at home; and, as the changing content of "Sharps and Flats" makes obvious, he increasingly and intentionally became detached from the rough-and-tumble journalism of a mass-circulation daily newspaper.

The last year of Field's professional life was devoted to the serial publication of two works: *The House* (1896), a humorous story partly based upon Field's own efforts to build a family home on Chicago's North Shore, and *The Love Affairs of a Bibliomaniac* (1896). A fictional autobiography, the latter is composed of loosely connected meditations on aspects of the book-collecting fever, reminiscent of *The Reveries of a Bachelor* (1850) by Ik Marvel (Donald Grant Mitchell). Matthew, the narrator, recounts anecdotes of the books he loved and pursued during his long life:

> For many, very many years I have walked in a pleasant garden, enjoying sweet odors and soothing spectacles; no predetermined itinerary has controlled my course; I have wandered whither I pleased, and very many times I have strayed so far into the tanglewood and thickets as almost to have lost my way. And now it is my purpose to walk that pleasant garden once more, inviting you to bear me company and to share with me what satisfaction may accrue from an old man's return to old-time places and old-time loves.

Matthew's meanderings in this garden of bibliophily amount to a sentimental summation of Field's own affection for books and the sorts of people they attract and inspire. *The New England Primer*, Daniel Defoe's *Robinson Crusoe* (1719), and the Brothers Grimm's *Household Stories* (1812) are among the volumes described in the narrative, but ballad verse and angling literature, as well as extra-illustrated copies and tall Elzevirs, also provided story-telling material. Through the voices of Matthew, Field also shares with his readers his recollections of famous bibliophiles, meditations on the fragrance of old books, and the pleasures of collecting.

Among his contemporaries Field was renowned for his own eccentric collection of more than thirty-five hundred volumes. Alongside his books were curious bric-a-brac, most notably William Gladstone's ax. Field's taste, though eclectic, was nevertheless quite conventional and heavily weighted toward English literature, Greek and Latin authors, humor, and memoirs. His book collection was dispersed in the 1920s; the value of the volumes sold derived primarily from their association with Field. This association was so highly valued that Field's son, Eugene Field II, entered on a lucrative career by forging his father's signature in books and providing a spurious certificate attesting to their presence in his father's library.

Much of Field's writing about books and book collecting asserts his belief that bibliophily is the reflection of personal values and, indeed, the values of an entire community. Concerning the 1891 sale of the Brayton Ives copy of the Gutenberg Bible to James W. Ellsworth of Chicago for $14,800, Field argued in a rare signed column of 5 March 1891 that the acquisition of a book of such extraordinary historical interest by a private citizen demonstrates the intellectual prominence, economic superiority, and social maturity of the entire city of Chicago. The recognition of the importance of rare books, Field argues, and their acquisition are the best results of a life of education, leisure, and financial security. The book trade, in turn, represents the assimilation of those cultural values by individuals and by society. Field thus concludes that bibliophily, while the recreation of the few, serves an exemplary social function, and book collectors, at their best, represent the productive alternative to the spectacle of Chicago parvenus. In a 6 September 1894 column Field included a paragraph about Ellsworth's home, reiterating his continuing emphasis on the potential public worth of private possessions:

The residence of Mr. James W. Ellsworth in Michigan avenue is an object of increasing interest to which we delight to refer intelligent visitors to Chicago. Its beautiful art gallery, its remarkable collection of books and manuscripts, its superb porcelains ... bespeak a taste and refinement of exceptional advancement. It is an education and an inspiration to see and to enjoy these rare, dainty, beautiful things, and it is the happy fortune of our public that Mr. Ellsworth is prompt and gracious in according access to his uniquely elegant home.

Field did not write loving descriptions of beautiful books to improve understanding or convey information in a pedantic sense, but to create a feeling for books as the carriers of great ideas and as wonderful objects and to convey the feelings which make and mark the bibliophile. In *The Love Affairs of a Bibliomaniac,* Field's commentary on *The New England Primer* reveals his insights into the enduring value found in books:

My Book and Heart
Must never part.
So runs one of the couplets in this little Primer-book, and right truly can I say that from the springtime day sixty-odd years ago, when first my heart went out in love to this little book, no change of scene or of custom, no allurement of fashion, no demand of mature years, has abated that love. And herein is exemplified the advantage which the love of books has over the other kinds of love. Women are by nature fickle, and so are men; their friendships are liable to dissipation at the merest provocation or the slightest pretext.
Not so, however, with books, for books cannot change. A thousand years hence they are what you find them to-day, speaking the same words, holding forth the same cheer, the same promise, the same comfort; always constant, laughing with those who laugh and weeping with those who weep.

The demands of Field's position as a columnist for an urban newspaper were often at odds with his artistic aspirations, and a great deal of his writing was the worse for the haste with which it was produced. Nevertheless, Field resolved the conflicts between the quotidian demands for copy for an indiscriminate mass readership and his desires to create finely crafted essays, stories, and poems for a genteel audience through his bibliographic journalism. His advocacy of the private pleasures of book collecting and reading reached a huge audience during his lifetime; the high value collectors continue to place on *The Love Affairs of a Biliomaniac* is the best evidence of Field's enduring literary legacy.

Biographies:
Clara Banta, *Eugene Field: The Story of His Life, for Children* (Kansas City, Mo.: Sweet, 1898);
Slason Thompson, *Eugene Field: A Study in Heredity and Contradictions,* 2 volumes (New York: Scribners, 1901);
Charles H. Dennis, *Eugene Field's Creative Years* (Garden City, N.Y.: Doubleday, Page, 1924);
Thompson, *Life of Eugene Field, The Poet of Childhood* (New York: Appleton, 1927);
Jeannette C. Nolan, *The Gay Poet: The Story of Eugene Field* (New York: Messer, 1940);
Robert Conrow, *Field Days: The Life, Times, & Reputation of Eugene Field* (New York: Scribners, 1974).

References:
Ida Comstock Below, *Eugene Field in his Home* (New York: Dutton, 1898);
Henry W. Fischer, *Abroad with Mark Twain and Eugene Field: Tales They Told to a Fellow Correspondent* (New York: Brown, 1922);
The Library of the Late Eugene Field: To Be Sold by Order of his Widow, Mrs. Julia Sutherland Field, Tuesday and Wednesday Evenings, December Eighteenth, Nineteenth, at Eight-fifteen O'Clock (New York: Anderson Galleries, 1923).
Francis Wilson, *The Eugene Field I Knew* (New York: Scribners, 1898).

Papers:
The major collections of Eugene Field's papers are at the Newberry Library, Chicago; University of Chicago Library; Chicago Public Library; New York Public Library; Jones Library, Amherst, Massachusetts; Denver Public Library; Harry Ransom Humanities Research Center University of Texas; Saint Joseph Public Library, Saint Joseph, Missouri; and Washington University Library, Saint Louis, Missouri.

Henry Clay Folger

(18 June 1857 – 11 June 1930)

William Baker
Northern Illinois University

SELECTED BOOKS: *A Tribute to the Memory of Charles Pratt: An Address at Pratt Institute, on Founder's Day, October 2, 1903* (N.p.: Privately printed, 1903);

A Unique First Folio, with photographs by George Dupont Pratt (New York: Outlook, 1907).

Henry Clay Folger was one of the preeminent book collectors of the last decade of the nineteenth century and the first three decades of the twentieth. He collected English titles and was particularly interested in Shakespeareana. This passion resulted in a Shakespeare library unrivaled for its quality and size — a library that he generously donated to be administered by the trustees of Amherst College for the use of scholars worldwide.

Henry Clay Folger was born to Henry Clay and Eliza Jane Clark Folger in New York City on 18 June 1857. He descended from Peter Folger, who had bought Nantucket Island from Native Americans. He attended the Adelphi Academy in Brooklyn, where he held a scholarship donated by Charles Pratt, president of the board of trustees of the academy, partner of John D. Rockefeller, and father of Folger's close friend, Charles M. Pratt. After graduating from Adelphi, Folger entered Amherst College. In his junior year his father's wholesale millinery business failed, forcing Folger to leave Amherst and enter the College of the City of New York. His Amherst classmates Charles M. Pratt and William M. Ladd, however, guaranteed the money that allowed him to complete his education at Amherst, from which he graduated in June 1879 after winning awards in English composition and being elected to Phi Beta Kappa.

After graduation he entered the Pratt-family oil business. While serving a clerkship at Charles Pratt and Company, he pursued a law degree at Columbia University. In 1881 he graduated cum laude from Columbia and was awarded a master's degree from Amherst for work done in absentia. In 1886 he became secretary of the Manufacturing Committee

of Standard Oil, and in 1898 he was named committee chairman. In 1908 he was elected to the Board of Directors of the Standard Oil Company of New Jersey, and by 1910 he had become relatively wealthy. In 1911 government action against Standard Oil under the Sherman Anti-Trust Act led to the breakup of the company, whereupon Folger became president of Standard Oil of New York (1911–1924) and then chairman of the board (1924–1928).

Folger's interest in Shakespeareana was first aroused in 1879 at Amherst after he heard a lecture delivered by Ralph Waldo Emerson titled "Superlative or Mental Temperance." Folger was so impressed that he began devouring Emerson's writings, including "The Tercentenary of Shakespeare's Birth," an excerpt from an address Emerson had delivered in 1864. Also in that year Folger bought the Handy Volume Edition of Shakespeare, published by Routledge. One or more of the thirteen volumes in this set would serve as a constant companion on Folger's future travels.

Folger's interest in Shakespeare was also furthered by his marriage to Emily Clara Jordan on 6 October 1885. A Vassar graduate whose master's thesis was titled "The True Text of Shakespeare," Emily Folger shared her husband's passion for book collecting, and she would help execute his plans to build a library to house the collection they assembled together. Shortly after their marriage Folger gave his wife a copy of the Halliwell-Phillipps facsimile of the 1623 First Folio, for which he paid $1.25. The facsimile called attention to textual variants in editions of Shakespeare's plays. In 1889 Folger attended an auction at Bangs in New York City, where the 1685 Fourth Folio was among the lots; he acquired the work for $107.50. It was the first of his thirty-six Fourth Folios. He would also acquire twenty-four Third Folios (1663–1664), fifty-eight 1632 Second Folios, and seventy-nine copies of the First Folio.

In 1891 Folger and his wife secured one of these First Folios during their first of many trips to

Henry Clay Folger, portrait by Frank Salisbury, 1927 (Folger Shakespeare Library)

Shakespeare's birthplace at Stratford-upon-Avon. This copy, known as the Vincent-Sibthorpe Folio, is the largest copy known. Its leaves are uncut, and text and portrait are in an early state; it may have been the first copy printed in 1623. The copy was presented by the printer, William Jaggard, to Augustine Vincent of the College of Arms for Vincent's defense of Shakespeare's right to acquire a coat of arms.

Folger and his wife scoured book catalogues for Shakespeareana and made many trips to England, visiting bookshops and auction houses. Folger had agents who worked for him, searching for books and bidding for them in his absence. Collecting Shakespeare's works and anything connected with the dramatist and his times became an obsession for the couple. They acquired promptbooks, manuscripts, playbills, paintings, costumes, music, and mementos relating to Shakespeare. The objects

became surrogate children to this childless couple. The Folgers lived simply, devoting to their collecting all money not needed for necessities. Some of the acquisitions they kept at home, but many were stored in bank vaults and warehouses.

The growth of Folger's library may be traced in letters to his 1879 Amherst class secretary. In 1889 he wrote of "gathering . . . a modest library." Five years later he admitted that although his days were devoted to Standard Oil, his nights were given to Shakespeare. He observed that he had "been signally fortunate . . . quite beyond my greatest hopes and have made a collection of material illustrating Shakespeare which I believe will soon be notable." In 1909 Folger wrote that he had "found the means of adding to my collection of Shakespeareana until it is the largest and finest in America, and perhaps in the world. That is really saying a great deal, for collecting Shakespeareana has been the life-work of

Portrait of Emily Jordan Folger by Salisbury, 1927
(Folger Shakespeare Library)

many students during the past one hundred years." Folger competed against avid and exceedingly rich collectors such as John Pierpont Morgan, Marsden J. Perry of Providence, and Henry E. Huntington. Yet Folger's willingness to do his homework, his thoroughness, his readiness to pay cash, and his single-mindedness often secured him the advantage against competitors with heavier purses.

Folger's first extensive purchase was the Shakespeare library at Warwick Castle in 1897. The eminent nineteenth-century Shakespeare scholar John Halliwell-Phillipps had assembled it, and in 1852 he had produced a preliminary catalogue of its treasures. According to A. S. W. Rosenbach, who often acted for Folger, "the library was housed in a beautiful old room in that historical structure [Warwick Castle] and it contained not only many interesting books, such as the quarto of *Romeo and Juliet* of 1599 and the *Merchant of Venice* of 1600, but it was particularly rich in manuscripts." Among these was a contemporary manuscript copy of the two parts of *Henry IV*, described by Rosenbach as "probably the only surviving one of any of Shakespeare's plays prepared during his lifetime." Folger bought the collection directly from Lord Warwick.

Perry's library also held Halliwell-Phillipps association copies. Halliwell-Phillipps had disposed of

some of his collection, but his will instructed that the rest be sold to the city of Birmingham, England, after his death, which occurred in 1889. Birmingham could not raise the necessary seven thousand pounds. In 1897 Perry paid ten thousand pounds for the library. Ten years later upheavals in the stock market forced him to sell the Halliwell-Phillipps Rarities – books, manuscripts, and portraits, including the Droeshoot portrait of Shakespeare in its first state.

Folger described the catalogue of Halliwell-Phillipps's collection "as fascinating as a novel, for the clever collector told how each item earned its place with other gems, and how he had tracked down his quarry with patience and skill." Among the gems was the first attempted publication of a collected edition of Shakespeare. In 1619 Thomas Pavier began reissuing Shakespeare's plays in quartos, printing ten plays before he was compelled to cease because of copyright violations. Perry owned a volume in contemporary binding including nine of the works reissued by Pavier. The acquisition of the Perry library directly from Perry placed Folger in the forefront of Shakespeare collectors in America.

Other important additions to Folger's collection came from Sweden and from the libraries of the bishop of Truro, Lord Howe, William A. White,

The Folger Shakespeare Library as seen from East Capitol Street, Washington, D.C. (Horydcuak, Rittase & Gottscho)

and Baroness Burdett-Coults. The manner in which Folger acquired these items reveals much about him as a bookman and collector. In December 1904 Folger learned from the *New York Sun* that a unique copy of the *Titus Andronicus* quarto of 1594 had emerged in Sweden. Gerard Langbaine had mentioned this imprint in 1691, but it subsequently vanished. Folger immediately telegraphed his London agent, instructing that someone should go to Lund to purchase this only known copy of Shakespeare's first published play. "What is the highest you are willing to pay?" the agent telegraphed back. Folger recalled, "it took three hours of tramping over city streets to clarify a bewildered mind sufficiently to cable the answer, two thousand pounds." Meanwhile, two London dealers also offered Folger the quarto at the same price, but they had not yet bought it. Folger instructed his agent to offer the money in cash and so secured the 1594 *Titus*. Folger described it as "a veritable nugget. It is in immaculate condition, clear, perfect, and in the original bluish-gray, soft paper covers, just as such plays were offered to the playgoers at the theaters for a few pence."

This acquisition was the result of Folger's determination to buy as many Shakespeare quartos as he could, despite the fact that the fashion in collecting had been to acquire folios. He would own four copies of the 1609 quarto of *Pericles* (though he sold one to Huntington) and seven of the 1619 edition. He also would buy three copies of the 1594 *Rape of Lucrece* and two of thirteen known copies of the 1609 *Sonnets*. He recognized the variant nature of the text of each copy and knew that scholars would profit from the ability to compare them.

The July 1906 purchase of sixteen quarto editions from the library of Dr. John Gott, bishop of Truro, illustrates Folger's persistence, luck, and clever use of cables and trusted agents. Folger learned from a footnote in an article by the Shakespeare scholar Sir Sidney Lee that Gott had a collection of quartos. Folger instructed his London representative, Sotheran, to visit the bishop to see whether the quartos were for sale. The reply was that British social protocol prevented such action without a letter of introduction. Folger refused to be put off and instructed, "Do send someone at my ex-

The Reading Room in the Folger Shakespeare Library (Horydczak, Rittase & Gottscho)

pense, and devise some way to get the books." Sotheran's agent discovered that Gott was ailing and needed money to repair his house. Folger cabled a generous offer and secured the books just before Gott died. Had Folger hesitated, the quartos would have been tied up in estate valuations and might have eluded him.

Folger's purchase of twenty-seven quartos in 1907 again was the result of his luck and perseverance. The quartos were owned by Lord Howe and had been assembled by Charles Jennens in the eighteenth century; in 1773 they had been bequeathed to W. P. A. Curzon, an ancestor of Lord Howe. Among these quartos was the 1604 *Hamlet,* the first authoritative text of the play. After two years of negotiations between Lord Howe and Folger, Howe finally set a price, but Folger thought it too high. Howe then decided to auction the books at Sotheby's in London, but just prior to the auction Folger reached private agreement with him.

Folger maintained cordial relationships with his competitors. At the Britwell sales, for example, Folger and Huntington withdrew their bids for the unique first edition of Christopher Marlowe's *Hero and Leander* (1598) to allow William A. White of

Brooklyn – a friend of Folger's – to buy it. When White died in 1927, the Marlowe volume went to Folger. He also secured from White's family a copy of *Greene's Groatsworth of Witte Bought with a Million of Repentance* (1592), the first book to refer to Shakespeare. The only other known copy was in the British Museum. From White's library Folger also acquired copies of the 1594 first edition of *The Rape of Lucrece,* the 1598 quarto of *Richard II,* and the first issue of the 1609 quarto of *Pericles,* which White had bought at the Perkins sale in London in 1889.

Despite heavy purchasing Folger for the most part kept his collecting out of the public eye. George E. Dimock, a close friend of Folger, claimed that when Folger had come to own fifty First Folios, Richard Savage, custodian of the Shakespeare library at Stratford-upon-Avon, doubted that Folger owned five. Folger's reticence was in part the consequence of shyness; yet he also feared that his business associates would look askance at his purchases. Folger's acquisition of Perry's 1619 Pavier edition of Shakespeare for one hundred thousand dollars received much publicity fostered by Rosenbach, who had handled the sale. Folger called Rosenbach to request that future purchases be kept quiet and went on to recount the elder Rockefeller's comments on reports of the purchase: "We – that is, my son and I and the board of directors – were disturbed. We wouldn't want to think that the president of one of our major companies would be the kind of man foolish enough to pay $100,000 for a book!" Folger disarmed the criticism by claiming that the newspapers had exaggerated the selling price but made certain to keep subsequent acquisitions as quiet as possible.

The precise date at which Folger began planning a library is uncertain, though Philip B. Knachel, who would serve as a director of the Folger Shakespeare Library, believed that by the end of World War I such plans were under way. There was pressure in England for him to choose Stratford-upon-Avon as the site for the collection, and Folger said that he had considered placing the library "near the bones of the great man himself, but I finally concluded I would give it to Washington; *for I am an American.*" Folger was committed to helping make the United States a center for literary study, and to that end he chose an area across from the Library of Congress at the heart of the nation's capital. He acquired land around the Library of Congress, the purpose of which remained unknown to all but his lawyer; his architect, Paul Philippe Cret of Philadelphia; consulting architect Alexander B. Trowbridge; and the builders, the James Baird Company. On 28 May 1930 the library cornerstone was laid; Folger died a few weeks later, on 11 June 1930. The building was dedicated on 23 April 1932, the anniversary of Shakespeare's birth and death. Emily Folger lived to see the library in operation, and when she died on 21 February 1936, she left the residual of her estate to the trustees of Amherst College to use "for the benefit of the Folger Library." This endowment included some three million dollars of her own money. Her husband had left a generous endowment, but the stock market crash of 1929 and the ensuing Depression had diminished its value. She thus assured the survival of the institution that embodied the vision she and her husband shared.

Joseph Quincy Adams, the first librarian of the Folger Library, wrote:

> Here . . . in almost unbelievable fullness and richness, we assembled books, pamphlets, documents, manuscripts, relics, curios, oil-paintings, original drawings, watercolors, prints, statues, busts, medals, coins, miscellaneous objects of art, furniture, tapestries, playbills, prompt-books, stage properties, actors' costumes, and other material designed to illustrate the poet and his times. The library is thus more than a mere library; it is also a museum of the Golden Age of Elizabeth, and a memorial to the influence that Shakespeare has exerted upon the world's culture.

Folger's collection has become a mecca for Shakespeare scholars. Its riches have allowed convenient and detailed study of the texts, of Shakespeare's sources and contemporaries, as well as of adaptations of his work. Instead of being scattered across the world, these riches are brought together in a way that makes them greater than even their individual rarity would suggest; for one sees in this library the finest results of dedicated and knowledgeable collecting.

References:
Joseph Quincy Adams, *The Folger Shakespeare Memorial Library: A Report on Progress, 1931–1941* (Amherst, Mass.: Trustees of Amherst College, 1942);

The Folger Shakespeare Library Washington (Amherst, Mass.: Trustees of Amherst College, 1933);

Henry C. Folger, 18 June 1857– 11 June 1930 (New Haven: Privately printed, 1931);

Louis B. Wright, *The Folger Library: A Decade of Growth 1950–1960* (Washington, D.C.: Folger Shakespeare Library, 1960);

Wright, *The Folger Library: Two Decades of Growth: An Informed Account* (Charlottesville: University Press of Virginia, for The Folger Shakespeare Library, 1968).

Papers:
The papers of Henry Clay and Emily Jordan Folger are at the Folger Library, Washington, D.C.

Warren Richardson Howell

(13 November 1912 – 11 January 1984)

Jennifer Larson
Yerba Buena Books

Warren R. Howell devoted his life to the antiquarian book trade, joining his father's downtown San Francisco business, John Howell – Books (also known as The Open Book Shop) in 1932. Except for three years spent in the armed services during World War II, he worked in the book trade without break until his death in 1984 at the age of seventy-one. His long and distinguished career was characterized by expertise in fine and rare books in all fields, meticulous research and description, restraint in pricing, and sound disinterested advice to collectors and librarians. He held to a standard of antiquarian bookselling more typical of the first half of the century than the second. He was instrumental in the formation and growth of many of the major private and institutional collections of his time and was gifted in transmitting his enthusiasm for great books to others, among them several collectors who purchased only from him and who ceased collecting rare books after he died. John Howell – Books was the publisher of seventy-five highly regarded works of history, literature, and bibliography, and issued fifty-four rare-book catalogues from 1923 to 1982. Howell was generous with his time and resources in furthering philanthropic projects, frequently serving on boards and committees, and as an officer of a variety of nonprofit book-oriented organizations. In its prosperous final quarter-century of operations, more than forty young employees received their introduction to the antiquarian book trade at John Howell – Books and went on to start their own rare-book businesses or to careers in related fields.

Howell's father, John Gilson Howell (1874–1956), founded the family book business in October 1912 after serving an eight-year apprenticeship at Paul Elder's elegant Arts and Crafts Book Shop in San Francisco. John Howell met his future wife, Rebecca Ruskin Richardson, at Paul Elder's shop. She was an actress and a New Zealander distantly re-lated to John Ruskin, a fact in which her son Warren took great pride. She played an active role in the direction of the book business, which operated under the motto, "Where there is no vision the people perish." John Howell – Books relocated twice: from 107 Grant Avenue to 328 Post Street in 1918; and in 1924 to 434 Post Street, an ideal two-thousand-square-foot Union Square location designed by architect Will C. Hayes to evoke, in the style of his teacher Bernard Maybeck, "a gentleman's library set down on a city street."

Warren Howell was born in Berkeley, California, on 13 November 1912 and graduated from Berkeley High School. He and his twin brother Ruskin were the middle two of four sons, but Warren was the only one to become a bookseller – although his younger brother Robert entered into related work as a partner in the publishing firm of Howell-North Press. Warren Howell's early plans for a career in engineering were curtailed by the Depression, which in 1932 compelled him to abandon his studies at Stanford University after two years and assist in the book business. He worked ten years as a bookseller, from July 1932 to July 1942, before joining the U.S. Navy. During this period there was very little activity in antiquarian books – the rare-book market remaining depressed until after the war. He attributed the survival of John Howell – Books to sales of new and secondhand books to people passing through San Francisco, consignments and trades with other dealers, and the fees earned by John Howell for a series of lectures on the history of the Bible delivered up and down the Pacific Coast.

John Howell was primarily a bookman rather than a businessman, and the firm's stock reflected his personal tastes rather than book-market trends. A disproportionate share of the bookshop's profits went into his personal collection of rare and important editions of the Bible, which also formed the

Warren Richardson Howell

basis of his lecture series. He maintained a large inventory of seventeenth-century English literature, for which there was little demand, and books on the Bacon-Shakespeare controversy, for which there was almost none. He had from his earliest years in business published and distributed the writings of his friends in attractive limited editions. He was sociable, well-liked and admired, and frequent visitors to the bookshop included his literary acquaintances: Gertrude Atherton, George Sterling, Charles Caldwell Dobie, Bruce Porter, Christopher Morley, Dr. Aurelia Henry Reinhart, Douglas Watson, Kathleen and C. G. Norris, Stewart Edward White, Wilmarth S. Lewis, and Joseph Henry Jackson.

Just as Warren Howell may be credited with instilling and nurturing a love of fine books in dozens of collectors and future booksellers, he in turn credited a single individual, Dr. Herbert McLean Evans, F. R. S., with inspiring his own lifelong passion. In the early 1930s, Howell met Evans, a distinguished biologist who discovered and isolated vita-

min E, and a dedicated book collector. He bought books because he knew and understood them, Howell recalled, and he formed at least eleven distinct collections, mostly of the history of science and medicine, but also of Americana. These libraries were sold periodically to various dealers and institutions in order to settle Evans's book debts and to allow him to continue buying.

The principal customers of John Howell – Books during Howell's first decade in the business – Dr. George D. Lyman, Thomas W. Norris, Thomas W. Streeter, and Henry R. Wagner – were buying Californiana. Nevertheless, Howell enthusiastically took on the task of building up the botanical and ornithological library of Edward E. Hills of Hills Brothers Coffee. That extensive collection, now at the California Academy of Sciences, included the splendid folio color-plate bird books of John Gould and D. G. Elliot. To fill a noticeable gap in this collection – the Audubon double elephant folio in four volumes – Howell struck his first big coup in a long career remarkable for its sensational rare-book triumphs: in 1940 he traced the set formerly owned by Mark Hopkins to the California School of Fine Arts (now the San Francisco Art Institute), which occupied the Hopkins mansion. Unbeknownst to the director of the school, the Hopkins Audubon was in the basement of the mansion. Hills promptly acquired the former Hopkins set through John Howell – Books for $8,000. Nearly forty years later, in 1979, Warren Howell sold another Audubon set for $435,000 and later witnessed the price climb to $1.5 million at public auction, just prior to his death.

Howell felt, both at the time and in retrospect, that his father's business was severely hampered by lack of capital. He very much regretted missing opportunities to purchase fine libraries like that of Edwin Grabhorn because of insufficient funds. He also noted that his father failed to adjust his asking prices to reflect the post-Depression marketplace, in which the value of certain types of books had fallen substantially. It was typical of John Howell's approach to business that he would refuse to lower the prices he asked for books he considered worthwhile simply because of market conditions. Yet, although more of a businessman than his father, by the end of his career some of Warren Howell's attitudes toward the book business were, in relation to those of his younger colleagues, as quixotic as his father's had ever been.

Even during his wartime service in the military, Howell dealt mainly with books and book production. He served as assistant flag secretary on the staff of Adm. R. K. Turner, commander of the amphibious forces in the U.S. Pacific Fleet. Howell's duties included the production and distribution of the navy's secret operating plans. Notable among these was the immense and complex *Operation Plan for Okinawa,* designed, edited, mimeographed, and collated aboard ship under the supervision of Howell. He also developed a model for the production of such plans that was adopted by other cruiser and battleship commanders and their staffs, and for which he received commendation. He was also rewarded the Navy Bronze Star with Combat Cluster.

By the end of the 1940s the rare-book business had picked up. In 1950 Howell became managing partner of John Howell – Books and began to expand the firm's specialties to include voyages and travels, science and medicine, Americana, fine printing, cartography, natural history, prints and paintings of the West, and photography, in addition to English and American literature, Californiana and rare editions of the Bible. He traveled frequently to purchase books but did not continue the practice of his father's generation of antiquarian booksellers, in which they would call on important collectors and librarians with a steamer trunk filled with rare books to sell. He frequently stated his preference for bringing great books to California to enrich local collections. In that he succeeded, but he was never loath to buy or sell a fine book when the opportunity presented itself, regardless of geographical considerations.

One of Howell's first acts as head of the business was to find a permanent home for the John Howell Bible collection, the sale of which would provide him with badly needed cash for the purchase of new stock. The Korean War, however, interfered with fund-raising efforts to place the collection – which had grown to seven thousand volumes of Bibles and works of biblical scholarship – in the San Francisco Theological Seminary. Eventually he arrived at a gift-purchase agreement with the Pacific School of Religion in Berkeley; scarcely ten years later he would exceed the agreed-upon figure in paying for a copy of the Coverdale Bible of 1535 at auction.

Throughout his career, Warren Howell displayed a predilection for the sensational. In 1960 he paid $148,000, then the highest price achieved at auction for a historical manuscript, to secure the original log and journal of Capt. James Cook's voyages in the Pacific Ocean from 1768 to 1775. He was proud of having sold more than twenty copies of what he was fond of calling the most common of all rare books, the Nuremberg Chronicle, that lavishly illustrated incunabulum published by Anton Koberger in 1493. Toward the end of his career he paid $285,000 at auction for a magnificent seventeenth-century English maritime atlas of 164 double-page manuscript charts by William Hack. Although he relished the attention and publicity these transactions attracted, Howell did not admire highspot collecting. He felt that the most satisfying and rewarding collections require an investment of time and attention, as well as money.

The profitability of such high-end transactions enabled the firm to provide an extraordinarily high caliber of service to its customers at all levels. John Howell – Books was remarkable for the size of its staff, which in the final decade of the business fluctuated between ten and twenty full-time employees. This large staff was at the service of all customers, except in most cases other booksellers, who were expected to help themselves. They were, in Howell's view, seeking to garner an additional profit on a particular book at the expense of a final purchaser

John Howell — Books, Post Street, San Francisco

who either was one of Howell's own customers, or, as he saw it, ought to have been. Nevertheless, a large volume of sales at John Howell — Books was to the trade. Similarly, a relatively chilly reception could be expected by anyone Howell suspected of being interested in rare books for investment potential or of lacking a proper appreciation of books. He did not subscribe to the proposition that the customer is always right. Those customers he respected, however, were accorded unparalleled consideration. Courtesies included in-house and outside refurbishing and restoration, virtually unlimited consultation and reference assistance, book searches, and unrestricted return and exchange privileges.

One of Warren Howell's most firmly held tenets was the necessity of obtaining a great book in the finest condition possible. He frequently repeated a philosophy of the rare-book business he unfailingly attributed to his father: "We don't sell books — we sell condition." Many of his favorite

phrases smacked of good salesmanship: "I haven't sold you that book — I've given you the opportunity to place it in your library," for instance, or, "We price our books in the back, because the price should always be the last consideration."

As a salesman of books, Howell considered his greatest achievement to have been his role in the 1964 sale of the Robert B. Honeyman, Jr., pictorial collection to the Bancroft Library at the University of California, Berkeley. Howell attributed much of the success of the sale to George Hammond, director of the Bancroft, and Susanna Dakin, who made a gift of fifty thousand dollars toward the purchase price. Yet, it was John Howell — Books that had been very active in forming this great collection of California lithographs, drawings, watercolor and oil paintings — and it was Howell who had worked hard to promote the collection.

The first publication to bear the imprint of John Howell appeared in 1913, just one year after John Howell — Books was founded. From the modest beginning of a Bohemian Club Grove Play, *The Fall of Ug,* by Rufus Steele, the firm went on to publish the outstanding bibliography in western Americana, Wagner's *The Plains and the Rockies* in 1921, as well as more than a dozen important contributions to the history of California and the West. John Howell – Books also published definitive editions of Robert Louis Stevenson, Bret Harte, and Mark Twain. These publications were not undertaken for profit, and they did not produce much financial return; indeed, several titles remained in print nearly ten years after the firm closed its doors. Nevertheless, their contribution to the growing international reputation of the bookselling business was considerable.

John Howell – Books Catalogue One did not appear until 1923, ten years after the first book publication. Given its prominence, the volume of its business, and the caliber of its merchandise, the firm issued surprisingly few rare-book sales catalogues. Many of the best books were sold privately to collectors with longstanding relationships with John Howell – Books. Howell often claimed that his chief reward in selling fine books was the satisfaction derived from having personally selected the most suitable future owner of a great book. The catalogues of John Howell – Books which nevertheless did occasionally appear were written by a series of talented scholars to a very high standard of scholarship and excellence of design.

The firm's first truly spectacular catalogue was compiled by John Swingle and issued as Catalogue 33 in 1961. It offered 113 items including an entire collection of 846 "First Editions of Epochal Achievements in the History of Science," formed by Dr. Herbert M. Evans and sold en bloc. Other offerings included a copy of the first book printed in California, Jose Figueroa's *Manifesto a la Republica Mejicana* (Monterrey: Agustin V. Zamorano, 1835); copies of the second and third editions of *Mr. William Shakespeares Comedies, Histories, and Tragedies* (London: Tho. Cotes for Richard Hawkins, 1632; London: Printed for Philip Chetwind, 1663); important autograph letters of Thomas Jefferson and George Washington; and an original Nahuatl manuscript on twenty leaves of coarse native *amatl* paper dated 1534.

Catalogue 40, *100 Rare Books* (1970) was compiled by Michael Horowitz and featured a celebrated edition of one of the earliest books to exhibit a pure Roman type, Aurelius Augustinus *De Civitate Dei* (Venice: Johann and Wendelin de Spira, 1470); the only complete copy of the first volume of the first California newspaper, the *Californian* (Monterey: Colton & Semple, 15 August 1846–6 May 1847); a fine illuminated French Book of Hours (Rouen, e. 1460–1480); portions of the autograph manuscripts of Washington Irving's "The Legend of Sleepy Hollow" (New York, 1824) and *Astoria, or Anecdotes of an Enterprise Beyond the Rocky Mountains* (c. 1835–1836); and two copies of the first edition of Sir Isaac Newton's *Philosophiæ Naturalis Principia Mathematica* (London: Joseph Streater, 1687), exhibiting variant imprints.

John Howell – Books Catalogue 50, *California,* was issued in five parts from 1979 to 1980 and offered 1,665 items carefully described by Jack Collins and Camilla Knapp. The offerings were primarily from the library of Jennie Crocker Henderson, granddaughter of Charles Crocker of the celebrated "Big Four," builders of the Central Pacific Railroad. Because of its focus and comprehensiveness, this catalogue became a standard reference work, consulted by dealers and collectors for price information and frequently cited in catalogue descriptions.

The most splendid of the John Howell – Books catalogues was compiled by Richard Reed and issued in 1982 "to commemorate the 70th anniversary of John Howell – Books and the 50th anniversary of Warren R. Howell's association with the firm." It offered 114 items ranging in price from $1,150 to $150,000, including 55 items priced over $10,000. Among these were the same copy of Figueroa's *Manifesto* previously sold from Catalogue 33; John Keats's three published books of poems, all in original boards (*Poems,* London: Printed for C. & J. Ollier, 1817; *Endymion: A Poetic Romance,* London: Printed for Taylor and Hessey, 1818; and *Lamia, Isabella, the Eve of St. Agnes, and Other Poems,* London: Printed for Taylor and Hessey, 1820); William Blake's *Illustrations of the Book of Job* (London: William Blake, 1825 [i.e., 1826]); one of 100 signed copies of James Joyce's *Ulysses* (Paris: Shakespeare & Company, 1922); a presentation copy of Johannes Kepler's *Tabulæ Rudolphinæ,* considered the foundation of all planetary calculations for more than a century (Ulm: Jonas Saurius, 1627); and the Henry Huth copy of Abraham Ortelius's *Theatrum Orbis Terrarum* (Antwerp: In Officina Plantiniana, 1592).

Howell was active in clubs and organizations from the beginning of his career in books. In 1949 he helped found the Northern California Chapter of the Antiquarian Booksellers' Association of America (ABAA) and participated in international antiquarian book fairs – the most visible activity of the ABAA in cities across the nation and overseas. In addition to local office and committee work, he served on the association's national board of gover-

Interior of the Post Street shop

nors and as president from 1976 to 1978. He was a founding and lifelong member of the Friends of the Bancroft Library and served on the Stanford University Libraries Visiting Committee. In 1982 Stanford University Libraries named him the first recipient of the Warren R. Howell Award in gratitude for his "continuing counsel and for his generous contributions to the collections of fine and rare books and manuscripts so needed for scholarship." He was active in the Gleeson Library Associates of the University of San Francisco, which elected him a fellow and honored him in 1982 with a program and an exhibit on the occasion of his fiftieth anniversary in the antiquarian book business. Howell was a director of the California Historical Society, a recipient of its Henry R. Wagner Award, and a life fellow of the Pierpont Morgan Library. He also served as president of the Book Club of California from 1973 to 1975.

Howell was a club man, active in social organizations, bookish and otherwise. He served as master of the press of Roxburghe Club of San Francisco and was an active member of the Grolier Club and the Association Internationale des Bibliophiles. He particularly valued his membership in the Bohemian Club, where he served on the library committee and as director. He was also a member of the Pacific-Union Club and the English Speaking Union.

The final two years of Howell's life were marred by the revelation that from 1976 to 1982 he was the unwitting agent of Joseph Putnam, a rare-book thief who stole hundreds of books from the John Crerar Library of Chicago and consigned them to John Howell – Books. Of a total of 247 titles valued at approximately $330,000, three were highly prized books, such as *De Motu Cordis* (Frankfurt: William Fitzer, 1628) by William Harvey; *De Revolutionibus Orbium Coelestium* (Nuremberg: Johannes Petreius, 1543) by Nicolas Copernicus; and *De Humani Corporis Fabrica* (Basel: Johannes Oporinus, 1543) by Andreas Vesalius. The true source of the books became known as a result of the transfer of the assets and holdings of the Crerar Library to the

University of Chicago. The university filed a lawsuit against the thief that also named Howell and John Howell – Books, alleging that Howell "knew or should have known" that the books were stolen. The accusation was one from which Howell never personally recovered, and he died before the case went to court. His widow, Antoinette Howell, opted for a settlement in which no punitive damages were paid. Howell was exonerated of wrongdoing by, among others, the Federal Bureau of Investigation.

John Howell – Books closed its doors in September 1984, nine months after the proprietor's death, when it became apparent to several prospective purchasers of the business that the return on so large and valuable an inventory of rare books was considerably out of proportion with the investment required. In 1985 and 1986 the inventory and reference library of John Howell – Books were dispersed in a series of auctions in San Francisco and New York, at which Howell's retail prices for books long in stock were frequently exceeded, often by Howell customers of long standing.

During its seventy-year history, John Howell – Books became a remarkably effective social and cultural institution and built a strong reputation for the quality, range, and quantity of its inventory; for the extent of its reference library; and for its large and multitalented staff. Above all, its proprietor, Howell, possessed an unmatched depth and breadth of experience as well as an international network of contacts in the antiquarian-book field gained in his drive to promote the understanding and appreciation of fine books of all kinds.

Papers:
The business records of John Howell – Books, the unpublished autobiography of John Howell, and the Howell Family Papers are at Stanford University. The Sally V. Zaiser Collection of John Howell – Books publications and memorabilia is at the Harry Ransom Humanities Research Center, University of Texas at Austin.

Henry E. Huntington

(27 February 1850 – 23 May 1927)

Donald C. Dickinson
University of Arizona

Many of Henry E. Huntington's obituaries referred to him as the greatest book collector the world had ever known. Certainly few could equal his determination or his willingness to commit huge amounts of money for individual volumes or whole collections. Between 1910 and 1926 he spent an estimated $17 million on books and manuscripts. During that period he completely dominated the auction rooms of New York and London and in the process amassed a library that rivaled the great collections of England and Europe.

Henry E. Huntington was born 27 February 1850 in the rural community of Oneonta, New York, the fourth child of Solon and Harriet Saunders Huntington. Solon Huntington, a descendant of an old Connecticut family, owned a general merchandise store and dabbled in real estate. Harriet Huntington, the daughter of a prominent New York physician, managed the household and raised the children in a close, church-oriented environment. The family lived in a pleasant eight-bedroom house that Huntington later donated to the town as a public library. The Huntington children were expected to work around the house and to attend both church and Sunday school. The work ethic was a force in their daily lives. The amusements that were available were simple and inexpensive – swimming in the summer and skating and sledding in the winter. Reading was a popular family activity. Harriet was an avid reader and introduced books and magazines to the children at an early age.

Huntington attended local schools to the age of seventeen and then took a full-time job. At first he clerked in his father's store, but at the age of twenty he decided to widen his horizons. After spending a few months with relatives in Cohoes, New York, he moved to New York City and found a job sweeping and stocking shelves in a hardware store. His father's brother, Collis P. Huntington, a successful railroad entrepreneur, lived in New York

and frequently invited his nephew to dinner and occasionally gave him financial support.

In 1871 Collis convinced Huntington to leave the hardware store and take a job working for him as the manager of a sawmill in Saint Albans, West Virginia. The mill was part of Collis Huntington's expanding railroad empire and supplied ties for his construction projects in the eastern states. This was the beginning of an important relationship, one that would extend over thirty years and involve Huntington in ever-increasing management responsibilities. In early 1892 Huntington moved to San Francisco to become his uncle's West Coast manager with the title of first vice-president of the Southern Pacific Railway Company.

While he was working in Saint Albans in 1873, Huntington had married Collis Huntington's niece, Mary Alice Prentice, and by the time they moved to San Francisco, the Huntingtons had four children. They settled into a comfortable three-story house on Jackson Street, a house that provided not only ample space for the family but space for books as well. Huntington had started to buy books while in Saint Albans, standard sets of literary and historical classics, but had to sell them to settle a business agreement. In San Francisco he found himself in a sophisticated cultural environment with a well-developed antiquarian book trade. He began to do a considerable amount of business with William Doxey, whose shop at the Sign of the Lark on Market Street specialized in literary sets and fine bindings, many of them imported from London. In a two-week period in 1898 Doxey sold Huntington a forty-two-volume deluxe set of Honoré de Balzac's works for $150, Leopold von Ranke's *History of the Popes* (London: Bell, 1884) for $20, *England under the Saxon Kings* (London: Murray, 1845) for $10, and several volumes with illustrations by George Cruikshank and Thomas Rowlandson. Huntington had begun to acquire a typical

Henry Edwards Huntington; photograph by Arnold Genthe (Henry E.
Huntington Library and Art Gallery)

gentleman's library. A person with means, Huntington believed, should surround himself with the signs of stability and position – good furniture, fine china, paintings, and books.

In 1900, at age seventy-nine, Collis Huntington died and left his favorite nephew more than $15 million in stocks and other assets. Political factors within the Southern Pacific Company, however, prevented him from inheriting his uncle's position as president. Having been involved in the management of the Market Street Rail Company in San Francisco, Huntington decided to take his knowledge of that system to southern California, where interurban service was still virtually unknown. His timing was perfect. Beginning in the late 1890s, workers and their families from the Midwest had moved to the Los Angeles area in a steady stream. New bedroom communities branched out from the central city in all directions. Between 1890 and 1920

Los Angeles grew from a dusty frontier town of 50,000 to an urban center of 576,000, greatly increasing the need for inexpensive housing, transportation, and utilities. Huntington bought undeveloped land cheaply, laid rail lines along it, and then sold the land to subdividers at a handsome profit. He also invested in electrical-power generation and distribution. His control over real estate, transportation, and electrical utilities made him one of the most powerful figures in southern California during the first decade of the twentieth century.

By 1910, after ten successful years of rail development in the Los Angeles basin, Huntington decided to withdraw from some of his day-to-day management responsibilities. He wanted to spend more time on both his four-hundred-acre ranch in San Marino, where he was building a spacious new home, and on his book and art collections.

Henry Huntington with his uncle Collis Huntington (left) and newsboy in New York City, 1895 (Henry E. Huntington Library and Art Gallery)

A book collector eager to expand his library had two options open to him – he could browse in the bookshops and attend auction sales personally or he could work through a dealer who knew the trade and had experience in working with the auction houses. As it had always been his practice in business to take advantage of the knowledge of specialists, Huntington chose to be represented by experienced book dealers. One of his first associates was Issac Mendoza, the proprietor of the Old Ann Street Book Store in New York. Mendoza sold Huntington three or four large collections between 1904 and 1910. Outstanding among these was the one-thousand-volume Charles Morrogh library made up of first editions, illustrated classics, fine printing, and sumptuous bindings. Huntington purchased the Morrogh library after a brief examination and without argument for the asking price of $15,000. This ability to make decisions quickly

would serve Huntington well in the process of building his library.

As a result of his purchases from Mendoza and several other dealers, Huntington became known in New York book circles as a wealthy new collector with an increasing appetite for rare books. Among the many who were interested in securing Huntington as a customer, the most aggressive was George D. Smith. Trained in the book business from the age of thirteen, Smith had worked first as a stock boy for Dodd, Mead, and Company and then as an assistant for the rare-book dealer William Benjamin. At the age of twenty-five he had established a shop of his own. As a book dealer he was known to be tough, determined, and, if need be, ruthless. Huntington, himself a resourceful businessman, appreciated Smith's expertise, his memory for prices and dates, and his direct, unassuming manner. Although Smith may not have appreciated the literary value of books and manuscripts, he had a knack for evaluating the commercial possibilities of rarities from the collector's point of view. Smith first appeared as Huntington's agent in 1908 at the Henry Poor sale at the Anderson Auction Company in New York. The Poor library was rich in the kind of books that interested Huntington at that time — limited editions, association copies, fine bindings, illuminated missals and Books of Hours. In all, Huntington secured some sixteen hundred lots at the Poor sale, nearly one-fourth of the entire offering.

The groundwork for the great Huntington library, however, was established in the spring of 1911 with his purchase of the Elihu D. Church library. Between 1890 and 1905 Church, a wealthy Brooklyn businessman with fastidious taste, had gathered an important library of Americana and English literature. Although the collection only numbered some two thousand volumes, each item represented the best possible copy of that particular work. The library contained such rarities as the manuscript of Benjamin Franklin's *Autobiography,* the *Bay Psalm Book* (Cambridge, Mass., 1640) and a unique copy of the *General Lawes of Massachusetts* (Cambridge, Mass.: Printed according to the order of the General Court, 1648). There were also prime copies of travel accounts by Bartolomé de Las Casas, Sir Martin Frobisher, and Amerigo Vespucci; colonial imprints representing the earliest presswork from Cambridge, Boston, and New York; pamphlets on Indian relations; and an array of Shakespeare quartos from the distinguished library of Frederick Locker-Lampson.

Smith told Huntington that the Church collection was available but that it would probably be broken up and sold by several dealers. Huntington, whose practice had always been to incorporate established, small rail lines under his direction, saw that in one swift move he could become the owner of a library that had taken years of discriminating bibliographic connoisseurship to develop. It was much too inviting a prospect to overlook. He told Smith he would buy the entire library for $750,000. This was one of the most important decisions Huntington ever made, for in securing such a superb group of books he had begun to define the scope of his collection. It would be a humanistic research library centered on Anglo-American culture.

Three weeks after the newspapers announced the Church purchase, Huntington and Smith were engaged in another important transaction — the auction of the Robert Hoe III library. Hoe, whose inherited fortune came from the family printing

press–manufacturing business, had gathered a notable library of illuminated manuscripts, early printings, English and French literature, Americana, and fine bindings. After his death the family placed the books up for sale at the Anderson Auction Company. Billed as the sale of the century, the Hoe auction attracted dealers from all over the United States and London, Paris, and Berlin. Huntington gave Smith almost unlimited commissions on many of the Hoe rarities. On the first day of the sale, 24 April 1911, Huntington paid $12,000 for the 1486 edition of Dame Juliana Berner's *Book of Hawking;* the so-called Book of Saint Albans, it was the first English book to use color printing. Almost immediately following that sale, the auctioneer introduced lot 269, the item that had been discussed in the newspapers for weeks, the Gutenberg Bible (Mainz, circa 1455), thought to be the first book produced in Europe from movable type. The sale had been preceded by much speculation on how much money the book would fetch and whether one of the European dealers would take it back to its place of origin. Huntington, however, had decided that the Bible would stay in America; Smith opened the bidding at $10,000 and never hesitated until he had secured the work for Huntington at the record-breaking price of $50,000, up until that time the highest amount paid for a printed book.

The purchase created a sensation, and its story was run by newspapers around the world. Some of the accounts took Huntington to task for spending so much money for a book he could not read, since it was in Latin. Most of the reports, however, expressed admiration for Huntington since he had beaten out the sophisticated European dealers and in so doing proved Americans could equal anyone in their appreciation of high culture. As the Hoe sale continued in the winter of 1911 and the spring and fall of 1912, Huntington continued to make substantial purchases. He bought William Blake rarities; early printings of Geoffrey Chaucer and Shakespeare; first editions of Edmund Spenser, Richard Steele, and John Suckling; and some notable Americana.

The Church and Hoe purchases launched Huntington's career as a serious collector. Other dealers besides Smith now began to offer rarities — prominent among them Charles Sessler and A. S. W. Rosenbach of Philadelphia, Gabriel Wells of New York, and Bernard Quaritch of London. From Sessler, Huntington bought first printings of Charles Dickens and William Makepeace Thackeray, and Wells supplied early editions of Alexander Pope, Thomas Carlyle, and George Meredith.

Arabella Huntington, circa 1890 (Henry E. Huntington Library and Art Gallery)

Rosenbach, just starting his career, sold Huntington ten William Blake pen-and-watercolor designs for John Milton's *Paradise Lost* for $17,000 – a steep price, but one the collector paid without complaint. Huntington's negotiations with Quaritch started on a somewhat unsatisfactory basis in 1911 at the first session of the Henry Huth sale in London when the collector made inquiries but offered no specific bids. Quaritch bought the choice items for other customers. At the second Huth sale in 1912 Huntington commissioned Quaritch to buy a large number of literary and historical items.

As the books poured into Huntington's suite in the Metropolitan Club in New York, adequate storage space became a serious problem. Books covered chairs, tables, and most of the floor. Some crates sat unopened. Huntington's new home in San Marino, however, was nearing completion, and Myron Hunt, the architect, had planned ample space for the library. Plans for the new home also benefited from advice provided by Collis Huntington's widow, Arabella Huntington, who it had been rumored would become the second Mrs. Henry Huntington. After living apart for years, Huntington and his first wife had settled divorce proceedings in 1906. The rumors of a second marriage proved to be correct when in July 1913 Henry and Arabella were united in a simple ceremony in

Paris. Arabella, a southern beauty with a taste for the grandiose in art and architecture, never felt at home in California and insisted on three-to-four-month annual visits to New York and Paris. Huntington, who would have been happy to spend the entire year on his beloved ranch, deferred to her wishes.

Shortly after their marriage Huntington moved his books to Arabella's mansion on New York's Fifth Avenue. There they filled the handsome third-floor library and spilled over into the basement workrooms. The flow continued unabated. In early 1914 Huntington bought the Chatsworth Library, a large theatrical collection owned by William Cavendish, sixth Duke of Devonshire. The library consisted of plays, playbills, and manuscripts, a veritable archive of sixteenth- and seventeenth-century theatrical history. Among the special items in the library were four Shakespeare folios, fifty-seven quartos, and the sixteenth-century manuscript of John Bale's *Kynge Johan*. Experts estimated that more than 90 percent of known English plays for the period 1660–1800 were represented by first editions in the collection. The second part of the library consisted of twenty-five examples of the work of England's first printer, William Caxton – among them *The Recuyell of the Historyes of Troye* (1474–1476), the first book printed in the English language.

Several private collectors, after seeing the high prices Huntington was willing to pay, offered their libraries to him directly. Beverly Chew sold Huntington his seventeenth-century English poetry collection for $230,000. It was a price Chew thought too high for anyone to pay, but Huntington agreed with hesitation. Huntington also bought Ward Hill Lamon's collection of Abraham Lincoln documents and Frederick Halsey's twenty-thousand-volume library of American and English literature.

By 1915 the Huntington library numbered some forty-five thousand volumes. With only an informal checking system managed by the secretarial staff, however, it had become extremely difficult to account for specific items and to avoid duplication. It was time to seek professional help. In late 1914 Huntington met George Watson Cole, the bibliographer who had catalogued the Church library. The two men took to one another immediately. The following spring Huntington offered Cole the position of cataloguer for the New York library. Cole arrived in October, and by Christmas he and three assistants had started to organize the vast accumulation. The checking process revealed a considerable number of duplicates that could be sold on the open

A page from the Ellesmere manuscript (circa 1410) of Geoffrey Chaucer's The Canterbury Tales, *one of Huntington's most celebrated acquistions (Henry E. Huntington Library and Art Gallery)*

The Huntington Library, San Marino, California

market. Huntington authorized Mitchell Kennerley, president of the Anderson Auction Company, to act as his agent. Between 1916 and 1926 Kennerley sponsored fifteen duplicate sales, netting Huntington approximately $600,000.

Smith was now representing Huntington in both London and New York. With Huntington's commissions he bought heavily at the sale of the library of George Herbert, Earl of Pembroke in 1914 and at the Huth and Britwell sales from 1915 to 1919. Although the library was an ongoing satisfaction, there were unsolved questions. Where should the books be located permanently? To what purposes would the collection be put? On the first question Huntington was adamant. The library would be located on his ranch in San Marino. He had already arranged for the construction of a separate library building adjacent to his home. The second question was more difficult. For several years George Ellery Hale, the director of the Mount Wilson Observatory, had urged Huntington to organize the library for scholarly research. Hale's plans included the development of research departments headed by distinguished specialists, a fellowship program to provide support for younger scholars, and a publication office – all supervised by a governing board of trustees. In 1919 Huntington put many of Hale's ideas into action by signing an indenture and placing various properties and collections under the administrative control of a five-man board of trustees. It was not until 1926, shortly before his death, that he set up a substantial endowment to carry forward the work he had started.

Perhaps Huntington's most spectacular purchase between 1916 and 1920 was the Bridgewater library. Begun in the seventeenth century by Sir Thomas Egerton, Baron Ellesmere, the library consisted of some forty-four hundred printed books and more than fourteen thousand literary manuscripts including the famed Ellesmere Chaucer.

The general reading room at the Huntington Library (Henry E. Huntington Library and Art Gallery)

There were Caxton imprints, Shakespeare folios and quartos, Americana, and a large gathering of eighteenth-century plays in manuscript. When Huntington secured the library for $1 million, the *New York Times* on 27 May 1917 referred to him as "the prince of collectors" and "the first bibliophile in the land." The Bridgewater purchase was to be Smith's last major transaction as Huntington's agent. In March 1920 he died of a heart attack in his bookshop.

Several dealers were ready to replace Smith at Huntington's side, but the victory went to Rosenbach. He had gained Huntington's confidence with small, successful transactions over the years, and now he moved in quickly as the collector's chief agent. In addition to a thorough knowledge of the book world, Rosenbach offered customers the benefits of his doctorate in English literature and a scholar's appreciation for literary and historic values. Rosenbach sold Huntington a portion of Marsden Perry's distinguished Shakespeare collection, made

substantial purchases for him between 1920 and 1926 at the Huth and Britwell sales in London, then sold him the Battle Abbey papers, the Wilberforce Eames Americana, the Robert Holford library of early printings, and selected items from the incunabula holdings of Sir Thomas Phillipps. At the time of his death in 1927 Huntington had invested approximately $4.3 million with the flamboyant Philadelphia dealer.

At about the same time that Rosenbach took over Smith's mantle, Cole was making final arrangements to move the books and manuscripts from New York to California. It was an extremely difficult task, but by October 1920 Cole and his staff of twelve had set up workrooms in the new library building in San Marino and started to list and shelve the vast and growing collection.

As he approached his seventy-fourth birthday in February 1924 Huntington had many reasons to be pleased with his life. His marriage to Arabella had been a happy one, and the development of the ranch grounds into a handsome flowering estate had progressed as he had planned. His books, manuscripts, and artworks were now together in California and secure under the careful administrative control of the trustees. Scholars had started to make regular use of the library materials.

While Huntington virtually stopped buying at auction sales during the last three years of his life, he continued to make important private purchases en bloc. He acquired the Otto H. F. Vollbehr incunabula; the Jack London papers; the Stowe manuscripts, consisting of British court records, deeds, and seals going back to the twelfth century; the Robert Howe papers on British naval history; the letters of Robert Morris, the financier of the American revolutionary war; and the Henry Stevens pamphlets on European politics. All of these acquisitions came at a time when Huntington's health was deteriorating. He had always been robust, but in 1925, after a series of debilitating illnesses, he underwent surgery for cancer. He died two years later in May 1927, when he failed to recover from a second operation.

From first to last, Huntington was a practical businessman, competitive and shrewd, a man who applied the business principles that he had learned in railroading to the process of building a distinguished library. What started simply as a rich man's accumulation turned into a scholar's archive. Huntington wanted his library to be outstanding and recognized as such. It was a matter of great pride that in only fifteen years he had been able to build a collection equal to those that had required centuries to develop in Europe and England. He was delighted when the *Short Title Catalogue of Books Printed in England, Ireland and Scotland and English Books Printed Abroad 1475–1640* (1927) reported that his library held more than one-third of the 26,143 items listed, a record far exceeding that of any other American library. Huntington admired expertise and placed his confidence in agents such as Smith and Rosenbach, bibliographers such as Cole, and advisers such as Hale. The library he

formed, with their help, is recognized today as one of the preeminent humanistic research centers in the world.

References:
W. N. C. Carlton, "Henry E. Huntington," *American Collector*, 10 (August 1927): 5–10;

Donald C. Dickinson, "Mr. Huntington and Mr. Smith," *Book Collector*, 37 (Autumn 1988): 367–393;

William Friedricks, *Henry E. Huntington and the Creation of Southern California* (Columbus: Ohio State University Press, 1992);

George Ellery Hale, "The Huntington Library and Art Gallery," *Scribner's Magazine*, 82 (27 July 1927): 31–43;

John E. Pomfret, *The Henry E. Huntington Library and Art Gallery* (San Marino, Cal.: Huntington Library, 1969);

Robert O. Schad, "Henry E. Huntington: The Founder and the Library," *Huntington Library Bulletin*, 1 (May 1931): 3–32;

George Sherburn, "Huntington Library Collections," *Huntington Library Bulletin*, 1 (May 1931): 33–106;

James Thorpe, "The Founder and His Library," *Huntington Library Quarterly*, 4 (August 1969): 291–308;

Louis B. Wright, "Huntington and Folger, Book Collectors with a Purpose," *Atlantic Monthly*, 209 (April 1962): 70–74.

Papers:
The major collection of personal and business correspondence, business papers, reports, book bills, catalogues, and ephemera relating to Henry E. Huntington as a collector is located in the Henry E. Huntington Library and Art Museum, San Marino, California. His correspondence with George Watson Cole is located at the American Antiquarian Society in Worcester, Massachusetts, and his correspondence relating to business negotiations with A. S. W. Rosenbach is located in the Rosenbach Museum in Philadelphia, Pennsylvania.

James Lenox

(19 August 1800 – 17 February 1880)

Francis J. Bosha
Kawamura Gakuen Woman's University

BOOKS: *A Bibliographical Account of the Voyages of Columbus* (New York: C. B. Richardson, 1861);

Shakespeare's Plays, in Folio (New York: 1861);

The Early Editions of King James' Bible in Folio (New York, 1861);

Letter of Columbus to Luis de Santangel, 1493 (New York, 1863);

The Voyages of Hulsius (New York: Printed for the Trustees, Lenox Library, 1877);

The Voyages of Thevenot, edited by George Henry Moore (New York: The Trustees, Lenox Library, 1879);

Bunyan's Pilgrim's Progress, edited by George Henry Moore and Samuel Austin Allibone (New York: Printed for the Trustees, Lenox Library, 1879);

The Jesuit Relations, edited by George Henry Moore (New York: Printed for the Trustees, Lenox Library, 1879).

OTHER: George Washington, *Washington's Farewell Address to the People of the United States of America*, edited by Lenox (New York, 1850);

Niccolo Scillacio, *De Insulis Meridiani atque Indici Maris Nuper Inventis*, edited by Lenox with a translation by John Mulligan (New York, 1859).

SELECTED PERIODICAL PUBLICATIONS – UNCOLLECTED: "Curiosities of 'American' Literature: No. 1, Smith's General History of Virginia, New England and the Summer Isles," *Norton's Literary Gazette and Publishers' Circular*, 1 (1854): 134–135;

"Curiosities of 'American' Literature: No. 2, Smith's General History of Virginia, New England and the Summer Isles," *Norton's Literary Gazette and Publishers' Circular*, 1 (1854): 218–219;

"Curiosities of 'American' Literature: No. 3, Works of Master Richard Hakluyt," *Norton's Literary Gazette and Publishers' Circular*, 1 (1854): 272–273;

"Curiosities of 'American' Literature: No. 3 Concluded, Works of Master Richard Hakluyt," *Norton's Literary Gazette and Publishers' Circular*, 1 (1854): 384–386;

"Curiosities of 'American' Literature: No. IV," Transcript of Oliver Cromwell's letter to John Cotton, dated 2 October 1651, *Norton's Literary Gazette and Publishers' Circular*, 1 (1854): 328;

"Shakespeare's Plays in Folio," *Historical Magazine*, 5 (February 1861): 1–5; reprinted in *Bibliopolist*, 2 (1870): 181–187.

From 1845 until his death, bibliophile and philanthropist James Lenox devoted most of his energy and significant financial resources to amassing one of the major collections of rare books and manuscripts in America. His collection included the first Gutenberg Bible to be brought to the Western Hemisphere, Shakespeare folios, the original autograph manuscript of George Washington's farewell address, as well as thousands of rare early editions and incunabula. In 1870 he incorporated the Lenox Library in his native New York, to which he gave his collection of some twenty thousand volumes. In 1895 the library was consolidated with the Astor Library and the Tilden Trust to form the New York Public Library.

James Lenox was born on 19 August 1800 in New York City, the ninth of twelve children and the third and only surviving son of Robert and Rachel Carmer Lenox. Robert Lenox immigrated to America from Kirkcudbright, Scotland, with two brothers shortly before the American revolutionary war and joined his maternal uncle, David Sproat, a Philadelphia merchant. When Sproat moved to New York, Robert accompanied him and often traveled on his uncle's behalf to the West Indies. After the war Robert married and in 1784 established his permanent residence in New York City, where he became an importing merchant in the West Indian trade in

his own right. He owned extensive tracts of land throughout New York City, including a three-hundred-acre farm near Central Park that ran from Sixty-eighth Street to Seventy-fourth Street and between Fourth Avenue and Fifth Avenue. This land would prove integral to his son James's plans decades later.

James Lenox graduated from Columbia College in 1818 and, after studying law, was admitted to the New York bar on 18 January 1822. He then traveled throughout Europe until 1826, when he returned to New York to become a partner with his father. In 1829 the firm became known as Robert Lenox and Son. Upon his father's death in 1839 James inherited most of the Lenox commercial and realty holdings, and in 1840 he changed the firm's name to James Lenox, Merchant.

Lenox also maintained an association with Princeton University throughout his life, as his father had done. In 1821 he was awarded an honorary A.M. degree, and he served as trustee of Princeton Seminary from 1831 to 1879. During that time he was also a director of Princeton Seminary (1835–1847) and a trustee of the College of New Jersey (1833–1857). In 1867 he was awarded an honorary LL.D. degree from Princeton. In addition, in 1875 Columbia awarded him another honorary LL.D. degree.

Lenox, a lifelong bachelor, worked in the family business, located at 59 Broadway, until 1845, when he retired to devote the remainder of his life to collecting books, manuscripts, and art objects and to philanthropy. Working out of an office in the basement of his mansion at 53 Fifth Avenue, Lenox in 1845 commissioned George P. Putnam to purchase for him in London some "old Bibles" listed in catalogues issued by Thomas Thorpe, along with three copies of Richard Hakluyt's *Principall Navigations* (London, 1589), one of which included the rare Wright-Molyneaux map of the world. From the outset Lenox had set his focus on some of the sort of books that appealed to him most: Bibles and accounts of great voyages. To these categories he would soon add another: books relating to North and South America.

Putnam referred his friend, the bookseller Henry Stevens, to Lenox in the fall of 1845. By the summer of 1846 Stevens — who had acted as London purchasing agent for the Library of Congress and the Smithsonian Institution as well as for such individual collectors as John Carter Brown — became one of Lenox's principal agents and, later, his biographer. Lenox would also come to rely on Obadiah Rich, another American bookseller established in London, for books and manuscripts.

Over the course of their business relationship, which lasted until 1871, Stevens "ransacked," as he termed it, all of Europe "for bibliographic rarities" for Lenox. On 29 June 1848, when Lenox agreed to become the first patron of Stevens's proposed study, "Bibliographia Americana" to the year 1700, Stevens in turn decided to begin granting Lenox "first choice" of his rare finds, a preferential arrangement which he had had up to that time with John Carter Brown. Stevens never completed his bibliographic project, but he greatly aided Lenox's book collecting efforts.

Beginning in 1845, Lenox single-mindedly but discreetly purchased volumes for what would become the Lenox Library; he worked ten hours a day examining each new consignment and maintaining detailed records of his transactions. Lenox "had a mind of his own," Stevens observed, "and a fortune to back it." The latter is hardly an exaggeration, for he inherited from his father one of the great fortunes of the day, some $2 million (each of his sisters received almost $100,000). The will also advised — though it did not stipulate — that the land be kept unsold and intact for James's heirs. James Lenox did hold onto the land until 1864 but then began to sell off parcels which, by his death in 1880, had earned him some $3 million. With his investments, the lucrative business his father established, and the real estate, James Lenox was, as Stevens wrote, well able to work on his collection "as he liked . . . without outside influence, interference or dictation."

For the most part Lenox kept his plans for the Lenox Library to himself until he felt his collection was ready. His reticence, however, led some to view him as too aristocratic or haughty. He disdained notoriety and quietly conducted himself in his other activities as well; a generous giver, he supported charities, chief among them being the Presbyterian Hospital, which he helped establish.

Lenox was so busy simply collecting the volumes as rapidly as possible that he generally did not arrange or catalogue his acquisitions. Instead he entered them in one of his working lists or made an interleaved entry in a sales catalogue. Except for the occasional book or manuscript which he would display in a bookcase in the gallery in his house along with the artworks he purchased, the great majority of his rare books were merely piled in one of his mansion's many empty rooms from floor to ceiling after being carefully examined and collated. When a room was filled, he would lock it and move on to fill another. Sometimes the books, as Stevens described it, would be "corded up like wood." Until the Lenox Library was established, it thus was virtually impossible for anyone to gain access to the ever-expanding collection. Furthermore, Lenox tended to be jealous of his treasures and nervously guarded them. He therefore rarely lent them, and then only when he had duplicate copies, which he often had acquired for that purpose. Such loans would usually be made through the Astor Library, since Lenox would almost never allow scholars to examine the material in his house.

What Stevens described as Lenox's "first absorbing penchant" was his dedication as a collector of what would amount to well over four thousand Bibles (approximately twenty-four hundred of them in English) in various early editions. According to London bookseller Bernard Quaritch, who also supplied Lenox with rare volumes, Lenox's "interest was concentrated in the landmarks that revealed the progress of Christianity, this being in his mind only another word for civilisation. To him the English Bible was the most important of all books."

At the Wilkes sale in London in 1847, Lenox bought an imperfect copy (missing four leaves) of the forty-two-line Latin Mazarin Bible, the first book printed from movable type. Gutenberg is believed to have printed it between 1450 and 1455. It would not be until 1922 that the New York Public Library received three of the four missing prologue leaves as a gift from a rare-book collector, replacing the type-facsimile pages that Lenox's copy contained. The price of five hundred pounds struck Lenox as unreasonable at first, since he had instructed his representative to bid three hundred pounds. The representative's handwritten *3* was misread by the auction agent as a *5,* resulting in the higher price. Even the London newspapers described five hundred pounds as a "mad price,"

Portrait of Lenox by Sir Francis Grant, 1848 (from Henry Stevens, Recollections of
James Lenox and the Formation of his Library, *1951)*

though Lenox eventually felt it was money well spent to have been able to bring the first Gutenberg Bible to America. Among other items at that sale he acquired was the first Latin Bible printed in France (Paris, 1476), for fifty pounds.

Another notable Bible which Lenox purchased was the 1631 octavo "Wicked Bible" (London: Printed by Robert Barker), so called for its many typographical errors, including one in the Seventh Commandment: "Thou shalt commit adultery." Although Charles I had ordered the king's printers Robert Baker and Martin Lucas to destroy all one thousand copies of the flawed volume, six copies survived. In 1855 Lenox bought one copy for fifty guineas.

Among the more literary works that Lenox collected was a wide selection of editions of his favorite author, John Bunyan, including a 1678 first printing of *Pilgrim's Progress.* In fact, all the early English editions of *Pilgrim's Progress* became desiderata

for him. Lenox also gradually acquired one of the great John Milton collections in the world.

Other fields which engaged Lenox's attention as a book collector were Americana — particularly pre-1700 materials — and books relating to early voyages, including those of Christopher Columbus, Amerigo Vespucci, Marco Polo, and Hernán Cortés. Early editions of voyages printed by Theodore De Bry and Levinus Hulsius were particularly prized by Lenox, and he also collected volumes printed by Giovanni Battista Ramusio and Melchisedich Thevenot. Despite Lenox's enthusiasm for early Americana, he was not especially concerned about acquiring rare books in or about the languages of the American Indians, which were offered to him.

To add to his collection of Americana, Lenox purchased for fifty guineas in 1847 a De Bry folio copy of Thomas Hariot's "Briefe and true Report of the new found land of Virginia" (Frankfort, 1590),

James Lenox, circa 1870

which is also known as "Virginia's First Folio." Nearly two years later in March 1849, in a trade with the British Museum for *Ames's Typographical Antiquities* (1785–1790), Lenox obtained an octavo original edition of "The Elvas Relation of DeSoto's Discoveries" (1557), in Portuguese. Of the works he collected regarding discoverers, those on Columbus most keenly attracted his interest. To that end Lenox purchased in 1849 Petrus de Alyaco's "Imago Mundi," which was printed around 1483 and is believed to have first directed Columbus's attention to the Western Hemisphere.

Lenox also acquired five of the nine 1493 Latin original editions of the letter Columbus wrote – dated 15 February–14 March 1493 – while shipboard, to Luis de Santangel, treasurer of Aragon. This included the only complete illustrated octavo copy with two cover leaves printed by Jakob Wolff of Pforzheim (Basel, 1493) plus a quarto Basel printing and three quartos printed in Rome. The following year in 1850, Lenox was also able to purchase a German quarto edition of the Columbus letter printed by Bartholomäus Küstler (Strasbourg, 1497). In this letter, which was translated from the original Spanish into Latin by Leander de Cosco and which Wilberforce Eames described as "the choicest and most valuable of all publications relating to America," Columbus gave an account of his first voyage. He wrote that he had discovered "not an island, but the continental country of Cathay."

In 1870, while he was designing the Lenox Library, the architect Richard Morris Hunt presented Lenox with an unique addition to his collection of discovery-related items: a small copper globe dating from 1510–1511. This was the oldest post-Columbian globe then extant, and it was valuable because of the light it shed on the state of contemporary geographical knowledge. Especially noteworthy was the fact that while South America was generally depicted accurately, the entire North American continent north of Yucatan was represented as open sea.

The acquisition of another noteworthy piece of Americana led to something of a controversy since Lenox bid against the Library of Congress to obtain it: his 1848 purchase, for twenty-two hundred dollars, of the original autograph manuscript of George Washington's farewell address. Despite the criticism leveled at Lenox for competing with the United States government to buy a national treasure, Lenox maintained that after the Library of Congress purchasing committee refused to tell him either what their bidding limit was or even if they actually intended to bid on it, he felt no need to defer to them when he made his bid. The following year he printed 54 folio copies and 175 quarto copies of the manuscript, with variorum notes and illustrations, which he then gave to his friends and other libraries.

In 1848, however, when George Washington's library of some three thousand books also came on the market, with one-tenth of them bearing their former owner's signature, Lenox declined to purchase even the autographed copies. Most of the collection proved difficult to sell at the time, and only at a reduced price was it eventually sold to the Boston Athenaeum. Lenox did, in time, purchase two of the autographed volumes for twenty pounds and fifty pounds.

What may well have been Lenox's busiest years as a collector in New York and abroad occurred between 1854 and 1857, as is evidenced by his extant correspondence. During 1854–1855 Lenox spent, through Stevens alone, more than fifty thousand dollars; for much of 1855–1856 Lenox traveled through Europe hunting rare volumes. In February 1854 Lenox purchased for forty pounds a holograph letter written by Oliver Cromwell to Rev. John Cotton of Boston, dated 2 October 1651. Later that year Lenox published the letter as part of his "Curiosities of 'American' Literature," in *Norton's Literary Gazette and Publishers' Circular* (1854). He also contributed two other bibliographical pieces to that volume: one concerned the various editions of John Smith's 1624 *General History of Virginia,* and the other dealt with the works of Richard Hakluyt.

A few months later Lenox was able to make significant progress in his quest for incunabula. On 6 July 1854 at Sotheby's auction he spent £105 for *The History of Jason* (1476 or 1477), one of the earliest works printed by William Caxton that he would acquire. At that same sale Lenox also purchased two manuscripts (circa 1410) of Wycliffe's New Testament, as well as his 1530 copy of Tyndale's Pentateuch. Another 1854 purchase was of the only extant copy of the first edition of the New Testament (London: Printed by Robert Baker, 1611), for a little more than £37.

Soon after, Lenox expanded the scope of his collection to include Shakespeare folios, beginning with his 1854 purchase of a First Folio for £163, which, according to Robert Metcalf Smith, "stirred the book-collecting world." In December 1855 he moved to acquire some forty quartos for £500, and for an additional £100 he purchased four folios. As Smith observed decades later in the *Shakespeare Association Bulletin* (1929), Lenox's "financial zeal . . . was agreeably equalled by his bibliographical acumen. He not only bought Shakespeare originals, but studied them closely for variants. Within the next twenty years he brought together thirteen Shakespeare Folios, including nearly every variant issue, leaf, or title-page of which he knew the existence, and twenty-nine quartos."

In 1855 Lenox also bought his copy of the first work printed in Anglo-America (excepting a broadside and a brief almanac), *The Whole Booke of Psalms Faithfully Translated into English Metre,* widely known as *The Bay Psalm Book* (Cambridge: Daye, 1640). Stevens purchased it for him for nineteen shillings at a Sotheby's auction after a seven-year hunt, and then he sold it to Lenox for eighty pounds.

Near the end of the decade, Lenox's interest in history extended to antiquity and, coupled with his philanthropic nature, it led to his extraordinary gift to the New York Historical Society: the Ninevah marbles. He purchased these twelve Assyrian sculptures in bas-relief, dating from the ninth century B.C. and weighing in total some seventeen tons, for three thousand dollars. In appreciation, on 7 December 1858 the society designated the gift as the Lenox Collection of Ninevah Sculptures and asked the donor to sit for a portrait for its gallery. Lenox declined, and he wrote the society on 20 December 1858: "My health permits me to leave the house only in fine weather, and I cannot therefore promise compliance." In 1937 the society sent the sculptures "on indefinite loan" to the Brooklyn Museum, which purchased them in 1955 and continues to display them.

During the Civil War Lenox, according to Stevens, "suspended generally his ardent foraging for rare books, and only occasionally had an intermittent attack of his old bibliographical fever." In fact, however, Lenox bought extensively during the war from London bookseller Edward G. Allen, as evidenced by the Lenox letters to Allen in the New York Public Library. Harry Miller Lydenberg has suggested that Stevens sought to explain his re-

The Lenox Library, circa 1890

duced sales to Lenox during this time as being war related. Yet, given the significant volume of Allen's sales, it may well have been due to what Lydenberg proposed were "personal differences between Stevens and Lenox."

Still, the war generally did pose a problem for international commerce due to risks to shipping and the fluctuations in world currency rates, and it is worth noting that during this time Lenox turned his attentions increasingly toward his various philanthropic projects. While this "did not represent any diminuation in Mr. Lenox's objectives as a bibliophile," Victor Hugo Paltsits observed, it may have been that Lenox's mind simply "found other more compelling objectives for the use of his wealth" during this period.

To that end, by 1864 Lenox began to sell off large parcels of the land he had inherited. In time he also gave additional tracts of land valued, totally, in excess of four million dollars, to build the Presbyterian Hospital, the Phillips Memorial Presbyterian Church, and the Presbyterian Home for Aged Women. He also set aside an entire block between Seventieth and Seventy-first streets on Fifth Avenue for his Lenox Library, which is today the site of the Frick Collection.

As Lenox approached both his seventieth year and the prospect of establishing his library, he slowed his once-almost-feverish pace. According to Stevens, Lenox had repeatedly conveyed messages to him, between 1865 and 1875, along these lines: "I have *almost* made up my mind to stop purchasing." Yet, as the extensive records Lenox maintained of all his transactions attest, once his plan for the Lenox Library matured, his expenditures, though relatively reduced, were still "considerable."

As is true of any serious collector, Lenox at times passed up opportunities to acquire certain works which, when they came around later at higher prices, he finally purchased. The sale of the library of George Brinley in March 1879 is a case in point. Among the items later purchased for the by-then-established Lenox Library was the Narragansett Declaration (Boston, 1645), signed by John Winthrop, for which Lenox paid nearly $200, or four times the price he had been offered in 1868. He also belatedly bought from the Brinley estate a copy of John Smith's 1624 "General History of Virginia" for $1,800 – having declined it years earlier for $1,275.

It should be noted that in the case of Lenox, unlike that of other competing collectors, some of his failures were attributable to the fact that he worked alone. As Stevens pointedly observed: "No one was permitted to assist him." Not only did he personally collate every book he bought, working in his basement office, but he meticulously annotated

The exclusionary policies of the Lenox Library are the subject of this 17 January 1884 cartoon in the satrical magazine Life.

the various catalogues he consulted, maintained detailed accounts of his purchases, and conducted a wide-ranging correspondence, writing his own letters. He found himself compelled to work into the night and, consequently, a sense of being overburdened is evident in many of his letters. In one letter, dated 10 May 1869, Lenox wrote: "I have been able to leave my room today for the first time. . . . My Physician forbids my talking. The cataloguing must, I fear, bear the blame."

His health began to deteriorate when he was in his late sixties. Indeed, when visiting Lenox in September 1868, Stevens could see the effect of the strain his work caused: "His memory began already to fail to tell him where particular books were deposited, and it was not always easy for himself to find his brief record of them, nor was it possible for anyone else to find either the books or the entry of them."

When Lenox's health worsened the following year, he decided it was time to proceed with the formal establishment of the Lenox Library. On 20 January 1870 the library's incorporation was approved by the New York Senate in bill number nine, which had been introduced earlier that month by Sen. William M. Tweed and supported by Sen. Henry C. Murphy. Until then, according to the 16 January 1870 issue of the *New York Times,* "Nothing, or next to nothing, had been heard of his intention until it

received publicity through a circumstance not to be avoided." The Lenox Library would be, the *Times* added, "a free . . . gift to the City of New York."

While Lenox proceeded for more than a quarter of a century to collect thousands of volumes for his library, he appears to have been operating on a general, vaguely defined master plan. According to David Bryson Delavan, who as a young physician knew the elderly Lenox, in the 1870s Lenox

intended to found a great library, of unusual character and scope; not a general public library in the ordinary sense but a collection of rare books and manuscripts not to be found elsewhere, invaluable for scholars and students of special subjects but far too precious for the use of ordinary readers whose wants could readily be met in other ways.

Yet, after the Lenox Library was incorporated and Lenox was elected president of the board of trustees, he became concerned over just how he should operate his institution. In a letter dated 11 February 1870 Lenox wrote, "I would like to get, if such a thing exist [sic], the regulations of the British Museum, as to the kind of books given to general readers in its Hall – is an introduction required? do they allow the use of pen and ink . . . what are the regulations as to *reserved* Books." The library went on to adopt most of the British Museum rules and followed them until 1895, when the Lenox Library was consolidated with the Astor Library and the Tilden Trust to become part of the New York Public Library.

In his last decade, beset by health problems that included a chronic bronchial condition, Lenox distanced himself from much of the daily operations of the library, which he entrusted to George Henry Moore, its first superintendent, and to Samuel Austin Allibone, its librarian. Still, the restrictiveness that had characterized Lenox's private library carried over into the Lenox Library, and for many years to follow public access remained extremely limited. On 18 May 1879 – eighteen months after the library's general opening – the *New York Times* was reporting that "some impatient people are constantly asking when the library 'will be opened to the public.' "

"In his last few days," according to his brother-in-law, John Fisher Sheafe, "he seldom spoke: on one occasion he remarked: 'My days are ended: I have had a long and happy life, and I am going to be with Christ.' " On 17 February 1880 James Lenox died in his Fifth Avenue home, where he had devoted his life to book collecting, and was buried in the New York City Marble Cemetery.

Lenox was described by Henry Stevens as "a man of few words and few intimate friends." His obituary in the 19 February 1880 issue of the *New York Times* stated, "Very few men in New York knew Mr. Lenox at all, and the number of his intimate acquaintances might be told on the fingers of one hand." The obituary also noted with considerable understatement that, while James Lenox "was also, like his father before him, a member of the Chamber of Commerce . . . it is probable that many of his associates did not know him by sight."

References:

David Bryson Delavan, *Early Days of the Presbyterian Hospital in the City of New York* (East Orange, N. J.: Abbey Printshop, 1926);

Wilberforce Eames, "The Lenox Library and Its Founder," *Library Journal,* 24 (May 1899): 199–201;

Eames, "Two Important Gifts by George F Baker, Jr.," *Bulletin of the New York Public Library,* 28 (August 1924); 595–598;

Harry Miller Lydenberg, *History of the New York Public Library, Astor, Lenox and Tilden Foundations* (New York: New York Public Library, 1923);

Victor Hugo Paltsits, "Proposal of Henry Stevens for 'A Bibliographia Americana' to the Year 1700, to be published by the Smithsonian Institution," *Papers of the Bibliographical Society of America,* 36 (1942): 245–265;

Robert Metcalf Smith, "The Formation of the Shakespeare Libraries in America," *Shakespeare Association Bulletin,* 4 (July 1929): 66;

Henry Stevens, *Recollections of James Lenox and the formation of his Library,* revised and elucidated by Victor Hugo Paltsits (New York: New York Public Library, 1951);

Sam P. Williams, *Guide to the Research Collections of the New York Public Library* (Chicago: American Library Association, 1975).

Papers:

The principal collection of James Lenox's papers, along with his annotated, interleaved catalogues and working lists, is in the New York Public Library. In addition, the New York Public Library administers an archive of Lenox's letters and personal papers (1825–1880) relating to his life and career. This includes his correspondence with and book lists and invoices from Henry Stevens and some 200 letters (1859–1873) from Lenox to Edward G. Allen relating to book purchases. Other frequent Lenox correspondents include Thomas Chalmers, a Scottish author; Charles Robert Leslie, an English painter and author; and George Livermore, an American authority on Bibles. Another collection of 195 Lenox letters, written to Edmund Bailey O'Callaghan (September 1852–December 1860), is in the Library of Congress; a microfilm copy of this collection is also in the New York Public Library.

Wilmarth Sheldon Lewis

(14 November 1895 – 7 October 1979)

William K. Finley
College of Charleston

BOOKS: *Tutors' Lane* (New York: Knopf, 1922);

Yale University. Class of 1918. A Memorial to the Men of the Yale College Class of 1918 Who Died in the Service of Their Country, 1917–1918 (New Haven: Yale University Press, 1924);

The Forlorn Printer: Being Notes on Horace Walpole's Alleged Neglect of Thomas Kirgate (Farmington, Conn.: Privately printed, 1931);

Bentley's Designs for Walpole's Fugitive Pieces (Farmington, Conn.: Privately printed, 1936);

Private Charity in England, 1747–1757 by Lewis, Ralph M. Williams, and A. Stuart Daley (New Haven: Yale University Press, 1938);

Three Tours Through London in the Years 1748, 1776, 1797 (New Haven: Yale University Press, 1941);

The Yale Collections: For the University Council on the Library and Museums (New Haven: Yale University Press, 1946);

The Layman and Libraries (Sydney: Public Library of New South Wales, 1947);

Collector's Progress (New York: Knopf, 1951);

Horace Walpole's Library (Cambridge: Cambridge University Press, 1958);

The Service Used at the Funeral of Annie Burr Auchincloss Lewis, 11th May 1959 (Farmington, Conn.: Privately printed, 1959);

Horace Walpole: The A. W. Mellon Lectures in the Fine Arts, 1960 (New York: Pantheon, 1961);

In Memory of Joseph Rockwell Swan, 1878–1965 (N.p.: Privately printed, 1965);

One Man's Education (New York: Knopf, 1967);

See For Yourself (New York: Harper & Row, 1971);

Thomas Gray, 1716–1771 (Cambridge: Pembroke College, 1971);

A Guide to the Life of Horace Walpole (New Haven: Yale University Press, 1973);

Bicentennial Address: July 4, 1976 (Farmington, Conn.: Farmington Historical Society, 1976);

Read As You Please (Cleveland: Rowfant Club, 1977);

Rescuing Horace Walpole (New Haven: Yale University Press, 1978).

OTHER: Horace Walpole, *A Selection of the Letters of Horace Walpole,* edited by Lewis (New York & London: Harper, 1926);

John Heneage Jesse, *Notes by Lady Louisa Stuart on George Selwyn and His Contemporaries,* edited by Lewis (New York: Oxford University Press; London: Milford, 1928);

Walpole, *Horace Walpole's Fugitive Verses,* edited by Lewis (New York: Oxford University Press; London: Milford, 1931);

Walpole, *On Modern Gardening: An Essay,* preface and biographical note by Lewis (New York: Young, 1931);

Walpole, *Anecdotes Told Me by Lady Denbigh,* edited by Lewis (Farmington, Conn.: Privately printed, 1932);

Philip Stanhope, second Earl of Chesterfield, *Some Short Observations for the Lady Mary Stanhope Concerning the Writing of Ordinary Letters,* edited by Lewis (Farmington, Conn.: Privately printed, 1934);

Walpole, *The Duchess of Portland's Museum,* introduction by Lewis (New York: Grolier Club, 1936);

Walpole, *Memoranda Walpoliana,* introduction and preface by Lewis (Farmington, Conn.: Privately printed, 1937);

Walpole, *The Yale Edition of Horace Walpole's Correspondence,* 48 volumes, edited by Lewis and others (New Haven: Yale University Press, 1937–1983);

Walpole, *The Impenetrable Secret, Probably Invented by Horace Walpole. An Explanation of the Secret,* note by Lewis (Farmington, Conn.: Privately printed, 1939);

Wilmarth Sheldon Lewis, 1966

Walpole, *Notes by Horace Walpole on Several Characters of Shakespeare,* edited by Lewis (Farmington, Conn.: Privately printed, 1940);

Allen Tracy Hazen, *A Bibliography of the Strawberry Hill Press, with a Record of the Prices at which Copies have been sold . . . Together with a bibliography and census of the Detached Pieces,* preface by Lewis (New Haven: Yale University Press; London: H. Milford, Oxford University Press, 1942); republished as *A Bibliography of the Strawberry Hill Press* (Folkestone, U.K.: Dawsons, 1973);

Walpole, *The Castle of Otranto: A Gothic Story,* edited, with notes, by Lewis (London & New York: Oxford University Press, 1964);

"The Beggar's Opera" by Hogarth and Blake: A Portfolio, edited by Lewis and Philip Hofer (New Haven: Yale University Press, 1965);

Hazen, *A Catalogue of Horace Walpole's Library,* 3 volumes, preface by Lewis (New Haven: Yale University Press, 1969);

"The Accord and Resemblances of Johnson and Walpole," in *Eighteenth-Century Studies in Honor of Donald F. Hyde,* edited by W. H. Bond (New York: Grolier Club, 1970), pp. 179–186.

SELECTED PERIODICAL PUBLICATIONS – UNCOLLECTED: "Horace Walpole's Library," *Library,* 2 (June 1947): 45–52;

"The Last Word," *New Colophon,* 2 (June 1949): 163–166;

"The Yale Edition of Horace Walpole's Correspondence, 1933–1973," *Yale University Library Gazette,* 48 (1973): 69–83.

"It doesn't matter what you collect as long as you do it passionately," Wilmarth Sheldon Lewis

Lewis with his wife, Annie Burr Lewis, and Rev. K. Cronin at Strawberry Hill, 1951

once said. "Passion," however, is perhaps too mild a term to describe Lewis's drive to collect. Few if any collectors have been as obsessed with their subjects or have pursued them as ardently as Lewis in his quest for everything related to the eighteenth-century man of letters Horace Walpole. A key figure in the latter half of the 1700s, Walpole fostered a Gothic revival in architecture with the remodeling of his Twickenham villa, Strawberry Hill. He wrote the first Gothic novel, *The Castle of Otranto* (1764), operated his own printing press at his estate, and wrote thousands of letters revealing of contemporary English culture. As Leslie Stephen observed, "The history of England throughout the eighteenth century is simply a synonym for the works of Horace Walpole." Having committed himself to pursuing Walpole, Lewis approached his subject with religious zeal; he called each of the Walpole-related books, letters, manuscripts, and other items in his collection "a piece of the true cross." Lewis became the chief promoter of Walpole in the twentieth century, though he frequently referred to himself as "merely Walpole's train bearer."

Lewis, called "Lefty" since childhood by his close friends, was born to Miranda Sheldon and Azro Nathaniel Lewis, a dentist and later a business

executive, on 4 November 1895 in Alameda, California. Lewis was the youngest of five sons, two of whom were his half-brothers by his father's previous marriage. Lewis received his early education at the Mastick Grammar School in Alameda and at the Thacher School at Ventura, where he developed a fascination for writing – especially short stories – and received an introduction to eighteenth-century literature. Although his parents maintained a well-stocked library and encouraged Lewis in his early reading, neither was a collector. As a child Lewis collected houseflies, seashells, stamps, coins, butterflies, and beetles. Lewis credited his half-brother Charles with stirring his interest in fine books; Charles took him as a young man to John Howell's bookstore in San Francisco. Charles was not a collector, but he imparted to Lewis his appreciation of beautiful books – an appreciation heightened by this early contact with the renowned Howell, who opened his vaults to the impressionable youth.

Lewis began studies at Yale University in 1914, coming into contact with several of the best literature professors in the country and the bookstores of New Haven, especially the Brick Row Bookshop, where Lewis was soon to become a steady customer. At Yale Lewis studied under Henry Seidel Canby, William Lyon Phelps, and Chauncey Brewster Tinker. It was Tinker who whet Lewis's appetite for learning about eighteenth-century life and literature.

At Yale Lewis joined the staff of the literary paper and was a member of Beta Theta Pi fraternity, the Scroll and Key society, and the Elizabethan Club, which held a famous collection of Shakespeare folios and quartos and other early texts. Lewis had the opportunity to meet William Butler Yeats, G. K. Chesterton, and John Masefield when they visited the Elizabethan Club. Lewis got to know Masefield rather well and searched the bookshops of New Haven for his books – Lewis's first focused collecting interest. By recommending William Makepeace Thackeray's *Four Georges: Sketches of Manners, Morals, Court and Town Life* (1860) Masefield also introduced Lewis to the topic of Walpole's correspondence.

World War I interrupted Lewis's education. In 1917 he joined the army, became a second lieutenant, and was sent to France. There he spent most of his time in an army hospital with mumps and arthritis. Discharged in 1918, he reentered Yale in the fall of 1919. Lewis graduated from Yale in 1920 with no clear career in mind. That same year he became an editor at the Yale University Press, giving him a connection that would later serve his plans for his Walpole collection. From Carl Rollins, the university printer, Lewis learned the various typefaces in quality printing and the skill required in producing truly fine books. In 1922 his dream of becoming a published author was realized with his *Tutors' Lane* (1922), a brief novel about life at a New England college (a Yale in thin disguise). The novel did not achieve great success, and it was the only one of four completed novels that Lewis was to have published.

Lewis's career as a premier collector began in 1922. His mother died that year, and his share of her estate made him self-sufficient. Although he did not immediately begin buying books on a grand scale, he now had the means to do so. On a trip to England with several friends in the summer of 1922, he rediscovered the fascinating world of old books. Although he had admired books of past centuries in the bookshops of Howell and others, he had not indulged, and his purchases from the New Haven book dealers had mainly been confined to contemporary literature. At an antique shop in Newbury, Lewis experienced the thrill of discovering unsuspected treasures at low prices. Although he had no thoughts

at the time of specializing in eighteenth-century literature, he purchased mostly eighteenth-century titles, thinking that such acquisitions would please and impress Tinker. During this visit Lewis purchased some 250 volumes for little more than ten pounds. The thrill of possession at a bargain price, he later claimed, started him on his career as a serious book collector; he was, as he put it, now "blooded." Before returning to the United States he sought out other bookstores throughout England and soon amassed a sizable library, though his overseas collecting was not focused.

Lewis's trip to England in 1923 was to have a lasting influence on him. At York he was persuaded by an antiquarian book dealer to purchase a copy of John Jesse's *George Selwyn and His Contemporaries: With Memoirs and Notes* (London: Bentley, 1843–1844) with copious notes by Lady Louisa Stuart. The many puzzling references to personalities and events of the eighteenth century, and especially the references to Walpole, piqued Lewis's curiosity, which he was to spend the rest of his life satisfying.

Afterward, each book dealer that Lewis encountered furthered his knowledge of the world of books and bookselling. In 1924 he met a London dealer, whom he calls "Mr. X" in his autobiographical *One Man's Education* (1967). Mr. X taught him the expensive lessons that not all booksellers are honest and that items are not always what they are purported to be. It was, however, this same book dealer who at the 1924 Milnes Gaskell sale at Hodgson's in London bought for Lewis his first Walpoliana: six letters to the Scottish historian John Pilkerton. These letters so fascinated Lewis that he bought and read the sixteen volumes of Helen and Paget Jackson Toynbee's edition of Walpole's correspondence, *The Letters of Horace Walpole, Fourth Earl of Oxford* (Oxford: Clarendon, 1903–1905). With Tinker's advice and blessing, Lewis determined to become a serious Walpole collector. On another trip to London in 1925 he focused on Walpole and bought everything he could find.

Lewis was insatiable. Determined to own even those items remotely related to Walpole and his circle, he purchased books, manuscripts, letters, diaries, scrapbooks, pictures, clippings, and artifacts of every kind. He became enamored of Walpole's Gothic home, Strawberry Hill. Over the years he would collect a huge research library on Gothic influence in the eighteenth century. An early focus in his Walpole collecting were books produced by the Strawberry Hill Press. Eventually he would own a copy of every Strawberry Hill title as well as vari-

HORACE WALPOLE'S
LIBRARY

BY

WILMARTH SHELDON LEWIS
FELLOW OF YALE UNIVERSITY

Cambridge
AT THE UNIVERSITY PRESS
1958

Title page for Lewis's history of Horace Walpole's Library

ants, often twenty or more, of most of these titles. One of the Strawberry Hill titles most desired by Lewis was Walpole's *Description of the Villa . . . at Strawberry Hill,* first published in 1774 and republished in 1784. Lewis was able to acquire thirty-five of the three hundred copies printed. As Lewis wrote in the preface to Allen Tracy Hazen's *A Bibliography of the Strawberry Hill Press . . .* (1942), "It is not enough to own a single copy of the same edition. . . . Mr. Hazen shows that 'duplicates' must be treated with respect — and caution, for they may turn out not to be duplicates after all."

His Walpole collection greatly facilitated his general study of eighteenth-century culture. Walpole's letters illuminated the human side of eighteenth-century life and the lives of the colorful personalities of the period. From the outset collecting Walpole correspondence was as great a priority

for Lewis, as was acquiring books from Walpole's library and titles published by Strawberry Hill Press. In his 1951 third-person autobiography, *Collector's Progress,* Lewis describes his obsession with Walpole and Walpole's era: "The panorama of the eighteenth century unrolled before him, the sweep of great events, the rise and fall of reputations, the lilacs and nightingales at Strawberry Hill and the mob loose in the streets of London. . . . He took on Walpole so thoroughly that he identified himself with him." Indeed, Lewis often took great delight in drawing parallels between their lives. So enthralled did Lewis become of all things Walpolian that he would "try to follow the subsequent history of each and every piece as if it were the Grail itself."

In 1926 he purchased a house built in 1784 on Main Street in Farmington, Connecticut, where he

Lewis's library in Farmington, Connecticut, 1966

had lived since 1922. The house was to remain his home and the repository of his Walpole collection for the rest of his life. In 1928 he married Annie Burr Auchincloss, a member of a wealthy New England family. Before they returned from their honeymoon, Lewis had the architect William Adams Delano design a large new library to house his burgeoning eighteenth-century collection.

In 1933 Lewis began preparing a new edition of Walpole's correspondence. Lewis had recognized the need for a new edition after having collated some of the letters in his collection with Toynbee's printed versions. Lewis found errors and omissions; furthermore, Toynbee had included no letters to Walpole. Lewis agreed to finance and edit a new edition, and Yale agreed to the project. Relying on his collection, or the "Walpole factory," as Lewis called it, for source material for the project, Lewis intensified his search for Walpole material.

In the preface to the first volume of *The Yale Edition of Horace Walpole's Correspondence* (1937)

Lewis wrote that he intended "to give a correct text, to include for the first time the letters to him [Walpole], and to annotate the whole with the fullness that the most informative record of the time deserves." Lewis estimated that the edition would require seventeen years to complete and would fill thirty volumes. As he noted in the introduction to volume forty published posthumously in 1980, he was "thirty years and twenty volumes off." Volume forty-eight, the final installment of the index, appeared in 1983, four years after Lewis's death. The *New York Times* hailed the edition as "one of the most notable literary projects of all time"; the *Spectator* termed it "one of the highest achievements of American scholarship." Many have referred to it as "the grandfather of scholarly editions," since it served as the model and inspiration for the publication of the papers of Benjamin Franklin, Thomas Jefferson, Sir Thomas More, and others. The forty-three volumes of text include all of Walpole's extant letters, some four thousand from Walpole – the ma-

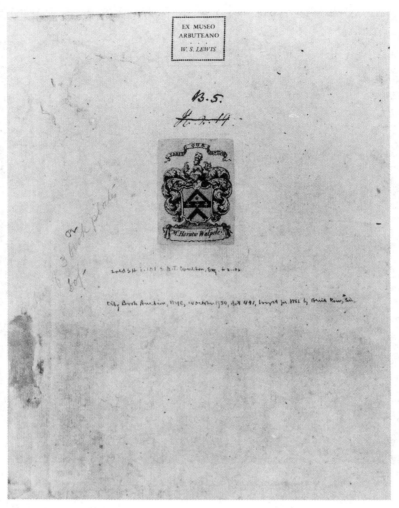

Horace Walpole's first bookplate for his library, with Lewis's bookplate above it
(Wilmarth Sheldon Lewis–Walpole Library, Farmington, Connecticut)

jority of them owned by Lewis — and about three thousand to Walpole. The five-volume index Lewis described as "the index to end all indexes"; it provides access to "the whole fabric of political, social, financial, artistic, military, and literary history so far as it is portrayed" in Walpole's letters. Many of the illustrations came from Lewis's collection. He wrote the introduction to each of the correspondences and secured a library of microfilm to assist with annotations.

As early as the 1920s, soon after he began collecting Walpole in earnest, Lewis contemplated writing a biography of the man; instead he shared his resources at Farmington with R. W. Ketton-Cremer, who wrote an excellent biography. Lewis did write much about his favorite subject, however. *Horace Walpole: The A. W. Mellon Lectures in the Fine Arts, 1960* (1961) was presented at the National Gal-

lery in Washington, D.C., in February and March 1960; Lewis dedicated the volume to his recently deceased wife. In his preface to the published lectures Lewis observes that rather than writing a complete biography he attempts to show Walpole "as I see him after thirty-five years of collecting, editing, and study. What was he like? What is the explanation of the contradictions and complexities of his character, behavior, and achievement? Why have so many found him baffling? I hope that this book will answer these questions." In the six lectures that comprise the volume, Lewis deals with Walpole's family and friends, his political career and his *Memoirs,* his house at Strawberry Hill, his writings, and, finally, his letters.

Another product of Lewis's passion was the charming *Rescuing Horace Walpole* (1978). The book opens with an imaginary conversation between

Lewis and God. God tells Lewis, " 'I am going to destroy every object in your house except one, and you have twenty minutes to choose it.' " Lewis at once selects Richard Bentley's drawings and designs for Strawberry Hill; this choice earns Lewis the right to save another twenty-five items. Although the autobiographical works of Lewis – *Collector's Progress* and *One Man's Education* – provide more complete descriptions of Lewis's library, *Rescuing Horace Walpole* presents detailed discussions of those objects Lewis held most dear. The prized material is presented in chronological order of composition, beginning with the seven-thousand-word manuscript "Short Notes of the Life of Horatio Walpole," which Walpole began in 1746 and finished in 1779. Lewis called this "the most important Walpole manuscript I know of." Other items treated in the book include a portrait of Walpole's parents, which hung in the Blue Bedchamber of Strawberry Hill; the journal of Walpole's private press; Walpole's letter to Lady Ossory dated 15 January 1797, six weeks before he died; and Allan Ramsay's portrait of Walpole. Lewis discusses the provenance of these works and the bypaths and curious ways by which many of them came to Farmington.

Lewis had interests other than Walpole. His love of art is reflected both in *See for Yourself* (1971), in which he discusses his ten favorite pictures, and in his extensive collection of prints and paintings. He was devoted to Yale; as a trustee of the university he encouraged the growth of the library. He also supported the Watkinson Library of Hartford and the Redwood Library at Newport, Rhode Island. Yet it was Walpole and the eighteenth century with which Lewis was most intimately identified. By the time of his death in 1979 he had accumulated a library far larger and more comprehensive than he had dared to contemplate when he first decided to become the world's foremost Walpoleon. Of the identified seventy-five hundred volumes in Walpole's library, over three thousand made their way to Lewis's collection; almost half of these – and an equal number of Walpole letters – were acquired in a six-year burst of collecting from 1933 to 1939. Lewis purchased the originals of over twenty-six hundred letters to and from Walpole and made photocopies of over twenty-five hundred others as the basis for the Yale edition of the *Correspondence*. Lewis's library contained over twenty-five thousand eighteenth-century titles – books, pamphlets, and manuscripts. His more than eight thousand satiric prints and caricatures comprised a collection second only to that of the British Library; he also owned one of the largest collections of Hogarth prints in the world. His file drawers, containing cards on all aspects of Walpole's life and on every item known to have belonged to him as well as on more-general eighteenth-century topics, bulged with more than nine hundred thousand cards.

Among the more valuable "supporting" documents collected by Lewis are the letters, manuscripts, and private papers of the marquise Marie de Vichy-Chambord du Deffand, who at the age of sixty-eight fell in love with the forty-eight-year-old Walpole and wrote many letters to him; the French translation by Louis XVI of Walpole's *Historic Doubts on the Life and Reign of King Richard the Third;* the papers of the eighteenth-century diplomat, politician, and member of parliament Sir Charles Hanbury Williams (filling ninety-four volumes); the official and private correspondence of Walpole's tutor Edward Weston; the papers of the British prime minister George Grenville; and manuscripts relating to Thomas Chatterton, the young poet whose suicide many blamed on Walpole for his refusal to offer Chatterton his patronage. A happier association existed between Walpole and the poet Thomas Gray; Lewis secured ten volumes of musical scores collected by Gray. Lewis also acquired many revealing eighteenth-century diaries, journals, and letters from British royalty and major contemporary figures such as the poet William Cowper; William Pitt, first Earl of Chatham; Pitt's son William 'the Younger'; writer William Beckford; and Whig political leader Edmund Burke.

Lewis's obsession provoked the scorn and ire of some critics. British writer and critic Cyril Connolly accused Lewis of "Walpoliolatry" and attacked him in print in 1943:

> Such an insatiable craving can clearly never be satisfied until all the copies of all Walpole's books either written or published by him have accumulated round their rightful owner, and Strawberry Hill has moved to Farmington. At this rate the books will soon be migrating of their own accord and only an act of Parliament, with the closing of our frontiers, can prevent the complete extinction, on this side of the Atlantic, of all remaining traces of Walpole.

Others, however, admired Lewis's assiduousness and determination. In reviewing *Collector's Progress* John Carter wrote:

> Perhaps his most impressive achievement in the purely technical sphere can hardly be appreciated by the layman. . . . It is that, in spite of being . . . known as the keenest Horace Walpole collector in the world he has managed to avoid putting prices up against himself. . . .

Only a combination of resolution and finesse with the power to attract and retain the trade's good will could have kept the tortuous course between the Scylla of an extortionate price and the Charybdis of a missed opportunity. . . . Even if bibliophiles as a class are not as curmudgeonly as their critics sometimes suppose, it is still eloquent testimony to Mr. Lewis' international reputation that his natural rivals, instead of swooping on some enviable piece and thus winning a trick from the maestro, tend rather to withdraw in his favor – and even to keep a spare eye open in his interest.

Early in his collecting career Lewis determined that his Walpole collection would one day be presented to his alma mater. At his death in 1979 Lewis left to Yale his collection, his home in Farmington, and a healthy endowment for preserving and augmenting his collection. After his death his collection has thus continued to grow. The library at Farmington, accessible to all serious scholars of Walpole and the eighteenth century, remains what it was during Walpole's lifetime: the finest collection on Walpole in the world and a monument to one man's insatiable quest.

References:

Geoffrey T. Hellman, "The Age of Wilmarth Lewis," *New Yorker* (15 October 1973): 104–106, 108–111;

Hellman, "Farmington Revisited," *New Yorker* (October 1959): 144–160;

Hellman, "The Steward of Strawberry Hill, I," *New Yorker* (6 August 1949): 26–37;

Hellman, "The Steward of Strawberry Hill, II," *New Yorker* (13 August 1949): 31–37;

W. W. Williams, "The Amateur Professional: A Personal View of W. S. Lewis," *Saturday Review of Literature,* 21 (16 March 1940): 11–12, 18;

Robin W. Winks, *Cloak and Gown: Scholars in the Secret War, 1939–1961* (New York: Morrow, 1987).

J. K. Lilly, Jr.

(25 September 1893 – 5 May 1966)

Joel Silver
Indiana University

BOOK: *A List of One Hundred Books Selected from the Collection Now in the Library of Josiah Kirby Lilly, Jr.* (Indianapolis: Privately printed, 1928–1929).

Josiah Kirby Lilly, Jr., assembled one of the finest general collections of books and manuscripts in the United States in the twentieth century. Amassed over three decades, Lilly's collection ultimately totaled more than twenty thousand books and seventeen thousand manuscripts, which were presented by the collector to Indiana University between 1954 and 1957. With special strength in American, British, and Continental literature; Americana; and science and medicine, Lilly's collection was remarkable for its consistently high standard of condition and its wide-ranging scope. Lilly was also the instigator and financial supporter of several bibliographical projects.

J. K. Lilly, Jr., was born on 25 September 1893 in Indianapolis, Indiana. He attended the Hill School in Pottstown, Pennsylvania, and graduated in 1914 from the University of Michigan School of Pharmacy. In that year he married Ruth Brinkmeyer of Indianapolis and then began work at Eli Lilly and Company, the pharmaceutical firm founded in 1876 by his grandfather, Col. Eli Lilly. With the exception of a period of military service in World War I, Lilly worked at the firm for the rest of his life. He became president in 1948 and served as chairman of the board of directors from 1953 until his death in Indianapolis on 5 May 1966.

Lilly began collecting books and manuscripts in the mid 1920s. He had been an avid reader as a child, and his later visits to Brentano's during business trips to New York resulted in the purchase of sets of the works of famous authors, as well as individual titles in literature and travel. None of these books, however, held any bibliographic distinction, and Lilly soon graduated to more discerning purchases. He began reading about book collecting and its principles, particularly in the writings of A. Edward Newton. Focusing his first serious efforts on American literature, he started with some of the works of popular Indiana authors, including James Whitcomb Riley, George Ade, and Lewis Wallace.

Lilly soon expanded beyond Indiana literature and collected Mark Twain's and Edgar Allan Poe's works – also the first authors whose works Lilly pursued in real depth. Working with a variety of booksellers Lilly solicited stock lists, made his selections, and evaluated each item individually when it arrived. He never hesitated to return a book or manuscript if it did not meet his standard of condition or if it failed to excite his imagination: all purchases throughout his collecting career were understood to be on approval.

Lilly eventually built up an enviable collection of Twain's works, including presentation copies of both *The Adventures of Tom Sawyer* (Hartford, Chicago, Cincinnati: American Publishing; San Francisco: A. Roman, 1876) and *Adventures of Huckleberry Finn (Tom Sawyer's Comrade)* (New York: Charles L. Webster, 1885), first American and first British editions of nearly all of Twain's works published during his lifetime, autograph letters, and the manuscript of the unfinished play, "The Quaker City Holy Land Excursion," dated 1867. Lilly was also extremely successful as a collector of Poe, forming an excellent library that contained several Poe rarities, including *The Prose Romances of Edgar A. Poe, No. I. Containing the Murders in the Rue Morgue, and The Man That Was Used Up* (Philadelphia: William H. Graham, 1843), *Al Aaraaf, Tamerlane, and Minor Poems* (Baltimore: Hatch and Dunning, 1829), and the small pamphlet that has traditionally been one of the most sought-after volumes of American literature, *Tamerlane and Other Poems* (Boston: Calvin F. S. Thomas, 1827).

Lilly's acquisition of *Tamerlane,* Poe's first published book, from Goodspeed's Book Shop in 1928, was by far his most important and ambitious purchase to date. As one of only a half-dozen copies then known, *Tamerlane* placed Lilly on the map as a

Josiah Kirby Lilly, Jr. (Lilly Library, Indiana University)

collector; the purchase price of more than twenty thousand dollars was far more than he had yet spent on any other book or manuscript. Word of the purchase soon spread, however, with newspaper stories announcing his acquisition of the book, as well as its price, teaching him a lesson about the mixed blessings of notoriety. While the deluge of offers that followed his public debut as a collector did lead to Lilly's acquisition of books such as the first edition of the Eliot Indian Bible (1663), the publicity was not welcomed by the Lilly family, and the lunatic letters which followed far outnumbered those with any promise. The most memorable offer received by Lilly as a result of the *Tamerlane* stories was contained in a handwritten note mailed to him at Eli Lilly and Company: "If you will put ten thousand dollars ($10,000) under the big white stone under the west end of the Eagle Creek Bridge just east of the Insane Asylum at midnight Nov. 18th just one night later at same time

and place you will find the original copy of the Ten Comandments." After this incident, with the exception of some privately printed checklists or keepsakes sent to friends, Lilly kept his collecting activities quiet.

Lilly's collecting interests extended beyond American literature, and the range of his collections grew rapidly. He developed a strong affection for the books printed at William Morris's Kelmscott Press, and he soon built up a complete collection of them. Lilly's interests in private presses never went beyond this, however, and other than an occasional purchase, Kelmscott was the only modern press from which Lilly collected. He joined the Grolier Club in 1928 and soon began to collect seriously in English literature, using as an initial guide the catalogue of the Grolier Club's influential exhibition *One Hundred Books Famous in English Literature with Facsimiles of the Title-Pages* (1902). Throughout his ca-

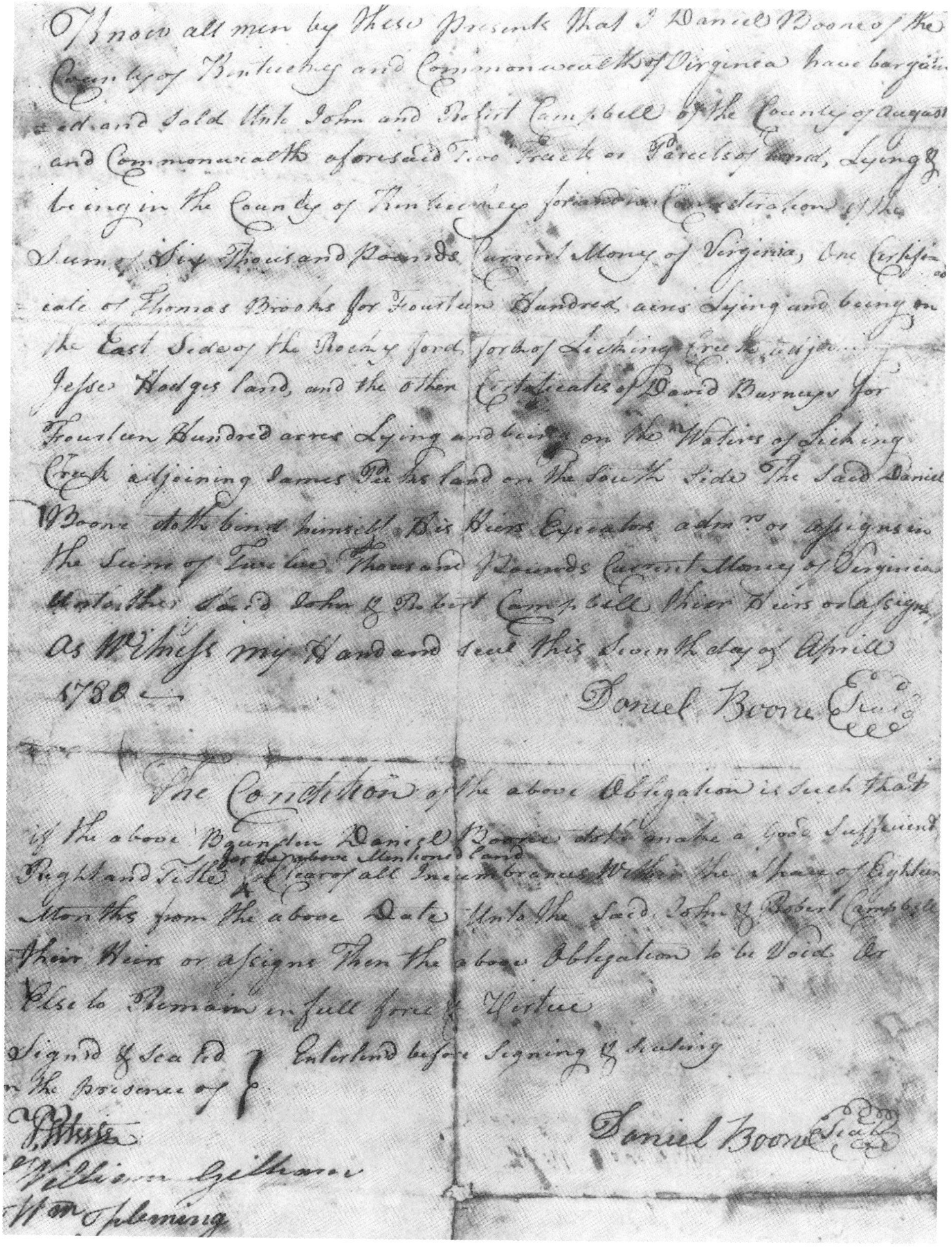

Know all men by these Presents that I Daniel Boone of the County of Kentucky and Commonwealth of Virginia have bargained and Sold Unto John and Robert Campbell of the County of Augusta and Commonwealth aforesaid Two Tracts or Parcels of Land, Lying & being in the County of Kentucky for and in Consideration of the Sum of Six Thousand Pounds Current Money of Virginia, One Certificate of Thomas Brooks for Fourteen Hundred acres Lying and being on the East Side of the Rocky fork, fork of Licking Creek adjoining Jesse Hodges land, and the other Certificate of David Burneys for Fourteen Hundred acres Lying and being on the Waters of Licking Creek adjoining James Parks land on the South Side The said Daniel Boone doth bind himself, His Heirs Executors admrs or assigns in the Sum of Twelve Thousand Pounds Current Money of Virginia Unto the Said John & Robert Campbell their Heirs or assigns As Witness my Hand and seal this Seventh day of April 1780

Daniel Boone {Seal}

The Condition of the above Obligation is such that if the above Bounden Daniel Boone doth make a Good Sufficient Right and Title for the above Mentioned land Clear of all Incumbrances Within the Space of Eighteen Months from the above Date Unto the Said John & Robert Campbell their Heirs or assigns Then the above Obligation to be Void Or Else to Remain in full force & Virtue

Signed & Sealed } Enterlined before Signing & Sealing
in the presence of }

J. Patteson
William Gilhamt
Wm Fleming

Daniel Boone {Seal}

Part of Lilly's Americana collection, this 1685 land deed signed twice by Daniel Boone was acquired in 1947 (Lilly Library, Indiana University).

The 1814 Baltimore edition of "The Star Spangled Banner," which book dealer David Randall sold to Lilly in 1948 (Lilly Library, Indiana University)

reer Lilly used the Grolier Hundred as a checklist. Although the checklist did not necessarily dictate his book hunting, it remained something of a scorecard; after three decades he had acquired the first editions of ninety of the hundred and the earliest obtainable editions of four others. He acquired a Shakespeare First Folio and a Caxton Chaucer, Charles Dickens's *The Posthumous Papers of the Pickwick Club* (London: 1836–1837) and William Makepeace Thackeray's *Vanity Fair* (London: Bradbury and Evans, 1847–1848) in parts, Robert Burns's *Poems, Chiefly in the Scottish Dialect* (Kilmarnock: Printed by John Wilson, 1786) in original boards, and a presentation copy of Edward FitzGerald's translation of the *Rubaiyat of Omar Khayyam, the Astronomer-Poet of Persia. Translated into English Verse* (London: Bernard Quaritch, 1859).

Some of the Grolier Hundred volumes that eluded Lilly, such as the 1611 King James Bible, had indeed been offered to him but were rejected by Lilly on the basis of condition. Condition became increasingly important to Lilly as he matured as a collector, and he would often trade a previously purchased copy for an-

other copy of a book if it represented a significant improvement in condition. He gradually limited his circle of dealers to those who understood his insistence on top condition and eventually worked mainly with Goodspeed's, Howard S. Mott, Jr., John S. Van E. Kohn, A. S. W. Rosenbach, and David A. Randall, who played an increasingly important role in finding Lilly books in several fields and in providing bibliographic advice.

Randall first met Lilly in 1932. In 1935 Randall became manager of the rare book department at the Charles Scribner's Sons' bookstore in New York and gradually became Lilly's chief bookseller and adviser. Randall and John Carter of Scribner's London branch were also Lilly's chief suppliers in the area of world literature. Lilly decided to collect first and early editions of significant works in languages other than English after reading Asa Don Dickinson's *One Thousand Best Books. The Household Guide to A Lifetime's Reading. A Variorum List Compiled from Many Authoritative Selections. With Descriptive Notes* (1924). Spurred on by Dickinson's list, which was a distillation of other "best books" lists, Lilly acquired

The Lilly Library at Indiana University

first editions in the original languages of the works of hundreds of authors ranging from Homer to Tolstoy.

Lilly pursued books on the Dickinson list throughout the 1930s. He was also continuing to work on the Grolier Hundred and was building depth in his American literary holdings. By the mid 1930s his library had outgrown his home, and his collection was sufficiently important for Lilly to want to house his books with greater security. Lilly had been concerned about proper storage conditions for his books from the time he began collecting, and many of them were kept in custom-made quarter-leather cases, made to Lilly's personally measured specifications. He also never loaned his books or manuscripts for exhibitions, not wishing the publicity and fearing loss or damage to his irreplaceable holdings.

In 1935 and 1936 he had a library building constructed in the country, northwest of Indianapolis. Incorporating the latest advances in security and fireproofing, the Eagle Crest Library housed Lilly's collections until their move to Indiana University two decades later. Lilly spent a great deal of his spare time at Eagle Crest, and it was to Eagle Crest that he took his bibliographic visitors.

With the beginning of the 1940s Lilly became more interested in American history, and he decided to form a collection of the highlights of Americana, from the voyages of Christopher Columbus through the Civil War. In 1947 Lilly unsuccessfully attempted to purchase at auction the Crowninshield-Stevens-Brinley-Vanderbilt-Whitney copy of the 1640 *Bay Psalm Book,* the first book printed in British North America. This defeat in the auction room further strengthened Lilly's resolve to form a prime collection of Americana.

As usual he preferred to buy books individually rather than in a group, but he made an exception in the case of the small and select Baron Hardt collection of early Americana, which he purchased in 1948. This collection contained the 1493 first printing in Latin of the letter from Columbus announcing the discovery of the New World, as well as strong holdings of *Jesuit Relations,* the annually published reports of Jesuit activities in New France.

Other purchases of Americana by Lilly during this period included important books and pam-

The reading room at the Lilly Library

phlets relating to the seventeenth-century English settlements in New England, a first printing of the Declaration of Independence of 1776, the first official printing of the Constitution (1787), documents signed by George Washington and Abraham Lincoln, Thomas Jefferson's copy of the first printing of the Bill of Rights (1789), and John James Audubon's *The Birds of America* (London: 1827–1838). Like his father, who had formed a collection of the sheet music of Stephen Foster, Lilly was interested in famous American music. He obtained several early printings of Francis Scott Key's "The Star-Spangled Banner," as well as manuscripts and early editions of Julia Ward Howe's "Battle Hymn of the Republic" and Daniel Decatur Emmett's "Dixie."

Scientific and medical books became the focus of his concentration late in his book collecting. Since the early 1930s Lilly on occasion had acquired items in science and medicine; he had also formed an excellent collection of the works of Sir William Osler but had not yet gone after the high spots in the field as he had in English literature and Americana. Unlike some of Lilly's other areas of collecting, there were no standard published lists of the key books in the areas of science and medicine

to use as guides. Bern Dibner's *Heralds of Science* was not published until 1955, and Harrison Horblit's Grolier Club catalogue, *One Hundred Books Famous in Science,* did not appear until 1964. As Lilly's holdings grew, he wanted to make certain that he was acquiring the major as well as the minor pieces.

Randall agreed to compile a list of important medical books for Lilly, but there was an air of uneasiness surrounding the project. Lilly had asked a bookseller for a "key books" list once before, and it was an experience that Lilly did not want to repeat. In 1944 Rosenbach had provided him with a list of what Rosenbach considered to be the one hundred most important books in Americana; the list contained an inordinate number of books that happened to be in Rosenbach's stock at the time. Lilly was Randall's best customer, and Randall had to tread warily. Finally, the noted medical librarian William R. Le Fanu was commissioned to compile the list. The Le Fanu medical list was completed in 1952 and was used by Lilly and Carter in the search for medical works. A similar list of scientific books, commissioned by Randall from I. Bernard Cohen of Harvard University, was completed in 1955, after Lilly had curtailed his book collecting.

The Lincoln Room at the Lilly Library

Beginning after World War II and continuing through the early 1950s, Lilly added landmark scientific and medical books to his collections, including *De Revolutionibus Orbium Coelestium* (Nuremberg: Joannes Petreius, 1543), by the astronomer Nicolaus Copernicus; the great anatomy of Andreas Vesalius, *de Humani corporis fabrica Libri septem* (Basel: Joannes Oporinus, 1543); Sir Isaac Newton's *Philosophiae Naturalis Principia Mathematica* (London: Joseph Streater for The Royal Society, 1687); and William Harvey's work on the circulation of the blood, *Exercitatio Anatomica de Motu Cordis et Sanguinis in Animalibus* (Frankfurt: 1628). He also added hundreds of other lesser-known books in the field, creating significant depth in the collection. As always, condition was a prime factor in his choices. Lilly was still upgrading copies of major books, like the Vesalius, and was still searching for presentation or association copies wherever possible.

With the acquisition of Harvey's *de Motu Cordis* in August 1953, Lilly felt that he had reached a milestone in his collecting. He had been collecting books and manuscripts for nearly three decades and had invested an enormous amount of energy and resources in the formation of a first-class library. Al-

though Lilly had had help from some of the best booksellers and bibliographers, all acquisition decisions had been his own, and he had collected what he wished. *Enthusiasm* was a word that Lilly used repeatedly in his book correspondence; and it was his own enthusiasm rather than those of his dealers that guided him.

He owned no illuminated manuscripts, despite pleas from booksellers, and illustrated books needed to qualify in some other way to be considered for inclusion in his collection. His own love for the sea was transformed into a strong collection of voyages and travels, nautical history, and piracy; a predilection for military history led to the acquisition of costume books and military memoirs. He purchased what he wished and consistently rejected any book or manuscript – no matter how highly recommended or how great a bargain – for which he could not muster enthusiasm.

By 1953 Lilly had built the kind of collection he had once envisioned. He owned first editions of thousands of the most significant books of literature, history, and science, and his manuscripts ranged from a holograph of Robert Burns's "Auld Lang Syne" to the original manuscript of James M.

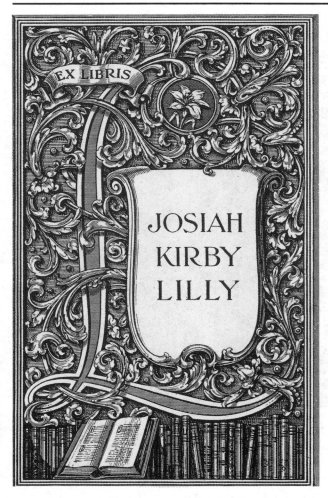

Lilly's bookplate (Lilly Library, Indiana University)

Barrie's *Peter Pan: or, the Boy Who Wouldn't Grow Up* (first performed in December 1904, Duke of York Theatre, London). In one of his initial enthusiasms, Indiana literature, he now owned good collections of all the major authors: he owned the largest Riley collection in the world and had acquired many manuscripts of Wallace, including that of *Ben-Hur: A Tale of the Christ* (1880). His holdings of American literature had grown to encompass the period from the early republic to the beginning of the twentieth century.

Those items he wished to add to his collection he felt were now out of his reach. Those Grolier Hundred titles or individual landmark books such as the Gutenberg Bible that his library lacked were unavailable in acceptable condition within his book budget. Lilly also had begun to form several other collections, including stamps, coins, firearms, edged weapons, nautical models, and military miniatures: his enthusiasm for these newer collections out-

weighed his desire to continue collecting books and manuscripts on a large scale.

In addition to his collecting, Lilly had established a program of support for bibliographical scholarship. In 1938 he initiated through the Lilly Endowment a series of grants to the Library of Congress for the support of bibliographical research, particularly in the area of American children's books. After a few false starts, Jacob Blanck was hired as project bibliographer, and a bibliography of Lilly's favorite nineteenth-century author of books for young boys, Charles Austin Fosdick, who wrote under the pseudonym of Harry Castlemon, was produced. Blanck was then brought to Indianapolis by Lilly to assist in the production of a series of bibliographies of Indiana authors – a project funded by a Lilly grant to the Indiana Historical Society. Eventually four bibliographies of important Hoosier authors were issued, having been compiled by Anthony J. Russo, Dorothy R. Russo, and Thelma L. Sullivan, and financed by the Lilly Endowment.

The *Bibliography of American Literature* (or *BAL*) is the largest and most widely used bibliographical work in its field. It owes its existence to Lilly, who had long felt the need for such a work in his collecting, as well as to Blanck, who had conceived the idea of a comprehensive bibliography that would supersede Merle Johnson's *American First Editions* and become a standard reference in the area of American literary study. Lilly agreed to fund the project through an annual grant from the Lilly Endowment. He also insisted that the bibliography not be a private undertaking and instead be carried out under the auspices of a recognized organization or institution. The Bibliographical Society of America agreed to oversee its production, and Blanck was installed as research director. The first volume of the *BAL*, published in 1955, would be dedicated to the "Directors of Lilly Endowment, Inc., of Indianapolis, and more particularly to the President of that organization, Josiah K. Lilly."

With the *BAL* well under way, and with his book collecting reaching a plateau, Lilly severely curtailed his book buying in late 1953 and in 1954. By the autumn of 1954 he had made the decision to keep the collection together rather than to disperse it, and to donate the collection to an institution rather than offer it for sale. He selected Indiana University, and in a letter of 26 November 1954 to university president Herman B. Wells, Lilly expressed his hope "that at Bloomington, Indiana there may be assembled ultimately in the custody of Indiana University the most outstanding institutional general collection of rare historical and literary material in the Middle West." The gift, which arrived in Bloomington in installments through late 1957, was formally announced by Indiana University on 8 January 1956.

Randall, Lilly's longtime bookseller, came to the university later that year as rare book librarian and professor of bibliography, and he supervised the construction on the Indiana University campus of the Lilly Library. The library was built to house not only Lilly's collection but also the other rare books and manuscripts formerly held in the university library's Department of Special Collections. The Lilly Library was officially dedicated on 3 October 1960. Lilly attended the dedication ceremonies, as he had the groundbreaking, but Randall could never persuade Lilly to return for another visit.

Following the donation of his collection to Indiana University, Lilly turned his attention to his other interests, but he continued for the rest of his life to read and to collect novels of the sea, working toward compiling a list of what he considered the best of such works. He remained connected to the *BAL* as the Lilly Endowment continued to support the project to some degree, although the majority of the financial backing came from the National Endowment for the Humanities. With the publication of the ninth and final volume in 1991, the project was completed under the editorship of Michael Winship.

After his death in 1966, Lilly's varied collections were dispersed. Above all, Lilly derived a great deal of enjoyment and fulfillment from his books and manuscripts, and he was eminently satisfied with the arrangements that he had made for their permanent disposition and use. The library that he gathered to suit his own taste stands today as the core of a great research library, and J. K. Lilly, Jr., remains one of the most accomplished collectors of the twentieth century.

References:

E. J. Kahn, Jr., *All In A Century: The First 100 Years of Eli Lilly and Company* (Indianapolis: Eli Lilly and Company, 1976?);

James H. Madison, *Eli Lilly: A Life* (Indianapolis: Indiana Historical Society, 1989);

David A. Randall, *Dukedom Large Enough* (New York: Random House, 1969);

Randall, *Eighty-Nine Good Novels of the Sea, the Ship, and the Sailor. A List Compiled by J. K. Lilly. An Account of Its Formation* (Bloomington, Ind.: Lilly Library, 1966);

Randall, *Grolier: or 'Tis Sixty Years Since. A Reconstruction of the Exhibit of 100 Books Famous in English Literature Originally Held in New York, 1903, on the Occasion of the Club's Visit to The Lilly Library, Indiana University, May 1, 1963* (Bloomington, Ind.: Lilly Library, 1963);

Randall, "J. K. Lilly: America's Quiet Collector," *Antiquarian Bookman,* 37 (27 June 1966): 2679–2681;

Randall, *The J. K. Lilly Collection of Edgar Allan Poe: An Account of Its Formation* (Bloomington, Ind.: Lilly Library, 1964);

Randall, "Josiah Kirby Lilly," *Book Collector,* 6 (Autumn 1957): 263–277;

Randall, *Medicine: An Exhibition of Books Relating to Medicine and Surgery from the Collection formed by J. K. Lilly,* (Bloomington, Ind.: Lilly Library, 1966);

Joel Silver, *J. K. Lilly, Jr., Bibliophile* (Bloomington, Ind.: Lilly Library, 1993).

Papers:
Much of Lilly's correspondence with his booksellers during the period from 1926 to 1954 is held by the Manuscripts Department of the Lilly Library at Indiana University, Bloomington, Indiana. Additional materials related to Lilly's business career are in the archives of Eli Lilly and Company, Indianapolis, Indiana.

James Logan

(20 October 1674 – 31 October 1751)

Mary Anne Hines
Library Company of Philadelphia

See also the Logan entry in *DLB 24: American Colonial Writers, 1606–1734.*

BOOKS: *The Charge Delivered from the Bench to the Grand-Jury, at the Court of Quarter Sessions, Held for the County of Philadelphia, the 2nd. Day of September 1723*... (Philadelphia: Printed & sold by Andrew Bradford, 1723);

The Antidote. In Some Remarks on a Paper of David Lloyd's, Called A Vindication of the Legislative Power... (Philadelphia: Printed by Andrew Bradford, 1725);

A Dialogue Shewing, What's Therein to Be Found. A Motto Being Modish, For Want of Good Latin, Are Put English Quotations... (Philadelphia: S. Keimer, 1725);

A More Just Vindication of the Honorable Sir William Keith, Bart. Against the Unparalleled Abuses Put Upon Him, In a Scandalous Libel Call'd, A Just and Plain Vindication of Sir William Keith, &c. (Philadelphia: Printed by Andrew Bradford, 1726);

De plantarum generatione experimenta et meletemata (Philadelphia, 1737); republished as *Experimenta et meletemata de plantarum generatione*... (Leyden: C. Haak, 1739); English translation by Samuel Fothergill (London: Printed for C. Davis, 1747);

Demonstrationes de radiorum lucis in superficies sphaericas... (Leyden: C. Haak, 1741);

To Robert Jordan, and Others the Friends of the Yearly Meeting... (Philadelphia: Printed by B. Franklin, 1741).

TRANSLATIONS: Dionysius Cato, *Cato's Moral Distiches Englished in Couplets* (Philadelphia: Printed & sold by B. Franklin, 1735);

Marcus Tullius Cicero, *Cicero's Cato Major; or, His Discourse of Old Age* (Philadelphia: Printed & sold by B. Franklin, 1744; London: Printed by S. Austen, 1750).

James Logan was one of the most active political figures in colonial Philadelphia. He was also a scholar and perhaps the most extraordinary bookman of his time. In 1731, when Benjamin Franklin and his friends needed guidance in formulating their first order of books for the fledgling Library Company of Philadelphia, they went to James Logan, described in the Library Company meeting minutes of 29 March 1732 as "a Gentleman of universal Learning, and the best Judge of Books in these Parts." For their purposes of forming a library for intellectual advancement, Logan was the best judge in all of colonial America. His bibliophilic passion was as much for the contents of the books as for the aesthetic beauty of their bindings and printing.

James Logan was born in Lurgan, Ireland, on 20 October 1674, the son of Isabel Hume Logan and Patrick Logan, a Scottish Quaker schoolmaster. Educated by his father and from books, Logan became fluent in Greek and Latin and knew the basics of Hebrew, French, Italian, and Spanish before the age of thirteen. One of the few volumes which bears his mark of ownership as a youngster is a copy of Johann Buxtorf's *Lexicon Hebraicum et Chaldaicum* (Basel: Johan Konig and Fil, 1676), attesting to his early penchant for languages. Other interests carried throughout his life include astronomy, mathematics, physics, history both ancient and modern, the Greek and Latin classics, as well as the later classicists, natural history, philosophy, and especially botany.

When Patrick Logan retired from his position at a school in Bristol, England, in 1693, nineteen-year-old James succeeded him. It was here that Logan began to assemble his first personal library. Over the next few years, according to Logan's later recollections, he managed to procure over seven hundred volumes, including a copy of Ptolemy's *Almagest* (Venice: Liechtenstein, 1515), on only his schoolmaster's salary.

In 1698 Logan resigned from his position at the school, sold his library in Dublin, and set out to

James Logan; portrait painted by Thomas Sully in 1831, after the circa 1735–1745 portrait of Logan by Gustavus Hesselius
(Library Company of Philadelphia)

make a fortune. Using the money earned from the sale of his library, he purchased a cargo of linen and returned to Bristol a cloth merchant. The business failed within a year, but during that time he met and became friends with William Penn. Penn asked Logan to join him on his return voyage to Pennsylvania in 1699 as his personal secretary.

In Pennsylvania his position was one of increasing honor, responsibility, and wealth. He acted as the Penn family's official representative and held various political offices, including mayor of Philadelphia, governor of Pennsylvania, chief justice of the Pennsylvania Supreme Court, and chief negotiator with the Native Americans. He again tried his hand as a merchant and made a sizable fortune in land speculation and the Susquehanna fur trade. To facilitate transportation of his trade goods and furs,

Logan invented the Conestoga wagon, or covered wagon.

It was not long before Logan's thirst for intellectual stimulation again became a passion. His papers from this period, including his personal correspondence and record books, provide a detailed picture of his personality and book-buying habits. He repeatedly complained about the dearth of intellectual companionship and the general unavailability of good books in the colonies. To stave off intellectual boredom he struck up correspondences with those he viewed as his equals. Among his correspondents were successive governors of New York Robert Hunter and William Burnet, Quaker scholar Josiah Martin, Johann Albrecht Fabricius, British mathematician William Jones, Quaker physician John Fothergill, and Peter Collinson. He also began

Stenton, the Logan country estate outside Philadelphia

to collect books again. "Books are my disease," Logan once stated, and his relapse was an all-consuming one.

In 1708 Logan made his first important purchase of books – a collection of works on astronomy by Johann Bayer, Boulliau, Tycho Brahe, Hevelius, Giambattista Riccioli, and others, bought from Mary Margaret Zimmermann, the widow of Johann Jacob Zimmermann, a German astronomer. These were the earliest known German works to have come to Pennsylvania. A new library now begun, Logan decided to concentrate on mathematics next, purchasing copies of Sir Isaac Newton's *Principia Mathematica* (London: Jussu Societatis Regiae ac Typis Josephi Streater, 1687), the first copy known in America, and Charles Hayes's *Treatise of Fluxions* (London: Edward Midwinter, 1704). With the help of these books he mastered the new concept of calculus.

Opportunities to purchase such books did not often present themselves in Philadelphia. Most transactions were transatlantic and often took months to complete. An urgent business trip for William Penn in 1710 allowed Logan to immerse himself in the book world of London. He spent time and money at all of the major booksellers – Midwinter, Bateman, and Innys – and made contact with London's great thinkers such as Newton, John Flamsteed, Charles Hayes, and Francis Hauksbee. He returned to the colonies in 1712 refreshed and had a "Great Chest of Books" shipped to him by his friend and agent John Askew.

Doing business with the English and Continental booksellers proved to be difficult for Logan. He rarely dealt with the booksellers directly, believing them to be dishonest, and attempted to cultivate relationships with like-minded gentlemen who would act as his agents. Correspondence with these men reveals a mind that knew exactly what it wanted regarding the condition and price of a book; he was even able to suggest booksellers who might have copies of something he had seen years before. His persnickety personality colored all of these relationships, however, and it seemed that no one ever truly pleased him.

His insatiable curiosity about the contents of all of the books he purchased made him by default a bibliographer. He inspected, collated, and read them all. The following portion of a letter to John

James Logan's library at Stenton

Whiston written in 1749 is typical of those written to many of his book scouts from London to Amsterdam:

> I return to thee that miserably blotted Basil in 3 Voll. which thou ought to have been ashamed to send me at any rate (Pray look to Vol. I) and what is most scandalous, the same words that are printed Text are Copied over again, for Greek is nearly as familiar to me as English, . . . I send thee also Eusebius de Praeparatione Evangelij, for it wants 3 leaves between pages 378 and 385 left out in the first binding which I discovered solely by my lately reading over that beautiful Edition of Robt Stephens with his Demonstr. which I bought of C Bateman in 1710, and with that I also send thee his Demonstr. both printed in the same vile Character in lieu of which send me the Paris Edition of 1628 charging me with the difference of the Cost if any. I send thee also thy Spenser which thou charged at a Guinea, tho' Tho Osborn had sent me before a much better, that is a fairer and cleaner one for 16 (s), at which rate thou may give me credit for this, by which I lose a Crown.

Toward the end of another letter to Whiston about defects and high prices, Logan states, "Thou may therefore well excuse me for finding fault with thee as I doe when thy prices are unreasonable, [I] who have been a buyer of Books above these 50 years and am not to be put off as a common American, as thou has divers times served me, for I know a book well."

He knew his books very well. In 1721 Logan wrote to Johann Fabricius to note an error in Fabricius's *Bibliotheca Graeca* (Hamburg, 1705–1728). Fabricius had identified the earliest copy of Ptolemy's *Almagest* as the Basel, 1538 edition; Logan remembered having a Venice edition of about 1500 in his first library, the one he sold in Dublin. He wondered if Fabricius might help him to obtain a copy of this edition or at least a copy of the Basel, 1538 for his new collection. Fabricius was unsuccessful. Undaunted, Logan made the same request of a friend in Dublin who was not only successful but produced the same copy Logan had sold years before.

Book dealers were not the only ones with whom Logan argued. Many of the surviving volumes in his library bear the literary scars of Logan's battles with their authors. Newton was criticized for his chronological system and for removing all mention of Gottfried Leibnitz from his *Principia;* Logan

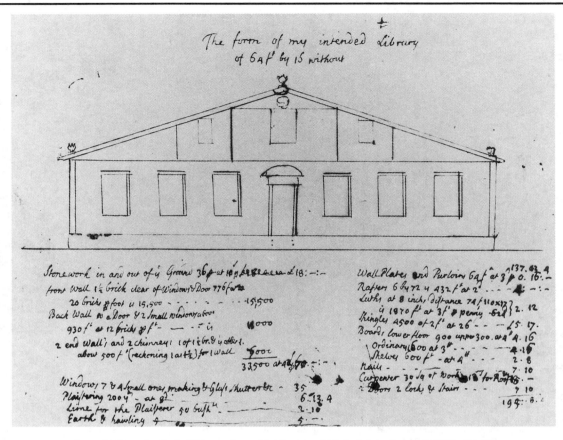

Logan's plans for the building to house his library, which he left to the city of Philadelphia

added words to foreign-language dictionaries and stars to John Flamsteed's *Celestial Atlas* (London, 1729); he suggested variant translations of Greek and Latin classics and corrected errors in Ephraim Chambers's *Encyclopedia* (London: James and John Knapton, 1728) and Philip Miller's *Gardeners Dictionary* (London: C. Rirington, 1733).

In 1714 James Logan had married Sarah Read, daughter of Charles Read, a prominent Philadelphia merchant. By October 1728 Sarah had given birth to seven children, three of whom died very young. His social position and the size of his family led Logan to draw up plans for a much larger house outside the city to accommodate his family and his books. Late in 1728, just before work began on his new home, Logan fell and damaged his hipbone, leaving him crippled. Two years later he began moving most of his growing collection to his new country estate named Stenton. He moved only books he deemed worthy of serious study, weeding out what must have been many early Philadelphia imprints. No pamphlets, official documents, or copies of his own writings were moved.

Away from the bustle of city life and forced to curtail his daily routine due to his physical ailments, Logan devoted more of his time and attention to his library and writing. He suffered two strokes a year apart, in 1739 and 1740, leaving his right side paralyzed. His mind remained active, and the years of his convalescence from his hip injury and strokes were also his most productive in terms of his nonpolitical writings. Two of his major works were translations – Dionysius Cato's *Moral Distiches* (1735) and Marcus Tullius Cicero's *Cato Major* (1744). Both were printed by Benjamin Franklin, and the *Cato Major* is considered by many to be Franklin's finest piece of printing. An interest in aerial germination of seeds sparked by reading William Wollaston's *Religion of Nature Delineated* (London: Samuel Palmer, 1726) and Richard Bradley's *New Improvements of Planting and Gardening* (London: W. Mears, 1726) led Logan to experiment with corn. He published his findings – the first to describe accurately the mechanization of plant fertilization – under the supervision of Dutch naturalist Johann Friedrich Gronovius as *Experimenta et meletemata de*

Title page for the catalogue of Logan's collection

plantarum generatione . . . (1739). An English translation by Samuel Fothergill was published in London by C. Davis in 1747. Several pieces of his correspondence with Hans Sloane from this period were published in the *Philosophical Transactions* of the Royal Society. His last major effort was a philosophical work entitled "The Duties of Man Deduced from Nature." It was the earliest nontheological treatise on philosophy attempted in America. He completed almost three of the six intended chapters before abandoning the project in 1742.

He also continued to augment his library. But as the collection grew and developed, so did his concern for its future. None of his children shared his passion for books, and he could see little point in leaving his collection to any of them. In 1742, in a letter to Josiah Martin, Logan first mentioned his intention "to bestow all my Latin, Greek, Oriental and Mathem[atical] Books on ye City of Philad[elph]ia." With the idea of public benefit in mind, Logan frantically added to the collection from this point until his death. He had Isaac Norris, his son-in-law, compile a catalogue of the library in 1743–1744. Though incomplete, it is the earliest of its kind with such complete bibliographical descriptions. Logan himself designed the building in which his library would be housed and set up an endowment for the collection. After his death in 1751 his family carried out his wishes, and in 1754 his collection of more than twenty-six hundred volumes was brought from Stenton to the Loganian Library on Sixth Street in Philadelphia.

Logan deeded his library to the city so that all educated persons would have access to it. Its reception and use by the public, however, was not what Logan expected, and the collection languished. In 1792 James Logan, Jr., took steps to transfer his father's treasures to the more active Library Company of Philadelphia. The Library Company's board of directors added an additional wing to a new building on Fifth Street to house the collection. Logan's original library and those volumes added to the Loganian Library after his death remain among the collections of the Library Company.

During his lifetime James Logan had amassed one of the finest collections of scholarly works known in America. He knew well the value of all the works he acquired and their value as a collection. He also knew the book trade, and took pride in his talents as a price negotiator and bargain hunter. In a letter to Peter Collinson, Logan once wrote, "I have made as good use of the best books on the Subject [of medicine] as many others who have ye honour of writing MD."

Biographies:

Wilson Armistead, *Memoirs of James Logan* (London: Gilpin, 1851);

Frederick B. Tolles, *James Logan and the Culture of Provincial America* (Boston: Little, Brown, 1957).

References:

Catalogus Bibliothecae Loganianae (Philadelphia, 1760);
Edwin Wolf II, *The Library of James Logan of Philadelphia, 1674–1751* (Philadelphia: Library Company of Philadelphia, 1974).

Papers:

There is a wealth of surviving material concerning Logan and his library, including much of the correspondence between Logan and his book agents. The papers of James Logan are housed in the Logan Family collection at the Historical Society of Pennsylvania. These papers include correspondence, among which are letters from William Penn, and some of Logan's scholarly, scientific, and biographical papers, 1681–1753; letter books, 1701–1750; correspondence copied by Deborah Logan, 1700–1747; letters on political and business affairs, 1698–1769; documents relating to Indian affairs, 1701–1802; archives of the Provincial Council, 1694–1755; Logan's "Justification" before the assembly, 1709; his receipt book, 1702–1709; his account book, 1712–1720; his ledger, 1720–1727; and his daybook, 1722–1723.

Amy Lowell

(9 February 1874 – 12 May 1925)

See also the Lowell entry in *DLB 54: American Poets, 1880–1945*, First Series.

BOOKS: *Dream Drops or Stories from Fairy Land by a Dreamer,* by Amy Lowell, Katherine Bigelow Lawrence Lowell, and Elizabeth Lowell (Boston: Privately printed by Cupples & Hurd, 1887);

A Dome of Many-Coloured Glass (Boston & New York: Houghton Mifflin, 1912);

Sword Blades and Poppy Seed (New York: Macmillan, 1914);

Six French Poets: Studies in Contemporary Literature (New York: Macmillan, 1915; London: Macmillan, 1916);

Men, Women and Ghosts (New York: Macmillan, 1916; London: Macmillan, 1916);

Tendencies in Modern American Poetry (New York: Macmillan, 1917; Oxford: Blackwell, 1921);

Can Grande's Castle (New York: Macmillan, 1918; Oxford: Blackwell, 1920);

Pictures of the Floating World (New York: Macmillan, 1919);

Legends (Boston & New York: Houghton Mifflin, 1921);

A Critical Fable (Boston & New York: Houghton Mifflin, 1922);

John Keats (Boston & New York: Houghton Mifflin, 1925);

What's O'Clock, edited by Ada Dwyer Russell (Boston & New York: Houghton Mifflin, 1925);

East Wind, edited by Russell (Boston & New York: Houghton Mifflin, 1926);

The Madonna of Carthagena (N.p.: Privately printed, 1927);

Ballads for Sale, edited by Russell (Boston & New York: Houghton Mifflin, 1927);

Selected Poems of Amy Lowell, edited by John Livingston Lowes (Boston & New York: Houghton Mifflin, 1928);

Poetry and Poets: Essays, edited by Ferris Greenslet (Boston & New York: Houghton Mifflin, 1930);

The Complete Poetical Works of Amy Lowell (Boston: Houghton Mifflin, 1955).

OTHER: "In a Garden," in *Des Imagistes: An Anthology,* edited by Ezra Pound (New York: A. & C. Boni, 1914; London: Poetry Bookshop, 1914), p. 38;

Some Imagist Poets: An Anthology, edited, with contributions, by Lowell (Boston & New York: Houghton Mifflin, 1915; London: Constable, 1915);

Some Imagist Poets, 1916: An Annual Anthology, edited, with contributions, by Lowell (Boston & New York: Houghton Mifflin, 1916; London: Constable, 1916);

Some Imagist Poets, 1917: An Annual Anthology, edited, with contributions, by Lowell (Boston & New York: Houghton Mifflin, 1917);

Fir-Flower Tablets: Poems Translated from the Chinese, English versions by Lowell, from the translations of Florence Ayscough (Boston & New York: Houghton Mifflin, 1921; London: Constable, 1922).

Amy Lowell of Boston was described by A. Edward Newton in his *The Amenities of Book-Collecting and Kindred Affections* (1918) as "A poet of rare distinction, a critic, and America's most distinguished woman collector." Having begun collecting at an early age, she ultimately assembled a literary library of some twelve thousand volumes, which included first editions, association copies, and autograph manuscripts of the great writers of English and American literature. She had a particular interest in John Keats and built one of the largest private collections of Keatsiana.

Lowell described herself to be "of thoroughgoing New England stock." She was a descendant of Percival Lowle, a merchant from Bristol who immigrated in 1639 to Newbury, Massachusetts. The Lowells of subsequent generations made their way to the pinnacle of Boston society, as the popular saying "the Cabots speak only to the Lowells and the Lowells speak only to God" attests. Amy Lowell's grandfathers, John Amory Lowell and Abbott Lawrence, were pioneers in the development of the cotton industry in New England. Lawrence also served as ambassador to the Court of Saint James's.

Amy Lowell, circa 1916

Her father, Augustus Lowell, followed in his father's footsteps in his business interests, in his love of horticulture, and in civic responsibilities. Her mother, Katherine Bigelow Lawrence, was an accomplished linguist and musician.

Amy Lowell was born on 9 February 1874 at Sevenels, the family's ten-acre estate in Brookline, Massachusetts. She was the youngest of five children. Her brothers, Percival and Abbott Lawrence, were in their sophomore and freshman years at Harvard University; her sisters, Katherine and Elizabeth, were sixteen and twelve at the time of her birth. Lowell was first tutored at home and later attended Boston private schools until the age of seventeen.

At the age of six, Lowell was given a copy of Jacob Abbott's *Rollo Learning to Read* (Boston: John

Allen, 1835). Her biographer S. Foster Damon recorded her recollection of the occasion:

> I perfectly remember the awakening of the acquisitive instinct for which it was directly responsible. The book... had been given to my mother when she was six years old.... I suppose it was brought out for my amusement, but it aroused such a passion of covetous desire in my small mind as to shake it to its foundations. The mere touch of that straight-grained morocco was a delight, the old wood-cuts, coloured with crayons doubtless by my mother, were to me gems of the purest art.

She did not rest until all the Rollo books, and there were many of them, made their way from a bookcase in the middle hall of their Boston home on Commonwealth Avenue to her private bookcase in her nursery. By the time she was fourteen, she had

Sevenels, Lowell's estate

read most of the novels of Sir Walter Scott, James Fenimore Cooper, Charles Dickens, Frederick Marryat, and Jules Verne. She moved on to the writings of William Makepeace Thackeray, Charlotte Brontë, Anthony Trollope, and Jane Austen.

In 1891 Lowell made her first "major" purchase of books: a set of the complete works of Scott, bought with her Christmas money. After her father's death in 1900 Lowell purchased Sevenels (her mother having died in 1895). Lowell remodeled the ground floor of the house to accommodate her expanding library. A wall was removed between two rooms, and she paneled the enlarged room in oak brought over from England. Large built-in bookcases were constructed with invisible shutters that could be pulled down and locked when the house was closed. One section was fitted with false backs to conceal the door to her room-sized airtight safe in which she kept her manuscript collection.

In his *A Magnificent Farce and Other Diversions of a Book-Collector* (1921), Newton describes the effect of Lowell's outspoken and forthright manner on her

collecting: "Miss Lowell began forming her library many years ago, under the direction of the elder Quaritch; and I can quite understand that, when she breezed into his shop in Piccadilly, he gave her the run of the place and allowed her to make her own prices." She visited the firm of Bernard Quaritch on her return from Europe in 1896 and Egypt in 1897–1898. But it was E. H. Dring with whom she dealt on a regular basis at Quaritch; their correspondence covers a period of over twenty-four years. From Quaritch in 1898 she bought several books illuminated by William Blake. In 1904 she acquired from the firm the largest portion of her collection of autograph letters of John Keats as well as early drafts in his holograph of "Song of Four Fairies" and "To J[ames] R[ice]." They had been part of the papers of John Taylor, who along with James Augustus Hessey had published Keats. The Taylor papers contained letters about Keats, among them Joseph Severn's letter to Taylor describing Keats's final days in Rome. Taylor's "Memoir of Richard Abbey" was also among the papers.

Lowell's library at Sevenels

Lowell added to her Keats holdings in 1905 when she bought from Dodd, Mead and Company the Rowfant Library Keats collection, which had belonged to Frederick Locker-Lampson. Included were early holograph drafts of "On First Looking into Chapman's Homer," "The Eve of St. Agnes," and "Otho the Great," and autograph letters to Severn, Fanny Keats, Jane Reynolds, and others. At the Harry Buxton Forman sale held at the Anderson galleries in 1920, she acquired a holograph draft with revisions of "Lines on Seeing a Lock of Milton's Hair." In 1921 she purchased a fragment of an early draft of "Isabella, or the Pot of Basil" from New York bookseller Gabriel Wells. At the William Harris Arnold sale in 1924, she bought letters written by Keats to his brother George and a fragment of a draft with revisions of "The Cap and Bells." Three letters from Keats to Fanny Brawne made their way into Lowell's collection from a variety of sources. She acquired an early draft with revisions of the ode "To Autumn" as a gift from Elizabeth Ward (later Mrs. Elizabeth Perkins), one of Lowell's Boston friends who had inherited the manuscript.

Of Keats's three published works, Lowell owned seven copies, five of which were presentation copies: two of the *Poems* (London: Ollier, 1817) – one of which was presented to Keats and annotated throughout – one of *Endymion: A Poetic Romance* (London: Taylor and Hessey, 1818), and two of *Lamia, Isabella, The Eve of St. Agnes, and Other Poems* (London: Taylor and Hessey, 1820). The volume prized most by Lowell was the copy of *Lamia* presented to Brawne with a modest inscription: "To F. B. from J. K." When it came on the market in the 1920 sale of the library of Harry Buxton Forman, Lowell was determined to have it. As recorded by Damon, Lowell engaged A. S. W. Rosenbach to bid for her at the Forman sale on the principle that "I have always found that it was necessary to stifle the opposition in auction sales, and the only way to do so is by getting the opposition on your side."

Rosenbach succeeded in acquiring the copy of *Lamia* for $4,050. Her enthusiasm for the book is evident in the correspondence with Rosenbach, "As you assured me that the book would be mine, I really have no fear in the matter, but mine it must and

Amy Lowell, circa 1920

shall be even if I buy nothing else for some years. I consider it necessary as the crown of my collection of Keats's autograph copies." Rosenbach also sold Lowell a copy of William Hazlitt's *Characters of Shakespeare's Plays* (London: Ollier, 1817), which had been owned by Keats. Other books in Lowell's collection that had been owned by Keats included Leigh Hunt's *Foliage* (London: Ollier, 1818), Zachariah Jackson's *Shakespeare's Genius Justified* (London: Major, 1819), John Selden's *Titles of Honor* (London: Dring, 1672), and the first volume of Edmund Spenser's *Works* (London: Tonson, 1715).

In a letter to Jeanette Marks, Lowell comments on the influence her Keats collection had on her verse: "I think the constant studying of his manuscripts with his corrections, and seeing why he made them, has taught me more about writing poetry than anything else in the world." The format for her first book of poetry, *A Dome of Many-Coloured Glass* (1912), was modeled upon that of *Lamia*. She

was so pleased with the results that she continued to use the same format for each of her books of poetry.

In addition to the Keats collection, Lowell built up an extensive literary library — with an emphasis on poetry — which included autograph manuscripts, letters, and first and other early editions of English and American authors. Represented in the collection were Matthew Arnold, Jane Austen, Richard Doddridge Blackmore, William Blake, the Brontë sisters, Elizabeth Barrett Browning, Robert Browning, Robert Burns, Lord Byron, Thomas Carlyle, Arthur Hugh Clough, Samuel Taylor Coleridge, Stephen Crane, Emily Dickinson, George Eliot, Ralph Waldo Emerson, Thomas Hardy, Nathaniel Hawthorne, Samuel Johnson, Ben Jonson, Rudyard Kipling, Charles Lamb, D. H. Lawrence, Herman Melville, George Meredith, Edgar Allan Poe, Percy Bysshe Shelley, Richard Brinsley Sheridan, Alfred Tennyson, William Makepeace Thackeray, Anthony Trollope, Walt Whitman, William

Wordsworth, and others. Among the contemporary poets were Rupert Brooke, E. E. Cummings, Hilda Doolittle, T. S. Eliot, Robert Frost, Vachel Lindsay, John Masefield, Edgar Lee Masters, Edna St. Vincent Millay, Harold Monro, Ezra Pound, Edward Arlington Robinson, Carl Sandburg, Siegfried Sassoon, Sara Teasdale, and William Butler Yeats.

Included in this wealth of material were Scott's own interleaved and annotated copy of *Anne of Geierstein* (Edinburgh: Printed for Cadell, 1829) and presentation copies of Hardy's *The Woodlanders* (London: Macmillan, 1887) and *Wessex Tales* (London: Macmillan, 1888) given by the author to A. C. Swinburne and Robert Browning. Perhaps the most fascinating of these association copies was Hester Lynch Thrale Piozzi's set of the eighth edition of James Boswell's *Life of Samuel Johnson, LL.D.* (London: T. Cadell and W. Davies, 1816). Piozzi, one of Johnson's biographers, acquired the book in Bath in 1816. The work later belonged to Abraham Hayward, who edited Piozzi's autobiography and letters; Lowell acquired the set from Quaritch. Newton, himself a mighty collector of eighteenth-century English books in general and of Samuel Johnson and James Boswell in particular, described Lowell's set as that "which, above all others, every Johnsonian would wish to own." The set contains some 575 marginal comments.

Lowell was a significant figure in the book-collecting world of the first quarter of the twentieth century. An occasion which typified both her passion for bibliophily and her powerful presence was a dinner held in her honor at Rosenbach's emporium in Philadelphia, an evening later recounted by Rosenbach in his memoir. Among the guests were Mrs. Alexander Hamilton Rice (the mother of Harry Elkins Widener), Newton, Americana collector Herschel Jones, artist Joseph Pennell, and Ada Russell, Lowell's companion. The evening began at eight o'clock and continued well into the morning hours. Lowell dominated the conversation, first arguing persuasively that her manuscripts of Keats's "On First Looking into Chapman's Homer" was earlier than the manuscript in the Morgan collection. She went on to insist that modern verse had a vital quality lacking in the old. Pennell took up the other side of the argument, and the two debated with occasional commentary from the others. As the discussion drew to a close, Lowell stubbed out her cigar and exclaimed, "I'm dying of hunger. It's four-thirty; time for something to eat!" In summing up the evening Jones commented: "Some dinner – some terrapin – some Amy – some cigar Amy smoked." Delighted with the occasion, Lowell later wrote to Newton, "I look upon Rosey's [Rosenbach's] dinner as one of the most extraordinary and interesting things I ever went to."

In addition to her writing and collecting, Lowell spent much of her time lecturing and reading before university audiences and at societies and clubs all over the country. In the spring of 1925, on the eve of a visit to England for a lecture tour, she suffered a severe hernia attack. An operation was scheduled for 13 May, but on 12 May Lowell suffered a cerebral hemorrhage and died at her home in Brookline. Her collections of books and literary manuscripts were left to Harvard University along with trust funds for purchasing additions to it and for a traveling-poet fellowship.

Biographies:
S. Foster Damon, *Amy Lowell: A Chronicle* (Boston & New York: Houghton Mifflin, 1935);
F. Cudworth Flint, *Amy Lowell* (Minneapolis: University of Minnesota Press, 1969).

References:
Winifred Bryher, *Amy Lowell, a Critical Appreciation* (London: Eyre & Spottiswoode, 1918);
Jean Gould, *Amy: The World of Amy Lowell and the Imagist Movement* (New York: Dodd, Mead, 1975);
Horace Gregory, *Amy Lowell; Portrait of the Poet in Her Time* (Edinburgh: Nelson, 1958);
Maxwell Luria, "Miss Lowell and Mr. Newton: The Record of a Literary Friendship," *Harvard Library Bulletin* (January 1981): 5–34;
A. Edward Newton, *The Amenities of Book-Collecting and Kindred Affections* (Boston: Atlantic Monthly Press, 1918);
Newton, *A Magnificent Farce and Other Diversions of a Book-Collector* (Boston: Atlantic Monthly Press, 1921);
A. S. W. Rosenbach, *The Unpublishable Memoirs* (New York: Kennerley, 1917);
Edwin Wolf II and John Fleming, *Rosenbach: A Biography* (Cleveland & New York: World Publishing, 1960).

Leonard L. Mackall

(29 January 1879 – 19 May 1937)

Carolyn Smith
Johns Hopkins University

BOOK: *Catalogue of the Wymberley Jones DeRenne Georgia Library at Wormsloe, Isle of Hope near Savannah, Georgia* (Wormsloe: Privately printed, 1931).

OTHER: *Goethes Gespräche, Gesamtausgabe,* second edition, 5 volumes, edited by Mackall, Flodoard Freiherr von Biedermann, Max Morris, and Hans Gerhard Graf (Leipzig: F. von Biedermann, 1909–1911);

"Servetus Notes," in *Contributions to Medical and Biological Research, Dedicated to Sir William Osler, in Honour of his Seventieth Birthday, July 12, 1919, by his Pupils and Co-workers,* 2 volumes, edited by William H. Welch and others (New York: Hoeber, 1919), pp. 767–777;

William Osler, *The Evolution of Modern Medicine,* edited by Mackall, Fielding H. Garrison, Harvey Cushing, and Edward C. Streeter (New Haven: Yale University Press, 1921);

Bibliotheca Osleriana; a Catalogue of Books Illustrating the History of Medicine and Science, Collected, Arranged and Annotated by Sir William Osler, Bt. and Bequeathed to McGill University, edited by Mackall, William W. Francis, R. H. Hill, and Archibald Malloch (Oxford: Clarendon Press, 1929);

"Goethe's Letter to Joseph Green Cogswell, Dated July 29, 1819, on Presenting a Set of his Works to Harvard College, Now Reprinted From the Original Manuscript," in *Essays Offered to Herbert Putnam by his Colleagues and Friends on his Thirtieth Anniversary as Librarian of Congress, 5 April 1929,* edited by William Warner Bishop and Andrew Keogh (New Haven: Yale University Press, 1929).

SELECTED PERIODICAL PUBLICATIONS – UNCOLLECTED: "The First Translation from the Rubáiyát of Omar Khayyám into a Modern Language," *Lamp,* 27 (December 1903): 314–316;

"Briefwechsel zwischen Goethe und Amerikanern; Goethes Geschenck an die Harvard University," *Goethe Jahrbuch,* 25 (1904): 3–37;

"Goethes Edler Philosoph," *Euphorion,* 11 (1904): 103–106;

"Thomas Carlyle's Translation of Faust's Curse," *Archiv für das Studium der neueren Sprachen und Literaturen,* 112 (1904): 388–391;

"Goethe and the Carlyles: Some Notes and Corrections," *Athenaeum,* no. 4424 (10 August 1912): 142;

"Sources of the Fantasmagoriana (1812)," *Englische Studien,* 49 (January 1916): 326–332;

"The Wymberley Jones DeRenne Georgia Library by Its Librarian," *Georgia Historical Quarterly,* 2 (June 1918): 63–86;

"Goethe's Quatrain 'Liegt dir Gestern klar und offen,' a Paraphrase from Maucroix," *American Journal of Philology,* 41 (1920): 379–383;

"A Letter from the Virginia Loyalist John Randolph to Thomas Jefferson, Written in London in 1779," *Proceedings of the American Antiquarian Society,* new series 30 (April 1920): 17–31;

"Sir William Osler," *Papers of the Bibliographical Society of America,* 14 (1920): 20–32;

"Edward Longworthy and the First Attempt to Write a Separate History of Georgia, with Selections from the Long-lost Longworthy Papers," *Georgia Historical Quarterly,* 7 (March 1923): 1–18;

"Coleridge Marginalia on Wieland and Schiller," *Modern Language Review,* 19 (July 1924): 344–346;

"A Manuscript of the 'Christianismi Restitutio' of Servetus, Placing the Discovery of the Pulmonary Circulation as Early as 1546," *Proceedings of the Royal Society of Medicine,* 17, Section History of Medicine (1924): 35–38;

"The Source of Force's Tract 'A Brief Account of the Establishment of the Colony of Georgia under Gen. James Oglethorpe February 1,

*Leonard L. Mackall (Special Collections, Milton S. Eisenhower
Library, Johns Hopkins University)*

1733,' " *American Historical Review,* 30 (January
   1925): 30–308;
"Six Books," *Bulletin of the Johns Hopkins Hospital,* 46
   (January 1930): 83–90;
"Authorship of the Original of Goethe's
   'Hochländisch,' " *Modern Language Notes,* 51
   (February 1936): 94–96.

On 21 September 1924 the *New York Herald
Tribune* began publishing a Sunday book review supplement which included a column called "Notes for
Bibliophiles." Leonard Leopold Mackall, a collector
and independent scholar living most of the time in
Savannah, Georgia, edited and usually wrote the
weekly column from the first issue of the supplement to 1937. He covered the news of the book
world and also wrote substantial articles about literature and aspects of book history and design, drawing on wide knowledge and an up-to-date network

of friends and acquaintances occupied with libraries, collecting, and the antiquarian trade.

Leonard L. Mackall was born in Baltimore on
29 January 1879. His father, Leonard Covington
Mackall, was from Maryland, and his mother, Louisa Frederica Lawton Mackall, was from Georgia.
They were socially well connected and had independent means. For a while the family lived in Philadelphia, but after her husband's death in 1890 Louisa
moved to Savannah with her three children.

In 1896 Leonard graduated from Lawrence-
ville School in New Jersey, then traveled in France
and Germany for nearly a year with his mother and
younger brother and sister. He entered Johns Hopkins University in 1897, planning to be an electrical
engineer, but failed mathematics. He did excel in
modern languages, however, and became greatly interested in German literature. Books fascinated
Mackall, even as an undergraduate, and he endeav-

ored to learn everything he could about them, not only their content but their production and history, and who had owned individual copies.

One of Mackall's student friends was William W. Francis, godson and cousin of William Osler, then physician in chief of the Johns Hopkins Hospital and professor of medicine at the university. A book collector, Osler bought *Essays on Physiognomy* (London: J. Murray and others, 1789–1810), by Johann Caspar Lavater, with whom he was not familiar. Francis mentioned the Lavater work to Mackall, who knew at once that the author was one of Johann Wolfgang von Goethe's correspondents. Mackall asked to see the book, and Francis introduced him to Osler, who accepted him as a fellow collector.

After graduating from Johns Hopkins, Mackall entered the Harvard Law School, but he left after two years. While at Harvard he had met Charles Eliot Norton, the retired professor of art history who had edited the correspondence of Goethe and Thomas Carlyle. Norton and Mackall became good friends. Through Norton's encouragement Mackall gave up his law studies and in 1902 entered the University of Berlin, where, in spite of serious illness, he began to work on his first scholarly publications, including a study of Goethe's relations with New England intellectuals. In a 27 December 1904 letter to Mackall, Norton described his friend as "one of the most thorough and exact of the students of Goethe's life and works."

Mackall reentered Johns Hopkins as a graduate student in German in 1904. In its emphasis on philology and attention to detail the department was well suited to Mackall. His interest as a student and collector focused on the background of intellectual history — the small facts that shape the larger picture: the influences on a writer's work, his sources, and the historical/cultural circumstances surrounding a book's printing and reprinting.

In May of 1906 Mackall was appointed a fellow in the German department, but he resigned in October to go abroad. His health again was poor, and he decided to continue his studies in Germany at a slower pace than would have been required at Johns Hopkins. From 1906 to the end of 1915 he lived mostly in Jena and took courses at the University of Jena but apparently did not try for a degree. Jena was convenient to Weimar, the location of important resources for Goethe studies. On the strength of his earlier work Mackall became one of the editors of the new collected edition of Goethe's conversations, published at Leipzig from 1909 to 1911. He contributed articles on literature to schol-

arly journals, using his own growing collection as well as the university library for his work.

Mackall traveled in Germany, France, England, and Scotland and sometimes returned to the United States for visits. Years later, in a memorial essay on Mackall, his friend Lawrence C. Wroth, librarian of the John Carter Brown Library in Providence, Rhode Island, recalled a story of Mackall in Paris. Two of his friends thought Mackall's bibliographical interests to be a useless affectation and decided to play a trick on him. That evening they began a dinner conversation about a variation on page 63 of a certain copy of a Renaissance book — information they had picked up from a dealer that morning and only partly understood. "You've got it all wrong," said Mackall to his friends. "That variation is not on page 63 because there are only fifty-two pages in the book." He went on to tell who owned the copy in question and who had owned it before, and he explained reprints, variants, and textual changes to his friends so thoroughly and lucidly that they never again questioned his knowledge or its value.

In England Mackall visited Osler, who had served as Regius Professor of Medicine at Oxford since 1905. Osler was building his library on the history of medicine (now at McGill University in Montreal), and Mackall helped him with acquisitions. Osler's collection included works by Michael Servetus, the Spanish theologian and physician, who, in a theological work, described for the first time the circulation of the blood through the lungs. Osler published a pamphlet on Servetus in 1909, and Mackall, having found the bibliographical problems of his rare works fascinating, began to collect them on his own.

Mackall was appointed honorary secretary for England and America of the Bibliophily Section of the Leipzig International Book Exhibition in 1914, with responsibility for arranging loans by collectors, among them Thomas J. Wise and Seymour DeRicci. After the outbreak of World War I, Mackall, indifferent throughout his life to politics on any scale, studied and traveled as before. In December of 1915 he went home for a visit, leaving his books and papers in Jena.

An acquaintance of Mackall's in Savannah, Wymberley Jones DeRenne, was a collector of books on the history of Georgia and the Confederacy and constructed a building on his estate, Wormsloe, to house the collection. In March 1916 DeRenne was still adding to his collection and hoped to publish a catalogue when, at his urging, Mackall became his librarian. Mackall had an assistant for

Leonard L. Mackall (right) and his friend Robert Bridges, editor of Scribner's Magazine, *at the Century Club; a pencil sketch by the club librarian (Leonard Leopold Mackall Collection, Special Collections, Milton S. Eisenhower Library, Johns Hopkins University)*

the cataloguing and worked on purchases with DeRenne, who was enthusiastic about the results he achieved. "I often think of the valuable additions you have acquired for the library through your energy and tact," DeRenne wrote Mackall from New York City on 16 April 1916.

DeRenne died on 23 June, but his son Wymberley wished the library work to continue, although he may not have understood it, and Mackall remained at his post. Mackall invited George Watson Cole, librarian of the Huntington Library, to catalogue the principal rarities. When the United States entered World War I, however, Wymberley DeRenne joined the army, and Mackall was faced with only limited support as a consequence. He began using part of his salary to make acquisitions. The library was finally closed in July 1918; in October of the same year Mackall was elected a member of the American Antiquarian Society for his work on Georgia history and bibliography. Despite their financial difficulties after the war, Wymberley DeRenne and his sisters wanted the catalogue of the li-

brary completed and published. Mackall found a copy editor to prepare his work for the press. He wrote a preface to the catalogue when it was published in 1931.

From 1919 to 1921 Mackall lived most of the time in New York City, where his mother and younger brother and sister, who were both married, also resided. With the help of his brother-in-law, the artist Gari Melchers, Mackall joined the Century and Coffee House Clubs, and George Watson Cole sponsored his membership in the Grolier Club. A sociable man, Mackall derived pleasure from his participation in the clubs, and the clubs provided him with contacts that furthered his book interests and certainly gave him his opportunity at the *New York Herald Tribune.*

In New York he wrote book reviews for the *Literary Review* of the *New York Evening Post,* and he continued the bibliographic work inspired by Osler's interest in Servetus. "Servetus Notes," Mackall's research discoveries in the bibliography of the physician/theologian, appeared in the collection of essays published in honor of Osler's seventieth birthday in July 1919. Mackall intended the notes to supplement and correct Osler's 1909 pamphlet.

Osler died in December 1919, leaving historical and bibliographic projects unfinished. Mackall was one of the editors of his lectures, *The Evolution of Modern Medicine,* which Yale published in 1921, and helped edit the catalogue of Osler's library, the *Bibliotheca Osleriana* (1929). He was one of the friends Osler himself had designated to complete it. The principal editor, William W. Francis, sent him proofs from Oxford as the work progressed. In 1923 Mackall went to Oxford at Lady Osler's invitation and found that there was tension between Francis and Lady Osler, who differed on the speed and detail with which the catalogue should be produced. Although, like Lady Osler, Francis was Mackall's friend, he was nervous at Mackall's presence; this is perhaps the reason why Mackall declined to be listed as an editor when the catalogue was published.

New York was becoming too expensive, so Mackall moved to Savannah in 1921 with his mother. Yet he continued to do business in New York. In September 1924 Mackall undertook his column, "Notes for Bibliophiles," for fifty dollars a week. There had been other book columns, notably "The Bibliographer," which George H. Sargent, a newspaperman, had been writing for the *Boston Evening Transcript* since 1903. Yet, unlike Sargent, who was a popularizer, Mackall took a scholarly approach. When possible Mackall was as careful in preparing his column as he was in his work for academic journals. His earliest columns, in fact, had footnotes. He invited outside contributors when a specialist was needed, and sometimes he dealt in great detail with bibliographic matters such as printers' marks, types, editions and issues, literary hoaxes, and the publishing history of *Candide.* Often he simply reported the news of books: sales, exhibitions, and events such as the opening of new libraries. He was a merciless reviewer of new books, reporting authors' factual errors and the resources they had ignored. In 1930 William Edwin Rudge of Mount Vernon, New York, reprinted Mackall's review of Wroth's *Abel Buell of Connecticut, Silversmith, Type Founder & Engraver* (1926) as an attractive small book limited to forty copies. A year later the Columbia University Press showed interest in publishing a group of the columns, and Mackall chose fifty-eight he considered his most successful; but the project did not go any further.

Writing was difficult for Mackall. His columns, although competent and informative in sub-

stance, were stiff and dry in tone and style. There is scarcely a hint in his published work of the attractive personality that drew people to him. Mackall inspires confidence in his readers, but he does not entertain them.

Mackall's library was his principal source for research, although he used institutional ones as well, frequently sending for photostats. As a scholar and newspaper writer he kept in touch with other researchers and anyone who might help him with information. He also gave more help than he received, sometimes volunteering it. He read and commented on articles being prepared for the new *Columbia Encyclopedia;* checked *American Book Prices Current* for its publisher, Dutton; advised biographers of people he had known; and helped with exhibitions at the Grolier Club and the New York Academy of Medicine, which named him its consultant in bibliography in 1930.

Mackall was a general collector, almost entirely of books but sometimes of manuscripts. Responding to a questionnaire for the 1922 edition of "Private Book Collectors in the United States," he listed his interests as "Antiquarian Bibliography, Superstition, Early Science, Servetus, Goethe, Byron, Georgia History, Comparative Literature." He steadily watched catalogues and used his money with caution. Mackall detested flamboyant dealers who inflated prices; he avoided high spots and developed a collection of rarities and books for reference which belonged together logically.

The books he had collected in Europe and America took up space in every room of his Savannah house and were arranged without noticeable order. Mackall's catalogue was his memory, which rarely failed. If he happened to be in New York and needed to consult a book, he would write to a cousin in Savannah with exact directions for finding and shipping it. The wooden house presented a risk, so Mackall stored his most valuable books in his Century Club locker, where, like the other members, he also kept a supply of alcohol during Prohibition.

Mackall did not forget, as he bought books and manuscripts, that they would belong to others after him, and he often gave them away, taking satisfaction in placing them appropriately. He was a member of the Grolier Club's library committee and presented more than three hundred titles of early bibliography to fill gaps in its collection. He gave books on the history of medicine to the new Welch Medical Library at Johns Hopkins when it opened. As a student in Germany, Mackall had published a letter Goethe had written to the American librarian Joseph Green Cogswell concerning a gift of the German poet's works to the Harvard College Library. Mackall had to use a draft for his publication. When the original letter came on the market in London twenty years later, he bought it and gave it to Harvard with the stipulation that he would be the first to publish it, and he did so in a Festschrift for Librarian of Congress Herbert Putnam in 1929.

Mackall was fond of the saying "Habent sua fata libelli" (books have their destinies), used by Terentianus Maurus, a second-century grammarian. He collected half a dozen editions of Terentianus published between 1503 and 1825 and presented them to the Pierpont Morgan Library, for at that time it owned the only copy in the United States of the first printed edition (Milan, 1497). In a 15 November 1930 letter to the director of the Morgan Library, Belle DaCosta Greene, he asked her to consider the books as "having come by bibliographical attraction or gravitation" to her library.

Early in 1936 Mackall failed in what he believed was an assured election to the presidency of the Georgia Historical Society – an acute disappointment because he had not been well for several years and believed he was running out of time. In March he was asked to direct the federal survey of archives in Georgia for the Works Progress Administration but was obliged to decline because the work would have been too strenuous. Shortly thereafter the president of the Bibliographical Society of America, Augustus H. Shearer, became ill, and Mackall as first vice-president assumed Shearer's duties. He completed the arrangements for the society's spring meetings in Richmond and Williamsburg. At Richmond, Mackall was elected president and was warmly applauded by the assembled bibliophiles.

The presidency allowed Mackall to combine his two greatest joys, books and people. He conducted meetings and handled administrative matters with aplomb. As president he was asked to speak to the Elizabethan Club at Yale and held their interest with a discussion of bibliographic history, theory, and anecdote. He also served ex officio on the American Historical Association's Committee for Americana in College Libraries.

In February 1937 Mackall was at last elected president of the Georgia Historical Society, but he was never able to act in the position, for his next

bout of illness ended with his death on 19 May 1937. His largest bequest was 9,693 books, including his excellent Servetus collection, to Johns Hopkins University.

Having shunned the life of a lawyer or academic, Mackall maintained enough means by which he could follow and develop his bibliophily. He might have gained more recognition for his work if he had had facility as a writer, but even composing short articles was for him a draining experience. A major scholarly article on George Gordon, Lord Byron, for which he did research never took shape, and some attempts to write for magazines proved futile. As a collector, however, he was remarkably skillful and made a virtue of his limited funds by seeking out valuable material that did not have general appeal.

Mackall's achievement was the sum of many accomplishments on a small scale. He added to the resources of intellectual history by discovering facts and sources and making them known, by contributing to major bibliographies and helping others in their research, and by his thoughtful attention to finding proper homes for his books. Through active participation he supported and often enlivened the book world of his time, and his newspaper articles record much of its history.

Biography:
William W. Mackall, *A Character Sketch of the Late Leonard Leopold Mackall* (Savannah, Ga.: Mason, 1938).

References:
John F. Fulton, "Humanism in Bibliography: An Appreciation of Leonard L. Mackall," *Special Libraries,* 28 (October 1937): 279–283;
Lawrence C. Wroth, "Career in Books," *Johns Hopkins Alumni Magazine,* 26 (1938): 81–86.

Papers:
Mackall's papers are in the Special Collections department in the Milton S. Eisenhower Library, at Johns Hopkins University. There is some correspondence in the Osler Library, McGill University, Montreal; in the Georgia Historical Society, Savannah; and among the DeRenne family papers in the Hargrett Rare Book and Manuscript Library, University of Georgia, and at the Grolier Club in New York City.

Cotton Mather

(12 February 1663 – 13 February 1728)

Kevin J. Hayes
University of Central Oklahoma

See also the Mather entries in *DLB 24: American Colonial Writers, 1606–1734* and in *DLB 30: American Historians, 1607–1865.*

SELECTED BOOKS: *Military Duties, Recommended to an Artillery Company; At their Election of Officers, in Charls-Town* . . . (Boston: Printed by Richard Pierce for Joseph Brunning, 1687);

Memorable Providences, Relating to Witchcrafts and Possessions . . . (Boston: Printed by R. Pierce & sold by Joseph Brunning, 1689); republished as *Late Memorable Providences Relating to Witchcrafts and Possessions* . . . (London: Printed for Thomas Parkhurst, 1691);

Work upon the Ark. Meditations upon the Ark As a Type of the Church . . . (Boston: Printed by Samuel Green, 1689);

The Wonderful Works of God Commemorated. Praises Bespoke for the God of Heaven, In a Thanksgiving Sermon . . . (Boston: Printed by S. Green & sold by Joseph Browning & by Benjamin Harris, 1690);

The Triumphs of the Reformed Religion, in America. The Life of the Renowned John Eliot; A Person justly Famous in the Church of God, Not only as an Eminent Christian and an Excellent Minister, among the English, But also, As a Memorable Evangelist among the Indians, of New-England . . . (Boston: Printed by Benjamin Harris & John Allen for Joseph Brunning, 1691);

A Midnight Cry. An Essay For our Awakening out of that Sinful Sleep, To which we are at This Time too much disposed: and For our Discovering of what peculiar things there are in This Time, That are for our Awakening . . . (Boston: Printed by John Allen for Samuel Phillips, 1692);

Preparatory Meditations upon the Day of Judgement, published with *The Great Day of Judgement,* by Samuel Lee (Boston: Printed by Bartholomew Green for Nicholas Buttolph, 1692);

The Wonders of the Invisible World. Observations As well Historical as Theological, upon the Nature, the Num-

Cotton Mather, 1727 (mezzotint by Peter Pelham)

ber, and the Operations of the Devils . . . (Boston: Printed by Benj. Harris for Samuel Phillips, 1692); republished as *The Wonders of the Invisible World: Being an Account of the Tryals of Several Witches, Lately Executed in New-England* . . . (London: Printed for John Dunton, 1692);

Early Religion, Urged in a Sermon, Upon The Duties Wherein, and the Reasons, Wherefore, Young People Should Become Religious . . . (Boston: Printed by Benjamin Harris for Michael Perry, 1694);

The Short History of New-England. A Recapitulation of Wonderful Passages Which Have Occurr'd, — First in the Protections, and then in the Afflictions, of New

England . . . (Boston: Printed by B. Green for Samuel Phillips, 1694);

Brontologia Sacra: The Voice of the Glorious God in the Thunder Explained and Applyed . . . (London: Printed by John Astwood, 1695);

Johannes in Eremo. Memoirs, Relating to the Lives, of the Ever-Memorable Mr. John Cotton, Who Dyed, 23.d. 10.m. 1652. Mr. John Norton, Who Dyed, 5.d. 2m. 1663. Mr. John Wilson, Who Dyed, 7.d. 6.m. 1667. Mr. John Davenport, Who Dyed, 15.d. 1.m. 1670 . . . (Boston: Printed for & sold by Michael Perry, 1695);

Piscator Evangelicus. Or, The Life of Mr. Thomas Hooker . . . (Boston: Michael Perry, 1695);

Humiliations follow'd with Deliverences. A Brief Discourse On the Matter and Method Of that Humiliation which would be an Hopeful Symptom of our Deliverance from Calamity. Accompanied and Accommodated with A Narrative Of a Notable Deliverance lately Received by some English Captives From the Hands of Cruel Indians . . . (Boston: Printed by B. Green & J. Allen for Samuel Phillips, 1697);

Pietas in Patriam: The Life of His Excellency Sir William Phips, Knt. Late Captain General, and Governour in Chief of the Province of the Massachusetts-Bay, New England . . . (London: Printed by Sam. Bridge for Nath. Hiller, 1697);

The Bostonian Ebenezer. Some Historical Remarks, On the State of Boston, The Chief Town of New-England, and of the English America . . . (Boston: Printed by B. Green & J. Allen for Samuel Phillips, 1698);

Eleutheria: Or, An Idea of the Reformation in England: And a History of Non-Conformity in and since that Reformation, With Predictions of a more glorious Reformation and Revolution at hand . . . (London: Printed for J. R., 1698);

Decennium Luctuosum. An History of Remarkable Occurrences, In the Long War, which New-England hath had with the Indian Salvages, From the year 1688 To the Year 1698 . . . (Boston: Printed by B. Green and J. Allen for Samuel Phillips, 1699);

Pillars of Salt. An History of Some Criminals Executed in this Land for Capital Crimes. With some of their Dying Speeches; Collected and Published, For the Warning of such as Live in Destructive Courses of Ungodliness . . . (Boston: Printed by B. Green & J. Allen for Samuel Phillips, 1699);

A Pillar of Gratitude . . . (Boston: Printed by B. Green & J. Allen, 1700);

The Religious Marriner. A Brief Discourse Tending to Direct the Course of Sea-Men, In those Points of Religion, Which may bring them to the Port, of Eternal Happiness . . . (Boston: Printed by B. Green & J.

Allen for Samuel Phillips, 1700);

Magnalia Christi Americana: Or, the Ecclesiastical History of New-England, from Its First Planting in the Year 1620, unto the Year of our Lord, 1698 . . . (1 volume, London: Printed for Thomas Parkhurst, 1702; 2 volumes, Hartford: Published by Silas Andrus, printed by Roberts & Burr, 1820);

Family Religion Excited and Assisted . . . (Boston, 1705); republished with an Algonquian translation by Experience Mayhew (Boston: Printed by B. Green, 1714);

The Negro Christianized. An Essay to Excite and Assist that Good Work, The Instruction of Negro-Servants in Christianity . . . (Boston: Printed by B. Green, 1706);

The Best Ornaments of Youth. A Short Essay, on the Good Things, Which are found in Some, and should be found in All, young people . . . (Boston: Printed & sold by Timothy Green, 1707);

A Memorial Of the Present Deplorable State of New-England, With the many Disadvantages it lyes under, by the Male-Administrator of their Present Governour, Joseph Dudley . . . (London: Printed by Benjamin Harris & sold by S. Phillips, N. Buttolph & B. Elliot in Boston, 1707);

Corderius Americanus. An Essay upon The Good Education of Children, And what may Hopefully be Attempted, for the Hope of the Flock, in a Funeral Sermon upon Mr. Ezekiel Cheever . . . (Boston: Printed by John Allen for Nicholas Boone, 1708);

The Deplorable State of New-England, By Reason of a Covetous and Treacherous Governour, and Pusillanimous Counsellors . . . (London: Printed by Benjamin Harris, 1708; Boston: Printed by Samuel Kneeland?, 1721);

Bonifacius. An Essay Upon the Good, that is to be Devised and Designed, By Those Who Desire to Answer the Great End of Life, and to Do Good While they Live . . . (Boston: Printed by B. Green for Samuel Gerrish, 1710);

Nehemiah. A Brief Essay on Divine Consolations . . . (Boston: Printed by Bartholomew Green, 1710);

Theopolis Americana. An Essay on the Golden Street Of the holy City: Publishing, A Testimony against the Corruptions of the Market-Place. With Some Good Hopes of Better Things to be yet seen in the American World . . . (Boston: Printed by B. Green & sold by Samuel Gerrish, 1710);

Perswasions from the Terror of the Lord. A Sermon Concerning The Day of Judgement; preached on a solemn occasion . . . (Boston: Printed by Timothy Green, 1711);

Duodecennium Luctuosum: The History of a Long War With Indian Salvages, And their Directors and Abet-

tors: *From the Year, 1702. To the Year, 1714 . . .*
(Boston: Printed by B. Green for Samuel Gerrish, 1714);

*Psalterium Americanum. The Book of Psalms, In a Trans-
lation Exactly conformed unto the Original; But All
in Blank Verse . . .* (Boston: Printed by S. Kneeland for B. Eliot, S. Gerrish, D. Henchman &
J. Edwards, 1718);

*A Voice from Heaven. An Account Of a Late Uncommon
Appearance in the Heavens. With Remarks upon it.
Written for the Satisfaction of One that was desirous
to know the meaning of it. By One of the Many who
observed it* (Boston: Printed for Samuel Kneeland, 1719);

*The Christian Philosopher: A Collection of the Best Discov-
eries in Nature, with Religious Improvements* (London: Printed for Eman. Matthews, 1720;
Charlestown, Mass: Published at the Middle-
sex Bookstore, printed by J. M. M'Kown,
1815);

*India Christiana. A Discourse, Delivered unto the Commis-
sioners, for the Propagation of the Gospel among the
American Indians . . .* (Boston: Printed by B.
Green, 1721);

*The Angel of Bethesda, Visiting the Invalids of a Miserable
World* (New London: Printed & sold by Timo-
thy Green, 1722);

*Coelestinus. A Conversation in Heaven, Quickened and As-
sisted, With Discoveries Of Things in the Heavenly
World . . .* (Boston: Printed by S. Kneeland,
1723);

*A Father Departing. A Sermon On the Departure of the
Venerable and Memorable Dr. Increase Mather,
Who Expired Aug. 23, 1723. In the Eighty Fifth
Year of his Age . . .* (Boston: Printed by T. Fleet
for N. Belknap, 1723);

*The Voice of God in a Tempest. A Sermon Preached in the
Time of the Storm; Wherein many and heavy and un-
known Losses were Suffered at Boston . . .* (Boston:
Printed by S. Kneeland, 1723);

*Parentator. Memoirs of Remarkables in the Life and the
Death of the Ever-Memorable Dr. Increase Mather . . .*
(Boston: Printed by B. Green for Nathaniel
Belknap, 1724);

*The Palm-Bearers. A brief Relation of Patient and Joyful
Sufferings; and of Death Gloriously Triumphed over;
In the History of the Persecution which the Church of
Scotland Suffered, from the Year 1660, to the Year
1688 . . .* (Boston: Printed by T. Fleet for S.
Gerrish, 1725);

*Manuductio ad Ministerium. Directions For a Candidate of
the Ministry . . .* (Boston: Printed for Thomas
Hancock, 1726); republished with *Gratulatio . . .*
by Samuel Mather, as *Dr. Cotton Mather's Stu-*

dent and Preacher . . . (London: Printed for
Charles Dilly, 1781);

*Ratio Disciplinae Fratrum Nov Anglorum: A Faithful Ac-
count of the Discipline Professed and Practised in the
Churches of New-England . . .* (Boston: Printed
for S. Gerrish, 1726);

*The Vial poured out upon the Sea. A Remarkable Relation
Of certain Pirates Brought unto a Tragical and Un-
timely End . . .* (Boston: Printed by T. Fleet for
N. Belknap, 1726);

*Agricola. Or, The Religious Husbandman: The Main In-
tentions of Religion, Served in the Business and Language of Husbandry . . .* (Boston: Printed by T.
Fleet for D. Henchman, 1727);

*Boanerges. A Short Essay to preserve and strengthen the
Good Impressions Produced by Earthquakes . . .*
(Boston: Printed for S. Kneeland, 1727);

*The Terror of the Lord. Some Account of the Earthquake
That Shook New-England In the Night, Between the
29 and the 30 of October. 1727 . . .* (Boston:
Printed by T. Fleet for S. Kneeland, 1727);

Diary, edited by Worthington C. Ford, Massachusetts Historical Society *Collections*, seventh series, 7 (1911), 8 (1912);

Narratives of the Indian Wars, 1675–1699, edited by
Charles H. Lincoln (New York: Scribners,
1913);

Paterna: The Autobiography of Cotton Mather, edited by
Ronald A. Bosco (Delmar, N.Y.: Scholars'
Facsimiles & Reprints, 1976).

The Mather library developed through several
generations. Richard Mather began the family book
collection, part of which descended to Increase, who
made it one of seventeenth-century New England's
most distinguished libraries. Building on the books
acquired by his father and grandfather, Cotton
Mather made the family library the greatest book
collection in colonial New England. No complete
record of the library's contents survives from Cotton Mather's lifetime. After his death the collection
was dispersed among his descendants, but contemporary testimony, combined with Mather's own
comments about the library and his vast erudition,
confirm its size and importance. With Thomas
Prince, Cotton Mather deserves distinction as one
of colonial New England's two greatest bibliophiles.

Cotton Mather was born on 12 February 1663
to Increase and Maria Cotton Mather. Under Benjamin Thompson and Ezekiel Cheever, Mather studied at the Boston Latin School, where his fondness
for languages became apparent. He read Cicero and
Virgil; composed themes and verses in Latin;
learned Greek by reading Homer, Isocrates, and the

Greek Testament; and began reading Hebrew. In 1675 at the age of twelve he entered Harvard College. While at Harvard he studied logic, ethics, metaphysics, mathematics, rhetoric, oratory, and divinity and continued his study of languages. After graduation in 1678, a speech defect hindered his entry into the ministry, and he began studying medicine.

The surviving books of Cotton Mather's library show that until the age of twenty he habitually inscribed each with his name and the year he acquired it. These early acquisitions suggest the breadth of his education and confirm his interest in languages. In the 1670s he acquired an English/Latin dictionary; a collection of aphorisms in Greek and Latin; Jean Tixier's *Epithetorum . . . Epitome* (London: ex officina Societatis Stationariorum, 1642); Wilhelm Schickard's Hebrew grammar, *Horologium Hebraeum* (London: typis Thomas Paine, venit apud Philemonem Stephanum and Christophorum Meredith, 1639); William Walker's *Phraseologia Anglo-Latina* (London: for R. Royston, 1672); and a recent Greek grammar. Mather took pleasure learning Latin by reading Terence's and Plautus's comedies, copies of which he received from his father. Increase Mather's home was destroyed by fire in 1678, but fortunately much of the library was saved. Cotton wrote, "by the Gracious Providence of God, he lost little of his Beloved Library: Not an Hundred Books from above a Thousand."

While Cotton's interest in medicine and natural philosophy continued throughout his life, by the end of the 1670s he had decided to pursue a career in the ministry and began work on his A.M. at Harvard, concentrating on languages and divinity. His acquisitions during the late 1670s and early 1680s include a variety of religious books, several volumes by Johann Heinrich Alsted, and various anatomical works. Among some of the "mercies of God" that Mather listed in an 8 October 1681 diary entry appears: "My convenient *Study,* with a well furnished *Library.*" Mather is referring to his father's library, but Cotton's own collection was rapidly growing.

Cotton Mather had begun assisting his father's ministry at Boston's Second Church in 1680, and, with an eye toward a permanent position there, he continued refining his oratorical abilities. To this end he acquired books concerning eloquence and oratory by Jacobus Lectius, Marc-Antoine Muret, John Rainolds, and Nicolas Caussin. In a 12 March 1683 diary entry Cotton listed some "Rules of Speech," including: "By *Read-*

ing, both of exemplary *Men,* and of profitable *Books,* which may teach mee, *the Government of the Tongue.*" In 1685 he was ordained at the Second Church and remained its minister until his death in 1728.

Like most colonial bibliophiles, Mather mostly depended on overseas booksellers for the volumes he wanted, and he frequently placed orders with English booksellers. Mather always wanted more books than he could afford, however, and the financial burden of supporting his large family often made book buying difficult. Chance acquisitions he considered acts of providence. In January 1697, for example, he wrote in his diary, "I had in my Prayers, particularly a strange Perswasion, that I should ere long have a notable Accession, made unto the Treasures of my *Library.* I wonder what should bee the meaning of *this.*" In an entry dated 16 October 1700 he recorded the following incident:

> I was this Afternoon making my *pastoral Visits* unto the Families in my Neighbourhood; a Service wherein I enjoy a strange Presence and Conduct of Heaven, but go thro' very spending Labour. In these Visits, after my Discourses, I left Books in each of the Families: and *four Books* had I thus given away this Afternoon. A Thought came into my mind; *Why should I putt myself to this Expence? Perhaps I overdo: no other Minister in the Land would do so: Perhaps it would not be amiss for me, to forbear this expensive Way of serving my Flock!* I check'd this Thought: And I had immediately an Impulse upon my mind, that I should quickly see something, to encourage my doing what I do, and to testify that God accepts it. Well; passing along the Street, a sudden Inclination took me, to step into an House of a Gentlewoman, who had been a long time in a disconsolate Widowhood; I thought it would be *pure Religion* to visit her. I did so; and she told mee, that she had a Parcel of Books, which once belong'd unto the Library of our famous old Mr. *Chancey;* and if I would please to take them, she should count herself highly gratified, in their being so well bestowed. I singled out, about *forty Books,* and some of them large Ones, which were now added unto my Library, that has already between two and three thousand in it, and several of them, will be greatly useful to me, in my Design of writing *Illustrations* upon the divine Oracles. Behold how the Lord smiles upon me!

He repeated the estimate of his holdings in a 21 November 1702 diary entry: "My Study, is tho' a large, yett a warm chamber . . . the hangings whereof, are Boxes with between two and three thousand Books in them." According to a 1719 entry, a young pupil of Mather catalogued the library, but no inventory of Mather's library survives, and it is unknown precisely how large it eventually became. Samuel Mather's late-eighteenth-century estimate of seven or eight thousand volumes is generally considered an exaggeration; four thousand seems more likely. In *Letters from New-England,* John Dunton called it "the Glory of New-England, if not all America." To be sure, Mather's library was superior to any in New England, as he once boasted to a correspondent, John Squire, in January 1716. With the library of William Byrd II, it was one of the two largest private collections in colonial America. In his "Great American Book Collectors to 1800," (*Gazette of the Grolier Club,* 1971) Edwin Wolf II declared the Mather and Byrd libraries "tied for the distinction of being the largest in colonial America."

Mather actively helped other New Englanders obtain books. While motivated by religious zeal, vanity, and self-aggrandizement, he had a genuine desire to expose others to religious writings and book collecting. More than any other individual of his time, Mather deserves credit for disseminating devotional literature throughout New England — and beyond. His diary records many instances of his ardor and generosity. He gave books to ocean-bound seamen (including his *The Sailour's Companion*), expectant mothers (including his *Elizabeth in her Holy Retirement*), farmers in distant settlements, soldiers in Canada, bedridden women, and young men studying for the ministry. In visiting the families of New England, as recorded in his diary, he resolved to "be speak little Studies and Bookshelves for the little Sons that are capable of conversing with such things; and begin to furnish their Libraries and perswade them to the Religion of the Closet." Mather's determination and erudition made him an annoyance to Boston booksellers. He frequently pestered them with advice about what books they should stock. He was disturbed by Harvard's inadequate library, and he sometimes donated books to the college.

While his ministry remained a primary concern throughout his life, Mather never neglected science and medicine. These interests led to his election to the Royal Society of London in 1713. In 1715 Mather completed *The Christian Philosopher: A Collection of the Best Discoveries in Nature, with Religious Improvements,* a work which attempts to harmonize science with religion, and it was published five years later. While few of Mather's science books survive, his sources for *The Christian Philosopher* may suggest the extent of his scientific book collection.

Mather also took a passionate interest in the history of America. His Americana collection included White Kennett's *Bibliothecae Americanae Primordia* (London: J. Churchill, 1713), the earliest published bibliography of Americana. English histo-

rian Daniel Neal highly respected Mather's work and sent him a copy of his *History of New-England* (London: J. Clark, R. Ford, and R. Cruttenden, 1720). Mather thanked him in a 5 July 1720 letter: "The *History of New England* whereof you have made a kind present unto me, obliges me to render you my thanks . . . Your performance is the Reverse of what was done by the malicious and satanic pen of one *Oldnixson* [John Oldmixon] . . . in his Account of the *English Empire in America,* whose history of New England has far more lies than pages in it, and the more unpardonable because contradicted in the very book." Clearly, Mather had little patience for carelessness.

Manuductio ad Ministerium. Directions For a Candidate of the Ministry (1726), Mather's guide to the education of ministers, indicates the stance he took toward books and learning near the end of his life. While intellectually grounded in seventeenth-century Puritanism, Mather evinces a liberal attitude toward eighteenth-century natural philosophy. He recommends that the minister be well schooled in not only religion but also the humanities and the sciences: he should know the standard scientific works, but he should also embrace modern experimental philosophy. While believing that a minister should know his Latin, Greek, Hebrew, and Syriac, Mather recognizes that a well-rounded education involved the study of modern languages as well. The minister should not be "an Odd, Starv'd, Lank sort of a thing, who had lived only on *Hebrew Roots* all his Days." Mather even recommends reading poetry, naturally giving Homer and Virgil his highest praise, but including Richard Blackmore among suggested poets.

In the preface to Samuel Mather's *The Life of the Very Reverend and Learned Cotton Mather* (1729), Prince eulogized Mather as "a Person of a wonderful *quick Apprehension,* tenacious Memory, lively Fancy, ready Invention, unwearied Industry: of vast Improvements in Knowledge." Prince was amazed at the depth and breadth of Mather's reading: "How many languages, Histories, Arts and Sciences, both ancient and modern He was familiarly vers'd in — What a vast Amassment of *Learning* He had grasp'd in his Mind, from all sorts of Writings." Prince's tribute also provides important comment on Mather's reading process. Mather preferred books "that were likely to bring him something *New,* and so increase his Knowledge. In two or three Minutes turning thro' a Volumn, he cou'd easily tell whether it wou'd make Additions to the Store of his Ideas. If it cou'd not, He quickly laid it by: If otherwise, he read it . . . perusing those Parts only that represented something *Novel,* which he Pencil'd as he went along, and at the End reduc'd the Substance to his *Common Places,* to be review'd at Leisure; and all this with wonderful Celerity . . . As he increased in Years, the less Time he had occasion to expend in running thro' an Author; til at length there were but few Books published that would take him *much* to read."

Letters:

Selected Letters of Cotton Mather, edited by Kenneth Silverman (Baton Rouge: Louisiana State University Press, 1971).

Bibliography:

Thomas James Holmes, *Cotton Mather: A Bibliography of His Works,* 3 volumes (Cambridge, Mass.: Harvard University Press, 1940).

Biographies:

Samuel Mather, *The Life of the Very Reverend and Learned Cotton Mather* (Boston: Printed for Samuel Gerrish, 1729); republished with a foreword by Babette Luvy (New York: Garrett, 1970);

Barrett Wendell, *Cotton Mather: The Puritan Priest,* edited by Alan Heimert (New York: Dodd, Mead, 1891);

Otho T. Beall, Jr., and Richard Shryock, *Cotton Mather: First Significant Figure in American Medicine* (Baltimore: Johns Hopkins Press, 1954);

David Levin, *Cotton Mather: The Young Life of the Lord's Remembrancer, 1663–1703* (Cambridge, Mass.: Harvard University Press, 1978);

Kenneth Silverman, *The Life and Times of Cotton Mather* (New York: Harper & Row, 1984).

References:

Henry Joel Cadbury, "Harvard College Library and the Libraries of the Mathers," *Proceedings of the American Antiquarian Society,* 50 (1940): 20–48;

Robert Middlekauf, *The Mathers: Three Generations of Puritan Intellectuals, 1596–1728* (New York: Oxford University Press, 1971);

Perry Miller, "A Note on the Manuductio ad Ministerium," in Thomas James Holmes, *Cotton Mather: A Bibliography of His Works,* volume 2 (Cambridge, Mass.: Harvard University Press, 1940), pp. 630–636;

Kenneth B. Murdock, Introduction to *Selections from Cotton Mather* (New York: Harcourt, Brace, 1926);

Winton U. Solberg, "Cotton Mather, *The Christian Philosopher,* and the Classics," *Proceedings of the American Antiquarian Society,* 96 (1986): 323–366;

Raymond Phineas Stearns, *Science in the British Colonies of America* (Urbana: University of Illinois Press, 1970);

Julius Herbert Tuttle, "The Libraries of the Mathers," *Proceedings of the American Antiquarian Society,* 20 (1910): 269–356;

Edwin Wolf II, "Great American Book Collectors to 1800," *Gazette of the Grolier Club,* new series 16 (June 1971): 1–70.

Papers:

The American Antiquarian Society contains the largest collection of Mather's surviving books and a major collection of Mather papers. Other Mather papers are at the Massachusetts Historical Society and the Boston Public Library.

Susan Minns

(21 August 1839 – 1 August 1938)

BOOK: *Book of the Silkworm: A Plea for the Cultivation of Silk and the Silkworm in the United States* (New York: National Americana Society, 1929).

Over a period of some seventy years, Susan Minns assembled the largest and most comprehensive private collection of material on the Dance of Death. In addition to books and manuscripts, her collection included prints, bookplates, coins, medals, and curios depicting Death.

Susan Minns was a descendant of William Minns of Great Yarmouth, who immigrated to Boston in 1737. Two of his sons became involved in the book trade as printers and later as publishers. William, the eldest son and Susan's great uncle, was a Loyalist who after 1779 made his home in Halifax, Nova Scotia, where he edited and published the *Weekly Chronicle* from 1786 to 1826. William's brother and Susan's grandfather, Thomas, established himself as a printer in Boston. In 1794 he became a partner of Alexander Young in the publication of the *Massachusetts Mercury* (later the *New England Palladium and Mercury*). In June 1796 the firm of Young and Minns was appointed official printer to the Massachusetts legislature.

Thomas's second son, Constant Freeman Minns, was Susan Minns's father. Although he had no formal training, he was fluent in several languages and translated business news from South American and European newspapers for his father. In 1825 Constant Freeman moved to New York, where he balanced his scholarly interest in languages with a mercantile career. Poor health forced him to retire in 1836. He returned to Massachusetts and settled in Lincoln, where he was much involved in community activities until his death in 1841.

Constant Freeman Minns and his wife, Frances Ann Parker, had three children: Thomas, Frances Antoinette, and Susan. Although Thomas attended private schools in the Boston area, no mention is made of his sisters' education. All three apparently inherited their father's linguistic abilities. As his father had done, Thomas balanced business and scholarship with civic responsibilities. He pursued a mercantile career in textiles and had interests in railways, particularly the Union Pacific. At the same time, he developed a reputation as an authority in the early history of Massachusetts. Thomas never married, and, as their sister Frances Antoinette had predeceased him, Susan was the primary beneficiary of his estate. At her brother's death in 1913 she inherited among other things a town house on Louisburg Square in Boston. There she lived alone, filling the house with her Dance of Death collection.

By her own account, Minns began collecting at an early age; a love for woodcuts provided the initial stimulus. In the foreword to the 1922 auction catalogue she recalled: "As a child I was given books illustrated by [Alexander] Anderson, [Thomas] Bewick, Birket Foster, [Carl August] Richter and others. I was shown how woodcuts were printed and even tried my hand at blocks. So that quite early I began to buy anything that had a woodcut."

She soon added a touch of the macabre to her general interest in woodcuts. She read Francis Douce's *The Dance of Death Exhibited in Elegant Engravings on Wood, with a Dissertation on the several Representations of that Subject, but more Particularly on those ascribed to Macaber and Hans Holbein* (London, 1833), which led her to other reference works on the subject. She obtained and studied Gabriel Peignot's *Recherches Historiques et Littéraires sur les Danses des Morts et sur l'Origine des Cartes à Jour* (Dijon and Paris, 1826); H. F. Massman's *Literatur der Todtentänze* (Leipzig, 1840); and E. H. Langlois's *Essai Historique, Philosophique et Pittoresque sur les Danses des Morts* (Rouen, 1852). From them she gleaned all that was known about the Dance of Death from its probable origins in the religious dramas of the late Middle Ages to the transmission of the theme into painting and print. She became familiar with the first of the European frescoes and carvings in churches and monasteries to employ the theme — as well as the manuscripts and early printed books of the fifteenth and sixteenth centuries.

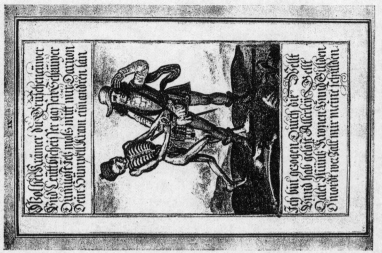

BASLE DESIGNS OF "DANCE OF DEATH"
ORIGINAL WATERCOLOR
Reduced Facsimile
[No. 33]

THE MINNS "DANCE OF DEATH" COLLECTION

First Session, Tuesday Afternoon, May 2nd

30. **BASLE DANCE OF DEATH.** MERIAN (MATTHAEUS). La Danse des Morts, pour servir de Miroir a la Nature Humaine. Avec le Costume Dessiné a la Moderne, et des Vers a chaques Figures. *Engraved title. 42 engraved plates and reversable portrait after Merian's designs, folding plate of the Crucifixion by Girardet;* L'ART de bien Vivre et de bien Mourir. Treizieme Edition . . . *Engraved frontispiece.* 2 vols. in one, 8vo, old boards, broken at joints, shaken.   Locle: Chez St. Girardet [1788]
VERY RARE. INTERIORLY A GOOD, CLEAN COPY, WITH FINE IMPRESSIONS OF THE PLATES. In this curious volume an unknown artist has copied Merian's plates, but arranged the figures in modern costume, producing some rather startling effects. The text is in verse.

31. **BASLE DANCE OF DEATH.** MERIAN (MATTHAEUS). La Danse des Morts, pour servir de miroir a la nature humaine. Avec le costume dessiné a la moderne, et des vers a chaques figures. *With engraved frontispiece, title, 41 plates and portrait, after Merian's designs.* 8vo, full maroon morocco, gilt, gilt top, BY PIERSON.   Locle: Chez St. Girardet [1788]
VERY RARE. IN EXCELLENT CONDITION.
With bookplate of the Viconte de Savigny de Moncorps.

32. **BASLE DANCE OF DEATH.** Der Todten-Tantz, wie derselbe in der Weitberühmten Stadt Basel als ein Spiegel menschlicher Beschaffenheit, ganz Künstlich mit lebendigen Farben gemahlet, nicht ohne nützliche Verwunderung zu sehen ist. *With woodcut title vignette and 41 large woodcuts of the Dance of Death, partly after the Basle paintings, partly after Holbein's designs, head-and-tail pieces.* 8vo, half morocco, gilt, red top, other edges uncut and partly unopened.
Basel, bey Gebrüdern von Mechel, 1796
FINE CLEAN EXAMPLE. PRACTICALLY UNHANDLED. EXCELLENT IMPRESSIONS OF THE WOODCUTS. Inserted as frontispiece is a view of Basle, entitled,—"Der Todten-Tanz zu Basel. Anno M. DLXXVI."
A modern reprint of old cuts first used in Frölich's edition of 1608, which see for full description.

33. **BASLE DANCE OF DEATH.** ORIGINAL WATERCOLOR PAINTINGS AFTER THE BASLE DESIGNS. *Series of 40 original watercolor paintings, averaging 4⅜ by 4⅜ inches, each with eight lines of German descriptive verse, written by hand in Gothic characters in black ink. Red and gilt ruled borders and dividing lines.* Each leaf trimmed to narrow margin, gilt edged and mounted on heavy paper, with hand-colored lavender border and black ruled frame, bound in 8vo, red velvet, gilt metal embossed corners and clasp, rose watered silk doublures and end-leaves, gilt goufred edges, velvet worn at edges and back, gilt skull and cross-bones lacking from front cover. Enclosed in black calf envelope folder.
Germany, *circa* Eighteenth Century

[See Illustration]

BEAUTIFUL SERIES OF ORIGINAL PAINTINGS, IN FINE STATE OF PRESERVATION, COLORS VIVID, LEAVES CLEAN. The first three leaves are slightly torn in margins, not injuring the paintings however, the other leaves being in good condition throughout. There is no text on the first two pictures.
The designs and the text follow Merian's plates and text very closely, but the pictures show slight variations throughout, and in the majority backgrounds of trees, houses and other outdoor views have been added. The pictures are differently arranged, four designs are omitted and two entirely new designs included. A VERY BEAUTIFUL WORK, AND QUITE EVIDENTLY EXECUTED BY AN ARTIST OF SKILL AND EXPERIENCE.

Pages from the Minns sale catalogue

Pages from Minns's copy of Geofroy Tory's Book of Hours (1527)

As depicted on the walls of the cemetery of the Church of the Holy Innocents in Paris, a convent and monastery in Basel, Saint Paul's Churchyard in London, and elsewhere, the Dance of Death was a procession of all ranks and orders of society. Hierarchically arranged, each person was shown in his or her encounter with Death, who took the form of a skeleton. The dialogues between Death and his victims were recorded in the accompanying text which varied somewhat from region to region. The authorship of the text was unknown, and the attribution to a mysterious German named "Macaber" was dismissed by Douce and other authorities. The message was a simple one: Death comes to the mighty as well as the humble; repent and lead a good life in this world if you wish to be saved in the next. The theme struck a chord in Minns, and using Douce and the other reference works as her guide, she set out in pursuit of Death. She received assistance from S. R. Koehler, curator of prints at the Boston Museum of Fine Art, who provided introductions to booksellers in Europe.

The earliest known book version of the Dance of Death was printed in Paris by Guyot Marchant for Godfrey de Marnef in 1485 under the title *Danse Macabre*. It contained seventeen woodcuts based on the paintings in the cemetery of the Church of the Holy Innocents. While Minns was unable to acquire a copy of this edition — only one copy is known to have survived — she did obtain a copy of the rare 1490 Marchant edition with twenty-four woodcuts and text in Latin. Death's victims in this version were all men, but later editions included images of women as well and added new trades or professions, among them that of the printer in his workshop. Minns owned a copy of the 1568 Lyon edition of *La grande danse macabre des homes & des femes hystoriee et augmentee de beaulx dictz en Latin*; several of the so-called popular editions printed in Troyes in the seventeenth and eighteenth centuries; and nineteenth-century reproductions of early editions.

Roughly contemporaneous with the early editions of the *Danse Macabre* were the illuminated manuscripts and printed versions of *Horae,* or

Woodcut from the title page for Minns's copy of Hieronymo Savonarola's Predica dellarte del Bene morire *(1496)*

Books of Hours. Minns acquired about seventy examples produced in the fifteenth and early sixteenth centuries. These prayer books, intended for use by the laity, included the "Office of the Dead," the prayers for the funeral service, with appropriate illustrations. The manuscripts contained drawings decorated with rich colors and illuminated with gold leaf. The wood or metal cuts in the printed books often were similarly adorned. The subject matter included death and burial scenes, the raising of Lazarus, and various depictions of Death Triumphant: Death as the Grim Reaper with his scythe, Death on a coffin, Death carrying a coffin, Death seated on an open tomb, Death riding an ox, Death on horseback, as well as the Dance of Death.

Minns especially prized a magnificent mid-fifteenth-century French manuscript containing a translation of Boethius's *De Consolatione Philosophiae*

(circa 524) and six other texts. The miniature illustrating the *Histoire du miroir du corps et de l'âme* shows Death hovering in the air and startling a young woman regarding herself in a mirror. This miniature was featured as the frontispiece in the 1922 auction catalogue. The text of Boethius obviously appealed to Minns; she also owned a Latin edition printed in Strasbourg in 1501.

The theme of Death appeared in devotional works not wholly devoted to the Dance of Death. These Minns acquired with equal pleasure. The *Ars Moriendi,* or the "Art of Dying Well," was intended to comfort the dying and assist them in their struggle against the temptation of the Devil. Minns had copies of the *Ars Moriendi* in Latin (Cologne, circa 1475; Nuremburg, 1512), Dutch (Cologne, 1520), and German (Diligen, 1569 and 1572). Of the *Cordiale Quatuor Novissimorum,* or "The Four Last

Things," she owned a fourteen-leaf fragment of an early Spanish translation and two Dutch translations, printed in Delft about 1499. She found room on her shelves for Girolamo Savonarola's *Predica dell'arte del bene morire* (Florence, 1496) with a striking woodcut of Death triumphant on the title page, and a Dutch translation of the *Imitatio Christi* (Lubeck, 1489) with a woodcut of Death holding a scythe.

Death figures as one of three blind guides to which all men are subject – the other two being Love and Fortune – in a poetic work by Pierre Michault entitled *La Dance des aveugles*. Minns owned a copy printed in Paris about 1495. The copy is illustrated with woodcuts of Death slaying men with arrows and Death on horseback with a coffin under his arm riding toward Hell's mouth. Minns also acquired editions of Sebastian Brandt's *Stultifera Navis,* or "Ship of Fools": the first Latin edition (Basel, 1497) containing two illustrations of Death; two sixteenth-century Lyon editions with the text in French and containing Dance of Death woodcuts; and a Dutch translation (Leyden, 1610). She acquired a copy of the 1554 London edition of John Lydgate's translation of Giovanni Boccaccio's *Fall of Princes* because it also contained Lydgate's translation of the *Danse Macabre* from the cemetery of the Church of the Holy Innocents. Although emblem books did not contain the Dance of Death designs as such, they appealed to Minns; she added the works of Andrea Alciati, Jakob Cats, Theodore de Bry, Georgette de Montenay, Otto Van Veen, and others to her collection.

To many the Dance of Death theme was best treated by Hans Holbein the Younger, whose interpretations were first published at Lyon in 1538 under the title *Les Simulachres & Historiees Faces de la Mort.* The book's illustrations provided the perfect balance between realism and imagination, resignation and fear. Following a woodcut of the Dance of the Dead, all ranks and orders of society are illustrated in their encounter with Death. Each is portrayed in a separate vignette rather than a procession. Some greet Death calmly while others, startled and fearful, attempt to escape his grip. The text accompanying the illustrations consists of quotations from Scripture in Latin and French rather than of dialogue between Death and his victims.

The popularity of the work is well documented in Minns's collection. From the Rosenthals in Berlin she obtained virtually every edition listed in Massman's bibliography. Included among these works were reinterpretations of Holbein's designs

done in the seventeenth and eighteenth centuries, including the famous version by Wenzel Hollar. Of the versions with the original Holbein designs she owned two copies of the first edition of 1538; multiple copies of editions printed at Lyon in Latin (1542, 1545, and 1547), in French (1547 and 1562), and in Italian (1549); a Basel edition in Latin (1554); Venice editions in Italian (1545 and 1546); Cologne editions in Latin (1555, 1557, 1566, 1567, 1572, and 1573); a Nuremburg edition in German (1560); and an edition in Bohemian (1563). Her copy of the 1547 Lyon edition in French was especially prized for it had belonged to Hollar. She also owned many fine examples of the series of ornamental initial letters designed by Holbein and known as his "Alphabet of Death."

In the seventeenth century the Basel *Todten-Tänzt* paintings were reproduced by Matthäus Merian, a celebrated engraver of Frankfurt. Minns owned two copies of the first edition of 1649, illustrated with forty-two copperplate engravings; a 1696 reprint of the first edition issued by Merian's heirs; and several eighteenth-century editions. The theme was taken up by Rudolf and Conrad Meyer, who issued their *Todten-dantz* with sixty copperplate illustrations (Zurich, 1650). J. R. Schellenberg took a playful approach in his *Freund Heins Erscheinungen in Holbeins Manier* (Winterthur, 1785). Death is caused by a ballooning accident in one illustration, while a cascading wall of books is Death's instrument in another. Minns had copies of these works as well as Thomas Rowlandson's *The English Dance of Death* (London, 1815–1816), with text by William Combe, and Isaac Cruikshank's *The British Dance of Death* (London, 1823).

To complement the books, Minns collected broadsides commemorating the deaths of famous people, invitations to funeral services, and bills of mortality from the London plague. She converted a portion of her house into a picture gallery where she displayed the thousand or more prints, drawings, and paintings. There were woodcuts and engravings by Albrecht Dürer, Holbein, Lucas van Leyden, and Hollar; caricatures by Rowlandson, James Gillray, and Cruikshank; a remarkable series of etchings by Alphonse Legros; and rare Russian, Chinese, and Japanese prints on the subject.

While the books and prints were her primary focus, Minns could not resist tarot and playing cards, coins and medals, carvings, and other curios associated with Death and its personification. Among the curios in Minns's collection were several Japanese carvings in wood and ivory of skeletons and skulls. Not to be forgotten were the poison cups, said to have been used by Lucrezia Borgia, from which Susan sipped her tea.

At the age of eighty-three Minns decided to sell her collection at auction. The sale took place at the American Art Association Galleries in New York on 2 and 3 May 1922. "I have had the pleasure of collecting," she stated. "Let others have the same." She made certain that the University of Louvain would have that pleasure. Having learned of the efforts of the Committee for the Restoration of Louvain to rebuild collections destroyed during World War I – particularly one similar to her own – Minns donated $12,500 to be used toward the purchase of books from her collection. As the sale totaled less than $18,000, she was in effect the chief buyer at her own sale. Much of the material that went to Louvain was destroyed in World War II. Some of Minns's books, however, have survived in North American collections. Manuscripts and early printed books were purchased by Joseph Martini, who sold several, including the *Ars Moriendi* and the Michault *La Dance des aveugles,* a year later to William M. Ivins, Jr., curator of prints at the Metropol-

itan Museum of Art. The magnificent manuscript of Boethius was bought by A. S. W. Rosenbach for $1,025, the highest price paid at the sale. He sold it to the Spencer Collection at the New York Public Library three years later. Five of the Book of Hours manuscripts were purchased by Philadelphia collector John Frederick Lewis; they are preserved in the Lewis Collection of European Manuscripts in the Rare Book Department of the Free Library of Philadelphia.

Following the sale Minns returned to her home in Boston where she devoted herself to the breeding of silkworms. She published a work entitled *Book of the Silkworm: A Plea for the Cultivation of Silk and the Silkworm in the United States* (1929). As if charmed against the subject she had pursued so relentlessly, Minns eluded her own dance with Death until the summer of 1938, a few weeks shy of her ninety-ninth birthday.

Reference:

Marie Korey, "Susan Minns and the Dance of Death," *Descant,* 22 (1991–1992): 87–98.

John Pierpont Morgan

(17 April 1837 – 31 March 1913)

and

John Pierpont Morgan, Jr.

(7 September 1867 – 13 March 1943)

Ruth Rosenberg
City University of New York

The 13 March 1943 issue of the *New York Times* described the banking house of J. P. Morgan and Company as having "attained a place of importance in international financial affairs that not even the house of Rothschild attained in the period of its greatest power." J. P. Morgan, the man responsible for the success of the Morgan enterprise, came to rival Henry Huntington as one of the greatest collectors of artworks, rare books, and manuscripts in the United States. His son, J. P. Morgan, Jr., succeeded him at the bank and continued to add to his father's collection. The rare books and manuscripts amassed by the Morgans are now available to scholars and the general public at the Pierpont Morgan Library in New York City. Much of the art is there as well, though large holdings are at the Metropolitan Museum of Art in New York City and the Wadsworth Atheneum in Hartford, Connecticut.

J. P. Morgan was born on 17 April 1837 in Hartford, the son of Junius Spencer and Juliet Pierpont Morgan. The family later moved to Boston, where Junius served as partner in a banking firm that acted as agent for George Peabody's investment bank in London. Peabody, an American, invited Junius to join him as his partner in London. When the Morgan family relocated to London, Morgan was enrolled at a school in Vevey, Switzerland. He subsequently studied for two years at the University of Göttingen in Germany, after which his father arranged a position for him with a bank in New York.

Soon after returning to the United States, Morgan fell in love with Amelia Sturges. They married in Paris in 1861. She was afflicted with tuberculosis, however, and she died four months after their wedding. Morgan continued to revere her memory for as long as he lived. He and his second wife, Frances Tracy, had four children: John Pierpont Morgan, Jr., Louisa (Satterlee), Juliet (Hamilton), and Anne, who remained unmarried and devoted her life to charitable and political causes.

Morgan's ties to his father's prosperous London firm enabled him to move ahead in the banking profession within the United States. By 1895 Drexel, Morgan and Company in New York had become J. P. Morgan and Company. Upon his father's death in 1890 Morgan became head of the London firm Junius S. Morgan and Company (which became Morgan, Grenfell and Company in 1910). He also headed Drexel and Company in Philadelphia and the Paris firm Morgan, Harjes and Company.

Morgan's great indulgence was collecting works of art and rare books and manuscripts. His collecting began on 5 August 1851 with his receipt of a card that he had sent to President Millard Fillmore for his signature. In the early 1880s his father gave him the manuscript of Sir Walter Scott's *Guy Mannering*. In 1883 Joseph Sabin put together a catalogue of Morgan's acquisitions; it included a set of autographed letters and documents from the signers of the Declaration of Independence, a letter from Robert Burns incorporating three poems, and the first Bible printed in North America, the *Eliot Indian Bible*.

After his father's death Morgan came into a large inheritance, which he used to build his collection. During the 1890s he bought several first editions of titles in English literature and the Sir Charles Fenn collection of European autographs. Among his acquisitions during this period were manuscripts of John Keats's *Endymion* (1818) and of Charles Dickens's *A Christmas Carol* (1843); Morgan also acquired manuscripts that George Gordon, Lord Byron had given to his mistress. He also purchased a Gutenberg Bible on vellum, the Mainz Psalter from 1459, the ninth-century Lindau Gospels with its elaborate jeweled binding, and the four

John Pierpont Morgan, Sr.

Shakespeare folios. He began to buy collections en bloc, reasoning, "What's the use of bothering about one little piece when I might get them all?" The first such purchase was of the books and manuscripts belonging to the English bookseller James Toovey; this included a set of Aldine imprints (this printing house was established in Venice in 1490) and a group of tooled leather bindings.

In 1900 Morgan purchased the collection of Theodore Irwin of Oswego, New York, consisting of books and manuscripts. This library was particularly rich in early illuminated manuscripts such as the eighth-century *Golden Gospels* (also known as *King Henry VIII's Gospels* because it had been presented to the king by Pope Leo X). In 1902 Morgan bought a library of manuscripts and early printed books, some seven hundred volumes, from Richard Bennett of Manchester. Much of this collection had come from English printer and designer William Morris and included one hundred illuminated manuscripts and works from all of the early sixteenth-

century printers. Morgan paid seven hundred thousand dollars for this library, which also contained thirty-two books from the shop of William Caxton, England's first printer.

Caxton had printed several volumes in English on the Continent before he set up his shop in Westminster. Like many of the early printers, he was learned and did his own translations into English from French of works that he wished to print. Among the Caxtons that Morgan obtained from Bennett was the first printing of Geoffrey Chaucer's *The Canterbury Tales* (1478) as well as a second edition (1484) of that same work. Twenty-four woodcuts were added to the second edition; Caxton writes in his prologue that since some readers had complained of "incorrectness" in the earlier edition and had lent him a more correct manuscript from which to work, he therefore went ahead with this second printing.

Other books in this batch of Caxtons included *Dictes or Sayings of the Philosophers* (18 November

John Pierpont Morgan, Jr.

1477), the first book printed in English with a day, month, and year indicated; Vincent of Beauvais, *The Mirror of the World* (1481), one of the first books printed by Caxton with illustrations; *Chronicles of England* (1482); *Order of Chivalry* (1484); *The Book Called Caton* (1484), the fourth edition of the orations of the Roman statesman Cato printed by Caxton, accompanied by a commentary translated by Caxton from the French; John Lydgate, *The Life of Our Lady* (1484); *The Royal Book or Book for a King* (1488), a translation by Caxton of *Le Livre des Vices et des Vertus,* and one of the finest specimens of Caxton's work in existence; *Doctrinal of Sapience* (1489), an instructional book for priests described by Caxton as "necessary for simple priests who do not understand the scriptures, for simple people and put into English translated out of French by William Caxton, Westminster"; and *Book of Divers Ghostly Matters, The Seven Points of True Love, The Twelve Profits of Tribulation,* and *The Rule of St. Benet* (1491). Morgan

continued to purchase Caxtons en bloc when they became available; the library now possesses fifty-seven printed in England as well as other copies produced on the Continent.

By 1900 Morgan was able to leave much of the daily business affairs of his bank in the hands of his partners and devote a large portion of his time to art and rare-book purchases. His custom was to make himself available to dealers at his New York home in the mornings. On trips to Europe and Egypt he was likewise besieged by dealers and others seeking to sell him treasures. During this period Morgan obtained three major collections of French literature: the chansons de geste sold by Edward Ker, the Burchard set of medieval romances, and the De Forest library of tales and sagas. In 1904 he obtained the manuscript of book 1 of John Milton's *Paradise Lost.*

Also by 1900 the room in which Morgan kept his treasures at the family home on the corner of

Madison Avenue and Thirty-sixth Street in New York had, according to family members, "become so crowded that it was difficult to get into it and find anything; books, pictures, and manuscripts were piled on the floor, after every table and chair had been filled." He therefore bought the property on Thirty-sixth Street adjacent to his house and commissioned Charles F. McKim of the renowned architectural firm McKim, Mead and White to build a library. Design and construction took almost six years. The result was a Renaissance palazzo built of fitted marble blocks in the classical Greek design.

Engaged by Morgan to manage the Library was twenty-one-year-old Belle da Costa Greene, who had trained at the Princeton University library as a cataloguer with a special interest in rare books. She worked for the Morgan family and later for the trustees of the Pierpont Morgan Library as director of the library from 1905 to 1948. Greene was instrumental in Morgan's last major block purchase. In 1908 she convinced the family of Lord Amherst to sell her a group of fourteen Caxtons that they had already announced would be put up for sale at public auction. The night before the auction was to take place she attended a dinner in London with some book dealers who wished to know if she might be bidding against them the next day. During the course of the dinner a telegram arrived for Greene. It was from the Amherst family, giving their final approval of her proposal that Morgan buy the Caxtons, thereby removing these volumes from the auction. Greene was thus able to tell the book dealers, in all sincerity, "You may now have your reply, gentlemen. I shall not bid against you tomorrow." For these Caxtons Morgan paid $125,000.

When Morgan wished to acquire a specific item for his collection, he would take whatever steps were necessary to achieve his goal. Francis Henry Taylor, in his *Pierpont Morgan as Collector and Patron, 1837–1913,* preserves this statement attributed to Morgan: "I was told in London that Byron manuscripts were in the possession of a lady, a relative of Byron, in Greece. Libraries in England were after them. I wanted them. I therefore, through the advice of an expert, engaged a man, gave him a letter of credit and told him to go to Greece and live there until he had gotten those manuscripts. Every once in a while, during several years, a volume would come which the relative had been willing to sell, until the whole was complete." Morgan was assiduous in the pursuit of rare and beautiful things because he believed, in his words, that it was the duty of the privileged few "to ensure the moral superiority of America" and elevate the asthetic standards of the nation as a whole. "Culture and art," he said, "were indexes of civilization."

To promote his convictions he privately published lavish catalogues of his collections. Compiled and written by experts in the field, the catalogues were beautifully made – some bound in tooled leather. The number of copies printed was often very limited. Morgan would present copies to institutions and heads of state, including the president of the United States and the king of England.

During the last four years of his life Morgan made several outstanding acquisitions. The large group of American nineteenth-century literary manuscripts belonging to Stephen Wakeman became his in 1909. In 1910 Morgan requested from Mark Twain the manuscript of *Pudd'nhead Wilson* (1894). This prompted Twain to write, "One of my high ambitions is gratified – which was, to have something of mine placed elbow to elbow with that august company which you have gathered together to remain indestructible in a perishable world." Also in 1910 Morgan bought the collection of master drawings belonging to C. Fairfax Murray, thereby greatly enlarging the library's holdings in this genre, which was also represented in the library by the William Blake series of *Job* watercolors. In 1911 Morgan purchased a large group of Coptic manuscripts, mostly from the ninth century, that had been found buried on the grounds of an Egyptian monastery. The manuscripts preserved nearly the whole of the Coptic New Testament, as well as the liturgy of the Coptic church, with many full-page colored illustrations. These texts were sent to the Vatican, though Morgan retained title to them, for conservation and reproduction.

Morgan made several other notable purchases in 1911. At the Hoe auction he won with a bid of $42,800 the only surviving complete copy of Sir Thomas Malory's *Morte d'Arthur* printed by Caxton in 1485. Competing with him to acquire this volume was Huntington. He also bought from the extensive Sir Thomas Phillipps collection of manuscripts the Gospels of Countess Matilda of Tuscany, written and decorated in Italy around 1100. Other acquisitions during this period included a perfect Gutenberg Bible on paper; manuscripts of Alexander Pope, Burns, Scott, Dickens, William Makepeace Thackeray, Emile Zola, George Meredith, John Ruskin, and Twain; the earliest manuscript of Aesop's *Life and Fables* in Greek; and a fine Persian manuscript, a bestiary from the late thirteenth century. In 1912 Morgan brought over from

The Morgan mansion at the corner of Madison Avenue and Thirty-sixth Street in New York. This house was torn down in 1928 to make room for an annex to the Pierpont Morgan Library.

England much of the art and the books that had been kept in the houses he inherited from his father. They were brought to the United States at this time for two reasons: Parliament was about to impose large death duties upon such items while, on the other hand, the U.S. Congress had just repealed the import tax on works of art.

When Pierpont Morgan died in Rome in 1913, Morgan, Jr., inherited his art collection along with the books and manuscripts in the library. Included in the collection were 19,175 printed volumes, 1,305 manuscripts, and 1,098 prints, appraised at a value of $7.5 million. The collection was unsurpassed in the Western Hemisphere for its illuminated manuscripts of the medieval period and Renaissance, its master drawings, early printed books, and bookbindings. An exhibition of original letters, manuscripts, and drawings of English authors from the Pierpont Morgan Library, most of them obtained by the elder Morgan, was held over a four-month period in 1924–1925 at the New York Public Library. Over 168,000 people came to view it. A similar exhibition of pictorial or illuminated

manuscripts was held in 1933–1934 and was viewed by more than 117,000 people.

Morgan, Jr., was born in 1867 in Irvington, New York. Within the family and to close friends he was known as Jack. He graduated from Harvard University and in 1890 married Jane Grew, with whom he had four children: Junius Spencer, Henry Sturgis, Jane (Nichols), and Frances (Pennoyer). He became a partner in his father's New York company and its associate houses in Philadelphia and Paris. In 1894 he was sent to J. S. Morgan and Company in London, where he and his family remained for eight years. Upon his father's death in 1913 he succeeded as head of all the Morgan enterprises. The following year the city of New York found itself unable to meet its financial obligations maturing in London and Paris; Morgan organized a bankers' syndicate to raise $100 million in gold for the city's benefit. Morgan and his firm financed a great part of the Allies' requirements for U.S. credits during the first years of World War I, and in 1917–1918 the firm organized sources of industrial supply for American participation in the war.

The Pierpont Morgan Library, built next to the Morgan mansion in 1900–1905

Morgan, Jr., shared much of his father's social and economic philosophies. The *New York Times* 13 March 1943 obituary article on Morgan, Jr., quotes him as saying that to destroy the leisure class would be to "destroy civilization." Asked to define the "leisure class," he replied that it "includes all who can hire a maid." His recipe for success was "Do your work; be honest; keep your word; help when you can; be fair." (Perhaps his father's most widely quoted aphorism was "Anyone who even has to think about the cost had better not get a yacht.")

The first gift to the library presented by Morgan, Jr., was the manuscript of Thackeray's *Vanity Fair* (1847–1848) that he had given to his father in 1905. In 1915 he bought for the library the manuscript of *The Rose and the Ring* (1855), which Thackeray had written in 1853 for Edith Story. The manuscript contains the author's own pen-and-ink sketches to illustrate the tale. Years later one of Morgan, Jr.'s sons gave him for a Christmas present the printed copy of *The Rose and the Ring* which Thackeray had inscribed, "With the author's most respectful compliments to Miss Edith Story Christmas 1854."

Morgan, Jr., in consultation with Greene, took a close interest in the acquisitions and activities of the library. He wrote, "I am endeavoring to complete as far as possible the undertaking that my Father began, of gathering in this Library as full as possible a collection of incunabula." He did not want to make purchases indiscriminately. In 1919 he wrote to Greene:

I believe we shall do better to spend the money we have available – which is not an unlimited amount – in continuing our policy of filling with special manuscripts and with printed books before 1520, than we shall by scattering it about in buying Shakesperian items which seem to me to be higher priced than one can justify. The same applies to the collection of bindings of which Pearson has written to me. Six or seven thousand pounds taken out of our available spending money for a lot of bindings collected by somebody else, does not appeal to me. . . . We have very good bindings, and I do not feel like adding to them in this wholesale way, though an occasional few may be very well when one has the loose change necessary.

Among the outstanding acquisitions made by Morgan, Jr., is the French thirteenth-century illuminated manuscript, "Old Testament Illustrations." He purchased it privately in 1916 from the Phillipps heirs. Early in the fourteenth century it had been at the Court of Naples; it passed later to Bernard Cardinal Maciejowski, bishop of Kraców and primate of Poland, who in 1608 presented it to Shah Abbas the Great of Persia. After World War I Morgan purchased what Frederick B. Adams in *An Introduction to the Pierpont Morgan Library* describes as "six exceptional manuscripts." Among these were "a sumptuous Greek Gospel Lectionary of the eleventh century, and a Spanish Apocalypse dated 926, majestic in size, and profusely illustrated with vivid miniatures transformed from a late classical prototype." In 1920 Morgan acquired from the Phillipps collection the tenth-century Greek illuminated manuscript of *De materia medica* by Pedanius Dioscorides. Adams refers to the manuscript as the "cornerstone of the Library's fine botanical collection."

During the 1920s Morgan, Jr., bought two richly illuminated manuscripts of the Gospels made in England before the Norman Conquest. These had been owned by Countess Judith of Flanders, sister-in-law of both King Harold III and William the Conqueror. Another volume he obtained, still in its jeweled silver-gilt binding, was the Missal of Abbot Berthold, generally considered the finest thirteenth-century German manuscript extant. Morgan, Jr., also acquired the twelfth-century *Life, Miracles and Passion of St. Edmund* with thirty-two miniatures, one of the earliest cycles of pictures illustrating the life of an English saint.

Other purchases by Morgan, Jr., during this period included an eighth-century collection of sermons in Anglo-Saxon called the "Blickling Homilies," an excellent *Lancelot du Lac* written and illuminated in France during the early fourteenth century, several Caxtons, and a fine copy of Ptolemy's *Cosmographia* printed in Bologna in 1477. Adams asserts that although Morgan, Jr., obtained for the library only about one-third as many illuminated manuscripts as had his father, the materials he brought to the library were of exceptional quality. As for incunabula, he purchased about half as many as had his father, bringing the library's total to about two thousand.

In 1949 the library sponsored an exhibition in honor of Greene, who had retired as director the previous year. On view were many of the treasures already mentioned, as well as many others acquired by Greene in consultation with Morgan. Among these was the *Chansonnier Provençal*, a manuscript written in Italy in the thirteenth century in the langue d'oc of Provence and providing an anthology of the songs of the troubadours. Here, too, were the

Sphaera Mundi of Joannes de Sacro Bosco, a fifteenth-century Austrian manuscript of the text in which John Holywood of Halifax, a thirteenth-century Englishman, had created a simplified syllabus of the astronomy of Ptolemy for his students at the University of Paris. Other acquisitions on display included *Livre des Merveilles d'Aise*, a fifteenth-century French version of the journey of Marco Polo to China, and the *Livre du Roy Modus*, a fifteenth-century illustrated French manuscript about hunting.

The incunabula on view at this exhibition included another Marco Polo text, the first edition published in German and printed in Nuremberg in 1477, and the rare first edition (Basel, 1494) of the *Narrenschiff*, or *Ship of Fools*, by Sebastian Brant. Also on exhibit were a copy of the revolutionary *De Revolutionibus Orbium Coelestium* of Nicolaus Copernicus, printed in Nuremberg in 1543 and the 1543 Basel edition of the important anatomical work by Andreas Vesalius, *De Humani Corporis Fabrica*. In the catalogue of this exhibit it is stated that the Morgan Library is something more than "an aggregation of rare, famous, and spectacular works, that it is, in fact, an integration of texts of dynamic characteristics, great records of human experience, great assertions of ideas." The manuscripts and books in the library "portray the common heritage of western man, the life of medieval Europe, in as many aspects as possible. Here are its religion, art, history, and literature; here are the doing and thinking of humble scribe, of illuminator, bookbinder, metal worker, and wood carver, of tellers of tales and chroniclers as well as of great princes and mitred lords."

In 1924 Morgan, Jr., gave the Pierpont Morgan Library — the great collection of books, manuscripts, and drawings begun by his father and added to by him — as well as the building that housed these treasures, to a board of six trustees, he being its president. The board was to administer it as a public research library, utilizing a considerable endowment that Morgan gave for this purpose. He wrote that his desire was "to increase the value of the whole for educational purposes." He estimated the value of the collections at the time to be about $8.5 million, though many experts considered this quite conservative. Purchases for the library made by Greene had to be authorized by the trustees rather than by Morgan alone.

Under the influence of Morgan, Jr., the library rendered service to the scholarly community throughout the world and, indeed, to all who appreciate beautiful objects. In 1925 Morgan, Jr., issued a

The Pierpont Morgan Library West Room, circa 1910

complete photographic reproduction of the library's Coptic illuminated manuscripts dating from the eighth to the eleventh century. Most of these had been obtained by his father and sent to the Vatican Library for repair and conservation. Ten sets of these reproductions were printed, consisting of sixty-three volumes each. These facsimiles were sent to American, English, and European libraries for use by scholars. Two years later Morgan, Jr., published a facsimile edition of the "Old Testament Illustrations" that he had acquired in 1916. In addition to the program of facsimile reproduction, which the library has continued, special exhibitions were sponsored by the institution, with impressive catalogues printed to accompany them. Unlike the expensive issues that had been prepared by Morgan, Sr., for royalty in years gone by, these catalogues were meant for the general public.

In 1928 Morgan, Jr., had the house in which his father had lived demolished and in its place erected an annex to the library. This along with the generous endowment supplied by Morgan allowed the library to expand its sphere of activities. The extra space has been well utilized, and public use of the library has much increased because of it. The discrete collections to be found in the library during the latter part of the 1930s were the following:

Assyrian and Babylonian Seals, Cylinders, and Cuneiform Tablets;

Egyptian, Greek, and Other Papyri;

Medieval and Renaissance Manuscripts (sixth to sixteenth centuries);

Authors' Autograph Manuscripts and Letters (sixteenth to twentieth centuries);

Historical Letters and Documents (eleventh to twentieth centuries);

Printed Books (fifteenth to twentieth centuries);

Bookbinding and Metal Bookcovers (eighth to twentieth centuries);

Drawings (fourteenth to nineteenth centuries);

Etchings by Rembrandt;

English and Other Mezzotints (seventeenth to nineteenth centuries);

Italian Bronze Plaquettes and Medals (fourteenth to seventeenth centuries);

Greek and Roman Gold and Silver Coins

Morgan, unlike his father, had a whimsical side that occasionally presented itself. In 1922 he was being importuned by the officials of the Russian Orthodox monastery on Mount Athos in Greece to buy a set of Greek manuscripts for what he thought was an absurd price. The archimandrite wrote a letter to Morgan regarding the manuscripts in a high-flown pietistic style. Morgan's reply was as follows: "May the grace of Rabelais be with you, Amen. . . . I regret to find the holy brethren of Athos are so deeply tainted with wordly wisdom and guile. . . . Surely it would ill become us of the sackcloth to lend ourselves willing victims of this holy larceny."

Morgan worked closely with Greene for thirty years, and an easy and unpretentious relationship developed between them. Greene had strong ideas about items that she liked or disliked for the library. She wrote to Morgan, Jr., "In regard to the Tennyson items which, personally I loathe, it is a question of perfecting your already large and fine collection of imbecilities." Morgan replied from London, "I reluctantly confirm that we ought to have the Tennyson idiocies." On another occasion Greene wrote, "The visitors, few or many, are so damn respectful, never speaking above a whisper, that I occasionally think of importing a hoodlum (I should say another hoodlum) to keep myself company." Morgan replied, "I do not think I should feel so badly as you seem to about the respectfulness of the visitors. They ought to feel that way whether they show it or not. . . . though of course I can quite understand your desire to have *some* hoodlumism around somewhere, for company's sake, now that I am abroad."

Morgan was awarded an honorary LL.D. by Cambridge University in 1919, primarily to show appreciation for the part his firm played in supplying funds and matériel to Britain during World War I. The citation referred to him as one "who, not unmindful of academic studies, not only collects books, but also reads them." In 1930 Oxford conferred upon him the honorary degree of Doctor of Civil Laws, this in thanks for his having arranged for the *Psalter and Book of Hours* of John, Duke of Bedford, and for the *Luttrell Psalter* to remain in England.

Morgan, Jr., died in Boca Grande, Florida, on 13 March 1943. The Pierpont Morgan Library, its contents, its publications, and its exhibitions, endure as a living memorial to both father and son.

References:

Frederick B. Adams, Jr., *An Introduction to the Pierpont Morgan Library* (New York: Pierpont Morgan Library, 1964);

The First Quarter Century of the Pierpont Morgan Library, a Retrospective Exhibition in Honor of Belle da Costa Greene (New York, 1949);

John Douglas Forbes, *J. P. Morgan, Jr. 1867–1943* (Charlottesville: University Press of Virginia, 1981);

In August Company: The Collections of the Pierpont Morgan Library (New York: Pierpont Morgan Library with Harry N. Abrams, 1993);

Stanley Jackson, *J. P. Morgan* (New York: Stein & Day, 1983);

Pierpont Morgan Library, *Review of the Activities and Acquisitions of the Library from 1936 through 1940* (New York, 1941);

Pierpont Morgan Library, *Review of the Activities and Major Acquisitions of the Library 1941–1948* (New York, 1949);

A. W. Pollard, general editor, *Catalogue of Manuscripts and Early Printed Books from the Libraries of William Morris, Richard Bennett, Bertram, Fourth Earl of Ashburnham, and Other Sources, now forming portion of the Library of J. Pierpont Morgan*, 4 volumes (London: Chiswick Press, 1906–1907);

Linda Horvitz Roth, ed., *J. Pierpont Morgan, Collector* (Hartford, Conn.: Wadsworth Atheneum, 1987);

Francis Henry Taylor, *Pierpont Morgan as Collector and Patron, 1837–1913* (New York: Pierpont Morgan Library, 1957).

A. Edward Newton

(26 August 1864 – 29 September 1940)

Richard E. Brewer
Monmouth College

BOOKS: *The Amenities of Book-Collecting and Kindred Affections* (Boston: Atlantic Monthly Press, 1918);

A Magnificent Farce and Other Diversions of a Book-Collector (Boston: Atlantic Monthly Press, 1921);

Doctor Johnson: A Play (Boston: Atlantic Monthly Press, 1923);

The Greatest Book in the World and Other Papers (Boston: Little, Brown, 1925);

This Book-Collecting Game (Boston: Little, Brown, 1928);

The Format of the English Novel . . . with Reproductions of Title-pages from Books in the Author's Library (Cleveland: Rowfant Club, 1928);

Thomas Hardy, Novelist or Poet? . . . with Facsimiles of Original Letters in the "Oak Knoll" Library (Philadelphia: Privately printed, 1929);

A Tourist in Spite of Himself (Boston: Little, Brown, 1930);

End Papers (Boston: Little, Brown, 1933);

Derby Day and Other Adventures (Boston: Little, Brown, 1934);

Bibliography and Pseudo-Bibliography (Philadelphia: University of Pennsylvania Press, 1936);

Newton on Blackstone (Philadelphia: University of Pennsylvania Press, 1937).

SELECTED PERIODICAL PUBLICATION – UNCOLLECTED: "E. V. Lucas: The Passing of a Wit," *Atlantic Monthly,* 162 (November 1938): 616–624.

OTHER: *William Blake, 1757–1827, A Descriptive Catalogue of an Exhibition of the Works of William Blake Selected from Collections in the United States,* with an introductory essay by Newton (Philadelphia: Philadelphia Museum of Art, 1939).

Over a collecting career that covered more than four decades, Alfred Edward Newton assembled a library especially rich in British literature of the seventeenth and eighteenth centuries. With Chauncey Brewster Tinker of Yale and Robert B. Adam of Buffalo he fostered an interest in the English neoclassical writers, especially Samuel Johnson and James Boswell, at a time when their works were largely ignored. Newton promoted them by writing about them and by purchasing first editions of their works. His love of books encompassed the sixteenth and the nineteenth centuries as well. As a prominent collector widely known for his magazine articles and colorful public persona, he played a central role in the great boom in book collecting, or "this book-collecting game," as he called it, which peaked between about 1910 and 1930. When his own collection was sold at auction in 1941, the book world looked on eagerly. Moreover, Newton's nine volumes of essays, published between 1918 and 1937, brought him international fame as a writer of witty and stylish prose, even as they helped strengthen, or revive, the fame of his favorite authors and encourage his thousands of readers to collect their works.

Alfred Edward Newton was born to Alfred Wharton Newton and Louisa Swift Newton in Philadelphia on 26 August 1864 at the northwest corner of Twentieth and Spruce streets. His ancestors had emigrated from Tunbridge Wells in Kent before the Revolutionary War. His family included two sisters, two aunts, and his uncle Swift, of whom he was particularly fond.

As a boy he read such staples of youth as *Sandford and Merton,* the Rollo books, *Swiss Family Robinson,* and *Robinson Crusoe.* He received a rudimentary education at a boarding school in Downingtown, Pennsylvania, and later he attended a business school in the evening. Though he never studied in a university, he was eventually awarded honorary degrees by Temple University (1919), Haverford College (1925), and the University of Pennsylvania (1935).

One of his earliest jobs was as office boy for the Curtis Publishing Company. An early exposure to literature may also have come from subsequent

experience in a fashionable stationery and book-store owned by Porter and Coates, two well-to-do Quakers. According to Newton's son, Swift, some fellow workers interested Newton in reading and collecting books. He was initially drawn to Napoleon, collecting everything he could on this subject.

One of Newton's first compositions was written in 1878 when he was fourteen and titled "When My Ship Comes In":

When my ship comes in I intend to take a trip across the ocean with my wife and children. I am going first to England, next to France, and after that to Switzerland and Italy. After I have traveled through all these places I intend to go to Egypt, and the Holy Land, and then I am going through India to China and Japan. After that to California and all the other places of interest in the United States. When I arrive at home I intend to go into business. I don't quite know what kind it will be, but I think it will have something [to do] with printing or stationery. When I get [to be] an old man I intend to retire from business with a large fortune, say $200,000.

Young Newton's agenda later in life was followed with remarkable consistency, as he pursued the nineteenth-century ideal of the Grand Tour, with the exception of the Far East. His shrewd business acumen would result in fruitful and varied ventures such as publishing, a chocolate factory, a fancy-goods business, and the manufacture of electrical

Newton in his library at Oak Knoll, 1935

equipment, from which he made a fortune later in life. He joined the Cutter Electrical and Manufacturing Company in 1895 and became its president in 1900.

Two events, however, which occurred in the decade following the penning of his ambitious program, were most responsible for shaping his personality. The first of these occurred when he was twenty; he traveled to England, where he became a confirmed Anglophile. What Newton loved above all was London. Its cultural ambience, its literary and historical associations, its bookshops, its civility, and even its music halls were sources of endless fascination for him from his youth until well into his seventies, when illness kept him from further travel. He felt cheated unless he made an annual or even semiannual pilgrimage to England.

The second and equally momentous event was his reading Boswell's *Life of Samuel Johnson* when he was twenty-one. From this time forward Newton's devotion to Johnson and to the *Life* fell little short of idolatry. Toward the end of Newton's life, his good friend Charles Grosvenor Osgood remarked that Newton "was, one might say, primarily educated upon one book – Boswell's *Life of Johnson* – which he had read from early youth and knew almost by heart. The vigor of his wit and style owed something no doubt to his long association with Johnson." If a man was a confirmed Johnsonian, he was sure to be Newton's friend; if not, then Newton had grave doubts as to his character. In time Newton acquired an eloquent portrait by Sir Joshua Reynolds of Johnson in his later years and even a teapot owned by the great lexicographer. In 1930 Newton was the first American to be elected president of the Johnson Society of Great Britain.

Newton's enthusiasm for eighteenth-century literature was evident relatively early in his life. Determined to have a representative library, at the age of eighteen he asked a friend where to begin and was urged to secure Alexander Pope's translation of Homer's *Iliad* and the *Odyssey,* both of which he devoured enthusiastically. Looking back at this event from the vantage point of more than fifty years, Newton amusingly noted, "I feel quite sure that I believed the original was written in just such rhyming couplets as Pope handled with such amazing skill." Other early purchases which helped form his neoclassic taste included Lemprière's *Classical Dictionary* and Horne Tooke's *Pantheon.*

In 1890 Newton married Babette Edelheim, who came from a German-Jewish family. The couple had two children: a daughter, Caroline Newton (1892–1975), whom Newton referred to as "Lina," and a son, Edward Swift Newton (1894–1974), who was called Swift. In 1901 Newton became engaged in what was to be a lengthy and expensive litigation involving a patent suit between his own electrical business and the Allied Westinghouse and General Electric Companies. The experience helped in making him increasingly disenchanted with the business world; he turned more and more to the solace offered by book collecting and literature. At Christmas in 1907 Newton privately printed and circulated among friends a calendar of the new year with a quotation from Walt Whitman and comments by himself. He thus inaugurated an annual series of Christmas gift publications that would continue until the year of his death. These charming little blue books, which covered an impressive variety of literary subjects, became, even in Newton's lifetime, highly prized by collectors, who would pay increasingly large sums for them at auctions, much to Newton's own amazement and delight. Nearly all of them were eventually gathered into one or another of Newton's volumes.

During this period he began to give more time to the Grolier Club in New York and spend more hours reading in the well-stocked library of his suburban estate, Oak Knoll, in Daylesford, Pennsylvania. By 1909 he was in the process of assembling a truly notable library and spent little time at the Cutter Electrical Company. The same verve and vigor which he once devoted to business was now being turned to book collecting and kindred pursuits.

Newton was also acquiring a wide circle of literary friends. It is fitting that in the Johnson bicentennial year of 1909 two of these friends were working on Johnson projects and were to become distinguished academicians. The first was Osgood of Princeton, whom Newton had known for a few years. Osgood was preparing a volume, *Selections from the Works of Samuel Johnson,* for which Newton supplied the illustrations. The second was Tinker, who also drew upon Newton's library for the Yale exhibition of Johnson and who was to dedicate his first book – a collection of Fanny Burney's reminiscences of Johnson – to "A. Edward Newton, Johnsonian." Newton himself was organizing yet another Johnson exhibition at the Grolier Club, for which Osgood agreed to prepare a long descriptive note. It was Osgood also who devised at this time Newton's famous Temple Bar bookplate with a Johnsonian mot from Boswell: "Sir, the biographical part of literature is what I love most."

Newton often asserted that, along with his book collecting, he "collected professors." In addition to Osgood and Tinker, with whom he exchanged letters and visits over a period of more than thirty years, he was also friendly with Francis B. Gummere of Haverford, Christian F. Gauss of Princeton, and Felix E. Schelling of the University of Pennsylvania. When one considers Newton's varied business enterprises, his frequent travel, his visits to auction rooms and bookshops, his letters to academicians, and his correspondence with many other friends, the sheer volume of his activity seems staggering.

Newton had a rare genius for friendship and firmly believed, in the words of Johnson, in "keeping his friendships in good repair." A partial list of these friends indicates something of the rich variety of his interests. Among book collectors were Beverly Chew; Adam; the young Harry Widener, who perished on the *Titanic;* Dr. A. S. W. Rosenbach, a fellow Philadelphian as well as a premier book dealer in the post–World War I era; Gabriel Wells, another great bookseller of the era; and James and Hugh Tregaskis, proprietors of the great Caxton Head Bookshop of London. There were also banker and antiquarian William McIntire Elkins; composer Jerome Kern, the sale of whose books in early 1929 yielded record prices that were not to be surpassed for decades; Mitchell Kennerly, president of the Anderson Galleries on Park Avenue; poet and collector Amy Lowell; artist and illustrator Joseph Pennell; Max Beerbohm, who created an amusing caricature of Newton; the prolific author Christopher Morley; Carolyn Wells, anthologist of humorous verse; editor of the *Atlantic Monthly* Ellery Sedgwick; and Agnes Repplier, whose graceful, witty essays were highly prized by Newton and his friends. While abroad he also befriended John Burns, the influential Labour politician; Lord and Lady Charnwood; the scholarly Sir Walter Ralegh; E. V. Lucas, essayist and biographer of Charles Lamb; and Augustine Birrell, the genial late-Victorian essayist who shared Newton's love of eighteenth-century authors and whose prose style influenced Newton's writing.

In the words of

Charles Lamb

"Yours ratherish unwell"

A. EDWARD NEWTON

*Title page for Newton's 1937 Christmas pamphlet. During his lifetime his
privately printed gift publications were sought by other collectors.*

As his essays began to accumulate and be received with increasing appreciation, Newton conceived of collecting them in a privately printed volume. In the fall of 1914 he sent a monograph on book collecting to Sedgwick. This essay was warmly accepted and published the following year. Others followed and met with the same enthusiasm. These pieces were to form the nucleus of Newton's first volume of essays, published in November 1918 as *The Amenities of Book-Collecting and Kindred Affections*.

For Newton as for many others, the advent of the war was traumatic. He sensed that the world which he had known and loved was in the process of passing away forever. His son, Swift, who served in the American Expeditionary Force in France, recorded Newton's reactions in August 1914 at Oak Knoll upon hearing that the war had actually started: "My father . . . instantly broke into tears and said, 'My friends, the England that I love, the England of Trollope, is gone forever!' " For Newton, as for his older contemporary Henry James, the ancient rituals and established hierarchies of England were irresistible — Monarchy and Church, abbeys and granges, vicars and rectors, lords and ladies, riding and hunting, and the country gentry who presided over it all. Newton sadly and accurately perceived that the picturesque and comfortable stabilities of Old England — the England of Anthony Trollope — were sure to be gravely jeopardized by the war.

Unable to travel during the war years, Newton increasingly turned to writing. He composed an essay on Bar for his Christmas pamphlet in 1915.

Newton holding R. B. Adam's Boswell notebook (photograph by Christopher Morley)

There followed in fairly rapid succession pieces on Boswell, Trollope, Piozzi, and other literary subjects. Some of these essays were published in the *Atlantic Monthly,* and all of them, as well as an Oscar Wilde piece and the two previously published articles on book collecting, were incorporated into *Amenities* at the end of 1918. At this time, as his friend Osgood noted, "Like Byron, he woke to find himself famous in literature." In three weeks *Amenities* sold more than one thousand copies, and by spring 1919 a second impression of five thousand copies had been ordered. The following year the second of ten eventual editions appeared. These included a volume in the Modern Library series in an inexpensive format.

Also at the end of the war Newton struck up a friendship and memorable correspondence with Lowell. He had been introduced to her by Sedgwick in 1915 and was captivated by her unusual personality as well as by her fine collection of books. He included her photograph in *Amenities* with the caption "Miss Amy Lowell, of Boston, Poet, Critic, and America's Most Distinguished Woman Collector."

Newton's letters to Lowell are surely among the most courtly and affectionate he ever wrote; but no less fascinating are those to other friends, such as Osgood, which are more confessional than those to Lowell. Perhaps the most literary of his correspondences are those with Tinker. It is as hard to categorize Newton's letters as it is his essays, however; he is by turns earthy and fanciful, modest and assertive, playful and serious. His letters were never dull, never pedantic.

The decade after World War I must have been for Newton one of the most satisfying and fruitful of his life. Despite a slight heart attack in 1919, his health remained good. Swift had returned home from the war unharmed. His finances were more than ample for the travel, writing, and book collecting that now occupied most of his time. Moreover, he had achieved a solid reputation as an author and was increasingly in demand as a lecturer. Even though he treated his success with a modicum of self-deprecation, there is no doubt that he relished the attention success brought him.

Newton continued to work at his electrical business (the chocolate works having been sold in 1917) after the publication and enthusiastic reception of *Amenities,* although his heart was elsewhere — chiefly in his writing, in his friendships, and in the auction rooms. In February 1919 he told Lowell, "When pleasure interferes with business, I cut out business." The four books that he produced during this decade include some of his finest, most characteristic work: *A Magnificent Farce and Other Diversions of a Book-Collector* (1921), *Doctor Johnson: A Play* (1923), *The Greatest Book in the World* (1925), and *This Book-Collecting Game* (1928).

With the cessation of the war, Newton was once again able to engage in travel, and every year thereafter he and Babette sailed to England — sometimes twice. Other journeys took them to the Continent and, on one occasion, to the Middle East. These travels are amply and charmingly recorded in his later books, especially *A Tourist in Spite of Himself* (1930) and *Derby Day and Other Adventures* (1934).

By April 1921 Newton had finished his second collection of essays, *A Magnificent Farce,* which was to be published in September. It sold one thousand copies in a week, greatly exceeding its author's expectations and requiring three impressions in its second month of publication. The large-paper edition was oversubscribed and, owing to its scarcity, sold in New York for as much as twenty-five dollars. Newton was inundated with letters, all of which he thoroughly enjoyed, praising his work and asking him questions about book-collecting matters.

Toward the end of the same year Newton's friend the eminent bookseller Gabriel Wells bought a defective Gutenberg Bible, which he proposed to break up and sell in sections of two leaves. These were to be bound up with a bibliographic essay by Newton. This project, too, proved to be a notable success.

In 1923 brisk sales of his play *Doctor Johnson* delighted Newton and his Johnsonian friends. The dialogue was drawn largely from Boswell's *Life* and from various letters and documents of both Johnson and his contemporaries. In a letter to Osgood, Newton wrote: "I take little credit to myself for this success. The cast is so brilliant that no kind of a play could be an utter failure in its hands." Despite the author's modesty more than four thousand copies were sold during the first three weeks of publication, and the play was ultimately performed by amateur groups in America and abroad. Reynolds's portrait of Johnson in his later years, which Newton owned, served as the frontispiece.

The success of *Doctor Johnson* and, two years later, *The Greatest Book in the World,* encouraged Newton to build an addition to Oak Knoll in order to house his growing collection of books. This room, dedicated by his friend Tinker with a suitable address for the occasion, contained Newton's first editions of virtually all major English and American authors, along with his remarkable collection of fine prints, which included several of William Blake's engravings as well as portraits of his favorite authors.

At book sales during this period, such as at the Adam sale of February 1926, Newton would arrange a private dinner for a few friends before — in some cases, after — an auction, with plenty of time after the sales were completed for smoking cigars and strolling the streets to enjoy good talk about authors and their books and the purchases that the group had just made. This genial practice, which Newton called "a Johnsonian frisk," was often accompanied by his muttered protestations of financial ruin. Newton also found book transactions to be at times an occasion for humor. Acting upon a suggestion by Tinker in the summer of 1926, he and Tinker decided to sell their unwanted books at auction. Their plans took on an atmosphere of facetious conspiracy as Newton assumed the lead in this scheme. He contracted Kennerley at the Anderson Galleries in New York to set up the most propitious date and suggested that all the items be presented as his own. The ensuing catalogue, with a characteristically impudent Newtonian preface, was entitled *The Books of a Busted Bibliophile.*

In the mid 1920s there had been rumors of a great trove of Boswell manuscripts in a castle outside Dublin. Newton urged his friend Tinker to go to Ireland and pursue the story, taking with him his impressive credentials (which included his recently published selection of Boswell letters) in order to secure this precious material. Tinker duly complied and in 1925 visited Malahide Castle, where he was shown an antique ebony cabinet stuffed full of unprinted Boswell manuscripts of every sort. In the flush of excitement he rushed off a cryptic postcard to Newton to confirm his glimpse of these treasures, which stated in part: "Sinbad and the Valley of Diamonds is the correct metaphor." Thus began one of the greatest literary discoveries of the century.

RARE BOOKS
ORIGINAL DRAWINGS
AUTOGRAPH LETTERS AND
MANUSCRIPTS

Collected by the late

A. EDWARD NEWTON

Removed from His Home
OAK KNOLL
Daylesford, Pa.

For Public Sale

*By Order of the Executors
Under the Will of A. Edward Newton, Deceased*
E. SWIFT NEWTON *and* BRANDON BARRINGER

AT THE

PARKE-BERNET GALLERIES · INC

30 EAST 57 STREET · NEW YORK

1941

Frontispiece and title page for the auction catalogue of Newton's collection. The photograph depicts Newton, Charles Osgood, Babette Newton, and Agnes Repplier having tea in Newton's Oak Knoll library.

Soon others, including Newton, made efforts to purchase the Boswell papers but met with no success. Then Newton suggested that his friend Col. Ralph Heyward Isham had both the temperament and the means to succeed where others had conspicuously failed. He was right. Since Newton had been close to all the principals in this exciting drama, he planned to write his own account of the acquisition and eventual publication of the materials; he never did, however. But he did remain busy making acquisitions for his own library. In 1927 he paid Wells sixty-two thousand dollars for the Carysfort copy of William Shakespeare's First Folio, which he called at the time the "capstone" of his collection.

At the end of the decade Newton published two small monographs issued in limited editions. The first of these, *The Format of the English Novel,* was printed by the Rowfant Club of Cleveland in 1928. The second, entitled *Thomas Hardy, Novelist or Poet?,* was privately printed in 1929 by Newton, who con-

tributed the proceeds for the erection in 1930 of a Thomas Hardy Memorial on Egdon Heath in Dorsetshire. Newton admired Hardy's work and owned a significant collection of his first editions.

When the market crashed in October 1929, Newton's business acumen enabled him to survive the crisis in better financial condition than many of his friends. Moreover, at the depth of the Depression in 1931 he managed to sell his business on terms distinctly advantageous to himself. Despite these successes, however, the deepening financial debacle, the rise of Adolf Hitler, and the failure of America and England to solve their problems left him distressed and anxious.

Even the "book-collecting game" seems to have lost some of its allure. In Cairo during the now-legendary Jerome Kern sale of January 1929, he recorded his amazement at the extravagant prices and in a letter to Tinker lamented: "I guess my collecting days are over. I can't stand the pace."

A year later a libel action was brought against him by the London firm of Quaritch on the basis of some critical remarks regarding auction practices he had made in an essay entitled "The Auction Room" published in his *This Book-Collecting Game*. As the 1930s wore on and the Depression deepened, other problems contributed to Newton's anxiety. The death of friends and his own sense of encroaching age troubled his spirit. The collapse of Adam's financial position and Adam's subsequent illness troubled him greatly, as did the exposure of the forgeries of his longtime friend T. J. Wise.

There were bright intervals amid the gloom. Newton reveled in the Johnsonian ceremonies at Lichfield, where he read his paper "Franklin and Johnson Meet at Mr. Strahan's," an imaginary dialogue much in the style of Walter Savage Landor. The occasion was his installation as president of the Johnson Society of Great Britain in September 1930. In December 1932 Newton tried to promote Repplier's new book *To Think of Tea!* by giving a Johnsonian tea part at which he, Babette, Repplier, and Osgood were photographed in Newton's library, with Repplier pouring from Dr. Johnson's teapot and Osgood standing beneath the Reynolds portrait.

The sale of his business interests in 1931 gave Newton even more time for travel and writing. He spent ever-larger parts of each year in England, maintaining a flat in Jermyn Street, Saint James's. Meanwhile the books issued forth at a steady pace: *A Tourist in Spite of Himself, End Papers* (1933), *Derby Day and Other Adventures*. A series of lectures he gave at the University of Pennsylvania were published as *Bibliography and Pseudo-Bibliography* (1936). These essays of the 1930s present Newton at his ripest, most expansive, most autobiographical. Skillfully crafted and diverse, they sold well even in times of economic uncertainty.

Newton's deepest literary passions did not falter in these last years of his life. In 1934 he founded a Trollope society, whose purpose was to secure the publication "of a complete, uniform, and legible edition of the Novels and Tales of one of the greatest of the Victorians." This project was to be based upon his own set of Trollope first editions and was to contain introductions by such Trollope enthusiasts as Shane Leslie, Henry S. Drinker, and Tinker. However, only two volumes had been published when the enterprise was cut short by Newton's failing health. (The project would be resumed after World War II.)

By the summer of 1937 Newton was gravely ill with cancer. His condition had deteriorated so badly by December that Swift advised Osgood to expect the worst and pleaded with him to prepare what would have been an obituary biography for the newspapers. But surprisingly Newton rallied and was to have three more years of alternate suffering and remission.

Understandably, his mood varied with his physical condition. At times his suffering was intense – so intense that he expressed a wish to die. In a letter of December 1939 to Tinker he confided, "For over two years my great longing was for death," and concluded, "This is from a lonely, heart-broken old man." In the midst of this anguish his friendships became stronger. If there is a Johnsonian vulnerability about his final years, there is also a Johnsonian candor and dignity.

Even while grappling with his illness he managed to write two noteworthy essays. One, his last *Atlantic Monthly* contribution, was a lengthy memoir on the passing of his friend Lucas in 1938. The other, an introduction to a descriptive catalogue of an exhibition of William Blake, was published in 1939 by the Philadelphia Museum of Art.

Newton died on 29 September 1940. Thousands in America mourned the passing of the man who had taught them the amenities of collecting books and the love of great literature and who had for many years enchanted them with the verve and wit of his essays. In Britain too, even in the dark days of the Blitz, time was found to remember Newton. Josiah Charles Stamp noted, "A Unique figure has passed from Anglo-American relations," and an obituary in the London *Times* lamented the loss of a "national humorist."

On Christmas of that year, the Library of Congress issued a small booklet of posthumous tributes by old friends in the same format that Newton had used every Christmas since nearly the beginning of the century. One of the most moving of these was the contribution of Osgood, who recalled many memorable hours spent in the Oak Knoll library:

> Never did I return to the academic shop from those ambrosial days and nights at Oak Knoll, where the time was not long enough to have our talk out, without access of new energy, a larger view, and renewed faith in the job. Not that we ever talked of such things. It was deeper than that. . . . Behind his many illustrious gifts was a very tender heart, not sentimental, but easily touched and moved. He was like Johnson in this also, and most of all, where friends were concerned. . . . One evening I sat alone with him at Oak Knoll. Each of us was deep, but not too deep, in a book, and neither of us spoke. After a bit he laid his book down and said:

"Charley, life cannot be better than this — two old friends sitting quietly together reading. Neither of them speaks unless he has something to say. Yet all the time, without a word, the exchange goes on."

In his will Newton echoed Edmond de Goncourt, stipulating that his books "be dispersed under the hammer of the auctioneer, so that the pleasure which the acquiring of each one of them has given me shall be given again, in each case, to some inheritor of my own tastes." Accordingly, in 1941 Newton's books were sold at auction at the Parke-Bernet Galleries in New York, the catalogue constituting yet another, though posthumous, Newtonian contribution to bibliography and bibliophily. Many of his old friends gathered at the sales to acquire a memento, though the offerings were of more than sentimental value. There were the autograph manuscript of Charles Lamb's poignant essay "Dream Children; a Reverie"; the rare first edition of Robert Burns's *Poems, Chiefly in the Scottish Dialect* (Kilmarnock, 1786) — purchased by Morley for $2,950; the first issue of Thomas Gray's *Elegy Wrote in a Country Churchyard* (London, 1751). There were many other treasures as well, including autograph letters by major authors. But the three sales yielded only $185,050.50, less than had been expected. The disappointing proceeds have been attributed to the continuing economic crisis and the depressing effects of the war, though the less-than-ideal condition of some of the items may have been partly responsible. The Newton provenance, however, atones for any bibliographic deficiencies. As Rosenbach notes: "It is what Newton wrote about his own beloved books, his spry and mellow comments, his humorous descriptions, that make each volume in his library a living thing. It is this that makes the books of Eddie Newton different from any in our land."

Letters:

Maxwell Luria, "Miss Lowell and Mr. Newton: The Record of a Literary Friendship," *Harvard Library Bulletin*, 29 (1981): 5–34;

Luria and Richard E. Brewer, " 'Dear Charley': A. Edward Newton's Letters to Charles Grosvenor Osgood," *Princeton University Library Chronicle*, 45 (1984): 230–255; 46 (1984): 4–48;

Luria and Brewer, "The Caliph and the Professor: A. Edward Newton's Correspondence with Chauncey Brewster Tinker," *Harvard Library Bulletin*, 33 (1985): 114–173;

Luria and Brewer, "From Oak Knoll to Great Russell Street," *Book Collector*, 36 (Spring 1987): 77–99.

Biography:

E. Swift Newton, *AEN/Remarks Made by E. Swift Newton on the Occasion of His Presentation of the Personal Library of His Father A. Edward Newton to the Free Library of Philadelphia* (Philadelphia: Free Library, 1954).

References:

Robert Fleck, "A. Edward Newton/A Collection of His Works," *Oak Knoll Books Catalogue*, no. 86 (New Castle, Del.: Oak Knoll Books, 1986);

The Rare Books and Manuscript Collected by the Late A. Edward Newton, 3 volumes and a prospectus volume (New York: Parke-Bernet Galleries, 1941);

Chauncey Brewster Tinker, "The Caliph of Books: A.E.N.," *Atlantic Monthly*, 172 (1943): 102–106;

A Tribute to A. Edward Newton, Christmas 1940 (Washington, D.C.: Library of Congress, 1940).

Papers:

The major collection of manuscript materials of A. Edward Newton is at the Free Library of Philadelphia. Other important collections include those at the Houghton Library, Harvard University; Beinecke Rare Book and Manuscript Library, Yale University; the University of Pennsylvania Library; and the Princeton University Library.

Carl H. Pforzheimer

(29 January 1879 – 4 April 1957)

Ruth Rosenberg
City University of New York

Carl H. Pforzheimer began his career as a four-dollar-a-week runner on Wall Street. He had established his own firm on the New York Stock Exchange by the age of twenty-three and went on to become an internationally known bibliophile. His library of English literature constituted one of the great rare-book and manuscript collections in private hands. The Percy Bysshe Shelley materials he acquired – print and manuscript – were more complete than any other holdings except for those of the British Museum.

Pforzheimer was born in New York on 29 January 1879, the son of Isaac and Mina Heyman Pforzheimer. He attended City College of New York. On Wall Street he became a specialist in trading shares of the Standard Oil Company after the dissolution of the old Standard Oil Trust in 1911. He was a charter member of the Curb Exchange, later to become the American Stock Exchange. He and his wife, the former Lily Oppenheimer, had two children. The Pforzheimers lived in a twenty-room English-style manor on a four-hundred-acre estate in Purchase, Westchester County, New York, to which he added a fine library to house his magnificent collection. Politically active in his town and county, Pforzheimer served at various times as member and chairman of the Westchester County Emergency Work Bureau, the Westchester County Commission on Government (whose recommendations led to the Home Rule Charter under which the county operates), and the Westchester County Planning Commission. In 1955 the National Municipal League, which he served as treasurer for more than thirty-five years, named its new building in New York for him. He served also for many years as chairman of the Board of Trustees of the Horace Mann School in Riverdale, the Bronx.

As his wealth grew, Pforzheimer began to acquire books and manuscripts. After some purchases at the Henry Huth, Robert Hoe, and Britwell Court sales, Pforzheimer emerged as a major buyer at the Henry Buxton Forman auction in 1920 at the Anderson Galleries, New York. There – guided by his friend and mentor Dr. A. S. W. Rosenbach, the Philadelphia bibliophile and dealer – he bought Robert Browning's *Pauline,* the rarest of the writer's works, for $2,560, then a record; Fanny Brawne's personal copy of John Keats's *Poems* for $1,750; one of the most curiously titled and elusive of Shelley's early works, *Posthumous Fragments of Margaret Nicholson: Being Poems found amongst the papers of that noted Female who attempted the life of the King in 1786, Edited by John Fitzvictor* (1810) for $6,750; and for the same price the tragedy *Oedipus Tyrannus* (1820), which Shelley withdrew from circulation and destroyed, except for a few copies. Shortly thereafter Rosenbach persuaded Pforzheimer to advance him $200,000 for the purchase of the Robert Schumann collection of French eighteenth-century books in fine bindings. Nothing of its elegance had ever before come across the Atlantic to the United States. Pforzheimer also acquired one of the largest Shelley manuscripts in existence, "A Philosophical View of Reform," on 201 pages, containing one of the best of the few landscape drawings made by the poet.

In 1923 a representative of the Rosenbach Company attended the Carysfort sale at Sotheby's in London and purchased the Mazarin Gutenberg Bible on behalf of Pforzheimer. So called because it had been in the library of Cardinal Mazarin, the Bible had resurfaced on the Continent about a century earlier and was purchased by James Perry, editor of the London *Morning Chronicle.* Perry sold it in 1822 for £168 to the duke of Sussex, who in turn sold it twenty-five years later for £190 to the bishop of Cashel. He sold it eleven years later for £596 to the earl of Crawford, who in turn passed it to the earl of Carysfort in 1887 for £2,650. Pforzheimer purchased it for £8,500 (about $60,000), setting a record for a Gutenberg Bible printed on paper. Rosenbach waxed lyrical about the Pforzheimer purchase and, indeed, about the collection of books

Carl H. Pforzheimer

and manuscripts that Pforzheimer was building. "The copy bought by Mr. Pforzheimer," stated Rosenbach in the *New York Times* of 9 November 1923, "is America's only perfect copy of the first issue of the Gutenberg Bible in an old binding. It adds another copy of the Gutenberg Bible to New York's Library treasures. I predict that within the next ten years this Mazarin Bible will be worth $100,000." Pforzheimer was himself quite emotional about his acquisition of this Bible. In a memoir he cites what had been written by the American bookseller Henry Stevens in 1847 when another Gutenberg was dispatched to America: "Not only is it the first Bible, but it is the first book ever printed. It was read in Europe half a century before America was discovered. Let no Custom House official, or other man in or out of authority, see it without reverently raising his hat. It is not possible for many men ever to touch or even look upon a page of a

Gutenberg Bible." The Gutenberg was not the only Bible that Pforzheimer purchased at the Carysfort sale. The second was a superb volume on vellum, the Fust and Schoeffer Bible dated 1462, the first Bible to include a printed date.

In the *Times* article Rosenbach mentioned several other noteworthy treasures in the Pforzheimer collection. They include the four folios of Shakespeare that had come from the Newdegate collection, the set having been in the Newdegate family from 1660 continuously until purchased by Pforzheimer. There was also an early quarto edition of Shakespeare with the only perfect copy known of the *Tragedy of Richard III* (1594). In Rosenbach's estimation, Pforzheimer possessed the finest collection of the works of Edmund Spenser then known, with the exception of that held by Henry Huntington. He also owned a copy of John Milton's *Comus*, "the celebrated one that once belonged to the Earl of

Page from William Godwin's proofs for Political Justice, *part of Pforzheimer's collection of works by Percy Bysshe Shelley and his circle of family and friends (New York Public Library)*

Bridgewater and which sold for $14,250 in the H. V. Jones sales, from which Mr. Pforzheimer purchased it in June, 1919." Rosenbach also lists Pforzheimer's recent acquisitions: "He recently purchased in a sale in London an autographed manuscript of Shelley's last will, written on three pages. He also purchased lately for the sum of $20,000 the original manuscript of Charles Dickens's Christmas book, *The Haunted Man,* which originally belonged to the Baroness Burdett-Coutts, to whom it was presented by Dickens."

At the 1923 Carysfort sale Rosenbach purchased for Pforzheimer the rare 1865 edition of Lewis Carroll's *Alice in Wonderland.* The price was £380. This led the *Evening Standard* to comment, "Alice certainly will sit up and rub her eyes if or when she hears of it." By this time Pforzheimer already owned seven books from the press of William Caxton, England's first printer. These included Jacobus de Cessolis's *Game of Chess* (1483); *Mirrors of the Worlde* (1481); Raoul Lef 'evre's *History of Troye* (1475); *The Festevall* (1483); and *Glanville* and *De Proprietatus* (1472). Of the Elizabethan dramatists, Pforzheimer owned first editions of George Chapman, Ben Jonson, Francis Beaumont and John Fletcher, Robert Greene, Samuel Daniel, Christopher Marlowe, and others. He also had a fine collection of autographed letters, including the Bulstrode correspondence of political and literary letters from the seventeenth century. He continued to build his collection with purchases at the Clawson sale of 1926 at the Anderson Galleries. Of the two hundred thousand dollars that he spent there, the most notable purchase was probably William Painter's *Palace of Pleasure* (1566–1567). This was a collection of ninety-four tales taken from Greek, Roman, and Italian authors. The Italian setting of many Elizabethan dramas is derived from this work and others like it; the plots of William Shakespeare's *All's Well That Ends Well* (circa 1602–1603) and *Timon of Athens* (circa 1605–1608) are taken from it. In 1929 Pforzheimer bought the manuscript of George Gordon, Lord Byron's *Marino Faliero* (1821) for $27,000.

The stock-market crash of 1929 and the ensuing Depression did not interrupt the continuing enhancement of Pforzheimer's holdings. In 1931 Rosenbach bought on order for him the only known perfect copy of the principal source for Shakespeare's *As You Like It* (circa 1599–1600), Thomas Lodge's *Rosalynde* (1590), for £2,400. In 1934 Rosenbach was chagrined that Pforzheimer was able to buy from him for a paltry $6,100 all of the following: thirteen plays by Chapman, Jonson's *Volpone,* eight John Marstons, and almost all of Thomas Nabbes's published work. In 1936

Pforzheimer bought the only surviving perfect copy of Spenser's translation of Plato's *Axiochus.* In 1938 he acquired a copy of Francis Bacon's *Essaies* (1612). In 1939, when Rosenbach purchased Elizabeth Barrett Browning's first book, *The Battle of Marathon* (1820), for $1,500, Pforzheimer recalled that the Jerome Kern copy had sold for $17,500 ten years earlier. He tossed a coin to decide whether he or another of Rosenbach's collector friends should get it. He won this prize, as he did another – one of the most attractive Byron manuscripts in existence, his farewell to his wife when she left him. In 1946 Pforzheimer bought Henry Howard, Earl of Surrey's *Songs and Sonnettes* (1559) for $8,200 from Rosenbach, who had acquired it in 1928 for £5,000.

Shelley was one of Pforzheimer's overwhelming interests. In 1896 Buxton Forman had paid a trifling £6 for Shelley's own copy of *Queen Mab* (1813). Rosenbach paid $6,000 for it at the Forman sale in 1920 and seven years later sold it for $9,500 to Kern. In 1929 it was sold to Gabriel Wells for $68,000 at the Kern sale at the Anderson Galleries. Wells's executors put it up for auction in 1951, and Pforzheimer got it for $8,000.

In 1940 Pforzheimer published a three-volume catalogue of his library's holdings titled *The Carl H. Pforzheimer Library: English Literature, 1475–1700,* compiled by Emma Unger and William A. Jackson. Jackson was Pforzheimer's librarian, subsequently moving on to become the librarian at Harvard University. He wrote extensive notes and provided impeccable descriptions of the books in the Pforzheimer collection, as well as comparative data on other copies located elsewhere. Published in a limited number of copies, beautifully printed and bound, this catalogue of rare books itself soon became a rarity. When it appears on the market now, it sells for thousands of dollars.

Pforzheimer himself wrote the introduction to the catalogue. It is for the most part a description of what were to him the great highlights of the collection he had put together. Besides his Bibles he mentions incunabula from the first press in Mainz, the *Philobiblon* of Richard de Bury printed in Cologne in 1473, the first edition of the *Imitatio Christi* printed by Gunther Zainer at the first press in Augsburg about 1473, and the first edition of Giovanni Boccaccio's *De claris mulieribus* printed in Ulm at about the same time by Gunther Zainer's brother Johann. From Venice, Pforzheimer had the *Sermones* of Augustinus from the press of Jacobus Paganinus in 1487 and the *Nine Comedies* of the classic Greek dramatist Aristophanes, printed by the scholar and humanist Aldus Manutius in 1498. Aldus had specialized during these early years in printing Greek classic texts; he gathered together Greek scholars and compositors, and Greek was the language of his household. The revival of Greek learning that took place in the Renaissance thus came to be disseminated, with the invention of printing, to an even wider audience. Pforzheimer also possessed the first printed edition of Homer, printed in Florence most probably by Bernardus Nerlius in 1488. Pforzheimer calls it "one of the most beautiful Greek books ever printed." Of his English incunabula he mentions the *Recuyell of the Historyes of Troye* (1475) by Raoul Le Fevre. This was the first book printed in the English language, though it was produced in Bruges, Belgium, by Caxton and Colard Mansion before Caxton had set up his press in England. Pforzheimer calls this "one of the most famous of all books."

Of later items Pforzheimer mentions Daniel Defoe's *Robinson Crusoe* (1719), in the original calf; Jonathon Swift's *Gulliver's Travels* (1726), the earliest issue; the first issue of Thomas Gray's *Elegy* (1751); Laurence Sterne's *Sentimental Journey* (1768); Robert Burns's *Poems* (1786); and Thomas Boswell's *Life of Johnson* (1791), uncut and in the original boards. From the nineteenth century he had such items as *Grimm's Tales,* illustrated by George Cruikshank, in the original boards; Walt Whitman's *Leaves of Grass,* printed in Brooklyn in 1855; and the London edition of Edward Fitzgerald's *Rubaiyat* (1859). Among the manuscripts in the library were the holograph of William Cowper's translations of the *Iliad* (1785) and the *Odyssey* (1791), Sir Walter Scott's *Quentin Durward* (1823), George Eliot's notebook for *Daniel Deronda* (1874–1876), and A. A. Milne's *When We Were Very Young* (1924), with the original drawings by E. H. Shepard.

Carl Pforzheimer, Jr., in his foreword to the first volume of *Shelley and His Circle,* set down his father's objective in collecting as "not to seek completeness of each author but rather to secure the important books of English literature and, when available, rarities and unique copies." The elder Pforzheimer in his introduction to the English-literature catalogue nonetheless pointed out that, in the case of some authors, he did seek insofar as possible to achieve a degree of completeness. Among such authors Pforzheimer includes John Skelton; Henry Howard, Earl of Surrey; Edmund Spenser; George Chapman; and Ben Jonson. Also in this category are some of the early English essayists. Of the works of Francis Bacon he writes, "It is with a thrill of pleasure that I glance from the Golden Treasury Series of *Bacon's Essays,* dated 1896, and purchased forty-four years ago, to a recent acquisition, the precious little octavo first edition of Bacon's *Essayes,* 1597 – the only copy in a private collection."

Pforzheimer always had a special affection for any and all materials relating to Shelley; it is thus not surprising that he was one of the authors for whom Pforzheimer sought completeness. He wrote, "The material relating to 'Shelley and his Circle' forms a separate entity in the Library. Here are manuscripts, autograph letters, corrected copies, and first editions in their original bindings, of Percy Bysshe Shelley and of his wife Mary Wollstonecraft Shelley, of his father-in-law William Godwin and Mary Wollstonecraft, of Claire Clairmont, Lord Byron, Thomas Jefferson Hogg, Leigh Hunt, Thomas Medwin, Thomas Love Peacock, and Edward John Trelawny. Here are many letters and documents relating to the will of Shelley."

When Carl Pforzheimer died in 1957, ownership and control of the library passed to the Carl H. and Lily Pforzheimer Foundation. In 1961 the library published the first volume of *Shelley and His Circle* with subsequent volumes following in later years. This is the catalogue that Pforzheimer had organized on chronological principles to portray the inter-relationships that had existed among the people whose writings are included. The Carl H. Pforzheimer Library, now housed in its own suite at the New York Public Library, continues to acquire materials germane to the Romantic period of English literature; further volumes in the *Shelley and His Circle* series will appear.

In 1978 the trustees of the Carl H. and Lily Pforzheimer Foundation determined to concentrate the library's support of scholarship and curatorial and collecting energies in the field of English Romanticism. Hence, a large number of the library's treasures that date from before that period were offered for sale at Sotheby's in London. The Gutenberg Bible was sold for $2.4 million and is now housed on the campus of the University of Texas at Austin.

References:

Kenneth Neil Cameron, *The Carl H. Pforzheimer Library: Shelley and His Circle* (Cambridge, Mass.: Harvard University Press, 1961);

Emma Unger and William A. Jackson, *The Carl H. Pforzheimer Library: English Literature 1475–1700,* 3 volumes (New York: Privately printed, 1940); revised by Bernard Quaritch (London, 1977);

Edwin Wolf II and John F. Fleming, *Rosenbach: A Biography* (Cleveland: World Publishing, 1960).

Abbie Hanscom Pope

(13 May 1858 – 24 August 1894)

Abbie Pope formed a remarkable library of between seven and ten thousand books. Her collection included illuminated manuscripts, incunabula, early English literature, Americana, first editions of English and American authors of the nineteenth century, autograph letters and manuscripts, extra-illustrated works, fine bindings, and bibliography. After her death her library was sold by her husband to Dodd, Mead and Company, which issued a prospectus in October 1895. Robert Hoe bought a large portion of the collection, while the remainder was offered for sale in Dodd, Mead catalogues of March and April 1896.

Abbie Hanscom was born on 13 May 1858 in Raynham (now Prattville), Massachusetts, the daughter of Charlotte Ellen Pratt (born Raynham) and John Hanscom. Little is known of Abbie Hanscom's early life or education. In the census of 1880 she is listed as a member of her father's household in Chicago with the designation "musical student."

In 1872 Hanscom had moved to Chicago. His initial listings in the Chicago directories describe him as a contractor, carpenter, or builder; later as a travel agent; and finally as a commission merchant. In 1873 Abbie Hanscom's future husband, Norton Quincy Pope, moved to Chicago, where he became involved in grain trade with John Hanscom; he later resided with the Hanscoms. Hanscom and Pope seem to have been involved in brokerage profiteering in the notorious "bucket shops." Unlike a reputable brokerage house the bucket shops essentially were gambling operations. They ostensibly dealt in stocks, grain, cotton, and other commodities but did not execute trades and manipulated sale prices to their advantage. The bucket shops were the focus of court cases in 1883–1884. These events may have provided the incentive for Hanscom and Pope to leave Chicago for more respectable life in Brooklyn in the spring of 1885. John Hanscom is listed in an 1886 Brooklyn directory as a banker in New York City with his residence at 241 Park Place, Brooklyn, which also is given as the residence of Norton Quincy Pope. He and Abbie Hanscom married in

1887. How and why Pope began collecting books is also a mystery, but her library was well established before her marriage. She had, in fact, acquired the greatest printed book in her collection shortly after moving to Brooklyn in 1885, when at the age of twenty-seven she outbid the British Museum at the Osterley Park sale to buy the unique complete copy of the first edition of Thomas Malory's *Morte d'Arthur,* printed in 1485 by William Caxton. The history of Abbie Pope's copy of the *Morte d'Arthur* can be traced back to the celebrated library of Dr. Francis Bernard, physician in ordinary to King James II, whose collection was sold in 1698. At the sale Bernard Alfred Quaritch had two commissions: one from the British Museum of £1,800 and one from a fellow dealer, B. F. Stevens, of £2,200. It sold for £1,950. After the sale it was learned that Stevens was acting for a young American woman, Abbie Hanscom. Her triumph in obtaining the volume was regarded by her contemporaries as a mark of her discrimination and determination as a book collector.

In the years following her marriage, New York newspapers reported on her love of art, her taste in collecting paintings, as well as her knowledge of the industrial arts. Her work for organizations that advanced the education of women was also noted in contemporary newspapers. Interested in music, she served as vice-president of the Seidl Society, a position she held at the time of her death. In addition, Abbie Pope was devoted to animals, especially dogs and horses. The purchase in 1890 of a considerable estate in Poland, Maine — where her parents also acquired summer property — allowed her to indulge her love of animals. White Oak Hill Farms, as the Popes' 530-acre estate was known, included a palatial two-story kennel housing pedigreed dogs and two fine-haired monkeys as well as luxurious stables for their horses.

But it was her books that brought Abbie Pope the greatest renown. She was considered an authority on bookbinding and in 1892 headed the Bookbinding Committee for the World's Fair. Her obitu-

A page from Abbie Pope's copy of Sir Thomas Malory's Morte d'Arthur,
printed by William Caxton in 1485 (Pierpont Morgan Library)

ary notice in the 28 August 1894 issue of the *Brooklyn Daily Eagle* stated that "it was her delight to encase [her books] in bindings as sumptuous and beautiful as they deserved. In this department of embellishment Mrs. Pope was an expert of recognized merit and authority."

Her library, housed in a wing of the Brooklyn residence at 241 Park Place, was described in books and articles of the early 1890s that dealt with the private libraries in New York or Brooklyn. The items in her library most often mentioned were the copy of *Morte d'Arthur* and "the Famous Charles VI Missal." The fifteenth-century missal was then believed to have been executed for Charles VI of France, presented by him to Henry V of England on the occasion of his marriage to Catherine of Valois, Charles's daughter and subsequently owned by Henry VI, Henry VII, and Henry VIII. The splendid manuscript belonged to Ambrose Firmin Didot and brought the highest price (Fr 76,000) when his library was sold in 1879. Afterward it was bought by the comtesse Mniszeck, step-daughter of Honoré de Balzac, for Fr 100,000. It came into the market again after her death in 1887, presumably when

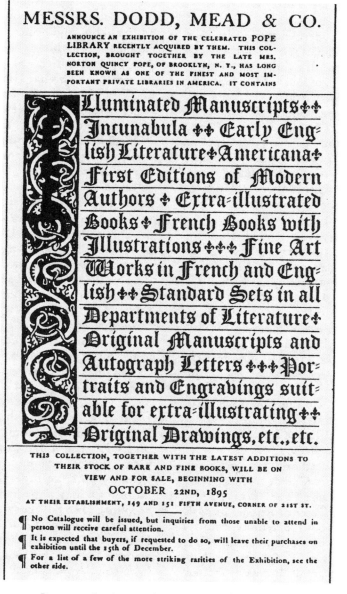

Prospectus for the sale of Pope's library (Grolier Club)

Pope purchased it. The missal was among the Pope books acquired by Robert Hoe and later sold in his sale for $18,700. It is now in the collections of Yale University.

At the Osterley Park sale Pope had acquired another Caxton: John Gower's *Confessio Amantis* (1483), one of five copies known, for £810. In the accounts of her library it usually was regarded as the second most important printed book in the collection. Mention was made of the fact that she owned books printed by Johannes Gutenberg, Wynken de Worde, Richard Pynson, and "other famous typographers," although individual titles

were not given. Her William Shakespeare holdings included a superb set of the four folios, with duplicates of the Third and Fourth Folios; thirteen quartos (among them the first edition, second issue of *Troilus and Cressida*); and the 1640 *Poems*. She owned copies of the first editions of both parts of Edmund Spenser's *Faerie Queen* (1590, 1596), as well as his *Complaints* (1591) and *Colin Clout* (1595); a copy of Michel de Montaigne's *Essays,* (1603) that had belonged to James I; a large-paper copy of Francis Bacon's *Advancement of Learning* (1605); the only known copy of Thomas Middleton's *Honourable Entertainment* (1621); and many other volumes of Elizabethan and Jacobean drama, poetry, and prose.

Her first editions of modern authors were also notable. She had a fine collection of Charles Dickens's works with original drawings by George Cruikshank, Hablot K. Browne, and others inserted. She also collected the writings of Robert and Elizabeth Barrett Browning, George Eliot, Leigh Hunt, John Keats, Charles Lamb, Andrew Lang, Percy Bysshe Shelley, and William Makepeace Thackeray. Her holdings of American authors included William Cullen Bryant, Ralph Waldo Emerson, Nathaniel Hawthorne, Oliver Wendell Holmes, Henry Wadsworth Longfellow, James Russell Lowell, and James Greenleaf Whittier.

Her collection of early Americana included a 1478 edition of Ptolemy's "Geography"; a copy of the Columbus Letter, probably the 1494 Basel edition of the letter written by Christopher Columbus describing the New World; early editions of the voyages of Amerigo Vespucci; and a copy of Juan de Zumárraga's *Doctrina Breve,* printed in Mexico City in 1544. She owned a large-paper copy of William Smith's *History of the Province of New York* (1757); John Filson's *Discovery, Settlement, and Present State of Kentucke* (1784), with the rare map; the works of the Mathers, John Cotton, and other early writers; and books printed by Benjamin Franklin, including an uncut copy of James Logan's translation (1744) of Cicero's *Cato Major.*

Those who commentated on New York's private collection usually reserved their highest praise for the grangerized sets in the Pope library. Their favorite was a large-paper copy of Robert Burns's works (Edinburgh, 1877–1879), extended from six to thirteen volumes with autograph manuscripts (among them, "The Five Carlins," "Bonnie Dundee," "Galloway Election" and "It was a' for our rightfu' king"), autograph letters, watercolor drawings, portraits and other illustrations, and facsimiles and specially printed title pages.

Other grangerized sets in the Pope library included Thomas Campbell's *Life of Mrs. Siddons* (1834), containing portraits and autograph letters; Miguel de Cervantes's *Don Quixote* (Edinburgh, 1879–1884), extended from four to eight volumes by the insertion of drawings and engravings; George Raymond's *Memoirs of William Elliston* (1844), with added portraits, autograph letters, and playbills; an 1881 edition of Shakespeare's works, expanded to forty volumes with engravings and watercolors; John Payne Collier's *An Old Man's Diary* (1871–1872), with autograph letters; and James Parton's *Life and Times of Benjamin Franklin* (1864),

expanded to eight volumes with portraits of Franklin and others, twenty-one autograph letters signed by Franklin, and copies of newspapers and almanacs printed by him.

Special notice was given to her collection of the works of Thomas Dibdin, especially his edition of *Typographical Antiquities.* Pope's large-paper copy contained a unique twenty-four-page vellum fragment of the text; letters from Dibdin to the printer, William Savage, regarding the printing of the book; and a volume of illustrations, including early woodcuts by Albrecht Dürer, Lucas Cranach, and others, collected to illustrate the "Disquisition on Early Engraving and Ornamental Printing."

Although Pope was considered the creator of the library, her husband apparently took an interest in it after their marriage. It was he with whom Quaritch attempted to deal when he was in New York in the winter and spring of 1890, although he did meet her. Contemporary accounts occasionally referred to the collection as "Mr. Pope's library." Nevertheless, Dodd, Mead described the library as having belonged to "the late Mrs. Norton Quincy Pope" when they announced its purchase.

The circumstances surrounding the death of Pope in the summer of 1894 are not entirely clear, but changes in the lives of her family followed the event. The Popes and the Hanscoms were enjoying themselves at their summer homes in Maine when on 24 August Abbie Pope died suddenly of apoplexy. Three days later her body was brought to Brooklyn for the funeral. In the following spring Norton Quincy Pope had the barn and the kennels at White Oak Hill Farms taken down. On 18 July 1895 the *Mechanic Falls Ledger* reported that the Hanscoms' summer home had been totally destroyed by fire and that Abbie Pope's library had been sold. A week later it carried an account of the marriage of Norton Quincy Pope to Jennie Barnes, a cousin of his late wife, on 18 July. What remained of the social or business ties between Pope and Hanscom came to an end in October 1895, when Pope brought a suit against his former father-in-law, accusing him of absconding with funds and failure to pay his creditors. By December 1895 the Hanscoms had Abbie Pope's remains moved from Brooklyn to the Hanscom family plot at Pine Grove Cemetery in Poland. Norton Quincy Pope died in 1897 from pneumonia while on a business trip in Toronto.

The sale of Abbie Pope's library "in its entirety" by her husband to Dodd, Mead in the summer of 1895 had been the first step in the dispersal of the collection. What Dodd, Mead paid for the library is not certain; the figures given in contemporary newspaper accounts range from $150,000 to $250,000. In their October 1895 catalogue the firm stated that she had brought the collection together "at an outlay of about $200,000." Dodd, Mead announced an exhibition of the "celebrated Pope library" from 22 October to 15 December 1895 in a separate prospectus. No catalogue was to be issued, but "a few of the more striking rarities" were listed in the prospectus.

A large portion of the Pope library was acquired by Robert Hoe, probably early in 1896, although how much he bought and what he paid for the books is not clear. Some accounts suggest that he bought it more or less en bloc, but it is evident from later Dodd, Mead catalogues that this was not the case. Hoe did acquire the Caxtons, the "Charles VI Missal," and Shakespearean quartos. The remainder of the Pope library was offered for sale, with books from "other sources," in Dodd, Mead catalogues of English literature and Americana is-

sued in March and April 1896. Although no mention of the Pope library is made in subsequent catalogues, the set of Dibdin's works listed in a catalogue of February 1897 includes her *Typographical Antiquities*.

Hoe placed his portion of the Pope library back on the market in 1911, and the Caxton "Malory" and other books once owned by Pope, who was described by the *New York Evening Post* as "the most notable woman book-collector America has produced," made the news once again. George D. Smith dominated the sale; buying the best books for Henry H. Huntington, Smith acquired the Caxton printing of Gower's *Confessio amantis*. But the Malory eluded him. It was acquired by another *femme bibliophile,* Belle da Costa Greene, at $42,500, for John Pierpont Morgan, Sr.

Reference:

Charles Ryskamp, "Abbie Pope: Portrait of a Bibliophile," *Book Collector,* (Spring 1984): 38–52.

Thomas Prince

(15 May 1687 – 22 October 1758)

Kevin J. Hayes
University of Central Oklahoma

See also the Prince entry in *DLB 24: American Colonial Writers, 1606–1734.*

BOOKS: *God Brings to the Desired Haven. A Thanksgiving-Sermon, Deliver'd at the Lecture in Boston, N.E., on Thursday, September 5, 1717. Upon Occasion of the Author's safe Arrival Thro' Many Great Hazards & Deliverances, Especially on the Seas, in Above Eight Years Absence from his Dear & Native Country* (Boston: Printed by B. Green, 1717);

A Sermon Delivered by Thomas Prince. . . . At his Ordination (Boston: Printed by J. Franklin for S. Gerrish, 1718);

An Account of a Strange Appearance in the Heavens on Tuesday-Night March 6, 1716. As it was seen over Stow-Market in Suffolk in England (Boston: Printed by S. Kneeland for D. Henchman, 1719);

Earthquakes the Works of God, & Tokens of His Just Displeasure. Two Sermons on Psal. XVIII.7. At the Particular Fast in Boston, Nov. 2, and the General Thanksgiving, Nov. 9. Occasioned by the late Dreadful Earthquake . . . (Boston: Printed by D. Henchman, 1727);

Morning Health No Security against the Sudden Arrest of Death before Night. A Sermon Occasioned by the very Sudden Death of Two Young Gentlemen . . . (Boston: Printed for Daniel Henchman, 1727);

A Sermon on the Sorrowful Occasion of the Death of His Late Majesty King George of Blessed Memory, and the Happy Ascension of His Present Majesty King George II to the Throne . . . (Boston: Printed for Daniel Henchman, 1727);

Civil Rulers Raised up by God to Feed His People. A Sermon at the Publick Lectures in Boston, July 25, 1728. In the Audience of His Excellency the Governour, His Honour the Lieut. Governour, and the Honorable Council and Representatives . . . (Boston: Printed for Samuel Gerrish, 1728);

The Departure of Elijah Lamented. A Sermon Occasioned by the Great and Publick Loss in the Decease of the

Thomas Prince

Very Reverend & Learned Cotton Mather . . . (Boston: Printed for D. Henchman, 1728);

The Grave and Death Destroyed, and Believers Ransomed and Redeemed from Them. A Sermon at Middleborough East-Precinct July. VII. 1728. Being the Lord's-Day after the Decease & Funeral of Samuel Prince . . . (Boston: Printed for S. Gerrish, 1728);

The People of New-England Put in Mind of the Righteous Acts of the Lord to Them and Their Fathers, And Reasoned With Concerning Them. A Sermon Delivered at Cambridge Before the Great and General Assembly of the Province of Massachusetts May 27th,

MDCCXXX. Being the Anniversary for the Election of His Majesty's Council . . . (Boston: Printed by B. Green for D. Henchman, 1730);

A Sermon at the Publick Lecture in Boston January VIII, 1729, 30. Upon the Death of the Honorable Samuel Sewall . . . (Boston: Printed by B. Green, 1730);

The Vade Mecum for America: or, a Companion for Traders and Travellers . . . (Boston: Printed by S. Kneeland & T. Green for D. Henchman & T. Hancock, 1731);

The Dying Prayer of Christ, for His People's Preservation and Unity. A Sermon to the North Church in Boston, January XXV, 1731, 2. Being a Day of Prayer for Divine Direction, in their Choice of Another Colleague Pastor to Succeed the Rev. Dr. Cotton Mather . . . (Boston: Printed by S. Kneeland & T. Green for S. Gerrish, 1732);

The Faithful Servant Approv'd at Death, And Entring into the Joy of His Lord. A Sermon at the Publick Lecture in Boston. July XXVII, 1732. Occasion'd by the Much Lamented Death of the Honorable Daniel Oliver . . . (Boston: Printed by S. Kneeland & T. Green for D. Henchman, 1732);

Young Abel Dead, yet Speaketh. A Sermon Occasioned by the Death of Young Mr. Daniel Oliver . . . (Boston: Printed for D. Henchman, 1732; Bungay, England, 1801);

Precious in the Sight of the Lord Is the Death of His Saints . . . A Sermon upon the Death of Mrs. Elizabeth Oliver . . . (Boston: Printed by S. Kneeland & T. Green, 1735);

Christ Abolishing Death and Bringing Life and Immortality to the Light in the Gospel. A Sermon Occasioned by the Death of the Honorable Mary Belcher . . . (Boston: Printed by J. Draper for D. Henchman, 1736);

A Chronological History of New-England in the Form of Annals. Being a Summary and Exact Account of the Most Material Transactions and Occurences Relating to this Country, In the Order of Time Wherein They Happened, From the Discovery by Capt. Gosnold in 1602, to the Arrival of Governor Belcher, in 1730. . . , volume 1 (Boston: Printed by Kneeland & Green for S. Gerrish, 1736); volume 2, numbers 1–3 published as *Annals of New-England . . .* (number 1, Boston: Printed & sold by S. Kneeland & by J. & T. Leverett, 1754; numbers 2–3, Boston: Printed by B. Edes & J. Gill for S. Kneeland & for T. Leverett, 1755);

A Funeral Sermon on the Reverend Mr. Nathanael Williams . . . (Boston: Printed by S. Kneeland & T. Green, 1738);

The Sovereign God Acknowledged and Blessed, Both in Giving and Taking Away. A Sermon Occasioned by the Decease of Mrs. Deborah Prince . . . (Boston: Printed by Rogers & Fowle for T. Rand, 1744);

Extraordinary Events in the Doings of God, and Marvelous in Pious Eyes. Illustrated in a Sermon at the South Church in Boston, N.E. On the General Thanksgiving, Thursday, July 18, 1745. Occasion'd by the Taking of the City of Louisbourg on the Isle of Cape-Breton, by New-England Soldiers, Assisted by a British Squadron . . . (Boston: Printed for D. Henchman, 1745; London: Printed & sold by J. Lewis, 1746);

The Pious Cry to the Lord for Help When the Godly and Faithful Fail Among Them. A Sermon Occasion'd by the Great and Public Loss in the Death of the Honorable Thomas Cushing Esq; Speaker of the Honorable House of Representatives . . . (Boston: Printed for T. Rand, 1746);

The Salvations of God in 1746. In Part Set Forth in a Sermon at the South Church in Boston, Nov. 27, 1746. Being the Day of the Anniversary Thanksgiving . . . (Boston: Printed for D. Henchman, 1746; London: Printed & sold by T. Longman & T. Shewell, 1747);

A Sermon Delivered at the South Church in Boston, N.E. August 14, 1746. Being the Day of General Thanksgiving for the Great Deliverance of the British Nations by the Glorious and Happy Victory near Culloden . . . (Boston: Printed for D. Henchman & for S. Kneeland & T. Green, 1746; London: Printed & sold by John Lewis, 1747);

The Fulness of Life and Joy in the Presence of God. A Sermon Occasion'd by the Decease of Mrs. Martha Stoddard . . . (Boston: Printed by Kneeland & Green, 1748);

The Natural and Moral Government and Agency of God in Causing Droughts and Rain. A Sermon at the South Church in Boston, Tuesday, Aug. 24, 1749. Being the Day of General Thanksgiving in the Province of the Massachusetts for the Extraordinary Reviving Rains . . . (Boston: Printed & sold by Kneeland & Green, 1749; London: Printed & sold by John Lewis, and by R. Hett & J. Oswald, E. Gardner, G. Keith, and P. Russell, 1750);

God Destroyeth the Hope of Man! A Sermon Occasion'd by the Inexpressible Loss in the Death of His Late Royal Highness Frederick, Prince of Wales . . . (Boston: Printed by S. Kneeland for D. Henchman, 1751);

Be Followers of Them who Through Faith and Patience, Inherit the Promises. A Sermon Occasioned by the Decease of Mrs. Hannah Fayerweather . . . (Boston:

Printed by Edes & Gill for D. Henchman, 1755);

An Improvement of the Doctrine of Earthquakes, being the Works of God, and Tokens of His Just Displeasure . . . (Boston: Printed & sold by D. Fowle & by Z. Fowle, 1755);

The Case of Heman Considered In a Sermon on Psal. LXXXVIII.15. . . . Occasioned by the Death of Mr. Edward Bromfield . . . (Boston: Printed by S. Kneeland for D. Henchman, 1756);

The Character of Caleb. In a Sermon Delivered at the South-Church in Boston, on the Lord's Day, after the Funeral of the Honorable Josiah Willard, Esq; Secretary of the Province . . . (Boston: Printed & sold by S. Kneeland, 1756).

Thomas Prince started what he called his New England Library when he entered Harvard College in 1703. The collection was designed to chronicle the establishment and growth of New England, and he eventually used the library as source material for his *A Chronological History of New-England in the Form of Annals . . .* (1736). The greatest collection of Americana assembled during the colonial period, the library contained histories, travels, and promotional tracts and included the manuscripts and published work of the most prominent writers in seventeenth-century New England. No other colonial book collector more tirelessly sought out and preserved documents concerning early American history. With Cotton Mather, Prince deserves distinction as one of the two greatest bibliophiles in colonial New England.

Thomas Prince was born on 15 May 1687 at Sandwich, Massachusetts, the son of Samuel Prince and Mercy Hinckley, daughter of Gov. Thomas Hinckley of Plymouth Colony. His parents sent him to live with his maternal grandfather, who supervised Prince's education until he entered Harvard. In the preface to *A Chronological History,* Prince recalled, "Next to the sacred History, and that of the Reformation, I was from my early Youth instructed in the History of this Country." His boyhood reading included Nathaniel Morton's *New-Englands Memoriall* (Cambridge, Mass.: S. Green & M. Johnson for John Usher of Boston, 1669), William Hubbard's *Narrative of the Troubles with the Indians in New-England* (Boston: John Foster, 1677), other histories of the seventeenth-century Indian wars, and several of Cotton Mather's biographies of prominent colonial leaders.

Prince's bookplate shows that upon entering Harvard he established the New England Library. In describing how he had reached his decision to assemble a great collection of Americana, Prince writes in his preface to *A Chronological History* that early in his first year at college he "chanced in my leisure Hours to read Mr. *Chamberlain's* Account of the *Cottonian Library:* Which excited in me a Zeal of laying hold on every Book, Pamphlet, and Paper, both in *Print* and *Manuscript* which are either written by persons who lived here, or that have any Tendency to enlighten our History." Throughout his college years he continued developing the collection.

Prince received his A.B. at Harvard in 1707 and then taught school at Sandwich and completed work on his A.M., which he received in absentia in 1710. In 1709 he had begun a two-year travel through the West Indies and Europe. He settled in England in 1711, where he held a partial ministry at Coombs in Suffolk. While abroad Prince read and acquired additional works he had never before seen concerning New England history. Most notable among them was Edward Johnson's *Wonder-Working Providence* (London: Printed for N. Brooke, 1654). Prince left England to return to Boston in 1717. Although he was invited to preach at several New England churches, Prince preferred to settle in Boston, and on 23 December 1717 Joseph Sewall asked him to join him as copastor at Old South Church. Prince was inducted as associate pastor in October 1718; he retained the office until his death forty years later. Upon his ordination Prince established a book collection at the Old South Church and had a bookplate made for the "South Church Library."

On 30 October 1719 Prince married Deborah Denny, a member of his Coombs congregation who had followed him to America. They had four daughters and a son. Prince made sure each received a thorough education. When his daughter Deborah died in 1744 at the age of twenty-one, Prince wrote in her funeral sermon, *The Sovereign God,* "As she grew up, he [Prince] was pleas'd to restrain her from youthful Vanities, to make her serious, and move her to study the BIBLE and the best of *Authors* both of *History* and *Divinity.*" Under her father's guidance Deborah Prince read works by Mather, Thomas Shepard, and John Flavel, among others. Thomas Prince, Jr., would gain distinction as editor of *The Christian History* (1744–1745), the first religious periodical published in America.

Prince's various writings reveal his religious zeal as well as his activities as historian and scientist. He published many sermons, of which his funeral sermons are the most notable; scientific works such as *An Account of a Strange Appearance in the Heavens,* a description of the aurora borealis he had witnessed in England, and *Earthquakes the Works of God,*

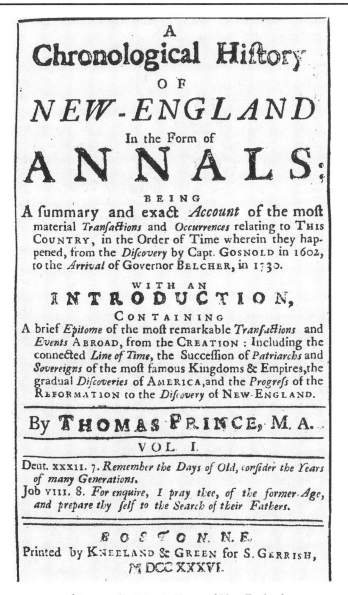

A
Chronological History
OF
NEW-ENGLAND
In the Form of
ANNALS;
BEING
A summary and exact *Account* of the most material *Transactions* and *Occurrences* relating to THIS COUNTRY, in the Order of Time wherein they happened, from the *Discovery* by Capt. GOSNOLD in 1602, to the *Arrival* of Governor BELCHER, in 1730.

WITH AN
INTRODUCTION,
CONTAINING
A brief *Epitome* of the most remarkable *Transactions* and *Events* ABROAD, from the CREATION : Including the connected *Line of Time*, the Succession of *Patriarchs* and *Sovereigns* of the most famous Kingdoms & Empires, the gradual *Discoveries* of AMERICA, and the *Progress* of the REFORMATION to the *Discovery* of NEW-ENGLAND.

By THOMAS PRINCE, M. A.

VOL. I.

Deut. XXXII. 7. *Remember the Days of Old, consider the Years of many Generations.*
Job VIII. 8. *For enquire, I pray thee, of the former Age, and prepare thy self to the Search of their Fathers.*

BOSTON. N.E.
Printed by KNEELAND & GREEN for S. GERRISH,
MDCCXXXVI.

Title page for Prince's history of New England

& *Tokens of His Just Displeasure* (1727), a work attempting to reconcile the most up-to-date scientific theories with the providential order of nature; *The Vade Mecum for America: or, A Companion for Trades and Travellers* (1731), a travel guide; and an edition of John Mason's *Brief History of the Pequot War* (1736). But his greatest effort was *A Chronological History,* which he had begun writing in 1728. Supplements to the history appeared in 1754 and 1755.

Both *A Chronological History* and his library reflect Prince's belief that he and his fellow colonists were enacting God's great historical design by carving a New Canaan from the American wilderness. His scholarship was meticulous. Cautious to avoid error, he refused to rely on secondary sources; and he scrupulously examined whatever original works he could find. His plan to tell the history of New England beginning with Creation caused him to search through a wide variety of historical works prior to Christopher Columbus; he read ancient chronologies from Ptolemy, Tacitus, Suetonius, and Dio Cassius. Prince became bogged down by the comprehensive scope of the project; the work and its supplements therefore only take the history of New England to 1633. Nevertheless, *A Chronological History* remains both an important early American history and a testament to Prince's thoroughness and erudition.

The New England Library contained several manuscripts and a wide variety of printed material concerning early America. Printed books relating to American history which survive from Prince's library include Jose Acosta's *Naturall and Morall Historie of the East and West Indies* (London: V. Simmes for E. Blount and W. Aspley, 1604); William Wood's *New Englands Prospect* (London: T. Cotes, for J. Bellamy, 1634); the *Bay Psalm Book* (Cambridge, Mass.: Stephen Daye, 1640); John Eliot's Indian Bible (Cambridge, Mass.: Samuel Green and Marmaduke Johnson, 1663); Mary Rowlandson's captivity narrative, *The Soveraignity and Goodness of God* (Cambridge, Mass.: Samuel Green, 1682); and an Algonquian translation of Richard Baxter's *Call to the Unconverted* (Cambridge, Mass.: S. Green, 1688). The most important manuscripts in the collection were William Bradford's "Of Plymouth Plantation" and John Winthrop's three-volume journal. Bradford's manuscript was stolen from the Old South Church during the revolutionary war and taken to England, but because Prince had pasted his bookplate into the manuscript volume, the history was identified in the nineteenth century and eventually returned to New England. Prince's other manuscript holdings included papers from his father-in-law, Governor Hinckley, John Cotton, and Increase and Cotton Mather.

In his will Prince made provisions for the library: "I have been many years collecting a number of Books, Pamphlets, Maps, Papers in Print, and Manuscript, either published in New England, or pertaining to its History and Public Affairs, to which I have given the name of the New England Library, and have deposited it in the Steeple Chamber in the Old South Church . . . I made the collection from a public View, and desire that the memory of many important Transactions might be preserved, which otherwise [would] be lost." Prince's collection was decimated during the revolutionary war. During the 1775 British occupation many books were destroyed, some used for kindling by British troops. Concern for the collection grew during the first half of the nineteenth century, and in 1866 the Old South Church agreed to place the Prince Collection on permanent loan to the Boston Public Library, where it remains. By the time Justin Winsor catalogued the collection in 1870, Prince's original distinction between the New England Library and his South Church Library had become blurred, and Winsor arbitrarily reorganized the two collections, placing works concerning America – any books printed in America, written by American colonists, or written about America – into one section and other books such as devotional works, ancient classics, schoolbooks, and European histories into the second section. The Winsor catalogue, listing 3,444 titles, does not necessarily represent Prince's own division of his library. The scope of *A Chronological History* suggests that anything relating to the history of the Christian people might rightfully belong with his New England Library.

The best way to understand how Prince used his library is to take a careful look at one particular volume – one of the most important surviving books in the Prince library – which he read often and valued highly. A volume which had been removed from the Prince library during the revolutionary war and recovered in 1814, the fourth issue of Capt. John Smith's *Generall Historie of Virginia, New-England, and the Summer Isles* (London: J. Dawson & J. Haviland, for M. Sparke, 1627) is heavily annotated by Prince. The annotations reveal his meticulous scholarship, his enthusiasm for the history of his birthplace, his joy of learning, and the seriousness with which he approached his task. Furthermore, they suggest that he read Smith with an eye toward writing his own history. As Prince's inscription on the verso of the title page shows, Prince acquired Smith's *Generall Historie* in Boston in March 1719.

In book 1 of the *Generall Historie* Smith mentions Madoc, the legendary Welsh voyager who had supposedly discovered and explored America during the twelfth century. On the flyleaf opposite the title page, Prince copied several quotations concerning the Madoc legend from James Howell's *Epistolae-Ho-Elianae* (London: Printed for Thomas Guy, 1673).

Prince's chronological approach in organizing his own history prompted him to pay close attention to the dates in his source material. To double-check Smith, Prince pulled down his copy of Samuel Purchas's *Purchas his Pilgrimage* (London: William Stansby for Henry Fetherstone, 1617) and compared the two accounts. He made Smith's easier to use with cross-references to and clarifications of places, people, longitudes, latitudes, and dates. Prince ignored book 2 of Smith's history. An expanded version of Smith's *Map of Virginia,* book 2 describes the Virginia Indians, but it is a static account – one in which time does not advance; and thus it contains nothing that Prince could use in his chronology. In books 3 and 4, which retell the first fifteen years of the Virginia experience, Prince underlined many additional passages, wrote more dates in the margins, and cross-referenced Smith's text with that of Purchas's.

Book 6, "The Generall Historie of New-England," was the most important book for Prince's purposes, and it is the most annotated. Prince recognized that Smith derived much of book 6 from his own *Description of New England* (London: H. Lownes, for R. Clarke, 1616), and Prince kept his copy of Smith's *Description* nearby as he read corresponding parts of the *Generall Historie.* When Prince read the part where Smith relates how he named New England, Prince wrote "New England" in the margin in big, bold letters. The map of New England included in Prince's copy of the *Generall Historie* differs from the map which originally appeared in Smith's *Description.* The *Description* gives Indian place-names whereas the *Generall Historie* map provides the English names which Prince Charles substituted. Onto the *Generall Historie* map Prince copied the corresponding Indian names. In Smith's text, which retained the Indian place-names, Prince wrote the corresponding English names.

Prince took note of where Smith stopped using his *Description of New England* as a source and began relying on other works such as his own *New Englands Trials* (London: W. Jones, 1622) as well as Edward Winslow's *Good Newes from New-England* (London: J. Dawson, for W. Bladen, 1624). Prince owned copies of both, and he continued his careful scrutiny of Smith's text. Comparing Winslow's *Good Newes* with Smith's *Generall Historie,* Prince even identified possible printing errors. Where Smith mentions "Scar a lusty Savage," Prince wrote in the margin: "But in Mr Winslow's account a wence this was taken, tis – There was a lusty Savage: & I suspect ye Printer mistook *There* for *Scar,* in Capt Smith's written abridgment." Prince also kept Bradford's manuscript "Of Plymouth Plantation" and Nathaniel Morton's *New-Englands Memoriall* nearby as he read Smith's sixth book, and he copied several lengthy passages from the two works into the margins of Smith's *Generall Historie.* Finally, on the back flyleaf of Smith's work, Prince wrote additional tidbits concerning Columbus, Ferdinand Ma-

gellan, and Hernán Cortéz which he derived from one of John Stow's historical accounts.

Prince boldly underscored Smith's remark: "of all the foure parts of the world I have yet seene not inhabited, could I have but means to transport a colony, I would rather live here then any where."

References:

Theodore Hornberger, "The Science of Thomas Prince," *New England Quarterly,* 9 (1936): 26–42;

Hornberger, "Thomas Prince, Minister," in *Essays on American Literature in Honor of Jay B. Hubbell,* edited by Clarence Gohdes (Durham, N.C.: Duke University Press, 1967), pp. 30–46;

Peter Knapp, "The Rev. Thomas Prince and the Prince Library," *American Book Collector,* 22 (October 1971): 19–23;

Samuel Eliot Morison, "Old School and College Books in the Prince Library," *More Books: The Bulletin of the Boston Public Library,* 11 (1936): 77–93;

Victoria Reed, "The New England Library and Its Founder," *New England Magazine,* 4 (1886): 347–363;

Lawrance Thompson, "Notes on Some Collectors in Colonial Massachusetts," *Colophon,* new series 2 (Autumn 1936): 82–100;

Justin Winsor, *The Prince Library. A Catalogue* (Boston: Alfred Mudge & Son, 1870);

Edwin Wolf II, "Great American Book Collectors to 1800," *Gazette of the Grolier Club,* new series 16 (June 1971): 1–70.

Papers:

Prince's books and miscellaneous manuscript material are at the Boston Public Library. Prince's almanac for 1736–1737 is at the American Antiquarian Society. A log kept by Prince during his voyages in 1709–1711 and several of his letters are held by the Massachusetts Historical Society.

David Anton Randall

(5 April 1905 – 25 May 1975)

Dean H. Keller
Kent State University

BOOKS: *Collecting American First Editions 1900–1933* (New York: Scribners, n.d.);

An Exhibition from the Indiana University Library of Original Printings of Some Milestones in Medical History and Natural Science, Aristotle (1476) to Salk (1951) With Emphasis on Biology – Botany (Largely from the J. K. Lilly Collection) On the Occasion of the Annual Meeting of the American Institute of Biological Sciences, August 24–28, 1958, Indiana University (Bloomington: Indiana University Library, 1958);

Dedication of The Lilly Library, Indiana University, October 3, 1960 (Bloomington: Indiana University, Lilly Library, 1960);

A. E. Housman: A Collection of Manuscripts, Letters, Proofs, First Editions, Etc. Formed by H. B. Collamore of West Hartford, Connecticut, Presented to The Lilly Library, Indiana University (Bloomington: Indiana University, Lilly Library, 1961);

Exhibition of Original Printings of Some Milestones of Science from Pliny (1469) to Banting (1922) (Bloomington: Indiana University, Lilly Library, 1963);

Grolier: or 'Tis Sixty Years Since. A Reconstruction of the Exhibit of 100 Books Famous in English Literature Originally Held in New York, 1903, on the Occasion of the Club's Visit to The Lilly Library, Indiana University, May 1, 1963 (Bloomington: Indiana University, Lilly Library, 1963);

The J. K. Lilly Collection of Edgar Allan Poe: An Account of Its Formation (Bloomington: Indiana University, Lilly Library, 1964);

Manuscripts Ancient-Modern: An Exhibition on the Occasion of the Manuscript Society's Annual Meeting. Held at The Lilly Library, Indiana University, October 1–4, 1964 (Bloomington: Indiana University, Lilly Library, 1964);

Three Centuries of American Poetry: An Exhibition of Original Printings (Bloomington: Indiana University, Lilly Library, 1965);

Eighty-Nine Good Novels of the Sea, the Ship, and the Sailor. A List Compiled by J. K. Lilly. An Account of Its Formation (Bloomington: Indiana University, Lilly Library, 1966);

The John Carter Collection of A. E. Housman (Bloomington: Indiana University, Lilly Library, 1966);

Medicine: An Exhibition of Books Relating to Medicine and Surgery from the Collection Formed by J. K. Lilly (Bloomington: Indiana University, Lilly Library, 1966);

The First Twenty-Five Years of Printing, 1455–1480: An Exhibition (Bloomington: Indiana University, Lilly Library, 1967);

American Patriotic Songs: Yankee Doodle to The Conquered Banner, With Emphasis on The Star Spangled Banner. An Exhibition Held at The Lilly Library, Indiana University, Bloomington, July–September, 1968 (Bloomington: Indiana University, Lilly Library, 1968);

Five Centuries of Familiar Quotations in Their Earliest Appearances in Print: September 1, 1968–January 1, 1969 (Bloomington: Indiana University, Lilly Library, 1968);

Dukedom Large Enough (New York: Random House, 1969);

An Exhibit of Seventeenth-Century Editions of Writings by John Milton (Bloomington: Indiana University, Lilly Library, 1969);

The Beginnings of Higher Education in Indiana: An Exhibit Commemorating the Sesquicentennial of Indiana University (Bloomington: Indiana University, Lilly Library, 1970);

Biology. An Exhibition at The Lilly Library in Honor of the Meetings of The American Institute of Biological Sciences and The American Psychological Society (Bloomington: Indiana University, Lilly Library, 1970);

An Exhibition of Books from the Firm of Lathrop C. Harper, Inc., Presented to The Lilly Library by Mrs. Bernardo Mendel (Bloomington: Indiana University, Lilly Library, 1970);

David Anton Randall

The Ian Fleming Collection of 19th–20th Century Source Material Concerning Western Civilization together with the Originals of the James Bond-007 Tales (Bloomington: Indiana University, Lilly Library, 1970);

An Exhibition on the Occasion of the Transfer of Public Papers of the Honorable Joseph W. Barr to The Lilly Library, Indiana University (Bloomington: Indiana University, Lilly Library, 1971);

An Exhibition of American Literature Honoring the Completion of the Editorial Work on the 100th Volume Approved by the Center for Editions of American Authors, together with Eighteenth-Century American Fiction Published Abroad, Eighteenth-Century American Editions of Some English Fiction, Eighteenth-Century American Drama, The First Quarter Cen-tury of Fiction written and Published in America: 1774–1799 (Bloomington: Indiana University, Lilly Library, 1973);

The First Hundred Years of Detective Fiction, 1841–1941, by One Hundred Authors on the Hundred Thirtieth Anniversary of the First Publication in Book Form of Edgar Allan Poe's "The Murder in the Rue Morgue" Philadelphia, 1843. An Exhibition Held at The Lilly Library, Indiana University, Bloomington, July–September, 1973 (Bloomington: Indiana University, Lilly Library, 1973);

Printing and the Mind of Man (Bloomington: Indiana University, Lilly Library, 1973);

An Exhibition Honoring the Seventy-Fifth Birthday of Hoagland Howard Carmichael, L.L.B., 1926,

D.M., 1972, Indiana University (Bloomington: Indiana University, Lilly Library, 1974);

Science Fiction/Fantasy: An Exhibition of Books Relating to Science Fiction and Fantasy from the Lilly Collection (Bloomington: Indiana University, Lilly Library, 1974);

The Adventures of the Notorious Forger (San Francisco: Randall & Windle, 1978).

SELECTED PERIODICAL PUBLICATIONS –
UNCOLLECTED: "The Legion of the Lost," *Colophon, A Book Collectors' Quarterly,* 7 (September 1931): 5–12;

"Waverly in America," *Colophon, A Quarterly for Bookmen,* new series 1 (Summer 1935): 39–55;

"Kipling and Collecting," *Publishers' Weekly,* 129 (25 January 1936): 379–380;

"Footnote on a Minor Poet," *Colophon, A Quarterly for Bookmen,* new series 3 (Autumn 1938): 587–597;

"Doyle, A. Conan (1879–1928). *Memoirs of Sherlock Holmes* . . . ," *Papers of the Bibliographical Society of America,* 34 (Second Quarter 1940): 190–191;

"Thackeray, W. M. (1811–1863). *Vanity Fair* . . . ," *Papers of the Bibliographical Society of America,* 34 (Second Quarter 1940): 191–192;

"Lever, Charles (1806–1872). *Our Mess* . . . ," *Papers of the Bibliographical Society of America,* 34 (Third Quarter 1940): 274–276;

"Thackeray, William Makepeace (1811–1863). *Vanity Fair* . . . ," *Papers of the Bibliographical Society of America,* 34 (Third Quarter 1940): 276–278;

"Brooke, Rupert (1887–1915). *The Collected Poems* . . . ," *Papers of the Bibliographical Society of America,* 36 (First Quarter 1942): 68;

"Grey, Zane (1872–1939). *Riders of the Purple Sage* . . . ," *Papers of the Bibliographical Society of America,* 36 (First Quarter 1942): 68;

"The Adventures of Two Bibliophiles," *New York Times Book Review* (6 August 1944): 14, 16;

"The Hogan Sale of American Literature," *Publishers' Weekly,* 146 (25 November 1944): 2068–2070;

"A Study of *A Study in Scarlet,* London: Ward Lock & Co., 1888; or, A Scandal in Bibliography," *The Baker Street Journal,* 1 (January 1946): 103–106;

"*The Valley of Fear* Bibliographically Considered," *The Baker Street Journal,* 1 (April 1946): 232–237;

"The Battle of Books, Or The Auction is the Payoff," *Publishers' Weekly,* 149 (11 May 1946): 2576–2577;

"A Plea for a More Consistent Policy of Cataloguing By Auction Galleries," *Papers of the Bibliographical Society of America,* 40 (Second Quarter 1946): 107–126;

"A Census of the Known Existing Original Manuscripts of the Sacred Writings," *The Baker Street Journal,* 1 (October 1946): 504–508;

"George Washington, Father of His Country and Governor Posey?," *The Indiana Quarterly for Bookmen,* 2 (October 1946): 122–128;

"A Tentative Enquiry into the Earliest Printings, In Book Form, of the First Four Sherlock Holmes Short Stories: A Scandal in Bohemia, The Red-Headed League, A Case of Identity and The Boscombe Valley Mystery, With a Conclusion Tending to Prove That in the Case of Two of Them Certainly, and Two of Them Possibly – America First!," *The Baker Street Journal,* 2 (October 1947): 491–496;

"Notes Towards a Correct Collation of the First Edition of *Vanity Fair,*" *Papers of the Bibliographical Society of America,* 42 (Second Quarter 1948): 95–109;

"Book-Collecting As a Hobby," *Antiquarian Bookman,* 11 (11 April 1953): 1283–1285;

"Josiah Kirby Lilly," *Book Collector,* 6 (Autumn 1957): 263–277;

"A Backward Glance Over Travel'd Roads," *Indiana University Bookman,* 3 (December 1958): 3–79;

"The J. K. Lilly Collection of Edgar Allan Poe," *Indiana University Bookman,* 4 (March 1960): 46–58;

"The First American Edition of Brontë's *Poems,*" *Book Collector,* 9 (Summer 1960): 199–201;

"Housman Manuscripts," *Book Collector,* 9 (Winter 1960): 456;

"*A Shropshire Lad* with a Variant Title-Page," *Book Collector,* 9 (Winter 1960): 458–459;

"Two States of 'Two Lives,' " *Papers of the Bibliographical Society of America,* 54 (Fourth Quarter 1960): 295;

"Bruce Rogers' First Decorated Book," *Papers of the Bibliographical Society of America,* 55 (First Quarter 1961): 40–41;

"Mr. Muir and Gabriel Wells: A Rejoinder," *Book Collector,* 10 (Spring 1961): 53–55;

"A Dedication Grolier Discovered Recovered," *Book Collector,* 10 (Spring 1961): 66–68;

Randall and Percy Muir, "How We Found the Manuscript," *Publishers' Weekly,* 179 (19 June 1961): 37–39; reprinted in *Memoirs of James II, His Campaigns as Duke of York 1652–1660* (Bloo-

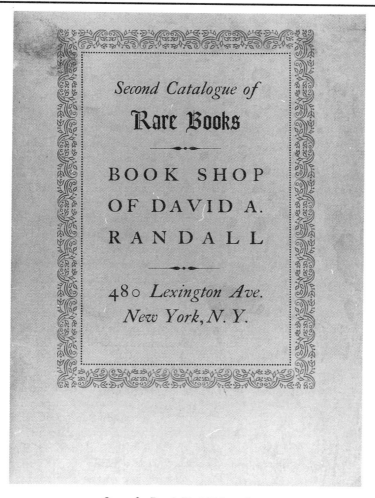

Cover for Randall's 1934 catalogue

mington: Indiana University Press, 1962), pp. 13–23;

" 'Dukedom Large Enough' I. Changing the Gutenberg Census," *Papers of the Bibliographical Society of America,* 56 (Second Quarter 1962): 157–174;

" 'Dukedom Large Enough' II. Hemingway, Churchill, and the Printed Word," *Papers of the Bibliographical Society of America,* 56 (Third Quarter 1962): 346–353;

" 'Dukedom Large Enough' III. Thomas Jefferson and the Declaration of Independence," *Papers of the Bibliographical Society of America,* 56 (Fourth Quarter 1962): 472–480;

" 'Dukedom Large Enough' IV. The Permanent Questionnaire," *Papers of the Bibliographical Society of America,* 57 (First Quarter 1963): 68–76;

"IPEX," *Antiquarian Bookman,* 32 (30 September 1963): 1199–1201;

"Check List: Andrew Lang Fairy Books," *Antiquarian Bookman,* 34 (31 August 1964): 805;

"The First American Edition of *1914 and Other Poems*," *Book Collector,* 13 (Autumn 1964): 359;

"The Gondoliers," *Papers of the Bibliographical Society of America,* 59 (Second Quarter 1965): 193–198;

"Gilbert and Sullivan's 'Princess Ida,' " *Papers of the Bibliographical Society of America,* 59 (Third Quarter 1965): 322–326;

"Copies of Conrad's *Chance,* Dated '1913,' " *Book Collector,* 15 (Spring 1966): 68;

"J. K. Lilly: America's Quiet Collector," *Antiquarian Bookman,* 37 (27 June 1966): 2679–2681; reprinted [Indianapolis, 1966?]; *Indianapolis Star Magazine* (2 April 1967): 20, 22, 24; *Oregon GP,* 15 (August 1966): 8–9, 21; *Report of the Rare Book Librarian, The Lilly Library, Indiana Univer-*

sity, July 1, 1965–June 30, 1967 (Bloomington: Indiana University, Lilly Library, 1967), 1–7;
"Booksellers and Collectors: A Dealer's Apprenticeship," *Publishers' Weekly,* 196 (21 July 1969): 35–38;
"Ian Fleming's First Book," *Book Collector,* 21 (Autumn 1972): 414–415;
"*A Shropshire Lad* Label Variants," *Book Collector,* 22 (Summer 1973): 176.

OTHER: *Henry William Herbert (Frank Forester): A Bibliography of His Writings 1832–1858,* compiled by William Mitchell Van Winkle with the bibliographic assistance of Randall (Portland, Maine: Southworth-Anthoensen Press, 1936);
A Primer of Book Collecting, by John T. Winterich in collaboration with Randall, newly revised and enlarged edition (New York: Greenberg, 1946); third revised edition (New York: Crown, 1966; New York: Bell, 1966; London: Allen & Unwin, 1966);
Carroll A. Wilson, *Thirteen Author Collections of the Nineteenth Century and Five Centuries of Familiar Quotations,* 2 volumes, edited by Jean C. S. Wilson and Randall (New York: Privately printed by Scribners, 1950);
"The Sadleir Collection," in *The Sadleir Collection: Addresses Delivered by Frederick B. Adams, Jr. and David A. Randall at the Dedication Ceremonies, University of California at Los Angeles Library, November 13, 1952* (Los Angeles: Friends of the UCLA Library, 1952), pp. 13–19;
"Institutional Collecting of Books and Manuscripts," in *Proceedings of the Conference on Materials for Research in American Culture, October 25–27, 1956, The University of Texas* (Austin: University of Texas, 1956), pp. 13–19;
"Frank J. Hogan, 1877–1944," in *Grolier 75: A Biographical Retrospective to Celebrate the Seventy-fifth Anniversary of The Grolier Club in New York* (New York: Grolier Club, 1959), pp. 200–202;
"Sherlock, Tobacco, and a Gold-Headed Cane," in *The Last Bookman: A Journey into the Life & Times of Vincent Starrett (Author-Journalist-Bibliophile)* by Peter Ruber (New York: Candlelight Press, 1968), pp. 77–79.

In a span of forty-six years, David A. Randall successfully engaged in two careers. From 1929 until 1955 he was a dealer in rare books in New York City, and from 1956 until his death in 1975 he was the head of a rare-book library, the Lilly Library at Indiana University. While the two careers are obviously related, moving from one to the other is not always easy, but David Randall had the talent and temperament to be able to make considerable contributions in both areas.

Dave Randall was born on 5 April 1905, in Nanticoke, Pennsylvania, the son of David Virgil and Harriet Witt Randall. Randall attended Harrisburg Academy, and he was graduated cum laude from the school in 1924. He then entered Lehigh University in nearby Bethlehem, Pennsylvania, where he received his B.A. in English in 1928 with an undergraduate thesis on Sir Thomas Malory's *Morte d'Arthur* (1485). At Lehigh he was a member of Phi Delta Theta fraternity and Phi Beta Kappa. It was also at Lehigh that his interest in books, and especially rare books, was stimulated, for he worked in the university's library as an assistant to Dr. Robert Metcalf Smith. A professor of English, Smith was conducting research on the Shakespeare folios which were in Lehigh's library collection.

Involved in Smith's research as he was, Randall was exposed to the names, at least, of the great collectors, scholars, book dealers, and libraries whom Smith contacted, cited, and discussed in his monograph. Years later, in 1945, Randall would be instrumental in helping his former professor have his somewhat controversial book, *The Shelley Legend,* published by Scribners, a favor which Smith duly acknowledged in his preface. Formal recognition of Smith's influence was made when Randall named him one of the dedicatees of his memoirs, *Dukedom Large Enough* (1969).

Immediately upon graduation from Lehigh, Randall turned down a Rhodes scholarship and entered Harvard Law School. He soon found that he could not give his full attention to the study of law and he increasingly was drawn to the world of books. He spent his time at Harvard in the Widener Library and as an auditor in a course called the "History of the Printed Book" taught by George Parker Winship. Winship, a distinguished Harvard librarian, bibliographer, and author, taught this popular course between 1915 and 1931, and is credited with stimulating the book-collecting instincts of many Harvard undergraduates. By January 1929 Randall had withdrawn from Harvard and was employed by E. Byrne Hackett at the Brick Row Book Shop in New York. His immediate supervisor at Brick Row was Michael Papantonio, later the partner of John S. Vane E. Kohn in the distinguished Seven Gables Bookshop. Randall's first assignment was to attend the Jerome Kern sale which went through ten sessions beginning on 7 January 1929. Thus Randall was thrust into the rare-book busi-

SCRIBNERS PRESENT

THE

MODERN LIBRARY

in

FIRST EDITIONS

1938

HEMINGWAY, ERNEST. The Sun Also [132] Rises.

New York: Charles Scribner's Sons, 1926.

12mo, First Edition, original black cloth, gold paper labels. $50.

Published October 22, 1926, in an edition of 5090 copies. The first issue, with the typographical error "stoppped" on page 181, line 26. As new, in the original dust wrapper in its first state, with the error, listing "In Our Time" as "In Our Times." A contemporary presentation copy inscribed on the fly-leaf: "To Sylvia with great affection. Ernest Hemingway. Paris, November 1926." The recipient was Sylvia Beach, publisher of Joyce's "Ulysses."

Ernest Hemingway startled the world with *The Sun Also Rises*, his first full-length novel. The disinherited and disillusioned survivors of the World War discovered in him their spokesman, a writer free of cant who could paint characters true to their own experience and way of life. *The Sun Also Rises* is a chronicle of a lost generation drifting, frustrated and demoralized, to its doom.

The Modern Library edition contains an Introduction by Henry Seidel Canby. The English title under which this book is published is *Fiesta*. The title, *The Sun Also Rises*, comes from *Ecclesiastes*—the same passage which supplied Sara Teasdale with her title *Rivers to the Sea*. The Verso of the dedication leaf prints the quotation from *Ecclesiastes* as well as Gertrude Stein's famous remark to Hemingway: "You are all a lost generation."

Title page and page from Randall's catalogue of first editions of works in the Modern Library series

ness at the highest level; he was introduced to the great collectors, dealers, and rare-book librarians of that exciting era.

While the era was an exciting one for the rare-book business, it also was the beginning of the Great Depression, and soon less attention and financial resources could be given to book collecting. Book shops were retrenching, and in 1931 Hackett told Randall that his services would no longer be needed. Randall had made a good beginning in the trade at Brick Row and he had cultivated a wide acquaintance in the trade, but the fact was that no one in the book business was hiring.

An alternative to returning to the coal fields of eastern Pennsylvania, and the one which Randall chose, was to become a book scout. Working out of his home on East Tenth Street just off Fourth Avenue in New York, he combed the secondhand bookshops that line Fourth Avenue between Eighth and Fourteenth streets for books needed by the tonier

dealers in the trade. With the knowledge he had gained at Brick Row, his considerable innate ability, and a good deal of luck, Randall was a successful scout. He realized, however, that his future would be limited and the work was not certain enough on which to raise a family. On 12 July 1929 Randall and Margaret Rauch were married, and their first son, Bruce Emerson, was born on 17 August 1931. A second son, Ronald Rauch, was born 24 January 1933. The Randalls' marriage would end in divorce after twenty-six years, and on 23 November 1956 he would marry Mary "Polly" Altmiller. Younger son Ronald would follow in his father's footsteps and would become a dealer in rare books.

Near the end of his first year as a book scout, Randall was discussing his ambitions with Max Harzof, the owner of G. A. Baker and Company, Booksellers, at 480 Lexington Avenue in New York, when Harzof, with the generosity which evidently marked his dealings with other aspiring bookmen, offered Randall a desk in his shop and access to his stock. In return, Randall helped with cataloguing, ran errands, and performed other chores. Years later Randall, in *Dukedom Large Enough*, called Harzof "the finest all-around bookman I have been privileged to know," and he further stated that "I worked harder, earned less and learned more in the three years I spent with him than any other comparable period."

From his desk at G. A. Baker and Company, Randall issued his first two catalogues, filled mostly with books from Harzof's stock, and it was there that he met Frederick B. Adams, Jr., John Carter, H. Bacon Collamore, William Jackson, J. K. Lilly, Jr., William Mitchell Van Winkle, and John T. Winterich, all of whom would have considerable influence on his career. It was during this period, too, that he began to write book reviews and articles on bibliography and book collecting, including "American First Editions 1900–1933," in a groundbreaking collection of essays edited by Carter called *New Paths in Book Collecting* (1934).

Carter was employed by Scribners as their London buyer of rare books, and he had been urging the firm to reorganize the rare-book department at the New York shop along the lines he advocated in his book. He believed a new clientele of younger collectors with a little money and a lot of imagination could be attracted. Charles Scribner agreed with the idea, and a search was begun for a manager of the reorganized department. The great collector of Horace Walpole, Wilmarth Lewis, whom Randall had met at Harzof's, it seems recommended Randall for the job, seconded by Carter.

Scribner was quick to decide, and in 1935 Randall began his twenty-year tenure as manager of the rare-book department of the Charles Scribner's Sons' bookstore. This also marked the beginning of what Randall later dubbed the "Carter-Randall-Scribner axis" that resulted in the location and sale of so many great, rare, and unusual books and manuscripts in the next two decades. From the beginning Randall and Carter determined to offer books that illustrated the philosophy demonstrated in *New Paths of Book Collecting*. While they did not neglect the more traditional areas of collecting, a review of the catalogues they issued reveals a determination to pursue new paths as well.

Randall's first catalogue, number 102 in the Scribner series issued in 1935, was *Familiar Quotations: A Collection of Their Earliest Appearances*, perhaps inspired by one of Carroll Atwood Wilson's favorite collecting areas; the last major catalogue was *Fifty Distinguished Books and Manuscripts*, number 137

issued in 1952, the only dealer's catalogue in this century, Randall believed, to list a Gutenberg Bible. In between there were many exciting, unusual, and groundbreaking catalogues, including one devoted to first editions of books published by Charles Scribner's Sons from 1847 to 1936 (number 108), and a 1936 catalogue titled *First Editions of Juvenile Fiction, 1814–1924* (number 107) with a Harry Castlemon item. This started Lilly on his great Castlemon collection, which later became the basis of Jacob Blanck's bibliography of Castlemon. There was *The Modern Library in First Editions*, 1938 (number 117) in that series' famous format, followed by a less successful *The Limited Editions Club in First Editions*, 1939 (number 123), an excellent *Catalogue of Original Manuscripts, and First Editions and Other Important Editions of the Tales of Sherlock Holmes . . .*, 1937 (unnumbered), two catalogues devoted to science and medicine (numbers 113 and 124), and seven catalogues of music material (numbers 105, 112, 119, 120, 121, 127, and 133).

While Randall began to publish articles and book reviews from his desk at Harzof's, the more stable and certain situation at Scribners encouraged him to become even more involved in writing. From 1935 to 1939 he was the American editor of *Bibliographical Notes and Queries*, which was published in London by the firm of Elkin Mathews, and he contributed a substantial number of notes to it. He and several others jointly conducted the "Bibliographical Notes" department of the *Papers of the Bibliographical Society of America* beginning with the second quarter of 1940 through 1941. He edited "Bibliographical Notes" for six issues of *The Baker Street Journal* in 1946–1948, and he was a contributing editor of the *New Colophon* during 1948–1950. He continued to review books for *Publishers' Weekly* and he collaborated with Winterich on a series called "One Hundred Good Novels," which ran in that journal from May 1939 to March 1942. He also assisted Winterich in revising his *A Primer of Book-Collecting* in 1946 and again in 1966; it remains one of the most readable and stimulating handbooks of its kind.

In the *Papers of the Bibliographical Society of America* for the second quarter of 1946, Randall contributed a provocative essay called "A Plea for a More Consistent Policy of Cataloguing by Auction Galleries." Although Randall later recalled in a letter to the editor of *Antiquarian Bookman* for 3 October 1966 that the article "had about as much effect as a feather dropped in the Grand Canyon would have towards filling it up," he received appreciative letters from Collamore, Arthur A. Houghton, Jr., Parkman D. Howe, Percy H. Muir, Howard

Peckham, Carl H. Pforzheimer, Donald G. Wing, and John Cook Wyllie regarding it.

During the Scribner years Randall's bibliographical abilities were engaged to produce a major bibliography and a collection catalogue in collaboration with collectors with whom he had worked for many years. In 1936 he was listed on the title page of Van Winkle's *Henry William Herbert (Frank Forester): A Bibliography of His Writings* for providing "bibliographical assistance." Van Winkle, a prominent New York lawyer and important collector of sporting books, had met Randall at Harzof's, and their friendship and business relationship continued at Scribners.

Randall knew Wilson during nearly all of his collecting career, roughly from 1925 until Wilson's death in 1947. His widow Jean and Randall assembled and edited Wilson's notes and descriptions of his books. Scribners published the book privately in 1950 in two volumes as *Thirteen Author Collections of the Nineteenth Century and Five Centuries of Familiar Quotations.*

During his career as a book dealer, Randall developed strong opinions about book collecting and book collectors, about libraries and librarians, and about the book trade. He also had the ability to get the right book to the right person at the right time, an ability, it should be said, that characterizes the best librarians as well as the best book dealers. Much of Randall's knowledge and many of his opinions are distilled in *Dukedom Large Enough* which covers the period from 1929 to 1956. But this knowledge and his opinions were developed, tested, and displayed in a steady stream of publications which he contributed to the popular and scholarly press not only during his career as a book dealer but also as the head of the Lilly Library at Indiana University.

From the rare-book department at Scribners there flowed books and manuscripts, singly or as collections, to America's greatest collectors and libraries. Collectors C. Waller Barrett, Mrs. Edward Doheny, Frank J. Hogan, H. Bradley Martin, Morris L. Parrish, Robert H. Taylor, Lilly, Houghton, and Wilson, libraries such as the Houghton, Huntington, Morgan, New York Public, the University of California at Los Angeles, the University of Virginia, and many others acquired major books and manuscripts through Randall at Scribners. He handled such individual treasures as the Shuckburgh copy of the Gutenberg Bible; the Declaration of Independence; a copy of the Thirteenth Amendment to the Constitution signed by President Abraham Lincoln, 33 senators, and 114 representatives;

Edgar Allan Poe's *The Murders in the Rue Morgue;* the manuscript of the earliest known version of Robert Burns's "Auld Lang Syne"; the manuscript of Wolfgang Amadeus Mozart's *Haffner* Symphony; William Blake's *Jerusalem* (1804); Michael Sadleir's incomparable collection of nineteenth-century fiction; Maj. J. R. Abbey's collection of illustrated books; A. E. Housman's manuscripts; and Wilson's collection of nineteenth-century American literature.

Randall first met Lilly in 1932 when Harzof sent Randall to Indianapolis with a case of books to offer to the collector. Most of the books that were offered were historical Americana, not one of Lilly's strong interests at the time, but there were also some good literary items in the case and these Randall was able to leave in Indiana. It was not until Randall had moved to Scribners that his relationship with Lilly flourished. Lilly concentrated on English and American literature; he bought one book at a time and usually inspected everything personally before making a purchase. Lilly bought very little during the war, but in 1946 he began to collect again with an interest in medicine, science, and Americana. Complementing Lilly's book-collecting passion was his interest in bibliography. Over the years he involved himself as a sponsor of several projects, to which Randall mostly was connected in one way or another.

In 1954 Lilly confided in Randall that he was thinking of giving up book collecting and donating his books and manuscripts to Indiana University. Would Randall consider giving up the trade to become the curator? Randall described the factors that went into his decision in *Dukedom Large Enough:*

> I had been in the business for over a quarter-century and thought that was enough. I had had some years of commuting (from New York to Cos Cob, Connecticut, then an hour and a half each way from door to door), apartment living, Long Island living, club living, a private home in the heart of New York — all of which made a beautiful university campus seem infinitely attractive. Besides, I had gone into my profession in the first place because I liked to be around books which, individually, I could never have aspired to. But the trouble was (or so I rationalized), someone was always buying them and taking them away just as we were becoming friends. Here I could get them and keep them — and what a lot of old friends I had to begin with. I never regretted my decision.

On 1 July 1956 Randall became rare-book librarian and professor of bibliography at Indiana University in Bloomington, thus beginning his second career in the world of books.

Randall at the Lilly Library

Indiana University already had a significant rare-book collection located in rooms in the main library building. But by 1975, the year in which Randall died, the collection had more than doubled and was housed in its own building, the Lilly Library. The Lilly Library opened its doors to the public on Saturday, 4 June 1960, and its formal dedication took place on 3 October 1960, with Indiana University President Herman B. Wells presiding and with an address by Adams, director of the Pierpont Morgan Library. For the dedication Randall assembled approximately five hundred books and manuscripts representative of the library's major fields of collecting at that time.

In the five years between his arrival on the Bloomington campus and the opening of the Lilly Library, Randall set his stamp on the future direction of the library's collections. In addition to Lilly's great collection, Randall acquired the fine collection of early printed books of George A. Poole, Jr., of Chicago, which included the New Testament portion of the Gutenberg Bible; the first William Caxton printing of Geoffrey Chaucer's *The Canterbury Tales;* the archives of the Howard Shipyards and Dock Company of Jeffersonville, Indiana, consisting of more than a quarter of a million pieces spanning the period from 1841 to 1941; and the papers of Upton Sinclair numbering nearly two hundred thousand items, among other large and important collections. He also acquired such important individual books and manuscripts as the first Bible in English to be printed in America, the rare first issue of Lewis Carroll's *Alice's Adventures in Wonderland* (1865), a manuscript translation in French of the memoirs of James II, the manuscript of Harold Pinter's *The Caretaker* (1960), and Ann S. Stephens's *Malaeska: The Indian Wife of the White Hunter* (1862), the first in Beadle's Dime Novels series.

After the opening of the Lilly Library and during the final fifteen years of his tenure at Indiana

University, Randall maintained this almost incredible record of quality and quantity of acquisitions. Among the many major collections he secured were the Bernardo Mendel library of material on Latin American discovery, history, and culture; the Starr collection of more than one hundred thousand pieces of American popular music; the stock of the New York bookseller Lathrop C. Harper, which increased the Lilly Library's holdings of incunabula by more than four hundred titles; Ian Fleming's library of nineteenth-century science and thought, together with the manuscripts and personal copies of the James Bond 007 stories; the Bobbs-Merrill publishing company archives containing more than fifty thousand letters; the papers of Wendell Willkie; and C. R. Boxer's collection of books and manuscripts relating to the history of the Portuguese in the Orient during the seventeenth and eighteenth centuries, historical works on Japan from 1542 to 1800, and the Dutch East India Company and the seventeenth-century Anglo-Dutch naval wars.

The Lilly Library always welcomed collections relating to Indiana writers – great favorites of Lilly's – Indiana political figures, and distinguished Indiana University professors. Individual items acquired during these years included Tycho Brahe's *Astronomiae Instauratae Mechanica* (1598); all four editions, each substantially revised, of Robert Burton's *The Anatomy of Melancholy* (1621) published during the author's lifetime; the manuscript of "The Adventure of the Red Circle," a Sherlock Holmes story by Sir Arthur Conan Doyle, a personal favorite of Randall's who was a member of the Baker Street Irregulars and a devoted Holmesian; a diary of Theodore Dreiser covering the period of October 1902–February 1903, the personal gift of Randall who made several important donations to the Lilly Library over the years; the manuscript of John Millington Synge's *The Playboy of the Western World* (1907); an autograph letter of George Washington, dated 14 April 1789, in which he accepts the presidency of the United States; and the first edition of William Butler Yeats's first book, *Mosada* (1886). Randall was also very proud of what turned out to be his last major purchase, a first edition of John Bunyan's *The Pilgrim's Progress* (1678).

To carry out the work of the Lilly Library, Randall was fortunate in the support he received from president and later chancellor Wells; librarians Robert A. Miller, Cecil K. Byrd, and W. Carl Jackson; a rare-book staff already in place that included Doris Reed, Elfrieda Lang, and Geneva Warner; Josiah Q. Bennett (whom Randall brought to the Lilly Library from the Parke-Bernet Galleries

in New York in 1965); and William R. Cagle, now head of the Lilly Library, who came from Indiana's main library. Together they acquired, catalogued, and made available to the scholarly community a vast array of books and manuscripts, and in the process the Lilly Library became known as one of the country's premier rare-book libraries. Further evidence of Randall's acquisitions work can be found in the series of *Reports* he issued from 1957 through 1969 and in the series of exhibition catalogues he produced for the Lilly Library, some of which should be singled out for special comment.

The opening of the Lilly Library focused a considerable amount of national attention on Indiana's strong holdings in many fields of study, and many groups and organizations made arrangements to visit. When possible, special exhibitions were arranged to suit the interests of the visitors. In 1963, for example, the Grolier Club visited Bloomington and the members were treated to an exhibition and catalogue entitled *Grolier: or 'Tis Sixty Years Since. A Reconstruction of the Exhibit of 100 Books Famous in English Literature Originally Held in New York, 1902.* The following year the Manuscript Society held its annual meeting at Indiana University and viewed an exhibition titled *Manuscripts Ancient-Modern.* Catalogues of exhibitions of *Three Centuries of American Poetry* (1965), *Medicine* (1966), *The First Twenty-five Years of Printing, 1455–1480* (1967), *American Patriotic Songs* (1968), *The Ian Fleming Collection of 19th–20th Century Source Material Concerning Western Civilization together with the Originals of the James Bond-007 Tales* (1970), *The First Hundred Years of Detective Fiction, 1841–1941* (1973), and *Science Fiction/Fantasy* (1974), Randall's last, are important scholarly contributions and are worthy of study today.

In 1973 Randall mounted an exhibition titled *Printing and the Mind of Man* based upon an exhibition with the same title which had been held in London ten years earlier. The Lilly Library lent thirty-one books to the London exhibition – more than half the total sent from the United States – and was fourth in the number of items contributed overall. The noted English collector and novelist Ian Fleming was third with forty-four contributions, and since Fleming's collection later came to the Lilly Library that brought the total of actual copies exhibited owned by Lilly to seventy-five. The speaker at the opening of the 1973 exhibition at Bloomington was Nicolas Barker of Oxford University who characterized the Lilly collection and exhibition as the summit of Randall's notable career and called it an achievement that few could ever hope to emulate.

Bennett, one of Randall's colleagues at the Lilly Library, called attention to Randall's "incredible skills in locating books" in *The David A. Randall Retrospective Memorial Exhibition: Twenty Years' Acquisitions,* and it is quite clear that his greatest contribution as Lilly librarian was the development of the collection.

One of Randall's innovations was the sale of duplicates from the Lilly Library's collection, the first sale of books of this magnitude by an institution since the Huntington sales over four decades earlier. Still another innovative program in which Randall was involved was the Lilly Library Fellowship Program, a training opportunity for rare-book librarians established in 1960 by Indiana University's Director of Libraries Robert Miller and Associate Director Cecil K. Byrd with the support of the Lilly Endowment of Indianapolis. The program trained fourteen librarians in rare-book work from 1961 through 1970.

Randall was a member of the Bibliographical Society of America, the Grolier Club, the University Club of New York, and the Caxton Club of Chicago, and in 1959 he received the Sigma Delta Chi "Leather Medal" for outstanding contribution by a faculty member to Indiana University. In 1975 he selected 241 books and manuscripts representative of acquisitions made by the Lilly Library during his tenure. Meant for an exhibition and catalogue to mark his retirement, it became a memorial exhibition when Randall died on 25 May 1975, a month before that retirement was to take place.

On 10 September 1975 friends of Randall met in Bloomington to pay tribute to one of the great bookmen of his time. A copy of the Coverdale Bible, the first printing of the complete Bible in English, was presented to the Lilly Library on behalf of his friends and the university by Randall's son Ronald, and it was accepted by Dean of Libraries W. Carl Jackson. Indiana University's Chancellor Wells, longtime colleague and friend Papantonio, and Ronald Randall spoke eloquently the evening of 10 September, but perhaps Chancellor Wells gave voice to the thoughts that were in the minds of many that evening when he said, in remarks reported in *AB Bookman's Weekly* for 10 November 1972:

> The founding and development of the Lilly Library were occurrences of unexcelled importance during my administrative years with the University. Its beginning and its successful evolution are jewels without measure. It was and it is Dave Randall's work.
>
> It was indeed a lucky day for Indiana University and for me when Dave Randall decided to direct this great enterprise at Indiana University.

References:

The David A. Randall Retrospective Memorial Exhibition: Twenty Years' Acquisitions. (Bloomington: Indiana University, Lilly Library, 1975);

Dean H. Keller, *David Anton Randall, 1905–1975* (Metuchen, N.J.: Scarecrow Press, 1992);

Pete Martin, "He Finds Fortunes in Forgotten Corners," *Saturday Evening Post,* 224 (22 March 1952): 42–43, 111–112, 114–116, 118;

Michael Papantonio, "David Anton Randall (1905–1975)," *AB Bookman's Weekly,* 56 (11–18 August 1975): 533–534;

Avery Strakosch, "David Randall of Scribner's," *Avocations, A Magazine of Hobbies and Leisure,* 2 (April 1938): 53–56;

Herman B. Wells and Ronald R. Randall, "Lilly Library Tributes to Dave Randall," *AB Bookman's Weekly,* 56 (10 November 1975): 2217–2120.

Papers:

Correspondence, manuscripts, and other material relating to Randall are located at The Lilly Library, Indiana University, Bloomington, and in the collection of Ronald R. Randall, Santa Barbara, California.

Gordon Norton Ray

(8 September 1915 – 15 December 1986)

William Baker

Northern Illinois University

See also the Ray entry in *DLB 103: American Literary Biographers, First Series.*

SELECTED BOOKS: *The Buried Life: A Study of the Relation between Thackeray's Fiction and His Personal History* (Cambridge, Mass.: Harvard University Press, 1952; London: Oxford University Press, 1952);

Nineteenth-century English Books: Some Problems in Bibliography (Urbana: University of Illinois Press, 1952);

Thackeray: The Uses of Adversity, 1811–1846 (New York: McGraw-Hill, 1955; London: Oxford University Press, 1955);

Thackeray: The Age of Wisdom, 1847–1863 (New York: McGraw-Hill, 1958; London: Oxford University Press, 1958);

New York University Founders Day Address . . . 'The Undoctored Incident' (New York: New York University, 1961);

Is Liberal Education Still Needed? (Syracuse, N.Y.: Design Center, Syracuse University, 1962);

Bibliographical Resources for the Study of Nineteenth Century English Fiction (Los Angeles: School of Library Service, University of California, 1964);

French Lithographs, 1820–1860, from the Collection of Gordon N. Ray: An Exhibition at the Grolier Club, New York City, January, 1965 (New York: Privately produced for distribution at the Grolier Club, 1965);

Tennyson Reads "Maud," Sedgewick Memorial Lecture, 1968 (Vancouver: Publications Centre, University of British Columbia, 1968);

H. G. Wells & Rebecca West (New Haven: Yale University Press, 1974; London: Macmillan, 1974);

The Illustrator and the Book in England from 1790 to 1914, preface by Charles Ryskamp, bibliographical descriptions by Thomas V. Lange, and photography by Charles V. Passela (New York: Pierpont Morgan Library & Oxford University Press, 1976);

The Art of the French Illustrated Book, 1700 to 1914, 2 volumes, preface by Ryskamp; bibliographical descriptions by Lange and photography by Passela (New York: Pierpont Morgan Library, 1982; Ithaca, N.Y.: Cornell University Press, 1982);

The Rare Book World Today: An Address to the Annual Meeting of the Fellows of the Pierpont Morgan Library, 28 April 1982 (New York: Pierpont Morgan Library, 1982);

Books as a Way of Life: Essays by Gordon N. Ray, with an introductory essay and a checklist by G. Thomas Tanselle (New York: Grolier Club, Pierpont Morgan Library, 1988).

OTHER: William Makepeace Thackeray, *The Letters and Private Papers of William Makepeace Thackeray,* 4 volumes, collected and edited by Ray (Cambridge, Mass.: Harvard University Press, 1945–1946; London: Oxford University Press, 1945–1946);

Thackeray, *The Rose and the Ring: Reproduced in Facsimile from the Author's Original Illustrated Manuscript in the Pierpont Morgan Library,* introduction by Ray (New York: Pierpont Morgan Library, 1947);

Thackeray, *The History of Henry Esmond, Esquire,* introductory essay by Ray (New York: Modern Library, 1950);

"The Importance of Original Editions," in *Nineteenth-Century English Books: Some Problems in Bibliography,* Third Annual Windsor Lectures in Librarianship (Urbana: University of Illinois Press, 1952);

"Thackeray, William Makepeace," in *The New Century Cyclopedia of Names,* edited by Clarence L. Barnhart and others (New York: Appleton-Century-Crofts, 1954), p. 3830;

Gordon Norton Ray (photograph by Blackstone–Shelburne, New York)

Thackeray, *Contributions to the "Morning Chronicle," Now First Reprinted,* edited, with an introduction, by Ray (Urbana: University of Illinois Press, 1955);

Nuel Pharr Davis, *The Life of Wilkie Collins,* introductory essay by Ray (Urbana: University of Illinois Press, 1956);

H. G. Wells, *The Desert Daisy,* introductory essay by Ray (Urbana, Ill.: Beta Phi Mu, 1957);

Henry James and H. G. Wells: A Record of Their Friendship, Their Debate on the Art of Fiction, and Their Quarrel, edited, with an introduction, by Leon Edel and Ray (Urbana: University of Illinois Press / London: Hart-Davis, 1958);

Masters of British Literature, edited by Robert A. Pratt, D. C. Allen, F. P. Wilson, James R. Sutherland, Carlos Baker, Francis E. Mineka, Richard Ellmann, and Ray, with an introductory essay by Ray (Boston: Houghton Mifflin, 1958; revised and enlarged, 1962);

Masters of American Literature, edited by Edel, Thomas H. Johnson, Sherman Paul, and Claude Simpson, with a prefatory note by Ray (Boston: Houghton Mifflin, 1959; revised, 1959);

An Introduction in Literature, edited by Herbert Barrows, Hubert Heffner, John Ciardi, and Wallace Douglas, with a prefatory note by Ray (Boston: Houghton Mifflin, 1959);

"Conflict and Cooperation in American Higher Education," in *Financing Higher Education 1960–70: The McGraw-Hill Book Company 50th Anniversary Study of the Economics of Higher Education in the United States,* edited by Dexter M. Keezer (New York: McGraw-Hill, 1959);

"H. G. Wells Tries to Be a Novelist," in *Edwardians and Late Victorians,* edited by Ellmann (N.p.: English Institute Essays, 1959; New York: Columbia University Press, 1960);

Wells, *The History of Mr. Polly,* edited, with an introduction, by Ray (Boston: Houghton Mifflin, 1960);

"Excellence in Public Higher Education: Problems and Opportunities," in *The Dedication and Symposium at Harpur College of State University of New York, Binghamton, September 29th, 1960* (Binghamton: State University of New York at Binghamton, 1960);

Selected Non-Dramatic Writings of Bernard Shaw, edited by Dan H. Laurence, with an introductory essay by Ray (Boston: Houghton Mifflin, 1965);

"The Private Collector and the Literary Scholar," in *The Private Collector and the Support of Scholarship:*

MR. AND MRS. RICHMOND THACKERAY AND THEIR SON WILLIAM IN 1814
From a water-color sketch by George Chinnery

THE LETTERS AND PRIVATE PAPERS OF

William Makepeace
THACKERAY

Collected and edited by
Gordon N. Ray

In four volumes
Volume I: 1817–1840

HARVARD UNIVERSITY PRESS
Cambridge, Massachusetts
1945

Frontispiece and title page for the first volume of Ray's major editorial project

Papers Read at a Clark Library Seminar, April 5, 1969 (Los Angeles: William Andrews Clark Memorial Library, 1969);

The American Writer in England: An Exhibition Arranged in Honor of the Sesquicentennial of the University of Virginia, foreword by Ray (Charlottesville: University of Virginia Press, 1969);

Victoria R. I.: A Collection of Books, Manuscripts, Autograph Letters, Original Drawings, Etc., by the Lady Herself and Her Loyal Subjects, Produced during Her Long and Illustrious Reign, 3 volumes, prefatory essay by Ray (San Francisco: David Magee Antiquarian Books, 1969–1970);

"Indiana University Library Dedication Address," in *Papers Delivered at the Indiana University Library Dedication, Bloomington Campus, October 9–10, 1970* (Bloomington: Indiana University, 1971);

"A Retrospective View," in *American Libraries as Centers of Scholarship: Proceedings of a Convocation Held at Dartmouth College on June 30th, 1978,*

Marking the Fiftieth Anniversary of Fisher Ames Baker Memorial Library, edited by Edward Connery Lathem (Hanover, N.H.: Dartmouth College, 1978);

Thackeray, *The Heroic Adventures of M. Boudin: Reproduced in Facsimile in Honor of William Pearson Tolley,* introductory essay by Ray (Syracuse, N.Y.: Syracuse University Library Associates, 1980);

Books and Prints, Past and Future: Papers Presented at The Grolier Club Centennial Convocation, 26–28 April 1984, introductory essay by Ray (New York: Grolier Club, 1984).

SELECTED PERIODICAL PUBLICATIONS –
UNCOLLECTED: "Thackeray and *Punch:* 44 Newly Identified Contributions," *Times Literary Supplement,* 1 January 1949, p. 16;

"The Love of Thackeray for Mrs. Brookfield: Gordon N. Ray on the 'Unwritten Part' of *Pen-*

Ray, circa 1950

dennis and Henry Esmond," *Listener*, 42 (4 August 1949): 196–198;

"*Vanity Fair:* One Version of the Novelist's Responsibility," *Essays by Divers Hands*, no. 25 (1950): 87–101;

"The Bentley Papers," *Library*, fifth series 7 (September 1952): 178–200;

"Seeing Dickens Plain," *Virginia Quarterly Review*, 29 (Spring 1953): 297–302;

"The Bennett Problem," *Accent*, 13 (Summer 1953): 187–188;

"Dickens Versus Thackeray: The Garrick Club Affair," *Publications of the Modern Language Association of America*, 69 (September 1954): 815–832;

"Thackeray's 'Book of Snobs,' " *Nineteenth-Century Fiction*, 10 (June 1955): 22–33;

"H. G. Wells's Contributions to the *Saturday Review*," *Library*, fifth series 16 (March 1961): 29–36;

"Helping the Superior Individual," *Journal of Proceedings and Addresses of the . . . Annual Conference of the Association of Graduate Schools in the Association of American Universities*, 13 (1961): 81–87;

"Impossible Loyalties? The Social Responsibility of the Humanist," *Journal of Higher Education*, 33 (February 1962): 61–71;

"Literature and the Darkness Within," *College English*, 24 (February 1963): 339–344;

"The University and the Community," *Tulanian*, 36 (July 1963): 6–8; *American Council of Learned Societies Newsletter*, 14 (October 1963): 1–8;

"In Memoriam: John D. Gordan," *Papers of the Bibliographical Society of America*, 62 (1968): 175–176;

"Trollope at Full Length," *Huntington Library Quarterly*, 31 (August 1968): 313–340;

"The Idea of Disinterestedness in the University," *Graduate Journal*, 8 (1971): 295–309;

The

Illustrator

and the Book

in England

from

1790 to 1914

Gordon N. Ray

The Pierpont Morgan Library

Oxford University Press

Drawn from his own collection, the catalogue of Ray's exhibit of English illustrated books provided a history of illustration as well as a dictionary of illustrators.

"A Galaxy of Poets," *Columbia Library Columns*, 26 (February 1977): 13–16;

"The Opening of the New Rare Book and Manuscript Library: Remarks at the Dedication and Reception," *Columbia Library Columns*, 34 (February 1985): 5–7.

Gordon Norton Ray was a passionate and discerning book collector; his collecting habits serve as a reflection and representation of his scholarly interests. He collected for institutions, such as the University of Illinois at Urbana Library, and for himself. His personal books, manuscripts, and papers have been left to the Pierpont Morgan Library in New York, which has held two exhibits representing his collecting interests. The exhibits of the English illustrated book held in 1976 and of the French illustrated book held in 1982 were drawn from his collection. In his introduction to *The Illustrator and*

the Book in England from 1790 to 1914 (1976) Ray notes, "Two things are needed to keep a collector interested in a chosen specialty: he must be continuously absorbed in the field and the material must be there to collect."

Gordon Norton Ray was born to Jessie Norton and Jesse Gordon Ray in New York City on 8 September 1915. Much of his childhood was spent on the shore of Lake Michigan in northern Chicago; he attended New Trier High School in Winnetka, Illinois. His love of books and book collecting developed at an early age. He writes in "A 19th-Century Collection: English First Editions" (1964): "I found myself buying out of my allowance my own copies of favorite books. After a while, I had all of 'Sherlock Holmes,' the Waverley Novels, and sets of Dickens, Stevenson and Mark Twain." He felt a particular passion for both English and French literature and illustrated books.

Ray attended Indiana University, where he was elected to three honorary societies: Phi Beta Kappa, Beta Gamma Sigma, and Phi Eta Sigma. He graduated in 1936 with an A.B. and A.M. in French literature. From 1937 to 1938 he held an Austin Scholarship at Harvard University, where he did graduate work in English literature. In 1938 he received his A.M. and decided to do his doctoral work on William Makepeace Thackeray, the subject of much of Ray's major scholarship. He writes, "In 1939 a doctoral dissertation on 'Thackeray and France' brought me the friendship of Hester Fuller and Mr. W. T. A. Ritchie, Thackeray's granddaughter and grandson, who entrusted to me the editing" of his letters. He visited Europe just before the outbreak of World War II and arranged for the microfilming of Thackeray's letters. Ray received his Ph.D. in 1940, and by 1 December 1942 he had completed his edition of the letters. He was an instructor at Harvard from 1940 to 1942. Between 1940 and 1 December 1942, when he received his call-up papers for active duty in the navy, Ray received a Dexter Scholarship and two Guggenheim Fellowships. Ray's friend Howard Mumford Jones agreed to read proofs and check references for him while he was serving in the navy. Ray comments: "My four years in the Navy were a blank in my collecting history. Only when I returned to academic life at the University of Illinois [as Professor of English in 1946] did I begin collecting again."

The Guggenheim Fellowship allowed him upon his discharge from the navy to return to London and, with Fuller to continue his explorations into primary Thackeray material. His six months in London formed the basis for his work on Thackeray, which divides into his editions of the letters, editions of works, an anthology, a critical study, and a biography. Ray's meticulous attention to detail and thorough research is seen in his four-volume *The Letters and Private Papers of William Makepeace Thackeray*, the first two volumes of which appeared in 1945; the third and fourth volumes were published in 1946. Although many Thackeray letters not included by Ray have subsequently emerged, his edition remains important for its extensive introduction, illustrations, "memoranda concerning certain persons who figure in Thackeray's Correspondence," extensive appendices, a thorough index of correspondents in each volume, a general index, and an index of Thackeray's writings. Ray extensively annotated the nearly sixteen hundred Thackeray letters printed. Ray also included more than one hundred letters to and about

Thackeray, as well as many of his diaries and account books. Ray's extensive connections with rare-book dealers and his familiarity with auction records revealed several hundred additional letters, the originals of which he was unable to trace.

An anonymous reviewer in the 17 October 1952 issue of the *Times Literary Supplement* wrote: "Mr. Ray's work is not only an admirable example in the compact construction of a large assortment of new facts . . . it is itself exhilarating in its portrait gallery of distinctive people." In *The Buried Life: A Study of the Relation Between Thackeray's Fiction and His Personal History* (1952) Ray draws upon the Thackeray letters. Ray exhibits his ability to uncover factual foundations for Thackeray's fiction and pursues biographical clues to reveal hidden secrets. Ray's two-volume biography, *Thackeray: The Uses of Adversity, 1811–1866* and *Thackeray: The Age of Wisdom, 1847–1863,* appeared in 1955 and 1958, respectively, having been approved by the Thackeray family. Using family archives, it is full of previously unpublished details, yet these are interwoven with Ray's central vision of Thackeray's genius. Frank Kermode wrote succinctly in the 9 May 1958 *Spectator*, "It would be difficult to overpraise [Ray's] skill, or to give an adequate idea of the quality or the extent of the new material he has made available." Ray's biography remains standard. In 1950 his introduction to the Modern Library edition of *The History of Henry Esmond, Esquire* was published. Four years later he began his general editorship of the Houghton Mifflin Riverside Series of literary classics; Ray's contribution would be his edition of H. G. Wells's *The History of Mr. Polly* (1960). Although Ray's critical and scholarly writings focus on Thackeray and Wells, he admired others, praising Anthony Trollope, who "was a great, truthful, varied artist, who wrote better than he or his contemporaries realized, and who left behind him more novels of lasting value than any other writer in English."

During his 1948 British sojourn, Ray had visited the bibliographer and bibliophile Michael Sadleir. Ray writes, "The experience of seeing his library was a revelation. Here were the novels to whose study I was devoting myself as they first appeared in boards, in wrapped parts, and in cloth. . . . And the copies for the most part, were as fresh as when they had left the publisher's shelves. The unspoken lesson of the master could not be missed: original editions in original condition add a dimension to literary study. For the first time I was shaken in my conviction that collecting rare books was an essentially frivolous pursuit." From 1948

The Art of the
French Illustrated Book
1700 to 1914

VOLUME I

Gordon N. Ray

The Pierpont Morgan Library

Cornell University Press

Title page for the first volume of Ray's last book

until his death Ray visited England and France most summers, buying books for his own collection, most of which is now at the Pierpont Morgan Library in New York, and, from 1950 until 1957, buying for the University of Illinois Library. He unsuccessfully endeavored to bring the Sadleir collection to his university. The University of California, Los Angeles, eventually gained this prized collection. Four major collections at Urbana are the fruits of Ray's activities. Some twelve thousand letters and manuscripts of the Richard Bentley papers of the nineteenth-century publishing house were acquired in 1951. A year later he acquired for Urbana the Grant Richards papers, some fifteen thousand letters written to the late-nineteenth- and early-twentieth-century London publisher, and forty-five volumes of copies of his replies. The next year saw the addition of the literary library, some eight thousand volumes, of the English book collector Tom

Turner. The strength of the collection "lies in first editions of books published in England between 1890 and 1949." Ray wrote in "The Tom Turner Library," which appeared in the Winter 1953 issue of the *Book Collector,* "It is better in poetry than in fiction and better in fiction than in other prose." In 1954, in what may well be Ray's most significant long-term purchase, for having shown faith in the enduring reputation of a modern master he acquired the H. G. Wells papers; about sixty thousand letters and manuscripts came to Illinois. The Wells collection reflected Ray's own research interest. He edited Wells's *The Desert Daisy* (1957) and collaborated with the Henry James scholar Leon Edel to write a comparative study, *Henry James and H. G. Wells* (1958). With Edel, Ray drew upon the Urbana collection to provide the record of the argument between James and Wells in *Henry James and H. G. Wells: A Record of Their Friendship, Their Debate on the Art of Fiction and Their Quarrel* (1958). Full documentation, an extensive introduction, and annotations to the letters are provided.

Ray's mother had died in 1954, and with his father's death in 1956 Ray inherited stock to the Independent Limestone Company (founded by his father in 1927). Eventually becoming the company's president in 1976, Ray spent much of his company income on his passion for collecting. Ray's book-buying activities enriched the coffers of English booksellers and developed a great collection at Urbana. In 1960 he left Urbana for the associate secretary generalship of the Simon Guggenheim Memorial Foundation in New York. In 1963 he became secretary general, holding this powerful position as a patron of excellence until he retired just prior to his seventieth birthday in 1985. He also served on twelve governing boards, ranging from that of the American Council of Learned Societies (treasurer, 1973–1985) to that of the Modern Language Association of America (1966–1985). Beginning in 1962–1963 Ray also served as professor of English at New York University, teaching and directing dissertations in Victorian literature; he became professor emeritus in 1980. In the summer of 1969 he was Beckman Professor of English at the University of California, Berkeley.

Until about 1970, with a few exceptions, illustrated English books were not collected. Major collections could be acquired for comparatively modest amounts, and English illustrated books were cheaper than French ones. Until 1958 Ray's book collecting had concentrated "on first editions of English and French literature, chiefly of the nineteenth century." He then extended the scope of his collections to fine bindings and illustrated books. Certain fundamental principles had always determined his collecting: condition, the necessity to keep "in touch with all major sources of supply," knowledge of the stocks of leading dealers, judicious bidding at auction sales, quick action regarding book dealers' catalogues, "the special interest of exceptional copies," the importance of association copies, the impracticality of title-by-title collecting, and the opportunity to buy collections. Bidding by cable and sight unseen, on 21 December 1964 he bought from Sotheby's in London J. N. Hart's collection of "426 proofs of wood engravings of English artists of the third quarter of the nineteenth century." The purchase formed the basis for the February–April 1965 Grolier Club exhibition, "Illustrated Books of the 1860s."

Two other purchases illustrate Ray's techniques of acquisition extending beyond the auction room. Selections from the library of the publisher and patron of original woodgraving, Thomas Balston, were sold at Christie's London auction rooms on 17 July 1968. In the summer of 1970 Ray found "in the basement of [his] principal London dealer a large collection of English illustrated books." They were the remainder of the Balston collection "deemed unsuitable for disposal at the auction." Ray made an offer on the spot and then purchased a treasure trove of private presses, three-color-process illustrated books, and other riches. Extensive contacts among dealers and purchases at auctions resulted in the acquisition of "twenty-two sketchbooks, 474 drawings . . . many lithographs and proofs of process illustrations, much manuscript material," and annotated and decorated materials by the book illustrator Edmund J. Sullivan.

More than twenty years of collecting is represented in Ray's *The Art of the French Illustrated Book, 1700–1914* (1982). French books generally were more costly than English ones, "although until the early 1970s a favorable exchange rate for the dollar kept them within range," and they were more widely dispersed geographically. The basis of his collection was the purchase in 1962 from the estate of Sadleir three hundred albums of French lithographs. Ray's interest in French illustration, and especially the work of Honoré Daumier, went back to his student days at Indiana University in 1935, when he pored "over Loys Delteil's ten-volume catalogue of his more than 4000 lithographs, each with its illustration." Lithographic albums and French illustrated books could be obtained in the 1960s in the United States, where there was a surplus of such books, many of which had been brought into the country in 1920 and 1922 by the great dealer A. S. W. Rosenbach for his wealthy clientele.

His work during those years, including many speeches, was an offshoot of his collecting interests: "English illustrated books of the nineteenth century and French illustrated books and bindings from 1700 through the 1930's." *The Illustrator and the Book in England from 1790 to 1914* appeared in 1976, and the two-volume, sumptuous *Art of the French Illustrated Book, 1700–1914* in 1982. Both these works formed the foundation for exhibitions at the Pierpont Morgan Library. As G. Thomas Tanselle observes, "These two books demonstrate the interconnections between scholarship and collecting, are masterpieces of trenchant commentary," continually revealing Ray's "comprehensive knowledge of the history of book illustration and his lifetime of reading in the literature that inspired the illustrations. They are monuments as solid in their field as his Thackeray work is in Victorian literary study."

Ray's Lyell lectures at Oxford in May 1985 surveyed French Art Deco books, "bringing his analysis of French bookmaking up to the chronological limit of his own collection."

The Illustrator and the Book in England from 1790 to 1914 is a catalogue of the 1976 Pierpont Morgan Library exhibition of Ray's comprehensive collection of illustrated books. Ray's concern in developing his collection was with the primacy of the image. Formal bibliographic description of the 333 numbered entries and other items has been supplied by Thomas V. Lange, but Ray provides descriptive text that places each book in its artistic and historical context. His last book, *The Art of the French Illustrated Book, 1700 to 1914,* with formal bibliographic description by Lange, again draws upon his own collection; the work accompanied an exhibition at the Pierpont Morgan Library and exhibits Ray's knowledge of the techniques of illustration, provides bibliographic sketches of the artists, and sets their work in their context.

Tanselle's selection of Ray's essays in *Books as a Way of Life* (1988) is divided into five sections. The first contains essays; the second, Ray's "Surveys of the Rare Book World"; the third, essays on "Collecting and Scholarship"; the fourth, "Books and Life." The fifth section is a four-part appendix containing Ray's 1953 review of Sadleir's *XIX Century Fiction;* his account of Turner; his "In Memoriam: John D. Gordan [1968]" — Gordan was chief of the Berg Collection of English and American Literature at the New York Public Library; and Ray's foreword to *The American Writer in England: An Exhibition Arranged in Honor of the Sesquicentennial of the University of Virginia.* Each of these represents and typifies his eclecticism as a bookman. Ray's writings on bibliophilic issues are biographical: they survey the state of the rare-book world, discuss the close relationship between scholarship and collecting, analyze bibliographic resources for nineteenth-century English fictional study, and "demonstrate the importance of books to each individual's formation of a view of life."

Ray's contributions to the study of nineteenth-century English literature; to Thackeray, Trollope, and Wells studies; and to the study of French and English illustrated books are significant. His bookmanship benefited from his various professional positions and activities: university professor, scholar and biographer, analyst of trends in rare-book librarianship, book and manuscript collector, and president of the Guggenheim Foundation. As Ray said in his July 1966 keynote address to the eighty-fifth annual conference of the American Library Association, "books offer a way of staying human."

Reference:

G. Thomas Tanselle, "Introduction and the Publications of Gordon N. Ray," in *Books as a Way of Life: Essays by Gordon N. Ray* (New York: Grolier Club, Pierpont Morgan Library, 1988), pp. vii-xxxiii, 383–393.

A. S. W. Rosenbach

(22 July 1876 – 1 July 1952)

Leslie A. Morris
Houghton Library, Harvard University

BOOKS: *A Catalogue of the Books and Manuscripts of Robert Louis Stevenson in the Library of the Late Harry Elkins Widener with a Memoir by A. S. W. Rosenbach* (Philadelphia: Privately printed, 1913);

The Unpublishable Memoirs (New York: Kennerley, 1917; London: Castle, 1924);

A Catalogue of the Books and Manuscripts of Harry Elkins Widener, 2 volumes (Philadelphia: Privately printed, 1918);

A Catalogue of the Works Illustrated by George Cruikshank and Isaac and Robert Cruikshank in the Library of Harry Elkins Widener (Philadelphia: Privately printed, 1918);

A Catalogue of the Writings of Charles Dickens in the Library of Harry Elkins Widener (Philadelphia: Privately printed, 1918);

An American Jewish Bibliography Being a List of Books and Pamphlets by Jews or Relating to Them Printed in the United States from the Establishment of the Press in the Colonies until 1850 (New York: American Jewish Historical Society, 1926);

Books and Bidders: The Adventures of a Bibliophile (Boston: Little, Brown, 1927 / London: Allen & Unwin, 1927);

Early American Children's Books (Portland, Maine: Southworth Press, 1933);

The All-Embracing Doctor Franklin (Philadelphia: Privately printed, 1932);

A Book Hunter's Holiday: Adventures with Books and Manuscripts (Boston: Houghton Mifflin, 1936).

OTHER: *Samuel Johnson's Prologue Spoken at the Opening of the Theatre in Drury-Lane in 1747 with Garrick's Epilogue: A Facsimile of the Hitherto Undiscovered First Edition, with Preface by Austin Dobson and Introduction and Notes by A. S. W. Rosenbach* (New York: Dodd, Mead, 1902).

SELECTED PERIODICAL PUBLICATIONS – UNCOLLECTED: "Aaron Levy," by Rosenbach and Isabella H. Rosenbach, *American Jewish*

Historical Society, Publications, 2 (1894): 157–163;

"The Curious-Impertinent in English Dramatic Literature before Shelton's Translation of Don Quixote," *Modern Language Notes,* 17 (1902): 179–184;

"The Influence of the 'Celestina' in the Early English Drama," *Jahrbuch der deutschen Shakespeare-gesellschaft* (1903): 43–61.

Dr. A. S. W. Rosenbach was called the "Napoleon of Books" by the *New Yorker,* the "Terror of the Auction Room" by the London tabloids, and "the most scholarly bookseller in [America]" by the writer and collector A. Edward Newton. He bought and sold the Gutenberg Bible five times. He bought and sold the First Folio of Shakespeare, in prime condition, six times, when no other twentieth-century dealer ever had more than one copy in comparable condition. Rosenbach, or "Dr. R," as he was known to collectors and friends, was, in short, the most successful and certainly the most famous bookseller of the twentieth century. He has been described by Edwin Wolf II as "an apple-cheeked, fun-loving, scholarly, bawdy, ungrammatical, tale-spinning, elephant-memoried supersalesman of great books." As a result of his involvement in the book trade, he amassed an important personal collection of books and manuscripts.

Abraham Simon Wolf Rosenbach was born in Philadelphia on 22 July 1876 and was the youngest of the seven children of Morris and Isabella Polock Rosenbach. His father had run a successful soft-goods store and was for many years one of the leading Jewish merchants of the city. In the year of Rosenbach's birth, however, his father went bankrupt, having overinvested in a catalogue of his goods for the Philadelphia Centennial Exposition.

As a child Rosenbach spent much time in the shop of his uncle, Moses Polock, a well-known and somewhat eccentric antiquarian bookseller. Through his uncle he became familiar with the

A. S. W. Rosenbach

book trade and bibliophily and met many Philadelphia collectors. At the age of eleven he made his first purchase at auction, an illustrated edition of *Reynard the Fox.* Further evidence of his bibliophilic development is found in his first publication, an article written for the Central Manuel Training School paper, *Argus,* entitled "Bibliomania." It told the story of the sale of Giovanni Boccaccio's *Decameron* and the battle over it in the auction room between the marquis of Blandford and Earl Spencer in 1812 during the sale of the library of John Ker, third Duke of Roxburghe. Printed by Christopher Valdarfer in 1471, it sold for the phenomenal sum of £2,260, a record which stood for many years.

Rosenbach attended the University of Pennsylvania, receiving his B.S. in 1898 and a Ph.D. in 1901 with a dissertation on the influence of Spanish literature on Elizabethan and Jacobean drama. It was in 1901 that Rosenbach made his first important discovery as a collector: in a volume of pamphlets he purchased at auction he found what was

then the unique copy of the *Prologue and Epilogue Spoken at the Opening of the Theatre in Drury-Lane, 1747* by Samuel Johnson and David Garrick.

In June 1903 Rosenbach went into business with his older brother Philip. Their firm, the Rosenbach Company, was located at 1320 Walnut Street in Philadelphia and sold not only rare books and manuscripts but also antique furniture, silver, prints, and drawings. The two brothers' temperaments were complementary. Philip desired an extremely comfortable lifestyle and viewed the business as a means to achieve it. Rosenbach, left to his own devices, might have remained a scholar and collector. Urged on by Philip to sell books rather than collect them, however, Rosenbach evolved into a scholarly, persuasive, and highly successful salesman who also happened to collect.

Two Philadelphia collectors, friends of Rosenbach, agreed to back the company. Joseph M. Fox provided twenty-five thousand dollars in capital; Clarence Bement offered his rich collection of

CATALOGUE ONE

A CATALOGUE

OF

RARE BOOKS

AND

MANUSCRIPTS

RELATING TO

AMERICA.

FOR SALE BY
THE ROSENBACH COMPANY
1320 WALNUT STREET
PHILADELPHIA

The first catalogue issued by Rosenbach, 1904

books and manuscripts to be sold on consignment by the fledgling firm. In August 1903 Polock died, and with financial help from his mother Rosenbach purchased heavily at the 1904 sale of his uncle's books and manuscripts. While most of what he purchased went into stock, a few volumes passed into his own collection, including a volume of tracts from George Washington's library with manuscript annotations.

For two years the Rosenbach Company struggled. Then in late 1905 Rosenbach was introduced by Bement to the Widener family of Philadelphia. Three generations of Wideners, collected paintings, tapestries, silver, and prints. The youngest Widener, Harry, was beginning to collect books. He and Rosenbach became close friends, and the rest of the Widener family soon began collecting books and manuscripts as well. As many collectors were to tes-

tify later, there was no one who could match Rosenbach when he set his mind to selling a book. His academic credentials were impressive; he had an endless supply of anecdotes which made the books he handled come alive; and he had the irresistible enthusiasm of a salesman convinced that what he was selling was better than anything else on the market. The Wideners were Rosenbach's first significant patrons, and they put the financially struggling Rosenbach Company on solid ground. Through them Rosenbach also gained entry to a small circle of wealthy Philadelphia customers. Following Harry Widener's death on the *Titanic* in 1912, Rosenbach undertook his first major bibliographical publication, a five-volume catalogue of Widener's collection.

Throughout the 1910s Rosenbach's customers were largely Philadelphia collectors: the Wideners,

Rosenbach (seated at table, fourth from right) at the sale of the Alice's Adventures Under Ground *manuscript at Sotheby's in London, 1928*

William M. Elkins, George C. Thomas, Newton, John B. Gribbel, and John B. Stetson. Gradually his clientele broadened, and he made sales to collectors such as Henry C. Folger, Henry E. Huntington, J. P. Morgan, Jr., Marsden J. Perry, Harry B. Smith, and William A. White. In 1920 the Rosenbachs felt confident enough to expand, and they opened a store at 273 Madison Avenue in New York City.

In that year the bookseller George D. Smith died. Smith had dominated the book trade, and his death left a vacuum that Rosenbach was determined to fill. Two of Smith's most important customers were Huntington and Folger, both of whom collected sixteenth- and seventeenth-century English literature, though Huntington did not limit himself to these periods. Fortunately for Rosenbach, this was the area of his greatest scholarly expertise. In Rosenbach's day, at least until the very end of his career, individual collectors were far more important than institutional ones. These collectors, while often quite knowledgeable about what they collected, tended to rely upon the expertise of professional dealers. Rosenbach knew more about the books he sold than most of his customers – and more than most other dealers – and this gave him an important advantage. He convinced both Folger and Huntington to trust him as their agent.

Rosenbach represented Huntington at the first of the sales of the Christie-Miller books from Britwell Court in 1921 at Sotheby's in London. This library was a large and superb collection of early English literature. Backed by bids from Huntington on almost every lot, Rosenbach dominated the sale. His purchases accounted for more than 80 percent of the total sold; three-fourths of these purchases were for Huntington. Beginning with this sale, newspaper reports on book auction sales opened with the succinct statement that all books were bought by Dr. Rosenbach of Philadelphia unless otherwise noted. The accounts almost invariably noted that the highest-priced item in the sale was bought by Rosenbach. As always, a few of his Britwell purchases ended up in his private collection.

The first of the Britwell sales marked the beginning of a string of Rosenbach triumphs in the auction room. Many collectors soon learned that if they wanted a book they should entrust their bid to Rosenbach; otherwise, he would undoubtedly be bidding against them.

The 1920s were a golden age for American book collecting and the Rosenbach Company. Almost without exception Rosenbach purchased every important book or manuscript to appear in the auction room. At the John Quinn sale in 1923 he demonstrated remarkable foresight in purchasing the manuscript of James Joyce's *Ulysses* (1922). Only one other dealer bid against him, and Rosenbach bought it for what now seems the ridiculously low price of $1,975. He offered it for sale only once; then it went into his own collection. At the same sale he purchased Joseph Conrad manuscripts, including the manuscripts of *Almayer's Folly* (1895), *Nostromo* (1904), and *Lord Jim* (1900). Again, several of these went into his private library.

The list of Rosenbach customers during this period reads like an honor roll of American collectors: Robert B. Adam, Frank B. Bemis, William K. Bixby, Charles and William A. Clark, John Clawson, Edward and Mary Harkness, Herschel V. Jones, Amy Lowell, Carl H. Pforzheimer, John Scheide, Owen Young, Folger, and Huntington. Throughout the 1920s Rosenbach set a series of auction records. In 1925 he paid $106,000 for a copy of the Gutenberg Bible, the highest price ever paid for a printed book at auction. The following year he paid $51,500 for a document of Button Gwinnett, signer of the Declaration of Independence, a record price for an autograph. In 1928 he paid $14,000 for a first edition (not inscribed) of Rudyard Kipling's *The Smith Administration* (1891), one of six known copies. It was the highest sum ever paid for the work of a living author. These highly publicized purchases cemented his reputation as the greatest book dealer of his day.

Rosenbach's most famous auction-room exploit came in 1928, when the manuscript of *Alice's Adventures Under Ground* (1886) was sold at Sotheby's for the benefit of the original Alice, Alice Liddell Hargreaves. The public, by now accustomed to hearing Rosenbach's name associated with the purchase of anything famous, expected him to buy it. His major competitors were two London firms: Quaritch, bidding for the British Museum; and Maggs, bidding for the American dealer Gabriel Wells. Rosenbach did not bid against the British Museum. He bid only after Maggs had bid. At £12,500 Quaritch dropped out. At £15,400 the manuscript was Rosenbach's. No other purchase he made attracted so much publicity. Ever after in the public mind Rosenbach was "the man who bought Alice." He offered to sell the manuscript to the British Museum for what he had paid for it – and to contribute toward the purchase himself – but despite thousands of small contributions the museum was unable to raise the money. Two months later Rosenbach sold the manuscript to the American collector Eldridge Johnson.

This period of American book collecting peaked in 1929 at the sale of the Jerome Kern collection – a library of the "high spots" of English and American literature. Conducted at the Anderson Galleries in New York, the sale was the ultimate vindication of Rosenbach's long-held contention that great books were worth great prices. Buyers paid ten to twenty times Kern's original purchase prices. The sale realized more than $1.7 million; Rosenbach's purchases totaling $410,000 were not quite a quarter of the whole.

Rosenbach's fame in the auction room made him a national figure. With the assistance of Avery Strakosch he wrote a series of articles about book collecting for the *Saturday Evening Post* beginning in January 1927. The articles, covering topics ranging from "Old Bibles" to "Some Literary Forgeries," preached the Rosenbach philosophy that great books only increase in value and that they are a good investment. The articles were later collected and published as *Books and Bidders: The Adventures of a Bibliophile* (1927), with a second series of articles later collected as *A Book Hunter's Holiday: Adventures with Books and Manuscripts* (1936).

His expensive auction purchases for the most part were made on behalf of a customer, not for stock. While they provided much publicity, they yielded little profit. Rosebach said quite rightly, "how can you make a decent profit if the world knows exactly how much you paid for a book or manuscript?" The financial success of the Rosenbach Company was due in large part to Rosenbach's private-treaty purchases. During the course of his career he bought more than seventy libraries privately and a host of individual books and manuscripts. The libraries he bought include the following: the Smith collection (1915); the Perry collection (1919); the Robert Schuhmann (1920) and Louis Olry-Roederer (1922) collections of French books, bindings, and drawings; the James Ellsworth collection (1923); the Frederick Trowbridge collection (1925), described by the newspapers as "the largest private collection in America ever sold to a single purchaser"; the Robert Holford collection (1925); a portion of the collection of Sir Thomas Phillipps (1923–1930); the Cortes family archive (1928); the library of the duke of Westminster (1929); and the Jones collection (1939).

His most controversial private purchase involved a group of books from the library at York Minster in 1930. Rosenbach financed this deal by arranging to sell two extremely rare books – printed by William Caxton and owned by the Minster – to Morgan. Assured of a 10 percent commission on the sale, Rosenbach then purchased sixty-nine more titles from the Minster library. These volumes included the famous "Book Lions of York," Erasmus's version of the New Testament, one of three copies printed on vellum, in its original binding; the *Eliot Indian Bible,* the first Bible printed in America, in an original Boston binding; two more Caxtons; and some rare Elizabethan pamphlets. The Erasmus and the *Eliot Indian Bible,* along with a few other items, ended up in Rosenbach's own collection. The transaction was called the "rape of York" by Rosenbach's biographers, Edwin Wolf II and John Fleming, because Rosenbach had purchased the books at a relatively low price. Yet more recent research in the files of the Minster reveals that Rosenbach paid what the Minster asked; the purchases would thus seem a case of seduction rather than rape.

At first the stock market crash of 1929 had little effect on the Rosenbach Company. Rosenbach continued buying, privately and at auction. Yet Rosenbach customers slowly cut back on their buying, and the fabulously expensive sales became rare. In an effort to revive confidence and prices Rosenbach relied heavily on publicity; not a major holiday went by without a special Rosenbach exhibition, accompanied by a newspaper story. While Rosenbach complained about how slow business was during this period, his volume of business compared to most other rare-book dealers was respectable. Furthermore, during the 1930s and 1940s new, important customers emerged: Estelle Doheny, Raymond Hartz, Frank Hogan, Harrison Horblit, Mary and Donald Hyde, Clara Peck, Victor Rothschild, Lessing J. Rosenwald, and Arthur A. Houghton.

Rare-book prices reached their nadir after the bombing of Pearl Harbor, forcing even the Rosenbach Company to set its prices a bit lower. The decline in prices was mirrored by a serious decline in the health of Rosenbach, who had always been a heavy eater and drinker. Philip assumed control of the book side of the business as Rosenbach's energy waned. While there was an occasional high-priced, publicity-laden auction purchase, for the most part the Rosenbach Company survived on the sale of the residue of the great libraries purchased in the 1920s. Rosenbach's last years were punctuated by a series of diabetic comas, kidney infections, and complications caused by high blood pressure. On 1 July 1952, just short of his seventy-sixth birthday, Rosenbach died.

As a collector Rosenbach sought books and manuscripts that met three criteria, roughly in order of preference: importance, rarity, and condi-

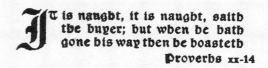

It is naught, it is naught, saith the buyer; but when he hath gone his way then he boasteth
Proverbs xx-14

Rosenbach used this motto in his catalogues.

tion. Most items he collected exhibited all three characteristics. Because of his position in the trade, he was often able to improve the quality of the books in his collection, as when he replaced a first edition of Cervantes' *Don Quixote* bound in nineteenth-century morocco with one of two surviving copies in a contemporary binding. He collected primarily in four areas: American children's books published before 1841, American Judaica, English literature, and Americana.

The core of his children's book collection was given to him by Polock in 1900. Polock had taken over the business of the Philadelphia printers and publishers M'Carty and Davis, who had absorbed the business of Johnson and Warner. Many of the children's books published by these firms passed as remainders to Polock, who decided to form a collection. Both Rosenbach and his sister Rebecca, who shared his interest in these small volumes, added to the collection over the years. They had little competition until the 1930s; it was a field of collecting that Rosenbach's interest helped to develop.

In the introduction to the bibliography of his collection Rosenbach explained the attraction of these books for him:

> Children's books have such a many-sided appeal that they are strangely satisfying to the collector. Not only do they have as much scholarly and bibliographical interest as books in other fields, but more than any class of literature they reflect the minds of the generation that produced them. Hence no better guide to the history and development of any country can be found than its juvenile literature.

When a catalogue of his collection of some eight hundred volumes was published in 1933, it immediately became the standard reference work in a field which until that point had been largely neglected. In 1947 Rosenbach presented the collection to the Free Library of Philadelphia.

His collection of American Judaica was similarly groundbreaking and was a natural outgrowth of his background and interests. Throughout his life he was involved in Jewish organizations: he served as president of the American Jewish Historical Society, Gratz College, and the American Friends of the

· *CATALOGUE THIRTY-NINE*

Shakespeare
QUARTOS

For Sale by
THE ROSENBACH COMPANY
1320 Walnut Street
Philadelphia
and
273 Madison Avenue, New York
1920

"WHEN HE IS GONE
AND HIS COMEDIES OUT OF SALE,
YOU WILL SCRAMBLE FOR THEM"
—*Troilus & Cressida*, 1609

The introduction to this catalogue states that "at present" the Rosenbach company has "the largest collection ever offered for sale of books related to Shakespeare."

Hebrew University; as honorary vice-president of the Jewish Publication Society of America; and as a trustee of Congregation Mikveh Israel in Philadelphia and Dropsie College for Hebrew and Cognate Languages. He received an honorary H.L.D. from the Jewish Theological Seminary in 1945.

His Judaica collection included *Evening Service of Roshashanah, and Kippur* (1761), the first Jewish prayer book printed in America; the first appearances of Hebrew type in the various American colonies; and many others, a large number in unique copies. All are listed in the bibliography of his collection *An American Jewish Bibliography . . .* (1926), which remains a valuable reference book in the field. Additionally, he collected manuscripts: records of trials of Jews by the Inquisition in Mexico; the papers of the Sheftall family

of Georgia; a series of letters from Alexander Mayer describing the California gold rush; and letters of the educator and philanthropist Rebecca Gratz. The collection was presented to the American Jewish Historical Society in 1931.

As a collector of English literature, however, Rosenbach was faced with something of a dilemma. As a businessman he knew he could make large sums of money from selling this material; yet it was precisely the kind of material he would like to collect himself. He resolved this dilemma in various ways, but usually by pricing the items he wished to keep so high that they would fail to sell.

Given his position in the trade, it is hardly surprising that Rosenbach managed to amass a remarkably fine collection of books and manuscripts en-

Rosenbach in his library, circa 1932

compassing English literature from the fifteenth to the twentieth centuries. From the late medieval period his collection includes two fifteenth-century manuscripts of Geoffrey Chaucer's *Canterbury Tales* and a manuscript of John Lydgate's translation of Boccaccio's *The Fall of Princes* (1554). Sixteenth-century material includes such rarities as the only known copies of the first printings of *Jacke Jugeler* (London: William Copland, 1562), *Gammer Gurtons Nedle* (London: William Copland, 1575), and *The First Rape of faire Hellen* (London: William Copland, 1595), and a manuscript bill of fare from the Mermaid Tavern, 1588. A strong collection of commonplace books, a unique copy of Robert Herrick's *A Description of the King and Queene of Fayries* (London: Richard Harper, 1634), and a first edition of *Pilgrim's Progress* once owned by John Bunyan's cell mate are representative of the seventeenth-century holdings. Drawings, books, a watercolor, and a manuscript by William Blake; manuscripts by John Keats, Percy Bysshe Shelley, and George Gordon, Lord Byron; letters and manuscripts of Charles Dickens, William Makepeace Thackeray, Lewis Carroll, Robert Louis Stevenson — as well as printed holdings for all these authors — are souvenirs of some of Rosenbach's most important purchases. This collection, along with hundreds of literary items left in the Rosenbach Company stock at the Rosenbach brothers' deaths, was inherited by the Rosenbach Foundation, now the Rosenbach Museum and Library.

The collection closest to his heart was his Americana. In his later years Rosenbach told the story of his first involvement with Americana at the age of sixteen. " 'My boy,' " his bookseller uncle had exclaimed, " 'Americana! That's the stuff to collect!' " As Polock went on to gloat over some newly acquired Americana, young Rosenbach listened and "was thrilled – thrilled to the marrow . . . I stood there transfixed." That which can be purchased cheaply is often undervalued; with the exception of "great name" Americana, the works had been largely ignored. Rosenbach's enthusiasm for American historical material helped to create a solid mar-

It was claimed that the value of the material in Rosenbach's vault was greater than that of the inventory in Macy's department store.

ket. He called Americana "the collector's best bet" and believed that demand would "increase in the same way as a stone gathers moss. . . . It is only meet and proper that Americans themselves should tenderly cherish the primal, honest, unpretentious things to which this country owes its greatness."

Rosenbach never had a customer who bought American documents at the same pace as Huntington and Folger bought early English literature. He sold to many buyers, a document at a time, but the bulk of his important purchases remained in stock for many years. With printed Americana, many of his important purchases went to Herschel V. Jones. Rosenbach bought his collection in 1939, securing many rare items of English Americana for his personal collection. Perhaps because he had fewer active Americana collectors among his customers, he treated his Americana collection as fairly sacrosanct; the English literature collection, on the other hand, was frequently raided for books to be sold to a customer.

Book for book and manuscript for manuscript, the Rosenbach collection of Americana is one of the finest. It includes books printed by Juan Pablos — the first three books printed in the Western Hemisphere of which complete copies are known; an important group of records documenting the earliest years of the Spanish settlement in Central and South America, including documents of Hernán Cortés and Francisco Pizarro; extremely rare early Virginia tracts, including Robert Johnson's *Nova Britannia* (London: Samuel Machan, 1609); a copy of the *Eliot Indian Bible* (Cambridge, Mass.: Samuel Green and Marmaduke Johnson, 1663) in its original binding; the only known copy of the first issue of Benjamin Franklin's *Poor Richard* almanac (Philadelphia: Benjamin Franklin, 1732); the earliest extant letter written by George Washington; Franklin's manuscript essay "On Wives and Old Mistresses"; the only recorded copy of the first printing of "Yankee Doodle" (Massachusetts, 1775?); Robert E. Lee's letter of resignation from the U.S. Army; the manuscript of Abraham Lincoln's "Baltimore Address"; and Ulysses S. Grant's draft of his telegram announcing Lee's surrender at Appomattox. During his last years, when illness prevented him from participating actively in the business, Rosenbach compiled a catalogue of his collection, now in the Rosenbach Museum and Library.

One of Rosenbach's most repeated stories about his Americana collection was that of his acquisition of what he considered the "jewel" of his collection, the *Bay Psalm Book* (1640), the first book printed in America. At the time, only ten other copies of the book were known, and all but two were in institutional collections. Rosenbach related the story of the acquisition of the book to Wolf. In 1933 a letter from a bookseller in Belfast, Ireland, named James Weatherup arrived, offering a *Bay Psalm Book* for sale. Weatherup had read of Rosenbach's exploits as a dealer and a collector and thought he might be interested in the book, even though it was missing a few leaves. The dealer described it in careful bibliographical detail and offered to send it for Rosenbach's inspection. Although certain that it must be a late English edition, hence valueless, Rosenbach was intrigued by the description and cabled Weatherup that he would have to see the book. Much to Rosenbach's delight, it turned out to be the real thing. If Rosenbach had been surprised to find the book was authentic, he was even more surprised at the price: £150. A check was quickly made out and dispatched. Fourteen years later, in 1947, Rosenbach bought a complete copy of the *Bay Psalm Book* for Yale for $151,000, which in the Rosenbach tradition again set a record as the highest price paid for a printed book at auction.

In 1950 the Rosenbach brothers established the Philip H. and A. S. W. Rosenbach Foundation. With the death of Philip Rosenbach – eight months after the doctor – the foundation inherited the brothers' collections of books, manuscripts, prints, drawings, and furnishings as well as their house at 2010 DeLancey Place. In the brothers' home in Philadelphia, now the Rosenbach Museum and Library, are many of the greatest items purchased by Rosenbach – the books and manuscripts he could never bring himself to sell. The first trustees of the foundation also transferred to the library many of the books and manuscripts which were part of the stock of the Rosenbach Company at the time of Philip Rosenbach's death.

Rosenbach's influence extends far beyond the walls of the collection he formed in Philadelphia. Rosenbach passionately believed in the importance of original source material. It was that passion which made him such an effective salesman and which led to the creation of some of America's greatest book collections. When Rosenbach began in the book business in 1903, research in many fields had to be conducted in Europe, for that was where the raw materials of scholarship were. By the time of his death in 1952, the libraries of America had become the beneficiaries of a vast westward flow of material – a flow which Rosenbach stimulated both through his purchases and through the cultivation of private collectors whose collections were ultimately to enrich the public research libraries of America.

Interviews:

Jefferson G. Bell, "Demands for rare books forces prices skyward," *New York Times,* 16 December 1923, VIII: 9;

Avery Strakosch, "Profiles: Napoleon of Books," *New Yorker,* 4 (14 April 1928): 25–28;

"Merchant to Collectors: Dr. A. S. W. Rosenbach, whose inventory is larger than Macy's," *Fortune,* 5 (1932): 60–69, 114–119.

Bibliography:

John Fleming, "A Bibliography of the Books, Contributions and Articles Written by A. S. W. Rosenbach," in *To Doctor R.: Essays here collected and published in Honor of the Seventieth Birthday of Dr. A. S. W. Rosenbach, July 22, 1946* (Philadelphia: Privately printed, 1946).

Biography:

Edwin Wolf II and John F. Fleming, *Rosenbach: A Biography* (Cleveland: World Publishing, 1960).

References:

Leslie A. Morris, *Rosenbach Abroad: In pursuit of books in private collections* (Philadelphia: Rosenbach Museum & Library, 1988);

Morris, *Rosenbach Redux: Further book adventures in England and Ireland* (Philadelphia: Rosenbach Museum & Library, 1989).

Papers:

Rosenbach's personal papers, the records of the Rosenbach Company, and material used by Edwin Wolf II and John F. Fleming in writing *Rosenbach* are held by the Rosenbach Museum & Library, Philadelphia.

Leona Rostenberg
(28 December 1908 –)

and

Madeleine B. Stern
(1 July 1912 –)

Ruth Rosenberg
City University of New York

BOOKS (by Rostenberg and Stern): *Old and Rare: Thirty Years in the Book Business* (New York: Schram, 1974; London: Prior, 1974); revised and enlarged as *Old and Rare: Forty Years in the Book Business* (Santa Monica, Cal.: Modoc, 1988);

Between Boards: New Thoughts on Old Books (Montclair, N. J.: Allanheld & Schram, 1978; London: Prior, 1978);

Bookman's Quintet: Five Catalogues about Books (New Castle, Del.: Oak Knoll, 1979);

Quest Book – Guest Book: A Biblio-Folly (Santa Monica, Cal.: Modoc, 1993);

Connections: Ourselves – Our Books (Santa Monica, Cal.: Modoc, 1994).

BOOKS (by Rostenberg): *English Printers in the Graphic Arts 1599–1700* (New York: Franklin, 1963);

Literary, Political, Scientific, Religious and Legal Publishing, Printing and Bookselling in England, 1551–1700, 2 volumes (New York: Franklin, 1965);

The Minority Press and the English Crown: A Study in Repression 1558–1625 (Nieuwkoop, Netherlands: De Graaf, 1971);

An Antiquarian's Credo, Lilly Library Chapbook Series, 1 (Bloomington: Indiana University Libraries, 1976);

Bibliately (State College, Pa.: American Philatelic Society, 1978);

The Library of Robert Hooke: The Scientific Book Trade of Restoration England (Santa Monica, Cal.: Modoc, 1989).

BOOKS (by Stern): *We Are Taken* (New York: Galleon, 1935);

The Life of Margaret Fuller (New York: Dutton, 1942; revised edition, Westport, Conn.: Greenwood Press, 1991);

Louisa May Alcott (Norman: University of Oklahoma Press, 1950; London & New York: Nevill, 1952);

Purple Passage: The Life of Mrs. Frank Leslie (Norman: University of Oklahoma Press, 1953);

Sherlock Holmes: Rare-Book Collector (New York: Schulte, 1953);

Imprints on History: Book Publishers and American Frontiers (Bloomington: Indiana University Press, 1956);

We the Women: Career Firsts of Nineteenth-Century America (New York: Schulte, 1963 [i.e., 1962]; revised edition, New York: Franklin, 1974);

So Much in a Life-Time: The Story of Dr. Isabel Barrows (New York: Messner, 1964);

Queen of Publishers' Row: Mrs. Frank Leslie (New York: Messner, 1965);

The Pantarch: A Biography of Stephen Pearl Andrews (Austin & London: University of Texas Press, 1968);

Heads and Headlines: The Phrenological Fowlers (Norman: University of Oklahoma Press, 1971);

Books and Book People in 19th-Century America (New York & London: R. R. Bowker, 1978);

The Game's A Head: A Phrenological Case-Study of Sherlock Holmes and Arthur Conan Doyle (Rockville Centre, N.Y.: Greene, 1983);

Antiquarian Bookselling in the United States: A History from the Origins to the 1940's (Westport, Conn.: Greenwood Press, 1985).

OTHER (by Rostenberg): "The Pamphlet as a Source for French History, 1559–1572," in *Renaissance Society and Culture: Essays in Honor of Eugene F. Rice, Jr.,* edited by John Monfasani and

Leona Rostenberg and Madeleine B. Stern displaying their wares at a New York book fair

Ronald G. Musto (New York: Italica Press, 1991), pp. 281–288.

OTHER (by Stern): *Women on the Move,* 4 volumes, edited by Stern (Nieuwkoop, Netherlands: De Graaf, 1972);

The Victoria Woodhull Reader, edited by Stern (Weston, Mass.: M & S, 1974);

Behind a Mask: The Unknown Thrillers of Louisa May Alcott, edited, with an introduction, by Stern (New York: Morrow, 1975; London: Allen, 1976);

Louisa's Wonder Book: An Unknown Alcott Juvenile, introduction and bibliography by Stern (Mount Pleasant: Central Michigan University, 1975);

Plots and Counterplots: More Unknown Thrillers of Louisa May Alcott, edited, with an introduction, by Stern (New York: Morrow, 1976; London: Allen, 1977);

Publishers for Mass Entertainment in Nineteenth Century America, edited by Stern (Boston: G. K. Hall, 1980);

A Phrenological Dictionary of Nineteenth-Century Americans, compiled by Stern (Westport, Conn. & London: Greenwood Press, 1982);

The Hidden Louisa May Alcott: A Collection of Her Unknown Thrillers, edited by Stern (New York: Avenel, 1984);

Critical Essays on Louisa May Alcott, edited by Stern (Boston: G. K. Hall, 1984);

Louisa May Alcott, *A Modern Mephistopheles and Taming a Tartar,* introduction by Stern (New York: Praeger, 1987);

The Selected Letters of Louisa May Alcott, edited by Joel Myerson and Daniel Shealy, associate editor Stern, with an introduction by Stern (Boston: Little, Brown, 1987);

A Double Life: Newly Discovered Thrillers of Louisa May Alcott, edited by Stern, Myerson, and Shealy, with an introduction by Stern (Boston: Little, Brown, 1988);

The Journals of Louisa May Alcott, edited by Myerson and Shealy, associate editor Stern, with an introduction by Stern (Boston: Little, Brown, 1989);

Louisa May Alcott: Selected Fiction, edited by Stern, Shealy, and Myerson, with an introduction by Stern (Boston: Little, Brown, 1991).

SELECTED PERIODICAL PUBLICATIONS –
UNCOLLECTED (by Rostenberg and Stern): "The Aldine Collection," *Friends of the Brigham Young University Library Newsletter,* 14 (Winter 1977): 1–14;

"American Bookselling: Historical Perspectives," *1976 Bookman's Yearbook,* part 2 (December 1977): 36–44;

"Uncommon Collectibles," *AB Bookman's Weekly* (3 April 1978): 2364–2405;

"The Significance of Ephemeral Tracts in Library Development," *Friends of the Brigham Young Library Newsletter,* 17 (Summer 1980): 1–24;

"Zeitgenossische amerikanische Antiquare und ihre Memoiren," *Aus dem Antiquariat* (September 1980): 382–391;

"Catalogues and Collections," *Professional Rare Bookman,* 2 (1980): 132–150;

"The Libri Affair: A Study in 'Bibliokleptomania,' " *AB Bookman's Weekly* (22 June 1981): 4901–4905;

"Sarah Clarke's Copy of *Memoirs of Margaret Fuller Ossoli:* A Double Association," *Manuscripts* (Summer 1991): 301–315;

"A Backward Glance by Leona Rostenberg and Madeleine Stern," *Antiquarian Booksellers Association of America Newsletter* (Summer 1992): 1–6;

"An Antiquarian Bookseller's Ode to Joy," *AB Bookman's Weekly* (22 March 1993): 1170–1194.

SELECTED PERIODICAL PUBLICATIONS –
UNCOLLECTED (by Rostenberg): "The Printers of Strasbourg and Humanism, from 1501 until the Advent of the Reformation," *Papers of the Bibliographical Society of America,* 34 (1940): 68–77;

"The Printing of Hebrew Text Books in Strasbourg 1544–1549," *Journal of Jewish Bibliography,* 2 (April–July 1940): 1–5;

"Margaret Fuller's Roman Diary," *Journal of Modern History,* 12 (June 1940): 209–220;

"Mazzini to Margaret Fuller, 1847–1849," *American Historical Review,* 47 (October 1941): 73–80;

"Some Anonymous and Pseudonymous Thrillers of Louisa M. Alcott," *Papers of the Bibliographical Society of America,* 37 (1943): 131–140;

"The Libraries of Three Nuremberg Patricians 1491–1568," *Library Quarterly,* 13 (January 1943): 21–33;

" 'The Sign of Basle': The Reformation Activities of a Paris-Basle Publishing House, 1519–1540," *Lutheran Church Quarterly,* 16 (July 1943): 1–12;

"Moses Pitt, Robert Hooke and the English Atlas," *Map Collector* (1980): 2–8;

"Liberté, Egalité, Bibliophilie," *American Book Collector,* new series 2 (September–October 1981): 2–18;

"Book Collecting in 17th-Century England," *AB Bookman's Weekly* (3 October 1983): 2027–2044;

"Tracking Down Pilgrim Press Books," *AB Bookman's Weekly* (21 November 1983): 3507–3520;

"Portrait from a Family Archive: Leon Dreyfus, 1842–1898," *Manuscripts,* 37 (Fall 1985): 283–294; 38 (Winter 1986): 43–52;

"Letters from New Orleans, 1902," *Manuscripts,* 41 (Spring 1989): 113–121.

SELECTED PERIODICAL PUBLICATIONS –
UNCOLLECTED (by Stern): "Margaret Fuller's School-Days in Cambridge," *New England Quarterly,* 13 (June 1940): 207–222;

"Margaret Fuller and *The Dial,*" *South Atlantic Quarterly,* 40 (January 1941): 11–21;

"The House of the Expanding Doors: Anne Lynch's Soirées, 1846," *New York History,* 23 (January 1942): 42–51;

"Louisa Alcott, Trouper: Experiences in Theatricals, 1848–1880," *New England Quarterly,* 16 (June 1943): 175–197;

"The Witch's Cauldron to the Family Hearth: Louisa M. Alcott's Literary Development, 1848–1868," *More Books: The Bulletin of the Boston Public Library,* 18 (October 1943): 363–380;

"Louisa M. Alcott's Contributions to Periodicals: 1868–1888," *More Books: The Bulletin of the Boston Public Library,* 18 (November 1943): 411–420;

"Approaches to Biography," *South Atlantic Quarterly,* 45 (July 1946): 362–371;

"Louisa M. Alcott: An Appraisal," *New England Quarterly,* 22 (December 1949): 475–498;

"Poe: 'The Mental Temperament' for Phrenologists," *American Literature,* 40 (May 1968): 155–163;

"William Henry Channing's Letters on 'Woman in her Social Relations,' " *Cornell Library Journal,* 6 (Autumn 1968): 54–62;

"Mark Twain Had His Head Examined," *American Literature,* 41 (May 1969): 207–218;

"Elizabeth Peabody's Foreign Library (1840)," *American Transcendental Quarterly,* 20 (Fall 1973): 5–12;

"A Biographer's View of Margaret Fuller: 30-Year Survey," *AB Bookman's Weekly,* 53 (4 February 1974): 427–430;

A CATALOGUE
for the
EASTER TERM

containing divers matters
relating to the
History of the
BOOK

LEONA ROSTENBERG
Rare Books
152 EAST 179th STREET
NEW YORK 53, N. Y.

1946

Rostenberg's first catalogue

"Louisa M. Alcott in Periodicals," *Studies in the American Renaissance* (May 1977): 369–386;

"The Alcotts and the Emerson Fire," *American Transcendental Quarterly,* 36 (Fall 1977): 7–9;

"Louisa Alcott's Feminist Letters," *Studies in the American Renaissance* (November 1978): 429–452;

"Margaret Fuller and the Phrenologist-Publishers," *Studies in the American Renaissance* (May 1980): 229–237;

"The English Press and Its Successors, 1793–1852," *Papers of the Bibliographical Society of America,* 74 (October–December 1980): 307–359;

"A Feminist Association," *Manuscripts,* 35 (Spring 1983): 113–117;

"Louisa Alcott's Self-Criticism," *Studies in the American Renaissance* (1985): 333–382;

"A Calendar of the Letters of Louisa May Alcott," *Studies in the American Renaissance* (1988): 361–399.

The doyennes of the rare-book business in America, most in the field would agree, are Leona Rostenberg and Madeleine B. Stern. These talented and energetic women have been business partners in New York City since 1945. Their reputation for scholarship and integrity and their love for the books they have bought and sold are known and appreciated among dealers and bibliophiles the world over.

In the "Bookseller's Credo," which serves as the concluding chapter of their book *Between Boards: New Thoughts on Old Books* (1978), Rostenberg wrote that the most important component of success is "a sound academic education." The daughter of Dr. Adolph Rostenberg and Louisa Dreyfus Rostenberg, she earned her master's degree from Columbia University in New York in 1933 and began work toward her doctorate in history. Rostenberg had proposed a dissertation on the role of Strasbourg printers in the dissemination of humanistic learning during the sixteenth century. After months of scanning hundreds of printers' prefaces in Alsatian libraries, she had compiled sufficient evidence to show the influence they had exerted between 1500 and 1530. Late in 1938 she completed the dissertation. In spite of the rich documentation she offered, it was summarily rejected by her adviser, Lynn Thorndike, as "invalid," although he had initially, albeit reluctantly, approved the project. In *Old and Rare: Thirty Years in the Book Business* (1974) Rostenberg relates how Thorndike had declared the printers' prefaces to have been written by "professional hacks and merely signed by them," since printers were merely "uneducated artisans driven by economic incentives," not by scholarship or by involvement with the ideals of the Reformation.

Madeleine Bettina Stern, Rostenberg's friend, was the daughter of Moses R. and Lillie Mack Stern. She earned her master's degree at Columbia in 1934 with a thesis on the role of Mary Magdalene in literary history. Rostenberg then convinced Stern to begin work on a biography of Margaret Fuller. The two of them took time from their other research to gather material on Fuller at the Boston libraries. Stern achieved her objective of reconstructing "the life of a nineteenth-century American woman of genius by applying some fictional techniques to a mass of substantiated fact." Upon the publication of *The Life of Margaret Fuller* in 1942, Van Wyck Brooks praised its masterly presentation of concrete details, which, he asserted, rendered it an "authentic picture."

According to the "Bookseller's Credo," the serving of an apprenticeship is an important next step after completing one's academic training. The future bookseller should "assume an internship with a specialist dealer" to learn "the various phases of antiquarian activity: buying, collating, cataloguing, selling, customer idiosyncrasies, values, needs and specialties of other dealers, auction mores." For five years Rostenberg learned all these details from rare-book dealer Herbert Reichner at 34 East Sixty-second Street, New York City. His was a "dismal brownstone," whose second-floor apartment was crowded with "periodicals, cartons, crates, catalogues and bookcases." Her employer was a Viennese refugee who had published a journal, the *Philobiblon,* for collectors in Austria.

She was paid $7.50 a week to type author, title, imprint, dealer, and price on index cards; to prepare three thousand labels for Reichner's first catalogue; and to clear books through customs. She observed her employer's negotiations with such customers as Lessing Rosenwald, collector of early illustrated books; the Harvard librarian Philip Hofer; the Houghton librarian William Jackson; the librarian of the Boston Public Library Zoltan Haraszti; and the botanical-book collector Rachel Hunt. Because of Reichner's specialization in early scientific treatises Rostenberg became familiar with the works of Sir Isaac Newton, René Descartes, and Antoine-Laurent Lavoisier and "the prices their books commanded."

While Rostenberg was absorbing the minutiae of the antiquarian's trade, Stern was teaching high-school English. What sustained them was their joint research on the Fullers, which resulted not only in Stern's book but also in several published articles by Rostenberg on Timothy's journals and Margaret's Roman diaries.

On 30 March 1943 Stern was awarded a Guggenheim Fellowship to research Louisa May Alcott. Both the project and the grant application had been suggested by the Alcott collector Carroll A. Wilson. As described in *Between Boards,* Rostenberg and Stern researched in the Houghton Library: "seated at a desk, side by side, we delved through piles of manuscript and mountains of family letters, reading, copying, searching, checking, comparing, connecting." Rostenberg found five letters written between 1865 and 1866 by a Boston publisher; they revealed Alcott's pseudonym, A. M. Barnard, the titles of the lurid thrillers she had written under that disguise, and the name of the periodical in which these stories had been published. The discovery was printed in 1943 and led to a biography (*Louisa May Alcott,* 1950), two books (*Behind a Mask: The Unknown Thrillers of Louisa May Alcott,* 1975, and *Plots and Counterplots: More Unknown Thrillers of Louisa May Alcott,* 1976, a compilation of letters (*The Selected Letters of Louisa May Alcott,* 1987), an anthology of Alcott's journals (*The Journals of Louisa May Alcott,* 1989), and many articles.

On 25 December 1943 Stern presented Rostenberg with embossed business cards, shipping labels, and stationery, "all bearing a copy of the printer's device from Jost Amman's *Book of Trades*" under the emblem "LEONA ROSTENBERG – RARE BOOKS." The firm was launched. Rostenberg opened her rare-book business at her family's home in the Bronx, a fourteen-room house at 152 East 179th Street. Downstairs her physician father, a dermatologist,

Rostenberg and Stern at the Thomas W. Streeter sale, held at Sotheby Parke-Bernet Galleries, New York City, between 1966 and 1969 (Sotheby Parke-Bernet, Inc.)

met his patients. Upstairs in a second-floor bedroom the rare-book business established its office — its stock of sixty volumes alphabetically arranged in a discarded encyclopedia bookcase. Rostenberg copied names of potential customers from a variety of membership lists of literary, historical, and bibliographical societies. Using this list of two thousand names, in September 1944 she mailed out copies of the firm's first trade announcement. Seven months later, on 10 April 1945, Stern joined Rostenberg as a partner in the business.

Each chose a particular area of collecting in which she had special expertise. This focus corresponds to the fourth principle stated in the "Bookseller's Credo": "Each bookseller should seek a specialty. He cannot embrace all disciplines and in his choice of a specialty should follow the interests aroused by his education and training. Having studied in the field of the Renaissance, I chose to special-

ize in its books and tracts. My partner, a graduate in English literature, turned toward belles-lettres." The shared common element in these apparently divergent interests was the partners' sense of being on a rescue mission, Rostenberg of undervalued Renaissance tracts, Stern of unappreciated nineteenth-century feminist works. Rostenberg has written eloquently in defense of pamphlets. Although "seemingly unimpressive [they] should not be denigrated," for, as she asserted in an October 1975 talk, "there are individual tracts of such magnitude that they have changed the world." She cited Lenin's 1902 pamphlet *What IS To Be Done?* and a letter written 409 years earlier by Christopher Columbus to Luis de Santangel describing the first voyage to the New World. As Rostenberg observed, after she and Stern had identified Alcott's authorship of those sensational stories of drug addiction and bloody violence, they had changed the status of a pamphlet to that of a rare book: "Librarians, finding the ten cent novelette 'V. V.' by 'A. M. Barnard' bound in durable cloth with 'Pamphlets Various' promptly disbound it and deposited it in their rare book rooms under the name of Louisa May Alcott." Rostenberg took pleasure in the salvation of a pamphlet, but Stern's focus was on the resourcefulness of the feminine mind. She found it heroic that a respectable author (Alcott) of wholesome juvenile tales could rescue her family from poverty by disguising her identity.

The small stock of Leona Rostenberg – Rare Books included some of Stern's purchases from the mid 1930s, such as a seventeenth-century Ovid acquired on the Quai d'Orsay for Fr 40, an Erasmus with Hans Holbein drawings for Fr 140, and a Charles Baudelaire translation of Edgar Allan Poe that cost Fr 3. Realizing that they needed to supplement their stock, they set out on a book-buying tour of New England. In Maine they found a rare copy of *Nacoochee* (1837), a long poem by Thomas Holley Chivers, friend of Poe, celebrating the American Indian; Charles T. Jackson's *Second Annual Report of the Geology of the State of Maine* (1838); and twenty scattered parts of the 1840 London edition of Charles Dickens's *Master Humphrey's Clock*.

Their most momentous early find came through an English book catalogue. Rostenberg immediately cabled for number 188, which was David Calderwood's *Perth Amboy* (1619). This item proved to be one of the twenty books printed by the Elder Brewster, one of the Pilgrim fathers, at his secret press in Leyden just before he set sail on the Mayflower. It was sold to John Fall, acquisitions chief of the New York Public Library. In the early 1960s, in a basement in Cecil Court off Charing Cross Road, Rostenberg and Stern found among William Fletcher's books another issue of the clandestine Pilgrim press. *Ad Responsum Nic. Grevinchovii Rescriptio Contracta,* written by William Ames and printed by Brewster in 1617, is a duodecimo of 240 pages bound in eighteenth-century calfskin. It bears Brewster's name in the imprint and contains the signature of George Baillie, Lord of the Treasury, who acquired the book in the early eighteenth century. Yale University now holds it in its treasure room.

As well as adding to stock through the conventional means of buying trips and catalogue purchases, Rostenberg happened on the first edition of Arthur Young's *A Six Weeks' Tour through the Southern Counties of England and Wales* (London: Nicoll, 1768) in the Columbia University discarded-book bin. Rostenberg's description of the book indicates its importance: "The present volume incorporates material gathered by Young during his first famous Tour. The work contains the only extant information relative to produce and stock in 18th-century England," and it is rare enough to have been absent from the extensive Kress Library of Business and Economics at Harvard, which owned the second edition. The Rostenberg-Stern copy of Young's book went to the New York Public Library. Another discard that Leona Rostenberg – Rare Books secured was the first Latin edition of Descartes's landmark psychological work *Passiones Animae,* which Yale purchased.

By March 1946, after a year's intensive work, Rostenberg and Stern were ready to issue their first catalogue. It was a five-century history of the printed book entitled *A Catalogue for the Easter Term containing divers matters relating to the History of the Book; its Printers, Technique, Art, Collectors, Compilers, Repositories and Forgers and its Unusual Delights.* The title reveals the partners' sense of humor as well as their connection with the Renaissance. The catalogue's recipients sent warm congratulations on this achievement. To Stern and Rostenberg nothing has equaled that first stunning success.

The following year they issued a catalogue on the Elzevier Press. The press had been established in 1580 in Holland and continued to flourish until the close of the seventeenth century, printing trim pocket-sized books on the arts, the history, and the science of the time. The Elzevier format enabled students to carry books easily and encouraged the increase of literacy. Rostenberg and Stern traveled to an auction in Philadelphia to purchase several lots of Elzeviers in anticipation of the orders that they expected would follow from the release of their 1947 catalogue, *The House of Elzevier – A Seventeenth Century Retrospect.*

Their next project was a buying tour of British bookshops. In London they encountered the booksellers whose names they knew from letterheads or catalogues. They met Irving Davis, who had an important Italian collection. With great trepidation they interviewed E. P. Goldschmidt, author of *Gothic and Renaissance Bookbindings* and owner of the greatest assemblage of Renaissance books in the world. They bought some Aldine Press books at Quaritch's and a first edition of Benedict de Spinoza at Harding's. At Seligman's they bought sixteen sermons by Martin Luther, one of them adorned with a 1519 woodcut portrait of the reformer. From Ernest Well of Golders Green they purchased a fifteenth-century Franciscan Flemish manuscript. Their third catalogue offered the eighty-five sixteenth-century books they garnered on this trip.

LEONA ROSTENBERG
and
MADELEINE B. STERN

Old & Rare

Thirty Years in the Book Business

*Dust jacket for Rostenberg and Stern's 1974 account of their years in the
book business*

In addition to their annual catalogues they issued bimonthly *Book Notes* covering the sixteenth and seventeenth centuries. They spread knowledge of early printed books and were highly praised in *Antiquarian Bookman*. Their addiction to tracts led to such catalogues as *One Hundred Years of France, 1547–1642,* featuring 755 pamphlets and 466 Mazarinades serving as a documentary history. Their thirty-seventh catalogue described 1,659 tracts of revolutionary France. The *Aldine Press* catalogue returned to books, offering 239 titles produced by the great firm founded by Aldus Manutius in Venice.

Graduating as both had during the worst years of the Depression, Rostenberg and Stern were intensely aware of the difficulty in finding meaningful work. As Rostenberg wrote in *Old and Rare,* she was "disillusioned and jobless after college in the early nineteen thirties, when 'careers' were WPA [Works Progress Administration] makeshifts and hope was met with rebuff." Furthermore, a condescending professor had warned her of the barriers women faced, especially if they were Jewish. The feisty Rostenberg shot back that she would have to take her chances, since there was nothing she could do about either. Stern, in a subsequent chapter of the book, echoed this recognition: "For any Baccalaureate, class of 1932, few fields were open. For a Baccalaureate, Female, Jewish, still fewer." She feared that the only thing for which her higher education had equipped her was "writing unpaid articles for learned journals."

Both did, indeed, become prolific contributors to academic periodicals. At the invitation of Victor Hugo Paltsits of the manuscript division of the New

York Public Library, Rostenberg addressed the Bibliographical Society of America on the relation of Alsatian printers and humanism. This lecture in 1940 became her initial publication. Stern's first articles were literary analyses in the *Sewanee Review* (1935, 1936, 1938). Over twenty books, more than 150 catalogs, and many essays have followed. The women work on their scholarly and creative writing during weekends in their Manhattan apartment at 40 East Eighty-eighth Street and during summers at their East Hampton, Long Island, house.

Much of their scholarship has been prompted by their business. Referring to each other interchangeably as Holmes and Watson they solve bibliographic mysteries in an enterprise that at once enhances the value of their stock and increases the fund of bibliographic knowledge. For example, Leona Rostenberg – Rare Books acquired an undistinguished, privately published 1726 military history with unsigned engravings, *Compendium of Military Discipline,* written by John Blackwell. Research revealed that this otherwise unremarkable volume contained plates by the great eighteenth-century artist William Hogarth. Antonio Campo's 1582 *Cremona* proved to have Judaic significance because two of its maps were by the Jewish engraver David Hebrews. A Latin declaration of war by the English Commonwealth against Holland in 1652 was unsigned. But stylistic identification, coupled with the knowledge that its printer, William Dugard, was a friend of John Milton's, confirmed that Milton was the document's author. The scholarship of Rostenberg and Stern enabled them to add value to a 1607 book of poems by Thomas Segethus, which had been dedicated to Sir Henry Wotton. The dedication was a mark of appreciation for Wotton's securing Segethus's release from a Venetian prison, the poet having been jailed for libeling a nobleman. Their knowledge of printers allowed them to see value in the third edition of William Wollaston's *Religion of Nature Delineated* (1725) because they recognized that its apprentice compositor was Benjamin Franklin.

Through their hands have passed books that have changed society, books such as Hugo Grotius's *De Ivre Belli ac Pacis Libri Tres* (Paris: Buon, 1625), which set the foundation of international law, or Jean Henri Dunant's *Souvenir de Solferino* (Geneva: Fick, 1862), which that through its description of the deaths of untended wounded on the battlefield led to the founding of the Red Cross. A third was Theodore Herzl's 1896 Warsaw publication *Der Iudenstaat,* which would lead to the establishment of the state of Israel.

In 1983 Rostenberg and Stern shared the American Printing History Award for "their important services in advancing understanding of the history of printing and its allied arts." This honor was bestowed at Columbia, and Rostenberg could not resist stating in her acceptance remarks, "It seems ironic that Columbia University is granting me this honor in light of the fact that forty years ago this institution denied me my degree." Ten years earlier Columbia had awarded her the Ph.D. she so richly deserved, though they did so not on the basis of her dissertation but because of her many subsequent publications.

In 1992 Rostenberg and Stern finished an adventure set in their summer home in East Hampton involving a long-lost copy of Erasmus's *Praise of Folly* (1511). Called *Quest Book – Guest Book: A Biblio-Folly,* its publication date coincided with the 1993 Antiquarian Book Fair. It tells of the four-centuries-long search for this rare volume and its final recovery through the assistance of their houseguests, some of whom are booksellers. It retells the events narrated in the opening chapter of *Between Boards,* in which the partners conclude that "there never was a better conversation piece than that fascinating copy of Erasmus' *Praise of Folly.*"

Truly committed antiquarians have a sense of mission. Rostenberg and Stern regard themselves as rescuers of cultural treasures from the scrap heap of history – and sometimes from the literal scrap heap as well – and as saviors of the remnants of humanism. They have succeeded in redeeming the old and the rare, in discerning its value and transmitting it to future bibliophiles. Through their perception and persistence they have earned the encomium "Trustees of the printed work," a phrase which derives from Rostenberg's monumental two-volume study, *Literary, Political, Scientific, Religious and Legal Publishing, Printing and Bookselling in England, 1551–1700* (1965). Their legacy to posterity is to have served as trustees of civilization "through the mastery of their profession."

George D. Smith

(1870 – 4 March 1920)

Donald C. Dickinson
University of Arizona

The playwright John Drinkwater once described George D. Smith as "The Napoleon of Bookdealers." In pursuit of a large collection or of a single volume Smith could be bombastic, determined, confident, fearless, and, if necessary, utterly ruthless. When Smith entered the auction room to bid on the behalf of a special customer, his battle strategy was simple – annihilate the competition. To go against Smith, as the Chicago book dealer Walter Hill once remarked, was like attacking a brick wall.

Little is known of Smith's early years or his family background. He grew up in New York City and at the age of thirteen in 1883 left school and went to work as a sweeper and stock boy for the Manhattan bookshop of Wiley and Son and later for the publisher and rare-book dealer Dodd, Mead. Surrounded by such knowledgeable bookmen as Robert H. Dodd, James F. Drake, George H. Richmond, and William E. Benjamin, Smith quickly became familiar with the qualities that make books valuable. In 1886, when Benjamin left Dodd to set up a business for himself, he took the energetic young stock boy with him as his first assistant. In Benjamin's shop at 744 Broadway, Smith met many of the prominent collectors of the day – Beverly Chew, E. Dwight Church, Augustin Daly, Robert Hoe, and Frederic Halsey, among others. He came to know their collecting interests, and they came to respect his memory for prices, dates, and provenance.

While working for Benjamin, Smith started to buy a few books for himself with a view to entering the trade as an independent dealer. It was a long-cherished plan. In a memorial printed in the 13 March 1920 issue of the *New York Evening Post,* Frederick Hopkins remembered the book dealer saying, "I had not been with Dodd, Mead a month when I began to dream of having a business of my own and I used to lie awake nights wondering how I should be able to earn the money to begin with." By 1890

George D. Smith (photograph by Genthe)

Smith had gathered enough stock so that he and his partner, A. J. Bowden, were able to open a shop at 830 Broadway under the name Mitchell's Rare and Standard Books. A prospectus promised that "Careful and diligent attention will be used in procuring books not in stock, and in attending to our customers' wants."

Smith and Bowden offered an impressive array of book and library services, as well as experienced agents in London ready to procure foreign publications and a professional staff in New York

At the start of his bookselling career, Smith (right) was in partnership with Alfred J. Bowden.

available to make appraisals and pay "spot cash" for desired items. Another branch of the Smith/Bowden enterprise, recognizing the difficulty of keeping a large collection in good order, would provide "experienced workmen to catalog, dust, clean and look after a library at a moderate charge per annum." Finally, fine bookbinding, "executed with dispatch, neatness and taste," could also be obtained on request.

Over the next several years the partners issued attractive, carefully edited catalogues featuring travel, biography, costume, reference works, bindings, and autographs. Smith and Bowden claimed that rare books were a sound investment and that the value of books bought from them would continue to rise. To prove their point they offered customers the right to return any book or manuscript after six months of purchase for the price they paid, less 10 percent. In 1890, in order to promote book buying in general and their shop in particular, Smith and Bowden brought out the first number of the *Literary Collector,* a journal that featured articles, notes on collecting, and advertisements for the trade. The journal ran successfully for over five years.

Although the partnership worked well enough, Smith was determined to go into business independently. In the spring of 1896 he opened a small shop at 69 Fourth Avenue. His first catalogue

offered George Cruikshank's *Humourist* (London: J. Robins, 1819–1822) with a series of colored plates, full calf, for $150; Edward Donovan's *The Naturalist's Repository of Exotic Natural History* (London: Printed for the Author and W. Simpkin and R. Marshall, 1823) with seventy-two elegantly colored plates, half morocco, gilt tops, for $8.50; Ralph Waldo Emerson's *Poems* (Boston: James Munroe, 1847) for $4.50; and the Boston bibliophile George Bancroft's copy of Samuel Smith's *The History of the Colony of Nova Caesaria, or New Jersey* (Burlington, N.J.: James Parker, 1765), original calf, first edition for $37.50. These and 447 other titles made up what was described on the cover of the catalogue as a selection of "A Few Beautiful, Rare, Curious and Valuable Books."

Smith first demonstrated his forceful style in the auction room in March 1900 at the Augustin Daly sale. As a prominent New York theatrical producer Daly had gathered an impressive library of stage history and biography, scripts, playbills, and manuscripts. Many of Daly's prize volumes were enhanced with sumptuous bindings and, in a process known as extraillustration, interleaved with prints, letters, and watercolors. The Daly copy of the Douay Bible (the first English translation for Catholics), for example, had been expanded to forty-one lavish volumes. With the hope that New York buyers would rush to own the Daly treasures,

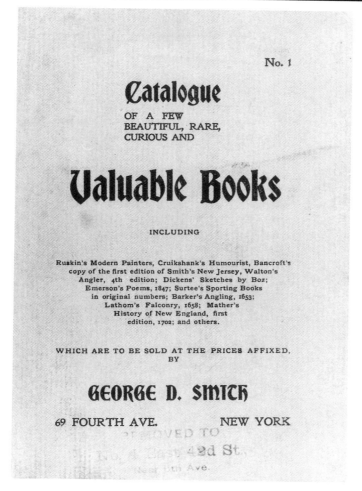

Smith's first catalogue (Bruccoli Collection)

Smith bought over one-third of the entire library. When the rush failed to materialize, he simply crated the books, shipped them to Chicago, and offered them there. Once New York collectors found that Smith was not going to cut his prices for their benefit but was in fact selling books rapidly out west, they flooded his shop with orders. It was a satisfying victory for the ebullient Smith. In the three years following the Daly sale Smith continued to make substantial purchases as the libraries of Brayton Ives, William H. Arnold, Frederick French, and Thomas Jefferson McKee came on the market.

During the summer of 1908 Smith met the railroad entrepreneur Henry E. Huntington, and from that meeting sprang one of the most notable dealer/collector relationships in the history of American book collecting. Huntington was eager to build a substantial rare-book library in a short period of time, and Smith was eager to sell books for a profit. The first transaction between the two men

appears to have taken place in the fall of 1908, when Henry Poor, whose inherited fortune had come from the family brokerage firm, placed his library up for sale at the Anderson Auction Company in New York. The library consisted of incunabula, fine bindings, illuminated manuscripts, private-press books, and limited editions — a lavish assortment. Smith, bidding for Huntington, took some sixteen hundred lots, one-fourth of the entire offering. These books provided the base for Huntington's soon-to-be-acclaimed rare-book collection.

In 1911, two years after the close of the Poor sale, Smith and Huntington made two more spectacular acquisitions. Smith purchased for Huntington the matchless E. Dwight Church rare-book library of Americana and English literature en bloc for $750,000. That year Smith also entered Huntington's bid of $50,000 for the Robert Hoe copy of the Gutenberg Bible, a sum that was up to that time the highest price paid for a printed book. As the Hoe

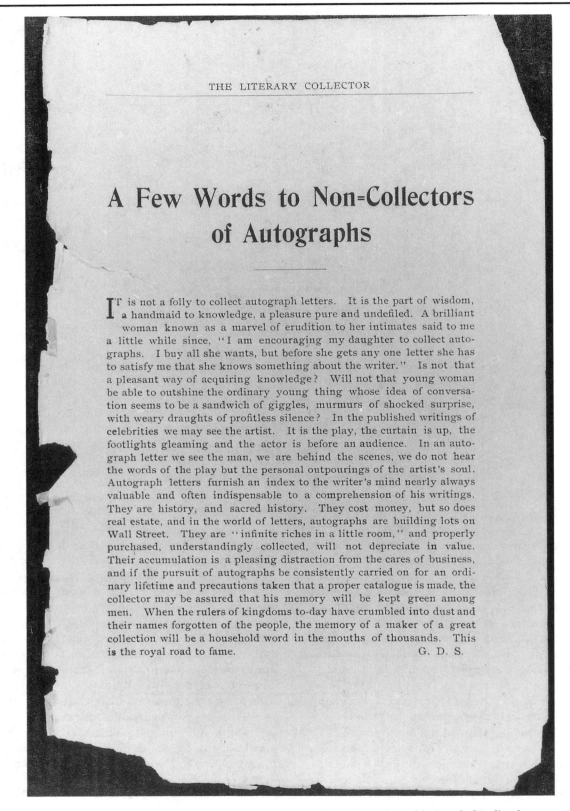

THE LITERARY COLLECTOR

A Few Words to Non=Collectors of Autographs

IT is not a folly to collect autograph letters. It is the part of wisdom, a handmaid to knowledge, a pleasure pure and undefiled. A brilliant woman known as a marvel of erudition to her intimates said to me a little while since, "I am encouraging my daughter to collect autographs. I buy all she wants, but before she gets any one letter she has to satisfy me that she knows something about the writer." Is not that a pleasant way of acquiring knowledge? Will not that young woman be able to outshine the ordinary young thing whose idea of conversation seems to be a sandwich of giggles, murmurs of shocked surprise, with weary draughts of profitless silence? In the published writings of celebrities we may see the artist. It is the play, the curtain is up, the footlights gleaming and the actor is before an audience. In an autograph letter we see the man, we are behind the scenes, we do not hear the words of the play but the personal outpourings of the artist's soul. Autograph letters furnish an index to the writer's mind nearly always valuable and often indispensable to a comprehension of his writings. They are history, and sacred history. They cost money, but so does real estate, and in the world of letters, autographs are building lots on Wall Street. They are "infinite riches in a little room," and properly purchased, understandingly collected, will not depreciate in value. Their accumulation is a pleasing distraction from the cares of business, and if the pursuit of autographs be consistently carried on for an ordinary lifetime and precautions taken that a proper catalogue is made, the collector may be assured that his memory will be kept green among men. When the rulers of kingdoms to-day have crumbled into dust and their names forgotten of the people, the memory of a maker of a great collection will be a household word in the mouths of thousands. This is the royal road to fame. G. D. S.

Smith's credo in the 1 November 1900 issue of the Literary Collector, *a journal he launched earlier that year*

CATALOGUE

.OF.

A Loan Exhibition

OF

RARE BOOKS

Illuminated MSS. etc.

(The Property of Mr. George D. Smith)

IN

The Palm Court
SELFRIDGE'S

From July 8th to July 21st, 1914

ADMISSION FREE.   NO TICKETS REQUIRED.

SELFRIDGE & CO., LTD., OXFORD STREET, W.

After his triumph at the Pembroke sale, Smith exhibited his acquisitions at Selfridge's department store in London.

sale continued through the winter and spring of 1912, Smith bought many other rarities for his special customers. In all, Smith invested just over $900,000 in the Hoe books and manuscripts – some $500,000 of that total spent specifically against Huntington's commissions. Writing about Smith's activities in the May 1931 issue of the *Huntington Library Bulletin,* Robert O. Schad, Huntington's curator of rare books, said,

> He knew little about the contents of books and probably cared less, but his experience had given him a knowledge of the rarity and value of books, accurate to a remarkable degree. His courage in buying, loyalty to his patrons and unaffectedness of manner were traits attractive to Mr. Huntington, who trusted Smith's judgement of book prices and valued his advice.

By 1910 Smith had moved out of his restricted quarters on Fourth Avenue and opened a larger store at 70 Wall Street. Four years later, as his success continued, he moved his valuable stock of early printed books to what he called his uptown branch at 547 Fifth Avenue. By that time Smith's list of customers had come to include some of the most affluent bibliophiles in the country, among others, William L. Clements, William Loring Andrews, Henry Clay Folger, William K. Bixby, and Cortlandt Field Bishop. These men understood that Smith could get them what they wanted. Although the prices might be high, books bought from Smith could almost always be resold for more than one had paid for them.

To maintain his position in the sometimes cutthroat New York book market, Smith cultivated friends in the right places. He was an active member of the Grolier Club, a prestigious organization of book collectors that dated back to 1884, and he was admired by the collector-writer A. Edward Newton and praised in Newton's books *The Amenities of Book Collecting* (1918) and *This Book Collecting Game* (1928). He also was on excellent terms with Mitchell Kennerley, the flamboyant president of the Anderson Auction Company. Other dealers knew from experience that it would be futile to bid against him with any hope of success.

With the New York market well in hand Smith shifted his sights to London. His first encounter with the British book world came in early 1914, when he acted as Huntington's agent for the purchase of two major collections from William Cavendish, sixth Duke of Devonshire. The contract drawn between Smith and C. A. Montague Barlow of the Sotheby, Wilkinson, and Hodge auction house in London was negotiated in New York. It outlined the details for payment of $750,000 for the Kemble-Devonshire plays, some 7,500 plays and 111 volumes of playbills covering the sixteenth and seventeenth centuries, and the Devonshire Caxtons, 25 books from England's first printer.

Smith sailed for England in June 1914, his briefcase packed with commissions from Huntington and other American collectors. On the first and second day (25 and 26 June) of the earl of Pembroke's Wilton House Library sales, Smith spent almost $100,000 buying nearly half of the 211 lots, many of them notable incunabula.

In a 26 June 1914 dispatch to the *New York Times* he jubilantly reported his success: "Eighty percent of the Pembroke collection is lost to England. I'm rather sorry I didn't get the whole shooting match. It would have caused such a howl to go up here. . . . I get a lot of fun out of my business. The squeal of the English is highly amusing, as when I acquired the Devonshire library." As if this jibe were not enough, he continued, "Incidentally I discovered that tea drinking can be a pretty expensive hobby. I went into a bookstore this afternoon fully prepared to spend $500 or even $1000 or more, and was told that the proprietor and his right hand man were both out to tea, so I walked out and bought nothing."

Smith followed his success at the Pembroke sale by dominating the July 1914 fourth session of the Henry Huth auction and then by seizing most of the first editions of works of Jonathan Swift, Percy Bysshe Shelley, and John Keats at the T. G. Arthur sale. At the conclusion of the Arthur sale Smith astounded the book world by sending an 18 July 1914 cable to the *New York Sun* denouncing the fraudulent price-fixing practices indulged in by some British dealers who were operating what he referred to as the London book ring. Smith stated that he had been invited to join the ring but declined and instead sought to defeat it. "My high prices," he declared in his press release, "caused the rest of the dealers to lose heart and they do not know yet what I am capable of." The event was important enough to be covered in a 19 July 1914 *New York Times* editorial; the writer praised Smith for "his faith in the continuance of American prosperity" and for beating the ring "in the familiar American way, by high bidding."

After returning to America Smith managed to sell many of his recent purchases by exhibiting them in his new Fifth Avenue store and by featuring them in a series of carefully annotated catalogues. One such catalogue, *Monuments of Early Printing in Germany, the Low Countries, Italy, France and England, 1460–1500* (1916), featured 136 incunabula. Smith

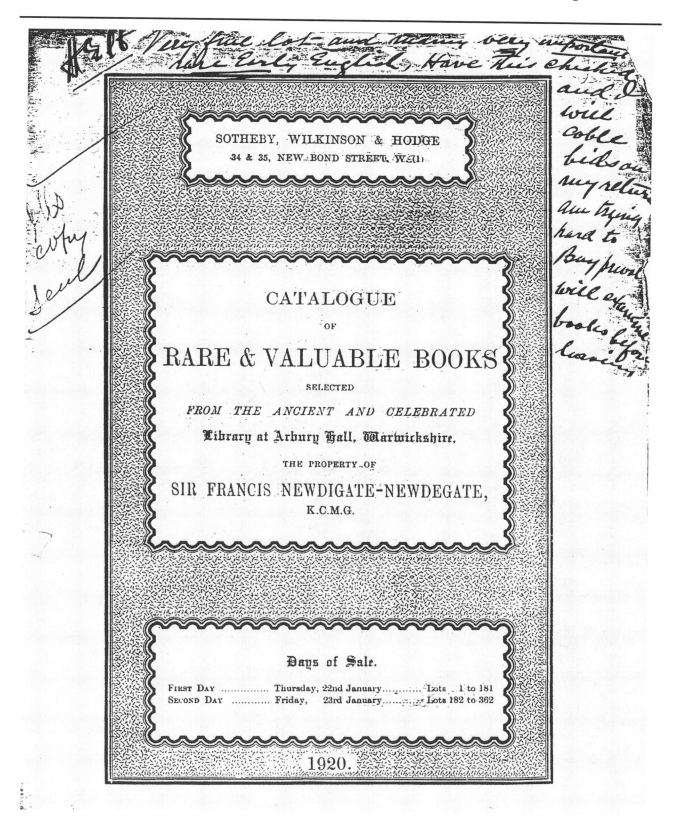

Smith sent this annotated catalogue to Henry E. Huntington in January 1920 (J. R. Maguire Collection).

defined the appeal of the "Cradle Books" in the preface:

> Attention must be paid to the fact that the Opportunity to acquire these Noble Monuments of the Early Printers is becoming of immensely greater difficulty every day. The private Libraries of Europe who assiduously collected the Glories of the First Presses are practically all sold out and there is absolutely no chance of their ever being dispersed by the Great National and Public Libraries which now contain the only Specimens of them extant.

Huntington took Smith's advice and purchased the entire block of incunabula for the remarkably low price of ninety thousand dollars.

After war broke out in Europe in 1914, and particularly after the United States entered the conflict in 1917, collectors had less money to invest in illustrated first editions and less time to devote to auctions and catalogues. Trade with overseas dealers came to a virtual standstill, affecting Smith's business as well as all the other members of the antiquarian book trade. Yet, he continued to do business – albeit on a somewhat limited basis – with regular customers such as Folger, Huntington, Clements, Bishop, and Herschel V. Jones.

Apart from the book trade, Smith lived the life of a wealthy businessman – which in fact he was. In the brief period of twenty years the Dodd, Mead, stock boy had become a legendary success in the tradition of the self-made American hero. He invested heavily in the stock market and in various real estate ventures, drove luxurious cars, and liked to entertain friends with expensive parties at New York hot spots Delmonico's and the Plaza Hotel. He bet large sums of money at the racetracks and owned a stable of thoroughbred horses. None of these investments brought him financial rewards on the scale realized from his book business, however, and slowly he divested himself of all but the books. In a letter of 28 September 1918 Huntington congratulated Smith on selling his string of horses and returning his attention to books.

During World War I he seemed to work harder than ever to maintain his status as New York's leading dealer. In the summer of 1916 Smith sailed for England to take part in the disposal of the Britwell Court library. This collection had been formed in the early decades of the nineteenth century by William Henry Miller and eventually had come into the hands of Sydney R. Christie-Miller, who had decided to put it up for auction. The plan for the sale called for twelve auction sessions, the first to be given over to the Britwell Americana – a distinguished gathering that included thirteen incunabula and a splendid set of the Theodor De Bry *Voyages* (Frankfurt, 1590–1630), which recount early European explorations of the New World. Smith made a private presale arrangement with Sotheby's and took the entire collection for himself. When a *New York Times* reporter asked Smith about the other American dealers who had traveled to London expressly to participate in the sale and now had to return home empty-handed, Smith replied slyly that they had no right to complain since they had enjoyed a pleasant sea voyage. By the time the books arrived in New York, Huntington had agreed to buy them all.

In the years leading up to and immediately following the end of World War I Smith continued to buy actively at the New York and London auctions. He also negotiated for the purchase of entire private libraries. In what may have been his single most important transaction, he secured the Bridgewater House Library for Huntington in 1917 at a cost of $1 million. This was a collection of some forty-four hundred printed books and over twelve thousand manuscripts, the most celebrated of all being the early-fifteenth-century Ellesmere Chaucer, often regarded as the best manuscript of *The Canterbury Tales*. Smith followed that purchase by dominating the Huth and Christie-Miller sales as they progressed in London through 1918 and 1919 and the Herschel Jones and Winston Hagen sales in New York in 1918. Bidding against Edmund Dring of Quaritch's in 1919, Smith paid $75,000 for the 1599 edition of William Shakespeare's *Venus and Adonis,* eclipsing the highest previous price given for a printed book.

Those who knew Smith best felt that he took on much more work than any one person could handle. Although he employed loyal assistants, Smith's approach was to do everything himself – correspondence, pricing, store management, buying trips, customer requests. He would often work all night after a big sale or after he returned to the city from a day at the races at Saratoga Springs. As the pressures of the business mounted, any mistake on the part of a staff member would throw him into a rage. If a binder trimmed an eighth of an inch too much from the edge of a valuable seventeenth-century pamphlet, Smith's ire would descend like a thunderstorm. Furthermore, he stored most of the details of the business in his head; with Smith out of the store no one knew the answers to business-related questions. Customers could not understand why books were not delivered as promised. Dealers fought with Smith over long-overdue bills.

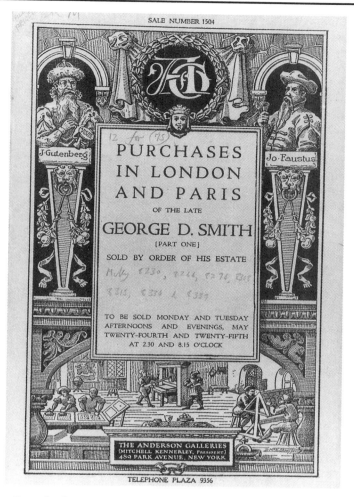

*Cover for the catalogue of one of the series of auctions of Smith's stock
after his death*

The pace of Smith's activities accelerated in early 1920 as he made preparations to bid on the literary treasures in the H. Buxton Forman sale. His control of the bidding for the most important items in that collection was taken for granted. On 4 March 1920, ten days before the sale, Smith and W. Lanier Washington, an alleged descendent of George Washington and occasional trader in Washington relics, were conducting business in Smith's office when the book dealer collapsed on his desk and died of a heart attack. Collectors and dealers were stunned by the news, which caused considerable speculation over what would happen to the American rare-book market without Smith.

Friends wrote letters of praise to the New York newspapers while enemies plotted to take over Smith's customers. Gabriel Wells, a prominent New York dealer, wrote the literary editor of the *New York Post* on 13 March 1920, "The book world has lost its most picturesque figure. . . . Beyond ques-

tion he was the most phenomenal exponent in the field there ever was, and I have no hesitation to assert, there ever is likely to be." An editorial in the 21 March 1920 issue of the *Nation* called Smith a "Broker in Books" and "a victorious scout" who had shifted the emphasis in book selling and book collecting. Perhaps the fondest tribute of all came from Kennerley, who in the 6 March 1920 issue of the *New York Evening Post* called Smith "the greatest book dealer the world has ever known. He lived books eighteen hours a day for the last thirty-seven years. . . . His passion for books was irresistible and contagious and many of the great collectors of today owe it to him that they collected books. . . . He is one of the rare few whose name will forever remain a tradition in the history of the times."

Those who tried to continue Smith's business found the financial records in chaos. The book stock was valuable, but it represented only a fraction of the amounts owed to auction houses and other dealers. As Smith's chief creditor, Kennerley was appointed executor and immediately mounted a series of sales. The results were disappointing. Between 1920 and 1927 various managers sold off the remaining stock and finally closed all accounts.

Smith was a shrewd salesman with a gift for seeing the commercial possibilities of a book or manuscript from the collector's point of view. He never pretended to understand literary values but with his remarkable memory for dates, prices, and condition could speak about every book he owned in great detail. He was competitive to an extreme degree, enjoying the chase and exalting in winning the prize.

References:

Matthew J. Bruccoli, "George D. Smith and the Anglo-American Book Migration," *AB Bookman's Weekly,* 91 (14 June 1993): 2524–2538;

Belden Day, "Anecdotes of G. D. Smith," *Publisher's Weekly,* 45 (10 April 1920): 1179–1180;

Donald C. Dickinson, "Mr. Huntington and Mr. Smith," *Book Collector,* 37 (Autumn 1988): 367–393;

John Drinkwater, "A Memory of George D. Smith," *Bookman,* 53 (January 1921): 308–311;

Charles F. Heartman, "George D. Smith, 1870–1920, Gentleman Bookseller" [originally printed privately in 1945 as a Yuletide Greeting from Book Farm, Beauvoir Community, Mississippi], *American Book Collector,* 23 (May–June 1973): 3–26;

Frederick Hopkins, "George D. Smith, the World's Greatest Bookseller," *New York Evening Post,* 13 March 1920, pp. 17–19.

Papers:

A collection of Smith's correspondence and files of book bills are held in the Henry E. Huntington Library in San Marino, California. Other letters are located at the Pierpont Morgan Library, New York City, and Folger Shakespeare Library in Washington, D.C. Smith's marked set of the Anderson Galleries catalogues are in the Special Collections Department of the Pennsylvania State University Library.

Henry Stevens

(24 August 1819 – 28 February 1886)

Susan Davis

BOOKS: *Catalogue of My English Library* (London: Whittingham, 1853);

Catalogue Raisonné of English Bibles, New Testaments, Psalms and Other Parts of the Holy Scriptures, from the Earliest Editions to the Year 1855 (London: Whittingham, 1855);

Historical Nuggets. Bibliotheca Americana, or a Descriptive Account of My Collection of Rare Books Relating to America, 2 volumes (London: Whittingham & Wilkins, 1862); second series published as *Historical Nuggets. Bibliotheca Americana or a Descriptive Account of Our Collection of Rare Books Relating to America,* 2 volumes, by Stevens and Henry Newton Stevens (London: Henry Stevens & Son, 1885);

The Humboldt Library: A Catalogue of the Library of Alexander von Humboldt with a Bibliographical and Biographical Memoir . . . (London: Henry Stevens, 1863);

Catalogue of the American Books in the Library of the British Museum at Christmas MDCCCLVI (London: Whittingham, 1866);

Bibliotheca Historica: or a Catalogue of 5000 Volumes of Books and Manuscripts Relating Chiefly to the History and Literature of North and South America . . . (Boston: Houghton, 1870);

Bibliotheca Geographica & Historica, or a Catalogue of a Nine Days Sale of Rare & Valuable Ancient and Modern Books, Maps, Charts, Manuscripts, Autograph Letters et cetera . . . (London: Henry Stevens, 1872);

The Bibles in the Caxton Exhibition MDCCCLXXVII . . . (London: Henry Stevens; New York: Scribner, Welford & Armstrong, 1878);

Photo-bibliography: or, A Word on Printed Card Catalogues of Old Rare Beautiful and Costly Books . . . (London: Henry Stevens; New York: Scribner, Welford & Armstrong, 1878);

Catalogue of the Percival Library . . . (London: C. Whittingham, 1879);

Benjamin Franklin's Life and Writings. A Bibliographical Essay on the Stevens' Collection of Books and Manuscripts Relating to Doctor Franklin. (London: Davy & Sons, 1881);

Stevens's historical collections. Catalogue . . . of rare books and manuscripts relating chiefly to the history and literature of America (London: Davy & Sons, 1881);

The Dawn of the British Trade to the East Indies as Recorded in the Court Minutes of the East India Company, 1599–1603 . . . (London: H. Stevens & Son, 1886);

Recollections of Mr James Lenox of New York and the Formation of His Library (London: Henry Stevens & Son, 1886); revised by Victor Hugo Paltsits as *Recollections of James Lenox and the Formation of His Library* (New York: New York Public Library, 1951);

Thomas Hariot, the mathematician, the philosopher and the scholar . . . (London: Privately printed, 1900).

An important American bibliographer and bookseller who lived in and worked out of London, Henry Stevens achieved his greatest success in Europe, where over the course of approximately fifteen years, he single-handedly brought to market many pivotal works dealing with the New World. One of the most remarkable book scouts ever, Stevens had an eye for rarities at a time when Europeans had not yet recognized the potential value of Americana. In his book *Recollections of Mr James Lenox of New York and the Formation of His Library* (1886), Stevens sums up his own career: "I found that a very large number of the choicest historical and bibliographical nuggets relating to the 'Age of Discovery,' with the exploration and development of the New World, occurred but once in my time, in the market for sale." Stevens had been the prospector who had panned out a sizable number of these nuggets.

The published works of Stevens were mostly book catalogues which often served in the short term as sales catalogues and in the long term as bibliographies. The major exception was his memoir of

the book collector James Lenox of New York. It has rightly been said that this work is more autobiography than biography. As portrayed in this book, the career of Stevens seems largely to have involved one momentous bibliographical find after another. His career was indeed highly successful, but it was a success that was hard earned.

The third of eleven children, Stevens was born on 24 August 1819 to Henry and Candace Stevens of Barnet, Vermont. To support a large family, the parents were necessarily vigilant of their money. In his *Bibliotheca Historica* (1870) Stevens describes his father's activities as "historical mousings" in which the elder Stevens searched through "garrets," "hen-coups," and "old Barrels" for books and paper ephemera relating to American history. Stevens's father was also a founder and the first president of the Vermont Historical Society. Before Stevens entered Middlebury College in 1838 he sold his mother's cheeses in order to defray education costs; he even-

tually had to interrupt his stay at Middlebury due to a lack of family funds.

To earn money, Stevens in 1840 went to Washington, D.C., where he found work as a Treasury Department clerk. Later he was transferred to a clerkship with a joint congressional committee investigating contractual claims involving the American Archives, a special collection of Americana within the Library of Congress. During this period he met Peter Force of the American Archives. When Stevens left Washington for Yale College the following year, he promised Force to scout New England for books and papers on behalf of the archives. He received his B.A. at Yale in 1843 and entered Harvard Law School in 1844. During his years at Yale and Harvard he had continued his scouting; the resulting knowledge and experience Stevens gained piqued his desire to go to Europe and scout for old books and papers relating to America.

Stevens early in his career

Stevens arrived in England in July 1845 on his own money and initiative. In *Recollections* he described himself then as "a self-appointed missionary, on an antiquarian and historical book-hunting expedition." He planned to offer his finds to institutions and private collectors in the United States. John Carter Brown of Providence, Rhode Island, whose acquaintance Stevens had made in the States, was one of Stevens's early private collectors. G. P. Putnam, who was then in London, was engaged as Stevens's agent to handle the shipping and invoicing of books.

Upon arriving in London Stevens attempted to arrange an interview with Antonio Panizzi, the Italian-born librarian of the British Museum. Panizzi was on leave, however, and was not to return for six months. When he did return, it was he who approached Stevens, asking the young man to evaluate the museum's holdings in American history and literature with an eye to improving the collections

and supplying works on the New World the library lacked. At that time the museum library contained about 160,000 total volumes. But Panizzi, like Stevens, was highly ambitious, and he had just completed a report proposing the expansion of the library to more than 600,000 volumes in the next few years. Stevens had originally planned a stay of approximately a year in England; the opportunity presented by Panizzi, however, persuaded him to take up residence there. He would live in London from 1845 until his death in 1886.

His association with Panizzi was most profitable: within a year and a half he had placed 10,000 items with the British Museum Library. Yet even before he met Panizzi, Stevens had begun offering some of his Americana to James Lenox, a wealthy New Yorker who up until that time primarily had collected American Bibles. Stevens's relationship with Lenox was also crucial to his success, although his dealings with Lenox were not as warm as with

Letter to Edward A. Crowninshield in which Stevens announces his appointment as consultant to the British Museum
(Manuscript Division, William L. Clemens Library, University of Michigan)

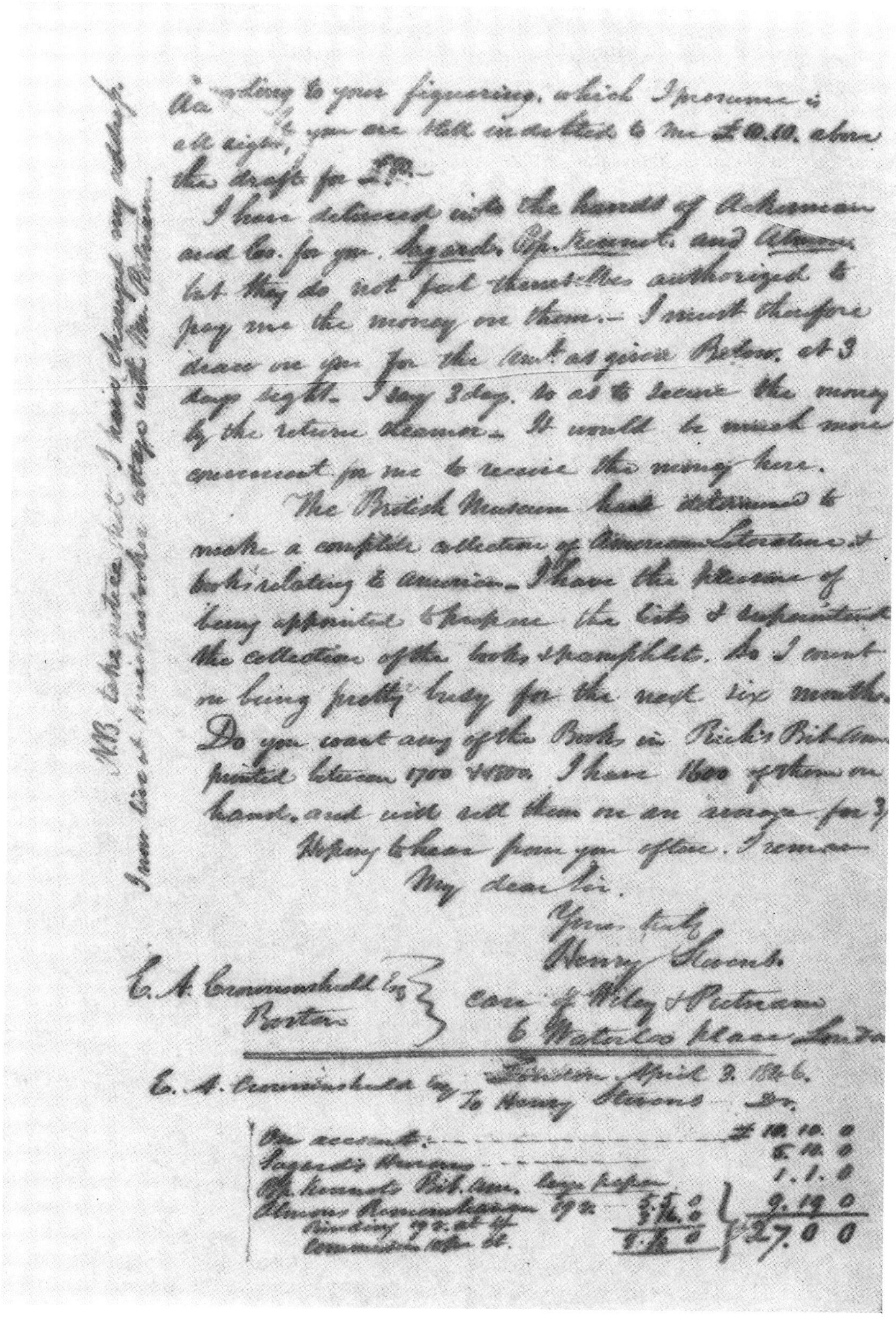

Panizzi. Lenox was a reserved and private man who preferred not to confuse business with friendship.

Buying interests frequently overlapped among Stevens's clients; Stevens, nevertheless, adroitly served his customers' interests. If a buyer refused an item, he would normally then be instructed to forward the book to a second buyer and, if he too passed, would send it on to a third buyer, and so on. Often a book would be well traveled by the time it finally found a home.

The first great bibliographical event in which Stevens played a part was the sale of a Mazarin Bible, today known as the Gutenberg Bible. The two-column, forty-two-line Bible printed in Germany in 1450–1455 by Johannes Gutenberg was the first book to be printed from movable type. Stevens informed Lenox that the Bible was coming onto the market and warned Lenox to be prepared to bid at least £190 ($950), the price another copy had brought at auction. Because Stevens was to be in Paris at the time of the London sale, he suggested that Putnam bid on behalf of Lenox. Putnam won the book at £500. Lenox was appalled by the cost: when the expenses were tallied in, the total price came to $3000. Yet Lenox eventually decided to keep the Gutenberg. In his memoir of Lenox, Stevens reflected that, in the end, "the result of this campaign was all in my favor." Victor Hugo Paltsits, who produced a revised edition of the *Recollections* in 1951, states that this copy was the first Gutenberg Bible to come to the Western Hemisphere.

Soon after engaging Stevens as his scout, Lenox was persuaded to expand his field of collecting from Bibles to early American exploration. Thomas Hariot's *Briefe and true Report of the new found land of Virginia* (1590), which describes the "commodities" and "natural inhabitants" of Virginia, was one of the first important works Stevens offered to Lenox. How Stevens obtained this item provides a good example of his capability as a deal maker and also illustrates the extent to which, two years after his arrival in London, Stevens had established his reputation as a savvy and respected book buyer.

Lenox had informed Stevens that he would like very much to possess the Hariot. Stevens, who had procured a copy of this work for Brown, cautioned Lenox that he felt it doubtful a second copy of so rare a work would turn up in the same decade. In June 1847, however, Panizzi approached Stevens about a certain rarity, the "Dati Columbus," which was soon coming to auction in Paris. The "Dati Columbus" was the Italian verse edition of the letter written by Christopher Columbus describing the New World. Knowing Stevens would undoubtedly

bid on the Dati on behalf of his American collectors, Panizzi asked him if there was not some way the British Museum could acquire the item. Stevens in turn suggested a deal: if Stevens won the Dati, he would pass it on to the British Museum in exchange for their duplicate and imperfect copy of Hariot's *Virginia.* Stevens in fact possessed the three leaves that the British Museum's copy lacked; he would thus be able to present Lenox with a complete copy. Panizzi agreed to the deal, and Lenox, while deprived of the Dati, was most pleased to add the Hariot to his growing collection.

In late 1847 Stevens returned to America to visit his family, make goodwill calls upon Brown and Lenox, buy Americana for the British Museum, and solicit new customers. In the spring of 1848, while still in the United States, he caused a stir by buying a portion of George Washington's library and then offering it to the British Museum. The collection included about three hundred volumes with Washington's ownership signature on the title page. Many Americans, including Henry's father, felt strongly that this historical collection should remain in the United States. Fortunately for Stevens's reputation, the British Museum passed on the collection, and Stevens with much difficulty finally sold the library to a civic-minded group of Bostonians. This was a bitter experience for Stevens, who, instead of doubling his initial investment of $3000 as he had hoped, realized a net profit of only $250 on this important library.

While in America Stevens conceived of the idea for a major bibliography of Americana. This "Bibliographia Americana" would list and describe all books either relating to or printed in America up to 1700. He submitted the proposal to the Smithsonian, and the institution agreed to publish one thousand copies of the bibliography as part of its Contributions to Knowledge series. Stevens in turn was to deliver the manuscript within eighteen months. Yet Stevens never completed the project, and it was not until Joseph Sabin began publishing his multivolume *Dictionary of Books Relating to America* twenty years later that a thorough bibliography of Americana was compiled.

One of Stevens's greatest coups was his acquisition of Benjamin Franklin's manuscripts. In 1850 H. A. Pulsford approached Stevens about the manuscripts – some three thousand in all – which had been left to his father, a London tailor. William Temple Franklin, grandson of Benjamin, had roomed over the tailor's shop in Saint James, and after his death his widow had given the manuscripts to Pulsford. Measurements were scribbled in some

IBLIOTHECA HISTORICA

R A Catalogue of 5000 volumes of
books and manuscripts relating chiefly
to the history and literature of North
and South America among which is in
cluded the larger proportion of the extra
ordinary library of the late HENRY STEVENS Senior of
Barnet Vt Founder and first President of the Vermont
Historical & Antiquarian Society　The whole compris
ng such a collection of ancient and modern books rich
nd rare useful and common as seldom occurs for sale
n any country including many titles never before re
corded in an American catalogue

EDITED WITH INTRODUCTION AND NOTES
BY HENRY STEVENS G M B F S A etc
SOMETIMES STUDENT IN YALE COLLEGE　NOW RESIDING IN
LONDON AT 4 TRAFALGAR SQUARE

To be sold by auction by Messrs LEONARD & Co at their Library Sales Room Nº
50 Bromfield Street in Boston on Tuesday the 5th Wednesday the 6th Thursday
the 7th and Friday the 8th day of April 1870　Sale each day to commence at
10 in the forenoon and 2 o'clock in the afternoon

BOSTON: H O HOUGHTON AND COMPANY
Cambridge: Riverside Press
1870

The catalogue in which Stevens pays tribute to his father's bookmanship

of the margins, and one manuscript had actually been cut to a sleeve pattern. Stevens purchased the collection with great delight and added to the collection over the years. He was not to sell the collection for some thirty years, during which time the manuscripts served as collateral on Stevens's many loans. When he finally sold them to Congress in 1881, he realized $35,000 on the sale and subsequently issued a "bibliographical essay" of the collection; a forty-page work, *Benjamin Franklin's Life and Writings* (1881), recounts the history of the collection and provides a useful Franklin bibliography.

In 1853 Stevens put out his first signed work, a one-hundred-page book entitled *Catalogue of My English Library*. One thousand copies were privately printed at Chiswick Press, London; the catalogue listed 5,751 works by major English authors. Like many of his published works, this catalogue was a superficial guide for Americans who wished to build up their own "English Library"; more important, it was to serve as an implicit advertisement for Stevens's book business. Stevens also included in the work an essay on the American import tax on English books, which, unsurprisingly, he deemed unfair. The catalogue paid off well for Stevens; according to Wyman W. Parker in *Henry Stevens of Vermont* (1963), Stevens received orders totaling almost £2,000 ($10,000) in the first ten days the catalogue was out.

A Bible that came on the market in 1855 caused a delicious stir: the so-called Wicked Bible of 1631 (it was apparently Stevens who coined the appellation). It had been believed that all one thousand copies had been destroyed shortly after its printing due to an error which altered the Seventh Commandment to read, "Thou shalt commit adultery." So little was known about the book that no one was even certain of its publication date. An in-

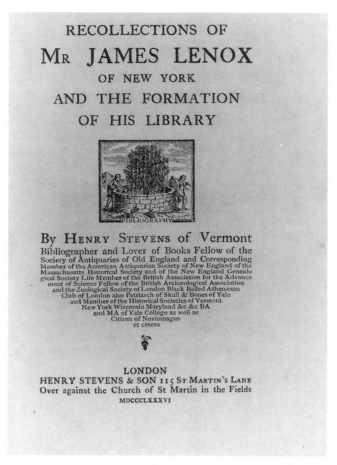

RECOLLECTIONS OF
Mr JAMES LENOX
OF NEW YORK
AND THE FORMATION
OF HIS LIBRARY

By HENRY STEVENS of Vermont
Bibliographer and Lover of Books Fellow of the
Society of Antiquaries of Old England and Corresponding
Member of the American Antiquarian Society of New England of the
Massachusetts Historical Society and of the New England Genealo
gical Society Life Member of the British Association for the Advance
ment of Science Fellow of the British Archæological Association
and the Zoological Society of London Black Balled Athenæum
Club of London also Patriarch of Skull & Bones of Yale
and Member of the Historical Societies of Vermont
New York Wisconsin Maryland &c &c BA
and MA of Yale College as well as
Citizen of Noviomagus
et cetera

LONDON
HENRY STEVENS & SON 115 St Martin's Lane
Over against the Church of St Martin in the Fields
MDCCCLXXXVI

Title page for Stevens's memoir of collector James Lenox

dividual possessing this Bible approached Stevens in June 1855, pressing him for an immediate commitment to purchase this evidently unique book. Stevens managed to stall the seller and dash off a letter to Lenox, who was staying in Paris at the time. Lenox's instruction came back that he was to buy the book immediately. Stevens, however, had discovered while collating the volume that he already possessed this Bible, although his was an incomplete copy. When the seller came to collect payment, Stevens informed him that the Bible was not, after all, a unique item and was able to negotiate the price down accordingly.

Another great find of Stevens's came that same year. Since his arrival in London Stevens had been searching for a copy of the *Bay Psalm Book* (1640), the first book printed in British North America, for Lenox. Stevens reports that during these ten years he had been able to locate only one copy in Europe, a fine copy in the Bodleian Library. The Bodleian did not realize what it had, and Ste-

vens did not wish to inform his friend Dr. Bandinel, the Bodley librarian, about his rarity until Stevens had located a copy of his own.

In January 1855, at a Sotheby's sale, Stevens found in one lot a *Bay Psalm Book* lying unnoticed within the parcel. Stevens had time only to glance at the volume before tying the parcel back up and moving back, stunned, to bid. He managed to bid casually and won the lot at nineteen shillings.

In 1859–1860 Stevens purchased two major libraries and, as usual, published catalogues of each. The private library of Edward A. Crowninshield came on the market after Crowninshield's death in 1859. This library, for which Stevens had supplied many volumes over the years, consisted of books about the New World; Stevens bought the collection for ten thousand dollars. The following year he bought the library of explorer Alexander von Humboldt. Stevens paid twenty thousand dollars for the seventeen thousand volumes, most of which dealt with science and exploration. Practically all the

Stevens among his books

Humboldt collection burned in a warehouse fire in 1865, before Stevens was able to dispose of them.

The Humboldt material burned unsold. The Civil War profoundly affected Stevens's book business as American customers either grew leery of the reliability of overseas shipments, were deterred by the exchange rate, or had more pressing concerns. Always resourceful, Stevens became an arms broker for U.S. general John C. Frémont, taking delivery of English cannon and shells and shipping them to America. However, when the colorful Frémont was relieved of his command by President Abraham Lincoln, this exciting new business withered for Stevens.

The diminution of his book business and the loss of his career as an arms dealer forced Stevens to concentrate on publishing. He had always found it drudgery but now had no other choice; he had never been very careful in managing his own finances and was hard hit by these reversals.

In 1862 he had his two-volume *Historical Nuggets,* which had been sitting in type at Chiswick for five years, printed. The "nuggets" were priced Americana from Stevens's own stock, most of which had already been sold at the time of printing. Nonetheless, it generated some income to justify its printing and was one of the more useful bibliographies Stevens produced. Another ambitious project of Stevens which had also been languishing at Chiswick for years was the *Catalogue of the American Books in the Library of the British Museum at Christmas MDCCCLVI* (1866). Stevens finally wrote the preface and had the work printed.

In 1867 Stevens's father died, leaving behind his own substantial collection of American history and literature. Stevens sold what he could to the

British Museum and then spent some time cataloguing the remainder to dispose of by auction, scheduled for April of 1870. The accompanying sale catalogue, known as Stevens's *Bibliotheca Historica,* is particularly notable for his "Explanatory," in which he pays tribute to his father and relates his family background. He also chides American collectors and librarians for being overcautious in their book-buying habits and charges that they all too often judge books not on their own merits but rather on whether or not they are mentioned in a favored bibliography. This lecturing of the book establishment helped stimulate the sale of some of the more obscure works of the *Bibliotheca Historica.*

One of the most notable accomplishments of his later years was his arranging of a Bible department to complement the 1877 Caxton Exhibition in South Kensington organized to commemorate the four hundredth year of English printing. Stevens came up with the idea of a Bible exhibit, put the show together in a short time, and produced an excellent catalogue to accompany the exhibition. *The Bibles in the Caxton Exhibition MDCCCLXXVII . . .* (1878) was a descriptive bibliography of approximately one thousand Bibles and included a history of the printed Bible from 1450 to 1877.

Stevens's best-known work, *Recollections,* was completed shortly before his death in 1886. Subsequently published by his son, the book has become a classic memoir of the book trade. Richard Garnett, in his *Essays in Librarianship and Bibliography* (1970), calls the book "one of the most racy of literary monographs, affording an excellent idea of the writer's quaint, shrewd, and anecdotal conversa-

tion." While Lenox may have been Stevens's best customer, in many ways the men were opposites: Lenox was austere and reserved, while Stevens was ebullient and warm; Lenox was patient, meticulous, and cautious, while Stevens could be impulsive, overconfident, and careless. Yet like many opposites these two intriguing individuals served to balance one another, and this perhaps accounted for the success of their business relationship and the enduring interest of Stevens's memoir.

Garnett refers to the mid 1800s as the "golden days" for Americana, when rarities still could be found – and inexpensively. "Mr. Stevens," writes Garnett, "probably contributed more than any other man to terminate this happy state of things." But perhaps Parker sums up Stevens's success best when he writes that Stevens "could find the books, and he would be remembered chiefly for this ability."

Biography:
Wyman W. Parker, *Henry Stevens of Vermont* (Amsterdam: N. Israel, 1963).

Reference:
Richard Garnett, "The Late Henry Stevens, F.S.A.," in his *Essays in Librarianship and Bibliography* (New York: Burt Franklin, 1899).

Papers:
Business correspondence of Henry Stevens is held at the Clements Library, University of Michigan. Other Stevens letters are in the Force Papers at the Library of Congress and in the Reserve Collection of the New York Public Library.

Thomas Winthrop Streeter

(12 June 1883 – 12 June 1965)

Katherine J. Adams
University of Texas at Austin

BOOKS: *Americana – Beginnings: A Collection from the Library of Thomas W. Streeter Shown in Honor of a Visit of the Hroswitha Club on May 3, 1951* (Morristown, N. J.: Thomas W. Streeter, 1952);

Bibliography of Texas, 1795–1845, 5 volumes (Cambridge, Mass.: Harvard University Press, 1955); revised and enlarged by Archibald Hanna, Jr., with a guide to the microfilm collection, *Texas as Province and Republic: 1795–1845* (Woodbridge, Conn.: Research Publications, 1983);

The Celebrated Collection of Americana Formed by the Late Thomas Winthrop Streeter Morristown, New Jersey Sold by Order of the Trustees, 7 volumes (New York: Parke-Bernet Galleries, 1966–1969).

SELECTED PERIODICAL PUBLICATIONS – UNCOLLECTED: "Texas, 1836–1936: An Exhibition," *Bulletin of the New York Public Library,* 41 (February 1937): 71–94;

"Notes on North American Regional Bibliographies," *Papers of the Bibliographical Society of America,* 36 (1942): 1–16;

"The Rollins Collection of Western Americana," *Princeton University Library Chronicle,* 9 (June 1948): 1–14;

"Henry R. Wagner, Collector, Bibliographer, Cartographer and Historian," *California Historical Society Quarterly,* 36 (March 1957): 165–175;

"Henry R. Wagner and the Yale Library," *Yale University Library Gazette,* 32 (October 1957): 71–76.

One of the outstanding collectors of Americana and the author of the landmark *Bibliography of Texas, 1795–1845* (1955), Thomas Winthrop Streeter matched his successful career as an attorney and business manager with a passion for American history and the books, pamphlets, maps, periodicals, and broadsides that documented it. Through a combination of knowledge, taste, enthusiasm, and financial means, Streeter assembled a private collection of Americana unsurpassed during the twentieth century. His family home and library on the outskirts of Morristown, New Jersey, where he lived from 1922 until his death, drew fellow collectors, booksellers, scholars, and librarians for three generations. As his collections grew, Streeter sought the help of a succession of assistants and librarians, one of whom was Howell J. Heaney, hired in 1947. In his address to the Rare Book Section of the Association of College and Research Libraries in 1970, Heaney described Streeter's house and library in Morristown:

> Its large, quiet library [was] shelved to the ceiling on two sides, the lower shelves projecting to provide a convenient surface for consulting reference works. In one wall a door led to the vault. The shelves there and those in the library must once have been adequate for the collection and Mr. Streeter's reference books, but as time went on, and both collections grew, they began to invade the living room.... Reference books infrequently used were stored in a room on the third floor, and long runs of government documents were shelved in the basement. The breakfast room was largely abandoned to canals and railroads, with certain periodicals added, and here, in piles of books and pamphlets, the practiced eye could trace, in almost geological drifts, the results of periodic "orderings" of the library proper in preparation for visits of distinguished groups – the Hroswitha Club, the Walpole Society, the booksellers and collectors attending some major sale.

Streeter was born to Frank Sherwin and Lilian Carpenter Streeter on 12 June 1883 in Concord, New Hampshire. He attended Dartmouth College, graduating with honors in history in 1904, and Harvard Law School, receiving a degree in 1907. Streeter was admitted to the New Hampshire and Massachusetts bars that same year. He practiced law in Boston with the firm of Choate, Hall, and Stuart. In 1912 he opened his own law office in Boston and then formed a partnership with Robert J. Holmes, creating the firm of Streeter and Holmes.

Streeter married Ruth Cheney in 1917. The couple had four children: Frank Sherwin, Henry

Thomas Winthrop Streeter

Schofield, Thomas Winthrop, and Lilian Carpenter. After about 1915 Streeter spent increasingly less time practicing law and more acting as a corporate manager. He moved to New York in 1917, where he became treasurer then vice president of the New York–based American International Corporation, a financial and development company. From 1923 to 1930 he served as chairman of the board of Simms Petroleum Company, and from 1931 to 1935 he represented the New York State Superintendent of Banks in the liquidation of the Bank of the United States. Streeter became president of the Mortgage Certificate Loan Corporation in 1935 and in early 1938 became director, then president, of the Prudence Bond Company. Streeter resigned in 1939 and thereafter — with the exception of his management until 1956 of the Ungalik Syndicate, a gold-dredging enterprise operating in Alaska — devoted himself to his historical and book-collecting interests.

Streeter was known by his friends and colleagues as a true gentleman bibliophile — bookseller Charles F. Heartman once called him a "prince of collectors and true book lovers." Honored by election as officer or trustee in many historical societies, research libraries, and book organizations, Streeter was especially active in the Bibliographical Society of America, the American Antiquarian Society, the Library of Congress Advisory Council, the Board of Fellows of the Pierpont Morgan Library, the Associates of the John Carter Brown Library, the New York Historical Society, and the Grolier Club. His substantial support of research libraries over the years also included many benefactions, such as the donation of portions of his vast collection of railroad ephemera to the American Antiquarian Society (pre-1841 imprints for Massachusetts, Rhode Island, and Connecticut), the University of Virginia (southern railroads), Dartmouth (post-1841 materi-

THE CELEBRATED COLLECTION

of

AMERICANA

FORMED BY THE LATE

Thomas Winthrop Streeter

Morristown, New Jersey

Sold by Order of the Trustees

VOLUME ONE

DISCOVERY AND EXPLORATION ⚹ ATLASES ⚹ NEW FRANCE
SPANISH SOUTHWEST ⚹ MEXICO
THE MEXICAN WAR ⚹ TEXAS ⚹ NEW MEXICO ⚹ ARIZONA
INDIAN TERRITORY AND OKLAHOMA

Public Auction
Tuesday · October 25 at 8 p.m.
Wednesday · October 26 at 1:45 p.m. and 8 p.m.

PARKE-BERNET GALLERIES · INC
[*Affiliated with* SOTHEBY & Co *London*]
New York · 1966

THOMAS WINTHROP STREETER

Frontispiece and title page for the first volume of the catalogue for the sale of Streeter's library

als on Vermont, New Hampshire, and Maine) and Princeton (mid-Atlantic railroads).

Streeter's fascination with history and books developed early. In 1904 he read a paper before the New York Historical Society; he made book purchases from Goodspeed's in Boston as early as 1916; and he attended his first auction in 1920. His early collecting centered on New England, but his interests quickly broadened as important regional bibliographies, such as Henry R. Wagner's *The Plains and the Rockies* (1920) and *The Spanish Southwest 1542–1794* (1924), and auctions of primary materials on the West opened new avenues for collecting. In developing his collections he sought the advice from and worked closely with many of the great bookmen of his day, including collector and bibliographer Wagner, librarian Lawrence C. Wroth, and booksellers Lathrop C. Harper, Edward Eberstadt, and Michael Walsh.

Streeter's collecting was characterized by unifying themes of subject, region, or chronology: American historical and cultural beginnings, rail-roads, California history through the gold rush, Texas history until 1845. His Americana collection was distinguished by selectivity rather than by depth and by excellent condition whenever possible. His was a collector's collection of great books in many fields rather than an exhaustive coverage of one field intended for research purposes.

Jewels in the crown of Streeter's American-beginnings collection included the second Plannck edition of Christopher Columbus's account of his discoveries, written on the homeward voyage (Rome: Stephan Plannck, 1493); Antonio Pigafetta's *Le Voyage et Navigation* (Paris: Simon de Colines, circa 1525), the account of an Italian nobleman who accompanied Ferdinand Magellan on his voyage and circumnavigation; *A Platform of Church Discipline. . .* (Cambridge, Mass.: Samuel Green, 1649), one of the earliest books printed in English America; Increase Mather's *Ichabod* (Boston: printed by Timothy Green, sold by the Book-sellers, 1702), which contains the first portrait engraving done specifically for a book in English America; *An Ordinance for the Government of the Territory of the United States, Northwest of the River Ohio* (New York: 1787), or the "Northwest Ordinance," which provided the plan for U.S. westward expansion; Meriwether Lewis and William Clark's *History of the Expedition* (Philadelphia: Bradford and Inskeep, 1814), actually written by Nicholas Biddle, an uncut copy in original boards, the most significant of all overland narratives; Gov. Ninian Edwards' *Communication to both Houses of Illinois Legislature* (Kaskaskia: printed by Matthew Duncan, 1814), the only known copy of the first Illinois imprint; and *Oration of Abraham Lincoln at the Dedication of the Gettysburg National Military Cemetery* (1863), the first separate printing of the Gettysburg Address.

In 1952 Streeter described the unifying theme of his Americana collection in his brief pamphlet *Americana – Beginnings: A Collection from the Library of Thomas W. Streeter Shown in Honor of a Visit of the Hroswitha Club on May 3, 1951.* In its introduction he named some of the "classes" of historical American beginnings that appealed to him: contemporary accounts of voyages to America, the beginnings of settlement in America, and cultural foundations as expressed in first or early imprints in colonies, states, and regions. Streeter envisioned *Americana – Beginnings* as an informal catalogue, one based on the brief exhibit labels he had written to accompany his display of books for the Hroswitha Club and planned as a souvenir of the members' visit. In preparing the catalogue for publication, however, he decided to expand the labels to include fuller annotations as well as collations and the locations of copies of each book in other libraries. As a result, *Americana – Beginnings* both reflects Streeter's painstaking thoroughness as a bibliographer and demonstrates his ability to write critical notes, two hallmarks of his famous *Bibliography of Texas, 1795–1845.*

Streeter's fascination with Texas history began as a boy when he spent time in Texas on a ranch in the Davis Mountains. He later made frequent visits to the state as part of his management of various Mexican oil interests. By 1922 he was a self-described "ardent" collector of Texana whose interest focused on the state's early colonization, the "drama" of its revolution from Mexico, and its history as a republic. As he wrote in the catalogue to the New York Public Library's "Texas, 1836–1936: An Exhibition," there are "few, if any, of our states whose history is so full of interest to the collector and the student as Texas." Streeter enjoyed remarkable success as a collector of Texana, acquiring more than two thousand items in all, covering the full span of Texas history and more than half of the items listed in his *Bibliography of Texas, 1795–1845.*

By 1927 Streeter had conceived the idea of continuing Wagner's *Spanish Southwest 1542–1794* by preparing a bibliography relating to Texas from 1795 to 1845. In his "Notes on North American Regional Bibliographies" (1942), Streeter writes that he made the decision to begin such a project in a "state of complete bibliographical innocence"; what he envisioned as a comparatively simple task "for the spare time of a busy life" quickly turned into a near-thirty-year project. In the preparation of his Texas bibliography Streeter sought the aid of and began friendship with many librarians, book collectors, and historians who were knowledgeable about Texas history and imprints. Foremost among these were bibliographer Wagner and librarian Ernest W. Winkler of the University of Texas, whose library housed the most extensive public collection of Texana in existence. To each Streeter laid out his ideas for a critical Texas bibliography covering 1795 to 1845 and received the necessary encouragement. His February 1927 correspondence with Winkler indicates his ideas and plans for the bibliography – including which types of materials to include and which to exclude – and these plans are remarkably true to the final publication.

Although the stock market collapse in 1929 and the Depression that followed meant that Streeter was preoccupied with business until his retirement in 1939, he was able to remain active in his Texas collecting and bibliographic work. In 1936, the year of the Texas centennial, for example, he helped prepare the exhibit and catalogue for the New York Public Library's "Texas, 1836–1936: An Exhibition," (1937) which displayed many of his Texas imprints. Following that exhibit, Streeter loaned materials from his collection for display in the Texas Hall of State during the Texas Centennial Exposition in Dallas. In 1939 portions of his Texas collection were displayed at opening ceremonies at the San Jacinto Monument, located on the battlefield where Texas had gained its independence from Mexico in 1836.

In 1942, when he was well into building his Texas bibliography, Streeter wrote "Notes on North American Regional Bibliographies," in which he commented on the various types of regional bibliographies he had studied. In "Notes" he also poses the question of whether a regional bibliography should be a mere list of titles without critical notes or a list so focused by subject or period that it allows for comprehensive coverage and critical treatment of the titles listed. Streeter clearly preferred

Mrs. Thomas W. Streeter with Gabriel Austin, Warren R. Howell, A. R. A. Hobson of Sotheby's, and Michael J. Walsh of Goodspeed's Book Shop after the final Streeter sale, November 1969

the latter version, and his article enumerates the points he felt essential to such a bibliography: that the contents of the books should be listed and their significance described; that books should be sufficiently described to identify perfect copies; and that the period dealt with should have unity and significance. Streeter cited Wagner's *Spanish Southwest* and Henry Harrisse's *Notes pour servir a l'Histoire, a la bibliographie . . . de la Nouvelle-France 1545–1700* (Paris: Truss, 1872) as two regional bibliographies that fulfilled all these essentials and that served as his inspirations and models.

Streeter's project to compile a critical bibliography of books, pamphlets, folders, broadsides, and maps relating to Texas from 1795 to 1845 took twenty-seven years to complete. During that time he corresponded with more than sixty librarians, collectors, and historians about Texas imprints and researched some eighty libraries to locate copies. Published by Harvard University Press in an edition of six hundred copies, *Bibliography of Texas* appeared in five volumes issued between 1955 and 1960. Its 1,661 entries are divided into three sections: Texas imprints, Mexican imprints, and United States and European imprints. Entries are fully annotated to place the piece in historic context or to describe its historic significance, and important details such as the presence of maps and printed wrappers are noted. Entries are supplemented by Streeter's history of printing in Texas through 1845 and a series of informative appendices on topics such as Texas

newspapers through 1845, official government periodicals of Coahuila and Texas, and the speeches on Texas in the U.S. Congress from 1836 to 1845.

Bibliography of Texas was hailed by scholars as a meticulous, definitive, and monumental achievement and as an outstanding contribution to southwestern history and scholarship. In the words of bookseller Edward Eberstadt, who reviewed it in a 1956 *Antiquarian Bookman,* it was "the foremost work yet accomplished in the field of American regional bibliography." Streeter's work easily supplanted Caldwell Walton Raines's groundbreaking *A Bibliography of Texas: Being a Descriptive List of Books, Pamphlets, and Documents Relating to Texas in Print and Manuscript since 1536* (Austin, Texas: Published for the Author, 1896), which covered a considerably longer time period but which had never been intended as a comprehensive treatment.

A second edition of Streeter's *Bibliography of Texas,* revised and enlarged, was published by Research Publications in 1983 as a single volume and was accompanied by a reproduction on microfilm of the full text of each imprint. With the original edition long out of print and demanding high prices in the antiquarian book market, the new edition was viewed as a means of updating the bibliography and making the Texas rarities widely available. It is a measure of Streeter's thoroughness that the new edition, published more than twenty-five years after the original, contained fewer than 150 additions, most of which were Mexican imprints. Prized by librarians, booksellers, and researchers, Streeter's *Bibliography of Texas, 1795–1845* remains an indispensable reference book on Texas imprints for the period.

In 1942 Yale University Associate Librarian James T. Babb wrote Streeter about Streeter's plans for his Connecticut railroad items. This contact eventually led to Streeter's Texas collection being acquired by Yale in installments beginning in 1956. The acquisition was made possible by a group of Yale's library associates, who were able to raise the $275,000 necessary for the purchase. Archibald Hanna, Jr., curator of western Americana at Yale, described the acquisition of Streeter's Texas collection in the 1957 *Yale University Library Gazette* as marking "a great step forward for the Western Americana Collection," one that provided "tremendous strength in one of the most interesting and important regions of the American West." In February 1957 the Yale library celebrated its acquisition with a display of 140 books, pamphlets, and broadsides, each the only copy located in Streeter's *Bibliography of Texas*. Of those shown, 114 were from the Streeter collection.

The Streeter Texas collection consisted of 232 Texas imprints, 199 Mexican imprints, and 449 U.S. and European imprints for the period between 1745 and 1845. The collection also included 575 Texas items for the period after 1845, 18 for the period before 1795, 370 manuscript collections, 95 Texas railroad items, 70 Texas and Pacific railroad items, 550 reference items, and Texas newspapers. Highspots included Álva Núñez Cabeza de Vaca's *La Relación y Commentarios* (Valladolid, Spain: por Francisco Fernandez de Cordova, 1555), which recorded the journey of the first European to come to present-day Texas; Stephen F. Austin's 1823 address *To the Settlers in Austins* [sic] *settlement,* printed as a broadside and marking the beginning of Anglo colonization of Texas; the *Municipal Ordinance for the Government of the Municipality of Austin* (1829), the earliest surviving imprint after the permanent establishment of a press in Texas; and an 1836 letter by William Barret Travis written from the Alamo in which he states, "I shall never surrender or retreat." For the Yale Library, the addition of Streeter's Texas collection to its existing western Americana, Texana, and southwestern holdings made it a preeminent repository for Texas imprints and one of the country's largest collections of primary sources on the history of the American West.

Streeter was one of the collectors whose interest in western Americana helped carve out a new field of collecting. Launched with the acquisition of the Hubert Howe Bancroft Collection of Western

Americana by the University of California in 1905, the development of the American West as a fertile collecting area received powerful stimulus from the publication in 1920 of Wagner's bibliography of western travel narratives, *The Plains and the Rockies,* and a series of auction sales of primary materials on the American West held in 1922. By the time Streeter's *Texas Bibliography* was published, rarities in the field were commanding widespread interest and high prices. Two men whose interest in and collections of western Americana were contemporaneous with Streeter were Philip Ashton Rollins and Wagner. Streeter wrote brief articles on Rollins in the *Princeton University Library Chronicle* in 1948 and on Wagner for the *California Historical Society Quarterly* and the *Yale University Library Gazette* in 1957. He considered both men old and dear friends, and his articles, laced with admiration for their acumen as collectors, described some of the exceptional rarities in their respective collections, including Rollins's ranch life and cattle trade titles and Wagner's Philip Nolan papers.

With the sale of his Texas books to Yale and the publication of the fifth and final volume of *Texas Bibliography* in 1960, Streeter began planning for his final contribution to the book world: the dispersal of his Americana collection through auction following his death. This was not a morbid undertaking. Streeter had planned the sale for more than twenty years as a means both of offering libraries an opportunity to strengthen their collections and of giving his fellow enthusiasts a chance at a public sale. He even assured eighteen libraries and institutions with which he had a special connection – including the American Antiquarian Society, the John Carter Brown Library, Harvard and Yale Universities, the New York Historical Society, and the California Historical Society – the means to acquire items at the auction through bequests totaling $414,000 from the proceeds of the sale.

Thomas W. Streeter died on 12 June 1965. The Streeter sale of Americana took place in sessions held between October 1966 and October 1969 at the Parke-Bernet Galleries in New York City. More than five hundred bookmen attended the opening session on 25 October 1966. Bidding was spirited throughout the entire Streeter sale, with prices so spectacular that *Antiquarian Bookman* printed successful bids and bidders in various of its May and November issues for 1966 through 1969. In all, 4,421 lots sold for a total of $3,104,982, breaking every Americana record.

The 7 November 1966 issue of *Antiquarian Bookman* described reactions to the "fantastic" prices offered at the first round of the auction: "Many an old-timer shook his head unbelievably at the brisk bidding in thousands and five thousands, but we noted that it was the old-time hard-headed professional dealers who were paying the prices since they knew that the Streeter sale was a once-in-a-lifetime opportunity." Among the sale's highspots were the Antonio Pigafetta's *Le Voyage et Navigation*, selling for $56,000; the second Plannck edition of the Columbus account for $30,000; the *Constitution of the State of New Mexico* (1850) for $8,500; the Cambridge *Platform* for $80,000 (purchased by Goodspeed's for Harvard, this was at the time the second-highest price ever paid for an American book); the "Northwest Ordinance" for $33,000; Edwards' *Communication* (the first Illinois imprint, 1814) for $30,500; George Washington's *The President's Address to the People of the United States* (1796) for $11,000; Lewis and Clark's *History of the Expedition* for $33,500 (a sale which *Antiquarian Bookman* called "a beautiful price for a beautiful copy!"); and an album of thirty lithographic views of California published by Kuchel and Dressel (1855–1858) for $19,000.

Though dispersed, Streeter's extraordinary Americana collection has been immortalized in the monumental catalogue prepared for the sale: *The Celebrated Collection of Americana Formed by the Late Thomas Winthrop Streeter Morristown, New Jersey Sold by Order of the Trustees* (1966–1969). It stands as both tribute to and legacy of Streeter's collecting, study, energy, and taste during a period of some forty-five years. Its seven volumes, arranged into Streeter's own categories, cover the full canvas of discovery, exploration, settlement, and development of the United States as shown through its imprints. Descriptive notes were based on Streeter's own, drawn from the eighty-seven loose-leaf notebooks, now held by the American Antiquarian Society, that he compiled over the years as he built his famous collection.

Streeter, enormously respected and admired by his friends and colleagues, is remembered as an extraordinary scholar-collector. His collecting and scholarship helped open the American West and Southwest as collecting areas. His Americana collection surpassed all other private American libraries of his day in size, scope, and unifying purpose, and his Texas collection was remarkable for its depth of treatment. His landmark work, *Bibliography of Texas, 1795–1845*, continues to be recognized as a major work in American bibliography and as a preeminent example of regional bibliography.

References:

Archibald Hanna, Jr., "The Thomas W. Streeter Collection," *Yale University Library Gazette*, 31 (April 1957): 147–153;

Howell J. Heaney, "Thomas W. Streeter, Collector, 1883–1965," *Papers of the Bibliographical Society of America*, 65 (1971): 243–256;

Charles F. Heartman, *Thoughts Upon Reading Thomas W. Streeter's North American Regional Bibliographies* (Hattiesburg, Miss.: The Book Farm, 1943);

Kenneth Nebenzahl, "Reflections on Brinley and Streeter," *Papers of the Bibliographical Society of America*, 64 (1970): 165–175;

The Only Located Copies of One Hundred Forty Texas Pamphlets and Broadsides: An Exhibition Marking the Gift of the Thomas W. Streeter Texas Collection by Friends of the Yale University Library (New Haven: Yale University Library, 1957);

"Personal Appreciations of T. W. S.," containing "A Personal Appreciation of T. W. S. by John Carter"; "A Memorial to T. W. S. by Lindley Eberstadt"; "A Memoir of T. W. S. by Archibald Hanna, Jr."; "A Few Recollections, by Michael J. Walsh"; and "Streeter Americana Highlights," *The 1970 AB Bookman's Yearbook, Part Two: The Old & The New* (1970), pp. 5–28;

"Record Highs at Streeter Sale," *AB Bookman's Weekly*, 38 (7 November 1966): 1802;

William S. Reese, "The Bibliographers of Texas," *AB Bookman's Weekly*, 63 (May–June 1979): 4623–4646;

Frank S. Streeter, "Some Recollections of Thomas W. Streeter and His Collecting," *Gazette of the Grolier Club* (1980): 40–50;

Lawrence C. Wroth, "The Americana Library of Thomas Winthrop Streeter," *The 1970 AB Bookman's Yearbook, Part Two: The Old & The New* (1970), pp. 3–4.

Papers:
The Beinecke Library at Yale University houses the Thomas W. Streeter papers, which include research notes, drafts, and proofs relating to his *Bibliography of Texas, 1795–1845*. The American Antiquarian Society holds Streeter's eighty-seven notebooks describing the contents of his Americana collection.

George Ticknor

(1 August 1791 – 26 January 1871)

Laura V. Monti
Boston Public Library

SELECTED BOOKS: *Syllabus of a Course of Lectures on the History and Criticism of Spanish Literature* (Cambridge, Mass.: Hilliard & Metcalf, 1823);

Outlines of the Principal Events in the Life of General Lafayette (Boston: Cummings, Hilliard, 1825);

Remarks on the Life and Writings of Daniel Webster of Massachusetts (Philadelphia: Carey & Lea, 1831);

Lecture on the Best Methods of Teaching the Living Languages. Delivered before the American Institute, August 24, 1832 (Boston: Carter, Hendee, 1833);

History of Spanish Literature, 3 volumes (New York: Harper, 1849; London: John Murray, 1849);

Union of the Boston Athenaeum and the Public Library (Boston: Dutton & Wentworth, 1853);

Papers Discussing the Comparative Merits of Prescott's and Wilson's Histories. Pro. and Con., as Laid before the Massachusetts Historical Society (Boston & Philadelphia, 1861);

Life of William Hickling Prescott (Boston: D. Estes, 1863; Philadelphia: Lippincott, 1863; London: Routledge, 1863).

OTHER: *The Remains of Nathaniel Appleton Hewen*, edited, with a memoir of his life, by Ticknor (Boston: Hilliard, Gray, 1827);

Johann Wolfgang von Goethe, *The Sorrows of Young Werther*, translated by Ticknor, as *George Ticknor's The Sorrows of Young Werther*, University of North Carolina, Studies in Comparative Literature, no. 4, edited, with introduction and critical analysis, by Frank G. Ryder (Chapel Hill, N.C., 1952).

SELECTED PERIODICAL PUBLICATIONS –
UNCOLLECTED: "Annotations on Milton's Paradise Lost," *General Repository and Review*, 2 (1812): 66–84;

"Griscom's Tour in Europe," *North American Review*, 18 (January 1824): 178–192;

"Free Schools of New England," *North American Review*, 19 (October 1824): 448–457;

"Works of Chateaubriand," *American Quarterly Review*, 2 (December 1827): 458–482;

"Memoirs of the Buckminsters," *Christian Examiner*, 47 (September 1849): 169–195;

"Joshua Bates," *American Journal of Education*, 7 (1859): 270–272.

George Ticknor's response to his teaching demands at Harvard College and the needs presented to him when writing his *History of Spanish Literature* (1849) was to assemble a library of some four thousand books and manuscripts dealing with Spanish and Portuguese literature from the fifteenth to the nineteenth century, one of the finest collections in this field assembled in his lifetime. Ticknor bequeathed his library to the Boston Public Library, which he helped establish and which his books did much to enrich.

Born 1 August 1791, the only son of Elisha and Elizabeth Billings Curtis Ticknor, George Ticknor was privileged to be part of a well-established and well-educated family. His father, a successful businessman, and his mother had both been teachers. Ticknor never attended school but was prepared by his father to enter Dartmouth College, where his father had attended. At Dartmouth Ticknor was a serious student of Latin and Greek, and after graduating in 1807 he continued studying these two subjects with Dr. John Gardiner, the rector of Trinity Church in Boston. In 1810 he began reading law at the law office of William Sullivan, son of Gov. James Sullivan, and in 1813 he was admitted to the bar. He practiced for only one year; he was unenthusiastic about a law career, which did not suit his love of learning.

He decided to go to Europe – and especially to Germany – where he planned to continue his study of the classics and of German. After a few weeks in London he began his studies at the University of Göttingen. During his stay in Germany, Harvard offered Ticknor the Smith Chair in Romance Languages. Up until then, however, Ticknor had

George Ticknor; portrait by Thomas Sully, 1828 (Dartmouth College)

not revealed even a slight interest in Romance languages, including Spanish. He wrote to his father from Göttingen on 9 November 1816, discussing how he felt about the offer and asking for his consent. In the letter he reveals his unfamiliarity with Spanish, speaking of it "as a new subject of study to which I have paid no attention since I have been here, and which I have not taken into the plan of my studies and travels in Europe. If I am to be a professor in this literature I must go to Spain." This trip would change his life.

From Germany he went to Italy. In Rome in 1817 he accepted Harvard's offer and began to take instruction in Italian and visit other cities of Italy. From Italy he traveled to Madrid. On 23 May 1818 Ticknor wrote to his father, mentioning that he had read Miguel de Cervantes's *Don Quixote* to his traveling companions from an edition that he presumably bought in Perpignan. It is sometimes said that the cornerstone of the Ticknor collection was the Antwerp 1672–1673 *Don Quixote* given to Ticknor by

James Freeman of King's Chapel as early as 1806; but in fact it was the *Don Quixote* he bought in Perpignan. To this first book were added all the other precious titles in the collection.

On this trip his love for Spain and its books was born. In Ticknor's letter to Mrs. Walter Channing from Madrid dated 25 July 1818 he writes, "There is more national character here, more originality and poetry in the popular manners and feelings, more force without barbarism and civilization without corruption, than I have found anywhere else." He had come to learn Spanish, and he applied himself diligently to his task. Ticknor had a letter of introduction to Jose Antonio Conde, an important member of the Academy of History of Madrid, and convinced him to help him with his Spanish. Conde spent four hours a day with him reading a large portion of the Spanish classics.

In Madrid he saw the rare books and manuscripts at the Escorial, which he described as "a great mine which is yet but imperfectly explored." When

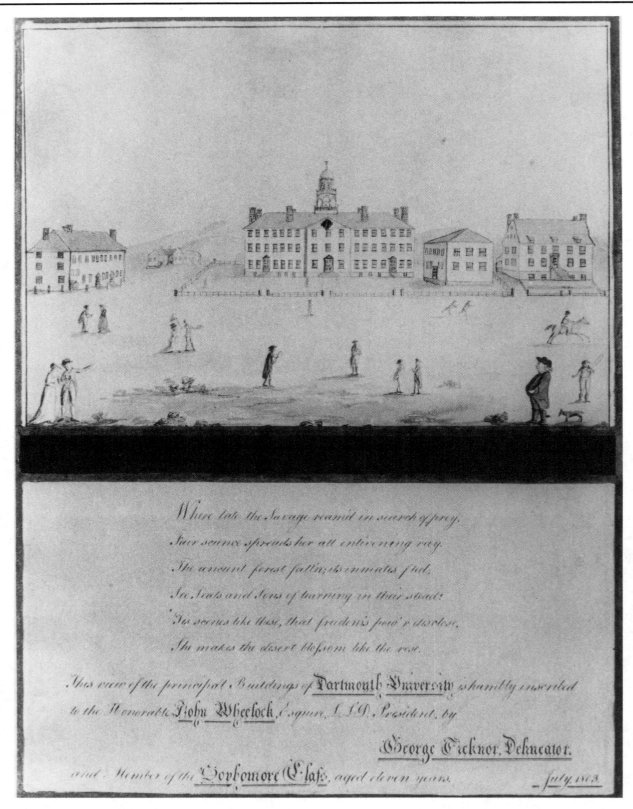

Watercolor of the Dartmouth campus, painted by Ticknor when he was an eleven-year-old sophomore (Dartmouth College)

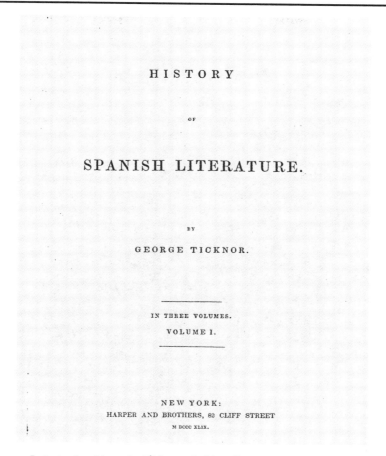

HISTORY

OF

SPANISH LITERATURE.

BY

GEORGE TICKNOR.

IN THREE VOLUMES.
VOLUME I.

NEW YORK:
HARPER AND BROTHERS, 82 CLIFF STREET
M DCCC XLIX.

*In preparing this work, Ticknor relied heavily on his own collection of
Spanish literature.*

visiting the Archivo de Indias he was again impressed by the wealth of stored material that included letters of Hernán Cortés, Sebastian Cabot, and Diego Columbus, son of Christopher Columbus. He also visited the Biblioteca Nacional de Madrid, the library of Seville, and the collections of the count of Osuna, the marquis of Pidal, and many others. He needed books for his classes, and he began to collect the most desirable and rare books with the help of Conde, who, according to Ticknor, "knew the lurking places where such books and their owners are to be found; and to him I am endebted for the foundation of a collection of Spanish literature which without help like his I shall fail to make." Ticknor also described a trip to southern Spain and Portugal, where, he wrote, he purchased "a collection of books in Portuguese belles-lettres and literary history as complete as I could get, because I knew I never could hope to have anything in this language and literature which I did not bring with me."

He returned to Boston in April 1819 and in August assumed his post at Harvard. On 18 Sep-

tember 1821 he married Anna Eliot. In America he continued to increase his Spanish library. When the local book dealers were not able to fill his book orders, he relied on professors and friends not only in Spain but also in England, France, Germany, or any other country from which he received notices about volumes he desired. His persistence in pursuing certain books for his library is evident in his letters to the London bookseller Obadiah Rich and to Pascual de Gayangos. Gayangos was a Spanish intellectual doing research in the British Museum when Ticknor met him during his second trip to London in 1835, the year he resigned from Harvard. From that meeting was born a friendship which brought about years of correspondence that provided notes, books, and information while Ticknor was writing his *History of Spanish Literature,* which he began after his return from his second trip to Europe in 1838.

Nothing illuminates Ticknor's passion for book collecting more than the letters of Ticknor to Gayangos. After *History of Spanish Literature* was pub-

George Ticknor, 1867

lished in 1849, Ticknor wrote a letter dated 26 May 1850 to Gayangos on the subject of Spanish books to be added to his library: "I would say two things. The first is, that of course, I feel less anxiety to buy them than I did before I had finished my *History* . . . still [there] are certain books that must be bought, whenever I can lay my hands upon them if the prices be not what the French called *des prix foux*." On 4 January 1851 Ticknor wrote to Gayangos, "I have determined to stop purchasing Spanish books for a time, and so shall relieve you from my little commissions. . . . The truth is, I am increasing my library in another very different direction." This is a puzzling statement because if he did change direction, it does not appear in his library. It is certain that he continued to buy Spanish works, for as late as 17 August 1869 he was discussing with Gayangos prices of certain Spanish titles.

When the Boston Public Library received Ticknor's library it contained 3,907 volumes including 598 pamphlets and 32 manuscripts that are mostly transcripts from originals found in Europe. Undoubtedly he encountered difficulties in assembling his library, and most of the time he was able to buy only a part of what he wanted, as is revealed in his notes written in the catalogues he used when ordering. In addition to the usual problems of competition and scarcity that all collectors face, Ticknor had to reckon with the consequences of the Inquisition in Spain and Portugal as well as public and even authorial indifference to the fate of important works. Among Ticknor's books are rarities that show traces of burning, cutting, or other expurgations, and he also owned official accounts of auto-da-fé.

In spite of the obstacles, the scope of the collection is amazing. At the time of his collecting, Ticknor's library was surpassed only by the British Museum and the private library of Lord Hollander, which Ticknor visited and admired during his trips to England. His library covers history and letters in editions from the fifteenth to the nineteenth century in a variety of subjects. In the field of early Spanish history he owned editions of the *Cronicas* beginning with the first edition of *Las Siete Partidas* (Zamora: Augustin le Paz and Juan Picardo, 1541), a work originally composed by Alfonso X de Leon y Castilla. Geography and navigation are well represented in the collection. Novels include the first edition of *Don Quixote* (1605-1615) and the long list of works of the prolific writer Cervantes in multiple editions and translations. Ticknor also owned Fernando de Rojas's *La Celestina* (Venice: E. da Sabio, 1534), a highly influential and popular work.

Ticknor's collection of poetry included the 1588 edition of Jorge Manrique's *Coplas* (Alcala de Henares: H. Ramirez), Luis de Góngora y Argote's *Obras* of 1627 (Madrid: Luis Sanchez), as well as other sixteenth- and early-seventeenth-century works by major and minor poets. Spanish drama is represented in the Ticknor collection by Lope Félix de Vega Carpio and Pedro Calderón de la Barca and their multiple *Autos Sacramentales, Dramas,* and *Comedias* in single titles, in early and later compilations. Titles in bibliography, literary history, heraldry, arts and sciences, law and politics, linguistics, and theology were also present in his library. The section of Portuguese literature contains the most distinguished names such as Luíz Vaz de Camoes and his 1613 *Lusiads* (Lisbon: Pedro Crasbeek). This collection also contains compilations in early and later editions of multiple volumes, compilations of the *obras* of a single author or multiple authors and of the *cronicas, autos sacramentales, comedias, dramas,* and *poesia,* such as the *Biblioteca de Autores Espanoles* (1846-1872) in sixty-four volumes or the *Coleccion de Documentos ineditos para la Historia de Espana* (1842-1873) in fifty-four volumes edited by Martin E. De Navarrete, Vincente Salva, and Pedro Saintz de Baranda. Among the manuscripts is the original of *El Castigo sin Venganza* (Madrid, 1631), by Lope de Vega, signed by the author.

One of the rarest books in the Ticknor collection is a copy of the *Cancionero General,* known by the name of the compiler Fernando (or Hernando) del Castillo. Published for the first time in 1511 in Valencia, it contains poems by or attributed to authors from the fifteenth century up to the time of its publication. Representative of the periods it embraces, the *Cancionero General* opens with devotional verses, followed by verses of individual poets and more secular poetry classified by subject matter. The editions before 1540 are of great rarity, as is the one in

the Ticknor collection. Ticknor gives to this copy, which is incomplete, the date of 1535 based on manuscript colophon, but Leo Wiener, who has studied the volume, maintains that it is the 1517 edition, of which only one other copy is known; the other copy is housed in the Bibliothéque Nationale. Adding to the rarity of Ticknor's copy is the fact that it had been expurgated by the Office of the Inquisition. Half of the first and all of the folios, up to folio 17, have been excised. On the first blank of the first folio is an inscription in a contemporary hand, "Este libro esta expurgado por el expurgatorio de Santo Oficio. J. Baptista Martinez." These early editions were destroyed by the Inquisition because the first section of the devotional poems contained works that, while of an ostensibly religious character, offended the church.

The *Obras de Devotion* have disappeared from Ticknor's copy, but they are followed by the verses of well-known poets such as the marqués de Santillana, Juan de Meba, Lopez Perez Guzman, Gómez Manrique, Lope de Zuniga, Diego Lopez de Haro, and Jorge Manrique. The individual poets are followed by the *canciones,* where the names of the most distinguished Spanish gentlemen and poets of the fifteenth century appear. Next come the *romances,* the *invenciones,* a particular form of verses pertaining to chivalry, the *villancicos* of rustic character, the *preguntas,* a series of riddles solved in verse, and the *obras menudas,* verses of minor poets.

Ticknor's varied and comprehensive collection remains one of the most famous for Spanish books. Ticknor's goal as a collector was to build a library responsive to the needs of teaching and writing a history of Spanish literature. His was a working library for scholarly reading; he therefore did not pay attention to the condition of a copy, caring only about what edition he had in his hands and the content of the edition. Almost all of Ticknor's books contain notes written in his own hand which enrich the collection with excellent bibliographic references.

Named to a board of trustees created on 24 May 1852 to study the feasibility of a library in the city of Boston, Ticknor was appointed immediately to a committee of three members. As a member of this committee Ticknor wrote a report with a draft delineating the goals and administration of the library. The report was sent to Baring and Company of London and attracted the attention of Joshua Bates, formerly of Massachusetts and then a member of the company. Bates sent a gift of fifty thousand dollars that was followed by other donations that secured the building and future of the library. It opened on 20 March 1854. Ticknor had been giving books to the library, so Bates asked for his help in selecting the books in Italian and German; Bates himself would secure the French books. The board then sent Ticknor to Europe with the available funds. He met Bates in London and traveled to Leipzig, Berlin, Vienna, Florence, Rome, and Paris, making important purchases. Ticknor made other book-buying trips to Europe, arranging for agents to take charge of acquiring the foreign books needed by the institution and at the same time making connections with distinguished European librarians. A member of the library's board of trustees until 1862, he was elected its president in 1865. He directed his energies to creating a new structure for the Boston Public Library, the McKim Building. It opened its doors in March 1871, two months after the death of its great benefactor on 26 January 1871. Ticknor had appointed his wife in charge of fulfilling his bequest of his collection to the library he was instrumental in building.

Letters:

Life, Letters, and Journals of George Ticknor, edited by George S. Hillard, Mrs. Anna Eliot Ticknor, and Miss Anna Eliot Ticknor, 2 volumes (Boston: J. R. Osgood / London: Sampson Low, 1876);

West Point in 1826, edited by H. Pelham Curtis (Boston, 1886);

George Ticknor's Travels in Spain, edited by George T. Northrup (Toronto: University Library, 1913);

Briefwechsel König Johann von Sachsen mit George Ticknor, edited by Johann Georg (Leipzig & Berlin: Teubner, 1920);

Letters to Pascual de Gayongos; from Originals in the Collection of the Hispanic Society of America, edited by Clara L. Penney (New York: Printed by order of the Trustees, 1927);

"Three Unpublished Letters of George Ticknor and Edward Everett," edited by Arnold Goldman, *British Association for American Studies Bulletin,* 8 (1964): 21–26.

Biographies:

Charles Henry Hart, *Memoir of George Ticknor, Historian of Spanish Literature* (Philadelphia: Numismatic and Antiquarian Society of Philadelphia, 1871);

David B. Tyack, *George Ticknor and the Boston Brahmins* (Cambridge, Mass.: Harvard University Press, 1967).

References:

Ezra S. Gannett, "The Christian Scholar," *Old and New,* 3 (May 1871): 516–522;

Prudence Hannay, "An American Man of Letters," *History Today* (1978): 633–642;

Michael H. Harris and Gerard Spiesler, "Everett, Ticknor, and the Common Man: The Fear of Societal Instability as the Motivation for the Founding of the Boston Public Library," *International Library Review,* 24 (1974): 249–276;

Tommaso Pisanti, "Ticknor in Europe," *Nuova Antologia* (1973): 46–52;

G. S. Plumley, "George Ticknor's Spanish Collection," *Harper's New Monthly Magazine,* 43 (June 1871): 893–896;

Chandler Robbins and George H. Hillard, *Tributes of the Massachusetts Historical Society to the Memory of the Hon. David Sears and George Ticknor* (Boston: Massachusetts Historical Society, 1871);

E. P. Whipple, "George Ticknor," *International Review,* 3 (July/August 1876): 441–461;

James Lyman Whitney, *Catalogue of Spanish and Portuguese Books Bequeathed by George Ticknor* (Boston: Trustees of Boston Public Library, 1879).

Papers:

Dartmouth College owns the largest collection of Ticknor's papers. Other important holdings are located at the Massachusetts Historical Society, Boston Public Library, and the Houghton Library of Harvard University.

Chauncey Brewster Tinker

(22 October 1876 – 16 March 1963)

Susanna Bartmann Pathak
Johns Hopkins University

BOOKS: *The Translations of Beowulf: A Critical Bibliography* (New York: Holt, 1903);

Catalogue of an Exhibition of Manuscripts, First Editions, Early Engravings and Various Literature Relating to Samuel Johnson, 1709–1784 (New Haven: Yale University Library, 1909);

The Salon and English Letters: Chapters on the Interrelations of Literature and Society in the Age of Johnson (New York: Macmillan, 1915);

Young Boswell: Chapters on James Boswell, the Biographer, Based Largely on New Material (Boston: Atlantic Monthly Press, 1922; London: Putnam, 1922);

Nature's Simple Plan: A Phase of Radical Thought in the Mid-Eighteenth Century (Princeton, N. J.: Princeton University Press, 1922);

The University Library: An Address on Alumni Day (New Haven: Yale University, 1925);

Rasselas in the New World (New Haven: Yale University Press, 1925);

The Wedgwood Medallion of Samuel Johnson: A Study in Iconography (Cambridge, Mass.: Harvard University Press, 1926);

A New Portrait of James Boswell, by Tinker and Frederick Albert Pottle (Cambridge, Mass.: Harvard University Press, 1927);

The Good Estate of Poetry (Boston: Little, Brown, 1929);

Addresses Commemorating the One Hundredth Anniversary of the Birth of William Morris, Delivered Before the Yale Library Associates in the Sterling Memorial Library, XXIV October MCMXXXIV, by Tinker and Carl P. Rollins (Stamford, Conn.: Overbrook, 1935);

Painter and Poet: Studies in the Literary Relations of English Painting: The Charles Eliot Norton Lectures for 1937–1938 (Cambridge, Mass.: Harvard University Press, 1938);

The Poetry of Matthew Arnold: A Commentary, by Tinker and Howard Foster Lowry (London & New York: Oxford University Press, 1940);

Essays in Retrospect: Collected Articles and Addresses (New Haven: Yale University Press, 1948).

OTHER: *Select Translations from Old English Poetry,* edited, with prefatory notes, by Albert S. Cook and Tinker (Boston: Ginn, 1902);

Select Translations from Old English Prose, edited by Cook and Tinker (Boston & New York: Ginn, 1908);

John Ruskin, *Selections from the Works of John Ruskin,* edited, with an introductory essay and notes, by Tinker (Boston & New York: Houghton Mifflin, 1908);

Fanny Burney, *Dr. Johnson & Fanny Burney; Being the Johnsonian Passages from the Works of Mme. D'Arblay,* introductory essay and notes by Tinker (New York: Moffat, Yard, 1911);

Letters of James Boswell, collected and edited by Tinker, 2 volumes (Oxford: Clarendon, 1924);

Oration & Poem Delivered at Yale University on the One Hundred and Fiftieth Anniversary of the Society of Phi Beta Kappa, oration by Tinker (New Haven: Yale University Press, 1927);

Henry Cockeram, *The English Dictionarie of 1623,* prefatory note by Tinker (New York: Huntington Press, 1930);

A Catalogue of the Altschul Collection of George Meredith in the Yale University Library, compiled by Bertha Coolidge, with an introduction by Tinker (Boston: D. B. Updike, Merrymount Press, 1931);

James Boswell, *Boswell's Life of Johnson,* introductory essay by Tinker (New York: Oxford University Press, 1933);

Chauncey Brewster Tinker; portrait by Deane Keller (Yale University)

Collection of Rare Books, Manuscripts, and Autograph Letters in English Literature, introductory essay by Tinker (New York: Edgar H. Wells, 1940);

Presentation of the Gold Medal of the American Academy of Arts and Letters to Bruce Rogers, 21 May 1948, address by Tinker (Portland, Maine: Anthoesen Press, 1948);

Matthew Arnold, *The Poetical Works of Matthew Arnold,* edited by Tinker and Howard Foster Lowry (New York: Oxford University Press, 1950); revised as *Arnold: Poetical Works* (New York & London: Oxford University Press, 1963);

Anthony Trollope, *The Duke's Children,* preface by Tinker (London & New York: Oxford University Press, 1954);

John Milton, *Il Penseroso; With the Paintings by William Blake, Together with a Note Upon the Paintings,* note by Tinker (New York: Limited Editions Club, 1954).

TRANSLATION: *Beowolf, Translated out of the Old English* (New York: Newson, 1902; revised, 1912).

SELECTED PERIODICAL PUBLICATIONS –
UNCOLLECTED: "Walpole and Familiar Correspondence," *Yale Review,* 4 (April 1914): 578–589;

"In Praise of Nursery Lore," *Unpopular Review* (October 1916): 338–347;

"The Poetry of Christina Rossetti," *American Church Monthly,* (June 1918): 266–279;

"Authors Who 'Go Out,'" *Atlantic Monthly* (August 1918): 231–234;

"The Asperities of Book-Collecting," *Yale Review,* 9 (1919): 207–209;

Robert B. Adam II, Tinker, William Harris Arnold, and William F. Gable, circa 1920

"The Poet, the Bramble, and Reconstruction," *Atlantic Monthly* (November 1919): 670–673;

"British Poetry Under the Stress of War," *Yale Review,* 9 (July 1920): 714–726;

"The Fall of the Curtain," *Yale Review,* 11 (October 1921): 130–138;

"Pre-Raphaelites and Labor," *Literary Review* (29 July 1922): 833–834;

"The Significance to Yale of the Gift of the Gutenberg Bible," *Yale University Library Gazette,* 1 (1926);

"Arnold's Poetic Plans," *Yale Review,* 22 (June 1933): 782–793;

"The Caliph of Books: A. E. N.," *Atlantic Monthly* (December 1943): 102–106;

"Religion After the War," *Rippon College Alumnus,* 18 (1944): 7–15;

"Newman's Secession, 1845," *Holy Cross Magazine* (October 1945): 302–304;

"Reflections of a Curator," *Yale University Library Gazette,* 23 (1948).

The career of Chauncey Brewster Tinker as a literary scholar fed and directed his passion for book collecting. His books, essays, and articles and the range of his collecting activities illustrate a profound commitment to teaching English literature, a subject he found sublime. He believed books were the means of sharing the best and most pleasurable productions of civilized society. Tinker collected thousands of books not merely to exhibit them but to unite books and scholars. "Is a book a thing to be read," he asked in a 1943 tribute to friend and fellow collector A. Edward Newton, "or is it to be enclosed in a glass case and 'exhibited' like a rare hummingbird for stupid spectators to gape at?" Tinker reasoned that to a scholar, the rare book was "a living voice"; to a rich man it might be no more

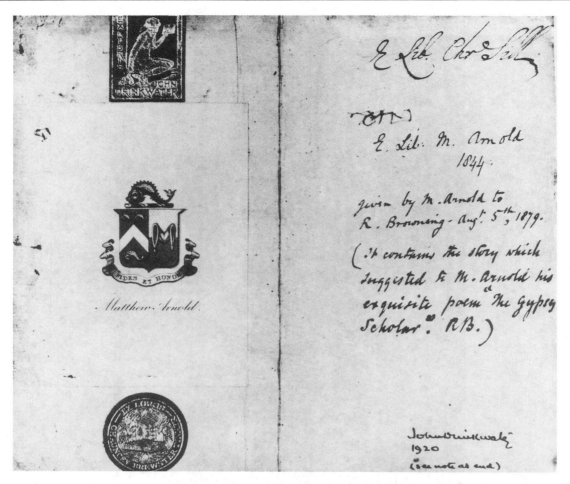

Tinker's bookplate is below those of Matthew Arnold and John Rinkwater in this copy of The Vanity of Dogmatizing *(1661) by Joseph Glanville (Sterling Memorial Library, Yale University).*

than "a costly souvenir." Newton's great triumph, Tinker wrote, was that he understood and shared the enthusiasm of a scholar: "he showed that the men who handle great books must have great abilities."

Chauncey Brewster Tinker was born to Rev. Anson Phelps Tinker and Martha Jane White Tinker in Auburn, Maine, on 22 October 1876. Both parents suffered from tuberculosis, and the family moved to Colorado to improve the parents' health when Tinker was an infant. His mother died of tuberculosis when Tinker was three, and his first stepmother died of a fever six months after her marriage to Tinker's father. Raised by his father's third wife, Tinker grew up in Colorado and attended East Denver High School. "I was by no means an heroic little boy," he wrote years later in a *Saturday Review* article on the subject of ancestor worship. "My great ambition was to be a conductor on the Boston & Maine railway." His announcement that

he would go to college in Boulder was thwarted by his stepmother's reply, "You will go to Yale."

Following family tradition, Tinker entered Yale in 1895 (his father had been a member of Yale's class of 1868). Tinker had in fact been named for one of his father's Yale classmates, Rev. Chauncey Brewster of Connecticut. Tinker's interest and capacities in the study of English literature were evident early in his undergraduate career. He took courses on Geoffrey Chaucer and seventeenth-century English literature taught by William Lyon Phelps. Tinker would later succeed Phelps as the most popular professor of English at Yale. Phelps, a renowned teacher and lecturer, recalled Tinker as being "one of my most brilliant and original pupils."

After receiving a B.A. degree with honors in English literature in 1899, Tinker pursued literary studies at Yale, earning an M.A. degree in 1901. Although intensely interested in the eighteenth century, he followed the advice of his mentor, Albert S.

A page from Tinker's copy of William Wordsworth's Poems *(1807), with revisions by the poet (Sterling Memorial Library, Yale University)*

Tinker in A. Edward Newton's Oak Knoll library, 1935

Cook, and chose *Beowulf* for the subject of his dissertation. *Beowulf* was a sensible choice, Cook reasoned, because "No one will find out anything new about *him*." In 1902 Tinker received his Ph.D in English literature. He returned to the English department as a member of the Yale faculty in 1903 after serving a year as an associate in English at Bryn Mawr College. His teaching career at Yale, interrupted only by service in the Red Cross and military intelligence during World War I, would last more than forty years. It was marked by Tinker's "happy distinction" to excel in both teaching and research.

In the 1920s and 1930s, courses in nineteenth-century poetry and the age of Samuel Johnson would clinch his reputation as one of the century's greatest and most inspiring Yale teachers. Reports of his extraordinary teaching style are abundant, for he had among his many students a plethora of talented future scholars and writers including H. D. Leavitt, Sinclair Lewis, Thornton Wilder, Philip

Barry, Archibald MacLeish, and Stephen Vincent Benét. Wilmarth S. Lewis claimed Tinker could have taught the telephone book and produced an electric effect. A glass eye contributed to Tinker's slightly formidable appearance, and his grave and often dramatic entrance into the lecture hall produced a tension in the classroom and in the lecturer himself that, as Herman W. Liebert observed in his remembrance of Tinker, "made all his lectures memorable."

Tinker took even the most valuable books and manuscripts from his collection to the undergraduate lecture hall and to the seminar room for students to inspect and savor. Graduate students would be given manuscripts or letters from Tinker's personal collection and asked to report on the bibliographic problems they posed or some other scholarly point. "What, pray, are the books for?" Tinker would ask of anyone who might question his practices.

The first of the dozens of scholarly books and editions Tinker produced were on Old English literature and emphasized his determination to make books more accessible to readers. *Beowulf, Translated out of the Old English* (1902) appeared the same year he received his Ph.D. The aim of his translation, Tinker states in his preface, was to make a simple, less archaic, and more readable version of the poem which would nonetheless be consistent with the character of the original. In a preface to the 1912 revised edition Tinker explains that he has added footnotes and altered the text "to increase the simplicity and intelligibility of the rendering." *The Translations of Beowulf: A Critical Bibliography* (1903), based on Tinker's dissertation, was written to be a useful contribution to bibliography by giving a historical and critical account of all nineteenth-century translations of Beowulf.

Next Tinker was engaged in producing the first of several editions of Old English literature, *Select Translations From Old English Prose* (1908), which he and Cook edited together. Later, the popularity of their Old English prose volume and the wish to make pre-Chaucerian poetry accessible to intelligent and curious students resulted in Cook and Tinker's bringing out a revised edition of *Select Translations From Old English Poetry* in 1926 (first published in 1903). The editors state in their preface that Old English poetry, which at its best was characterized by a sense of reality and a sense of reverence, should be translated and "drawn from the cabinets of professional scholars into the light of day." The desire of Tinker the scholar to democratize literature by making it accessible and intelligible to students and general readers was shared by Tinker the collector.

In November 1909 Tinker arranged an exhibition at the Yale University Library for the bicentennial of Johnson's birth and wrote his first exhibition catalogue for the event. The Johnson exhibition, along with Tinker's course on "The Age of Johnson," were ultimately responsible for a growing interest in Johnson and his circle in the United States. While planning the 1909 exhibition of Johnson materials, Tinker had gone to Buffalo, New York, to meet Robert B. Adam, owner of an enviable collection of Johnson and James Boswell materials. Adam had obliged by lending Tinker books from his collection for the exhibition. Tinker's interest in collecting eighteenth-century books and manuscripts grew with their friendship during the next decade. Tinker counseled Adam and alerted him to purchases; Adam lent Tinker books and manuscripts, some of which helped Tinker with his work on Boswell's correspondence.

After World War I Tinker was at work on *Young Boswell: Chapters on James Boswell, the Biogra-*

pher, Based Largely on New Material (1922), which he dedicated to Adam. The endeavor led to his remarkable contributions to Boswell studies in the 1920s and secured his reputation as a scholar. His reputation and instincts as a collector were further developed during these years as well. He became acquainted with such book dealers as A. S. W. Rosenbach, James F. Drake, and Edgar H. Wells as he added to his eighteenth- and nineteenth-century book and manuscript collection.

In 1920 Tinker placed an advertisement in the *Times Literary Supplement* in an effort to substantiate the existence of a collection of papers Boswell had reportedly placed in an ebony cabinet. Tinker received an anonymous tip that he "try Malahide castle" outside of Dublin. At the urging of friend and fellow book collector Newton, Tinker in 1925 traveled to Dublin to meet with the sixth lord Talbot de Malahide, a Boswell descendant. Lord Talbot and his wife, however, were not moved by Tinker's plea to make the papers available to scholars. "It is sometimes difficult for . . . a scholar to avoid a feeling of resentment that a man should have got his hands upon a book of which he knows next to nothing . . . and can make no intelligent use," wrote Tinker in 1943, no doubt recalling his visit with Lord Talbot. Eventually Newton was able to help Lt. Col. Ralph Heywood Isham purchase a large share of the papers for £13,000. Litigation, however, prevented the bulk of Boswell's papers from becoming easily accessible to scholars until 1949, when Yale University Library purchased the collection for $450,000.

In 1925 seventy-five copies of *Rasselas in the New World* were printed. In this small but important work Tinker speaks as both critic and collector in his attempt to reevaluate Johnson's didactic romance, *The History of Rasselas, Prince of Abyssinia* (1759), in light of what new Boswell scholarship had revealed. Tinker gives an account of various descriptions of American editions of Johnson's moral fable in order to substantiate his claim that *Rasselas* has "triumphed over its shortcomings, and achieved immortality in spite of a number of defects, which, it might seem, would have consigned it to oblivion."

The greatest benefactor of Tinker's passion for uniting books and readers was the Yale University Library. In 1924 Tinker addressed Yale alumni, urging them to work to build the library's collections. The crux of his argument was powerfully and succinctly phrased: "Without books — without, that is, the recorded thought of the past — no university and, indeed, no civilization is possible." Yale had been "cradled in a library," and if the library, as center and source of Yale's intellectual life, was to become one of the best in the country, it needed to contain "millions of volumes, with strange books in it, out-of-the-way books, rare books, expensive books." After stating that the financial status of the library required "instant attention," Tinker challenged his audience: "if you do not wish Yale to be lost in the crowd, you must spend more annually for books." He recounted the library's strengths in history, classics, and Oriental and German literatures and then suggested that each alumnus become personally responsible for discovering one of the weaker sections of the library and filling it – a "human and romantic" approach to strengthening Yale's malnourished collections. The alumni, led by Frank Altshul, responded by forming the Yale Library Associates.

Though Tinker enjoyed building his private collection, he was more enthusiastic at the thought of developing Yale's collections, for as he writes in his 1948 essay, "Reflections of a Curator," he "recognized their peculiar value to scholars." In the 1926 first issue of the *Yale University Library Gazette,* Tinker commented on the library's acquisition of one of nine known Gutenberg Bibles in America. He called the gift significant in part because Yale had become a custodian of the precious book "on behalf of posterity," and, just as important, because it would prompt "an ever-increasing flow of gifts of this sort." Ultimately, the combination of strong scholarly interests and a love of teaching made him a brilliant curator for the university library, a role which made the fullest use of his singular personality and talents. Shortly after the library's Rare Book Room opened in 1931, he was appointed keeper of rare books, a title he retained after he retired from teaching in 1945.

In assessing his role as keeper of rare books, Tinker stated that he was "obliged to serve the library as best I could with my left hand." Tinker describes his service in the Rare Book Room in "Reflections of a Curator": "I come crashing in at any hour of the day [and] suddenly demand that Mr. Wing cable for a book costing fifty pounds or so. Work must be interrupted to keep me quiescent . . . bibliographies and lists must be examined to find out whether [a book] is really as rare and important as I have represented it." Marjorie Wynne, who worked with Tinker in the Rare Book Room in the 1940s, claimed that "for sheer charm, amusement, inspiration, and style, laced with a touch of drama, nobody could equal CBT."

In addition to helping the library acquire rare and important books, Tinker saw to it that the books were properly cared for and that no one, not even the "ardent researcher," be permitted to "use them up." Yet he disliked the notion that the Rare Book Room was a treasure room, claiming instead that "it is only a symbol and a segment of a vast institution charged with preserving and transmitting to others the means of scholarly activity." As keeper he did everything in his power to bring scholar and book together.

The scholars, collectors, and alumni Tinker urged to give their collections to university libraries had no greater example than Tinker himself. His dictate was simple: "Great collections formed by individuals must ultimately come into libraries like our own." The Tinker collection, coming as it did to Yale in snatches over the years, comprises much more than the thirty-five hundred items. The collection was particularly strong in Matthew Arnold, Oliver Goldsmith, Robert Browning, John Ruskin, Percy Bysshe Shelley, George Gordon, Lord Byron, Dante and Christina Rosetti, Alfred Tennyson, Algernon Charles Swinburne, William Morris, and, naturally, Johnson and Boswell. Of the hundreds of authors represented in the Tinker collection, however, some of the editions were rare and important, and others simply were needed to fill gaps in Yale's literature collections. The Tinker collection is invaluable too for its decades of correspondence between Tinker and the leading American and British booksellers and collectors of the day. These letters, often sparkling with wit, record transactions which always seem to transcend mere business.

By 1933, when an edition of Boswell's *Life of Johnson* with an introduction by Tinker was published by the Oxford University Press, Tinker's work as a Boswell scholar for the most part had come to a close, and he became occupied with the study of poetry. This shift in his scholarly interests was reflected in his intense efforts to build the library's collection of nineteenth-century British writers, including Swinburne, Browning, Byron, scores of minor writers, and most emphatically, Arnold, whose solitary spirit and quest for self-knowledge Tinker found compelling. Among Tinker's most impressive acquisitions were Arnold's diaries for 1845–1847. Tinker did not entirely abandon his interest in Johnson, however.

In 1937 Tinker went to Harvard to give the Norton lectures on the subject of poetic painting in England. These much-admired lectures were on the close relation of poetry to works by seven English painters, including William Hogarth, Sir Joshua Reynolds, Thomas Gainsborough, Richard Wilson, and William Blake. The lectures and nearly seventy illustrations were published by Harvard University Press the following year. In 1940 Tinker published *The Poetry of Matthew Arnold: A Commentary,* a companion volume to the complete *Poetical Works of Matthew Arnold* he hoped to bring out with Howard Foster Lowry the following year; but the edition of Arnold's poetry did not appear until 1950. Tinker also wrote an introduction to a 1940 exhibition-and-sale catalogue of rare English books, manuscripts, and letters for Edgar Wells. The introduction, which is essentially a treatise on the modern collector, was written as "a trifling expression of gratitude" for the many courtesies shown Tinker by the seven London booksellers offering their collections for sale.

In 1945 Tinker retired as Sterling Professor of English Literature after fifty years of teaching, writing, and lecturing. He continued to play an active role as keeper of rare books for some years, however. Yale bestowed on him an honorary doctorate in 1946. In 1948 Tinker presented a gold medal to Bruce Rogers for the American Academy of Arts and Letters. Rogers had produced Tinker's most beautiful book, *The Wedgwood Medallion of Samuel Johnson: A Study in Iconography* (1926). Rogers was also instrumental in planning a Limited Editions Club edition of John Milton's "Il Penseroso" and "L'Allegro" (*Il Penseroso; With the Paintings by William Blake, Together with a Note Upon the Paintings,* 1954), with Tinker writing the notes on Blake's illustrations. Tinker's writings, especially the essays and scores of book reviews, are characterized by wit and grace. The 1948 collection *Essays in Retrospect: Collected Articles and Addresses* is but a sample of the clarity and eloquence of his prose and intellect.

In 1955 Tinker was awarded the Yale Alumni Medal for his outstanding contributions to the university. The citation read in part: "He has embellished the Library, made Yale the leading center of studies in the 18th Century – and when need arose, even taught us our manners. . . . He taught us so well that he changed our lives." It was at this event, Tinker's last major public appearance at Yale, that he make his famous statement when asked how he would like to be remembered: "My students are my jewels."

Tinker's health declined gradually. Arteriosclerosis disease thwarted his intellectual vigor and dimmed his forceful personality, although he remained a Fellow of Davenport College until 1958. His final years were spent with his sister in Wethersfield, Connecticut; he died of a stroke on 16 March 1963 at the age of eighty-six. As his friend and colleague Herman W. Liebert recalled: "Tink was a better scholar than many collectors, a better collector than most scholars, and a better teacher than anyone of his time. His influence in all three of these roles continues to bear fruit."

Bibliography:

Robert F. Metzdorf, *The Tinker Library: A Bibliographical Catalogue of the Books and Manuscripts Collected by Chauncey Brewster Tinker* (New Haven: Yale University Library, 1959).

References:

The Age of Johnson: Essays Presented to Chauncey Brewster Tinker, edited by F. W. Hilles (New Haven: Yale University Press, 1949);

David Buchanan, *The Treasure of Auchinleck: The Story of the Boswell Papers* (New York: McGraw-Hill, 1974);

Allen T. Hazen and Edward L. McAdam, *Catalogue of an Exhibition of First Editions of the Works of Samuel Johnson in the Library of Yale University* (New Haven: Yale University Library, 1935);

Mary Hyde, "Adam, Tinker, and Newton," in *Johnson and His Age,* edited by James Engell (Cambridge, Mass.: Harvard University Press, 1984), pp. 285–307;

Hyde, "Boswell's Ebony Cabinet," in *Studies in the 18th Century III,* edited by R. F. Brissenden and J. C. Eade (Toronto: University of Toronto Press, 1976), pp. 21–35;

Wilmarth S. Lewis, "Chauncey Brewster Tinker, *Yale Library Gazette,* 170 (July 1963): 1–2;

Herman W. Liebert, "Chauncey Brewster Tinker 1876–1963," *Yale Alumni Magazine* (May 1963): 18–20;

Maxwell Luria and Richard E. Brewer, "The Caliph and the Professor: A. Edward Newton's Correspondence with Chauncey Brewster Tinker," *Harvard Library Bulletin* (Spring 1985): 114–173;

William Lyon Phelps, "Chauncey Brewster Tinker, '99," *Yale Alumni Weekly* (1926): 423–424;

Marjorie G. Wynne, *The Rare Book Collections at Yale: Recollections, 1942–1987* (New York: Trustees of Columbia University, 1988).

Papers:

Tinker's papers and much of the Tinker Collection are at the Beinecke Rare Book and Manuscript Library, Yale University.

B. George Ulizio

(2 February 1889 – 29 September 1969)

Dean H. Keller
Kent State University

and

Matthew J. Bruccoli
University of South Carolina

B. George Ulizio's copy of the first edition of *Sister Carrie* (1900) bears Theodore Dreiser's inscription citing the collector's "vigorous and forthright approach to life." Dreiser indulged in understatement. Ulizio's capacity to dominate all of his endeavors is documented by his bibliophilia. A self-made man, he was a self-made bookman.

Born in New Haven, Connecticut, on 2 February 1889, Ulizio attended parochial schools. After working as a waiter in New York he became a Wall Street runner. He was wounded in World War I and in his late years required the use of two canes. During the 1920s he was operating in Atlantic City, New Jersey, and Philadelphia as a real-estate and bond broker. His other activities included play bookings (*What Price Glory?*), sports promotion (he built the stadium at Boyle's Thirty Acres for the Dempsey-Carpentier "Battle of the Century"), and the Republican party (he was campaign manager for Sen. Joseph Freylinghuysen of New Jersey). He was also the subject of newspaper headlines: "Ulizio Held Bankrupt," "New Marital Web Entangles Ulizio," "$25,000 Is Awarded in Alienation Suit," "Dempsey's Manager Sued." He was arrested and released after beating a man who was abusing a horse.

There is no record of how Ulizio caught the book-collecting virus, but the endeavor obviously appealed to his highly developed competitive instinct. The 1920s were an era of great collectors and great book auctions. Philadelphia was a bookselling center with the shops of Charles Sessler and A. S. W. Rosenbach; however, Ulizio was not a Rosenbach customer because, as he said, "Rosenbach thought I was a sucker." The notable collectors A. Edward Newton, John C. Eckel, and Morris Parrish resided in the area, and Ulizio was on friendly terms with them. Newton wrote in *This Book Collecting Game* (1928):

I had unsuccessfully sought this edition [Herman Melville's *The Whale*] for years, and had just about made-up my mind to live and die without a copy of this excessively scarce book when I heard that a rival collector, B. George Ulizio of Atlantic City, had one. Knowing that money would not tempt him to part with it, I wrote and suggested an exchange. He declined what I offered, but added, "Since you want *The Whale* so badly, I am sending it to you with my compliments." I believe this incident to be unique in book-collecting annals.

In 1932 Ulizio donated some sixty volumes of Newton's writings to the Library of Congress and almost immediately began to collect his works again; there were thirty-one Newton items in the Ulizio collection in 1969. Ulizio's collecting rationale was typical of the time. He acquired what his friends and rivals were collecting: high spots of English and American literature, association copies, books signed by presidents, historical letters, first books, Charles Dickens, and the then-fashionable moderns. He did not depart from the traditional paths of book collecting, but Ulizio was not simply a book buyer. He knew his books thoroughly and could discuss their bibliographic significance.

His most extraordinary acquisition was a collection of duplicate copyright deposit copies. By law publishers are required to deposit in the Library of Congress two copies of each book published in America. The curator of rare books at that time, V. Valta Parma, decided to dispose of duplicate deposit copies in exchange for volumes that the Library of Congress lacked. Ulizio thereby acquired such deposit copies as Ralph Waldo Emerson's *Nature* (1836), Walt Whitman's *Two Rivulets* (1876), Louisa May Alcott's *Hospital Sketches* (1863), Bret Harte's *The Luck of Roaring Camp* (1870), and Robert Montgomery Bird's *Nick of the Woods* (1837). The Whitman has three inked-in corrections. Fifty-six of

B. George Ulizio (Kent State University Library)

those deposit copies were retained by Ulizio; they testify to his taste as well as to his understanding of their bibliographic value.

During his lifetime Ulizio disposed of four libraries – in whole or in part. His most distinguished library was the English literature material sold at the American Art Association/Anderson Galleries in January 1931. It has not been determined whether the decision to sell was dictated by postcrash financial considerations or that he decided that it was time to cash in. This sale was touted as the most important since the legendary Jerome Kern sale in 1929. The foreword by Eckel, a Dickens bibliographer, emphasizes the strength of Ulizio's Dickens holdings:

> Undeniably the outstanding book by Dickens is the "Pickwick" in parts. It is one of the fourteen prime copies which thus far have been stamped with the approval of bibliographers and experts in that field of rare book knowledge. It was the first "Pickwick" owned by the late George Barr McCutcheon and was traded by him to Gabriel Wells, who made the improvement which has given it deserved classification. It has the rare earliest

advertisement in Part VI (a belated bibliographical discovery made when the Kern copy came under observation). A fuller collation is given in the catalogue description of this noted book. An added feature in Mr. Ulizio's copy is a fragment of the manuscript. Of close secondary interest is the American Edition in parts. This is complete in every detail, in remarkably fine condition, and of the utmost rarity – far rarer, in point of actual fact, than its more famous English brother.

A collection of Dickens which includes all the great novels in parts, including "A Tale of Two Cities" and "Oliver Twist," carries an assurance which obviates extravagance of description. Such an aggregation of books supplies its own eloquence. Unusual rarities are present: "The Library of Fiction," in the fourteen parts; a very fine copy of Dickens' first book, "Sketches by Boz"; "Evenings of a Workingman" with a letter from Dickens to John Overs, the author, referring him to a publisher, and naming Newby, who issued the little volume; the "Christmas Books" in original cloth; the rare pamphlets of the General Theatrical Fund; "No Thoroughfare," privately printed, a Presentation Copy from Wilkie Collins, with notations by him; the real First Edition of "Hunted Down" in red cloth: these are among the leaders. Altogether there are ninety-seven catalogue numbers in this comprehensive collection.

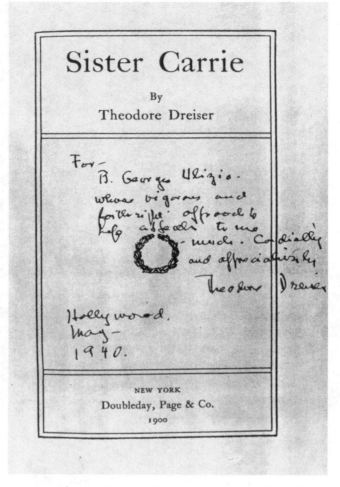

Copy of Theodore Dreiser's first novel, inscribed to Ulizio (Kent
State University Library)

Although it included many great volumes, the Ulizio collection did not have the concentration of association items that were the glory of the Kern sale. Moreover, the timing was bad: the big spenders of 1929 had retrenched in 1931. The 1,084 lots brought a disappointing total of $60,724: an average of $56 against the Kern average of $1,165. Since the lots were grouped, there were some 2,900 books in the Ulizio sale. Only five items broke $1,000: Dickens's *Library of Fiction* (1836–1837) in parts, $1,600; *The Pickwick Papers* (1836–1837) in parts, with a fragment of the manuscript, $13,000 (the Kern copy brought $28,000); the first American *Pickwick* (1836–1838) in parts, $2,500; *Oliver Twist* (1837–1838) in parts, $1,400; and Edward Gibbon's *The Decline and Fall of the Roman Empire* (1776–1788), $1,150. The 97 Dickens lots totaled $23,838. This sale had representative groups of the late-nineteenth- and early-twentieth-century English authors

then in collecting vogue: James M. Barrie, 42 lots (including one of the 50 copies of *The Allahakbarrie Book of Broadway Cricket,* 1899); Joseph Conrad, 28; John Galsworthy, 31; George Gissing, 24; Thomas Hardy, 48; Rudyard Kipling, 110 (*Departmental Ditties,* 1886, brought $925); George Moore, 22; Bernard Shaw, 55; James Stephens, 21; Oscar Wilde, 24; Robert Louis Stevenson, 81 (*The Penland Rising,* 1866, brought $875 and *The New Arabian Nights,* 1882, $700).

At the time of the 1931 sale it was announced that an auction of the Ulizio American literature library would follow that year, but he cancelled it. The second Ulizio auction was held at American Art/Anderson in 1935. The 344 lots of English and American literature brought only $4,625.50 ($13.45 per lot). The star item was Samuel Clemens's *Tom Sawyer* (1876) at $230. Oliver Wendell Holmes's *History of the American Stereoscope* (1869) – the first

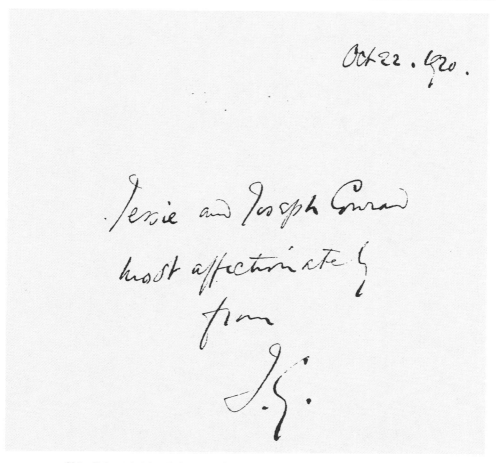

John Galsworthy's inscription to the Conrads in the dedication copy of In Chancery

copy ever auctioned – brought $110. A two-page Thomas Jefferson ALS attacking Alexander Hamilton and commenting on the first New York financial panic reached $120. Washington Irving letters went begging. Ulizio undoubtedly bought some of his own books at the sale, for some of the catalogued items were in his last collection. These two sales did not mark the termination of Ulizio's collecting activities. He continued to acquire extraordinary items. In 1940 he unsuccessfully negotiated for the purchase of Dreiser's manuscripts. *Moby-Dick* (1851) was acquired at the 1941 Newton sale. The dedication copy of Galsworthy's *In Chancery* (1920) inscribed to Joseph and Jessie Conrad, was purchased in the 1950s. There was a third Ulizio sale after World War II – in New Jersey – at which he was compelled to stop the slaughter. No copy of the catalogue has been located.

Ulizio recovered from his financial difficulties in the 1930s and was well off in his later years. His library and study occupied one floor of his Haddonfield, New Jersey, house. In addition to the

books and prints, there was a wall of bottles in straw wrappings, from the purchase of the cellar of an Atlantic City hotel when Prohibition was enacted.

Like all serious bibliophiles, Ulizio was concerned about the placement of his last library, which held some fifteen hundred volumes and many treasures. In 1969 Hyman W. Kritzer, director of the Kent State University Library, and Dean Keller, curator of special collections, successfully negotiated for the acquisition of the books and literary material in the Haddonfield house. This purchase formed the basis for an expanded effort to support the university's drive to establish itself as a major research institution in Ohio. The Ulizio books matched the university library's plan to concentrate on nineteenth- and twentieth-century literature in the English language.

It is remarkable that so many distinguished books remained after the auctions. There were 24 Willa Cather volumes; 18 volumes of Stevenson; a copy of *Huckleberry Finn* (1884) with a letter from Clemens to Ulysses S. Grant; 31 volumes of Lewis

SALE NUMBER 3883
PUBLIC EXHIBITION FROM THURSDAY, JANUARY TWENTY-SECOND

THE LIBRARY OF

B. GEORGE ULIZIO
PINE VALLEY, N. J.

SOLD BY HIS ORDER

[PART I]
FIRST EDITIONS OF
ENGLISH AUTHORS

UNRESTRICTED PUBLIC SALE
WEDNESDAY & THURSDAY
JANUARY 28, 29, AT 8:15
AND FRIDAY, JANUARY 30
AT 2:15 AND 8:15

AMERICAN ART ASSOCIATION
ANDERSON GALLERIES · INC.
30 EAST 57TH STREET
NEW YORK CITY
1931

Title page for the catalogue of the Ulizio collection auctioned in 1931
(Kent State University Library)

Carroll, reflecting the influence of Morris Parrish; 25 volumes of Robert S. Frost, mainly collected by Ulizio's daughter Patricia who also collected Pulitzer Prize volumes; 35 Kate Greenaway books, including a complete run of the *Almanacks* from 1883 to 1897. The Ulizio-Kent copy of Edgar Allan Poe's *Tales of the Grotesque and Arabesque* (1840) may be the dedication copy. Poe dedicated the work to Philadelphian William Drayton; on the title page of both volumes is written – but not in Poe's hand – "From the Author to Wm. Drayton."

When B. George Ulizio died on 29 September 1969, his last collection had been transferred to Kent State University in Kent, Ohio, where they are housed in the library's Department of Special Collections and Archives. These books were integrated with remarkable ease into the recently established collection policy for special collections. They substantially augmented collections of nineteenth- and twentieth-century English and American literature already begun by the library or formed the basis for collections in those fields that were to be developed to support the mission of the university.

A selection of 104 titles from the Ulizio collection formed the exhibition that was held in April 1971 to mark the dedication of Kent's new library building. The catalogue that was published on that occasion was arranged in six sections: "Copyright Deposit Copies"; "Association and Presentation Copies"; "English Literature"; "American Literature"; "First Books"; and "Miscellaneous Works."

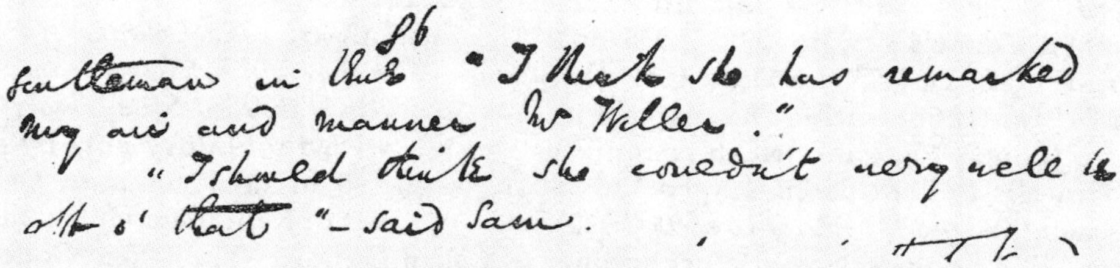

[handwritten manuscript fragment]

REDUCED FACSIMILE OF
A FRAGMENT OF THE ORIGINAL AUTOGRAPH MS.

[NUMBER 193]

A MAGNIFICENT COPY OF THE FIRST ISSUE OF "PICKWICK" WITH A FRAGMENT OF THE ORIGINAL AUTOGRAPH MANUSCRIPT

193 [DICKENS (CHARLES).] The Posthumous Papers of the Pickwick Club. Edited by "Boz." *With illustrations by Robert Seymour, R. W. Buss, and H. K. Browne.* London, 1836-7

13,000 *JBr.*

20 parts in nineteen, 8vo, original wrappers, uncut (backs repaired; name on front wrapper of Part XVIII and small ink spot on front wrapper of Part VIII). In a red crushed levant morocco solander case, gilt tooled; the whole enclosed in a second red morocco solander case.

A MAGNIFICENT COPY OF THE FIRST EDITION OF "PICKWICK", IN THE ORIGINAL PARTS, WITH ADVERTISEMENTS, MEETING ALL OF MR. ECKEL'S ELEVEN REQUIRED POINTS, WITH FURTHER POINTS OF ISSUE AS DESCRIBED BELOW. This was the first McCutcheon copy, sold by him because of the difficulty experienced in perfecting Part II, then defective. Since then, A PERFECT PART II HAS BEEN SUBSTITUTED, AND THE FIRST McCUTCHEON COPY TAKES ITS PLACE HIGH AMONG THE RANKS OF MR. ECKEL'S FAMOUS FOURTEEN.

ALL OF THE WRAPPERS ARE IN THE EARLIEST STATE, all are dated 1836, and those for Parts I-III bear the correct wording relating to the illustrations. The inside back wrapper of Part VIII has the very scarce John Horner advertisement, removed in later printings. The front wrappers of Parts IV and VI are inscribed in a contemporary hand: "*With the Publisher's Compliments*".

THE TEXT IN PARTS II, III, XII, XIII, AND XVI IS IN THE EARLIEST STATE, OR FROM THE FIRST PRINTING, revealing the errors and variants noted by Mr. George W. Davis. That of Part I has the pecularities noted by Mr. Davis as those of a later printing. In Part VI the two lines of the refrain, in the first verse of Mrs. Hunter's poem, are set in alignment.

ALL OF THE PLATES (except Nos. 28 and 41, "The Card Room at Bath" and "Mr. Weller and his Friends") ARE IN THEIR FIRST STATES. Plates 26 and 27 ("The Valentine" and "The Trial Scene") are present in both First and Second State, the First States laid in.

THE ADVERTISEMENTS IN PARTS I, II, IV, VIII, XI, XIII, XIV, XVI, AND XVIII AGREE IN EVERY DETAIL WITH MR. ECKEL'S COLLATION OF THE BRUTON COPY. (Part IV, of course, contains the First "Pickwick Advertiser". THIS IS IN ITS FIRST STATE, with the street-number in Murray's address missing. Part XI, in the "Pickwick Advertiser", contains THE FIRST MENTION OF DICKENS' NAME AS THE AUTHOR OF THE "PICKWICK PAPERS".)

The remaining parts present the following variations from the Bruton collation (chosen by reason of its accessibility):

Part III: Contains the Toilet advertisement, THE FIRST PAID ADVERTISEMENT TO APPEAR IN "THE PICKWICK PAPERS".

Part V: The "Pickwick Advertiser" is present in duplicate. THE VERY RARE FOLDING ADVERTISEMENT OF ROWLAND'S PRODUCTS IS PRESENT.

Part VI: CONTAINS GRATTAN'S 4-P. ADVERTISEMENT IN THE NEWLY DISCOVERED FIRST STATE, as in Part V of the Kern Copy. Later, to prevent duplication of copy, p. 4 was cancelled and announcements of the Memoires of Bourrienne and Mme. Junot substituted for that of Gilbert's map. (The second state of this advertisement may be seen in Part V of the present copy.) THE PRESENT COPY AND THE KERN COPY APPEAR TO BE THE ONLY

[DESCRIPTION CONCLUDED ON SECOND PAGE FOLLOWING]

28

Catalogue entry for Ulizio's copy of The Pickwick Papers *by Charles Dickens which brought $13,000 at the American Art Association /Anderson Galleries, New York, in 1931*

Like many of the collectors of his time, Ulizio enjoyed collecting authors' first books, and a section of the catalogue was devoted to them. He had Cather's *April Twilights* (1903), a fine unopened copy of Stephen Crane's *Maggie* (1893), Hardy's *Desperate Remedies* (1871), William Dean Howells's *Poems of Two Friends* (1860) – which he shared with fellow Ohioan John F. Piatt and which contains a letter from Howells to Platt dated 2 April 1867 – and W. Somerset Maugham's *Liza of Lambeth* (1897), among others. The books selected for exhibition not only demonstrated the scope and depth of Ulizio's work as a collector, but they pointed the way in which they would be used by scholars.

In the history of book collecting it is often the case that the intelligent and persistent private collector is out in front of institutional collectors in building important collections. B. George Ulizio was an example of that kind of personal collector, and the use of his collection since it came to Kent State University is testimony to that phenomenon.

References:

The B. George Ulizio Collection of English & American Literature: An Exhibition on the Occasion of the Dedication of the Kent State Library, April 9 & 10, 1971, with a prefatory note by Hyman W. Kritzer and an introduction by Dean H. Keller (Kent, Ohio: Kent State University Libraries, 1971);

Paul DuBois, "The Ulizio Collection: A Catalogue of Deposit Copies," *Serif,* 7 (September 1970): 35–51;

First Editions of English and American Authors . . . , sale #3883 (New York: American Art Association/Anderson Galleries, 1935);

The Library of B. George Ulizio. Part I: First Editions of English Authors, sale #4194 (New York: American Art Association/Anderson Galleries, 1931).

Henry R. Wagner

(27 September 1862 – 28 March 1957)

Ward Ritchie

BOOKS: *Irish Economics: 1700-1783. A Bibliography with Notes* (London: Davie, 1907);

The Plains and the Rockies: A Contribution to the Bibliography of Original Narratives of Travel and Adventure, 1800-1865 (San Francisco: Howell, 1920; revised, 1921); revised and enlarged by Charles L. Camp as *Henry R. Wagner's The Plains and the Rockies: A Bibliography of Original Narratives of Travel and Adventure, 1800-1865* (San Francisco: Grabhorn Press, 1937); revised by Camp as *The Plains and the Rockies: A Bibliography of Original Narratives of Travel and Adventure* (Columbus, Ohio: Long's College Book Co., 1953);

California Imprints, August 1846–June 1851 (Berkeley, Cal.: Privately printed, 1922);

The Spanish Southwest, 1542-1794, an Annotated Bibliography (Berkeley: Gillick, 1924; revised edition, 2 volumes, Albuquerque: Quivira Society, 1937);

Sir Francis Drake's Voyage around the World: Its Aims and Achievements (San Francisco: Howell, 1926);

Spanish Voyages to the Northwest Coast of America in the Sixteenth Century (San Francisco: California Historical Society, 1929);

Spanish Explorations in the Strait of Juan de Fuca (Santa Ana, Cal.: Fine Arts Press, 1933);

The Cartography of the Northwest Coast of America to the Year 1800, 2 volumes (Berkeley: University of California Press, 1937);

Mexican Imprints, 1544-1600, in the Huntington Library: An Exhibition (San Marino, Cal.: Huntington Library, 1939);

Collecting, Especially Books (Los Angeles: Anderson, 1941);

Juan Rodríguez Cabrillo, Discoverer of the Coast of California (San Francisco: California Historical Society, 1941);

Bullion to Books: Fifty Years of Business and Pleasure (Los Angeles: Zamorano Club, 1942);

The Rise of Fernando Cortés (Los Angeles: Cortés Society, 1944);

Nueva Bibliografía Mexicana del Siglo XVI: Suplemento a las Bibliografías de Don Joaquín García Icazbalceta, Don José Toribio Medina y Don Nicolás León, translated by Joaquín García Pimentel and Federico Gómez de Orozco (Mexico City: Editorial Polis, 1940 [i.e., 1946]);

Sixty Years of Book Collecting (Los Angeles: Zamorano Club, 1952);

The First American Vessel in California: Monterey in 1796 (Los Angeles: Dawson, 1954);

Peter Pond, Fur Trader and Explorer (New Haven: Yale University Press, 1955);

Journey to Arizona in 1876 (Los Angeles: Zamorano Club, 1962);

The Life and Writings of Bartolomé de las Casas, by Wagner and Helen Rand Parish (Albuquerque: University of New Mexico Press, 1967);

A Checklist of Publications of H. H. Bancroft and Company 1857 to 1870, by Wagner, Eleanor A. Bancroft, and Ruth Frey Axe (Berkeley & Los Angeles: Friends of the Bancroft Library and Friends of the UCLA Library, 1987).

OTHER: "Sixteenth-Century Mexican Imprints," in *Bibliographical Essays: A Tribute to Wilberforce Eames* (Cambridge, Mass.: Harvard University Press, 1924), pp. 249-268;

"The Portolan Atlases of American Interest in the Henry E. Huntington Library and Art Gallery," in *Essays Offered to Herbert Putnam by William Warner Bishop and Andrew Keough* (New Haven: Yale University Press, 1929), pp. 498-509;

Letters of Captain Don Pedro Fages & the Reverend President Fr. Junipero Serra at San Diego, California, in

Henry R. Wagner

October, 1772, translated by Wagner (San Francisco: Grabhorn Press, 1936);

Bound for Sacramento: Travel-Pictures of a Returned Wanderer, translated by Ruth Frey Axe, introduction by Wagner (Claremont, Cal.: Saunders Studio Press, 1938);

George William Beattie and Helen Pruitt Beattie, *Heritage of the Valley,* foreword by Wagner (Pasadena, Cal.: San Pasqual Press, 1939);

Francisco Hernández de Córdoba, *The Discovery of Yucatan,* edited and translated by Wagner (Berkeley: Cortés Society, 1942);

Juan de Grijalva, *The Discovery of New Spain in 1518,* edited and translated by Wagner (Berkeley: Cortés Society, 1942);

José Martín, *Memorial and Proposals of Señor Don José Martín on the Californias (Mexico, mdcccxxii),* translated by Wagner (San Francisco: Grabhorn Press, 1945);

"The House of Cromberger," in *To Doctor R . . . Essays in Honor of Dr. A. S. W. Rosenbach* (Philadelphia, 1946), pp. 227–239;

"Hispanic Americana in the John Carter Brown Library," in *Essays Honoring Lawrence C. Wroth* (Portland, Maine, 1951), pp. 423–455;

Edward Bosqui, *Memoirs,* introduction and bibliography by Wagner (Oakland, Cal.: Holmes, 1952);

Robert Ernest Cowan, *A Bibliography of the History of California and the Pacific West, 1510–1906,* introduction by Wagner (San Francisco: Book Club of California, 1952);

Cowan, *Booksellers of Early San Francisco,* foreword by Wagner (Los Angeles: Ward Ritchie Press, 1953);

Henry L. Oak, *A Visit to the Missions of Southern California in February and March 1874,* introduction by Wagner (Los Angeles: Southland Press, 1981).

SELECTED PERIODICAL PUBLICATIONS –
UNCOLLECTED: "The Discovery of California," *California Historical Society Quarterly,* 1 (1922): 36–56;

"California Voyages, 1539–1541," *California Historical Society Quarterly,* 3, no. 4 (1924): 262–267;

"Apocryphal Voyages to the Northwest Coast of America," *Proceedings of the American Antiquarian Society,* 41 (April 1931): 179–234;

"The Last Spanish Exploration of the Northwest Coast and the Attempt to Colonize Bodega Bay," *California Historical Society Quarterly,* 10, no. 4 (1931): 313–345;

"The Manuscript Atlases of Battista Agnese," *Papers of the Bibliographical Society of America,* 25 (1931): 1–110;

"Biblio-cartography," *Pacific Historical Review,* 1 (March 1932): 103–110;

"The Names of the Channel Islands," *Publications of the Historical Society of Southern California,* 15 (1933): 16–23;

"Fr. Morcos de Niza," *New Mexico Historical Review,* 9 (April 1934): 184–227;

"Joaquin García Icazbalceta," *Proceedings of the American Antiquarian Society,* new series 44 (1934): 103–153;

"An Exploration of the Coast of Southern California in 1782," *Historical Society of Southern California Quarterly,* 17 (1935): 135–142;

"The First Book Printed in America," *Colophon,* new series 1 (1936): 453–454;

"Journal of Tomas de Suria of His Voyage with Malaspina to the Northwest Coast of America in 1791," edited and translated by Wagner, *Pacific Historical Review,* 5 (1936): 234–276;

"New Mexico Spanish Press, 1834–1845," *New Mexico Historical Review,* 12 (January 1937): 1–40;

"The Journal of Jacinto Caamaño, Translated by Captain Harold Grenfell," edited by Wagner and W. A. Newcombe, *British Columbia Historical Quarterly,* 2 (1938): 189–222, 265–301;

"Captain John Cook's Second Expedition," *Pacific Historical Review,* 8 (1939): 465–466;

"Commercial Printers of San Francisco from 1851–1880," *Papers of the Bibliographical Society of America,* 33 (1939): 69–84;

"Early Silver Mining in New Spain," *Revista de Historia de América,* 14 (June 1942): 49–71;

"Two Unknown American Incunabula," *Papers of the Bibliographical Society of America,* 39 (1945): 318–319;

"Peter Martyr and His Works," *Proceedings of the American Antiquarian Society,* 56 (October 1946): 239–288;

"Saints' Names in California," *Historical Society of Southern California Quarterly,* 29 (1947): 49–58;

"The Descent on California in 1683," *California Historical Society Quarterly,* 26 (1947): 309–319;

"Henri Ternaux Compans: The First Collector of Hispanic-Americana," *Inter-American Review of Bibliography,* 4 (October–December 1954): 283–298;

"Dispersal of American Imprints of the Sixteenth Century," *Yale University Library Gazette,* 32 (1957): 22–26;

"Henri Ternaux Compans, A Bibliography," *Inter-American Review of Bibliography,* 7 (1957): 239–254.

Henry R. Wagner had an incredible memory. Names, dates, and events lodged in his mind to be sorted and used in the scores of books and articles he wrote during the long afternoon of his life. In explaining why he had left an important and well-paying position at the comparatively early age of fifty-five, he wrote in his autobiography *Bullion to Books: Fifty Years of Business and Pleasure* (1942), "The real reason was I wanted to divorce pleasure from business. I have been combining the two for a good many years and my dislike for business kept growing all the time while my interest in bibliographical and research work kept increasing."

Henry Raup Wagner was born in Philadelphia on 27 September 1862. In 1880 he matriculated at Yale University, where he was a member of Delta Kappa Epsilon fraternity, a founding member of Wolf's Head, and one of the men who incorporated the fabled Mory's restaurant. He graduated from Yale Law School in June 1886 and went to Kansas City, where he began the practice of law. After about a year he bought shares in a silver mine in New Mexico and worked there for a short time. His interest shifted from law to mining, and for the next few years he moved from place to place and from job to job in that industry. On one sojourn in Mexico he became curious about a primitive method of smelting ore; known as the Patio process, it had apparently been introduced into Mexico in the sixteenth century but had never been used in the United States.

Up to this point Wagner had no interest in collecting books; soon after stumbling on evidence of the Patio process, however, he found a book describing it in a bookstall in Mexico City. This discovery piqued his curiosity, and he began searching

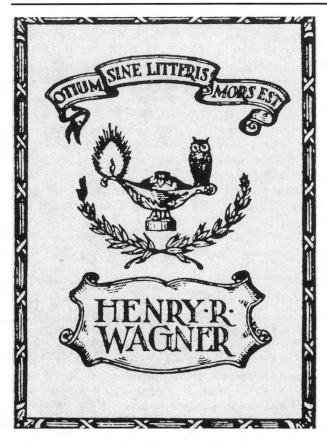

Wagner's bookplate

for other material on the subject. He was able to find little in the bookstores of Denver, where he was headquartered at the time. Soon thereafter he was offered a managerial position with the Guggenheims' American Smelting and Refining Company and was sent to places that proved to be more productive in his search for books. During a stay in Chile he found quite a few works on mining and smelting, and he came upon even more in London. It was not a field in which there was much competition, so he was able to pursue his interest uncontested. What was to be the first of his many collections grew to more than six hundred items; he eventually gave them to Yale.

Wagner became addicted to books and began to enjoy the lure of the search. During a three-year stay in London beginning in 1903 he haunted the bookstores and auction houses. He wrote of his experience in *Bullion to Books:*

> The number of these bookstores in London is incalculable. I certainly must have visited over one hundred, usually with no other result than to get my nose, clothes

and hands full of dust. At that time I had the idea this was the proper way to buy books. It is true that if you have nothing else to do and plenty of time to do it in you can extract a lot of pleasure from this peripatetic book-hunting, but it is a filthy job and brings very few rewards. After the first year I practically stopped going to more than one or two bookstores." He goes on to say: "The game of buying books is a great deal like a poker game. When you start playing poker a bet of fifty cents or one dollar looks like real money, but after you have played a year or two it looks like so much chicken-feed. Just so with buying books. When you begin $5 looks like a lot of money for a book, but after you have contracted the habit and the virus has thoroughly infected your system you do not even shudder at $50.

The relative scarcity of books on the narrow aspect of mining and metallurgy in which he was interested turned Wagner's collecting into a new direction: books on money. This pursuit resulted in an enormous collection of more than ten thousand items, which was eventually deposited at Yale. He became interested in Irish writers on money and economics, especially those of the eighteenth century. He went to Dublin to inspect the Trinity College collection and also examined those at Oxford and Cambridge. On the basis of this information and of his own collection he compiled and had printed *Irish Economics: 1700–1783. A Bibliography with Notes* (1907).

Just before his first book appeared in London, Wagner was transferred to Mexico. His interest soon shifted to books on the history and literature of the revolutionary period in that country. This collection, also containing books about Chile grew to twenty thousand items. He sold it to Yale for twenty-five thousand dollars, and it constitutes the major portion of the collection catalogued by Frederick Bliss Luguiens in *Spanish American Literature in the Yale University Library* (1939).

In 1917 Wagner retired, married Blanche Henriette Collet, and moved to Berkeley, California, to devote the remainder of his life to historical research. He was not wealthy, but he had sufficient funds to buy the books he needed for his research. His collecting priorities were usually influenced by his place of residence, and since he was located in the western United States, his interest shifted to that region. He began collecting narratives of the western migration, and when his collection had grown to sufficient proportions, he completed a bibliography, *The Plains and the Rockies: A Contribution to the Bibliography of Original Narratives of Travel and Adventure, 1800–1865* (1920). He was called to New York while the book was being printed and relied on the printer to do the proofreading. When he returned, he found more than three hundred errors in the book. He immediately withdrew it, offering to exchange any copies that had been purchased for a copy of the corrected edition; all but about twenty copies of the first edition were recovered. (An advantage of owning the original edition of 1920 over the revised edition of 1921 is that in the former the titles of the books owned personally by Wagner are marked with an asterisk: of the 349 books and pamphlets described, all but 47 were in his collection.) This bibliography has been augmented and reprinted several times; the most handsome edition, revised and extended to 428 items by Charles L. Camp, was printed in 1937 by the Grabhorn Press. Of it Wagner remarked, "It is more beautiful than a bibliography ought to be." Wagner subsequently sold his western collection to Henry E. Huntington; it comprised more than three thousand items.

In 1928 Wagner moved south to San Marino to be close to the Huntington Library. Not long afterward he required a translation from the German of some material on Hernán Cortés; seeking help from the University of California at Los Angeles, he was referred to a young student in the German department, Ruth Frey (later Ruth Frey Axe). She did such a satisfactory job that he requested that she come to work as his secretary after her graduation. While she had planned to go to graduate school and become a teacher, she accepted his offer. Though she did continue with graduate school, she served as Wagner's secretary from 1929 until his death. She wrote in her reminiscences of Wagner (1981):

> Mr. Wagner was always seated at his desk when I arrived.... He had always been working for some time before I arrived and we plunged immediately into the day's program as he had planned it. He told me that at Berkeley he usually worked until midnight or later, but after moving to San Marino his habits changed and he became a much earlier riser. His practice was to dictate directly to the typist. He expressed his thoughts so clearly and his work was so well planned that it was sometimes possible to use the first draft with few or no corrections.

In 1931 Wagner became a member of the Zamorano Club, a group of fifty or sixty bibliophiles, librarians, and printers. There was a monthly dinner meeting at which a member or guest speaker would give a talk on a bookish subject; in addition, there was an informal luncheon gathering in the club's rooms each Wednesday. Wagner seldom missed either the evening or luncheon meetings. The club's rooms and library were on the fourth floor of the University Club, a down-

town Los Angeles building handy to the many bookstores that at that time were clustered around Sixth Street and Grand Avenue. Following the Wednesday luncheons, many of the members – usually led by Wagner – would trek around the corner to visit the bookstores, finally converging on the fabled store of Ernest Dawson at the corner of Wilshire and Grand avenues.

After Wagner had finished writing about a subject, he lost interest in keeping the books he had collected on it. Also, he found that after he had published a bibliography, other collectors became interested in the subject, and he could sell his collection at a profit. In this way he not only made room for new books but also acquired money to buy them. As a result, his library turned over almost completely every few years. He said that the only books he regretted having parted with were those on which he had not compiled a bibliography. He collected everything he could find on a given subject and also did much research in libraries in Spain, England, Mexico, and the United States. Some of his more important collections were those on sixteenth-century Mexican imprints, sold to Huntington; Spanish explorations on the Northwest coast; books published by Grabhorn Press; and the Cortés collection. In 1937 the University of California Press published Wagner's *The Cartography of the Northwest Coast of America to the Year 1800* in two volumes. This work, along with *The Plains and the Rockies* and *The Spanish Southwest, 1542–1794* (1924), comprise Wagner's most enduring and important contributions to bibliography.

The Zamorano Club's evening meeting for September 1947 was a surprise celebration for Wagner's forthcoming eighty-fifth birthday. Wagner was seated, surrounded by friends and with a glass of sherry in his hand, when into the room were escorted his wife; his secretary; his former secretary from Berkeley, Signe Harding; and Dorothy Huggins, a close friend from San Francisco. At that time there were no women members, and it was against the rules of the University Club for women to be entertained anywhere except in special quarters on the first floor. Wagner's immediate reaction was one of shock at this improper intrusion, but it quickly turned into a wide smile upon having these women who were so dear to him joining in the occasion. There were many short talks in praise and friendship, and Francis Farquhar presented Wagner with a handsome book printed by the Grabhorn Press, *Essays for Henry R. Wagner,* that included pieces by Farquhar, Camp, Huggins, George L. Harding, and Carl I. Wheat, all friends of Wagner's from San Francisco. Finally, Wagner replied with a few

SIR FRANCIS DRAKE'S
VOYAGE AROUND THE WORLD

ITS AIMS AND ACHIEVEMENTS

BY

HENRY R. WAGNER

JOHN HOWELL
SAN FRANCISCO, CALIFORNIA
1926

*Title page for one of Wagner's contributions to knowledge of
sixteenth-century America*

words of advice from his position as an elder statesman. He admonished the club never to go into debt. He warned it against becoming just a social organization, saying that it should have some projects; he suggested that indexing the seven volumes of Hubert H. Bancroft's *History of California* (San Francisco: History Company, 1884–1890) would be of great service to scholars. Also needing indexing were the publications of the Historical Society of Southern California and Charles Lummis's *Land of Sunshine: The Magazine of California and the West* (1894–1901). (His suggestion was immediately followed in regard to the *History of California*. Chapters were allotted to various members, but with amateurs attempting to do a professional's work the project lingered on until it was finally turned over to two professional indexers, Everett and Anna Marie Hager. It was completed and published in two volumes in 1985, thirty-eight years after Wagner's initial suggestion.)

The Zamorano Club celebrated each succeeding birthday in the garden of Wagner's home in San Marino. His eyesight gradually failed; he remarked, "My mind has outlived my body. It's a pity they couldn't have gone together." He continued to work, however, arriving at his desk at 8:00, working until noon, and, after a twenty-minute lunch break, continuing until 4:40. His routine included dictating without notes and reading the material he had gathered (or being read to after he became blind). He usually carried on three projects at the same time, explaining that it kept him from going stale on any of them. He continued to buy books, ordering some the day before he died on 28 March 1957 at the age of ninety-four.

Henry R. Wagner was not a book collector in the strict sense; he bought books not to collect them but to use them. While he gave books to several institutions, especially Yale, he remained skeptical of the practice. According to Axe, he said, "Giving

Wagner in 1931

books is a very pleasant enterprise but I have always found it more grateful to the giver than the receiver. I have come to the conclusion that especially libraries do not appreciate gift books. What they want to do is to pay a high price for them, if they have the money, and then they think they have a prize which they exhibit in a glass case. If you happened to give them the same book it would disappear on the shelves and no one would hear about it."

The first bibliography of Wagner's writings (1934) listed 68 items. In his autobiography *Bullion to Books,* Wagner listed 97 items. *The Published Writings of Henry R. Wagner* (1955) included 167 books and articles. The definitive bibliography of Wagner's writings, compiled by Axe and published in 1988, lists 193 items.

In the preface to the 1955 bibliography Farquhar wrote: "More than once Henry Wagner

has remarked that his published works have never made a profit either for himself or for the publisher. They were designed for scholars in specialized fields and were not expected to be popular. That does not mean, however, that they are not important. As a matter of fact, many of them are so important that they will affect the writing of history for a long time to come. No greater contribution has been made in the past hundred years to the knowledge and understanding of the Sixteenth century in America than is contained in *The Spanish Southwest, Spanish Voyages to the Northwest Coast of America, Sir Francis Drake's Voyage Around the World, The Cartography of the Northwest Coast of America, Juan Rodrigues Cabrillo,* and the three Cortés Society volumes — *The Discovery of Yucatan, The Discovery of New Spain,* and *The Rise of Fernando Cortés.* Equal in value to almost any one of these books would be a volume embracing the shorter essays and reviews relating to this period. Nor is the Sixteenth Century the only period illuminated in Wagner's great scholarship. The comments in *The Plains and the Rockies* and in *California Imprints* exemplify his remarkable ability to perceive the significance of items passed over or misunderstood by others."

Bibliographies:

Published Writings of Henry R. Wagner (Santa Ana, Cal.: Fine Arts Press, 1934);

The Published Writings of Henry R. Wagner: Issued by the Zamorano Club of Los Angeles at the First Far Western Meeting of the Bibliographical Society of America, Held at the Henry E. Huntington Library on August 27, 1955, in Honor of Henry R. Wagner (Los Angeles: Ward Ritchie Press, 1955);

Ruth Frey Axe, *The Published Writings of Henry R. Wagner* (New Haven, Conn.: Reese, 1988).

Biography:

Ruth Frey Axe, *Henry R. Wagner: An Intimate Profile* (Clifton, N.J.: AB Bookman Publications, 1981; revised, 1993).

References:

Charles L. Camp, "Our Founder, Henry R. Wagner, Is Dead," *California Historical Society Quarterly*, 36 (1957): 79–82;

Edwin H. Carpenter, *Henry R. and Blanche C. Wagner* (Santa Ana, Cal.: Orange County Historical Society, 1964);

Stephen A. Colston, "Henry Raup Wagner: Bookman and Scholar Extraordinaire," *Brand Book Number Seven: The San Diego Corral of the Westerners: People of the Southwest and Pacific Coast* (San Diego, 1983), pp. 160–166;

Everett D. Graff, *Henry Raup Wagner, 1862–1957* (Chicago: Newberry Library, 1962);

Lawrence Clark Powell, *Bibliographers of the Golden State* (Berkeley: University of California Press, 1967);

Powell, *Viva Wagner* (Los Angeles: Press in the Gatehouse, 1964);

Ward Ritchie, *Bookmen & Their Brothels: Recollections of Los Angeles in the 1930's* (Los Angeles: Zamorano Club, 1970);

Thomas W. Streeter, "Henry R. Wagner, Collector, Bibliographer, Cartographer and Historian," *California Historical Society Quarterly*, 36 (1957): 165–175.

Papers:

Henry R. Wagner's papers are widely dispersed. The Bancroft Library has the most extensive collection, especially in the area of Wagner's research into the history of the Southwest. Yale has his collections pertaining to Irish and British writings on economics. California State University at San Diego holds the George Harding collection of Wagner's works, including some of his account books and ledgers. The Huntington Library, University of Califonia, Los Angeles, and the John Carter Brown Library also house significant portions of Wagner's extensive correspondence. This information was provided by his longtime secretary, Ruth Frey Axe.

Henry Walters

(26 September 1848 – 30 November 1931)

Elizabeth Burin
The Walters Art Gallery

WORK: Preface to *Incunabula Typographica: A Descriptive Catalogue of the Books Printed in the Fifteenth Century (1460–1500) in the Library of Henry Walters,* by Leo S. Olschki (Baltimore: Walters, 1906).

One of the great American art collectors of his day, Henry Walters purchased manuscripts and printed books with the same passion that led him to acquire some twenty-three thousand works of art dating from about 3000 B.C. to his own time. His more than 730 medieval and later manuscripts, the second largest collection of its kind in the United States, was complemented by more than twelve hundred incunabula and almost as many later titles. His interest in rare books must be seen as an integral part of his life as an art collector: the illuminated manuscripts, illustrated books, and fine bindings are works of art in their own right, and his collecting of unadorned volumes of diverse medieval, classical, and modern texts reflects a broad interest in the civilizations from which his other acquisitions emerged.

Henry Walters was born in Baltimore on 26 September 1848 to William Thompson and Ellen Harper Walters. William Walters had collected art since his youth. At the outbreak of the Civil War the elder Walters, a Southern sympathizer with investments in both Northern and Southern railroads, took his wife and two children, Henry and his younger sister Jennie, to Europe. Paris was their home for the next four years, and it was no doubt this stay that made Henry (or Harry, as he preferred to be called) a lifelong Francophile.

William Walters devoted considerable time in Paris and on his travels around Europe to collecting; Henry Walters frequently accompanied his father, especially after his mother's sudden death from pneumonia on a visit to London in November 1862. Little is known about the boy's formal education, although a visiting card of "Louis Samson, Inspecteur à l'Institution Bonnefous," found in a book

he acquired in 1865, suggests that he may have attended this school. William Walters supplemented his son's education and honed his connoisseurship by involving him in collecting and making him write essays on artistic subjects.

After the family returned to the United States at the end of the Civil War, Walters attended Loyola College in Baltimore; earned a bachelor's degree in 1869 and a master's in 1871 from Georgetown University; and studied engineering at the Lawrence Scientific School at Harvard, qualifying for a B.S. in 1873, (he did not receive the degree until 1906). There followed a year or so in Paris, visiting galleries and collecting with his father.

Walters began his railroad career in the engineering corps of the Valley Railroad in Virginia, moving on to the Pittsburgh and Connellsville Railroad. He then joined the Atlantic Coast Line, founded by his father, rising to vice-president and general manager by 1889. He was responsible for expanding and consolidating the line, building it into the chief artery of the Southeast by negotiating a merger with the Plant system in Florida and purchasing control of the Louisville and Nashville Railroad. By 1902 Walters was chairman of the board and the largest stockholder in both the Atlantic Coast Line and the Louisville and Nashville. He also became chairman of the board of the Safe Deposit and Trust Company of Baltimore.

During the lifetime of William Walters, Henry's artistic concerns coincided with his father's: nineteenth-century painting, the sculpture of Antoine-Louis Barye, and Far Eastern and French porcelains. The collection of manuscripts and early books did not begin to take shape until after the elder Walters's death, but Henry's interest in fine books was not without antecedent in his father's life. Beyond assembling a typical gentleman's library and a collection of reference works relating to his artistic interests, William Walters launched publishing ventures on subjects dear to his heart: Percheron horses, which he imported from France and bred;

Henry Walters

his collection of paintings: the work of Barye, whom he championed from 1861 until his own death; and oriental ceramics, of which he was perhaps the first serious collector in America. From 1886 these publications increasingly reflect a preoccupation with fine bookmaking for its own sake. It was no doubt his concern with fine printing and experimental illustration that led to William Walters's election to the Grolier Club in 1893, and Henry's participation in his father's publishing endeavors won him membership in the club immediately following William's death in November 1894. At this time he took charge of the completion of two publications initiated by his father: R. B. Gruelle's *Notes Critical and Biographical: Collection of W. T. Walters* (1895), designed by Bruce Rodgers in the style of William Morris's Kelmscott Press books, with the ornate initials, headbands, and title page rubricated

by hand in a few of the copies; and even more important, *Oriental Ceramic Art,* the landmark work by S. W. Bushell. The abundant illustrations in the latter include, in addition to more than 400 halftones throughout the text, 116 color lithographs by Louis Prang depicting examples in the Walters collection. Their execution and printing in five hundred copies took five years and necessitated multiple stones for each plate. The elaborate assemblage, in ten separate sections enclosed within five portfolios of Chinese silk, was itself a major undertaking, although fewer than half the copies were completed in this way. The work was at last published in 1897.

Meanwhile, Walters had come into his inheritance and had begun collecting in earnest, broadening his interests to include a wide range of civilizations and art forms and frequently spending as much as three months of the year buying art in Europe. His wealth also permitted him to entertain lavishly and to indulge in his other main hobby, yachting. Walters's attitude toward money in his earlier years is revealed in an unsigned inscription in his hand on the flyleaf of *Art and Scenery in Europe, with Other Papers,* by Horace Binney Wallace (Philadelphia, 1857): "Money is a very good thing if you have it – I can answer for that, because of what it does in advantages gained for social and literary cultivation of time, ease and tastes – But the '*getting of money*' (with few exceptions) does so *dwarf* and *stultify* the soul, that I always shrink from a community where it is the prevailing passion." A copy of Jules Michelet's *The Insect* contains a later flyleaf inscription: "We cannot extoll too much the virtue of industry – or labor – if physical or mental – but it is not the *toil* itself which enobles [*sic*] – but the spirit and the aim with which it is undergone." This respect for work is palpable in a letter written by Walters in old age to his nephew Lyman Delano, conveying advice on embarking on a career in the railroad industry with the warning that "there is no short cut or easy way to any position of trust and responsibility."

Far from directing his cultural and artistic interests strictly toward the enhancement of his own collection, he served as trustee of the Metropolitan Museum of Art from 1905 and as vice-president from 1913. He was also a trustee of the New York Public Library. An active member of the New York and Newport yacht clubs, he became a member of the syndicates formed to build defenders of the America's Cup. During World War I he served on the staff of the United States as director general of railroads and maintained the Passy military hospital near Paris, which earned him the Médaille de la Reconnaissance and the Legion of Honor. His many other acts of philanthropy included funding a home for destitute women in New York, presenting Baltimore with its public baths, endowing the Department of Art as Applied to Medicine organized by Max Broedel at the Johns Hopkins School of Medicine, donating works of art to the Metropolitan and other museums, and contributing generously to charities and cultural and educational institutions. Most of these donations and benefactions are hard to trace because Walters preferred to give anonymously.

This modesty resulted in a scarcity of information on his personal life; when he succeeded John D. Rockefeller, Jr., on the steel board in 1910, the *Wall Street Journal* (5 March) identified him as the richest man in the South in an article titled "Who is Henry Walters?": "Walters might be called the Wall Street mystery if enough were known about him to stimulate general curiosity. But he has succeeded so completely in effacing his personality and his acts, that he is not even a mystery. He is an unknown."

His loathing of journalists and of the limelight in general notwithstanding, Walters was an affable, charming, and hospitable man in private. His closest friends were the financier Pembroke Jones and his wife, Sarah Wharton Green Jones. The friendship had begun in Wilmington, North Carolina, where Walters had been based during his early years with the Atlantic Coast Line and had lived in the Jones's house. Beginning in the 1890s Walters spent most of his time in New York, paying frequent visits to Baltimore to attend to business concerns and to the family art collection. In New York he resided with the Joneses, who had moved there. In the winter the threesome spent time in Wilmington, and in the summer in Newport, Rhode Island, where Walters entertained on his oceangoing yacht, the *Narada.* In 1922, at the age of seventy-four, Walters married Sarah Jones, who had been widowed four years previously.

Walters's reticence and abhorrence of publicity make the details of his collecting activities difficult to trace. He kept few records, and to thwart any vulgar curiosity as to the prices he paid, he made a habit of promptly cutting the price column off his invoices. He once explained to the dealer Germain Seligman, "I don't want anybody in later years to talk of my collecting in terms of money spent. . . . That is my business. They'll have the works of art and their pedigrees." All too frequently, however, his scissors destroyed descriptions of other objects listed on the back of the invoice.

The few surviving documents indicate that Walters was collecting Egyptian and Near Eastern art by 1897 and had substantial holdings in medieval sculpture and ivories by 1903. The 1902 purchase in Rome of the entire collection of Don Marcello Massarenti, assistant almoner to the Holy See, formed the nucleus of Walters's ancient and Renaissance collections and led to the building of a palazzo-style gallery adjoining the family home in Baltimore to replace William Walters's more modest wing.

Walters's collecting of rare books may have been inspired by his membership in the Grolier Club. His first manuscript was, according to an autograph inscription, a late-fifteenth-century French Book of Hours of mediocre quality, perhaps purchased in the 1890s. In 1897 he bought his first Islamic manuscripts from Dikran Kelekian in Paris;

The Walters Art Gallery, Baltimore

Kelekian provided Walters with many important works over the following decades, including Armenian manuscripts and Near Eastern art. Also in 1897 George H. Richmond of New York supplied Walters with Americana and incunabula; in 1901 Richmond sold him some forty books from the Lefferts collection, including more Americana, English chronicles and literature, Geoffroy Tory's *Champ Fleury* (1529), fifteenth-century French Books of Hours, and nine illuminated manuscripts, among them a magnificent Florentine antiphonary of about 1380.

By the early 1900s Walters was in correspondence with the leading booksellers in Europe and had begun to collect manuscripts in larger quantities, sometimes selecting thirty or forty at a time from general stock or from items set aside by his regular suppliers; only a few itemized invoices survive. Usually he seems to have done his buying in person during his annual European trips, which were significantly disrupted only by World War I.

Payment, binding, and shipping arrangements for many Paris purchases were entrusted to George Lucas, who had been instrumental in William Walters's Paris collecting. Besides Richmond and Kelekian, Walters's suppliers included Jacques Rosenthal of Munich, Bernard Quaritch of London, Techener and Morgand of Paris, Julius Ichenhauser of New York, Ferdinando Ongania of Venice (who dedicated his 1902 publication on the Grimani Breviary to Walters), Léon Gruel of Paris, and Leo S. Olschki of Florence.

Gruel played a major role in forming the Walters collection of manuscripts. An invoice for a thirteenth-century illuminated French Psalter that Walters purchased from him survives from the 1890s, and by 1900 he was providing Gothic Books of Hours, Romanesque and earlier codices, early bindings, and other medieval objects. On his trips to Paris, Walters visited Gruel's shop on the rue St. Honoré regularly. Gruel's accounts have not been located, but an account book from Lucas's estate records large payments to Gruel for unitemized groups of manuscripts and books. Some 210 Walters codices can be identified as coming from Gruel by bookplates, by Gruel's handwritten description slips, or by boxes from his bindery. The majority are illuminated manuscripts of fine quality and of Western, often French, origin; several Byzantine codices also came from this source.

Eighty-one of the manuscripts bought by Walters from Gruel contain bookplates with the initials G. E., indicating joint ownership with Gruel's stepfather and business partner Jean Engelmann. It has been suggested that these manuscripts were acquired by Engelmann: Gruel was known more as a bookbinder than a bookseller, and his activity in the art market was limited; Walters appears to have been his chief client for manuscript sales. Perhaps this relationship grew out of Gruel's position as the American's favorite binder. Walters had many books elegantly bound in antiquarian and modern styles, often with his monogram, by Gruel's workshop. These books included a series of Grolier Club publications, which Walters could have had bound at the club's own bindery but preferred to entrust to Gruel's skillful craftsmen. A copy of William Matthews's *Modern Bookbinding Practically Considered* (1889), for example, is a sampler of the various techniques and styles of decoration on leather practiced by the workshop. No less unusual is the commemorative binding on a hand-illuminated copy of Gruelle's *Notes Critical and Biographical: Collection of W. T. Walters,* inlaid on the upper cover with an oxidized silver plaque by Victor Brenner with a double portrait of William and Henry Walters in relief and on the lower with two further plaques based on fine Chinese porcelain dishes in the Walters collection. Lucas's diaries include many references, particularly in 1895 and 1896, to having books bound for "HW" by Paris binders, most frequently Gruel.

The cordial nature of the relationship between Walters and Gruel is attested by an autograph dedication in a copy of the Grolier Club edition of Richard de Bury's *Philobiblon,* bound by Gruel in 1901 in a unique triple *dos-à-dos* binding as a souvenir for Walters. Another dedication by Gruel appears in the Walters copy of *La Madeleine depuis son établissement à la Ville l'Évêque* (Paris, 1910), a historical and archaeological study by Gruel. The business relationship continued even after Gruel's death in 1923, for the shop remained active under the direction of his son Paul until 1954.

In 1903 Walters arranged for purchases of illuminated manuscripts and early bindings from Olschki; in 1904 he paid a visit to the Florentine

dealer's shop. The following year Walters bought out Olschki's entire stock of incunabula, comprising more than a thousand titles, for which the dealer was preparing a catalogue. This purchase is a rare instance of Walters's buying in bulk, and, as in the case of the Massarenti collection, his aim was to form the basis of a collection that he could expand with carefully selected acquisitions. Walters purchased further incunabula from Olschki as they became available – including another seventy-four titles in 1905 – as well as from other dealers such as Quaritch and Martini and from the Trau sale in Vienna, where Olschki acted as his agent. He sent descriptions of the books purchased elsewhere to Florence for inclusion in the catalogue, which was finished in 1906 and bound in calf. Walters presented copies to major libraries in America and Europe.

The collection of incunabula testifies to Walters's recognition of the importance of early printing; because it was largely formed by Olschki, however, it does not give specific insights into Walters's tastes and interests. Italian books are most heavily represented, followed by German; French editions are remarkably few, considering Walters's Francophile bent, and the selection includes no English books.

Olschki, delighted with Walters's patronage, made every effort to satisfy his customer in the openly expressed hope of becoming his sole supplier of rare books. He drew Walters's attention to the finest early imprints available, both in his shop and at auction, recommending items for Walters's collection and sometimes acting as a consultant. Most of Walters's more than 150 Italian manuscripts and some 50 of other nationalities contain Olschki's penciled inventory numbers. The bookseller's friendship and gratitude are expressed in the Latin dedication to Walters of *Le Livre en Italie à travers les siècles,* a finely printed and illustrated catalogue of books exhibited by Olschki at the international exhibition in Leipzig in 1914. The following year Olschki presented Walters with a vellum copy of his facsimile edition of a Giovanni Boccaccio manuscript in the Laurentian Library, complete with a handwritten and decorated title page and dedication to Walters.

After forming the core of his collections of manuscripts and rare books, Walters continued to build on his holdings. He bought large groups of sixteenth-century illustrated books in 1905 from Breslauer and in 1908 from Quaritch. He collected further incunabula, including superior copies of some of the titles he had acquired from Olschki in 1905.

The printed books of the centuries after 1500 reveal Walters's taste for fine printing, illustration, and binding. His broader cultural interests are reflected by ancient texts and literary classics in rare editions, liturgical and philosophical works, travel books, and, of course, art books. Some of the volumes had been re-bound in the nineteenth century in mock period style, such as a group in extravagant imitation French Renaissance bindings by Hagué. Walters was doubtless aware of what he was buying, for many bindings made for him on commission by Gruel and others were also pastiches; he valued the craftsmanship they displayed. Similarly, he purchased from Gruel two nineteenth-century illuminated manuscripts made as prototypes for chromolithographic editions and was aware of at least one actual forgery in his manuscript collection.

In contrast with his bulk purchases of incunabula, Walters selected his manuscripts individually, aiming for a broad range of subjects and styles. The greatest strength of the collection lies in religious works, especially books of private devotion from late medieval and Renaissance Europe. Some two hundred Books of Hours form the largest, most representative group of their kind in the United States, complemented by other prayer books and nearly forty Psalters. Many of Walters's contemporaries also found Gothic art appealing and felt an affinity for the fervent personal piety of the late Middle Ages.

Walters's taste in manuscripts ranged in date from the ninth century to the nineteenth and in geographical origin from Spain to India. The 530 Western manuscripts that form the bulk of the collection, including more than 200 of French origin, mostly date from before 1550 and include literary, historical, and legal works. Some, notably among the Italian codices, were chosen for the cultural importance of their texts, but most are illuminated. These illuminations complement other portions of his art collection; at the same time, while many connoisseurs collected medieval miniatures as independent paintings, Walters purchased few cuttings or single leaves apart from a collection of Persian and Mogul miniatures and clearly understood the illuminated codex as an integral whole combining text, illustration, decoration, and binding.

The few name pieces in the collection include a *Bible historiale* once in the collection of Jean, Duke of Berry, and a fragmentary but artistically important thirteenth-century Bible believed to have been made for Conradin von Hohenstaufen, the boy duke of Swabia. Another special case is that of the Malet-Lannoy Hours, associated with the ancestral family of Walters's sister's husband, Warren Delano III. Walters usually chose objects for their intrinsic quality rather than for their provenance, however, and sought representative pieces as much as exceptional ones. His aspiration to represent broadly the history of bookmaking and illustration prompted him to collect fine Byzantine, Armenian, Arabic, Persian, and Indian manuscripts as well as Western examples. He arranged for his superintendent in Baltimore to make manuscripts and printed books available for study by scholars.

The contents of Walters's will remained a secret until his death on 30 November 1931. Widespread surprise greeted the bequest of his Baltimore art gallery, with its entire contents, and one quarter of his estate as an endowment to the mayor and city council of Baltimore "for the benefit of the people." The gift was made in the spirit of William T. Walters, since whose time the art collection had been open to the public on certain days. Most of the manuscripts and early books had long been housed in Baltimore, and they became part of the holdings of the Walters Art Gallery, which opened in 1934 as a public museum and has continued to expand its collections. Nearly all volumes kept in the collector's New York home at the time of his death went to his widow, who, in her final years, sold large quantities of art and furniture. More than fifteen hundred books were auctioned at the Parke-Bernet galleries in April 1941, mostly nineteenth-and-early-twentieth-century editions but also many earlier books, including some incunabula and manuscripts. A few have since come into the Walters Art Gallery's collection by way of gifts and purchases.

Henry Walters collected art on a scale that is almost inconceivable today. He was perhaps the last American art lover able to acquire extensively in nearly all periods and media, and his was among the greatest private collections to enter the public domain in the twentieth century. The manuscripts and rare books form a collection of a type more commonly housed in a library than in an art museum. They testify to the owner's keen understanding of the importance of the book not only in the history of literature and thought but also in the history of art and technology. The collection of illuminated manuscripts, one of the foremost in the United States, constitutes one of many remarkable groups of objects in the Walters Art Gallery that reflect Walters's discriminating taste. The holdings in late-medieval and Renaissance manuscripts represent a special strength amid the art and writings of diverse civilizations.

References:
"Connoisseur's Haven," *Apollo,* (December 1966): 422–433;

"Foreword: The Founders of the Collection," *Journal of the Walters Art Gallery,* 1 (1938): 9–12;

Dorothy Miner, "The Book of Eastern Christendom: American Collections of Near-Eastern Manuscripts," *Gazette of the Grolier Club,* new series 3 (February 1967): 14–22;

Miner, "The Collecting of Islamic Manuscripts in America," in *Acts of the Seventh International Congress of Bibliophiles, 29 September–13 October 1971* (Boston, Philadelphia & New York: Association Internationale de Bibliophilie, 1974), pp. 69–79;

Miner, "The Collection of Manuscripts and Rare Books in the Walters Art Gallery," *Papers of the Bibliographical Society of America,* 30 (1936): 104–109;

Miner, "The Publishing Ventures of a Victorian Connoisseur," *Papers of the Bibliographical Society of America,* 57 (1963): 271–311;

Miner, "The Rare Book Collections at the Walters Art Gallery," *Maryland Libraries,* 33 (Winter 1967): 7–11;

Parke-Bernet Galleries, Inc., *Four Centuries of French Literature, Mainly in Superb Bindings by Old and Modern Masters, Illuminated Manuscripts, Incunabula, Drawings, Miniatures, Americana, and Other Choice Items: Collection of Mrs. Henry Walters,* sale catalogue, 23–25 April 1941 (New York: Parke-Bernet, 1941);

Lilian M. C. Randall, *The Diary of George A. Lucas: An American Art Agent in Paris, 1857–1909* (Princeton, N. J.: Princeton University Press, 1979);

Randall, "Henry, Son of William: The Walters Rare Book Collection. A Talk at the Opening of the Exhibition at the Grolier Club, 20 December 1977," *Gazette of The Grolier Club,* new series 26–27 (June–December 1977): 46–57;

Randall, "Henry Walters and the de Lannoy Connection," *Bulletin of the Walters Art Gallery,* 33 (May 1981): 4–5;

Randall, *Medieval and Renaissance Manuscripts in the Walters Art Gallery,* volume 1 (Baltimore: Johns Hopkins University Press, 1989), pp. xi–xiv;

Randall, "A Nineteenth-Century 'Medieval' Prayerbook Woven in Lyon," in *Art the Ape of Nature: Studies in Honor of H. W. Janson* (New York: Abrams, 1981), pp. 651–668;

Bernard M. Rosenthal, "Cartel, Clan, or Dynasty? The Olschkis and the Rosenthals, 1859–1976," *Harvard Library Bulletin,* 25 (1977): 381–398;

Cristina Tagliaferri, *Olschki: un secolo di editoria, 1886–1986,* volume 1: *La libreria antiquaria editrice Leo S. Olschki (1886–1945)* (Florence: Olschki, 1986).

Gabriel Wells

(24 January 1862 – 6 November 1946)

William Baker
Northern Illinois University

BOOKS: *Lest We Forget!: A Declaration of Independence* (New York: Privately printed, 1921);

Life's Treat (New York: Privately printed, 1922);

Gentle Reactions (Garden City, N.Y.: Doubleday, Page, 1923);

A Layman's Peace Plan (Garden City, N.Y.: Country Life Press, 1924);

What Is Truth? (London: Heinemann, 1924);

Arbitration (Garden City, N.Y.: Country Life Press, 1925);

An Interpretation of Life: An Address by Gabriel Wells, Esq. Given before the Members of the Westside Men's Bible Class at the Third Annual Dinner February Seventeenth Nineteen Hundred Twenty-five (Philadelphia: Westside Presbyterian Church, 1925);

The Inwardness of Unemployment (London: Mathews, 1925);

The Tennessee Cause Celebre (Garden City, N.Y.: Doubleday, Page, 1925);

Life Eternal (New York: Wells, 1925);

The Correlation of Capital and Labor (Garden City, N.Y.: Doubleday, Page, 1926);

The Great English Strike, Its Three Lessons (Garden City, N.Y.: Doubleday, Page, 1926);

If I Were France (Garden City, N.Y.: Doubleday, Page, 1926);

Life Temporal (Mount Vernon, N.Y.: Printed by William Edwin Rudge, 1926);

Are We a Democracy? (Garden City, N.Y.: Doubleday, Page, 1927);

Intimations (London: Constable, 1927);

The Menace of Divorce (Garden City, N.Y.: Doubleday, Page, 1927);

These Three . . . (New York: Privately printed, 1927); republished with preface by André Maurois (London: Rudge, 1932; London: Kennerley, 1932);

The Way to Peace (Garden City, N.Y.: Doubleday, Doran, 1928);

On Capital Punishment (London: Heinemann / New York: Doubleday, Doran, 1929);

The World Crisis (Garden City, N.Y.: Doubleday, Doran, 1930);

To Be and to Have (New York: Rudge, 1930);

The Crisis: Its Causes and Remedies (London: Sotheran, 1931);

The Word (New York: Privately printed, 1931);

Now and After (New York: Privately printed, 1932);

Common Sense and the Crisis (Garden City, N.Y.: Doubleday, Doran, 1933);

Human Nature and World Disorder (Garden City, N.Y.: Doubleday, Doran, 1933);

If I Were Dictator (N.p., 1933);

Alone (New York, 1933);

The Carter-Pollard Disclosures (Garden City, N.Y.: Doubleday, Doran, 1934);

The Riddle of Being: A Theory of Correlativity (New York: Privately printed, 1934);

Life (New York: Privately printed, 1934);

Is Capitalism Doomed? (New York: Privately printed, 1935);

This Confused World (Garden City, N.Y.: Doubleday, Doran, 1935?);

The Money Muddle (New York: Privately printed, 1935);

A Plea for Common Sense (New York: Privately printed, 1935);

The Quest of Happiness (New York: Privately printed, 1935);

Can Peace Be Maintained in Europe? (New York: Privately printed, 1936);

Affinity (New York: Privately printed, 1936);

Appeal to Common Sense (London: Macmillan, 1937);

The President's Court Proposal (New York: Privately printed, 1937);

The One Certainty (New York: Privately printed, 1937);

Faith (New York: Privately printed, 1938);

Gabriel Wells on Education (New Brunswick, N.J.: Rutgers University Press, 1939);

Consciousness (New York: Privately printed, 1939);

What Is Wrong with the Human World? (N.p., 1940);

Duty (New York: Privately printed, 1940);

Good and Evil (New York: Privately printed, 1941);

Gabriel Wells; bust by Jo Davidson, 1928 (from Gabriel Wells, These
Three . . . , *1932)*

*Rare and Valuable Books, Important Autograph Letters and
Mss., Drawings and Paintings: Final Liquidation of the
Stock of the Late Gabriel Wells, by Order of the Executors of His Estate. Public Auction Sale, Nov. 12 Nov.
13* (New York: Parke-Bernet Galleries, 1951).

SELECTED PERIODICAL PUBLICATIONS –
UNCOLLECTED: "Beginning of a New Century,"
    New Haven (Connecticut) *Register,* 28 December
    1900;
"The Evolution of the Book Collector," *Bookman,* 51
    (April 1920): 180–186;
"The Case of Collecting," *American Book Collector,* 1
    (February 1932): 104–107;
"Poe as a Mystic," *American Book Collector,* 3 (February
    1936): 54–55;

"College Education and the Collecting Activity," *Yale
University Library Gazette,* 2 (July 1936): 7–9.

Gabriel Wells was one of the foremost American
book dealers during the period of extensive buying by
wealthy collectors from the early twentieth century
through the post-Depression years. The citation accompanying the honorary doctorate awarded him on 8 June
1935 by Rutgers University celebrates his importance
as a bookman, author, philanthropist, international authority on rare books, and, above all, a man of integrity.

Wells was born Gabriel Weiss in Balassa-
Gyarmat, Hungary, on 24 January 1862 to Moritz and
Helene Pissk Weiss. Educated in Budapest, Wells mas-
tered eight languages – he was particularly interested in
German, which he learned in order to read the Ger-

man philosophers in the original – but when he arrived in Boston at the age of thirty he could speak barely a word of English. Wells became a protégé of Harvard professor of psychology, William James; he would dedicate his *Gentle Reactions* (1923) "To the Memory of William James: A man who has faith in the other man." For three years Wells tutored in psychology and German at Harvard.

Wells's bookselling career began with John Lawson Stoddard's *Lectures* (Boston: Balch, 1897–1909), which was available only through subscription: Wells bought every set that he could find, rebound them, and resold them to dealers. He repeated this procedure with other subscription books and limited editions. His success is reflected in the changes of his business addresses: from a furnished room to an office at 128 East Twenty-third Street in Manhattan; then to larger quarters at 489 Fifth Avenue, opposite the New York Public Library; then, after a decade, to offices at 145 West Fifty-seventh Street. Wells never put out a catalogue of his stock; according to the antiquarian bookseller H. P. Kraus, when asked about this curious behavior Wells replied, "Let other dealers catalogue their books. I sell mine."

Wells shifted the focus of his business to fine and rare books, first editions, fine bindings, color plates, and sporting books. Later still he specialized in world literature, the Elizabethan period, incunabula, and manuscripts. He found innovative ways to make money. A great success was his purchase in London of a copy of the Gutenberg Bible that was missing more than 50 of its 541 leaves. Wells – to use his own word – "disseverated" the defective copy, had the separate leaves bound in blue tooled morocco leather by Stikeman, and sold them individually with a brief introductory essay by Wells's friend A. Edward Newton, whose extensive library Wells helped to build. *A Noble Fragment: Being a Leaf of the Gutenberg Bible 1450–1455 With a Bibliographical Essay by A. Edward Newton* (1921) sold for $150 to $500, depending on the leaf included. Newton's preface defended Wells's action, while acknowledging that it seemed "an act of vandalism to remove the leaves from the almost contemporary leather covers which have for . . . many centuries protected them." Wells's treatment of the Gutenberg Bible represents his entrepreneurial side, but it also demonstrates his generosity, since he gave some of the leaves to the New York Public Library to complete the defective James Lenox copy, the first Gutenberg that had been brought to America.

Wells's other publishing adventures included the thirteen-volume Autograph Edition of the works of Booth Tarkington (Garden City, N.Y.: Doubleday, Page, 1918–1919), the twenty-four-volume Sun Dial Edition of the works of Joseph Conrad (Garden City, N.Y.: Doubleday, Page, 1920–1928), the ten-volume Temple Bar Edition of James Boswell's *Life of Johnson* (New York: Wells, 1922), the ten-volume Standard Edition of the works of Herman Melville (London: Constable, 1922–1924), the thirty-seven-volume edition of the works of Mark Twain (New York: Wells, 1922–1925), the thirty-volume Autograph Edition of the works of Anatole France (New York: Wells, 1924), the sixteen-volume Norwich Edition of the works of George Borrow (London: Constable / New York: Wells, 1923–1924), a twelve-volume large-paper edition of the works of Oscar Wilde (New York: Doubleday, Page, 1923), the ten-volume Halliford Edition of the works of Thomas Love Peacock (London: Constable / New York: Wells, 1924–1936), and the twenty-volume Bonchurch Edition of the works of Algernon Charles Swinburne (London: Heineman / New York: Wells, 1925–1927). These limited editions are printed on special all-rag paper in fine levant morocco tooled bindings. Wells provided the ideas and sometimes also acted as publisher. All of the subscription sets sold out.

Wells had transactions with most of the major book buyers of his day. Occasionally he supplied books to Henry E. Huntington, who secured most of his wants through George D. Smith of New York and Charles Sessler of Philadelphia. During the Klein library sale at the Anderson Gallery in New York on 15–16 February 1911, Wells received a 10 percent commission for acting as Huntington's agent in purchasing Swinburne and Robert Louis Stevenson first editions.

After trying in March 1921 to interest Huntington in William Blake's original drawings for the *Book of Job* (London: Printed by William Blake, 1826), Wells sold most of the illustrations to Grenville L. Winthrop, who bequeathed them to the Fogg Art Museum at Harvard in 1943; *Satan before the Throne of God* was purchased by Templeton Crocker; Newton secured *When the Morning Stars Sang Together*. The latter drawing is now at the Fogg, as is *Job and His Daughters,* which Wells sold to Herbert L. Rothschild in 1924. The final drawing, *Job and His Family Restored to Prosperity* went to W. A. White. Lessing J. Rosenwald later added it to his collection of early illustrated books, and now it belongs to the National Gallery of Art in Washington, D.C.

Wells was more successful in dealing with J. K. Lilly, Jr., the shrewd book buyer who was head of an Indianapolis pharmaceutical company. Lilly's correspondence with Wells (now at the Lilly Library of Indiana University) reveals that between 1923 and 1941 Wells offered Lilly approximately sixty-five items. Though Lilly bought only a few of these, they were important additions to his collection. The most remarkable books Wells sold Lilly were copies, formerly owned by Mrs. John Rylands, of William Shakespeare's First (1623), Second (1632), Third

(1663), and Fourth (1685) Folios, bound in full red levant morocco; Lilly bought them in January 1935 for sixty-five-thousand dollars. Wells probably obtained the volumes through Henry Sotheran and Company, the London bookstore Wells had bought to rescue from collapse after the accidental death of the owner, who had sold John Rylands the copies. According to Robert Metcalf Smith, Wells "doubtless holds the record for importing to America more First Folios of Shakespeare than any other dealer. In 1928 Wells purchased six Folios, and during his career he sold a total of thirty."

Another noteworthy title that Wells sold Lilly is a quarto *Merchant of Venice* (London: Printed by William Jaggard and Thomas Pavier, 1619), part of Pavier's attempted quarto edition of Shakespeare's works, falsely dated 1600 to avoid detection as a piracy. Lilly paid $550 for the book in October 1934. For $1,200 Lilly also bought a presentation copy of Edgar Allan Poe's *Tales* (New York: Wiley & Putnam, 1845), given by the author to Mary Gove; Wells had secured it at the Miller sale at the American Art-Anderson Galleries in New York, 5–6 December 1934, at which he acted for Lilly. A 17 August 1934 invoice shows Wells selling Lilly presentation copies of books by Heinrich Heine, Johann Wolfgang von Goethe, Immanuel Kant, Eugene Sue, and Anatole France; John Galsworthy's first book, *From the Four Winds* (London: Unwin, 1897) – the author's own copy, with an autograph poem on the flyleaf and the highest priced of the items at $675; a first edition of Oliver Goldsmith's *The Deserted Village* (London: Printed for W. Griffin, 1770), re-bound by Riviere; and George Gordon, Lord Byron's *Childe Harold's Pilgrimage* (London: Printed for John Murray, 1812–1818) in original boards, uncut. A first edition of René Descartes's *Discours sur la Methode* (Leyden: I. Maire, 1637) was coveted by another of Wells's customers, the scholar, bibliophile, and librarian Chauncey Brewster Tinker of Yale; but Tinker relinquished his claim, and in May 1939 the book went to Lilly for $260, a price that included "a fine case, for which there is no charge."

Most of Lilly's correspondence was with William Hobart Royce, Wells's manager. In June 1937 Lilly sent Royce a rare medical book as a present for his daughter. Royce was, according to E. Prest Drogan's introduction to Royce's *Balzac Bibliography* (1929), "Gabriel Wells's *alter ego,* he has command of every item that is likely to interest bookmen"; he was also an important collector in his own right. According to David A. Randall, Royce was recommended to Wells by the book dealer Max Harzof, who had trained Royce, as one who "could be implicitly trusted with bags of uncounted gold."

In 1939 Wells sent Lilly a copy of the manuscript for James M. Barrie's *The Little Minister* (Boston: Estes, 1891); in a 22 May letter Royce explained that "it was understood by everybody that it was a transcript, *and not the original manuscript*" of the play that Lilly was buying. Wells wrote Lilly two days later that the Barrie "is the original manuscript, the printer's copy, and that it bears every mark of its being that." Lilly replied on 15 November in a letter addressed to Royce that "there is only one way in the world that I would be interested in reconsidering the Barrie manuscript and that would be following the actual comparison of the two manuscripts at first hand by a disinterested, competent person." Lilly did not buy the manuscript.

Another important collector who had extensive dealings with Wells was Carl H. Pforzheimer; Wells sold Pforzheimer George Eliot's holograph notebooks, as well as items by Byron, Percy Bysshe Shelley and their circle. Wells bought nineteenth-century fiction and manuscripts for Albert A. Berg, and Wells and Berg gave the New York Public Library the manuscript for Byron's *The Curse of Minerva* (London: Privately printed by T. Davison, 1812) for the Henry W. Berg Collection (named for Albert Berg's brother). They also donated the manuscripts for Barrie's *The Little Minister,* Sir Walter Scott's "The Siege of Malta," and Bernard Shaw's first play, *Widowers' Houses* (London: Henry, 1893).

Another Wells customer of long standing was Henry Clay Folger; their correspondence runs from 1912 to 1930, the year of Folger's death. Wells sold Folger many items related to Shakespeare, including a made-up copy of the First Folio; Folger was eager to get First Folios in any condition. Wells also sold Folger seven pictures with Shakespearean associations. The first was the so-called Kneller Portrait, which Folger bought in September 1918 for $2,100. In June 1922 the Lumley Portrait of Shakespeare sold for 300 guineas at the Burdett-Coutts sale at Christie's in London; Folger bought it from Wells for $1,750 after Wells convinced him of its importance. In December 1923 Folger bought for $550 a portrait of the eighteenth-century actor David Garrick that Wells had acquired from Harry Spurr, a London dealer. An oil on canvas depicting Portia and Shylock, dated 1835, was bought by Folger in January 1927 for $2,000, with Wells acting as agent for the owner, A. H. Halberstadt, of Pottstown, Pennsylvania. In August 1927 Folger bought the most expensive of his painting acquisitions, paying $51,075 for *The Infant Shakespeare Attended by Nature and the Passions,* by George Romney. Another Romney, a study for *Titania, Puck and the Changeling,* was bought by F. Sabin at the

SHELLEY'S OWN COPY OF "QUEEN MAB" WITH HIS MANUSCRIPT REVISIONS

1077 SHELLEY (PERCY BYSSHE). [Queen Mab; A Philosophical Poem: With Notes.]   [London: Printed by P. B. Shelley, 1813]

8vo, original boards, uncut (shaken, rebacked, and back worn). In a sage green levant morocco silk-lined box, with snap.

FIRST EDITION, AND WITHOUT DOUBT THE MOST VALUABLE AND DESIRABLE SHELLEY VOLUME WHICH HAS EVER OCCURRED FOR SALE BY AUCTION. IT IS SHELLEY'S OWN COPY, PROFUSELY FILLED WITH HIS MANUSCRIPT NOTES from Canto VIII to the end of the Poem, which he terms the "Second Part."

This is the copy Shelley used for an abridged and amended text of the poem, which he entitled "The Daemon of the World", and which he printed in 1816 in the volume "Alastor and other Poems". It lacks the title and dedication leaves and, of course, the lower portion of the leaf (pp. 239-240) containing the imprint, which Shelley himself cut from the copies he distributed among his friends.

This book was once the property of H. Buxton Forman who used it for completing "The Daemon" in his edition of Shelley's Poetical Works, and is fully described there. It contains many deletions and very many alterations and additions all in Shelley's hand.

Until 1905 it was believed that this copy was the only one in existence, containing such alterations and additions, but in that year another copy came to light which proved to be a transcript from this copy made for the printer to follow, the first copy—this copy—evidently, being kept by Shelley.

In the case enclosing this book are letters which passed between H. Buxton Forman and Dr. Thomas J. Wise who acquired the second copy. These letters tell the story of the discovery and the acquisition of the copy now in the Ashley Library.

It is evident that Shelley used this copy for his first attempt at forming the text of "The Daemon", and that when he came to prepare the printer's "copy" he made the copy now in the Ashley Library.

When Mr. Forman was afforded the opportunity to collate and compare the two volumes, he dealt with the respective differences in a communication to "The Athenaeum" of October 14, 1905. Dr. Wise, describing his copy in his "A Shelley Library" (1924), makes this note: "In the main the changes made in both agree, but to a certain extent each carries revisions peculiar to itself." It is interesting to learn, from the correspondence which passed between Dr. Wise and Mr. Buxton Forman, that after the former had acquired the second copy of Shelley's book, he offered the latter one thousand pounds for his copy, and another Shelley book. Mr. Forman declined the offer.

68,000.00

Catalogue description of an item in the Jerome Kern Collection, sold at auction in 1929. Wells placed the highest bid, $68,000, but he was unable to resell the book.

London Christie's Raphael sale on 29 May 1927 for £304.10.0 and obtained by Folger from Wells in March 1928 for $3,850.

Wells cultivated personal contacts with Tinker, keeper of rare books in the new Sterling Library at Yale, and with Yale trustee Wilmarth Sheldon Lewis, for whose private collection Wells obtained Horace Walpole materials. When Tinker was developing a George Eliot collection at Yale, Wells kept him supplied with materials. Wells had extensive contacts in Europe, particularly in England, France, and his native Hungary. His connections with the trade in England extended from his part ownership of Sotheran's bookshop in London and a close relationship with the bookselling brothers Lionel and Philip Robinson (in whose apartment Wells stayed when in London) to buying at Sotheby's and other English auction houses. In Paris in 1925 Wells was instrumental in saving Honoré de Balzac's house from being razed. Some of his writings were translated into Hungarian in 1929, and he received the Hungarian Cross of Merit in

1931. Wells died in his apartment at the Hotel Mayflower in New York on 6 November 1946.

Opinions of Wells in memoirs written by fellow booksellers are divided. Randall, who became the Lilly librarian at Indiana University, repeats in his *Dukedom Large Enough* (1969) remarks that he made in the spring 1961 issue of the *Book Collector* in response to Percy H. Muir's observations in the autumn 1960 number. For Muir, Wells was "a dear, pathetic, ridiculous little man ... brash, unjust," and Wells's chief rival, A. S. W. Rosenbach, was "by far the greatest bookseller." Randall points out that Rosenbach "bought almost exclusively in the sale room or privately. Gabriel was in and out of bookshops all the time." He admits that Rosenbach "was the more scholarly and better educated person and the more skillful manipulator" but says that during the period from 1930 to 1945 Wells "was by far the greater and more wholesome influence on the entire antiquarian book-world." During the Depression, Randall says, Wells supported the auction market and collaborated with fellow dealers; he "desired nothing more than to sell books to the trade and was a constant buyer for stock both from the trade and at auction." Rosenbach, on the other hand, did not collaborate with the trade and purchased "the most expensive item in a sale – invariably with someone else's money." Wells was consistently an underbidder and purchased more at a given sale. He would lend money to a dealer who "had the opportunity to purchase something he couldn't finance." Further, Wells helped dealers when they got into financial trouble, especially in the 1930s. He assisted Harzof and Randall himself, and he helped rebuild confidence in the trade following the 1929 stock market crash. Randall observes, "In the years of the Depression [Wells] was the strong right arm of the small (and some not so small) dealers and of the American auction market. His death at that time would have been a shattering blow to the antiquarian trade," whereas Rosenbach's death would have been "merely a matter of gossip."

Randall notes that "many people took cruel advantage of [Wells's] ignorance and vanity." During the Jerome Kern sale at the Anderson Galleries in New York on 21 January 1929 Wells and Rosenbach were competing for Kern's copy of *Queen Mab* (London: Printed by P. B. Shelley, 1813); apparently Shelley's personal annotated copy, the book had been sold to Kern by Rosenbach for ninety-five hundred dollars. Rosenbach pushed Wells to a bid of sixty-eight thousand dollars, which was then the second highest American auction record for a book. The book was still in Wells's stock at his death; it was sold by his executors at auction in 1951 and purchased for eight thousand dollars by Pforzheimer.

Among Wells's gifts to libraries was the holograph for Thomas Wolfe's *Look Homeward, Angel* (New York: Scribners, 1929) to Harvard; he had secured the manuscript at auction in 1936 for what was then regarded as the absurdly high price of $1,750. Aline Bernstein, to whom Wolfe had dedicated the book, had put the manuscript on sale to raise money for the Spanish Republicans. In his will Wells gave certain libraries first choice of what they wanted from his stock.

Kraus regarded Wells as "a George D. Smith kind of bookseller," that is, one who was ignorant of all but the price of his merchandise: "Wells had perhaps some limited knowledge of rare books but no personal taste for them and no desire to learn." Kraus adds that Wells made no apologies for this lack, nor did he consider it a handicap. He cites Wells's response when Kraus asked to consult his reference library. "We don't need a reference library. . . . We do good business without one. . . . Believe me, Kraus,

you cannot sell a book easily when you know too much about it."

Not surprisingly, references to Wells in Edwin Wolf and John Fleming's biography of Rosenbach (1960) are unflattering. Wells is described as one of Rosenbach's "assassins," and Wells's success in purchasing the manuscript for Conrad's *Under Western Eyes* (London: Methuen, 1911) at the 1923 Quinn sale is referred to as Wells's managing to prevent its acquisition by Rosenbach, who had bought all the other important manuscripts at the auction. The two continually bid against each other, with Rosenbach usually winning. Wells sometimes triumphed, though, as in the case of the Conrad manuscript and as when, in 1933, the banker George Blumenthal gave Wells his excellent collection of Poe manuscripts that Rosenbach had held on consignment for several years without being able to find a buyer. Yet Rosenbach, Wells, and the collector Owen D. Young were on the same side as defendants in a case brought against them by Lord Rothschild. Young had bought from Rosenbach the Kern copy of the first edition of Henry Fielding's *Tom Jones* (London: Printed for A. Millar, 1749), said to be the only known copy in original, uncut condition. In 1937 Wells had sold the copy on Young's behalf, with a portion of Alexander Pope's holograph *An Essay on Man* (London: Printed for J. Wilford, 1733–1734), to Lord Rothschild. In the spring of 1940 it was discovered that the *Tom Jones* was defective. Young's librarian had collated the volumes in July 1931 and had found that leaves had been tampered with, so that the set was not in the pristine condition claimed for it. Young's librarian had informed Rosenbach, but neither Wells nor Lord Rothschild had known. Young and Wells settled with Rothschild, and the book was returned to Rosenbach.

Though innocent of intentional wrongdoing, Wells had not collated the book himself, as he should have. Another example of his failure to engage in bibliographical homework is found in his pamphlet *The Carter-Pollard Disclosures,* in which Wells defends Thomas J. Wise out of loyalty based on a long-term friendship. John Carter and Graham Pollard had recognized that Wise had been producing fabrications of nineteenth-century works and passing them along to collectors. Although the evidence was overwhelmingly against Wise, Wells refused to believe the charges.

Though sometimes gullible and occasionally vindictive, Wells reveals in his publications an idealistic approach to collecting and dealing. "The collector assembles and treasures, whilst the dealer stimulates and purveys," he wrote in *American Book Collector* for February 1932. "It is eminently the part of the antiquarian dealer to offer and distribute his stock with a preferential regard for destinations most adapted to serve the cause of culture." Johann Carl Buettner and Temple Scott praised Wells's publishing endeavors and commended his activities "as a producer of fine books, as a publisher of the best edition of standard authors," and as a philosopher and commentator on current events. They also cited the pithy epigrams in his beautifully designed Christmas keepsakes. Scott cites keepsakes titled "Life Eternal" (1925) and "Life Temporal" (1926). The one for 1925 was printed on Dutch watermarked paper manufactured by Van Gelder, included a colophon designed by Bruce Rogers, and was printed at the fine press of William Edwin Rudge. The keepsakes' enduring interest rests on their Rogers and Rudge associations rather than Wells's sentiments, which seem dated and overmoralistic.

Charles F. Heartman, who edited and published the *American Book Collector,* and other friends of Wells's published as a Yuletide gift a limited edition of *Bibliography of Wells's Writings and Speeches* (1939). In his preface Heartman draws attention to Wells's activities as a publicist, as a critic of contemporary society, and as a writer: "For a man who came to this country with a smattering knowledge of the English language, he has achieved, to an unbelievable degree, the distinction of being today a master of this medium of expression to an extent truly enviable." Heartman's emphasis is on Wells as a successful bookseller but one with a "disregard of commercial gain." Wells "considered himself a temporary trustee of treasures, which really should go to a more definite resting place."

Wells wrote profusely over many years on many subjects. His preferred form was the short, pithy comment, and he delighted in writing letters to newspapers, especially on topics of public concern such as Prohibition, the chances for peace in Europe after World War I, the consequences of the 1929 stock market crash, and the formation of the League of Nations. He continually advocated "mediation," cautioned "that direct action never settles anything permanently," and attacked American isolationism in the 1920s. He wrote a letter on Germany and the Jews in December 1935, but, as might be expected from his changing his name, he was not involved in Zionist causes.

Wells was a member of the Historical Society of New York, an honorary member of the Elizabethan Club of Yale and of the Johnson Club of London, and a member of the Council of Friends of British Libraries. He knew Shaw, Barrie, and other major literary figures of his time. He was a prime participant in the book trade and at book auctions for more than two decades. He was not a collector but a dispenser and placer of books, manuscripts, and paintings. Materials he sold, gave, or bequeathed are found in institutions in the United States and Europe. His business died with him, yet his position as a major figure in the rare-book and manuscript world of the period 1918 to 1945 is secure.

Bibliography:

Charles F. Heartman, *Bibliography of The Writings and Speeches of Gabriel Wells, LHD* (Hattiesburg, Miss.: Privately printed, 1939).

References:

Johann Carl Buettner, "The Publishing Activities of a Dealer in Rare Books," *American Book Collector,* 2 (1926): 268–270;

H. P. Kraus, *A Rare Book Saga: The Autobiography of H. P. Kraus* (New York: Putnam, 1978), pp. 84, 92–95, 139–142;

Harold M. Otness, *The Shakespeare Folio Handbook and Census* (New York: Greenwood Press, 1990);

William L. Pressly, *A Catalogue of Paintings in the Folger Shakespeare Library: "as imagination bodies forth"* (New Haven: Yale University Press, 1993);

David A. Randall, *Dukedom Large Enough* (New York: Random House, 1969);

William Hobart Royce, *A Balzac Bibliography* (Chicago: University of Chicago Press, 1929), p. xvi;

Temple Scott, "Gabriel Wells, The Philosopher," *American Book Collector,* 3 (March 1927): 229–235;

Robert Metcalf Smith, *The Shakespeare Folios . . . With a List of Folios in American Libraries* (Bethlehem, Pa.: Lehigh University Publications, 1927);

Edwin Wolf and John F. Fleming, *Rosenbach: A Biography* (Cleveland & New York: World, 1960).

Papers:

The major collections of Gabriel Wells's business correspondence are at the New York Public Library; the Folger Shakespeare Library, Washington, D.C.; and the Lilly Library, Indiana University at Bloomington. Among other collections are those at the British Library; the Harry Ransom Humanities Research Center, University of Texas at Austin; the Huntington Library, San Marino, California; Rutgers University Library; and Yale University Library.

Harry Elkins Widener

(3 January 1885 – 15 April 1912)

Leslie A. Morris
Houghton Library, Harvard University

Harry Elkins Widener once remarked of his family to fellow bibliophile A. Edward Newton: "We are all collectors. My grandfather collects paintings, my mother collects silver and porcelains, Uncle Joe collects everything, and I collect books." Given his background, it was perhaps inevitable that Widener became a collector. His grandfather, P. A. B. Widener, had made a considerable fortune through varied investments in streetcars, oil, steel, and tobacco, and he built Lynnewood Hall, an enormous, Versailles-like mansion in Philadelphia, which he filled with Old Master paintings. His eldest son, George, eventually took over the management of the family investments and married Eleanor Elkins, the daughter of his father's close business associate William Elkins.

Harry Widener, born in Philadelphia on 3 January 1885, was the eldest of the three children of George and Eleanor Widener. The family all lived at Lynnewood Hall, and Widener grew up in a protected and privileged environment. He attended the DeLancey School in Philadelphia and the Hill School in Pottstown, Pennsylvania, before entering Harvard in 1903.

At Harvard Widener's course work focused on history. It was not his historical bent which led him toward book collecting, however; it was his involvement in the Hasty Pudding Club. While researching costumes for various productions of this theatrical group, he became fascinated by the colorful depictions of English life by artists George Cruikshank and Thomas Rowlandson. The young collector purchased his first book for his collection in 1905 – a presentation copy of Charles Dickens's *Oliver Twist* (London: Chapman and Hall, 1841), illustrated by Cruikshank – which he bought from Campion for two hundred dollars.

Widener bought only that one book in 1905. It was during Christmas vacation that year that he first met fellow Philadelphia collector and bookseller A. S. W. Rosenbach. Rosenbach's first sales to Widener were modest, but the two quickly became close friends, corresponding about bibliographic topics and browsing bookshops together when Widener was home from college. Eleanor Widener was anxious to encourage her son's collecting, and she soon began buying from Rosenbach: in January 1906, for Widener's nineteenth birthday, she spent twenty thousand dollars on color-plate books for him.

This was a good beginning for Widener's first year of collecting. During 1906 Widener expanded his collection by purchasing fifteen sets of extra-illustrated volumes, many from the collection of Philadelphia collector Clarence S. Bement, whose collection was being sold on consignment by Rosenbach. These sets, which included Issac Walton's *Compleat Angler* (London: William Pickering, 1836), Samuel Pepys's *Diary* (London: Bickers and Son, 1877), and Samuel Johnson's *Life of Pope* (London: 1874), cost the young collector upward of three thousand dollars each. He bought close to fifty Rowlandson prints and drawings from Rosenbach; additional Cruikshank prints and illustrated books, again largely from Rosenbach, but also from the English dealers Maggs and Robson and the Boston dealer Charles E. Lauriat; and William Blake engravings. The collecting fever had indeed begun to take hold.

Widener once said that he collected only books he had read and liked, and some of the writers he liked best were the great nineteenth-century British authors: Dickens, William Makepeace Thackeray, Alfred Tennyson, and (perhaps his greatest enthusiasm) Robert Louis Stevenson. According to Rosenbach, Widener said that he had read Stevenson's *Treasure Island* (1883) no fewer than nineteen times. In 1906, along with his purchases of color-plate books, he began adding first editions of these authors to his growing collection.

While Widener certainly purchased from booksellers other than Rosenbach, his friendship with that persuasive dealer started to influence the direction of his collecting. Rosenbach urged Widener to

Harry Elkins Widener (Harvard University Archives)

collect not only the books he liked but also all the great books of English literature. Rosenbach promoted this new direction by appealing first to Widener's mother. In March 1906 Rosenbach convinced Eleanor Widener that if her son was to be a serious collector, he had to have a set of the four folios of William Shakespeare. This was a major leap for a beginning collector. Rosenbach did not have the First Folio in stock, but he did have the second, third, and fourth. Eleanor Widener bought them for eighty-seven hundred dollars. Thus, not so subtly, was the young collector's delight in books that he liked – the colorful prints of Cruikshank, the adventure stories of Stevenson – channeled toward a more serious purpose. However Widener, while he could be persuaded, kept true to one basic principle throughout his collecting career: "No matter how important a book or manuscript may be I only want those which interest me." He collected because he loved literature.

His mother's gift of the Shakespeare folios did succeed in making Widener think of collecting beyond the nineteenth century. In September 1906, as he was starting his final year at Harvard, Widener bought the folio works of Ben Jonson and Francis Beaumont and John Fletcher. It was his first purchase outside his early interests in color-plate books and nineteenth-century literature. At the same time he purchased Johnson's Bible, and shortly afterward Eleanor Widener bought for him a presentation copy of Dickens's *David Copperfield* (London: Bradbury and Evans, 1850). That Christmas his mother gave him Dickens's agreement with his publishers for *Sketches by Boz,* some Rowlandson drawings, and a few other items.

In March 1907 the collection of William Van Antwerp was sold at Sotheby's in London. Included in the collection was a good copy of the First Folio of Shakespeare, a key piece missing from Widener's collection. With the encouragement of Widener's mother (who was providing the cash), Rosenbach went to London to bid on Widener's behalf. Wisely, he decided to entrust the bid to the London bookseller Bernard Quaritch, who would otherwise have been a competitor, and the First Folio went to Widener for thirty-six hundred pounds. It was the highest price the folio had brought. Later, Widener bought the 1640 edition of Shakespeare's *Poems* from Rosenbach for twenty-five hundred dollars. He did not neglect his earlier enthusiasms, however. That same year he further expanded his collection of illustrated books by purchasing a complete set of Randolph Caldecott's children's books and forty Kate Greenaway titles from Pickering and Chatto in London. He also bought more than sixty nineteenth-century costume books from Rosenbach and continued to purchase heavily in books and manuscripts of Dickens, Thackeray, Stevenson, and George Cruikshank.

Shortly after adding the First Folio to his shelves, Widener graduated from Harvard and joined his grandfather, father, and uncle in managing the family's myriad financial interests. Now that he was a workingman with an income of his own, Widener began approaching his collecting more systematically. During his student years all of the major purchases for his collection were gifts from his mother. Once he was earning a salary, he became more willing to buy, although he would often remark, as he did to bookseller Luther Livingston in 1909, "I could not touch anything at present as I want just to pay off my debts." When an important sale was announced, he would stop buying from dealers to start saving his money for what he wanted in the auction.

The Rosenbach Company's files contain a list of 165 desiderata from the collection of Philadelphia collector Bement (being sold on consignment by Rosenbach) drawn up by Widener in February 1908, with his scrawled instructions to Rosenbach to "fill in the prices" of the books. The items range in importance and price from Raphael Holinshed's *Chronicles* (London: John Hunne, 1577) – his mother bought this for him in 1909 for $750 – and the first English translation of Miguel de Cervantes's *Don Quixote* (London: E. Blount, 1620), which Widener bought for $577.50, to the sequel to George Gordon, Lord Byron's *Don Juan* (London: Pagett, 1819); he bought it for $7.95. In all, it is an extremely ordered approach to collecting.

In 1908 Widener bought heavily at the sale of the Stevenson collector George M. Williamson, adding some eighty titles to his Stevenson collection

that year. Additional Thackeray and Dickens items found their way to his shelves; he bought many firsts of Algernon Charles Swinburne and Walter Pater; and he began amassing a major collection of Robert Browning's works, largely purchased from Maggs, Quaritch and Ernest Dressel North.

Widener was proposed for membership in the Grolier Club in 1907 by George F. Kunz (and seconded by J. P. Morgan and George B. DeForest), a mark of his acceptance by his peers as a collector. As part of the membership process, he was asked to write about his collecting. He was then twenty-four years old and had been collecting seriously for a little more than three years:

> My object is to have eventually as complete a collection of nineteenth century writers and illustrators as possible, while of course I hope to have a few of the great works of the earlier periods – such as Milton, Burton, and Shakespeare.
>
> At present the finest part of my library consists of Shakespeare, Extra-Illustrated Books – largely from the Daly Collection, and almost complete sets of the first issues of Swinburne, Pater, Reade, Stevenson and Robert Browning. Also some of my illustrators are fairly complete especially Rowlandson.

His nomination to the Grolier Club came at a time when he was planning to compile a catalogue of his collection. The catalogue was published, in an edition of one hundred copies on paper and two on vellum, in 1910; his friend Rosenbach helped compile the descriptions. His collection then numbered more than fifteen hundred volumes.

It was while working with Rosenbach on this catalogue that Widener bought from him one of the treasures of his collection, the countess of Pembroke's own copy of *Arcadia* (London: H. L. for Mathew Lownes, 1613), the poem written for her by her brother Sir Philip Sidney. The book had passed through Rosenbach's hands four years earlier and Widener had coveted it, but, at twenty-two hundred dollars, it had been beyond his budget. Now Rosenbach had it again. The price had doubled, but no collector will pass up a second time a book that he has wanted and lost. It went into his collection, and Rosenbach claimed that it was Widener's favorite book. But the nineteenth century was not neglected: Widener purchased the manuscript of an unpublished autobiography of Stevenson; forty-nine volumes illustrated by John Leech were purchased from Robson; and a new direction was taken with the purchase of twenty-nine William Morris books, including *Lectures on Art* (London: Macmillan, 1882) and *The Story of the Glit-*

A CATALOGUE

OF

SOME OF THE MORE IMPORTANT
BOOKS, MANUSCRIPTS
AND DRAWINGS

IN THE LIBRARY OF
HARRY ELKINS WIDENER

PHILADELPHIA
PRIVATELY PRINTED
MDCCCCX

Title page for the catalogue of selected items in Widener's collection
(Houghton Library, Harvard University)

tering Plain (Hammersmith, U.K.: Kelmscott Press, 1896–1897). For Christmas that year his mother gave him Sidney's copy of Francesco Guicciardini's *Dell'istoria d'Italia* (Vinegia, Italy: Gabriel Giolito, 1569); eight presentation copies of Dickens; and an illuminated copy of the Magna Carta printed on vellum for George IV. Widener particularly sought presentation copies of the books he loved.

The purchase of the *Arcadia* seems to have primed the pump as far as Widener's collecting was concerned. To that point, he had generally spent modest sums on books at any one time; most of the large purchases had been gifts from his mother. Now his limits were expanding. In January 1910 he spent nearly $17,000 on works by Dickens, Cruikshank drawings, a portion of the manuscript of Thackeray's *Pendennis* (1848–1850) with Thackeray's drawings, and first editions of Edmund Spenser's *The Faerie Queene* (1590) and John Milton's *Paradise Lost* (1667). Later that year he bought a first

edition of Daniel Defoe's *Robinson Crusoe* (1719) for $2,000 and a presentation copy of Dickens's *Pickwick Papers* (1837) for $1,650, both from Rosenbach.

In the spring of 1911 the library of American collector Robert Hoe was to be sold at auction in New York. This was one of the greatest collections of books in the United States, and it was to be one of the most important sales ever held in this country. The books were just the type for Widener's expanding collection, and he hoped to be a major buyer in the sale. But it was not to be. It was at the Hoe sale that California millionaire Henry E. Huntington emerged as an irrresistible force, sweeping all before him. Bidding through George D. Smith, Huntington bought the crown jewel of the collection, a copy of the Gutenburg Bible on vellum, for a record price of fifty thousand dollars; P. A. B. Widener was the underbidder. And so it went, with Huntington persistently outbidding the Wideners on everything they wanted.

Harry Widener was not only disappointed in not getting the books he wanted, he was appalled at the prices: "Are these awful prices going to keep up?" he complained to Livingston. This did not stop him from going into Rosenbach's in Philadelphia four days later and spending twenty-five thousand dollars on a William Caxton, some drawings for the *Pickwick Papers,* and Dickens's contract for the same. On a trip to England in the summer of 1911, the young collector carried letters of introduction to fellow bibliophiles Clement Shorter, Edmund Gosse, and T. J. Wise.

At the second Hoe sale, in January 1912, Widener fared somewhat better than at the first. As he remarked to Livingston:

> Indeed the only very high books were such in English Literature as Mr. Huntington did not happen to possess. On all such he was apparently unlimited and it made me very angry at not being able to buy the "Dunciad" and two of the Middletons. Still I had the small satisfaction of making him pay for them.

In this sale was a second copy of the Gutenberg Bible, and P. A. B. Widener still wanted one. On this occasion Rosenbach, who had handled the bid in the first sale, told Widener that he thought they would have a better chance of getting it if the bid were entrusted to Quaritch. Quaritch bought the Bible for $27,500. Harry Widener wrote excitedly to Livingston:

> Now I will tell you a secret only you *must tell no one* until it is out – Grandfather has bought the Hoe copy of the Mazarin Bible. Is it not great? I wish it was for me but it is not.

As a loyal Harvard alumnus Widener continued to be deeply interested in the college and particularly in the library. During his time at Harvard the college library was in badly cramped quarters, and a new one had been talked of for several years. In the spring of 1912, according to Harvard librarian George Parker Winship, Widener discussed with a friend how he could help raise the money for a new library; he wanted to have some influence in making it the best possible library for scholars to use. Nothing was to be done quickly, however, and in mid March Widener left for Europe with his parents. George and Harry Widener had been deputed by P. A. B. to look at some paintings he was thinking of acquiring, and Eleanor Widener was to make some purchases for her daughter's trousseau. Harry Widener wrote to a friend shortly before embarking that he did not expect to do much buying, as he was

saving for the Huth sale in London that June. However, he did leave bids for the final Hoe sale with Rosenbach – it was scheduled to begin 15 April, when Widener still would be en route from England on board the *Titanic.*

While in London Widener viewed the books for the upcoming Huth sale and made some purchases in the shops. He bought nine books from Quaritch, including the 1598 edition of Francis Bacon's *Essays,* on 1 April 1912. The Bacon he took away with him, requesting that the other books be shipped. A few days later he was back at Quaritch and bought the first edition of Edward Gibbon's *Decline and Fall of the Roman Empire* (1776–1788). Just before catching the train to board the *Titanic,* he stopped in at J. Pearson and Company and purchased a small, four-leaf pamphlet entitled *Hevy news of an horryble erthquake which was in the Citie of Scarbaria* (1542). This too he took with him.

The *Titanic* left Southampton on 10 April 1912 on her maiden voyage to New York. Five days later she crashed into an iceberg in the north Atlantic; more than sixteen hundred lives were lost. The *Boston Herald* on 24 April reported Eleanor Widener's account of the disaster:

> "Mr. Widener and I had retired to our cabin for the night," she said, "when the shock of crashing into the iceberg occurred. We thought little of it, and did not leave our cabin. We must have remained there an hour before becoming fearful. Then Mr. Widener went to our son Harry's room and brought him to our cabin. A short time later Harry went to the deck and hurried back and told us that we must go on deck. Mr. Widener and Harry a few minutes later went on deck and aided the officers who were then having trouble with those in the steerage. That was the last I saw of my husband or son."

News of the wreck of the *Titanic* reached New York the morning the third of the Hoe sales started. Rosenbach bid for Widener, even when it seemed certain that the young collector was lost. He was twenty-seven years old at the time of his death.

Much has been written about Widener's "last book." The story is perhaps one of the most famous of twentieth-century book stories. Fellow Philadelphian A. Edward Newton devoted a chapter in his book *The Amenities of Book Collecting* (1918), published six years after Widener's death, to what he called "in all the history of book-collecting . . . the most touching story." In his account Harry Widener's last purchase in London was the 1598 Bacon, and Harry presciently remarked to Quaritch, "I think I'll take that litttle Bacon with me

Harry Elkins Widener Memorial Library, Harvard University (Houghton Library, Harvard University)

in my pocket, and if I am shipwrecked it will go with me."

In his memoir of Widener, published with the catalogue of the Widener Stevenson collection in 1913, Rosenbach related what he called "the most touching, most pathetic, withal the most glorious incident in the romance of book collecting":

> He had purchased from Mr. Quaritch the rare second edition of Bacon's Essays (1598), of which only a few copies are extant. He said he would take it with him, as he did not want to trust it with the other volumes that he had bought. He would keep it in his dispatch box, with which he always traveled. Just before the "Titanic" sank he said to his mother: "Mother, I have placed the volume in my pocket; little 'Bacon' goes with me!"

Here Widener is not morbidly anticipating his own watery death – rather, if he is saved, the precious book will be saved too, rather than lost with his luggage. It seems unlikely that Rosenbach would have put into print a story about Eleanor Widener's last moments with her son unless the account had come from her and had her approval.

In Widener's will his collection was left to his mother with the request that it be given to Harvard when suitable accommodations could be found for it. There was great excitement at Harvard when news of the will was heard, for the university was hopeful that the Widener family might do something substantial, such as replace the inadequate college library building.

As the weeks after the death of her son passed, Eleanor Widener decided that there were two things that needed to be done for Harry. The first was to make his collection what it would have become had he lived to continue with it. This job she entrusted to Rosenbach. Second, a building needed to be provided for the collection. By August 1912

Harry Elkins Widener Memorial Room, Widener Memorial
Library (Harvard University Archives)

she had made up her mind that providing Harvard with a new college library would serve as the right memorial. In a letter to Harvard's president, A. Lawrence Lowell, Eleanor stated firmly:

> . . . the only thing I . . . want emphasized is, that the library is a memorial to my dear son & to be known as the "Harry Elkins Widener Memorial Library" & given by me & not his Grandfather . . .

The agreement was signed by Eleanor Widener and Harvard on 31 December 1912.

In his parallel course Rosenbach was tending to the growth of Widener's collection. Seven weeks after the sinking of the *Titanic,* the second Huth sale began. Eleanor Widener instructed Rosenbach to see that all Widener's commissions for the sale, left with Quaritch before his departure, were acted upon and every volume secured. These – which might truly by called the last books Widener purchased – included the unique copy of Robert Chamberlaine's

The Booke of Bulls (1636), the only perfect recorded copy of Richard Pynson's 1526 edition of Geoffrey Chaucer's works, and works by Samuel Daniel, Thomas Dekker, Michael Drayton, and William Drummond.

By the end of June 1912 – ten weeks after her son's death – Eleanor Widener had spent more than $120,000 adding to his collection. She bought along the lines Widener had collected: more Dickens, Cruikshank drawings, Thackeray, Blake's *Songs of Innocence and of Experience* (1794), George Chapman's translations of Homer (1598–1615), Alexander Pope's correspondence with his legal advisor, and many other volumes. P. A. B. Widener contributed by ordering the manuscript of Tennyson's "Charge of the Light Brigade," several of Robert Burns's manuscripts, and later the Vailima letters of Stevenson. In July Eleanor Widener bought a group of presentation copies of books by American authors that Rosenbach had been collecting over the last few years – $27,490 for Henry

Wadsworth Longfellow, Ralph Waldo Emerson, Nathaniel Hawthorne, Edgar Allan Poe, and others. As Eleanor wrote to a friend in August 1912, "[Dr. Rosenbach and Harry] always talked everything over together." Now that Harry was gone, she talked everything over with Rosenbach.

Eleanor Widener asked Rosenbach to publish a catalogue of the Harry Elkins Widener collection. The plan was to produce individual volumes for the three largest collections – Stevenson, the Cruikshanks, and Dickens – and then everything else. By Christmas 1913 the first volume of the Stevenson collection was finished.

During 1914 the building of the Harry Elkins Widener Memorial Library increasingly consumed Eleanor Widener's attention, and the pace of her purchases from Rosenbach diminished. But she frequently consulted Rosenbach about the library, and the depth of her attachment to him is summed up in a letter she wrote to him in July 1914:

> When the Library is finished I want all the books installed there. Then I will feel happiness and know I have done as my dear boy wished. Over two years have gone since I lost him, and I am no more reconciled than I was at first, and never will be again. All joy of living left me on April 15, 1912. Forgive me for writing you like this but you loved Harry, and can understand my sorrow.

The dedication of the library took place on 24 June 1915.

References:

Arthur Freeman, "Harry Widener's Last Books: Corrigenda to A. E. Newton," *Book Collector* (Summer 1977): 173–185;

William A. Jackson, "Notes: Hevy newes of an horryble erthquake in Scarbaria," in *Harvard Library Bulletin,* 6 (1952): 148–150;

A. Edward Newton, "A Word in Memory," in *The Amenities of Book Collecting* (Boston, 1918);

A. S. W. Rosenbach, *A Catalogue of Some of the Most Important Books, Manuscripts and Drawings in the Library of Harry Elkins Widener* (Philadelphia: Privately printed, 1910);

Rosenbach, *A Catalogue of the Books and Manuscripts of Robert Louis Stevenson in the Library of the Late Harry Elkins Widener with a Memoir by A. S. W. Rosenbach* (Philadelphia: Privately printed, 1913);

Rosenbach, *A Catalogue of the Books and Manuscripts of Harry Elkins Widener,* 2 volumes (Philadelphia: Privately printed, 1918);

Rosenbach, *A Catalogue of the Works Illustrated by George Cruikshank and Isaac and Robert Cruikshank in the Library of Harry Elkins Widener* (Philadelphia: Privately printed, 1918);

Rosenbach, *A Catalogue of the Writings of Charles Dickens in the Library of Harry Elkins Widener* (Philadelphia: Privately printed, 1918);

George Parker Winship, "The Harry Elkins Widener Memorial Library," *Harvard Alumni Bulletin,* XVII: 36 (16 June 1915): 668–670.

Papers:

Harry Widener's letters to Luther Livingston and two ledgers which record his purchases through 1910 are in the Widener Memorial Library at Harvard; his and Eleanor Elkins Widener's correspondence with A. S. W. Rosenbach is part of the Rosenbach Company archive, Rosenbach Museum and Library, Philadelphia. Information about Harry Widener's Harvard career is in the Harvard University Archives.

John Henry Wrenn

(11 September 1841 – 13 May 1911)

Richard W. Oram
University of Texas at Austin

The names of the Chicago book collector John Henry Wrenn and the English bibliographer and fabricator Thomas J. Wise will be linked forever in the annals of bibliophily. Their association began in the early 1890s and lasted almost twenty years, and it was Wise, acting as Wrenn's adviser and agent, who was responsible for acquiring most of the six thousand volumes of English literature in the Chicago industrialist's library. After Wise was unmasked in 1934, a nearly complete set of his faked pamphlets was discovered in the Wrenn Library. The publication a decade later of a portion of Wise's correspondence with Wrenn revealed that the latter had been systematically deceived and defrauded by his friend. Still later, the revelation that Wise had assembled made-up copies of Restoration plays using leaves stolen from the British Museum emerged from an examination of the Wrenn books. The Wise counterfeits constitute a relatively small percentage of the Wrenn Library, however, and even those who abhor Wise's criminal activities concede that without his assistance Wrenn could not have assembled such an important collection.

Little is known about Wrenn's origins, business career, and early book-collecting habits. Born in Middletown, Ohio, on 11 September 1841 and descended (according to family tradition) from the great English architect Sir Christopher Wren, Wrenn was first employed as a bookkeeper in the family's paper mill. He attracted the attention of his uncle, a Chicago banker, who brought him to that city. Wrenn married Julia Griggs in 1866; they had two daughters, Alice and Ethel, and a son, Harold. Becoming a partner in his uncle's firm, Wrenn was a pioneering member of the Chicago Board of Trade and other exchanges. Successful both as a banker and a broker, he eventually founded John H. Wrenn and Company. Wrenn became a member of the Grolier Club of New York in 1893. In 1903 he moved into the Robert W. Patterson mansion at 1500 Astor Street; a particularly attractive feature

of the house was a large library (twenty-two by thirty-eight feet, according to Wise) which housed his treasures. He retired as president of John H. Wrenn and Company in 1910 and died of a heart attack on 13 May 1911 while visiting his son in Los Angeles.

Thomas J. Wise, who frequently defrauded Wrenn by selling him fabricated copies of supposedly rare books

George Chandler. During a visit to England in the summer of 1892 he was introduced to Wise by the Chicago publisher and bibliophile W. Irving Way. Like Wrenn, Wise was a successful businessman — he was an executive in the essential-oils trade — though he was a far "sharper" and less scrupulous personality than the genteel and rather diffident Wrenn. Texas rare-book librarian Fannie E. Ratchford, who edited Wise's letters to Wrenn (1944), has reconstructed this fateful first encounter: "it was the host, self-assured, shrewd, and aggressive, who took the lead in conversation. He discussed with enthusiasm his various bibliographical activities ... even boasting of acquaintance with [Algernon Charles] Swinburne and [Robert] Browning. He brought out the crown jewels of his collection for the admiration of his visitor, enhancing their interest by stories of their acquisition."

The pattern of the relationship was thus established at the outset: Wise, although several years younger than Wrenn, invariably assumed a dominant, almost paternal role. He was the owner of the Ashley Library, which was soon to become one of the most important collections of English poetry and drama in England, and had already established a reputation as an editor and bibliographer. Wise was particularly well known in the book world for his republications and facsimiles of pamphlets by the Romantics and Victorians. In late 1893 Wrenn wrote to Wise, sending him a book as a present. Their surviving correspondence — which consists of about twelve hundred letters from Wise but only a few from Wrenn — makes it possible to trace the course of a fascinating dealer/collector relationship over more than fifteen years. During 1894 Wise responded to several inquiries from Wrenn and sent him William Morris's *Letters on Socialism,* one of several privately printed pamphlets Wise had seen through the press. But it was not until late 1896 that Wise and Wrenn begin to correspond regularly. On 14 December Wise wrote: "If you are collecting [Alfred] Tennyson, I daresay I can help you a bit during the next few months," and he promised to send Wrenn any duplicates he might acquire in the process of compiling a bibliography on the poet. From this point on Wise subtly began to incorporate offers of books, usually described as duplicates from his own library, into nearly every letter to Wrenn.

In April 1897 Wise sold Wrenn a copy of the first edition of John Milton's *Paradise Lost* (London: Printed and sold by Peter Parker, Robert Boulter, and Matthias Walker, 1667) for seventy pounds after some haggling over the price. Later he offered Tennyson's *Idylls of the Hearth;* when Wrenn asked

"From youth upwards a lover of good literature, he gradually developed into a collector, but not until shortly before our first meeting did his taste lean in one particular direction, and his mind become fixed on the class of books which interested me and eventually fascinated him," Wise wrote of his friend's early inclinations. Wrenn first began to collect books seriously — American literature in particular — around 1885. Most of his important acquisitions over the next twenty-five years came from England, though he is known to have had transactions with the Chicago dealers Walter M. Hill and

George Eliot. "Agatha". A poem. Privately printed. 1869.

Wm Wordsworth" Ode to the Queen"; Privately printed at Kendal in 1846. The rarest of all Wordsworth's pieces.

H. Rider Haggard. "Allan's Wife". An extremely rare little booklet. Uncut in original wrappers. Printed privately to secure copyright in the title of the (then forthcoming) novel of same name.

Matthew Arnold. "Geist's Grave"; privately printed, 1881.

Matthew Arnold. "Saint Brandan". 8vo. 1867.

John Ruskin. "The Opening of the Crystal Palace". 1854. In Wrappers. First. Ed.

John Ruskin. "Pre-Raphaelitism"; first edition in original covers.

W. M. Thackeray. "An Interesting Event". 8vo. 1849. One of the rarest of the First editions of W. M. Thackeray.

Page from Wise's 8 December 1900 letter to Wrenn (Harry Ransom Humanities Research Center, University of Texas at Austin)

Wrenn's library (Harry Ransom Humanities Research Center, University of Texas at Austin)

for an explanation of the book's history, Wise explained that it was a suppressed early version of *Enoch Arden, etc.* (London: Moxon, 1864) with a cancel title page. Bibliographical investigation has determined that the title page was a fabrication produced by Wise himself and inserted in the copy. Thus the first of Wise's manufactures – a relatively minor one – entered the Wrenn library. It was to be followed by many more. In August 1897 Wise coyly let out that "it is just possible that in a week or two I may be able to get hold of a Tennyson book" – namely, the true first edition of "The Last Tournament." It was, Wise claimed, one of the poet's "Trial Books," privately printed in advance of the official publication, and it was authenticated in a book of literary anecdotes by Wise's friend Harry Buxton Forman. It is now known that Forman was Wise's partner-in-crime, having collaborated with him on a series of fabricated pamphlets since 1887. These fakes had been carefully introduced into the book market little by little to avoid arousing the suspicion of collectors and bibliographers. Having established the value and desirability of the Tennyson item in several letters, Wise wrote Wrenn in October 1897 that he had obtained a copy for his correspondent at twenty-eight pounds, ten shillings; he added that "the book may be considered a bargain," and Wrenn apparently agreed. He could not have known that the source was Wise's stockpile of fabrications. Wise dangled a series of similar rarities before the collector in 1898, always carefully building up their desirability in advance. He invariably managed to "locate" an elusive copy, which he then shipped to Chicago. Wrenn's purchases helped to establish the pamphlets' authenticity and encouraged other American buyers to accept them at face value.

In his preface to the Wrenn Library catalogue (1920) Wise characterized his relationship with Wrenn as a mutually beneficial one; he claimed that he located scarce items for Wrenn in London and that Wrenn reciprocated by giving him leads on rare material in the United States. In truth, the flow of books was mainly from east to west, and it was accompanied by a steady flow of money in the opposite direction. Sometimes Wise did serve in a purely advisory capacity, making little or nothing from a transaction in which he participated.

Ratchford points out that he never charged an outright commission, but he usually stood to make a tidy profit from Wrenn's business in one way or another. He was, in fact, dealing in antiquarian books, though he would have disdained the ungentlemanly sound of that word. Well-to-do from his regular employment, Wise still needed supplemental income to support his large-scale book buying for the Ashley Library. Wise once told his associate Herbert Gorfin that Wrenn was "worth a thousand pounds a year to me." That sum was derived not so much from the fabricated pamphlets – it has been estimated that Wrenn spent eight hundred or nine hundred pounds on those acquisitions over the course of about thirteen years – as from the sale of "duplicates" and other books Wise had acquired from various sources; D. F. Foxon has established, for example, that Wise charged more than double the going auction price for twelve plays that Wrenn purchased between 1901 and 1903. In sum, Wise acted unethically by regularly misrepresenting the sources of the books he sold and by frequently (though not in every instance) overcharging his client; his other business practices, such as the sale of fabricated pamphlets, must simply be regarded as criminal.

Many examples of Wise's misrepresentation of the sources of his merchandise can be found in his letters to Wrenn. On 23 November 1900, for example, Wise announced that he was about to visit a "Mr. Arthur Hake" in search of Tennyson and Pre-Raphaelite poetry. Five days later he described in loving detail the deal he had concluded for £190, "a price which I should be prepared to pay were I buying the books for myself." In return for his efforts Wise asked only that Wrenn allow him to keep a minor Victorian novel, for which he proposed to deduct £5 from the sale price. In reality there never was any "Mr. Hake," most of the books were almost certainly assembled by Wise himself, and five of the pamphlets Wrenn acquired in the lot were actually Wise fabrications.

On other occasions Wise would whet Wrenn's appetite by referring to the imminent availability of important books that would fill major gaps in Wrenn's collection. After the passage of days or weeks Wise would triumphantly declare that he had viewed the items in question, and still later that he had concluded a deal on Wrenn's behalf, usually paying a figure substantially below what was originally requested by the seller. Ratchford's research has shown that the purported sellers can rarely be associated with the books they were supposed to have owned and in many cases cannot be

identified at all. Beginning in the early 1900s, Wise frequently cited "Herbert Gorfin, Dealer in Rare Books" as the source of some of the prizes he shipped to Chicago. His negotiations with Gorfin were described in detail, and if Wrenn had chosen to question the dealer's bona fides, an authentic-looking invoice accompanying the purchase would have silenced any doubts. The actuality was that Gorfin was Wise's clerk and principal factotum; he had no independent existence as a book dealer.

The original owners of some of the books that found their way to Wrenn's library can be identified. In 1901 Wise purchased sixty-four quarto plays on Wrenn's behalf from his friend the distinguished man of letters Edmund Gosse for thirty pounds; other books in the Wrenn collection were Gosse duplicates. The volumes of eighteenth-century poetry supplied by Wise were, for the most part, previously owned by the scholar-collector George Aitken, whose library, like Wrenn's, now resides at the University of Texas. Many of the best Pre-Raphaelite items were from W. M. Rossetti, also a Wise acquaintance; and Swinburne first editions, along with many presentation copies and manuscripts from the author's library at the Pines, came to Wise via Theodore Watts-Dunton, Swinburne's longtime companion. Forman supplied Wise with books from his library to send abroad. Though Wise took great pleasure in haunting bookshops himself – his coups are lovingly described in the letters to Wrenn – and seeking out bargains in London and elsewhere, he eventually needed additional sources of books as the pace of Wrenn's purchasing accelerated. From 1902 onward he required the services of William Calder, a dealer and book scout whose name appears inside the back cover of many Wrenn Library books.

The relationship of Wrenn and Wise was not entirely based on exploitation, and it cannot be denied that Wrenn derived many benefits from the association. For one thing, Wrenn was a passive personality who could not have put together a major library without aggressive assistance. Wise knew the auction records and "where the books were." Sometimes he was able to make a profit for himself and still pass along a bargain to Wrenn. Further, he performed several services for Wrenn, including handling the financial transactions and rebinding books and shipping them to America. Wrenn was almost always satisfied with his purchases, and his appreciation of Wise's efforts and advice grew stronger over the years. Wrenn visited the Wise home on several occa-

Wrenn's bookplate depicting his house in Chicago, his copy of
Rembrandt's Three Trees, *and a corner of his library*

sions. Beginning in 1904, the Wrenns and the Wises frequently vacationed together on the Continent, and Mrs. Wise and Mrs. Wrenn became good friends.

Around 1901 Wrenn's collecting interest turned somewhat away from the Victorians and the Romantics and toward the Elizabethans and Restoration drama. "I did not know that you were going in much for the earlier literature. I am doing so myself very largely," Wise wrote Wrenn in April of that year. The news must have been welcome to Wise, for it meant that he had a perfect market for duplicates and inferior copies of early plays in the Ashley Library. Wise began to ship quartos by such authors as James Shirley, Thomas Dekker, Philip Massinger, and Thomas Heywood to Chicago, the bulk of them at prices ranging from five to twenty-five pounds. He later directed Wrenn's attention to what he regarded as the overlooked pamphlet literature of the early eighteenth century, particularly works by Daniel Defoe and Jonathan Swift, explain-

ing that he was collecting in this area and had an opportunity to collect for Wrenn as well. In this case, as in others, Wise's sound judgment and knowledge of the contemporary book market made it possible for Wrenn to acquire unfashionable but important books at relatively reasonable prices.

It now appears that Wrenn's growing interest in quarto plays may have incited Wise to commit new acts of bibliographic larceny and fraud. Wise's letters show plainly that he was untroubled by the sophistication of books (that is, supplying leaves missing from an imperfect copy or substituting leaves in an inferior one to make it more desirable), and at the turn of the century the practice was not as frowned upon as it is today. A substantial portion of the quartos sold to the American collector were "repaired" with supplied half-title or title pages from incomplete copies in Wise's possession. Some books arrived in Chicago containing inferior leaves that Wise had removed from Ashley Library copies; Wise had kept for himself the better leaves from the copies he had purchased on Wrenn's behalf. In 1956 the British Museum announced that certain leaves were missing from quarto plays in its collections and that Wise was the chief suspect; subsequent research by Foxon and William B. Todd proved that Wise had stolen 206 leaves from the British Museum's copies of pre-Restoration plays and placed at least 75 of these leaves in books he sent to Wrenn. Furthermore, Wise habitually charged more for the made-up copies, as if to compensate for his labors. Since Wise always delivered shabby copies to the firm of Riviere and Son for rebinding in uniform tan morocco or calf before they were sent abroad, the substitution of stolen or inferior leaves was easily concealed.

After Wrenn's death the family was approached by dealers who wished to break up and sell his collection. These appeals were resisted, and in 1912 Wrenn's son began to compile a catalogue of the collection for publication. In late 1917 the library came to the attention of Prof. R. H. Griffith, an eighteenth-century scholar in the English department of the University of Texas. Griffith and the university's president prevailed upon Maj. George W. Littlefield, a member of the board of regents and one of the institution's chief benefactors, to purchase the Wrenn collection for $225,000 and donate it to the university. The price was a bargain, considering that it had recently been appraised at between $500,000 and $1 million. Under the university's auspices 120 copies of a deluxe five-volume catalogue of the collection as it stood at Wrenn's death were produced in June 1920. The descriptions were compiled by Harold Wrenn from information supplied by Wise, who added an introduction. Contemporary reviewers and later scholars have pointed out hundreds of errors in the Wrenn catalogue. Many are attributable to Wise's habit of ascribing anonymous items to particular authors without solid evidence. Wise blamed the catalogue's poor reception on the incompetence of the Wrenn family.

The University of Texas's first major acquisition of rare books, the Wrenn Library was housed in a special room of the university library. The arrival of the books in Austin attracted international attention and enhanced the university's image in the scholarly world. The Wrenn Library was moved to the tower of the university's Main Building in the 1930s, along with other special collections, and in 1971 to the new Harry Ransom Humanities Research Center building. Since the publication of *An Enquiry into the Nature of Certain Nineteenth-Century Pamphlets* (1934), by John Carter and Graham Pollard, the Wrenn Library has gained considerable celebrity for its extensive collection of Wise's fabrications. They include some eighty-five pamphlets (including four proof copies), whose title pages bear the names of Tennyson, Swinburne, Elizabeth Barrett and Robert Browning, William Makepeace Thackeray, and a host of other nineteenth-century authors. The market value of many of the Wise fakes now exceeds that of many genuine nineteenth-century pamphlets in the library. Moreover, because of the presence of the fabrications in the Wrenn Library, the University of Texas has become the leading center for studies of Wise.

The fabrications and Wise's sophisticated copies of Restoration plays, however, make up only a fraction of the Wrenn Library, which must be regarded as among the more impressive private American collections of its day. According to Carter, "the Wrenn Library may be hardly more than a partial carbon copy of the Ashley; but it was the top carbon from a great original." The Wrenn Library, about 80 percent of which Wise supplied, was in every respect more Wise's creation than Wrenn's. Wise's collecting philosophy was more forward-looking than that of many other contemporary collectors. Unlike his rival book collector Robert Hoe, Wrenn, acting on Wise's sound advice, avoided familiar high spots of English literature such as the William Shakespeare First Folio (1623) or the Kilmarnock Burns (1786). The Wrenn Library and Wise's Ashley Library attempted to document the history of English literature through both major works and less well known items; the model for both was, in all likelihood, Sir Frederick Locker-Lampson's Rowfant Library. Wise urged Wrenn to purchase "books of real literary value for which the pages of any other catalogue will be searched in vain," and he also sought out items that had never appeared on the shelves of an American library. As a bibliographer, Wise was well aware of the importance of collecting variant texts, and this practice accounts for the presence in the Wrenn Library of many editions and printings other than the first. A clear statement of Wise's goals for the Wrenn collection may be found in a letter to Wrenn of 13 March 1910:

But the main point is this, that it is not composed of a mere accumulation of mixed "rarities" of all kinds, but of a carefully selected series of the works of the Poets and Dramatic-Poets from the time of Elizabeth onwards — that is, it is [a] fine and representative collection of pure literature. This is the object I have had in view throughout, and that is the end I am attaining both for you and for myself. I do not believe that in any other library in America, either Public or private, can such collections be found of either (1) Mid-Seventeenth

Century Poetry: the 4to poems of 1640–1675; (2) The Eighteenth-Century Folio Poetry; and (3) The late Eighteenth-Century Octavo Plays.

As a result, the Wrenn Library contains important collections of works by many authors regarded as unfashionable at the turn of the century alongside works by such major figures as Shakespeare, Edmund Spenser, and John Dryden. Any accounting of the riches of the collection must begin with the works of the major Elizabethan and Jacobean dramatists, including Massinger, Dekker, and Ben Jonson. Wrenn made a point of collecting obscure Royalist pamphlet literature from the English civil war; along with a group of royal proclamations, these pamphlets make up a portion of the library known as "The King's Collection." Not only are there works by Dryden, William Congreve, and Richard Brinsley Sheridan, but also those by such lesser Restoration figures as Edward Brown and Charles Durfey. Thanks to Wise, Wrenn acquired unusually complete runs of works of Queen Anne and Augustan authors such as Defoe, Swift, Alexander Pope, and Henry Fielding before their prices soared; the early eighteenth century is, therefore, one of the library's strongest suits. In the nineteenth century the most significant author collections are those of Percy Bysshe Shelley – including the extremely rare *Original Poetry; by Victor and Cazire,* by Shelley and Elizabeth Shelley (Worthing: Printed by C. and W. Phillips and sold by J. J. Stockdale, London, 1810); Tennyson; Swinburne; and Robert Browning. Most of the productions of Morris's Kelmscott Press are represented. In his early days as a collector Wrenn purchased American literature, and so there are substantial holdings of works by Nathaniel Hawthorne, Henry Wadsworth Longfellow, and James Russell Lowell.

The presence of Thomas J. Wise in the Wrenn Library is almost palpable. The large group of Wise's fabrications and the quarto plays containing stolen leaves remind one of the unscrupulous entrepreneur's ruthlessness and greed. From a somewhat different perspective, however, the library as a whole may be regarded as a monument to Wise's bibliographical knowledge and skill at developing notable collections of English literature. Wrenn himself is much less manifest in the library he purchased, and it is nearly impossible to get a clear picture of Wrenn as either a man or a collector. It can, at least, be said that John Henry Wrenn was a collector with intelligence and taste but that it was his destiny to be dominated and overshadowed by a far more intriguing and imposing personality.

Letters:

Fannie E. Ratchford, ed., *Letters of Thomas J. Wise to John Henry Wrenn: A Further Inquiry into the Guilt of Certain Nineteenth-Century Forgers* (New York: Knopf, 1944).

References:

Carl L. Cannon, *American Book Collectors and Collecting from Colonial Times to the Present* (New York: Wilson, 1941), pp. 200–205;

John Carter, "John Henry Wrenn 1841–1911," in *Grolier 75: A Biographical Retrospective to Celebrate the Seventy-fifth Anniversary of the Grolier Club in New York* (New York: Grolier Club, 1959), pp. 31–34;

Carter and Graham Pollard, *An Enquiry into the Nature of Certain Nineteenth-Century Pamphlets* (New York: Scribners, 1934);

John Collins, *The Two Forgers: A Biography of Harry Buxton Forman and Thomas James Wise* (New Castle, Del.: Oak Knoll, 1992);

D. F. Foxon, *Thomas J. Wise and the Pre-Restoration Drama: A Study in Theft and Sophistication* (London: Bibliographical Society, 1959);

William B. Todd, "Unfamiliar Collections II: The Wrenn Library," *Library Chronicle of the University of Texas at Austin,* new series 8 (Fall 1974): 73–81;

Harold B. Wrenn, *A Catalogue of the Library of the Late John Henry Wrenn,* 5 volumes, edited by Thomas J. Wise (Austin: University of Texas, 1920).

Papers:

The Harry Ransom Humanities Research Center, University of Texas at Austin, owns Thomas J. Wise's letters to John Henry Wrenn and a few replies by Wrenn, as well as a few letters from Wrenn to correspondents including Edmund Gosse and Henry Buxton Forman.

John Cook Wyllie

(26 October 1908 – 18 April 1968)

Matthew J. Bruccoli
University of South Carolina

BOOKS AND PAMPHLETS*: and Randolph W. Church, *A Spenser Bibliography for 1928–1930* ... (Charlottesville: The Nutherpoms Press, 1931);

A Spenser Bibliography for 1928–1932, Together with an Index to the Same ..., compiled with Church (Charlottesville: University of Virginia, 1932);

An Appeal to the Women of Virginia to Assist in the Preservation of Historical Manuscripts (Sponsored by the Historical Societies and Civic Clubs of Charlottesville, Va., 1938);

and Randolph W. Church, *Preliminary Checklist for Abingdon,* Virginia Imprint Series Number 1 (Richmond: Virginia State Library, 1946);

The Tracy W. McGregor Library, Ad Interim Report ... A Summary of Ten Years, with a Draft of a Description of the McGregor Library (Charlottesville: McGregor Library, 1947);

Description of the Tracy W. McGregor Library University of Virginia (Charlottesville: The Tracy W. McGregor Library, 1949). Unsigned;

Preliminary Finding List of Writings on the Kentucky Book Trade, (Charlottesville: Bibliographical Society of the University of Virginia, 1949);

McGregor Library Reading List in American History, March 1950 (Charlottesville: McGregor Library, 1950). Unsigned;

Some Needs of the University of Virginia Library Prepared by the Librarian at the Request of the Alumni (Charlottesville, 1960);

Two Conventional Proposals for the Improvement of Access to the Technical Report Literature (Charlottesville, 1962);

and W. Reed Johnson, *Proposal for the Development of a Beta-Ray Radiography Instrument and Its Application to the Reproduction of Watermarks* (Charlottesville: University Library and Research Laboratories for the Engineering Sciences, 1964);

Science-Technology Subject-Heading Lists in English, Recent or Still Useful in Programming Information Retrieval Systems (Charlottesville: Science Reference Division, University of Virginia Library, 1965);

and Richard H. Austin, *List of Recent Reports of Interest to Technical Information Retrievers* (Charlottesville: Science Reference Division, University of Virginia Library, 1965).

OTHER: *Publications and Research, University of Virginia,* edited by Wyllie (November 1932);

University of Virginia Abstracts of Dissertations, 1935, edited by Wyllie (Charlottesville, University of Virginia, 1936);

Handbook of Virginia Libraries, 1936, edited by Wyllie, with N. Imogene Copps and Sarah White Jackson (Charlottesville: University of Virginia, 1936);

C. H. Quenzel, *Preliminary Checklist for Fredericksburg, 1778–1876,* Virginia Imprint Series Number 4. Wyllie was joint series editor (Richmond: Virginia State Library, 1947);

Secretary's News Sheet, edited by Wyllie (Charlottesville: Bibliographical Society of the University of Virginia, 1947–1967);

Abstracts of Dissertations Accepted in Partial Fulfillment of the Requirements for the Degree of Doctor of Philosophy, 1945–1947, edited by Wyllie (Charlottesville: The University of Virginia, 1948);

Abstracts of Dissertations Accepted in Partial Fulfillment of the Requirements for the Degree of Doctor of Philosophy, 1946, edited by Wyllie (Charlottesville: The University of Virginia, 1948);

Index to the Papers of the Bibliographical Society of America ..., edited by Wyllie (New York: Published by the Society, 1954);

Andres Bello, *A Georgic of the Tropics,* translated by Wyllie (Charlottesville: King Lindsay, 1954).

* Wyllie did not take credit for all of his work; this list includes the most important of his identified publications.

SELECTED CONTRIBUTIONS TO BOOKS AND PERIODICALS†: "Gordon, William

*John Cook Wyllie (courtesy of the John Cook Wyllie Library,
Clinch Valley College of the University of Virginia)*

Fitzhugh," *Dictionary of American Biography,* volume 7 (New York: Scribners, 1932), pp. 426–427;

"Lyons, Peter," *Dictionary of American Biography,* volume 11 (New York: Scribners, 1933), pp. 536–537;

"Lynch, Charles," *Dictionary of American Biography,* volume 11 (New York: Scribners, 1933), pp. 519–520;

"Levy, Uriah Phillips," *Dictionary of American Biography,* volume 11 (New York: Scribners, 1933), pp. 203–204;

"Manuscripts in Virginia," *University of Virginia News Letter* (1 January 1937): 1;

"Contemporary Virginia Literature," *University of Virginia News Letter* (1 April 1938): 1;

"Virginia, The University of," *Dictionary of American History,* edited by James Truslow Adams and R. V. Coleman (New York: Scribners, 1940), p. 375;

"A List of the Texts of Poe's Tales," *Humanistic Studies in Honor of John Calvin Metcalf* (Charlottesville, 1941), pp. 322–338;

"Foreword," *Early English Books at the University of Virginia,* by C. William Miller (Charlottesville: Alderman Library, 1941);

"An Invitation to Historians to Use the McGregor Library," *Dunmore's Proclamation of Emancipation, with an Invitation to the McGregor Library & An Account by Francis Berkeley of the Publication of the Proclamation* (Charlottesville: The Tracy W. McGregor Library, University of Virginia, 1941), pp. v–vi;

"Virginia, University of," *Encyclopedia Americana,* volume 28 (New York: Americana, 1946), p. 125;

"The printing of the proclamation," *By the King: A proclamation for settling the Plantation of Virginia* (Charlottesville: The Tracy W. McGregor Library, University of Virginia, 1946), pp. 31–39;

"Introduction" and notes, *Norfolk copyright entries, 1837, 1851-3, 1856-7, 1858-9, 1864, 1866-70,* transcribed by Barbara Harris (Charlottesville, The Bibliographical Society of the University of Virginia, 1947);

"University of Virginia Libraries," *The World Almanac, 1947* (New York: World-Telegram, 1947), p. 230;

"The Earliest Known American Verse, a Broadside Ballad from Virginia," *Virginia Magazine of History and Biography,* 56 (April 1948): 206;

"A Note on Virginia Transportation History," *Virginia Magazine of History and Biography,* 56 (July 1948): 368-370;

"A West Virginia Broadside," *Papers of the Bibliographical Society of America,* 42 (Fourth Quarter, 1948): 322-323;

"The Jefferson-Randolph Copies of an Anonymous Work Entered Three Ways by Sabin," *Virginia Magazine of History and Biography,* 56 (January 1948): 80-83;

"The Earliest Printing in Berryville, Virginia," *Proceedings of the Clark County Historical Association,* 9 (1949): 50-51;

"Early Albemarle, A Brief Historical Sketch Compiled from the Best Authorities," *Virginia and the Virginia County* (Charlottesville: League of Virginia Counties, 1949), pp. 9-10, 27;

"The Need," *Rare Books in the University Library* (Chicago: Association of College and Research Libraries, 1949), pp. 3-6;

"Library Acquires Finest Darwin Collection in U.S.," *University of Virginia Alumni News,* 37 (July 1949): 9;

"The Freedom of a Student Press," *The Virginia Spectator,* 110 (January 1949): 7, 40, 44-46;

"Introduction, Checklist, and Index," *Preliminary Checklist for Petersburg, 1786-1876,* Virginia Imprint Series number 9, edited by Edward A. Wyatt (Richmond: Virginia State Library, 1949), pp. 1-203, 312-358;

"The First Maryland Tract: A Reconsideration of the Date of Printing of the Maryland Charter," *Essays Honoring Lawrence C. Wroth* (Portland, Maine, 1951), pp. 475-83;

"Tracy W. McGregor and William L. Clements," *Antiquarian Bookman,* 7 (2 June 1951): 1849;

"Note on the Transcription," and "Bibliographical Note," *Memoirs of a Monticello Slave,* edited by Rayford W. Logan (Charlottesville: University of Virginia Press for The Tracy W. McGregor Library, 1951), pp. 8, 37-38; unsigned;

"Introduction," *A True Relation of the State of Virginia . . . ,* by John Rolfe (New Haven: Henry C. Taylor by C. P. R. at the Yale University Press, 1951), pp. 7-9; republished (University Press of Virginia for the Association for the Preservation of Virginia Antiquities, 1971);

Review of Hellmut Lehmann-Haupt, et al., *The Book in America, Antiquarian Bookman,* V III (25 August 1951): 469-470;

"The BSA and BSUV Joint Meeting," *Antiquarian Bookman,* 9 (31 May 1952): 1947-1948;

"Preface," *Thomas Jefferson's Prayer Book* (Meriden, Conn.: Meriden Gravure, 1952);

"Collector vs Keeper," *Antiquarian Bookman Yearbook* (1952): 33-34;

Reviews, columns, and articles as book-page editor, *Richmond News-Leader,* 1952-1962;

"The Forms of Twentieth-Century Cancels," *Papers of the Bibliographical Society of America,* 47 (Second Quarter, 1953): 95-112;

"Thomas Jefferson," Architect of American Democracy, *Compton's Pictured Encyclopedia* (Chicago: Compton, 1954), pp. 330-333;

"Pamphlets, Broadsides, Clippings and Posters," *Library Trends,* 4 (October 1955): 195-202;

"The Louisville Microcard Project," *Library Journal,* 81 (April 1956): 894-895;

Review of Jacob Blanck, *Bibliography of American Literature, The Book Collector,* 5 (Summer 1956): 183-187;

"Foreword," *Virginia's Role in America's History Told in Fifteen of its Most Important Books and Documents* (New York: John F. Fleming, 1958), p. 6;

"Rare Books," *The Concise Encyclopedia of American Antiques* (New York: Hawthorn Books, 1958), pp. 640-643, 656-663, 676-679;

"Tracy W. McGregor," *Grolier 75* (New York: Grolier Club, 1959), pp. 172-174;

"Prefactory," *A Brief Account of The Clifton Waller Barrett Library,* by Herbert Cahoon (Charlottesville: The University of Virginia, 1960);

"Introduction," The Tennyson Collection Presented to the University of Virginia in Honor of Edgar Finley Shannon, Jr. (Charlottesville: University of Virginia Press, 1961);

Review of P. M. Handover, *Printing in London from 1476 to Modern Times, Shakespeare Quarterly,* 12 (Summer 1961): 335-336;

with Atcheson L. Hench, "The 'Monte Carlo Method' of Atomic Energy Research," *American Speech,* 36 (October 1961): 233-234;

"Introduction," *Notes to Accompany a Facsimile of John Speed's Map of Virginia and Maryland 1676* (Charlottesville: McGregor Library/Univer-

A SPENSER BIBLIOGRAPHY FOR 1928-1930

₍to be used as a supplement to F.I.Carpenter's A REFERENCE GUIDE
TO EDMUND SPENSER and Alice Parrott's A CRITICAL BIBLIOGRA-
PHY OF SPENSER FROM 1923-28₎

compiled by
R.W.Church and J.C.Wyllie,
Fellows of English at the University of Virginia

*

with neither notes nor introduction by
THE AUTHORS

"Be bolde, Be bolde, and every where, Be bold."
THE FAERIE QUEENE Bk.iii,
Canto xi, Stanza 54.

FIRST EDITION
neither revised nor enlarged

Limited to 35 copies, mimeographed on ordinary paper, all stencils
having been destroyed.

Not signed by either author

All rights reserved, including that of translation into the Scandinavian.

Set up and carelessly printed at
UNIVERSITY, VIRGINIA
THE NUTHERPOMS PRESS
1931

Wyllie's first separate publication

sity Press of Virginia, 1962), pp. 1–4; "Intro-duction" signed by Anne Freudenberg, Arnold B. Levison, Sarah Dean Link, and Wyllie, who were presumably the editors;

"Proposals for Improving Access to the Technical Report Literature," *Proceedings of Conference on The Literature of Nuclear Science,* U.S. Atomic Energy Commission, 1962 (TID–7647), pp. 146–148;

"Meadow Branch, the Stream East of Monticello, Lately Called Tufton Branch, With Some Notes on the Nearby Surface Waters," *Virginia Place Name Society Occasional Papers,* number 4 (8 August 1962): 1–6;

"Totier Creek, A First-Families-of-Albemarle Place Name," *Virginia Place Name Society Occasional Papers,* number 2 [9] (8 October 1963): 1–8;

"Daniel Boone's Adventures in Charlottesville in 1781, Some Incidents Connected with Tarleton's Raid," *The Magazine of Albemarle County History,* 19 (1963): 5–18;

"The Bibliographer and the Collecting of Historical Materials," *Papers of the Bibliographical Society of America,* 48 (Second Quarter, 1964): 148–153;

"The Second Mrs. Wayland, An Unpublished Jefferson Opinion on a Case in Equity," notes by Wyllie, *American Journal of Legal History,* 9 (1965): 64–68;

"Introduction," Edward and Elizabeth Handy, *President Woodrow Wilson's Irish and Scottish Heritage* (Staunton, Virginia: Woodrow Wilson Birthplace Foundation, 1966), pp. iii–iv;

"New Documentary Light on Tarleton's Raid: Letters of Newman Brockenbrough and Peter Lyons," *Virginia Magazine of History and Biography,* 74 (October 1966): 452–461;

"The Forms of Culture, the Old and the New," *Report of the Virginia Cultural Development Study Commission, 1967,* written by the seventeen members of the commission, including Wyllie (Richmond, Va.); Senate Document number 9 (1967);

Introduction, "Thomas Jefferson on Higher Education, Documents Relative to the Founding of the University of Virginia," *Manual of the Board of Visitors of the University of Virginia, 1966* (Charlottesville: University of Virginia, 1967), pp. 31–36;

Review of T. H. Johnson, *The Oxford Companion to American History, Virginia Magazine of History and Biography,* 75 (January 1967): 117–119;

"The Role of the College Library," *The Virginia Librarian,* 14 (Summer 1967): 4–6;

"Observations Made During a Short Residence in Virginia: In a Letter from Thomas H. Palmer, May 30, 1814," edited by Wyllie, *Virginia Magazine of History and Biography,* 76 (October 1968): 387–414;

"Introduction, *William Faulkner: "Man Working," 1919–1962; A Catalogue of the William Faulkner Collections at the University of Virginia,* by Linton R. Massey (Charlottesville: Bibliographical Society of the University of Virginia, 1968), p. xv;

"Richmond's Library System needs Strong Queen Bee," *Richmond News Leader* (20 April 1968);

"Introduction," *An American Missionary to Meiji Japan,* by Robert L. Hilldrup (Privately Printed, 1970), pp. 1–2.

† Most book reviews and brief bibliographical notes are not listed.

The proper fulfillment of John Cook Wyllie's greatness was impeded by his refusal to recognize his greatness: he did not know how extraordinary his mind was. Wyllie did not achieve the high reputation accorded lesser librarians and bibliographers because he cared nothing for personal credit; he routinely gave away his ideas and discoveries. Wyllie's career inspires admiration and regret among those who worked with him because he accomplished so much but left so little of his mind on paper.

Wyllie was a double anachronism, joining old allegiances with an awareness of future requirements. One of those professionals who are described by amateurs as eccentric, he was a self-reliant man of principle who was too busy to be eccentric. Consistently truthful, he expressed apparently contradictory positions. Thus he was a generous benefactor of scholars and a dedicated preserver of research material who had reservations about promiscuous publication: "The frequent tooting of the tin horn of productive research is nothing more than the outward and visible sign of an inward and spiritual degeneration." This attitude no doubt influenced his reluctance to publish his work, which he regarded as work in progress. Accordingly, his 1960 Rosenbach Lectures were never prepared for publication.

Like many other great librarians he did not possess a library-school degree; his formal training in librarianship was limited to one summer at the University of Chicago. There was nothing about books that he could have learned from library schools or schools of information science or schools of media arts. He was a born bookman; working as

The Alderman Library, The University of Virginia

a librarian enabled him to devote his life to gathering books, preserving books, editing books, generating books, reviewing books, and facilitating the use of books. He functioned as an educator – not just as a librarian.

Addressing the Association of College and Reference Libraries in 1948, Wyllie admonished the group that "the mixture that still exists today of the librarian and the bibliophile is unfortunately a dying phenomenon." He defined rare books as "the unexpendable parts of a library's collection":

> One of the chief reasons for the need of rare book rooms in our university libraries today is the locust-like descent of great swarms of people on our collections. The locusts fall into two general categories: the student and the so-called trained librarian. Out of deference to the stated objectives of this association I pass over one of these categories lightly, but I will not forbear lamenting to this select group the wretched state of a profession, formerly one of dignity and character, which has so far fallen from the graces of the liberal arts and the natural sciences as to set up what can only be called trade schools. It is a dirty bird that fouls its own nest. You will forgive my bitterness if you have ever seen a class mark on a Ratcliffe binding, or if you have seen the Gaylord brand on a Zaehnsdorf inlay, or a punched page of an illuminated manuscript. Here surely are the marks of the beast.
>
> . . . .
>
> Most books, it is true, find their chief end in the noble function of being read, but the man who says that a book is only for reading is to me a pervert of the same order and only of a different kind as a man who says that a woman is only for sleeping with. Of course there are a great many books that are good only for reading, and some that are not good even for that, just as I dare say there are all kinds of women, but there is something in seeing a Gutenberg Bible or a first folio of Shakespeare or a Grolier binding or a Kelmscott Chaucer that has nothing at all to do with reading a book.

He believed that the chief responsibilities of a rare-books and manuscripts curator were to acquire research material to protect it from the atrocities of librarianship, and to make it usable by scholars.

Wyllie devoted his life's work to the University of Virginia, and it was his secret guilt that he was not an authentic Virginian. The son of the Rev. William Wyllie and Mabel Cook Wyllie, Episcopal Church missionaries, he was born in Palatka, Florida, on 26 October 1908. It may be a clue to Wyllie's character that he was a "missionary kid" — one of a group that has disproportionately distinguished itself in American life. He grew up in Santo Domingo, where he was educated mostly by tutors, and briefly attended two Virginia preparatory schools, Christchurch and St. Christopher's. In 1925 he was denied admission to the University of Virginia because he lacked necessary high-school credits. After a year at Lane High School in Charlottesville, he entered the University in 1926 and graduated with a B.A. in English in 1929. As an undergraduate he worked — paid and unpaid — for the library when it was located in the Rotunda.

After graduation Wyllie continued to work for the library while taking every advanced course offered by the English department, but he never took another degree. Having decided that the University was placing too much emphasis on graduate degrees, he declined to participate in what he regarded as the trend away from learning to diploma mills. Wyllie did not enjoy teaching in the classroom, but he was preceptor to a chain of students and colleagues. His preferred pedagogical technique was to initiate a project and then turn it over to someone else.

Wyllie was appointed assistant reference librarian in 1929; he was in fact the only reference librarian. In 1933–1934 he went, almost without funds, to Europe to visit libraries, binderies, and bookshops. Gerald Langford, Wyllie's graduate-school friend, has written that "on a trip to England, he picked up a copy of the 1636 edition of Kingsmill Long's translation of John Barclay's *Argenis,* which he gave me, with the suggestion that it would make a good Ph.D. dissertation subject for me, which indeed it did."

Upon his return Wyllie became curator of the Virginia Collection. When the Alderman Library opened in 1938 Wyllie was appointed director of the Division of Rare Books and Manuscripts. He created the rare-book division by examining every volume in the general stacks. At the Alderman Library dedication the first major gift to the new library was announced: the Tracy W. McGregor Library. McGregor had assembled a collection of 12,500 items dedicated to American history and had attempted to recruit Wyllie as his private librarian; after the collector's death the trustees of the McGregor Fund presented his library to the University of Virginia, at least partly in recognition of

McGregor's respect for Wyllie's abilities. Housed in the McGregor Room, this collection includes more than 2,000 Mather items.

After the army, navy, and marines turned him down because he was nearsighted, Wyllie joined the American Field Service as an ambulance driver in 1941 — before Pearl Harbor. He served with the British Eighth Army in North Africa, where he was the last man out of Tobruk and "heard the bagpipes at El Alamein." He received a field commission from the British, then returned to America and enlisted in the air corps. In 1944 he was communication chief for U.S. air-ground communication in Burma; in 1944–1945 he was an air-ground combat liaison and communications officer in China. Wyllie received a second field commission in the air corps and was discharged with the rank of first lieutenant, having been decorated by the British, American, and Chinese governments. The Legion of Merit citation read:

> For exceptionally meritorious service from 8 April 1943 to date as Senior Officer of an American Air-Ground Liaison Team operating with the Chinese 57th and Temporary 6th Division. Lt. Wyllie exhibited great courage and resourcefulness in establishing and maintaining observation posts in the most forward areas available from which he directed the extremely effective close air support of his unit which was credited with being one of the most contributing factors in the success of the Chinese Mission. When the 57th Division was relieved he immediately requested a new assignment to a forward area and proceeded to join the Temporary 6th Division where he continued to operate with great success making an enviable record and bringing great credit on the Military Service of the United States.

Wyllie was appointed Curator of Rare Books in 1946. When he married in 1949 he took a wife from the Alderman Library staff. He and the former Evelyn Dollens had two daughters, Elizabeth and Jane, who is a librarian. In 1956 he became university librarian, a promotion he accepted unenthusiastically because he felt that he could not work at the Alderman under any librarians other than his predecessors Harry Clemons and Jack Dalton; if he were to remain he would have to accept the librarianship. High administrative rank did not gratify Wyllie because he preferred books to committee work, yet he functioned effectively on an extraordinary number of committees. In 1966 he was appointed Director of Libraries of the University of Virginia with responsibility for all the libraries in the University of Virginia system. In this post he founded the Science and Technology Library at the University. The library at Clinch Valley College in

BIBLIOGRAPHICAL SOCIETY OF THE UNIVERSITY OF VIRGINIA

SECRETARY'S NEWS SHEET
No. 1

March 1947

The Society adopted a constitution on February 26, 1947 (a copy is attached), and elected the following officers:

Dr. Chalmers L. Gemmill
President

Dr. Fredson T. Bowers
Vice-President

Mr. John C. Wyllie
Secretary-Treasurer

Mr. Charles W. Smith
Councilor 1947-1950

Miss Lucy T. Clark
Councilor 1947-1949

Dr. Hugh M. Spencer
Councilor 1947-1948

Mr. Linton R. Massey
Councilor 1947

Professor Fredson Bowers then spoke on some problems and practices in bibliographical descriptions of modern authors. The scholarly deficiencies of certain descriptive bibliographies were pointed out, and suggestions were made concerning the prospects for work in the period of machine printing. Dr. Bowers made the point that if this work is to be of value, it must be done by or in collaboration with trained scholars.

In Dr. Bowers' opinion, a basic need is a study such as R. B. McKerrow's Introduction to Bibliography for the period after the passing of hand printing, with which McKerrow

Page from newsletter including the announcement of Wyllie's election as Secretary-Treasurer of the Bibliographical Society of the University of Virginia

Wise, Virginia, which he helped establish, was named for him in 1969.

John Cook Wyllie was five feet, ten inches tall with close-cut, wiry hair. His suits and ties were sprinkled with ashes. Wyllie was embarrassed by displays of emotion or self-revelation; but his close friends testified to his periods of doubt. During the war years he wrote, "Fact is in its simplest terms that I don't know what I want but have to depend upon my instincts to prevent me from getting it, and I can always in the last analysis count on my following the line of most resistance." He spent nothing on himself, except for two packs of cigarettes a day; he did not drink and was indifferent to food. Whatever spare money he had was spent on books which he gave to the Alderman. He was wholly unpretentious. As Curator of Rare Books in the 1950s he did not have a proper office; his desk was in a passageway behind bookcases, surrounded by piles of books. He frequently returned to the library after dinner. Many nights were spent with what he called "the book machine" — his system for processing gifts and acquisitions. Although he did not give the impression of being under pressure, Wyllie routinely worked on several projects at once and disliked time-wasting interruptions. He carried a book to read when he might be compelled to wait.

The mind of a scholar-librarian-educator is gauged by the books in his life. Wyllie was unostentatiously omnibibliophilic. There were twenty-eight books by his bed the night he died — all of which he was reading: Allen, *Love in the Making;*

Aiken, *Collected Criticism;* Adams, *John James Audubon;* Martinez, *Memoirs of a Medico;* Chekhov, *The Seagull and Three Sisters;* Deutscher, *Stalin;* Durrell, *Clea;* Eifert, *Louis Jolliet;* Freud, *Dictionary of Psychoanalysis;* Fromm, *May Man Prevail ;* *The Hazlitt Sampler;* Heimann, *History of Economic Doctrines;* Hobhouse, *Liberalism;* Hume, *An Enquiry Concerning Human Understanding;* Knapp, *A History of War and Peace, 1939–1965;* Labaree, *The Boston Tea Party;* Matthiessen, *American Renaissance;* Maxwell, *Ring of Bright Water;* Nucete-Sardi, *Aventura y tragedia di Don Francisco de Miranda;* Price, *A Generous Man;* Price, *A Long and Happy Life;* Quer, *The Physiology of Plants;* Shannon & Weaver, *The Mathematical Theory of Communication;* Tyler, *Anthropology;* Wade, *Slavery in the Cities, The South 1820–1860;* Wagenknecht, *John Greenleaf Whittier;* Waxell, *The Russian Expedition to America;* Wheare, *Legislatures.*

A university is an assemblage of books surrounded by people using them. Wyllie was highly receptive to technological developments; but his principal concern was in extending the use of the library to all classes of readers and researchers. When William Faulkner arrived at the University as writer in residence in 1956, there were not enough copies of his books in the Alderman stacks to meet the new demand; Wyllie placed a supply of uncatalogued Faulkner paperbacks in the lobby.

A librarian is best judged by his bookmanship and by the books and collections he builds or acquires. Wyllie's chief contribution to scholarship and librarianship was his work as Curator of Rare Books, which provided his chief gratification. During his tenure as head of rare books – with or without the title – the Alderman Library acquired the Tracy W. McGregor Library and the C. Waller Barrett Library of American Literature. He was partially or wholly responsible for the acquisition of these collections by gift or purchase:

Wilbur Cortez Abbott Collection of Seventeenth-Century English History and Literature (especially related to Oliver Cromwell);

Armed Services Editions Collection;

Samuel Bemiss Collection of Incunabula and Classics;

Joseph M. Bruccoli Great War Collection;

James Branch Cabell Papers;

Warren Chappell Collection;

Elizabeth Cocke Coles Collection of Virginiana;

Philip K. Crowe Collection (books about Ceylon);

John Dos Passos Papers;

William Faulkner Collection of Linton R. Massey;

Library of the Garnett Family of Elmwood (Essex County, Virginia);

Douglas H. Gordon Collection of French Renaissance Literature;

T. Catesby Jones Collection of Early Twentieth-Century European Graphic Art;

Edward L. Stone Collection on the Development of Printing;

Thomas W. Streeter Railroad Collection;

Marvin Tatum Collection of Contemporary Prose and Poetry;

Mrs. Robert Coleman Taylor Collection of First Editions of American Best Sellers;

Alfred Lord Tennyson Collection (of which the core was previously known as the Templeton Crocker Tennyson Collection);

Trollope Family Collection;

Victorius Evolution Collection;

Virginiana Collections;

Isaac Walton Collection;

Steven Watts Collection of Type Specimen Books;

James Madison Collection;

Alexander MacKay-Smith Collection (printed scores, primarily of eighteenth-century music);

Stephen McClellan Aviation Collection;

American Sheet Music Collection (part of which is called the Lynn T. McRae Collection);

Oscar Ogg Collection of Typography, Book Design, and Book Illustration;

Sabine Hall Library of Landon and Robert Wormeley Carter;

Sadleir-Black Collection of Gothic Novels;

Marion duPont Scott Collection of Sporting Books.

Wyllie's achievements as a collection builder were impeded by a puny budget and by his attitudes toward money. He was not stingy; but he did not comprehend how other people were motivated by money. He was personally indifferent to money – apart from providing for his family – and probably regretted the necessity of accepting any salary from the University. He declined consulting fees from libraries and other academic institutions because he believed that it was his duty to make his abilities available. Wyllie nurtured the conviction that dealers were insufficiently sensitive to the honor of donating material to the University. Great collections went elsewhere because he would not purchase anything for the library unless the funds were in hand. Adequate amounts were never in hand; in 1955 the total budget for rare-book and manuscript purchases was fifteen thousand dollars: ten thousand dollars from the McGregor Fund and five thousand dollars from the state. During the 1950s and 1960s

Wyllie (right) being congratulated on his appointment as Librarian of the University of Virginia by former librarians Jack Dalton and Harry Clemons, 1956; photograph by Ralph Thompson (courtesy of Special Collections Department, University Archives, The University of Virginia)

when the University of Texas was omnivorously paying big money for collections, and other institutions were attempting to compete, Wyllie felt that such conduct bordered on indecency. His achievements in collection development resulted from his ability to convince potential donors of the value of the University of Virginia and its library.

Wyllie's integrity as well as his technique in acquiring material are demonstrated by his response to James Branch Cabell's offer to donate some of his manuscripts to the Alderman Library and sell the rest of his papers elsewhere:

> there is a Calvinist streak in me requiring me to admit that these manuscripts ought not to be dispersed. In the interest simply of future Cabell scholarship, I would rather see the entire batch go to Bill Jackson at Harvard or Jim Babb at Yale (Either one can put their

hands on more money than I can) than that the manuscripts should be scattered from hell to breakfast with us getting some.

> If you scatter the manuscripts, there will be some disorganized flurries of notoriety at the wrong time in American literary history. But if you will just see to it that the manuscripts are kept together where they can be got at when the time comes for the real flowering of your literary fame, then you will have done something both for yourself and for American literature. I sadly admit that, unless I read the literary portents incorrectly, we will both long since have been underground when this day comes. But I have no shadow of a doubt that it will come, and for me to be a silent party to the dispersal of the manuscripts is to do less than justice to my own critical acumen.

> I admire your work and yet am hardheaded enough to know that its special bouquet is not for the present generation's mass market, where the prices are made. What would you think about getting yourself a

professional appraisal and then letting us try to find donors for half that sum? You could check the accuracy of the appraisal and the reality of our own interest by putting one of the manuscripts up at public auction in New York and letting us see if we could buy it in.

The Cabell Papers came to the Alderman Library through the generosity of the author's brother.

It is pardonable that most collectors are not bibliographers. It is unforgivable that some bibliographers are not collectors. But it is a capital offense for an alleged rare-books curator not to be a bookman. Wyllie formulated this code for his own bookmanship: "If you ask me why I looked for bookstores and libraries when I was in Cairo and Liverpool, my only answer is that I went to Cairo and Liverpool to look for libraries and bookstores. . . . I don't really claim to be a collector myself. I am only a keeper and admirer of other people's collections. Ownership of a book for most people like myself is a fugitive and transitory affair, lasting only a few years or decades. It takes a real book collector . . . to confer something of an immortality on their ownership."

During his term as book editor for the *Richmond News Leader*, Wyllie trained the editors to retain the array of printed material the paper received, which he fetched back to the University. He instructed the dubious journalists that even the "nut mail" constituted a record of the time that would be unrecoverable unless preserved. Wyllie's all-embracing acquisitions policy was not shared by some of his associates who claimed that "John's junk" was not worth the expense of cataloguing. His rationale extended to the rare-book stacks, which were populated with what lesser curators described as duplicate copies. Wyllie recognized that what appeared to be duplicates were not necessarily duplicates. Accordingly, he developed techniques for differentiating concealed printings on the basis of typographical evidence. For this purpose he bought the first Hinman Collator outside of the Folger Library. He may have originated the technique for using gutter measurements to identify impressions; and he was able to reconstruct the binding process for a printing from the thread colors in the copies. Wyllie's interest in cancels was connected with his work on differentiating printings; his 1953 article on "The Forms of Twentieth-Century Cancels" was the first published attempt to describe post-1825 examples.

Wyllie dismayed conventionally trained librarians by shelving later printings and editions of key works in his rare-book stacks. He believed that the proper function of bibliography is to construct the biography of a book and that books embody their own histories. He addressed the Grolier Club on the topic of "Second Editions"; characteristically he did not keep a copy of his remarks. Wyllie preserved everyone's work except his own.

In dedicating *The New Sabin* (1974) to Wyllie, Lawrence S. Thompson explained that he was "a sort of apostle of the rare book in America. His breviary was Joseph Sabin's *Dictionary of Books Relating to America,* and he dreamed of expanding it to a point at which it would dwarf the *National Union Catalog* in sheer bulk. He printed for very limited distribution six entries of a type which he conceived to be the ideal Sabin."

Wyllie was foremost a bookman, but he experimented with methods for applying technology to bibliographical research. In 1960 he rigged a television camera with a reading stand in order to transmit images of pages to other libraries at the University; in 1966 he collaborated with nuclear scientist W. Reed Johnson to reproduce watermarks by beta-ray photography and apply this technique to the Jefferson papers. Addressing the Bibliographical Society of America in 1964 — before the computer revolution — he forcefully called for new approaches to bibliographical work:

> With eighty-five per cent of the collectors who have ever lived still alive today, and with ninety-five per cent of the bibliographers who have ever lived still stalking the land, how do we create the conditions to get the two populations into useful juxtaposition for this presumably desirable heat transfer? How do we bring about the set of circumstances that will put great collections to great uses? How can worthy skills be applied to worthy ventures? How can great needs be supplied with great means?
>
> . . . .
>
> My suggestion is that the Society form a Council on Bibliographical Research and Development, and that this Council be handed as much money as can be scratched up and charged with finding as much more as it can, while it develops an approved dossier of research proposals to offer the eleemosynarily inclined.
>
> . . . .
>
> My only point, and I have now labored it enough, is that we are living in an age of machines, and we ought to learn to use them. The age is also one of corporate research, so I repeat my lugubrious warning, with what cheerfulness I can summon, that the great and solitary heroes like Bradshaw and de Ricci are gone, and we must all soon follow.

From 1952 to 1962 Wyllie was Book Editor for the *Richmond News Leader,* producing what was regarded as the best newspaper book page in the

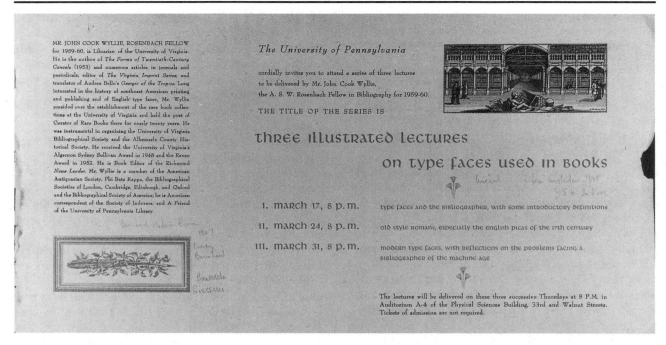

Wyllie's annotated announcement of the lectures he delivered in March 1960, while he was Rosenbach Fellow at the University of Pennsylvania (Bruccoli Collection)

South. He wrote hundreds of reviews, which were characterized by clarity and disdain for literary chitchat. Reviewing B. H. Liddell Hart's edition of the *Rommel Papers* (18 May 1953), Wyllie drew upon his experiences with the Eighth Army to expose the historian's pomposity and carelessness, concluding:

> It makes me a little mad for a stuffed shirt like Liddell Hart to have got his front feet in Rommel's trough. When Rommel is talking about the Blitzkrieg in France, Liddell Hart says Oh yes, he himself had invented it in 1920, and had a better name for it – the "expanding torrent."
>
> Nuts to us both, Mr. Liddell Hart. I invented this system of annotation before 1920 and I still call it "scratching my own back."

After attending a William Faulkner press conference at the 1955 National Book Awards ceremony, Wyllie wrote (31 January 1955):

> He is a small man, shy, sincere, nothing of the smart-aleck. He gets clothes-dummy frozen before banked cameras or a press-gang, thaws readily in a group of two or three people if one of them has a kind or an understanding word. The two Oxfords (Mississippi and England) are strong in him: rough edges of the country-store philosopher and the sophisticated reserve of the housebroken British; a Mississippi accent in Swinburnian rhythms, but too faint to hear unless you listen intently.

His eyes are black, his hair white. The sharp forward, ferret taper of his face and the fixed public stare give him a zoo-like appearance, something between a chicken and a fox, but he is handsome even in his mask. He carries a red bandanna handkerchief that he tucks up his left sleeve. His public voice is an inaudible, inexpressive monotone. As a public speaker he is a total loss, but what he writes to speak is golden.

. . . .

> This interviewer came away puzzled, but with an undiminished respect for Faulkner; and for his own part, still believes Faulkner has a right to be obscure, believes now that Faulkner moves under intense artistic compulsions, hovering between sophisticated coma and savage convulsion, of which your interviewer has only a dim and unsatisfactory comprehension.
>
> Here, at all events, is a fleeting impression of the most influential, the most original, and the most vilified novelist living, each of whose works has enriched all his others. Hemingway (Faulkner's closest rival in contemporary literary fame) has been too personal to support followers, too attractive not to produce imitators, but Faulkner has been sinking deep roots, while Hemingway has only been blooming and fading.

Wyllie denied that he was a man of letters, but a good case can be made for his literary qualifications. He wrote forceful prose that effectively expressed his critical judgments. His style was direct, almost journalistic, for he wrote against deadlines and had little opportunity to revise. Just as he was appalled by ostentatious or pretentious conduct, he

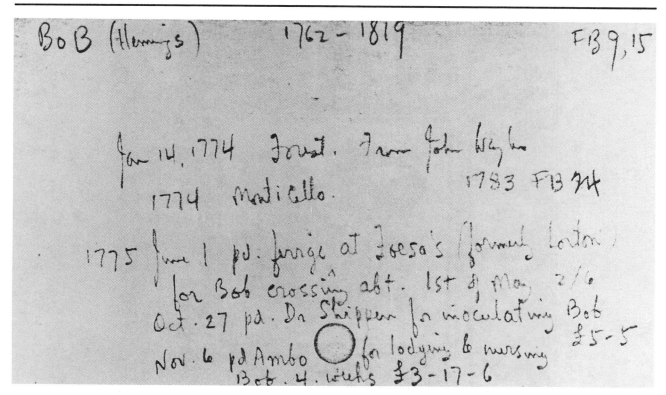

One of Wyllie's notes on Jefferson's slaves (courtesy of Special Collections Department, University Archives, The University of Virginia)

eschewed fancy writing. He read widely in literature, history, and biography and drew upon his extensive knowledge in his writings.

The earliest scholarly publication on which Wyllie's name appears is *A Spenser Bibliography for 1928–1930,* which he and Randolph W. Church — later the Virginia State Librarian — compiled and mimeographed in 1931. The parodic title page provides an indication of Wyllie's unsolemn approach to academic endeavors.

Dumas Malone said that Wyllie "knew more than any other living man about the slaves of Thomas Jefferson"; and his work grew to more than 950 file cards. Not a pious idolater of Jefferson, Wyllie pursued this subject because of the allegations that Jefferson had sired slave children; however, Wyllie found no evidence to support this claim. Wyllie also accumulated some seventy-five thousand citations for all reported Jefferson texts — in print or manuscript — which he made available to the Princeton University Jefferson Papers project. Wyllie's unpublished identification of the paper stocks purchased by Jefferson was undertaken to facilitate the dating of his writings.

What the Alderman Library staff refers to as the "Wyllie File" consists of seventy-two card trays containing some seventy-nine thousand three-by-five-inch cards and slips, mostly in his hand. The majority of the cards index *The University of Virginia Alumni Bulletin* and other University publications; but four trays hold more than four thousand cards with his notes on secondary Poe publications.

Wyllie's 1954 translation of Andres Bello's *A Georgic of the Tropics,* the first English translation of the 1826 poem, does not carry his name; the "Translator's Foreword" is signed J. C. W.

As a bibliographer Wyllie was chiefly interested in the identification of typefaces, the subject of his Rosenbach Lectures at the University of Pennsylvania in 1960 under the title "Three Illustrated Lectures on Type Faces Used in Books." His techniques for "fingerprinting" individual pieces of type from a font led him to question the accepted publication history of the *Bay Psalm Book* dated 1640. Wyllie suspected that what is held to be the first book printed in North America was actually printed in London:

> A) The type used for this *Bay Psalm Book* was used only for that book and a Harvard commencement broadside — and for no other surviving work printed in North America.

Wyllie's bookplate

B) This identical type was used in England before and *after* 1640.

Wyllie concluded that the 1640 *Bay Psalm Book* and the Harvard broadside were printed in England. He did not deny that a psalm book could have been printed in Cambridge, Massachusetts; but he contended that the volume dated 1640, which stipulates no printer or place of publication, was not printed in the Bay Colony. Because the same type was in use at the London shop of Isaac Jaggard, printer of the *First Folio* (1623) and Shakespeare quartos, Wyllie suspected that certain quartos dated before 1620 had been printed later.

In his Rosenbach Lectures Wyllie also revealed that although the Carter and Pollard disclosures about the Wise fabrications were correct, their typographical evidence was flawed. Carter and Pollard claimed that the pamphlets printed from kernless type were later than 1883; but Wyllie was able to identify kernless type in English printing of the 1870s.

Most bookmen or bibliographers are specialists; Wyllie, in addition to his work in typography and Virginia history, had an extraordinary range of research activities. But he was not a hobbyist, because he had no hobbies. Although he did not publish a book-length work of scholarship, he worked hard and seriously on his simultaneous research projects, intending to complete them in his retirement. He ran out of time.

Like all serious men, Wyllie disliked committee meetings, but he was an effective organizer of scholarly groups and projects. Wyllie was a founding member of the Albemarle County Historical Society and of the Virginia Place Name Society; he was an active member of other Virginia local-history organizations. It is difficult to rank his activities, but one of Wyllie's more significant endeavors was his role in the Bibliographical Society of the University of Virginia, of which he was a founding member, secretary-treasurer from 1947 to 1962, and treasurer from 1963 to 1968. He wrote or edited fifty-three numbers of the *Secretary's News Sheet* during those years.

The activities of the Bibliographical Society of the University of Virginia and the library were closely connected, and Wyllie assisted the launching of Fredson Bowers's *Studies in Bibliography*. Wyllie also reorganized the University of Virginia Press and was superintendent of the press from 1947 through 1949. He directed the McGregor Room Seminars (renamed the Peters Rushton Seminars) in Literature and Criticism and wrote most of the program notes.

Much of Wyllie's time was expended on editing other people's work and arranging for its publication or in organizing cooperative projects. After the death of Robert J. Turnbull, Wyllie salvaged the work in progress on Turnbull's *Bibliography of South Carolina, 1563–1950,* which was published in six volumes by the University of Virginia Press. He also edited and arranged the posthumous publication for Robert H. Webb's translations of Aristophanes. He supervised the Virginia Imprint Series and compiled in 1946 the first volume, *Preliminary Checklist for Abingdon, 1807–1876.* He encouraged Roger P. Bristol to undertake the Index to Evans's *American Bibliography* and helped to start the *Supplement to Evans.* In 1968, the year of his death, he initiated the Microfilm/Publications project, funded by the National Historical Publications and Records Commission, that produced microfilm and guides for research collections at the University. He served on the advisory boards for *The Papers of Thomas Jefferson* and *The Papers of James Madison.* He served on the boards of the Ellen Bayard Weedon Foundation and the William Faulkner Foundation.

There were book people in and out of Virginia for whom the most notable thing about the Alderman Library was the presence of John Cook Wyllie. When he received the Algernon Sidney Sullivan Award, a high honor bestowed by the University of Virginia, the citation written by Harry Clemons, the tenth University librarian, stated: "The full story of his generous and self-sacrificing efforts is known to no one else, and has been forgotten by him."

John Cook Wyllie suffered a heart attack at the end of his normal fourteen-hour workday and died on 18 April 1968. His death pauperized the University of Virginia libraries and the world of books.

References:

[Randolph W. Church], *John Cook Wyllie, 1908–1968: A Very Personal Remembrance* (Privately printed, 1972);

"John Cook Wyllie 1908–1968," *AB Bookman Weekly,* 45 (27 April 1970), 1439–1440. Tributes by Sol M. Malkin, C. Waller Barrett, Matthew J. Bruccoli, and Robert K. Black;

J.E.M., "John Cook Wyllie," *Proceedings of the American Antiquarian Society,* 78 (16 October 1968): 236–238;

Dumas Malone, "John Cook Wyllie, *The Century Association Year-Book 1973* (New York, 1973): pp. 371–372;

Jesse C. Mills, "Detective in the Book World," *Graphic Arts Review,* 23 (May 1960): 7–8, 46–48.

Checklist of Further Readings

Ahearn, Allen. *Book Collecting: A Comprehensive Guide*. New York: Putnam, 1989.

Bowers, Fredson. *Bibliography and Textual Criticism*. Oxford: Clarendon Press, 1964.

Bowers. *Textual & Literary Criticism*. Cambridge: Cambridge University Press, 1959.

Boynton, Henry Walcott. *Annals of American Bookselling, 1638–1850*. New York: Wiley, 1932; republished, with an introduction by Joseph Rosenblum, New Castle, Del.: Oak Knoll Books, 1991.

Brook, G. L. *Books and Book-Collecting*. London: Deutsch, 1980.

Brotherhead, William. *Forty Years among the Old Booksellers in Philadelphia*. Philadelphia: Brotherhead, 1891.

Burton, John Hill. *The Book Hunter*. Edinburgh: Blackwood & Sons, 1862.

Cannon, Carl L. *American Book Collectors and Collecting from Colonial Times to the Present*. New York: Wilson, 1941.

Carter, John. *ABC for Book Collectors*. New York: Knopf, 1951; sixth edition, with corrections and additions by Nicolas Barker, New York & London: Granada, 1980.

Carter. *Books and Book-Collectors*. Cleveland: World, 1957.

Carter. *Taste & Technique in Book Collecting: A Study of Recent Developments in Great Britain and the United States*. Cambridge: Cambridge University Press, 1948; republished, with an epilogue, London: Private Libraries Association, 1970.

Davis, Richard Beale. *A Colonial Southern Bookshelf: Reading in the Eighteenth Century*. Athens: University of Georgia Press, 1979.

Davis. *Intellectual Life in Jefferson's Virginia 1790–1830*. Knoxville: University of Tennessee Press, 1964.

Dickinson, Donald C. *Dictionary of American Book Collectors*. New York: Greenwood Press, 1986.

Dunbar, Maurice. *Books and Collectors*. Los Altos, Cal.: Book Nest, 1980.

Ettinghausen, Maurice L. *Rare Books and Royal Collectors: Memoirs of an Antiquarian Bookseller*. New York: Simon & Schuster, 1966.

Everitt, Charles P. *Adventures of a Treasure Hunter*. Boston: Little, Brown, 1951.

Farmer, Bernard J. *The Gentle Art of Book-Collecting*. London: Thorson's Publishers, 1950.

Farnham, Luther. *A Glance at Private Libraries*. Boston: Press of Crocker and Brewster, 1855; reprinted, with an introduction and annotated index by Roger E. Stoddard, Weston, Mass.: M & S Press, 1991.

Gaskell, Philip. *A New Introduction to Bibliography*. Oxford: Clarendon Press, 1972.

Goodrum, Charles A. *Treasures of the Library of Congress,* revised and expanded edition, New York: Abrams, 1991.

Greetham, D. C. *Textual Scholarship: An Introduction.* New York & London: Garland, 1992.

Greg, W. W. *Collected Papers.* Oxford: Clarendon Press, 1966.

Iacone, Salvatore J. *The Pleasures of Book Collecting.* New York: Harper & Row, 1976.

Jackson, Holbrook. *The Anatomy of Bibliomania,* 2 volumes. London: Soncino Press, 1930–1931.

Joline, Adrian H. *The Diversions of a Book-Lover.* New York & London: Harper, 1903.

Landon, Richard G., ed. *Book Selling and Book Buying: Aspects of the Nineteenth Century British and North American Book Trade.* Chicago: American Library Association, 1978.

Lehmann-Haupt, Hellmut. *The Book in America: A History of the Making, the Selling, and the Collecting of Books in the United States.* New York: Bowker, 1939.

Lewis, Roy Harley. *Antiquarian Books: An Insider's Account.* New York: Arco, 1978.

Littlefield, George Emery. *Early Boston Booksellers, 1642–1711.* Boston: Club of Odd Volumes, 1900.

Malclès, Louise Noelle. *Bibliography,* translated by Theodore Christian Hines. New York: Scarecrow, 1961.

Matthews, Jack. *Collecting Rare Books for Pleasure and Profit.* New York: Putnam, 1977.

McKerrow, Ronald B. *An Introduction to Bibliography for Literary Students.* Oxford: Clarendon Press, 1927.

Morley, Christopher. *Ex Libris Carissimis.* Philadelphia: University of Pennsylvania Press, 1932.

Muir, Percy H. *Book-Collecting as a Hobby: in a Series of Letters to Everyman.* London: Gramol, 1944.

Muir, *Book-Collecting: More Letters to Everyman.* London: Cassell, 1949.

Oliphant, Dave, and Robin Bradford, eds. *New Directions in Textual Studies.* Austin: Harry Ransom Humanities Research Center, University of Texas at Austin, 1990.

Peters, Jean, ed. *Book Collecting: A Modern Guide.* New York: Bowker, 1977.

Rees-Mogg, William. *How To Buy Rare Books: A Practical Guide to the Antiquarian Book Market.* Oxford: Phaidon Christie's, 1985.

Rogers, Horatio. *Private Libraries of Providence, with a Preliminary Essay on the Love of Books.* Providence: Sidney S. Rider, 1878.

Savage, Ernest Albert. *The Story of Libraries and Book-Collecting.* London: Routledge & Sons, 1909.

Schneider, Georg. *Theory and History of Bibliography,* translated by Ralph Robert Shaw. New York: Columbia University Press, 1934.

Sowerby, E. Millicent. *Rare People and Rare Books.* London: Constable, 1967.

Starrett, Vincent. *Penny Wise and Book Foolish*. New York: Covici Friede, 1929.

Stern, Madeleine B. *Antiquarian Bookselling in the United States: A History from the Origins to the 1940s*. Westport, Conn.: Greenwood Press, 1985.

Stern. *Books and Book People in 19th-Century America*. New York: Bowker, 1978.

Stillwell, Margaret. *Incunabula and Americana, 1450–1800*. New York: Columbia University Press, 1931.

Storm, Colton, and Howard Peckham. *Invitation to Book Collecting: Its Pleasures and Practices, with Kindred Discussions of Manuscripts, Maps, and Prints*. New York: Bowker, 1947.

Tanselle, G. Thomas. *A Rationale of Textual Criticism*. Philadelphia: University of Pennsylvania Press, 1989.

Tanselle. *Textual Criticism since Greg: A Chronicle, 1950–1985*. Charlottesville: University Press of Virginia, 1987.

Targ, William, ed. *Bouillabaisse for Bibliophiles*. Cleveland: World, 1955.

Targ, ed. *Carrousel for Bibliophiles*. New York: Philip C. Duschnes, 1947.

Thomas, Alan G. *Great Books and Book Collectors*. London: Weidenfeld & Nicolson, 1975.

Towner, Wesley, and Stephen Varble. *The Elegant Auctioneers*. New York: Hill & Wang, 1970.

Williams, William Proctor and Craig S. Abbott. *An Introduction to Bibliographical and Textual Studies*. New York: Modern Language Association of America, 1985.

Willoughby, Edwin Eliott. *The Uses of Bibliography to the Students of Literature and History*. Hamden, Conn.: Shoe String Press, 1957.

Wilson, Robert A. *Modern Book Collecting*. New York: Knopf, 1980.

Winterich, John T. *A Primer of Book Collecting*. New York: Greenberg, 1926; third edition, revised by Winterich and David A. Randall, New York: Crown, 1966.

Wroth, Lawrence C. "Good Booksellers Make Good Libraries," in *To Dr. R.: Essays Here Collected and Published in Honor of the Seventieth Birthday of Dr. A. S. W. Rosenbach July 22, 1946*. Philadelphia, 1946, pp. 263–272.

Wynne, James. *Private Libraries of New York*. New York: E. French, 1860.

Contributors

Katherine J. Adams ....University of Texas at Austin
William Baker ....Northern Illinois University
Francis J. Bosha ....Kawamura Gakuen Woman's University
Richard E. Brewer ....Monmouth College
Josephine Arlyn Bruccoli ....Columbia, South Carolina
Matthew J. Bruccoli ....University of South Carolina
Elizabeth Burin ....The Walters Art Gallery
Susan Davis ....Memphis, Tennessee
Glen Dawson...Dawson's Book Shop
Donald C. Dickinson..University of Arizona
William K. Finley ....College of Charleston
Kevin J. Hayes ....University of Central Oklahoma
Mary Anne Hines...Library Company of Philadelphia
Dean H. Keller ....Kent State University
Jennifer Larson ....Yerba Buena Books
Laura V. Monti..Boston Public Library
Leslie A. Morris ....Houghton Library, Harvard University
Annegret S. Ogden..Bancroft Library, University of California
Richard W. Oram ....University of Texas at Austin
Susanna Bartmann Pathak...Johns Hopkins University
Ward Ritchie..Laguna Beach, California
Ruth Rosenberg...City University of New York
Joseph Rosenblum..University of North Carolina at Greensboro
Alison M. Scott ....Bowling Green State University
Joel Silver..Indiana University
Carolyn Smith..Johns Hopkins University
Monsignor Francis J. Weber ....Archdiocese of Los Angeles
George Walton Williams ....Duke University

Cumulative Index

Dictionary of Literary Biography, Volumes 1-140
Dictionary of Literary Biography Yearbook, 1980-1993
Dictionary of Literary Biography Documentary Series, Volumes 1-11

Cumulative Index

DLB before number: *Dictionary of Literary Biography,* Volumes 1-140
Y before number: *Dictionary of Literary Biography Yearbook,* 1980-1993
DS before number: *Dictionary of Literary Biography Documentary Series,* Volumes 1-11

B

L

O

Y

Z

ISBN 0-8103-5399-7

90000

9 780810 353992